THE
MACHINERY OF JUSTICE
IN ENGLAND

THE
MACHINERY OF JUSTICE
IN ENGLAND

BY

R. M. JACKSON, LL.D.

Solicitor of the Supreme Court
Fellow of St John's College, Cambridge
Reader in Public Law and Administration
in the University of Cambridge

FOURTH EDITION

1964

CAMBRIDGE
AT THE UNIVERSITY PRESS
1964

PUBLISHED BY

THE SYNDICS OF THE CAMBRIDGE UNIVERSITY PRESS

Bentley House, 200 Euston Road, London, N.W. 1
American Branch: 32 East 57th Street, New York 22, N.Y.
West African Office: P.O. Box 33, Ibadan, Nigeria

THIS EDITION

©

CAMBRIDGE UNIVERSITY PRESS

1964

First Edition	1940
Second Edition	1953
Third Edition	1960
Reprinted	1963
Fourth Edition	1964

Printed in Great Britain at the University Printing House, Cambridge
(Brooke Crutchley, University Printer)

CONTENTS

CHAPTER I

HISTORICAL INTRODUCTION

CHAPTER II

CIVIL JURISDICTION

CHAPTER III

CRIMINAL JURISDICTION

CONTENTS

CHAPTER IV

THE PERSONNEL OF THE LAW

CHAPTER V

THE COST OF THE LAW

CHAPTER VI

SPECIAL TRIBUNALS

CHAPTER VII

THE OUTLOOK FOR REFORM

LIST OF TABLES

PREFACE TO THE FOURTH EDITION

Since the last edition of this book there have been several important changes in law and practice. To incorporate the new material and bring the account up to date I have substantially revised the text, with a fair amount of rewriting and some re-arrangement. The principal new legal provisions cover a wide field. Contempt of court and *habeas corpus* proceedings have been altered by legislation and I have added a new section on each of these matters: a new Table X is included to show the provision for appeals in cases of contempt. The section on courts with appellate criminal jurisdiction has needed heavy revision because of the Administration of Justice Act 1960, and Table V giving the system of criminal courts has been redrawn to show the new rights of appeal. There has been an increase of interest in the nature of a trial at common law, and I have added a section to Chapter 1 to bring some material together and relate it to the principle of open court and the position of the press. Legal aid has been made more widely available. In criminal cases the facilities appear more as a patchwork than a unified service, and I have included a new Table VI to show the arrangements for legal aid. The Ingleby Committee Report on Children and Young Persons has led to much discussion of juvenile courts and the services relating to families and children. Some changes have been made by legislation. It is difficult to appreciate the whole range of sentences and orders that a court may make in respect of offenders of various ages, and I drew a diagram that the Ingleby Committee found useful; it has been brought up to date and appears here as Table VIII. I have given a brief summary in the section on juvenile courts of some of the main questions and present views. The Streatfield Committee has reported on the organisation of the higher criminal courts and legislation has followed. Reorganised courts of Quarter Sessions and a revised arrangement of Assize Courts have come about, but the Streatfeild Committee also dealt with the method of providing courts with information about offenders, and that led to a review of the process of sentencing. The last of these major changes to be specially noted is that the Law Society has made great alterations in the examinations and training for becoming a solicitor. The account of these, and of many lesser changes, has been brought down to October 1963, with an indication that 1964 is expected to see a reorganisation of courts in Greater London, some powers to order re-trials in criminal cases,

ix

and some relief for unassisted litigants who succeed in legal combat against legally assisted plaintiffs.

A most difficult matter is to assess the general progress that has been made in bringing the administration of law nearer to the needs of the present day. In the realm of special tribunals and inquiries leading to decisions of ministers on acquisition of land, planning and similar matters, the legal empire has been greatly extended. I have rewritten much of Chapter VI to give what I feel to be a better description of the arguments and tendencies. Lawyers have succeeded in getting a large measure of 'judicialisation' of these processes, and they are pleased with what they have achieved. Whether the community has gained or lost is another question. One may have a distaste for the proselytising lawyer, whose arrogance about Whitehall and Townhall has little relation to the facts of life, or one may think he is a fine fellow who battles for freedom and justice, but the major point is whether the processes are in fact reasonably fair and reasonably quick. My finding is that any gains the lawyers may have brought to these processes are far outweighed by the delays, cost and uncertainties that have grown with the extension of legal practice. Both of the main political parties recognise that England needs great works to modernise our industrial and commercial equipment, but today England is probably the most difficult country for getting anything done. Our ancestors could get parliamentary powers, acquire land, build a railway and get it into operation in a shorter time than it now takes to get authority to begin on a project. The legal system has been more successful in allowing Rachmanism to flourish than in furthering the policies of decent national development.

In the Preface to the last edition I said that 'in matters that are the special preserve of the lawyers, dust and cobwebs have settled as thickly as ever before.... Turn to the core of the legal world, civil actions in the superior courts, and there is a sorry spectacle.... The talk about justice is admirable, but when people see what is really offered, they find that it is not what they want.' There have since been two independent reports that disclose realities behind the legal facade. In 1960 a Report on Chancery Chambers and Registrars' Offices showed a state of affairs that if it had related to administration other than that of the law would have been regarded as intolerable. In 1961 a Report of the Commercial Court Users' Conference showed why the commercial community has virtually no use for the High Court. The story is the same, all along the line, that the legal processes are not good enough for modern conditions. There is far more to this than a consumers' rebellion at being offered a poor article at a high price. The whole realm of lawyer and litigant is going through a silent revolution through the legal aid service. A vast amount of the work of the civil courts now depends on litigants being assisted persons; the defence of criminal charges is expanding, and virtually all the cost falls on public funds. An action for damages for personal injuries, with its cost and delay, its adversary handling of medical evidence, and its once-for-all lump sum for a successful plaintiff, can hardly be regarded as the best possible way to deal with these cases. The plaintiff these days is more likely than not to be an assisted person. We should not grudge him the money it costs, any more than we should complain about the medical and surgical care falling on the public purse; what we may very properly say is that the legal process should be as rational and well designed as the institutions for medical assistance.

The Lord Chancellor has referred to 'the wind of change being gently felt in the corridors of the law courts'. It is such a gentle wind that the accumulated rubbish of the law is in no danger of being blown away. The need, as great now as at any period of our history, is for the process of the superior courts to be recast and made fit for the kind of society in which we now live.

R. M. J.

CAMBRIDGE
November 1963

PREFACE TO THE FIRST EDITION

The object of this book is to explain the system of law courts and allied matters relating to the administration of justice. In the past the administration of justice has hardly been considered a 'subject'. Writers on constitutional law have included the system of the courts, but necessarily cannot give it much space; other law books are apt to assume that the reader is acquainted with the subject. Thought about law has changed a good deal in the last twenty years. The attempt to treat law as a pure science, isolated from the society it serves, is succumbing to a more sociological approach. To some extent this means that the lawyer must come down from his high perch and look at law in the light of its effects upon individuals and society. The best introduction to law is a study of the institutions and environment in which lawyers work. It is prescribed, under the title of 'The English Legal System', for the first year study in some law schools, although academic tradition has there succeeded in imposing a mass of historical study to satisfy the idea that it is cultural to know what happened in the middle ages and not cultural to know what happens in the twentieth century. My own impression, and I have been teaching this subject for some years, is that the needs of the law student and the needs of those interested in public affairs are here exactly the same— to know the present system for administering justice, how it really works, and what criticisms and suggestions have been made.

As this book is far from being an exhaustive treatise I have omitted a full documentation. References are confined to indicating further reading of a complementary nature, or to giving my sources for subjects that are not well known or statements that would otherwise appear merely dogmatic.

I give my grateful thanks to many people, including practising lawyers and teachers of law, who have helped me by discussion or by reading and criticising sections where their knowledge far exceeded mine.

R. M. J.

CAMBRIDGE
February 1939

CHAPTER I

HISTORICAL INTRODUCTION

I. THE COURTS

The present system of courts of law in England and Wales depends almost entirely on legislation passed during the last hundred years. Yet it is difficult to describe the present system without referring to older courts, since the functions of some of the newer courts were defined in terms of older institutions; the legislative changes did not so much sweep away the debris of centuries as take materials that were to hand and from them fashion a new design. When our superior courts were rehoused in the Strand, in 1882, they were given a huge neo-Gothic building. It would have symbolised our legal institutions much better if the architect had made a building out of all the styles and dates to be found in the country. The past history of our courts is also responsible for a curious distinction being made between courts of law (often called 'ordinary courts') and special tribunals. This is not a distinction of function, but a distinction of age. During the last half-century Parliament has entrusted judicial and quasi-judicial functions to various persons or bodies; if this process had occurred a hundred years or more ago, these tribunals would be 'ordinary' courts. To ignore these tribunals would lead to a lop-sided view of the administration of justice. There are, however, advantages in first discussing the system of 'ordinary' courts, for they are still the most important part of our system, and further because it is largely the limitation of 'ordinary' judicial process that has led to the creation of special administrative tribunals. This problem is discussed in chapter VI.

Today we generally assume that the administration of justice is a function of government to be exercised by the State. We express this in terms of the Sovereign, and speak of the King's (now the Queen's) judges, the King's or Queen's courts, and H.M. prisons, just as we speak of the Royal Mail and H.M. ships of war. But if we consider the early history of our courts we find entirely different conceptions. In the Norman period the King's Court was merely one of many courts. There were old local courts surviving from Anglo-Saxon times. These were the courts of the County[1] and of the Hundred,

---

[1] The ancient County Court must not be confused with the present-day County Court, on which see p. 28, below.

which was a subdivision of the County. Both County and Hundred courts had a wide jurisdiction over both civil and criminal offences. Feudal courts arose from the principle that any overlord who had tenants enough could hold a court for his tenants. In theory the feudal courts had no criminal jurisdiction, but in practice they dealt with minor offences. The King also had his court. All these courts were concerned with a great deal of business other than the trying of cases. In fact, the early King's Court was far more concerned with non-litigious matters than with litigation, for it was in effect the machinery of central government: it was composed of the great officers of State and such other men as the King chose to summon, and that assembly, sometimes large and sometimes small, legislated and administered and judged. The holding of courts was not thought of as being a public service. The right to hold a court, and take the profit to be made, was more in the nature of private property. It was on the same footing as the right to run a ferry and exclude anyone else from running a ferry in competition. These were called franchises, which always signified the exclusive right of a private person to exercise functions which we now consider should be in public hands. Privately run jurisdiction no more shocked the conscience of the Norman period than privately owned land shocks our conscience today.

The early development of the judicial machinery centred round one process: the King's Court gradually ousted most of the other courts and took over their work. This was not a sudden process. No frontal attack could be made, because the issues were those of property. A decree that feudal courts or franchise courts were to be abolished would have been an expropriation of property, hardly distinguishable from seizing rents due from other people's tenants. The success of the King's Court was due to the fact that the King offered better justice—his courts were selling a better and more reliable commodity. The first great steps were taken under Henry II, and the system he devised was good enough to withstand the upheavals under John. Magna Carta was, on the whole, an attempt to safeguard the rights of the propertied classes in the kingdom, and it included one clause designed to stop the King from taking work from feudal courts, but apart from this it accepted the existing judicial system. During the thirteenth century the King's Court steadily increased its jurisdiction, partly by inventing judicial remedies that no other court was able to offer. Royal justice was the most popular justice. The increasing business led to institutional changes. The old King's Court or Council split into several different institutions, with far more specialised functions. These divisions, or the germs of them, can all be seen in the thirteenth century, but it is easier to take stock of the changes when they are completed in the late fourteenth century.

The judicial activities of the King's Court were separated from the general governmental activities, and this separation led to a change in nomenclature. 'King's Court' then signified judicial institutions, and 'King's Council' was applied to the assemblies the King held for carrying on his government. The King's Council continued to be sometimes large and sometimes small; the small council was a group of officials and advisers in more or less continuous session; the large council was convened when matters of great importance arose. The beginning of Parliament in the late thirteenth century was in essence a strengthening of advisers to the King: the small council is reinforced by the great men of the realm, and this is reinforced by representatives of the counties and boroughs, that is, the commons. During the fourteenth century the great men are only summoned when the commons are summoned—the large council becomes the House of Lords. 'The Council' from the fourteenth century onwards is the small group of advisers and officials. The judicial work had been a council activity, but gradually it had come to be exercised in definite institutions which lost touch with the council and emerged as three independent law courts. There was overlapping of the jurisdiction of these courts, but the main line was that disputes between subject and subject should be brought in the Court of Common Pleas, cases where the King was particularly concerned (such as control over inferior tribunals and royal officials) went to the Court of King's Bench, and revenue cases went to the Court of Exchequer. These three were central courts sitting at Westminster, and they were staffed (by the close of the fourteenth century) by professional judges appointed by the King from the ranks of the practising barristers. They were known as the *common law* courts, to distinguish them from the ecclesiastical courts and other tribunals with special jurisdiction. The expression *common law* is discussed in the next section.

The common law system also included the Assize Courts. From early Norman times the King had sent trusted persons to visit the counties for various purposes. Domesday Book was compiled from the answers to inquiries made by itinerant commissioners. The purpose of a 'judicial visitation' and the authority for the activities of

the commissioners was contained in the terms of the royal commission; it might be a comprehensive overhaul of the administration
of a county or it might be limited to a few matters upon which the
King wanted information. At first these commissioners exercised
very little judicial authority, being far more concerned with making
inquiries into matters where the King might have a fiscal interest, but
eventually their judicial activities became the main purpose of their
visits: they became itinerant justices, and each county was visited
three or four times a year. The commission usually instructed the
itinerant to hear and determine allegations of serious crime, the
lesser offences being dealt with locally by the sheriff and later by
justices of the peace. Virtually all criminal trials therefore took place
in the county where the crime was committed. Civil litigation could
be in a local court if the sum in dispute were small,[1] but all cases of
importance tended to go to one of the common law courts at Westminster. Since trial was frequently by jury, and early juries were
essentially neighbour witnesses, the parties to the suit and the
jurymen would all have to travel to Westminster, which might be
a grievous burden on them. The comparative excellence of the central
courts was somewhat discounted by the distance that might separate
a litigant from the fountain of justice. To meet this it was provided
in 1285 that an action could be begun in one of the common law
courts at Westminster and would be set down to be tried there,
unless first (*nisi prius*) a justice of Assize should visit the county. The
practical working was that the action was started at Westminster,
the actual hearing took place in the county before the iterant
justice, and the formal judgment was made at Westminster; the
proceedings at Westminster could be conducted by attorneys and
counsel, so that the parties, witnesses and jurymen would have to
attend only at the Assize Court in the county town. Hence the
itinerant justices when they visited the counties had to do both
criminal and civil work. This is still the position, although since
1875 the whole of a civil case (that is, the commencement and judgment as well as the hearing) takes place in the Assize town, and we
talk of the 'civil side' instead of 'nisi prius'. The old language is
preserved in some Assize Court buildings, where one of the court
rooms bears the legend 'Crown Court' and is used for the trial of
prisoners, whilst the other is labelled 'Nisi Prius Court' and is used

---

[1] The Statute of Gloucester 1278 provided that cases under 40s. should not be
brought in the superior courts, but the judges interpreted this to mean that cases
involving more than 40s. could not be brought in inferior courts.

for civil cases. The expression 'itinerant justice' suggests that he is a professional judge: strictly speaking he was, and is, a person commissioned by the King. The hearing of civil cases at Assizes stressed the need for the itinerant to be a lawyer of adequate standing, and the practice grew up of giving such commissions to the judges of the common law courts. The Assize Court judge sits as commissioner, and not by virtue of his office as judge. This principle is useful, because judges, like other people, are apt at times to get bad colds and influenza, and there may not be enough judges to go on circuit; some eminent barrister who is named in the commission can then be asked to act as Assize Court judge.[1]

It thus appears that in the fourteenth century England had a fairly comprehensive judicial system, the Assize Courts being a happy compromise between centralisation and decentralisation: the best available justice was brought to the counties, points of law were chiefly argued at Westminster, and law throughout the realm tended to be uniform.[2] This was, however, achieved at the expense of flexibility. Our thirteenth-century judges considered that they were empowered to do what justice demanded: after the early fourteenth century the judges considered that their duty was to apply the law. 'Justice' and 'Justice according to the law' are different conceptions; a man has the latter if his case has been fairly tried and the law has been accurately ascertained and applied to the facts, even if the result offends the general idea of what is 'justice'. Common law was narrow, and dominated by technicality; the merits of a case might be totally obscured by a fog of procedure. Further, especially in the fifteenth century, a litigant might be deprived of remedies at common law through the activities of 'over-mighty subjects'; juries and even judges were often intimidated by powerful men. Many would-be litigants thought that common law would not or could not give them justice, and in such cases they adopted the expedient of petitioning the King. Since the King acted through his Council the petition might be addressed to the King, or Council, or to individual councillors. The Council was the government of the country, and was generally disinclined to waste its time considering petitions. Some petitions raised points in which the Council felt a real interest: piracy might lead to disputes with a foreign prince, and certain kinds

[1] In recent years there has been extensive use of commissioners for dealing with divorce cases (see p. 57, below).

[2] In addition to the courts already mentioned, there were many courts with special jurisdiction. Ecclesiastical courts were the most important.

of disorder may directly affect the government. But most of the petitions were disposed of by telling the petitioner to go to common law or by handing the petition over to the Lord Chancellor to investigate. At first the Chancellor investigated it with the help of a few councillors; later he did it alone, and reported his conclusion to the Council, who then made such decree as they saw fit. By the late fifteenth century, petitioners frequently sent their petitions direct to the Chancellor, and he investigated the case, and himself made the decree. When this stage is reached it becomes proper to speak of the Court of Chancery. The medieval Chancellor was the general secretary of state, and he was also an ecclesiastic; his idea of justice was very different from that of the common law judges. We do not know very much about the methods of the Chancellor in the earlier days, but in the sixteenth century there was a regular Chancery Court and its practice is fairly well known. The guiding principle of Chancery was 'conscience', which was of course no precise guide, but meant that relief would be given to a petitioner if the Chancellor thought that good conscience entitled him to a remedy. Within that vague limit, the work of Chancery was supplementary to that of common law.

During the sixteenth century the Council was re-organised. Some councillors were assigned to attendance on the King, and these formed what was later called the Privy Council. Others were to stay at Westminster to do routine work. Most of the routine work was of a judicial nature, being a continuation of the judicial activities of the Council: this became known as the Court of Star Chamber. Other courts closely connected with the Star Chamber were also set up. The political conflicts of the seventeenth century brought all courts connected with the Council into dispute, and in 1641 the Star Chamber and allied courts were abolished; the Court of Chancery survived.

A review of the law courts under Charles II shows the old three common law courts, Assizes, and the Court of Chancery dominating the scene.[1] The common lawyers, siding with the successful parliamentarians, had got rid of serious competition from Council courts, had captured the commercial work previously done in the Court of Admiralty, and prevented any extension of ecclesiastical courts. The old division of work between the Exchequer, Common Pleas, and King's Bench had broken down; by ingenious fictions litigants could bring ordinary actions in whichever court they preferred. The

[1] The Courts of Justices of the Peace are discussed later on p. 94.

King's Bench benefited most by this change, and became the most important of the common law courts. The Court of Chancery was no longer attacked: it was accepted, and invaded by the common lawyers. The old idea of 'conscience' slowly suffered an eclipse. Chancery was still said to be a court of 'equity', but equity ceased to be a fluid thing and became a set of rules. This is shown very clearly by the use of decided cases. Down to 1700 there are over a hundred volumes of reports of common law cases, and only eighteen volumes of Chancery cases, and few of these contain decisions earlier than 1660. For the eighteenth century there are almost as many Chancery reports as common law reports. Eighteenth-century Chancellors had received the same training as common lawyers, and they ran their court in much the same way, seeking for definite rules to be found in and deduced from previous decisions. In fact common law and equity (using this term in its technical sense of the rules applied in the Court of Chancery) were approaching each other so fast that Blackstone saw little difference between them. By the early nineteenth century a working partnership was well established. Equity was a gloss on common law: it was a set of rules which could be invoked to supplement the deficiencies of common law or to ease the clumsy working of common law actions and remedies.

During the nineteenth century other superior courts were set up. In 1857 the jurisdiction of ecclesiastical courts over wills and intestacies and matrimonial cases was abolished, and a Probate Court and a Divorce Court were established. Special provision was made for bankruptcy proceedings. Further, the elaborate and exceedingly inefficient system of appeal courts was mended piecemeal. There was no lack of superior courts: the trouble was mostly one of overlapping jurisdictions, varying procedure, and lack of co-ordination. A complete re-organisation was made by the Judicature Acts 1873-5. The courts numbered 1-12 in Table I were abolished. A Supreme Court of Judicature was established, divided into the High Court and the Court of Appeal. The jurisdiction formerly possessed by courts here numbered 1-8 was conferred on the High Court, and the former jurisdiction of courts 9-12 was (with modifications and additions) conferred upon the Court of Appeal. The High Court was divided into five divisions and Assizes, but in 1881 three of the divisions were consolidated: the High Court now consists of the Chancery, Queen's Bench, Probate Divorce and Admiralty Divisions, and the Assize Courts.

The scheme of the Judicature Acts 1873-5 has been retained; the

7

present authority is the Supreme Court of Judicature (Consolidation) Act 1925 together with subsequent amendments.

The Judicature Acts ended the separation of 'law' and 'equity'. The High Court succeeded to the jurisdiction of the old common law courts and the old Court of Chancery, and so can do anything that any of those could have done. The rules of common law and the rules of equity were not fused: the provision made was that *all* courts should apply and use both sets of rules. In a case of a conflict of rules, equity must prevail. The nature of common law and equitable remedies is retained. Suppose that *X* has a house on the edge of his land, with windows looking over land belonging to *Y*, and that *X* has acquired a right to light, sometimes called 'ancient lights'. If *Y* builds on his land so as to block *X*'s windows, then *Y* has infringed *X*'s rights: *X*'s remedy at common law is to sue *Y* and recover damages. The remedy in equity would be to ask the court to grant an injunction prohibiting *Y* from erecting the building, or, if the building is already erected, to command *Y* to pull it down. The court is not bound to grant an injunction. The judge will consider, among other things, whether the infringement is serious or trifling, and whether *X* has behaved reasonably; if *Y* had no reason to think that *X* had such a right, and *X* did not protest but waited until the building was completed, then the court might say that *X*'s conduct was such that he should not have an injunction. All equitable remedies are discretionary, but the discretion is exercised according to well-known principles. The common law remedy of damages is 'as of right'—if the right is infringed then damages *must* be given, but these may be very small if the plaintiff has not suffered substantially. Further, we still keep an ancient distinction between methods of enforcing a remedy. If damages awarded are not paid, the normal process is for the sheriff's officers to seize some property of the defendant, sell it, and hand the proceeds to the plaintiff. An equitable remedy is enforced by commanding the defendant to do or not do some specific act; if he disobeys the command, then he can be imprisoned for contempt of court, which means that he stays in prison until he apologises and 'purges his contempt' by being obedient. Since law and equity are now administered by all courts, an action for infringement of 'ancient lights' would normally be for damages for the past and an injunction for the future, both claims being made in the same action.

The growth and expansion of the King's Courts was doubtless an excellent thing for the building of a uniform law and standard

Table I. *Structure of superior courts of law*

Superior courts in the nineteenth century prior to the
Judicature Act 1873

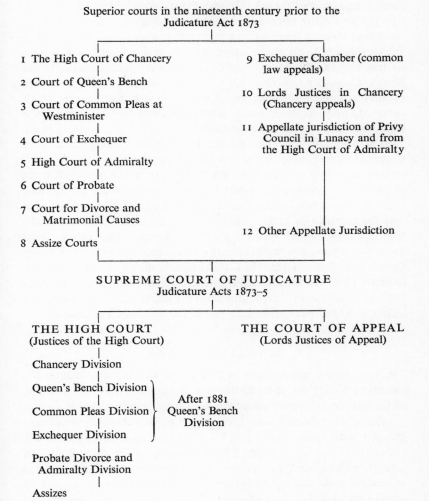

1 The High Court of Chancery

2 Court of Queen's Bench

3 Court of Common Pleas at
  Westminister

4 Court of Exchequer

5 High Court of Admiralty

6 Court of Probate

7 Court for Divorce and
  Matrimonial Causes

8 Assize Courts

9 Exchequer Chamber (common
  law appeals)

10 Lords Justices in Chancery
   (Chancery appeals)

11 Appellate jurisdiction of Privy
   Council in Lunacy and from
   the High Court of Admiralty

12 Other Appellate Jurisdiction

SUPREME COURT OF JUDICATURE
Judicature Acts 1873–5

THE HIGH COURT
(Justices of the High Court)

Chancery Division

Queen's Bench Division

Common Pleas Division

Exchequer Division

After 1881
Queen's Bench
Division

Probate Divorce and
Admiralty Division

Assizes

THE COURT OF APPEAL
(Lords Justices of Appeal)

HOUSE OF LORDS. Final Court of Appeal for Great Britain and (now
Northern) Ireland. (Lords of Appeal in Ordinary.) Appellate Jurisdiction Act
1876.

9

of justice in the country, but it was achieved at the expense of competing courts which were perhaps more suitable for poor litigants and small cases. The greatest number of disputes relate to small sums of money, and most of the inhabitants of this country have little money. The King's Courts offered trial at Westminster, or at Assizes held at most four times a year; neither proceeding was cheap. There had in Tudor times been an attempt by the creation of a Court of Requests to deal with small cases and poor litigants, but it was too close to the King's Council to survive the political storms of the seventeenth century. In many of the ancient towns there were local courts which survived, and some of these were improved by statutes of the eighteenth and early nineteenth centuries. There was no system at all. This was largely remedied by the creation of County Courts by statute in 1846. The passing of this Act was not easy. Lord Brougham's propaganda had to overcome an opposition which included most of the legal profession. Several changes have been made since 1846, but the main outline has not been altered.[1] The general idea was the creation of local courts to deal with small civil cases. The title 'County Court' was singularly ill-chosen, since these courts have no connection with counties. The organisation of County Courts is explained later. The County Courts may be likened to a new industry that is in broad outline planned from its inception, whereas the rest of our courts represent an old industry that has been subjected to a 'rationalisation scheme' at the hands of Parliament.

2. THE COMMON LAW

The expression *common law* originally came into use through the canonists. 'They use it to distinguish the general and ordinary law of the universal church both from any rules peculiar to this or that provincial church, and from those papal *privilegia* which are always giving rise to ecclesiastical litigation.'[2] The phrase passed from the canonists to the lay lawyers. The emergence of the three courts of Common Pleas, King's Bench and Exchequer gave England a system of courts with wide jurisdiction. The judges were appointed to administer the 'law and custom of the realm', which meant that (apart from the small amount of law enacted by the King and Council, or later Parliament) the judges built up their own set of

[1] The statutory provisions are now consolidated in the County Courts Act 1959.
[2] Pollock and Maitland, *History of English Law*, I, 176.

principles and rules. Their material consisted of general and local custom, and the juridical ideas of an age in which theology and law shared the hegemony of intellectual effort. The different 'laws' that had governed various parts of England tended to disappear. There emerged a general body of principles and rules that were applied in the King's Courts at Westminster and carried through the realm by Assize the judges on their circuits. This part of the law was 'common', and to be contrasted with anything that was particular, extraordinary or special, such as surviving local custom, canon law, or Roman law. The essence of common law was that it grew through judicial decisions recorded by lawyers.

The use of reports of decisions in past cases is not a phenomenon peculiar to English lawyers, although the actual technique they have developed is highly specialised. The tendency to look to past practice for guidance is prevalent in meetings and other organised activities. The appeal to the past minutes of clubs and societies is a familiar proceeding, and one would, for example, expect a local Jubilee Celebration Committee to begin its work by looking over the records of previous celebrations. The judicial use of precedents is a more formalised method of following what is really a widespread habit of mind. In the first place, the material is carefully selected and prepared. Every case in the superior courts has an official 'record', but that contains merely the bare bones of the case. It is only a few of the cases heard that raise any points of interest to lawyers, and these become the 'reported' cases. A report, unlike the record, contains the facts as found by the court, the arguments put forward, and the reasons given by the judge for coming to his decision. Law reports are essential for the working of the common law, and so it might be expected that law reporting would be an official activity, but this is not so: from the earliest times down to the present day the making of law reports has (with trifling exceptions) been left to private enterprise. For the fourteenth and fifteenth centuries we have a series of jottings made in court, known as the Year Books: they do not contain reports of cases as we understand that term, but are more notes of points that would be of use to practitioners. In the sixteenth century several volumes of reports were published, either because the author felt certain that if he did not publish the work someone would pirate the manuscript or because there was a market for such books. The following two centuries saw little change in the methods. Lawyers, learned and otherwise, collected accounts of cases and published them as they saw fit. The quality of the older reports varies immensely; for some years there are excellent reports, whilst other years produced no good reporting. Towards the end of the eighteenth century a firm of publishers began to issue reports at regular intervals. During the nineteenth century the proprietors of legal periodicals began to issue series of reports, some of which are still current. From 1866 onwards we have what are known simply as 'The Law Reports': these are produced by a co-operative system set up by the legal profession. The new co-operative system did not displace the older method of publishing for profit, and the then existing series of reports continued to be published. Enterprising law publishers have since started a new series of general reports and some further series on special subjects. The Law Reports have always been fully revised by the judges but publication has been somewhat slow; another series has offered speedy publication that is necessarily unrevised. No series is comprehensive, and the particular case one wants may not be in the series that one has available. The practitioner cannot afford all the series. A Committee[1] failed to find a satisfactory solution, but the problem may be solving itself. Recently three series of general reports have stopped publication, and The Law Reports now combine speed with accuracy by offering two versions, one weekly and the other fully revised.

The use of decided cases by our courts has changed in the course of time. No hard and fast system was possible until the days of printed books: before that time, judges were concerned to be consistent, and a barrister who could point to a course of judicial conduct would generally be able to convince a judge that he ought to follow the practice of his brethren or predecessors. After printed reports became available during the sixteenth century there was more precision in citation; cases are cited by name and the court is expected to follow them. But the judge was not *bound* to follow earlier decisions: the older view was 'that precedent is evidence, the

[1] In 1939 the Lord Chancellor appointed a Committee to 'report and advise him in regard to representations that had been made from several quarters to the effect that the great number of Law Reports which appeared to be increasing was causing difficulty to members of both branches of the profession engaged in the actual work of the Courts by reason of their multiplicity, of the expense occasioned by the necessity for purchasing them and the pressure on space available for the storage of books, and that similar difficulties arose in the case of those bodies which maintain Law Libraries and those who teach law'. The Committee reported in March 1940, and the result of their labours is contained in two sentences of their Report: 'That there are inconveniences, to say the least, in the present state of affairs, we are not prepared to deny. But we cannot recommend any cure for them which would not bring greater evils in its train' (para. 24 of the Report of the Law Reporting Committee, 1940).

best possible evidence, of rules of law, but *not more than that*; and that if the law which precedent purports to embody is erroneous, unreasonable, or even intolerably inconvenient, the precedent may be disregarded'.[1] This attitude lasted until about the middle of the last century, when a further hardening took place and our courts adopted a theory of 'absolutely binding' precedent. In the modern theory, the decisions of a court bind all inferior tribunals. In 1861 the House of Lords decided that it could not reverse its own prior decisions, so that a House of Lords' decision is binding on every court in our system, of which that House is the apex. Other decisions are binding or not according to the court that decided and the court in which they are cited: thus, a High Court decision is binding in a County Court, can be 'disregarded' by another High Court judge, and can be 'overruled' by the Court of Appeal.[2] This rigid system is in practice more flexible than it appears to be. What is binding is the principle on which a judgment is based, and a tiresome precedent can sometimes be circumvented by the casuistry known as 'distinguishing', or by saying that the 'decision must be regarded as having been given upon the peculiar facts'. The theory and practice of precedent is a highly controversial topic at present, and no short discussion can possibly do justice to the various contentions. The most curious thing about these controversies is that those who defend our present practice generally do so upon the ground that it is a well-tried technique that has been responsible for the growth of our common law: the historical fact is that our common law was created and fashioned by an older and more liberal tradition in which the notion of absolutely binding precedent was completely absent.

In a narrow sense common law is the result of the system of precedent used in the common law courts, that is, the old courts of Common Pleas, King's Bench and Exchequer, and in more modern times the King's Bench Division of the High Court. The place of statute law must, however, be considered. Our earliest enacted law was made by the King with the concurrence of his Council, and then, as Parliament became the accepted institution, by statute. The

---

[1] C. K. Allen in 51 *Law Quarterly Review* (1935), p. 333.

[2] There had been some doubt whether the Court of Appeal is bound by its own decisions, but, in *Young* v. *Bristol Aeroplane Co. Ltd.* [1944] K.B. 718, the Court of Appeal decided that it is absolutely bound by its prior decisions subject to certain exceptions. There are a number of difficulties, but the whole subject of precedent is fraught with difficulties which grow worse as the volume of legal writing increases. R. Cross, *Precedent in English Law* (1961), is a good guide to the mystique of case-law.

early form of statutes was amorphous, and the judges might query the existence of a statute or its exact terms. By Tudor times statutes had taken the form in which they are still cast, that is, an enactment by the King with the advice and consent of the Lords and Commons and by authority of the same. In fact the judges accepted the authority of statute law, although as late as Blackstone in the eighteenth century it was still customary to suggest that judges might disregard a statute that infringed natural or divine law. If the Stuarts had been successful in their controversies with Parliament we should have had a different legal order, but those controversies settled the question of the highest authority in the State: the common law judges, secure in the knowledge that their courts could not be overruled by prerogative courts, finally accepted the political fact of the dominant position of Parliament. It thus became an indisputable dogma that anything Parliament enacts will be accepted as law by our courts. Until after the Reform Act of 1832 the part played by statutes was not very great. The judges took the view that the law built up from precedents was the real body of the law, and that statutes were a kind of excrescence that, however useful, disfigured the otherwise harmonious form of their system. Statutes were construed to be in conformity with the common law whenever that was possible. The older statutes had been so construed, and had become surrounded with such a mass of case-law that lawyers usually thought of the case-law and not of the statute. The legislation of the last hundred years, and particularly of the last fifty years, has raised a difficult problem; this is discussed in chapter VI. The phrase 'common law' may be used to include statute, or to exclude it, according to context; it depends upon whether we are thinking of the whole body of law administered by the common law courts, or of the principles and rules that rest entirely upon precedent.

The growth of the Chancery Court has been mentioned in the last section. When the early nebulous character of this jurisdiction suffered a metamorphosis in the eighteenth century it came to look much like common law. 'Equity' came to mean the principles and rules acted upon in the Chancery Court; the essence of equity came to be precedent, although precedents in equity were worked in a more flexible way, since it was never possible to suppose that they were anything but relatively recent creations. The men who worked the Chancery system received what training they had in the Inns of Court, alongside those who practised in common law. The Lord Chancellor, being a political appointment, was frequently a man whose practice had been in common law. Since equity was a system complementary to the common law, and chiefly to be distinguished because it gave different remedies, the antithesis of 'law' and 'equity' is frequently used. When lawyers say that a remedy is 'legal' or 'equitable', they mean that the remedy in question has certain characteristics derived from the court in which it was devised.

Whatever court we turn to in our system, the authoritative sources of the law are confined to statute and reported decisions. The works of jurists, ancient or modern, may be of great assistance, and in practice a text writer of great standing may influence the court more than some obscure and ill-reported case, but in theory there is a definite line between the authoritative and the unauthoritative. The primary duty of a judge is, of course, to dispose of the case before him, and to do this he proceeds upon the supposition that the authoritative legal sources enable him to state the law. In most cases this is true, but when new points arise that supposition becomes a pious fiction. In form the judge then deduces some rule from the accepted material; in reality he consciously or subconsciously invents a rule that appears to be not inconsistent with accepted doctrine, and announces that that *is* the law of England, thus implying that judges merely declare the law and do not make it. This habit of mind is so ingrained that the common law is often thought of as a comprehensive body of law that has always existed, although every practitioner in searching precedents is engaged upon tracing the growth of some part of the law.

In a wide sense the expression 'common law' is used to mean the legal system and habits of legal thought that Englishmen have evolved. In this sense it is contrasted with systems of law derived from Roman law. It has been a principle of our law that when new lands have been settled by colonisation the settlers carry with them the law of England as far as it is applicable to the new conditions, whereas in territories acquired from a civilised power the existing law remains in force until the new sovereign alters the law. Hence in the Commonwealth the common law of England is the basis of the system where colonisation occurred, but where there was an existing system (as French law in Lower Canada and Roman-Dutch law in South Africa) the basis of the law is generally that of our predecessors, France, Holland or Spain. This principle led to the North American colonies having the common law, a heritage that was undisturbed when they became the United States. In the British Isles, the English system has dominated Wales and Ireland, but not Scotland, which retains a separate system of law in the Roman tradition and a separate system of courts. The Irish courts, although following the English pattern, are a separate system. The subject of this book is the English system in the narrow sense of that which applies to England and Wales, but since it is part of a wider conception it is relevant to consider the differences that exist between the common law systems and those founded on Roman law.

The common law or Roman law is the basis of most modern systems. The Roman law is not of course the law of the second century, but the law of Justinian overlaid with gloss and comment and comment on the comment until it sometimes has no apparent connection with the original texts. The tradition of codification has been largely responsible for the spread of modern Romanesque law. For instance, Japan, in the desire to modernise her law, would have preferred to adapt English law, but it was impracticable to import a system of law that could not be found in any concise form. The codes of France and Germany offered intelligible material in an accessible form, and so the Far East and the countries of South America turned to these Romanesque codes for study and adaptation. The division of countries into common law and Romanesque law is easy to make, but it is not a simple matter to be sure of the distinguishing marks. A distinguished jurist has explained that 'there is indubitably something which enables English and Irish and American and Canadian and Australian lawyers to read each other's books and understand each other's arguments and apply each other's judicial decisions and adapt each other's legislation as surely as they are unable to understand the arguments and read effectively the books and apply the authoritative texts of the non-English-speaking world. This is something we call the common law. But what is it?'[1] To some extent it is a matter of vocabulary. Technical legal terms can rarely be translated into a foreign language. Our word 'freehold' can be explained in French in a page or so of type, but it cannot be translated, for French law has no legal concept that is exactly equivalent. Many of our terms are Norman-French and Latin, but the same difficulties arise. On the other hand, the Roman law terms provide the Romanesque system with a common basis of reference. For instance, suppose that your neighbour is away on his Christmas holidays, and during his absence a storm damages his roof; you are

---

[1] Roscoe Pound in *The Future of the Common Law*. This volume contains addresses on this title given by distinguished lawyers in 1936 to a conference at the tercentenary celebrations of Harvard College.

unable to get in touch with him, and so act as a good neighbour and instruct a builder to repair the damage before further and more extensive damage occurs; then your neighbour refuses to pay the bill, and the builder says that you must pay since you instructed him to do the work. English law says that generally there is no obligation to indemnify a person who has voluntarily incurred expense in protecting the interests of another in his absence. Roman law recognised an obligation, called *negotiorum gestio*. So that, if we wished to make a symposium of foreign law on this matter, we could simply ask foreign jurists if their law recognises *negotiorum gestio*, and thereby avoid the pitfalls of rendering 'obligation', 'indemnify', 'voluntary' and 'interests' into several foreign languages. The problem of language must not be overlooked, but it does not supply a complete explanation.

Among suggested differences is the part that case-law plays in the common law, but the Romanesque systems make considerable use of precedent. French case-law is voluminous and essential to the working of their courts: there is no rule of absolutely binding precedent, but such a rule is only a recent addition to the English tradition. Again, jury trial has been singled out, but jury trial has spread widely in the Romanesque system. The 'rule of law' is often instanced. If this means merely public order and civil liberties, we can claim no monopoly: if it means the constitutional position of our Parliament and courts, it does not exist in the United States: if it means that the powers of the government are derived from law, then it is characteristic of every state.[1] It is a pity that such a high-sounding phrase, suggestive of a decent international and social order, should have acquired too many meanings to be of much use.

There is one distinction between the common law and the Romanesque systems that does, I think, give the key to the differences. It is the position of the judge. Where the Roman law tradition holds, a lawyer must choose at an early age whether he is going to practise before the courts or whether he is going on the bench. The judiciary is part of the administrative hierarchy; a young man starts as an assistant in a very inferior court and slowly works up to more exalted judicial status. This does not mean that he is a civil servant acting under the orders of a government department in all matters,

---

[1] The 'rule of law' as a characteristic of our system is principally associated with Dicey, *Law of the Constitution*, first published in 1885 and now edited by E. C. S. Wade. The phrase as used by many lawyers today has a different and less precise meaning; (see pp. 367–73, below).

but it does mean that the judiciary is a separate profession from the practising lawyer.[1] The English tradition, examined more fully in chapter IV, is that the legal profession is practically an autonomous body, the judges being drawn from its ranks when they are not less than middle-aged. The theory is that the best practising lawyers are ultimately elevated to the judiciary, where the terms of their appointment ensure that they shall be independent of administrative interference. Hence for the common lawyer the revered figure and the oracle is the judge. We should seek for the nature of English law not in its substantive rules but in its machinery of justice.

3. TRIAL AT COMMON LAW

It is generally accepted that there have been two main systems of trial in civilised law, the Accusatorial and the Inquisitorial. At the time of the foundation of our legal system in the twelfth and thirteenth centuries, common law procedure was accusatorial; the parties came before the court upon an equal footing, the court giving no help to either of them, it being the duty of the one party to formulate his grievance and of the other party to deny it. The mode of trial was some type of ordeal, which was *judicium dei*: the judgment was that of God, not that of the president of the court. A dislike of such proceedings was manifested by the Church. When, for instance, it was alleged that a priest was not conducting himself properly the ecclesiastical superiors showed little enthusiasm for a trial by *judicium dei*; the twelfth-century technique was to send a trusted person along to inquire into the allegations. This founded the inquisitorial concept of a trial, whereby the judge is expected to find out for himself what has happened, and he will do this by examining all persons, including the accused or suspected person, who may be able to enlighten him. In the thirteenth century the inquisitorial system represented the cause of progress, and eventually became the accepted theory on the Continent. The English kept to the accusatorial theory, partly because of an insular dislike for things foreign and partly because of the emergence of jury trial. Jury trial simply replaced trial by ordeal, the verdict of the jury having the same finality and the same inscrutability as the judgment of God. With a workable method of trial there was no need to import

---

[1] This does not prevent some appointments to the bench being made from practising lawyers or from academic lawyers. In England academic lawyers may have the formal qualifications for the bench, but they are not appointed.

foreign or ecclesiastical ideas, and, when the inquisitorial system resorted to torture, the English lawyer could feel that his system was superior. The emergence of the Chancery Court in the fifteenth century introduced the ideas of the inquisitorial system, for the Chancellor adopted the canon law theory of a trial. The Chancellors considered that their function was to get to the bottom of the cases submitted to them, and to do this they must interrogate those concerned, either by oral examination or by compelling one party to answer on oath a string of written questions. Further, a party could be compelled to give 'discovery', which means that he must disclose all documents he has that relate to the case. Now the Chancellor came to deal exclusively with civil actions, and here his notions have prevailed. Before the Judicature Acts 1873–5 a litigant at common law could seek assistance from the Chancellor in such matters as discovery, whereas, under our present system, all civil courts can order a party to answer interrogatories or make discovery of his documents. The Chancellor did not have occasion to touch our criminal law, and so in criminal trials there is none of this compulsory interrogating. English civil proceedings must, therefore, be classed as inquisitorial, and English criminal proceedings as accusatorial, whereas the Romanesque countries that invented the inquisitorial process use it for their criminal proceedings but retain a rigid accusatorial theory for civil litigation.

The distinction between the accusatorial and the inquisitorial system is one that has been made for centuries, and as a historical fact it has great importance, but it is perhaps of less use today than the distinction between what may be called the 'contest' theory and the inquisitorial theory of a trial. The interrogation of the defendant is the outward sign of the inquisitorial system, but it is historically no more than an incident in the performance of the judicial office: the fundamental idea of inquisitorial proceedings is that the judge must himself investigate a complaint, find out the facts for himself, and then do what ought to be done according to law. Early English Chancery proceedings show this; the petitions were often little more than an allegation that the defendant was 'a bad lot', with very sketchy accounts of his ill-doings, the request in the petition being that the Chancellor would investigate and do right in the matter. At common law we find a different conception. The judge is thought of as an umpire who must see fair play between two contesting parties. Whether the case was civil or criminal, it was the complainant who selected the precise ground of his complaint. The common law system of 'pleadings' was designed to reduce a case to one issue, either of fact or of law, so that when the case came before the court for trial the parties had already formulated the question that was to be answered; if the point was one of law it would be decided by the judges, whilst if it was one of fact it would go to the jury. The judges could, of course, see that the process of the court was not abused, but otherwise their function was confined to the issue that was before them. If the parties had selected the wrong issue, then the judge might point out what would have been the correct issue, but it was no part of the judicial duty to see that the court got to the bottom of a case and dealt with the true grounds of the dispute. Following the analogy of the judge as umpire, we can say that the parties selected the game that was to be played and the umpire saw that the game was properly played. The idea of a contest has survived in our law. Chancery actions slowly came to resemble common law actions in many respects; the pleadings, originally designed to assist the Chancellor in elucidating the facts, came more and more to formulate the issue that was to be decided by the court. The modern law of pleading in civil cases has given far more scope for amending pleadings so that the right issue is raised, but it is still true that the responsibility for selecting the proper grounds both for the plaintiff and the defendant rests on the parties. In criminal cases the basic rule is still that the defendant must be charged with a definite offence, and he must be acquitted if that offence is not proved even if it appears to the court that he has committed some other offence:[1] the judge is not an inquisitor who must find out whether the defendant has broken the law, but an umpire who is limited to the issue raised between the Crown and the defendant.

It was implicit in the common law conception of a trial that it was a culmination; the day comes when the issues that have been settled and defined by pleadings come before the court. Under an inquisitorial system the judge will collect evidence and material from the time when he becomes seized of the case, and hearings and final trial are essentially to make sure that the file or dossier is completed by representations on fact or law from those who are involved. In contrast the common law process was geared to jury trial. Once the pleadings showed an issue for a jury, the case had to be presented as a

---

[1] There are now many statutory exceptions, and where these apply it is possible for a man to be charged with offence A and convicted of offence B: these have been introduced where offences A and B are similar, or where B is less heinous than A.

whole, at one hearing. That was the 'day in court' which in a criminal case decided guilt or innocence and sentence and in a civil case decided liability and amount of damages. It was a public process, and it could hardly have been otherwise; the jury was traditionally the neighbours, and they were supposed to know about the facts. That slowly changed until juries were expected to decide on the evidence put before them, but the jury was still a man's 'country' to whose verdict he committed himself, and Assizes and Quarter Sessions were the periodical assemblies for the most important kinds of public business. A man might be hanged, or cast in damages, by the same process that could determine liability to remove an obstruction of the highway or repair a bridge. Open court was not derived from liberal thought but was an almost inevitable consequence of our system of courts and use of juries.

The contrast can be seen on the history of matrimonial proceedings. When these came before ecclesiastical courts the facts were ascertained by examiners who inquired in private and reported to the court, which gave judgment in public. The jurisdiction passed to a lay court in 1857 and became amalgamated with the other superior courts in 1873. It seems that the Divorce Court sometimes directed that evidence should be taken in camera. The legality of such a direction, given in a nullity suit in the interests of public decency, came before the House of Lords in 1913 in *Scott* v. *Scott*.[1] The Lord Chancellor and the Law Lords regarded the principle of open court as fundamental and proceeded to examine the exceptions. The affairs of wards of court and of lunatics were put into a special category because the jurisdiction was not contentious but a paternal administration which had always been private. Any justification for not sitting in open court must come from common law or statute. At common law the paramount duty of the court is to secure that justice is done, and therefore, if justice cannot be done except behind closed doors, the court must sit in private. Examples given were of litigation about secret processes where the court could not do justice if it sat in public and thereby destroyed the subject-matter, and circumstances of tumult or disorder that would make a public hearing impracticable. The interests of public decency would not affect the ability of a court to administer justice, and therefore a hearing in camera could not be ordered on those grounds. The Divorce Court promptly took the view that if a woman felt unable to give evidence in open court it was impracticable to do justice except in private, neatly citing

[1] [1913] A.C. 417.

Scott v. *Scott* as their authority for a new way of achieving customary results. A hearing in camera, apart from statutory authority, must still be justified in terms of the rule in *Scott* v. *Scott* and instances have been few. Some cases were heard in private during the First World War on security grounds and in 1920 the Official Secrets Acts were amended to allow private sittings in proceedings under those Acts. In 1958 the Court of Appeal allowed a witness in a bankruptcy case to be heard in private.[1]

One might expect that the principle of open court would carry a corresponding duty on the authorities to provide court houses with adequate accommodation for members of the public, but that is not so. Conditions vary from being tolerable to consisting of some seats from which little can be seen and almost nothing can be heard. Press reporters have in general no special right to be present; if the public can be in court, so can they, and on the same terms that there must be no photographing or making of sketches. Statutes have made some changes about the press and reporting, but this is by way of exception to common law. There are no requirements about law courts (as there are for meetings of local authorities) that special accommodation and facilities be made available for the press, and it is only by courtesy that some space is reserved for reporters.

The publication of 'indecent matter or indecent medical, surgical or physiological details being matter or details the publication of which would be calculated to injure public morals' in reporting judicial proceedings was prohibited by the Judicial Proceedings (Regulation of Reports) Act 1926. This applies to any proceedings, civil or criminal. Thus some four letter words may be freely bandied about a court as they were in the *Lady Chatterley* case but it does not follow that it is safe for a newspaper to use those words in describing the proceedings. Parliament has also had regard to the need to protect the parties in some proceedings from the strains of open court and the blare of newspapers. The Act of 1926 restricted press reports of Divorce Court proceedings to a bare statement of the parties and witnesses, the charges and defences, points of law, the judge's summing up if there is a jury, and the judgment together with any observations or reasons accompanying the judgment. Similar restrictions are imposed on reports of cases in Domestic Courts.[2] Juveniles are also protected against newspaper reports that would

---

[1] *Re Green (a bankrupt)* [1958] 2 All E.R. 57; an application was refused in *Re Agricultural Industries Ltd.* [1952] 1 All E.R. 1188.

[2] See p. 181, below.

reveal their names or school or would lead to their identification whether they were defendant in the case, or the victim or a witness; this applies automatically to all proceedings in juvenile courts[1] and in other courts a direction may be given when proceedings relate to conduct contrary to decency or morality. Restrictions have also been introduced as to the persons who may be present in court. Some proceedings, including charges of incest, evidence of sexual capacity in nullity suits and the making of adoption orders are heard in camera. For Domestic Courts and Juvenile Courts it is provided that no person shall be present except those specified, the effect of which is to exclude the public but to allow the press to be present.[2]

The common law practice of open court receives strong support from the newspapers with the claim that press freedom is the best safeguard against abuse of judicial process. That hearings should be in public is not universally accepted. If a person is injured in an accident and claims damages, negotiation is private and the press has no access to medical reports, financial reckonings and other personal matters; go to arbitration and it stays private; go to court and the more gruesome bits or any 'revelation' of private affairs may be reported. The business community prefers arbitration in private to the Commercial Court in public.[3] It may seem obvious that the trial of criminal charges should be in public and be reported, yet there are problems that are not yet settled, including committal proceedings[4] and detailed reports produced after conviction to help the court in sentencing.[5]

I have followed up these matters of the nature of a trial at common law because I think the machinery of justice in England has to be seen in its peculiar historical setting. It must not be regarded as a logical structure designed round basic principles. Procedures and practices led to a 'contest' conception of trial, in open court, but this gives it no special sanctity. We have to see how these ideas work out in the courts and processes of our own day.

---

[1] See p. 190, below.
[2] Magistrates' Courts Act 1952 s. 57 (2) and Children and Young Persons Act 1933 s. 47 (2); the provisions are not quite the same.
[3] See p. 90, below.   [4] See p. 147, below.
[5] See p. 224, below.

CHAPTER II

CIVIL JURISDICTION

1. CIVIL LAW AND CRIMINAL LAW

The division of the law into civil and criminal gives us the only two categories that are sharply distinguished for the administration of justice, for as a general rule civil cases are dealt with by one hierarchy of courts and criminal cases by another. The word 'civil' is unfortunate, since in connection with law it has four meanings. To those in the Armed Forces 'civil' generally denotes everything that is not peculiar to the Services; a civil court as contrasted with a court-martial then means a non-service tribunal irrespective of whether it has civil or criminal jurisdiction. To lawyers, the term 'civil' is sometimes used to mean the whole law of some particular state in contrast to international law. It may also signify Roman law: this comes from the medieval contrast between Justinian's compilation known as the *corpus iuris civilis* and ecclesiastical law known as the *corpus iuris canonici*. In this sense 'civilian' means a person learned in Roman law. The fourth sense, in which the word is generally used today, means that part of a country's law that is not criminal. The dichotomy here is really criminal and non-criminal, so that civil cases must be distinguished by settling the boundary of the criminal law.

Any attempt to define a crime in terms of acts or omissions leads to considerable difficulty. If, for instance, the driver of an omnibus drives recklessly and comes into collision with a private car, damaging that car and some of his own passengers, we shall find that the same act of reckless driving is a crime, also a tort (civil wrong) to his passengers and the owner of the private car, and also a breach of contract with the passengers in not using due care and skill in carrying them. The distinction is not between acts, but between the legal proceedings that are brought. If proceedings against the driver are aimed at punishing him, then those proceedings are criminal, whereas proceedings that aim at compensating the injured persons are civil. Criminal proceedings, usually called a prosecution, cannot (with certain exceptions) result in any pecuniary gain to the person injured, for if the defendant is fined the money goes into public funds. A person injured by a crime may start a prosecution, described in the next chapter, but as he can get nothing out of it, other than the satisfaction of his outraged dignity, he is likely to leave it to

24

the police if they are prepared to act. If what is wanted is compensation for injury, then civil proceedings are necessary, and these proceedings can be brought only by the injured person or his representative if he has died. Most criminal acts are also civil wrongs, but some crimes (such as treason and sedition) do not injure any particular person, and many civil wrongs (such as the majority of breaches of contract) do not amount to criminal acts. When the act is both a crime and a civil wrong, there is in general no reason why both a prosecution and a civil action should not be brought: the proceedings will be quite separate, coming before different courts, each court hearing the whole of the relevant evidence and deciding independently of the other court. It is in practice harder to get a conviction in a criminal court than to get judgment in a civil court in several types of case, so that it often happens that a motorist is acquitted of criminal charges arising out of his driving, whilst a civil court holds that he drove negligently and so must compensate the injured plaintiff. Assault is anomalous; the person assaulted must choose between criminal and civil proceedings. Libel is an instance where both proceedings lie, but in practice both will not be brought; if the writer or publisher of the libel has any money, a plaintiff will usually ask for compensation (damages) and be content if he gets a sum of money, but if the defendant has no money there is no point in trying to get any from him and the only course is to swallow the insult or institute a criminal prosecution.

In practice there is very little difficulty in distinguishing criminal and civil proceedings by the test of 'punishment' or 'compensation'; the general causes of confusion are certain peculiar cases.[1] *First*, there is a class of case called a 'penal action'. These were created by various statutes from the later medieval period onwards, enacting that certain conduct is prohibited under a penalty of a fixed sum of money generally recoverable as a civil debt. The idea of allowing anyone who notices the illegal conduct to sue for the penalty dates from the days before efficient police forces, the members of the public being in effect offered some substantial inducement to help in the enforcement of the law. The purpose of making the penalty rank as a civil debt is more curious. The Crown has the prerogative

---

[1] Kenny, *Outlines of Criminal Law*, ch. I; Winfield, *Province of the Law of Tort* (1931), ch. VIII; Allen, 'The Nature of a Crime', 13 (3rd series) *Journal of Society of Comparative Legislation* (1931), p. I, reprinted in Allen, *Legal Duties* (1931); Williams, 'The Definition of Crime', 8 *Current Legal Problems* (1955), p. 107; Hughes, 'The Concept of Crime: an American view' [1959] *Crim. L.R.* 239, 331.

of pardon, which allows the Crown to relieve a convicted person of any penalty that has been imposed, but this relates solely to criminal proceedings, the Crown being unable to interfere with the conduct or results of civil litigation. Some of these penal actions are the relics of religious differences: a Protestant House of Commons wanted to ensure that there should be no trading on Sunday and that certain oaths should be taken before some offices could be held. If these were backed by criminal sanctions only, then a wicked king could reverse the policy of Parliament simply by pardoning all offenders, thus profaning the Lord's Day and admitting Catholics to office. By making the penalty a civil debt the potentially wicked king was completely thwarted. Nearly all these penal actions were abolished by the Common Informers Act 1951, which schedules forty-seven statutes and takes away the element of private profit from proceedings under them; if the statute does not contain provisions for ordinary punishment, the 1951 Act makes the prohibited conduct an offence triable summarily and punishable with a fine of £100. Penal actions could still arise from disqualification for membership of the House of Commons, but the whole law was altered by the House of Commons Disqualification Act 1957 and new methods of enforcement have been provided. *Secondly*, damages in civil actions are usually assessed at a figure that is thought to be equal to the loss that the plaintiff has suffered, thus satisfying the notion that they are compensation. There are, however, a few cases where 'exemplary' or 'punitive' damages can be given. An example is trespass to land: in ordinary cases the physical damage to the land and things on it is the measure of damages, but where the trespass is wanton and insulting to the occupier of the land it is possible to get heavy damages. The legal theory is that these are to 'give a lesson' to the wrongdoer, but in reality they amount to compensation for the indignity and annoyance that has been suffered. The enormous damages sometimes given in libel actions are in theory compensation for the loss of reputation, but the recipients of these sums are the only people who have been satisfied with our law of libel. *Thirdly*, statute has assigned certain kinds of work to certain courts. It would be interesting to discuss whether divorce and separation rest on punishment of a guilty spouse or compensation of an innocent spouse, but this is unnecessary since Parliament so arranged matters that the rich and the officially poor could go to the Probate Divorce and Admiralty Division (indubitably a civil court) and thereafter remarry, whilst the rest of the community could go to the Magistrate's Court (normally a criminal court) and thereafter live in continence or adultery. Now that the social improvements of our age have brought divorce within the reach of everybody, the distinction continues on a somewhat different basis.

Table II. *System of courts exercising civil jurisdiction at the present day*

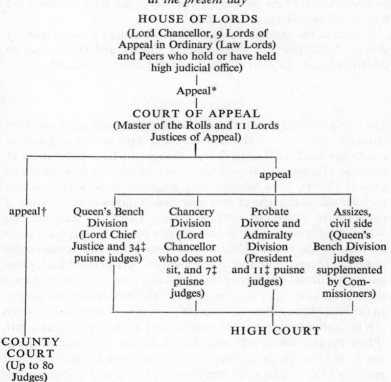

HOUSE OF LORDS
(Lord Chancellor, 9 Lords of
Appeal in Ordinary (Law Lords)
and Peers who hold or have held
high judicial office)

Appeal*

COURT OF APPEAL
(Master of the Rolls and 11 Lords
Justices of Appeal)

appeal†	Queen's Bench Division (Lord Chief Justice and 34‡ puisne judges)	Chancery Division (Lord Chancellor who does not sit, and 7‡ puisne judges)	Probate Divorce and Admiralty Division (President and 11‡ puisne judges)	Assizes, civil side (Queen's Bench Division judges supplemented by Commissioners)

appeal

HIGH COURT

COUNTY
COURT
(Up to 80
Judges)

There are in addition certain old courts exercising civil jurisdiction. The most important are: Liverpool Court of Passage, Tolzey Court of Bristol, Mayor's and City of London Court, Salford Hundred Court, Chancery Courts of Lancaster and of Durham; appeal lies to the Court of Appeal.

* Administration of Justice (Appeals) Act 1934 provides that no appeal shall lie to the House of Lords from the Court of Appeal except with the leave of that Court or of the House of Lords.

† Before the Administration of Justice (Appeals) Act 1934 appeals from County Courts (except in certain matters) lay to the High Court (Divisional Court of King's Bench Division), and thence, with leave, to the Court of Appeal.

‡ The maximum number of puisne judges is 53 and their assignment among the three divisions (given here as it stood in 1963) may be varied (see p. 36 below).

The customary divisions of the law, such as the law of contract, tort and property, are thought of as subdivisions of civil law, although it is obvious that much of the criminal law exists for the protection of property. Constitutional law, as generally understood, is partly civil, partly criminal, and partly not law at all as far as the courts are concerned. The division into civil and criminal is vital for an appreciation of the working of the courts, but it cannot form the basis of all classifications of law.

In outline the system of courts for civil matters is now relatively simple. Small cases go to the County Courts, and larger cases to the High Court. Table II shows the system diagrammatically.

2. COUNTY COURTS[1]

The ancient County Court became a court for small cases and then virtually died away. When in 1846 Parliament set up a system of courts for small civil cases it was thought to be a good thing to continue with such a hallowed name, and the new courts were named County Courts. They have nothing whatever to do with counties: they should be thought of as a new system rather than a revival of older courts. There are over 400 County Courts for England and Wales, the districts served by these courts being so arranged that in all parts of the country there is a County Court within reasonable distance. There are up to eighty County Court judges,[2] each judge having a 'circuit' which is a court or group of courts depending upon the amount of work to be done. Some of the circuits have two judges. In the nine Metropolitan districts the work is so heavy that the courts are in more or less constant session, and the circuit is one court. Where the population is thinner the circuit may mean that the judge has to hold courts in a dozen or more different towns:[3] the court must be held at least once every month, but it is possible for one judge to manage this because in the smaller town one or two days a month are sufficient to cope with the business. The judges are

[1] R. C. L. Gregory, *County Court Manual*, published in 1946 by H.M. Stationery Office, 4th edition 1962, is an admirable short account of County Courts and of the District Registries of the High Court. The legislation has been consolidated by the County Courts Act 1959.

[2] The County Courts Act 1934 provided for a maximum of sixty judges, and this was raised to sixty-five in 1950 and to eighty by the County Courts Act 1955. The Lord Chancellor can alter the number and boundaries of County Court districts and the places where courts are held.

[3] For example, circuit 35 (with Cambridge as the central point) has fifteen courts, the farthest being Peterborough, Luton and Bishop's Stortford.

appointed by the Crown on the advice of the Lord Chancellor[1] from barristers of at least seven years' standing, and may be removed by the Lord Chancellor for inability or misbehaviour. The retiring age is seventy-two, with a maximum extension to seventy-five. It is a full-time appointment, private practice or a seat in Parliament being expressly prohibited. The salary was raised from £1,500 to £2,000 in 1937, and since the war it has risen by stages to £4,400 in 1959:[2] a travelling allowance is made, and the office carries a pension.[3] Each court also has a registrar, who may be registrar of more than one County Court, appointed and removable by the Lord Chancellor. The registrar is a solicitor, and the Lord Chancellor decides in each case whether it is to be a full-time appointment or whether the registrar may also engage in private practice, and what salary is to be

---

[1] Within the Duchy of Lancaster the advice is given by the Chancellor of the Duchy. This anomaly was retained by the Administration of Justice Act 1956 and it also survives in respect of Justices of the Peace (see p. 160, below).

[2] It has been customary for all judicial salaries to be fixed by statute, so that any increase has needed new legislation. That is still the position for the superior judges, but the Judicial Officers (Salaries and Pensions) Act 1957 introduced a new provision: the salaries of the Recorders of the Crown Courts at Liverpool and Manchester (see p. 102, below), County Court judges and metropolitan stipendiary magistrates (see p. 174, below) can be increased by an Order made by the Lord Chancellor with the consent of the Treasury and approved by a resolution of each House of Parliament. Increases were made in 1959. The salary of a Metropolitan Stipendiary Magistrate and that of a County Court Judge used to be the same, but an Act in 1952 put a Metropolitan Magistrate £300 below a County Court Judge. The explanation given was that County Court judges had been receiving extra remuneration for acting as Commissioners to hear divorce cases (see p. 57, below) and that the new rate of salary was inclusive of those services. The difference has remained, and a Metropolitan Magistrate now receives £4,100.

[3] For many years judges and judicial officers have been entitled to a non-contributory pension of two-thirds of the salary on retirement with, however, certain requirements of length of service. This pension gave no protection to the holder except whilst he lived retired: if a judge died whilst in office, there would be no payment from public funds for his widow or children, and if he died in retirement the pension annuity would similarly cease without any provision for dependants. This was also the position in superannuation of public servants generally, until a new system was incorporated in the Superannuation Act 1949. The Administration of Justice (Pensions) Act 1950 follows the same principle of social security. In the first place, the rate of pension is reduced and a lump sum is payable on retirement or on death whilst still in office; this is simply a re-arrangement of pension money, since the amount saved to public funds by the lower annuities will go to pay the lump sums. Secondly, there is a contributory scheme which will provide some annuity to a widow and children, and for this the contributions fall about equally on the judges and on the exchequer. A table showing the financial effects upon the judges and officers concerned is given in Hansard for 24 November 1950. As regards retirement of the superior judges, see p. 264 below.

paid, the decision depending on the amount of business in the particular court. The registrar is the head of the office staff of the court, and he also acts as a lesser judge.

The jurisdiction of County Courts is strictly limited, for they may hear only those kinds of cases assigned to them by statute. There has been constant pressure for an extension of the jurisdiction, but the question has not usually been decided purely on the merits. Proposals for extension have always been mixed up with complaints about cost and delay and inefficiency in the High Court. In April 1947 the Lord Chancellor appointed two committees on Practice and Procedure, one for County Courts and the other for the Supreme Court. The County Courts Committee presented two Reports[1] making a number of recommendations, several of which have been carried out. Changes in County Court jurisdiction had to be considered by the Supreme Court Practice and Procedure Committee and are dealt with in an Interim Report in 1949.[2] Despite this legal addiction to looking through the wrong end of a telescope, the result, namely the County Courts Act 1955, has produced a more reasonable division of work between County Courts and the High Court.

A convenient division of jurisdiction is into that which is general and that which is special. The general jurisdiction, which is exercised by all county courts, corresponds to the ordinary actions that are brought in the Queen's Bench Division and in the Chancery Division. There is also jurisdiction in admiralty and bankruptcy which is 'general' in the sense that it corresponds to that of the High Court, but not all county courts have this jurisdiction. If the parties agree the Court has almost unlimited jurisdiction in these matters, but in the absence of agreement (and it is rarely forthcoming, for defendants are not often accommodating to the wishes of plaintiffs) there are limits both of subject and of the monetary amount of a claim. County Courts do not therefore cover the whole range of legal proceedings. They do not, for instance, deal with divorce and matrimonial cases or bastardy, and there is no criminal jurisdiction. The most important matters of general jurisdiction come under these headings:

(1) Actions founded upon contract and tort (except libel, slander, seduction and breach of promise of marriage) with certain monetary limits. Prior to 1939 the limit was £100, but in 1938 that was raised to

---

[1] Interim Report, Cmd. 7468 (1948); Final Report, Cmd. 7668 (1949). (The system of numbering used for Command Papers is explained on p. 441.)
[2] Cmd. 7764.

£200 subject to a proviso that a defendant who was sued for more than £100 could object to the jurisdiction, and so compel the plaintiff to transfer the action to the High Court. The County Courts Act 1955 has fixed the limit at £400. This may, however, be increased to £500 by Order in Council (thus avoiding the necessity for a new statute) provided that the draft Order is laid before Parliament and approved by resolution of each House.

(2) Equity matters such as trusts, mortgages and dissolution of partnership where the amount does not exceed £500.

(3) Actions concerning land, which includes houses and other buildings, where the net annual value for rating does not exceed £400. Most of these actions are by landlords to recover possession after serving a notice to quit, and the jurisdiction is commonly called possession actions.[1]

(4) Some Courts have limited Admiralty jurisdiction, and here a number of changes were made by the Administration of Justice Act 1956. The limitation is that a claim must not exceed £1000, except in the case of a claim for salvage, where the limitation is that the value of the property saved must not exceed £3500.

(5) Bankruptcies are dealt with in certain courts outside the London Bankruptcy District, and there is also jurisdiction in the winding up of companies with paid-up capital not exceeding £10,000.

(6) Proceedings transferred from the High Court. This is discussed later.

(7) The special jurisdiction arises under numerous statutes mostly of a type often called 'social' or 'collectivist'. This is an extremely important part of County Court jurisdiction, but it is impossible to make any adequate summary. The list includes Acts on Adoption of Children, Guardianship of Infants, Housing, Increase of Rent and Mortgage (Restrictions), Landlord and Tenant, Legitimacy and many other subjects. The legislation is largely since 1914, although in a few matters the authority is a late nineteenth-century statute with modern amendments. Many of the statutes represent a reversal of *laissez-faire* principles and the imposition of restrictions upon the freedom of contract. There has, for example, been a succession of statutes altering the law of landlord and tenant, virtually all intended to benefit or protect tenants. Thus, the Rent Restriction Acts gave tenants a high degree of security provided that the rent was duly paid, and there has also been much legislation about the condition of houses and the obligation to repair and to maintain in a satisfactory condition. Naturally such legislation is likely to produce a vast number of disputes, and jurisdiction over these fell almost entirely to the County Courts. When it appeared that the Rent Act 1957 might lead to serious hardships through some houses becoming decontrolled, the Landlord and Tenant (Temporary Provisions) Act 1958 promptly eased the position by giving County Courts a power to suspend dispossession for a transitional period. Another example of mitigating the effect of freedom of contract is the Hire Purchase Act of 1938, extended in 1954, designed to save people from the incidence of credit selling by unscrupulous firms. One very important special jurisdiction of County Courts was under the Workmen's

---

[1] Under the Small Tenements Recovery Act 1838 actions for possession of some premises can be brought in a magistrates' court; this jurisdiction is a survival from the period before the creation of County Courts.

Compensation Acts, but the law has been altered; under the National Insurance (Industrial Injuries) Act 1946 cases arising since that Act came into force are dealt with by tribunals[1] and County Courts have no jurisdiction.

The hearing of cases is divided between the judge and the registrar. It is possible in many matters for there to be a jury, but as may be seen in Table III litigants rarely ask for one. If there is likely to be delay at a court because of the amount of work, the Lord Chancellor can appoint a temporary judge. The registrar is in effect an assistant judge taking the lesser cases. These include cases where the defendant does not appear, or admits the claim. He could hear defended cases (in the absence of objection by the parties) where the claim did not exceed £10, but the County Courts Act 1955 increased the limit to £30, and also allows him to take cases beyond that figure if the parties consent to his doing so.

Table III shows proceedings in County Courts for some recent years. The large number of plaints entered before the war were mostly concerned with debt collecting of sums under £20,[2] and the common result was either that the actions were withdrawn because the commencement of proceedings induced the defendant to pay or that they were not defended and so were disposed of at a high speed in the absence of the defendant. The raising of the jurisdiction to £200 came into force in 1939, and the effect is apparent in the figure for plaints above £100. The total number of plaints declined rapidly during the war, the lowest level being reached in 1945. Since then there has been a steady increase in the volume of work, so that by 1957 the number of plaints is approaching the pre-war figure. Whilst the bulk of the claims are for amounts below £100, there has been a marked increase in claims for £100–£200. The effect of the 1955 Act in raising the ordinary limit from £200 to £400 is marked by a substantial number of claims for amounts over £200.

A high proportion of the cases are struck out or withdrawn, or there is judgment without a hearing or in the defendant's absence. These groups represent the cases in which the defendant pays up, and those where he does not pay or defend, and the plaintiff must get a judgment. In many cases the only question before the registrar is whether the defendant is to be allowed to satisfy the judgment by paying the sum by instalments. Table III shows that judgments on

---

[1] See p. 343, below. Workmen's Compensation cases often take a long time to settle, and County Courts are still dealing with cases that arose under the old law.

[2] Out of the 1,192,648 plaints for amounts not exceeding £100, 1,150,300 were for amounts not exceeding £20, and only 7652 were for amounts exceeding £50. This breakdown of the figures is not given in the post-war *Statistics*.

Table III. Proceedings in County Courts. The *Statistics* for 1939–48 have not been published, but some figures for those years are given in Comparative Tables in the *Statistics* for 1949 onwards

	1938	1939	1945	1950	1955	1957	1959	1961
Plaints entered:								
Total	1,262,402	1,094,770	212,483	496,439	727,154	1,078,097	1,322,117	1,677,738
Not exceeding £100	1,192,648	1,044,873	158,177	421,717	659,157	1,011,740	1,244,476	1,586,648
Above £100 but not exceeding £200	129	1,632	1,444	5,350	5,949	10,351	14,190	27,316
Above £200 but not exceeding £300				109		2,586	3,776	8,138
Above £300 but not exceeding £400						3,668	4,306	6,236
Above £400					140	125	165	189
Other plaints (recovery of land, etc.)	69,652	48,265	52,862	69,263	61,908	49,627	55,204	49,211
Struck out or withdrawn	435,517	Figures not available		193,434	254,615	341,858	348,900	451,470
Judgment without a hearing or in defendant's absence	783,746	688,095	92,470	268,722	442,721	679,121	935,036	1,161,905
Judgments on hearing:								
Before judge alone	19,414	16,262	16,431	23,865	18,307	15,819	21,654	19,783
Before judge with jury	4	—	—	—	1	—	2	1
Before registrar	11,407	10,668	2,525	4,818	5,866	8,555	11,841	13,557
Debtors sent to prison	3,452	2,593	221	489	1,215	2,539	5,355	6,323
Days of sitting:								
Judges	8,671	11,163	8,283	8,739	8,867	9,736	10,589	11,414
Registrars	2,716			1,775	6,583	7,444	8,143	8,907

hearings before judges and registrars, that is cases that are fought, are a small proportion of all the proceedings, and that their total number is much the same as it was before the war. Yet judges sat for many more days in 1961 than in 1938, whilst the sittings of registrars have increased threefold. Presumably the balance of County Court work is changing: the heavier or more difficult cases are increasing, so that the total load is heavier than it used to be. The bulk of County Court work nevertheless continues to be the vast amount of relatively small claims. If we consider that from a social point of view the importance of a court is the number of *persons* whose affairs it deals with, there can be no doubt that County Courts are the most important civil courts in the country. Except for a small section of the community, civil litigation means tradesmen, landlords and employers pursuing their actions, or more rarely being pursued, in County Courts.

In addition to County Courts there are borough and local courts with inferior civil jurisdiction. Halsbury, *Laws of England*, gives a list of 172 such courts, nearly all of them defunct or in abeyance. In most cases the County Court has a wider jurisdiction, and there is no conceivable reason why anyone should want to revive an ancient and often obscure court. But in a few cases the local court was flourishing at the time when County Courts were created, and where the local court had a wider jurisdiction it was of great use to its locality. The Bristol Tolzey Court and the Liverpool Court of Passage both have unlimited jurisdiction in ordinary actions. I am informed by local solicitors that many actions that would have to be brought in the High Court elsewhere are determined more quickly and cheaply in these courts. In 1962, 498 proceedings were commenced in the Bristol Court and 1,512 in the Liverpool Court. The Salford Hundred Court also has jurisdiction that is not possessed by County Courts, although here it is limited in amount; in 1962, 1,991 proceedings were commenced. The Mayor's and City of London Court is a combination of older courts. As the City of London Court it is deemed to be a County Court, and has the appropriate jurisdiction. As the Mayor's Court it has unlimited jurisdiction in actions of contract, tort and recovery of land when the cause of action arises solely within the City; it also has certain peculiar jurisdiction. In 1962 actions commenced numbered 12,491.[1] The Norwich Guildhall Court shows the vitality of local courts; it is being increasingly used,

[1] The figure for 1938 was 56,580, which included 53,314 plaints for less than £20.

having 286 plaints in 1958 and 673 in 1962. Apart from these local courts, all civil actions must be brought either in County Courts or in the High Court.

Many matters concerning County Courts, such as the relation to the High Court, nature of the trial, appeals and the enforcement of judgments are discussed in the following sections.

3. THE HIGH COURT

The High Court was created by the Judicature Acts, 1873–5, the general plan of which has been given in the last chapter. We speak of *the* High Court as if it were a single body like the House of Commons: actually it consists of over fifty judges who normally sit singly, proceedings before each of them (whether in London or on the civil side at Assizes) being proceedings in the High Court. The court is divided into three divisions. The Queen's Bench Division is the successor of the old common law courts of King's Bench, Common Pleas and Exchequer. The Chancery Division is the successor of the old Chancery Court. The Probate Divorce and Admiralty Division represents the jurisdiction of the three separate courts tha used to handle those topics. The idea of divisions is to secure some measure of specialisation. For all practical purposes we can regard each division as having a separate jurisdiction and the judges as being judges of a particular division, although strictly speaking the jurisdiction is that of the High Court and the judges are justices of the High Court; it is merely a matter of convenience that a judge usually does more or less the kind of work with which he is acquainted, and to ensure this, actions must be brought in the appropriate division.[1]

The ordinary judges of the High Court, that is, the judges other than the Lord Chief Justice, the Lord Chancellor and the President

---

[1] In 1938 E. was sculling a rum-tum on the Thames near Hammersmith Bridge when a collision occurred with an eight of the Westminister Rowing Club. E. sued Q., the secretary, and F., the treasurer, of the club in the King's Bench Division. The defendants filed a defence in Admiralty form and applied for transfer of the action to Admiralty. The Master refused transfer, but Asquith J. ordered transfer and the Court of Appeal upheld Asquith J. on the ground that the Judicature Acts transferred the jurisdiction of the Lord High Admiral and that that jurisdiction extended to wherever the tide ebbs and flows, and the waters of Hammersmith are tidal (*Edwards* v. *Quickenden and Forester* (1939) 187 *Law Times*, p. 111). At the hearing of the case [1939], P. 261, the judge held that the common law rule and not the Admiralty rule should prevail, as these craft, being propelled by oars, were not ships or vessels within the meaning of the Act.

of the Probate Divorce and Admiralty Division, are known as puisne judges. The number of judges that the Crown may appoint is fixed by statute. The Judicature Act of 1925 fixed the number of puisne judges at seventeen for the King's Bench Division, six for the Chancery Division, and two for the Probate Divorce and Admiralty Division. Delays in litigation led to the number being increased in 1935 to nineteen for the King's Bench Division and in 1927 to four for Probate Divorce and Admiralty, subject to the proviso that appointments above the 1925 establishment should not be made unless both Houses of Parliament presented an Address to the Crown requesting such appointment.[1] It was a very clumsy method of ensuring that there should not be too many judges, and fixing establishments by Divisions did not allow for adjustments between the Divisions to meet changes in the volume of work. Hence the Judicature (Amendment) Act 1944 repealed the earlier legislation and provided that the number of puisne judges of the High Court should not be less than twenty-five nor more than thirty-two. The maximum figure was increased by one in 1949, six more in 1950, three more in 1956, six more in 1960 and five more in 1962, so that the maximum is now fifty-three.[2] The 1944 Act (as amended) further provides that if the number of puisne judges is less than the maximum, but is twenty-five or more, new appointments may be made if the Lord Chancellor and the Treasury are satisfied that the state of business in the High Court requires additional judicial strength. On appointment a puisne judge is attached to whichever Division the Lord Chancellor directs, and he may (with his consent and the concurrence of the president of the Division) be transferred to another Division. Puisne judges must be attached to Divisions so that there are at least five for the Chancery Division, seventeen for the Queen's Bench Division and three for the Probate Divorce and Admiralty Division.

Anyone who wants to bring a civil action has to consider whether the appropriate court is a County Court or the High Court. A few special matters, such as claims under some statutes mentioned in the last section, *must* be brought in a County Court, but apart from such cases there is concurrent jurisdiction, the High Court being able to hear everything that can come before a County Court as well

---

[1] Supreme Court of Judicature (Amendment) Acts of 1935 and 1937.

[2] Patents and Designs Act 1949; High Court and County Court Judges Act 1950; Restrictive Trade Practices Act 1956; Administration of Justice (Judges and Pensions) Act 1960; Criminal Justice Administration Act 1962.

as everything that is outside County Court limits. But plaintiffs are discouraged from suing in the High Court when there is no reason why the County Court should not be used. If, for instance, a High Court action is commenced for an ordinary trade debt of less than £400, two things may happen: the High Court[1] may order the case to be transferred to a County Court, or the case may continue in the High Court at the plaintiff's peril as to costs; in the latter event, if the judgment at the trial shows that County Court proceedings would have been appropriate, the judge can say that the successful plaintiff shall only get such costs as he would have got in a County Court, which means that his litigation would be unprofitable. Whilst the sum in dispute is the normal criterion for choice of court, it does not always represent the real issue. If one of a group of underwriters of an insurance policy is sued for his contribution towards an alleged loss, the action may well be for a few pounds; it is known that all the other underwriters will abide by the decision, and hence the action may be well within County Court limits, yet a very proper case for the High Court. Test actions are brought in a considerable variety of cases where one decision will, in fact, govern the settlement of several claims. Cases relating to civil liberties may also involve a nominal or small money claim: if documents are said to have been illegally seized by the police it may be desirable to seek the decision of a High Court judge, and the plaintiff is not compelled to sue in an inferior court just because he cannot establish that the papers were worth more than £400. Hence if the action is a proper one for the High Court it will not be remitted to a County Court, and the plaintiff need not fear that costs will be used against him in a disciplinary fashion. It may happen that a plaintiff chooses to sue in a County Court but the defendant deems that the real importance of the action merits High Court proceedings; in such a case the defendant can apply to have the action transferred to the High Court. These rules are based upon good sense, but there is one rule that is hard to justify. If in a High Court action in tort it appears (from evidence submitted by the defendant) that the plaintiff has insufficient means of paying the defendant's costs in the event of the plaintiff losing, the court may remit the action to a County Court unless the plaintiff can give security for costs. This operates irrespective of the amount claimed, for the County Court has unlimited jurisdiction in the case of actions sent there from the High Court.

---

[1] This decision is made by a superior official (see p. 39), there being a right to take the matter before a judge.

It is, of course, a serious matter to be sued by an impecunious person, for a successful defendant will fail to recover costs from such a plaintiff, but it may be argued that it is a more serious thing to deprive a man of his opportunity of getting his case before a tribunal that is *ex hypothesi* the most appropriate court simply because he happens to be poor.[1]

In practice the distribution of work between the High Court and the County Courts does not always proceed according to the principles given in the last paragraph. In many cases an action is commenced without any expectation that the defendant will contest the matter.[2] Most solicitors when instructed to take proceedings for recovery of a debt of a substantial sum though less than £400 go to High Court rather than the County Court. The chance of the case being referred to a County Court, or of it being heard in the High Court but of costs being allowed only on the County Court scale, is not a discouragement when a case is not likely to be contested. The difference in cost is small,[3] and the procedure is in some ways less troublesome and more efficacious in the High Court. There is also the very important fact that debtors are more scared of a High Court writ than they are of a County Court summons. The result is that very many actions are commenced in the High Court that should on principle be commenced in County Courts; this does not affect the work of the judges, for the principle of division of jurisdiction is observed in the cases that reach contested trial.

Further consideration of the work of the High Court requires a discussion of the divisions.

The Queen's Bench Division and the civil side of Assizes

The judicial strength consists of the Lord Chief Justice of England and at present, in 1963, thirty-four puisne judges. The number of judges exceeds that of the other two divisions, partly because the Queen's Bench Division has the largest volume of work and partly because the judges are required to do work other than that of the work of their division. The jurisdiction is varied.

(1) *Ordinary civil actions* may be heard in the Queen's Bench Division or at Assizes. Certain classes of actions are assigned to the Chancery Division, and in others there is a choice between Chancery and Queen's Bench Division; this is discussed later. The civil side of

---

[1] 'Costs' are discussed below, pp. 295–304, together with a further analysis of 'speculative' actions.
[2] See p. 64, below.   [3] See p. 301, below.

Assizes can be regarded as a separate division in which High Court jurisdiction is exercised at a number of provincial towns, but in fact it is only certain kinds of High Court work that are taken on circuit. For many years the civil side of Assizes consisted almost entirely of common law actions corresponding to the ordinary actions of the Queen's Bench Division, and after a relatively short period of hearing divorce cases at Assizes (culminating in an avalanche in 1946 which made other arrangements necessary)[1] we are now back to conditions under which we can think of the civil side of Assizes as being primarily a perambulating sitting of the Queen's Bench Division though taking a few other High Court matters.

If a common law action is to be brought, the first step is to get a writ issued. Writs are issued from an office at the Law Courts in London, or the offices of the High Court (District Registries) that are established in 117 provincial towns; it is a formal step, the writ being drawn up by the plaintiff's advisers and stamped by an official on payment of a fee. The writ is then 'served' on the defendant by showing him the original and giving him a copy of it. The defendant must then 'enter an appearance', which means the filing of a document at the office, for unless he does this the plaintiff can proceed straight to judgment. In most cases the solicitors to both parties have been in correspondence before the action is started, and the writ is by arrangement served on the defendant's solicitors; the actual parties may have nothing to do until the case comes on for trial. Soon afterwards the respective solicitors go before an official, a 'master' in London[2] or the 'registrar' in the provinces, on a 'summons for directions'. After hearing what the parties have to say, the master or registrar makes an order about the place and mode of trial. The order may remit the case to a County Court, or it may direct trial in London or at some Assize Court. Remission to a County Court has been explained. As between trial in London or at Assizes, the governing principle is that of general convenience. If the parties and most of the witnesses all reside in one neighbourhood, then the most economical thing will be trial locally. The place where the matter arose does not of itself govern this decision; if a resident of Oxford and a resident of Cambridge have a car collision in the Lake District it is quite likely that civil litigation would be in London, for London would be equally convenient for both parties and it would

---

[1] See pp. 56–7 below.

[2] The office is described by Diamond, 'The Queen's Bench Master', 76 *Law Quarterly Review* (1960), p. 504.

probably be simpler to get witnesses to London than for the parties and witnesses to attend some north country Assize town. On the criminal side of Assizes the rule is different, for here the place where the offence is committed is the governing factor, and so a criminal charge arising out of the collision would be heard in the county where the events occurred. Whether a civil action is directed to be heard in London or at Assizes there will be the same sort of hearing. In 1962, 2,889 actions were tried or disposed of in Assize Courts, whereas 2,000 were so dealt with in London. The number tried in London is clearly not proportionate to the population: it is to be explained by the convenience of London and by the fact that so much commerce and industry is located there, either completely or by way of head offices or because the financial interest of the litigation is that of insurance carried on in London. The judge at Assize has to deal with a wide variety of cases, and so specialisation is impossible: the Queen's Bench Division in London has available all the judges who are not on circuit.

Specialisation is recognised to some extent by the assigning of London cases to different lists. The commercial list, instituted in 1895, is so well known that it is often called the 'Commercial Court'. This is discussed later.[1] Other civil actions are divided according to the mode of trial, as juries, non-juries and short cause; this merely assists the arrangement of work.

(2) *The Queen's Bench Division also has an appellate and a supervisory jurisdiction exercised by three and occasionally five or more judges sitting together, usually the Lord Chief Justice with a senior judge and one other, the court being known as a Divisional Court of the Queen's Bench Division.* It hears appeals on points of law from Magistrates' Courts[2] and from the appellate jurisdiction of Quarter Sessions.[3] The supervisory jurisdiction used to be exercised by prerogative writs, and in view of the language to be found in law reports prior to 1939, it is desirable to describe the old system for the changes are only procedural. The number of these cases is not large, only 87 applications being made in 1962, but the issues are generally important. Writs to commence actions are issued automatically by the appropriate office; no inquiry is made as to whether the plaintiff has a good case, for that will be ascertained at the trial. Prerogative writs were really orders made by the court. Originally these writs were peculiarly royal machinery, intended for use by the

[1] See p. 63, below.   [2] See p. 112, below.
[3] See p. 113, below.

Crown in the interests of the Crown. In the course of time they became available for use by ordinary citizens, often against servants of the Crown, so that they presented a complicated appearance. The best known of these writs is *habeas corpus*, whereby the courts can inquire into the legality of imprisonment or of private or domestic detention and secure the release of any person unlawfully detained.[1] *Mandamus* and proceedings of a like nature lie to command the performance of the public duties of persons, bodies and inferior courts. For instance, a borough council may be commanded to levy rates required by other authorities, and justices may be commanded to hear a case that they have declined to hear. *Prohibition* lies against an inferior tribunal and a party proceeding therein to prevent the hearing or further hearing of a case that for some reason, such as lack of jurisdiction, should not be heard by the inferior court. *Certiorari* also lies against inferior tribunals, the object being to bring the proceedings of the inferior tribunal before the High Court for review; if the original proceedings were in excess of jurisdiction, or irregular in some way, the purpose is to 'quash', for as the proceedings are found void they cannot be reversed;[2] in other cases the original proceedings may have been valid and regular, or a pending proceeding is within the inferior court's jurisdiction, but it is deemed desirable to get the case before the High Court either because proceedings in the original court or locality cannot be satisfactory or because the matter is thought to warrant a High Court trial.[3] The writ of *quo warranto*, for challenging the authority by which a person holds a public office, was not a prerogative writ, but the courts developed a procedure called an 'Information in the nature of the writ of *quo warranto*' which brought these proceedings into line with the true prerogative writs.

The normal method of prerogative writ procedure was to apply to the divisional court for a *rule nisi*; this was a direction to the effect that the writ asked for would be issued unless those concerned (who were given a copy of the *rule nisi*) showed cause why the writ should not issue. The matter was thrashed out at a subsequent sitting where the defendant 'showed cause' against and the applicant argued in favour of the writ being issued. The judgment of the court took the form of 'rule nisi discharged' or 'rule made absolute', the latter meaning that the writ be issued. In most cases the defendant

---

[1] See p. 228, below.
[2] The court has other powers (see p. 395, below).
[3] See p. 107, below.

was in a public position, and the writ was never actually issued because the defendant promptly did what the writ directed. If, however, the act or forbearance was disregarded, then the writ really did issue (after another application to the court); the defendant would then disobey it at his peril, for disobedience is contempt of court and (after further applications to the court) is visited with serious consequences. Special rules existed for *habeas corpus* to ensure speedy process.

The old procedure was unnecessarily complicated, and might involve several applications to the court. The language used to describe these cases was not easy to understand. Reform was at last made by the Administration of Justice (Miscellaneous Provisions) Act 1938. The writs of *mandamus, prohibition* and *certiorari* are abolished, their place being taken by orders of *mandamus, prohibition* or *certiorari*. The facts must now be put before the court, and the parties will argue for and against the making of the order; the proceedings will terminate by the court either making the order asked for or refusing to do so. Informations in the nature of a writ of *quo warranto* are also abolished and replaced by injunctions. There is really no good reason why the writ of *habeas corpus* should not have been abolished and reconstituted as an order, but it is understood that the framers of the statute did not care to run the risk of being thought subversive; they feared that any interference with *habeas corpus* would offend people, and that a sound bill might founder on this point. Hence *habeas corpus* remains a writ, with a special set of procedural rules. On the whole range of these ancient remedies the only substantive change is a slight increase in the scope of *mandamus*; for the rest there is no change in the substantive position.

If the operation of orders of *prohibition* and *certiorari* were confined to supervising the activities of inferior law courts the subject would be relatively simple, but in some ways the most important use of these orders is for judicial control of administrative bodies. The control of judicial or quasi-judicial activities of tribunals other than inferior law courts is discussed later.[1] Parliament has conferred upon various bodies, including the administrative departments, considerable power to make rules and regulations on specific topics. For instance, the Road Traffic Act 1930 s. 30, gave the Minister of Transport power to make regulations as to the use of motor vehicles on roads and the construction and equipment of motor vehicles. The motorist who sounds his horn between 11.30 p.m. and 7 a.m. on roads with street lighting by lamps not more than

---

[1] See pp. 394–405, below.

200 yards apart commits an offence under Regulation 84 of The Motor Vehicles (Construction and Use) Regulations 1955, made by the Minister pursuant to the Road Traffic Act. The motorist may commit innumerable other offences under the voluminous regulations. Delegated legislation is no new thing in our law, although extensive use of this device had not been made until relatively recently. In many matters today we must regard the statute as being authority for the carrying out of a policy, and look for the working details in rules that will be made by an administrative body acting under authority of the statute. A good example is the Legal Aid and Advice Act.[1] These statutes have come to be known as 'streamlined', and they certainly do resemble some modern motor cars in that the direction in which they are meant to go is not apparent at first sight. In these cases the minister is not given an absolutely free hand: his power is to make regulations within the scope allowed, or, as lawyers put it, he can only act *intra vires*; any regulations that are outside the provisions of the statute are *ultra vires* and so a nullity. If a minister makes a regulation that is felt to be unwise or oppressive to some section of the community, the law courts cannot review the regulation on that ground; the remedy here is political, in that the minister is politically responsible to Parliament. The law courts can be concerned merely with the *legality* of the regulation. The doctrine of *ultra vires* may be raised in various ways, but the most famous instances have been through the prerogative writs. Delegated legislation has been a controversial matter, largely because regulations have been associated with rationing and other controls and with the establishment of social services. Some legal writing reflects a dislike for the new ideas.[2] Now that the Conservatives support the welfare state the legal clamour has subsided.

3. *There are appellate functions exercised by a single judge.* Thus, appeals from masters are heard by a judge sitting in his room; this is known as 'in chambers', and takes up a substantial amount of time. Statute has of recent years provided for certain appeals to the High Court, as under the Housing Act and the Pensions Appeal Tribunals Act, and these matters come before a single judge of the Queen's Bench Division.

[1] See p. 309, below.
[2] Wade and Phillips, *Constitutional Law*, part VII, and particularly ch. 6, is the best of guides. See also Carr, 'Parliamentary Control of Delegated Legislation' (1956) *Public Law*, p. 200. C. K. Allen, *Law and Orders*, in its first edition (1945) is a delightful period piece; it should be read with 65 *Law Quarterly Review* (1946), pp. 58 *et seq.*

4. *The Queen's Bench Division has a wide original criminal juris-diction, which is, however, little exercised*; it is described in the next chapter.[1]

Complaints about law courts have a long history. We can feel some satisfaction that 'our one great judicial scandal'[2] happened in the reign of Edward I, but we have had a steady stream of lesser troubles. Most of the complaints can be brought under the heads of delay or of costs. Costs are discussed later.[3] Delay was, a hundred years or more ago, associated with Chancery rather than with common law: *Bleak House* should be read as part of legal history if the character of Esther prevents one from enjoying it as a novel. But our concern here is with the modern system, and during this century it has been common law business that has acquired the reputation for delays. It is still customary to talk about 'delay', but that is not a good word to describe the trouble. If we take the period that elapses between the date when the parties are ready with a case and the date of the hearing it will be found over the years that the period has varied greatly, yet, however short it may be (and in recent years it has been a matter of a few weeks),[4] there are still complaints. The real trouble is uncertainty as to when a case will be heard. The organisation of common law work is difficult because of the many calls upon the time of Queen's Bench Division judges. Common law actions on the civil side of Assizes have already been mentioned, but there is of course the criminal work of Assizes, which includes providing a judge for each session of the Old Bailey to take the most serious cases. Further, the Court of Criminal Appeal is staffed by Queen's Bench Division judges, and it may sit in three divisions of three judges each on one or two days a week. There are other needs for judges, as for the new Appeal Court from courts-martial.[5] Civil actions heard in London have to be fitted into this complicated pattern of the comings and goings of judges and their preoccupation with certain lists. Circuit work and the Court of Criminal Appeal have first claim on judicial time. If all the judges are in London, then an attack may be made upon all the lists, and litigants begin to count the days that are likely to elapse before their

---

[1] See p. 107, below.
[2] Maitland, in Selden Society edition of *Mirror of Justices*, p. xxiv.
[3] See p. 295, below.
[4] Lord Goddard L.C.J. in 1946 pointed out that the King's Bench Division was then trying cases set down in the same term (*The Times*, 17 April 1946), which was a far better state of affairs than there had been for many years.
[5] Courts-Martial (Appeals) Act 1951.

case is reached, but then there may come a rapid dispersal of judges until there is no judge available. If our case is next in a particular list on a Wednesday morning, we must be there, together with the witnesses, for the first case may collapse unexpectedly. All Wednesday, all Thursday and Friday morning we wait patiently; by lunch on Friday it may still be impossible to disperse, for if the obstinate case in front of us does end by three o'clock there is still an hour of judicial time to be filled in. It is expensive to keep many people waiting like that, and infuriating: when after waiting we learn that Mr Justice — cannot take our case at all because he must go on circuit, and no other judge is available because of this and that special list, I have often wondered why there are no recent instances under the Statute of Treasons of 1351, of 'slaying the Chancellor of the King's justices when in their places doing their offices'. Litigants may be too weary, for there is no atmosphere so enervating as that of a law court, or perhaps they realise that it is not really the fault of the judges. But it may be said that the cases in most lists do get heard at about the expected time and that no generalisations should be made from periods when there were too few judges. The answer is that even at its best the system is exasperating to parties, witnesses and lawyers. If one does not know the exact date on which a case is going to be heard it becomes unsafe to make engagements over any part of the period within which the hearing may occur: a good scouting system and plentiful use of telephoning may avoid much actual hanging about the court, but holding oneself in readiness is often destructive of other work, so that the time and energy that has to be given to the case is far greater than appears at first sight.

There were two inquiries in the 1930's which considered the state of business in the Supreme Court. The Business of Courts Committee, under the chairmanship of Lord Hanworth (then Master of the Rolls), was appointed at the end of 1932 with wide terms of reference as to the work and organisation of the Supreme Court: it produced three Reports between 1933 and 1936.[1] The recommendations of this Committee upon a large number of matters were adopted, but on the matter of despatch of business it cannot be said that much was achieved. The principal reason was that the Committee did not consider it feasible to adopt the fixing of a day for trial as a normal practice. That had for long been done in the commercial list, and in 1932 there had been established a New Procedure List with simplified procedure and fixed dates for trial

[1] Cmd. 4265 (1933), Cmd. 4471 (1934), Cmd. 5066 (1936).

which had been hailed in the law courts and in the press as a great reform. The Committee recommended some extension of New Procedure, along with other changes,[1] but by 1937 the New Procedure was quietly buried; its early success had been gained at the expense of less privileged cases, and a too widely extended preference ceases to be any preference. The second inquiry was the Royal Commission on Despatch of Business at Common Law, which was appointed late in 1934 and had Earl Peel as chairman; their Report was published in 1936.[2] The Royal Commission did recommend the fixing of dates for trials, but they were not prepared to recommend an increase of judicial strength; they thought that a number of changes could reduce the work of the judges and so provide sufficient judicial time. The total result of these two inquiries was that the despatch of business at common law was not markedly different from the state of affairs in previous years.

In April 1947 the Lord Chancellor appointed a Committee with Lord Evershed (Master of the Rolls) as chairman to inquire into Supreme Court Practice and Procedure: the terms of reference were very wide[3] and included specifically the consideration of the Reports of the Hanworth Committee on the Business of Courts and of the Royal Commission on Despatch of Business at Common Law. Three Reports were made,[4] and on this particular matter of the despatch of business there is no doubt that this Committee was more vigorous and radical in its outlook than any previous inquiry.

The Committee was emphatic about the need for introducing fixed dates for hearings.[5] That was in 1949, and it led many people to think that at last the superior law courts might become reasonably efficient and convenient for litigants. The hope of a brave new judicial world ebbed away: for seven years the customary sloth continued, until a falling volume of cases in the Queen's Bench Division made a change easier and indeed imperative if the flight from the courts was to be halted. In late November 1956 the Lord Chancellor announced that it had 'become possible to begin the

---

[1] The recommendation that there should be a business manager to look after the organisation of the work was particularly obnoxious to some judges. Lord Hewart referred to the proposed officer as a 'stage manager' and the proposal as being 'founded upon no evidence', in an address to the United Law Clerk's Society (*The Times*, 17 March 1936).

[2] Cmd. 5065 (1936).

[3] Proceedings in patents and designs and in matrimonial causes were not included as they had been the subject of other inquiries.

[4] Cmd. 7764 (1949), Cmd. 8176 (1951) and Cmd. 8617 (1952).

[5] Cmd. 7764 (1949), para. 63.

preparation' of a scheme for fixing dates of trials. The scheme began
in January 1957, and was amended in April 1957.[1] A review made at
the beginning of the new legal year in the autumn of 1957 showed
that it had been a great blessing and was working satisfactorily.[2]
This happy state did not last very long. By 1960 it was generally
not possible to get a fixed date assigned for less than eight months
ahead. By the beginning of 1963, with far more judges, the estimate
was much the same. The extra judicial time goes into Circuits and
putting in odd time on the ordinary lists, so that a case is reached
more quickly if it is put in an ordinary list than if it is given a fixed
date. For some years the position at Assizes was growing worse
and in some areas it became intolerable. Criminal work has priority
and there was often uncertainty as to whether a civil case might not
have to wait over until a subsequent Assize. The additional judges
and the changes introduced by the Criminal Justice Administration
Act 1962 should now allow sufficient judicial time for civil cases at
Assizes.[3]

More far-reaching changes raise questions of the whole structure
of the High Court and the organisation of its work, and consideration of these is postponed until after the sections on the other
Divisions of the High Court.

The Chancery Division

There are at present seven puisne judges in this division. The Lord
Chancellor is the President, but he is too busy elsewhere to take any
active part in this work. The Chancery Division judges do all their
work in London. There is in law no reason why the judges sent on
circuit for the Assize Courts should not be drawn from all the
divisions of the High Court, but in practice it is limited to the Queen's
Bench Division and some visits by Divorce judges. After the creation
of the High Court by the Judicature Acts 1873–5 some Chancery
judges were sent on circuit, but it was an unfortunate experiment and
had to be abandoned. Work on circuit has, for historical reasons,
been confined to the hearing of civil or criminal cases before juries, and
Chancery judges accustomed to work without juries were not successful in such an atmosphere. The result is that whereas Queen's Bench
work is both centralised in London and decentralised by the system
of circuits, the work of the Chancery Division is highly centralised:
if the parties to an action and their witnesses live in Cardiff, if the

---

[1] [1957] 1 W.L.R. 558.   [2] *The Times*, 20 November 1957.
[3] See p. 103, below.

case is to come before a Chancery Division judge the trial must be in London. For the north of England the position is a little different. The Counties Palatine of Lancaster and Durham each possessed ancient courts of wide jurisdiction. When the Judicature Acts 1873–5 abolished most of the superior courts in order to create the Supreme Court, the Chancery Court of Lancaster and the Chancery Court of Durham were left in existence. Their jurisdiction is limited geographically, but otherwise it is virtually that of the Chancery Division of the High Court. The Durham Court is very little used, but the Lancaster Court handles a fair volume of work, over 100 actions and matters being heard in court each year.

The genesis of the old Chancery Court was the need for a set of remedies to supplement the common law.[1] For this reason the jurisdiction has always appeared somewhat heterogeneous, being in effect a list of matters in which the common law either gave no remedy or did not give an adequate remedy or required some assistance of a procedural nature. The Judicature Acts 1873–5, replaced by the Judicature (Consolidation) Act 1925 s. 56, assigns various matters to the Chancery Division; the full provisions, too detailed to be given here,[2] result in the Chancery Division having exclusive jurisdiction in some matters and in others a concurrent jurisdiction with the Queen's Bench Division. Among the matters that always go to the Chancery Division are: the administration of the estates of deceased persons; the dissolution of partnerships; the redemption or foreclosure of mortgages; the execution of trusts, charitable or private; the wardship of infants and the care of infants' estates. These represent some of the branches of the law that were created and developed through the old Chancery Court, but the court, in developing a technique to deal with such matters, laid the foundations for jurisdiction in other matters. The old Chancery Court consisted of the Lord Chancellor as a working judge, assisted by the Master of the Rolls, an arrangement that became progressively inadequate and led to statutory changes in the nineteenth century. The chief effect, of course, of this insufficient judicial strength was that actions did not get heard for years after they were ready for trial, but a by-product of overworked Chancellors was the amount of work left to the officials known as masters. The masters were anciently high officials

---

[1] See p. 5, above.

[2] In addition to the list of matters set out in the Judicature Acts, a number of matters are assigned to the Chancery Division by other statutes. For details the White Book (see p. 64, below) should be consulted.

under the Chancellor, but with the growth of the Chancery Court their duties became connected with that court. The head of the masters was the Master of the Rolls, whose duties became so much judicial that by late Tudor times he acted as deputy for the Chancellor. The other masters acted as assistants to the court, their particular functions being to report to the Chancellor upon matters he submitted to them. Thus the Chancellor did not usually hear the whole of any complicated case, for he could delegate the hearing of certain points to a master, and then act on the master's report. If the subjects mentioned above as being assigned to the Chancery Division are considered, it will be seen that they offer considerable field for investigation and report by a skilled official; for instance, an account of any money involved will probably be needed, and the Chancellor could save a great deal of his time by delegating the taking of accounts to a master. So effective was this mechanism that the mere fact that accounts had to be settled was sufficient for the Chancery to be regarded as the proper court. This laid the foundations for assigning to the Chancery Division the affairs of limited liability companies. Bankruptcy law, which begins with a statute of 1542 and has remained a creature of statute, originally treated bankruptcy as virtually a crime. The common law courts dealt with bankruptcy, their jurisdiction passing to the Queen's Bench Division. Some bankruptcy jurisdiction was given to County Courts. The law of bankruptcy has long ceased to be akin to criminal law, although there are many criminal offences particularly connected with bankrupts. The modern conception is that bankruptcy serves the two purposes of securing an equitable distribution of the assets amongst the creditors and of enabling the bankrupt to get quit of the burden of debt. This changed conception led to bankruptcy jurisdiction being transferred in 1921 to the Chancery Division. A petition may be filed by a creditor or by the debtor himself. If an 'act of bankruptcy' is proved, a receiving order is made. The investigation is peculiar in that bankruptcy is partly administrative and partly judicial. The official receivers are officials of the Board of Trade and also officers of the court. In due course the bankrupt's property will be distributed and he will receive his discharge, the date of the latter depending upon the circumstances. Revenue cases used to go to the King's Bench Division (as the heir of the old Exchequer Court) but tax law is nowadays associated with companies, partnerships, settlements and so forth, and the Revenue List is taken by a Chancery judge.

To appreciate the nature of much of the work peculiar to the Chancery Division, it is helpful to notice a small point of language; for the Queen's Bench Division we usually talk about 'actions', denoting the idea of litigants who have a dispute to be determined, whilst in the Chancery Division we are more apt to speak of 'actions and matters'. Some of the causes in the Chancery Division are normal litigation between contesting parties, but 'matters' do not necessarily mean that there is a dispute. It often happens that trustees or executors under a will are in genuine doubt about their duties, and so, whether or not this has led to a dispute among themselves or with some beneficiary, the method is to get the matter before the Chancery Division. It does not matter particularly who commences proceedings provided that all those concerned are represented. The trustees or executors will probably take the line that they do not mind what happens because their sole desire is to do whatever the court says they ought to do. Many of the applications under the Companies Acts are for 'leave' for a company to do something, such as to reduce its share capital, restore its name to the Register, or for the court to 'sanction a scheme' of re-organisation. Hence in the Chancery Division we may find bitter opponents fighting to the best of their counsel's ability, or we may find a friendly atmosphere in which the common desire is that the judge shall approve of some proposal put forward by agreement among those concerned.

There is a considerable number of actions that can be brought either in the Chancery or the Queen's Bench Division. These are cases in which the choice would in the past have depended upon whether an equitable or a common law remedy was sought: for breach of contract a decree of specific performance could sometimes be obtained, or for various torts the plaintiff might seek an injunction restraining the defendant from further wrongful acts, both of these being equitable remedies available in the Chancery Court and more suitable in some cases than the remedy of damages obtainable in the common law courts. Now that all remedies, equitable and legal, are obtainable in all courts[1] the old reason for choice of courts does not apply to choice of division in the High Court. Hence in many cases of breach of contract and of tort the Chancery and the Queen's Bench Division have concurrent jurisdiction. It is difficult to describe the factors that influence practitioners in choosing the division in such cases. Until the decline in the use of juries in civil cases[2] the

---

[1] See p. 8, above. [2] See p. 66, below.

mode of trial was often the decisive consideration, for trial by jury could be had normally in the Queen's Bench Division and be avoided in the Chancery Division; this is of little importance now. The elusive factor is a difference of 'atmosphere' in these two divisions. Traditionally the notions of a trail are different,[1] and although law and equity learned to walk in harmony there are differences of outlook that have survived. The Chancery judges, and counsel appearing before them, are concerned with the elucidation of facts and the determination of the correct principle to be applied, working in a quiet and somewhat academic manner to build up their system. The common law judges are, of course, also concerned with facts and principles, but historically the determination of the facts has been a matter for the jury, and the law applicable has had to be stated so that a jury could at least appear to understand it. Since the distinctions might be called temperamental, we may say that the practitioner often feels that the Chancery or the Queen's Bench Division, as the case may be, will be more sympathetic, and in accordance with this estimate he selects the division.

The Probate Divorce and Admiralty Division

The lumping together of these three topics is often a source of wonder or amusement. Sir Alan Herbert has suggested that the idea is jurisdiction over wrecks—wrecks of wills, marriages and ships. The three topics represent the main parts of our law that were of non-native growth. Wills and intestacies and matrimonial matters were in the hands of ecclesiastical courts until 1857, so that the basis of the jurisdiction was canon law (which owed a good deal to Roman law) modified by English legislation. Admiralty law is essentially European, with a definitely Roman law basis. Hence the civilian, a man trained in Roman law, used to find that the ecclesiastical courts and the Admiralty Court were nearer to each other in ideas than they were to the common law or equity courts. The professional civilian has gone: he who practises in Probate Divorce or Admiralty has now received the usual legal education and has then specialised at some later time.

The judicial strength was for many years the President of the Probate Divorce and Admiralty Division and two puisne judges. The number was raised to four in 1937, and increases since the war have led to there being, in 1963, eleven puisne judges. The President is normally engaged upon the work of the division.

[1] See p. 18, above.

Probate

The function of this jurisdiction is to give a valid title to the property of a deceased person. If the deceased made a will, the court has to decide whether the document, or which of several documents, is a valid will, and whether there is under that will an executor to carry it out; the court 'grants probate' to executors, who may then take the necessary steps to deal with the estate. If the deceased died intestate, or left a will but there is no executor, then the court has to determine who should be appointed to wind up the estate, such a person being called an administrator and being authorised by 'letters of administration'. In the great majority of cases there is no dispute, and the function of the court is performed by officials; persons named as executors in wills, or near relations in the case of intestacies, apply to the Registry at Somerset House or to their local District Probate Registry, and by producing the necessary sworn statements receive probate or letters of administration. Over 200,000 grants are made in this way each year. Contentious work is relatively small. An action may be brought to establish the validity of a will, or to claim letters of administration, or to procure the revocation of probate or letters of administration. Under 100 such cases are heard each year in the Probate Division, the trial generally being without a jury. For small estates the jurisdiction may be exercised by a County Court, but few cases have been brought: in 1955 the limit was raised to £1000. There are special statutory provisions which enable Post Office Savings not exceeding £100 and some other forms of property to go to persons entitled without the need for probate or letters of administration.

Divorce

A better title is Matrimonial Proceedings, but as petitions of divorce constitute the bulk of the work the court is inevitably referred to as the Divorce Court. The law has been consolidated by the Matrimonial Causes Act 1950. Proceedings are commenced by filing a petition praying for the remedy required. The following decrees may be sought:

(1) *Dissolution of marriage*, commonly called divorce. This presupposes that the parties are bound by a valid and existing marriage. The grounds upon which the court can dissolve a marriage are entirely statutory, and are set out in section 1 of the 1950 Act, now amended by the Divorce (Insanity and Desertion) Act 1958.

(2) *A decree of nullity*. This differs from divorce in that the principle

here is that for some reason the apparent marriage is declared to be void or thereby avoided. In the case of a marriage void for incapacity, as where the parties are within the prohibited degrees, the theory is that there never has been a marriage. If through some strange accident *A* marries his sister *B*, there is no marriage, and therefore both *A* and *B* are free to marry again without getting any decree from the courts. A decree in such a case is merely a safeguard. In other cases the marriage may be declared to be no marriage, but until the matter has been before the court the marriage is still existing. A husband whose wife refuses to consummate the marriage is still her husband; he may now petition for a decree of nullity, but until he has done so successfully he may not marry again under the pains of the law of bigamy.

(3) *Restitution of conjugal rights.* This is a complaint that the other spouse has gone away and refuses to return. The decree directing the resumption of co-habitation cannot be enforced, but such decrees were a useful preliminary to other complaints. The position has been altered and there are now relatively few cases.

(4) *Judicial separation.* This decree does not entitle the parties to remarry: in effect it says that one party has behaved in such a way that the other party can refuse to co-habit without thereby breaking the obligations of matrimony. A petition for judicial separation may be on any grounds that are sufficient for divorce, or failure to satisfy a decree for restitution of conjugal rights, or for grounds recognised by the old ecclesiastical courts. The usual result is that if a wife petitions she will be enabled to live apart from her husband and at the same time get an assured income from him, whilst if a husband petitions[1] he can live apart and she will forfeit the right to be maintained by him.

(5) *A decree of presumption of death and of dissolution of marriage may be sought.* The court will presume death from evidence that shows that death is the only reasonable supposition, as when a person falls overboard from a ship at sea and is not rescued, or continual absence of a person for seven years without reason to believe that person is still alive will provide a presumption of death that holds good unless the contrary is proved.

(6) *Declaration of legitimacy, etc.* If it is thought that some

---

[1] Petitions by husbands are unusual; the aggrieved husband can refuse to have anything to do with his wife and refuse to give her any money, thus forcing the wife either to accept that situation or to bring a petition herself on the grounds that her husband's conduct is unjustifiable.

matters, such as legitimacy of some person, can be proved now but may be difficult to prove at a later date, the court may be asked to make a declaration. Such a step may well be taken when rights to property are involved, for then the expense of putting evidence into safe storage may be justified.[1]

Whether the law governing divorce is satisfactory or not is outside the scope of this book, but there are certain characteristics of the law that must be mentioned because they have affected the working of the courts. Our divorce law is classified as civil, but in principle it is perhaps nearer to the idea of a private criminal action. The basic theory of divorce is that there must be an innocent petitioner and a guilty respondent. The innocent party is to have relief and the guilty party is to suffer. If the guilty spouse is the husband, he must provide an income for life to his former wife irrespective of her capacity to earn her own living, and to pay for children of the marriage (whether or not the wife has ample means to do so) without having any say in their upbringing or education. If the guilty spouse is the wife, she will be punished by being deprived of any income from the husband. The husband petitioner may claim damages against the man with whom the wife has commited adultery (the co-respondent), and these damages will be found to depend upon the wealth of the co-respondent rather than the expense incurred by the husband through the disturbance of his household. Such issues may be tried by a jury, and if the jury care to find that the wife has committed adultery, but the co-respondent did not the court can accept such a verdict, thus accepting the proposition that A can have sexual intercourse with B without B having sexual intercourse with A. It follows from the notion of 'guilt' that if the petitioner has committed some matrimonial offence the right to relief has gone, and the court will only grant a divorce by exercising its discretion. Further, unlike other civil litigation, agreement between the parties may be fatal. Also, again contrary to the general theory of our law, in divorce cases the court regards everyone as a suspicious character. Every petitioner has to swear, usually twice over (once in writing and once orally), that he or she is innocent of any matrimonial offence. Not content with this, a period which was six months until 1946 and is now three months must elapse between the decree nisi and the

---

[1] There is also the possibility of a suit for jactitation of marriage. This arises (very rarely indeed) when a person boasts of being married to someone to whom he is not married so that a reputation of marriage may arise. The court orders the offender to keep perpetual silence in the matter.

decree absolute so that anonymous letter-writers may suggest to the Queen's Proctor that some petitioner has committed adultery; the honesty of litigants must then be checked by a detective service run on public money. These peculiarities led to an unnecessary restriction in the courts exercising jurisdiction in divorce. There have been great changes in the last few years, but a proper appreciation of these requires some account of the state of affairs in the period between the wars.

Until 1920 all divorce cases were heard in London. Parliament then provided that matrimonial causes could be heard at Assizes, subject to rules of court. Under the rules that were made this jurisdiction was exercised in certain Assize courts only, and was confined to the hearing of undefended cases or poor persons' cases.[1] A petitioner might, therefore, have to bear the expense of trial in London because the local Assize Court did not hear such cases or because the respondent defended the case. In 1936, out of 5915 petitions in matrimonial causes, 2192 (of which 1231 were Poor Persons) were tried at Assize towns. If a given King's Bench Division judge on circuit could try a case in one town he could presumably try it in another, and if he was competent to try a defended case for a Poor Person he was presumably competent to do the same for those who were not so poor. From the litigants' point of view it was obvious that anything that made the court more accessible in distance and cheaper in cost was a distinct gain. The opposition to any such change came from the judges and the legal profession. The London barristers and solicitors had a strong financial interest in centralised justice. If Assize facilities were extended the King's Bench Division judges would have had to do more divorce work, and some of them took the view that they ought not to be called upon to administer such a distasteful part of the law,[2] which was, of course, a sound argument if we think that law courts exist for the benefit of judges. The only plausible argument that was put forward for keeping divorce jurisdiction in a confined circle was that it

[1] See p. 305, below.

[2] This appeared from the evidence given to the Business of Courts Committee, Cmd. 4471 (1934), p. 12, and to the Royal Commission on the Despatch of Business at Common Law, Cmd. 5065 (1936), p. 59. Judges at Assize towns have sometimes criticised the system. In *The Times* of 11 March 1937, Lord Hewart L.C.J., after granting a decree nisi at Sussex Assizes, is reported to have asked: 'To what do I owe the advantage of having to deal with this rubbishy case at Lewes?' In the same issue Mr Justice Swift, at the Birmingham Assizes, is reported to have said: 'Do not let anybody say that I disapprove of divorce on circuit, because I don't.'

required specialists, or at least a body of judges who could consult together. It was said that divorce law must be administered on uniform principles, and that 'discretion' where both parties are 'guilty' cannot be worked properly by a large body of judges who are engaged primarily upon other work.[1] There was for long a tendency to regard matrimonial causes as a difficult branch of the law that is incomprehensible to all save the select few. The practice of the Divorce Court sustained this tradition by having rules that were obscure and self-contradictory.[2] Any mysteries that existed in divorce practice were due to the tendency of any small group of men engaged upon one type of work to lose their sense of proportion and erect their craft into a close guild. Lord Merrivale, formerly President of the Probate Divorce and Admiralty Division, on several occasions expressed the view that divorce could not be safely mixed with the everyday work of the common law judges, because divorce affects the public well-being as well as the individuals concerned. Common law judges may interpret the law so that men are hanged or imprisoned or set free, trade unions may be crippled or exalted, the whole range of civil liberty may grow greater or less through precedent upon precedent, but apparently 'discretion' in divorce was too important for the public welfare for it to be entrusted to such unreliable judges. The grotesque edifice built by Lord Merrivale and his predecessors might come toppling down if vulgar hands were to touch their work. Conditions after 1941, when petitions began to increase in numbers far above the pre-war level, made it impossible for the close guild attitude to be maintained, and a comparatively rational solution has been found for the problem of the bringing and trying of divorce suits. The substantive law is virtually unchanged. An observation made by Lord Hewart L.C.J. in 1935 is still pertinent: 'Perhaps it is not vouchsafed to everybody, whether in Holy Orders or out of them, to appreciate the full sublimity and beauty of the doctrine that if one of two married persons is guilty of misconduct there may properly be divorce, while if both are guilty they must continue to abide in the holy estate of matrimony.'[3]

The question of trial in the provinces was examined by a Committee[4] which reported in 1943 in favour of allowing all classes of divorce cases to be heard at certain Assize towns, and for all classes

[1] Cmd. 4471 (1934), pp. 10–13; Cmd. 5065 (1936), pp. 59–61. The exercising of 'discretion' is not confined to divorce; it is commonplace in all courts, civil and criminal. [2] Cmd. 5065 (1936), p. 60.
[3] The London *Daily Telegraph*, 21 October 1935.
[4] Matrimonial Causes (Trial in the Provinces) Committee, Cmd. 6480 (1943).

of divorce cases to be capable of being begun and prosecuted up to trial in certain district registries. The Committee also recommended that wherever practicable judges of the Divorce Division should go on circuit. These recommendations were carried out. Because of accommodation and other difficulties it was later provided that the divorce work at Assizes could be taken at some other time than the ordinary civil and criminal work.

The great congestion of divorce work led to the appointment in June 1946 of a Committee under the Chairmanship of Mr Justice (now Lord) Denning. This Committee worked rapidly and issued three Reports[1] in the following eight months. The major recommendation of the First Report was that the period of six months between decree nisi and decree absolute should be reduced to six weeks. This period is a matter of procedure within the province of the Rule Committee,[2] and the change was carried out within a few days.

The Second Report dealt with the important matter of jurisdiction. The Committee found that divorce as part of the ordinary Assize system had been a failure. The King's Bench Division judges had not had enough time, and trial by Divorce Division judges on circuit had been a success for the provinces at the expense of the London lists. It was recommended that divorce should stay in the High Court, but that judicial strength should be found by the appointment of Commissioners, and that the persons to be appointed Commissioners should be mainly (but not exclusively) County Court judges. The Commissioners should sit at selected provincial towns and in London, with all the jurisdiction of a High Court judge in divorce and matrimonial cases. In all respects, including robes, form of address and payment, they should be in the position of a High Court judge. These recommendations were carried out. As regards London, the arrears were soon cleared off, and the judges of the Probate Divorce and Admiralty Division can keep abreast of the current work. In the provinces the system of Commissioners now has some appearance of permanency. There are forty-two 'divorce towns' at which Commissioners sit, taking both defended and undefended cases. In 1962, 9,921 matrimonial causes were heard in London and 20,400 outside London, of which 19,624 were heard by Commissioners and only 776 were tried at Assizes. This Report also

[1] Committee on Procedure in Matrimonial Causes. First Interim Report, Cmd. 6881 (1946); Second Interim Report, Cmd. 6945 (1946); Final Report, Cmd. 7024 (1947).
[2] See p. 63, below. In 1957 the period was altered to three months.

made a number of recommendations for simplifying and cheapening the procedure. Some, but not all, of these recommendations have been carried out.

The Final Report is mostly concerned with matters that require statute. Reconciliation is discussed, and it is recommended that there should be a Marriage Welfare Service, sponsored by the State but not a State institution. The interests of children should be better represented to the Court. There should be changes in the law as to maintenance. Further procedural reforms are needed. Part of these recommendations has been further examined by a Departmental Committee appointed to consider the line of development of marriage guidance as a social service assisted by Exchequer grants, and a Report was presented in 1948.[1] Probation officers were attached to the Divorce Court in London in 1950 as welfare officers and to courts in the provinces in 1957, but other recommendations have not been carried out.

The great number of cases has led to matrimonial causes being an important part of general legal practice. The tiresome close guild attitude has been broken down, getting its obituary notice in the Second Report: 'The assumption that divorce involves a peculiar discretion which only a few know how to exercise is not valid.' The pressure of work has also had important effects on legal aid for poor people.[2]

There is not much more that could be done about jurisdiction and procedure within the present framework; it was hoped that the Royal Commission on Marriage and Divorce, appointed in 1951, would lead to a more rational law, but the Report[3] has had little effect.

It is generally assumed that the statistics of divorce show an increasing tendency for a disregard of the marriage bond. The number of petitions in 1914 was 1348, increasing during the war years and being 5749 in 1919 and 5184 in 1920; in 1921 the figure

---

[1] Cmd. 7566 (1948).   [2] See p. 309, below.

[3] Cmd. 9678 (1956). It has attracted some vigorous criticism; see O. R. McGregor, *Divorce in England* (1957), an excellent book. The principal result of the Report has been new provisions for securing the welfare of children. The Matrimonial Proceedings (Children) Act 1958 requires the court not to make any final decree unless and until the court is satisfied that satisfactory arrangements have been made for the care and upbringing of any child under sixteen years old (including a child of one party to the marriage if he has been accepted as one of the family), or that it is impracticable for the parties to make such arrangements, in which case the court can make arrangements if necessary by committing a child to the care of a local authority, or placing the child under supervision. Probation officers are attached as court welfare officers.

was down to 3464, and in subsequent years the figure gradually rose until in 1938 there were over 10,000 petitions filed. A full analysis of these figures cannot be made here, but one of the factors must be recognised. An undefended divorce suit cost on the average more than £50. Changes in the Poor Person's rules came into force after 1918, with the result that thousands of working-class people who previously were barred from a remedy because of their poverty became able to take proceedings. Whereas in 1914 there were only 99 petitions by Poor Persons out of the 1348 petitions filed, in the years after 1918 the Poor Persons' cases accounted for at least half and in some years nearly three-quarters of the total cases. Of the 'paying clients' it is probable that many could not have afforded the suit if it had not been for the 1920 legislation allowing trial at Assizes in some cases. From 1942 onwards there was a steady rise in the number of petitions filed, reaching a peak of some 48,000 in 1947 and falling to 29,000 by 1950. In this post-war spate of matrimonial proceedings there was a higher proportion of 'paying clients' than before the war; there was more money in peoples' pockets and the Poor Persons Procedure was somewhat strained. Now we have a new system of legal aid which looks as if it really does cover all the need for assistance for divorce cases, and the figures for petitions filed are a better guide to the number of broken marriages. But in looking back over past years one must always remember that figures for proceedings brought have been much influenced by ability to pay or facilities for free or cheap assistance.

Admiralty

In Tudor times the Admiralty Court was a general commercial court, dealing with all classes of commercial disputes, whether maritime or not. The common law courts were jealous of this thriving rival, and during the seventeenth century they succeeded in depriving the Admiralty Court of jurisdiction over any matter except those purely maritime. Now in the High Court this distinction can still be traced. Various matters affecting ships, such as a contract to purchase a ship or charter-parties by which a ship or the use of a ship is hired, come before the Queen's Bench Division and are determined by the common law. Where maritime law is applicable the cases go to Admiralty.[1] This is a highly specialised topic: apart

---

[1] The jurisdiction was laid down by the Judicature Acts, but it was redefined and now rests on the Administration of Justice Act 1956: it covers aircraft as well as ships.

from small cases in certain County Courts, the whole of the work is done in London, where the work is in the hands of a few firms of solicitors and a few barristers. In one sense the court is international, since it is frequently trying cases where foreign ships are concerned, and a high standard of judicial ability is needed. This is secured, despite certain difficulties discussed later, and greatly reinforced by the system of nautical assessors. Where the judge requires assistance in matters of nautical skill he is assisted by two Brethren of Trinity House, who sit on the Bench with the judge. A jury is never used. The system of a judge with technically qualified and disinterested assessors is alien to the common law, but it appears to work excellently in Admiralty; it certainly appears to be far better than the common law technique of listening to expert witnesses called by the parties at great expense to assert contradictory views. The procedure in Admiralty has several peculiarities when compared with other courts. The most noticeable difference is that some proceedings are *in rem*. In all other courts proceedings are necessarily *in personam*, that is, they are against some person or body like a corporation that is regarded as a fictitious person. If you have been run down by a motor-car you can sue the driver or his employer but you cannot sue the car itself. In Admiralty it is possible to sue a ship or a cargo. The writ may be served on the ship if in British waters by nailing it to the mainmast (or tying it on with string if the mast is of metal), whereupon the ship is not allowed to leave port unless security is given. Normally, of course, the owners defend the action. The purpose of this is to make sure that the plaintiff will recover damages if he wins, for the owners (particularly if they are foreign owners) may have no assets within the jurisdiction; proceedings *in rem* mean that either security is given or the ship is still in port, in which case she can be sold by order of the court and the judgment satisfied out of the proceeds.

The volume of work in Admiralty is not large; under 300 writs are issued a year, of which less than a quarter reach trial. The amount of money involved is often considerable. Since proceedings may mean that a ship is detained, and under modern conditions this may mean an expenditure of hundreds of pounds a day, the court has to keep abreast of the work. In most of the cases both parties (or their insurers) can afford the costs; the problem of litigation by poor people or those of modest means that has been such a difficulty in most of our courts hardly affects Admiralty. Also, when a substantial sum is in dispute the amount of costs incurred may appear reasonable.

If my motor-car is destroyed in a collision, High Court proceedings may cost an aggregate of say £600 for determining liability of say £450. A minor collision may easily cause £10,000 damage to a ship and a few hundred pounds of costs is more proportionate to the importance of the issue. It is perhaps these reasons, as well as the nature of the court and its proceedings, that make the Admiralty Court the least criticised tribunal.

In time of war the law of prize comes into operation and there are then sittings as a Prize Court. It takes some time to wind up these matters, and in 1949 fifty-six captured enemy vessels were condemned as prize. In 1957 there was one matter in the Prize Court.

The Organisation of the High Court

The divisions of the High Court and the allocation of work between them are explicable as a matter of legal history, but they are hard to justify as a rational structure. Thus, a Probate judge determines whether a document is a valid will, and a Chancery judge interprets the will and deals with the administration of estates. Admiralty is highly specialised, and nearer to commercial work than to probate or divorce, yet the commercial court is part of the Queen's Bench Division. Legal practice, appointments to the bench and an efficient use of judicial times are said to be affected by this inconvenient arrangement of Divisions.

There does seem a prima facie case for revising the divisions of the High Court and making a more rational allocation of the business. There is no dearth of views, for the High Court has been the subject of a series of official inquiries. The Business of Courts Committee (Hanworth Committee) recommended a dissolution of the Probate Divorce and Admiralty Division; the probate work should go to the Chancery Division and Admiralty to the Queen's Bench Division.[1] The commercial and admiralty work would then be grouped together, offering a better scope for specialised judges. These proposals were not adopted for a number of reasons. There was some misunderstanding of what was intended. Critics thought that admiralty work would go into the general run of common law work, so that cases might come before any judge irrespective of his particular knowledge, thus destroying the merits of the Admiralty Court. Actually it was intended to keep admiralty work separate, but linked with commercial work.[2] Further opposition was probably based on a disinclination to enter the fold of the Queen's Bench

[1] Cmd. 4471 (1934). [2] Cmd. 5065 (1936).

because the internal organisation in that Division in the period before the war did not commend itself to many observers.

The Royal Commission on the Despatch of Business at Common Law (the Peel Commission) took a somewhat strict view of their terms of reference[1] and considered the circuit system and the Divisions of the High Court merely as they affected the despatch of business. Hence when they came to consider the proposals of the Hanworth Committee the principal point was whether a rearrangement of Divisions would help the congestion in the King's Bench Division, and obviously it would not: the King's Bench judges on circuit were already carrying a large load of divorce work (which some judges much disliked), and if all divorce were to be transferred to the King's Bench Division the existing congestion would get far worse. On that argument the Peel Commission strongly opposed the proposals of the Hanworth Committee. The circuit system was referred to a special Committee.[2]

The Committee on Supreme Court Practice and Procedure spent six years, from 1947 to 1953, on examining and making Reports about the Supreme Court. The Committee was primarily concerned with practice and procedure as it affects efficiency and cost. Their interest is reflected in the Reports that they made,[3] but their terms of reference specifically required them to consider the Reports of the Hanworth Committee and of the Peel Commission.

Their conclusion was against any re-organisation of the Divisions, on the ground that the advantages would not be sufficient to warrant the great upset that would be caused. That may well be a sound estimate, though it is a stock argument for leaving things as they are. The great contribution of the Evershed Committee is not their assessment of the merits of a scheme of Divisions, nor the changes that they recommended in the many detailed rules of procedure that they discuss, but in their realisation that the decline in certain kinds of litigation is due to a failure of the courts to meet the requirements of litigants.

Most of these matters have arisen again over the Commercial

---

[1] Cmd. 5065 (1936), para. 11.

[2] Report of the Circuit Towns Committee, Cmd. 5262 (1936).

[3] Interim Report, Cmd. 7764 (1949), on County Court Jurisdiction and fixed dates for trials; Second Interim Report, Cmd. 8176 (1951), Procedure in Admiralty and Chancery, The Annual Practice, and Court fees; Third Interim Report, Cmd. 8617 (1952), Durham Palatine Court; Final Report, Cmd. 8878 (1953), Practice and Procedure generally (300 pages) and 5 pages on Distribution of Business in the High Court.

Court. For some years it was obvious that merchants and business-men had little use for the court, and in 1960 the Lord Chancellor took the unusual course of summoning a conference of consumers. Representatives of 21 separate industries or trade organisations met and their Report[1] is one of the most important documents about the working of the court and the reasons why people who can choose prefer to go to arbitration. The chief complaints were about expense, delays, elaboration of pleadings and procedure, and insistence on oral evidence. Arbitration was said to be better on all those aspects and in addition it is private, more acceptable to foreign businessmen and its awards are easier to enforce abroad than are judgments of courts. It was suggested that a judge should be enabled, at the request of the parties, to sit as an arbitrator. Rearrangement of the High Court to provide an Admiralty and Commercial Division was suggested. Mr Justice Megaw, who was appointed to take the Commercial Court, gave a Practice Direction in 1962 which is in effect a reversion to the earlier and simpler procedure.[2] Discussion is continuing on the other steps that may be taken. If the re-organisation of the High Court is to be undertaken, it might be desirable for the Restrictive Practices Court to be grouped with Admiralty and Commercial jurisdiction.

4. THE MODE OF TRIAL

Matters of procedure are governed almost exclusively by Rules of Court made under powers given by statute. For the Supreme Court the Rule Committee consists of the Lord Chancellor, the Lord Chief Justice, the Master of the Rolls, the President of the Probate Division, four judges of the Supreme Court, two practising barristers and two practising solicitors, the four judges and the barristers and solicitors being appointed by the Lord Chancellor. The Rules that are made must be published and laid before Parliament. County Court Rules are made by a committee of five County Court judges, two barristers, two registrars of County Courts, and two solicitors, all appointed by the Lord Chancellor. The Rules then have to be submitted to the Lord Chancellor, who may allow, disallow or alter them. In all cases the Rules are subject to the limitation that, being delegated legislation, they can be valid only within the scope of the powers given by Parliament, but since the rule-making power is

---

[1] Report of the Commercial Court Users' Conference, Cmnd. 1616 (1961).
[2] [1962] 1 W.L.R. 1216.

largely vested in judges, it is unlikely that judges will ever find that the statutory power has been exceeded. The code of procedure is arranged under about seventy Orders, each Order comprising a number of Rules. Law publishers issue annual volumes[1] containing the texts and copious annotations. More than 3800 closely printed pages of orders, rules, statutes, decided cases and comment are required for a complete account of procedure in the Supreme Court, and a volume of some 1700 pages for County Courts. The Rules are being revised, the first instalment coming into force in 1964. It is impossible to describe procedure within a short compass,[2] and I shall deal merely with certain salient points.

It is customary to think of 'procedure' as governing the steps that must be taken from the commencement of a case down to the trial, the trial itself, and subsequent steps for enforcing the judgment or order of the court, together with the bringing or defending of any appeal that may be made to a higher court. The centre of this picture is the trial, which means the hearing of the case before a judge or a judge and jury. In practice only a small number of the actions commenced ever result in a trial. Apart from matrimonial causes, which are exceptional in that all cases (whether defended or undefended) must come before a judge, the general rule is that a case will not reach trial unless it is contested. This is clearly shown in the Queen's Bench Division and in the County Courts. In 1962 in the Queen's Bench Division 62,970 proceedings were commenced, yet only 926 cases were actually tried; in the County Courts it is also only a small proportion of the cases that reach actual trial.[3] A certain number of proceedings are commenced and then withdrawn, either because the plaintiff comes to the conclusion that the case is not worth further costs or because the defendant settles the action by paying the sum claimed or an agreed sum by way of compromise. Often the issue of a writ is little more than a tactical move in negotiations for a settlement. The solicitors representing an injured pedestrian try to settle their client's claim against a motorist by dealing with the solicitors for the motorist's insurance company; if a deadlock is reached, then a writ is issued, suggesting that the plaintiff

---

[1] The *Annual Practice* (the 'White Book') and the *County Court Practice*.

[2] Odgers, *Pleading and Practice*, and Gibson's *Practice of the Courts* are useful to students. However, I remember Mr Weldon (of the firm of law coaches responsible for the latter book) impressing upon his class of students that procedure can never be learned from books alone, and that students could not expect to know all the stages of a lengthy chancery action because none of them had lived long enough. [3] See p. 32, above, and Table III.

means to fight. The defendant may take up the challenge, but it is more likely that a renewed effort will be made to reach an agreed sum. If the plaintiff insists upon claiming what is thought to be too much, the defendant may 'pay into court' what he thinks is a reasonable sum; this puts the plaintiff into a difficult position, for he must choose between accepting that sum and ending the action, or continuing the action on the terms that if he is awarded more than that sum he will get his costs in the ordinary way, but that if he is awarded less then he must pay his own costs and the costs of the defendant since the date of the payment into court. Actions may also fail to reach trial because there is no defence to the case. The defendant may allow the proceedings to continue without doing anything about them, with the result that the plaintiff obtains judgment by default. In certain types of case, both in the Queen's Bench Division and in County Courts, special provision is made for obtaining a speedy judgment where the case is likely to be uncontested. The plaintiff gives particulars of his claim and supports this with a sworn statement as to the claim, and stating that in his belief there is no defence to the action. The parties are then summoned to attend before an official of the court; if the defendant can show that he has some defence to the action he is given leave to defend, but if no apparent defence is put forward the plaintiff is forthwith allowed to enter judgment against the defendant. In the majority of these cases, known as Order 14 in the High Court and 'default summons' in County Courts, the defendant does not usually seek to defend the case, for he knows quite well that he has no defence. In such common matters as actions for the price of goods sold and delivered, or actions brought on negotiable instruments, this method of summary judgment is generally followed. For every action in the Queen's Bench Division that reaches trial there are more than a dozen actions terminated by judgments by default or under Order 14 without there having been any trial at all.[1] It is thus wrong to think of legal proceedings being synonymous with the trial of cases: the great bulk of the actions brought are settled or terminated by judgment without trial. In the background to all actions there is, of course, the possibility of a trial, and the nature of this necessarily conditions much of our system.

Confining ourselves here to civil cases, the purpose of proceedings

---

[1] For County Courts the distinction made in the Statistics is between cases 'Determined without Hearing or in Defendant's absence' and actions 'Determined on Hearing' (see Table III).

prior to the trial is to clarify the dispute. The steps are taken by the solicitors to the parties, often in consultation with a barrister who drafts the documents required, but for convenience these will be referred to as if the parties themselves were acting. After the writ has been issued and served on the defendant, a formal 'appearance' for the defendant is entered. The plaintiff then sends to the defendant a Statement of Claim setting out the allegations that he makes. The reply to this is a document called the Defence. Neither of these documents deals with the evidence upon which the allegations will be supported. For instance, in a libel action the Statement of Claim will allege that the defendant published certain matter concerning the plaintiff and that the words bear a defamatory meaning. The Defence may deny the publication, or admit the publication but deny that the words were defamatory, or plead that the words were fair comment on matters of public interest, or that the words were true. The general idea is that each party should know with some precision the case that he has to meet, and that this process must be complete before the parties go into court. The process of pleadings is under the control of officers of the court, with an appeal to a judge, and appropriate orders are made to see that each party has adequate information. Thus, if the defendant has published a 'life-story' of the plaintiff in which the plaintiff is described as having lived 'a life of crime', in a libel action the defendant may plead in defence that those words are true. This will enable the defendant to produce any evidence of the criminal activities of the plaintiff, and unless the plaintiff is further informed he will have no idea what charges he may have to meet. Hence an order will be made that the defendant produce Particulars, which means that he must give adequate information of the matters he proposes to prove so that the plaintiff can prepare to meet such allegations. As mentioned above, an order may be made for a party to answer interrogatories, or to produce for inspection any relevant documents he may possess. Eventually the pleadings are closed, and the case is ready for trial. In the course of these preliminary proceedings the place and the mode of trial will have been determined. The place of trial has already been discussed;[1] the mode of trial is determined in the same way, that is, by an official of the courts subject to an appeal to a judge. The usual choice as to mode of trial is between trial before a judge alone or before a judge and jury.

The traditional common law mode of trial was judge and jury,

[1] See p. 39, above.

whereas the Chancery Court did not use juries. The Judicature Acts 1873-5, in fusing the administration of law and equity, may be regarded as the triumph of Chancery ideas in civil suits. The normal mode of trial came to be a judge alone. Within a few years of the passing of these Acts, the use of juries in civil cases at common law declined drastically; from 1885 until 1917 roughly half the cases heard in the King's Bench Division were before a judge alone. The shortage of man-power during 1917 led to restrictive measures, and in the early 1920's jury trial was at a very low ebb. A small measure of recovery took place, aided by the repeal of the restrictive measures in 1925, but the popularity of jury trial again declined. The Administration of Justice (Miscellaneous Provisions) Act 1933 imposed some restrictions upon jury trial in King's Bench actions.[1] Under that Act jury trial is to be ordered where there is a charge of fraud, or the case is one of libel, slander, malicious prosecution, false imprisonment, seduction or breach of promise of marriage, unless the court is of opinion that the trial requires any prolonged examination of documents or accounts or any scientific or local investigation which cannot be conveniently made with a jury. In other cases the court has power to order a jury, and here it was decided in 1937 that the court's discretion is quite unfettered, there being no obligation on the applicant for a jury to show any special reason.[2] The result was that jury trial fell to less than 10 per cent of King's Bench cases.[3]

There were severe restrictions upon jury trial during the war,[4] and

---

[1] The Judicature Act of 1925 s. 99 (1) (h) provides that rules may be made for prescribing in what cases in the High Court the trial shall be by jury or by judge alone. It was thought more expedient that the substantial changes of 1933 should be made by Parliament rather than by the Rule Committee of the Supreme Court.

[2] *Hope* v. *G.W.R.* (1937) 53 T.L.R. 399. The effect of this decision is that the judges can give or refuse jury trial in any case. This is clearly shown in *Christen* v. *Goodacre* [1949] W.N. 234: in an action against a house surgeon for damages for negligence in surgical treatment the judge ordered trial by jury notwithstanding the fact that the hospital authorities who were co-defendants did not want jury trial, and that the case involved scientific and medical evidence and difficult legal questions; the Court of Appeal refused to interfere with the judge's discretion. Examples from cases reported in *The Times* are: 2 April 1958, an allegation of conspiracy of officials, jury refused; 9 February 1960, action by a child who had been injured by a bus, jury allowed; 31 January 1962, action on marine policy, underwriters alleging arson and false representation, jury allowed.

[3] I have analysed these changes in detail in 1 *Modern Law Review* (1937), p. 132.

[4] The Administration of Justice (Emergency Provisions) Act 1939 provided that there should be no juries in civil cases unless the judge ordered a jury. All juries in civil cases consisted of seven jurors. The limitation upon juries was revoked for actions begun after 4 April 1946, and the number of jurors was restored to twelve on 1 January 1947.

since these were revoked in 1947 there has been an even lower proportion of jury trials than before the war: in 1962, 926 cases were tried in the Queen's Bench, of which only 38 were before a jury. Juries have never been popular in County Courts, and changes in the right to jury trial were made on the same lines as for the King's Bench, the rules governing County Courts being enacted in the County Courts Act 1934. The result was a virtual end to jury trial in County Courts; figures for some recent years are given in Table III. Juries are not used in the Chancery Division or in the Admiralty Court. In defended divorce cases and in contested probate cases there are no restrictions and either party may apply for a jury, but this occurs in very few cases; the average is under one jury case a year in defended divorce and under two a year in contentious probate.

There was in the past a distinction between 'special juries' and 'common juries'. A special jury was drawn from more well-to-do people than a common jury, the theory being that they would be more intelligent and more able to understand a difficult case than their poorer neighbours. The qualifications for jury service are explained later.[1] In practice there was no difficulty in getting a special jury if the case was to be tried by jury at all, though the applicant had to pay the cost of £12. 12s. unless at the trial the judge certified that the case was suitable for a special jury, in which case the cost was paid by the losing party. The Juries Act 1949 abolished special juries except for special juries of the City of London in commercial cases, with the concomitant change that ordinary juries and jurors may no longer be called 'common'.

The group of cases where *prima facie* there will be jury trial is, of course, the happy hunting-ground of newspaper reporters, so that a public accustomed to reading accounts in newspapers may perhaps be excused for thinking that juries are usually used in civil cases. The decline in the use of juries in civil cases is not due entirely to lack of faith in this mode of trial. The effectiveness of jury trial depends largely upon the type of juror and the selection of matters that are left to juries; these problems are examined later.[2] Litigants are, however, more concerned with litigation being cheap and speedy and its results being fairly predictable than with the perfection of justice, and that suggests avoiding jury trial.

Trial by a judge with assessors is common in Admiralty, and

---

[1] See p. 276, below.
[2] See p. 281, below.

theoretically possible in the other divisions.[1] Cases are sometimes referred to those high officials, the Masters, either for general adjudication or for the decision of some particular point. Attached to the High Court are four Official Referees, appointed by the Crown on the advice of the Lord Chancellor.[2] A case may be sent to an Official Referee either for him to render a report upon some point, such as a question of accounts, or for him to try the case. The Official Referees have courts and chambers in the law courts, their court ranking as a sitting of the High Court. Nearly three hundred cases a year are tried in this way.

The pleadings and the other formal steps in the preparation of a case represent merely part of the work that has to be done. Often the most difficult part of the preparation is the securing of the necessary evidence. The solicitors interview all the possible witnesses, and make a full written note of what they will say. This may involve some travelling. In some cases it is necessary to submit a question to an expert; the extent of personal injuries may be more skilfully assessed by a specialist than by a general practitioner. The solicitor then prepares the 'brief' for the barrister (more often referred to as 'counsel'). This is a bundle of papers which includes a chronicle of the case made by the solicitor together with copies of all documents and of the statements made by witnesses. Counsel usually indicates which of the witnesses should be called, whereupon the solicitor must make arrangements for the witnesses to attend the trial. Some witnesses attend voluntarily, subject to their expenses being paid, whilst other witnesses are summoned by a *subpoena* which compels their attendance. In English practice the trial, or 'day in court', is a climax at which the whole case must be presented. The procedure at the trial varies somewhat according to the circumstances. In the now typical instance of a trial before a judge alone, the plaintiff's counsel 'opens the case' by giving an account of the facts and referring to any documents. The plaintiff's witnesses are then called, and give their evidence orally by being 'examined' by plaintiff's counsel. They may then be 'cross-examined' by defendant's counsel, and, if this leaves ambiguities, 're-examined' by plaintiff's counsel. If the defendant is going to call witnesses, the case for the defendant is then taken in the same way, defendant's

[1] An assessor helped the judge in *Southport Corporation* v. *Esso Petroleum Co. Ltd.* [1953] 3 W.L.R. 773, a Queen's Bench Division action on nuisance, trespass and negligence when oil escaped from a stranded ship and spoiled the amenities of the foreshore. Under the Patents Act 1949 there are scientific advisers to assist the Court.   [2] Administration of Justice Act 1956.

counsel opening his case, calling witnesses, and then summarising the evidence and presenting his arguments. Plaintiff's counsel then has the last say, because he may reply by comparing the evidence for the plaintiff with that for the defendant, and present his arguments. If the defendant does not propose to call any witnesses, then the final speech for the plaintiff is made after the plaintiff's witnesses have been called. The defendant's counsel will then comment on the evidence for the plaintiff and deal with any relevant points. In the case of a jury trial, the openings must be longer, the final speeches must be fuller, and the judge must sum up to the jury. Also, the evidence will be taken less speedily, because counsel will want to make sure that the jury have grasped certain points. The jury may be asked to give a general verdict for the plaintiff or for the defendant, or the judge may put specific questions to the jury. In the latter case there may be legal argument as to the meaning of the verdict. When a judge sits without a jury he is expected to state shortly the basis of his decision. In a difficult case he may reserve judgment, which means that he will consider his notes and consult legal works, finally writing a judgment which he will read in court. In jury trials there is generally little for the judge to do in giving judgment except direct judgment in accordance with the verdict of the jury and make an order as to costs.

Two points about this type of trial may be noted. *First,* the responsibility of the parties is not confined to settling the issue to be decided, but extends to the preparation of the evidence and its presentation. A good example is medical evidence. In the last few years judges have been inclined to urge litigants to submit an agreed medical report, but if the doctors do not agree the technique is to call the doctors for each party. One set of professional men, paid by the plaintiff, say one thing, and another set of professional men, paid by the defendant, say another thing. Under the inquisitorial system the judge would have been compiling a dossier of the case long before the trial, and he would himself have appointed some medical expert to make a report for the use of the court. In the same way, inspection of vehicles, plans of the scene of accidents, and other matters would be investigated and reported upon. The 'trial' would be far from a comprehensive review of everything in issue, for the court would want to hear evidence primarily on points not already covered by the dossier, which often means that the trial is no more than a completion of the dossier upon which the judges[1]

[1] Where the inquisitorial method of trial is used it is customary for the court to consist of more than one judge.

will come to a decision. The 'contest' theory of trial is seen at its worst when technical questions are involved. In practice it is necessary to counter the other party's experts by producing equally weighty (and equally expensive) experts; in selecting the experts it is better to be guided by 'newspaper-fame' than by learning and ability. The professions in England are so organised that there should be no difficulty in avoiding these troubles by a system of reports made at the request of judges, or by copying the Admiralty practice of a judge sitting with technical assessors.[1] *Secondly*, the evidence is presented in such a way that it imposes a considerable strain upon those who listen to it, which is particularly important in jury trials. The cross-examination of the plaintiff's witnesses is the only thing that gives any indication of the extent to which the defendant is going to contradict what is said for the plaintiff. The method of 'confrontation', which is not used in our courts, allows the immediate contradiction of evidence. Thus, if witness A says that he was not at a given place at a given time, confrontation allows A's evidence to be interrupted so that witness X may testify that A was at that place. Under our method the evidence of A may be contradicted by X some hours or days later, the jury aided by counsel being expected to remember what A said. The method of confrontation has its own drawbacks, and it is mentioned here simply to show that our method is not inevitable. The trained lawyer may make light of the burden of marshalling many apparently unconnected pieces of evidence, weighing them against similar fragments, and producing an ordered whole. To most minds a decision is facilitated by an early statement of both points of view so that there can be the least possible doubt about the bearing and relevance of the evidence. It is a curious thing that our law of evidence, primarily built up with jury trial in mind, should result in a system more suitable for those with a trained technique than for laymen. The rules as to what matters may be given in evidence are meant to exclude irrelevant and prejudicial matters. They succeed fairly well in doing this, but result in such circumlocutions that an impression of deliberately concealing information is frequently created. Unfortunately, the laws of evidence cannot be discussed without examining them at some length. A further result of jury trial has been the insistence upon oral evidence. Until relatively recently the jury were of course too illiterate to deal with documents. If we had had trial by judge alone at common law it is likely that we should be used to the idea of written evidence. In

[1] The topic of technical questions in jury trials is discussed at p. 283, below.

many cases there is no doubt that an oral examination of a witness is preferable to his written report; a report may be convincing but the man himself unconvincing, and *vice versa*. Yet we keep up this rule where it is plainly ridiculous: if, for instance, it is necessary to establish the wind velocity and rainfall on a given day, the written report of an official meteorologist as to the readings of his instruments is *prima facie* inadmissible as evidence, although if the meteorologist is called as a witness he can read out his records and may well not be cross-examined at all. Written reports are admissible if agreed to by the other party, and under the Evidence Act of 1938 the court may admit such statements, but, since the party who wishes to put in written evidence must get the order of the court before the trial or take a chance that the court will admit it at the trial, it still remains true that such evidence is considered an exception. The Evershed Committee was 'anxious that the [Evidence] Act should be as widely and liberally used as possible'.[1] Practice continues unchanged.

5. THE ENFORCEMENT OF JUDGMENTS AND ORDERS

The majority of judgments are for the payment of sums of money. If the defendant fails to pay, the plaintiff may resort to 'execution', which is the technical term for enforcing a judgment. The primary method of enforcing a judgment debt is to have the property of the defendant seized and sold. Property takes so many different forms that there can be no one simple method. Moveable goods can be seized by the appropriate officer and sold. The defendant's land may also be taken, but the complicated nature of our land law requires a further order of the court before it can be sold. Debts due to the defendant (which includes any credit balance he may have at his bank) cannot be physically seized, but the court may order the money to be paid to the plaintiff. Similarly, stocks and shares belonging to the defendant require special provisions. Where the defendant has an income-yielding asset that cannot be taken it is possible to get a receiver appointed to take the income and apply it to the judgment debt. The general effect is that all the assets a man has may be taken away by the appropriate process for the satisfaction of the judgment. If the defendant has no assets, then the plaintiff will get nothing. Of course the plaintiff ought to have made sure before he began the

[1] Final Report of the Committee on Supreme Court Practice and Procedure, Cmd. 8875 (1953), para. 274.

action that there was a fair chance of the defendant being able to meet any judgment that might be given. It does, however, happen that even with care a plaintiff finds himself with a favourable judgment and a defendant who does not pay and has no discoverable assets. When Dickens was writing the remedy was simple; imprisonment for judgment debts was the standard remedy. The Debtors Act 1869 severely curtailed imprisonment for debt, and introduced the present theory that no man may be imprisoned for debt unless his default is wilful: a committal to prison must not be made unless a judge is satisfied that the defendant has or has had since the date of the judgment the means to pay the sum. Committal to prison is designed to put pressure on the defendant; it does not extinguish the debt, and so it would be stupid cruelty if the debtor was unable to pay. Whether the present practice is in accordance with the theory is open to question.[1] There has been a great increase in the number of committals to prison by County Courts: the figures have risen from under 489 in 1950 to 6232 in 1961 and 7913 in 1962.[2] In the High Court the parties are likely to be professionally represented, and it is unlikely that abuses can arise except in rare cases. In the County Courts it depends upon the thoroughness with which the judge works, but even the most conscientious judge is at a great disadvantage. The plaintiff will produce evidence of means, and, remembering that some debt collectors are not the most scrupulous of people, it is easy to produce evidence that appears better than it really is. The poor and unrepresented defendant, who need not be present, may never get his version of the facts before the court. The plaintiff does not, of course, want to get the defendant sent to prison, his resort to a committal order being in the nature of a most unpleasant threat. Imprisonment is such a disaster to most people that they will succeed in raising the money somehow or other. The plaintiff's argument is that 'I know he cannot pay, but if I get a

[1] In an article 'In gaol for debt', *Quarterly Review*, January 1939, Sir Thomas Artemus Jones (a County Court judge) argued that imprisonment for debt on County Court judgments should be abolished; he had found that bad and unscrupulous trading rests ultimately upon the ability to get a committal order against the debtor. The Debtors Act 1869 had, as a Bill, no clause for retaining the power of imprisonment; the clause was inserted in the course of debate. It is suggested that the inclusion of this power was due to the representations made by a deputation of County Court judges. County Court judges had at that time little to do except debt-collecting cases, and they feared that if committal orders were abolished the work of their courts would decline and their jobs would disappear. H. Cecil, *Not Such an Ass* (1961), gives a realistic account of this jurisdiction.

[2] J. C. Wood, 'Attachment of Wages', 26 *Modern L.R.* (1963), p. 51, examines the scope for deductions from wage packets.

committal order his relatives or friends will pay up to keep him out of jail'. A County Court judge has ample powers to see that humane orders are made. He can order payment by instalments, and it is in fact unusual to make a committal order on the first judgment summons except in default of an instalment order.[1] The whole trouble is that the judge may be misinformed or partially informed and that the technique for seeing that he is properly informed is so defective. Imprisonment for default in payments of fines[2] has shown that the services of an investigating officer are really necessary; someone like a probation officer, who can visit the home of the defendant and ascertain the true state of affairs, is the soundest method. There is no such service for County Courts. He who owes a small sum may be harassed by various means, whereas the debtor on a grander scale, that is, of £50 and upwards, can as a last resort file his own petition in bankruptcy and eventually secure his discharge and make a fresh start with the old debts extinguished.

A judgment for the possession of land is enforced specifically by an officer entering upon the land and putting the plaintiff in possesssion. A judgment for possession of a moveable object may be enforced in much the same way. In the case of the equitable remedies, now available in all courts, the judgment directs the defendant to do something or to abstain from doing something. The acts (other than an order to pay money) or forbearances are then enforced by application to the court for committal to prison: usually the court directs committal to prison, suspending the operation for a little time so that the party in default may have an opportunity of obeying the directions of the court. A refusal to obey will result in imprisonment for contempt of court. There are also other forms of execution designed to meet particular cases. In the case of judgments that affect status there is no need for execution: thus a decree of divorce is immediately effective, and execution is inapplicable.

In the matter of execution the powers of a County Court are substantially less than that of the High Court. The most commonly used are the seizure of the judgment debtor's goods, the committal order, and the specific recovery of land. The Administration of Justice Act 1956 improved some of the forms of enforcing judgments, and it provided that High Court and various other judgments or orders for payment of money can be enforced in a County Court.

---

[1] The principles were confirmed by the Court of Appeal in *Barefoot* v. *Clarke* [1949] I All E.R. 1039.

[2] Cmd. 4649 (1934), and pp. 183 and 227, below.

6. THE RESTRICTIVE PRACTICES COURT[1]

The creation of this court in 1956 marked a complete change in national policy. In the first place, the tendency had previously been to get away from specialised courts in favour of a system of courts of general jurisdiction. Thus the various superior courts of a hundred years ago, some of them of specialised jurisdiction, were transmuted into the High Court.[2] One may think of the present organisation of the High Court as providing in effect a separate Chancery Court or a Divorce Court, but the unity of the High Court is a reality: a decision by, say, a Divisional Court of the Queen's Bench Division is a High Court decision and therefore the matter cannot be re-opened in the Chancery Division either by a single judge or a Divisional Court of that Division.[3] There have been plenty of instances since the Judicature Acts of 1873-5 where statute has created a special body to deal with a particular subject. Most of these have been regarded as special tribunals, although there has never been any very clear distinction between such tribunals and law Courts.[4] The Railway Rates Tribunal, now the Transport Tribunal,[5] is a court of record, yet it has never been regarded as part of the ordinary system of civil courts. The Restrictive Practices Court ought, on any reasonable classification by scope and function, to be put among the special tribunals, but it is by statute 'a superior court of record' and that phrase, using the word *superior*, is used by statute to describe the High Court. Hence we must put the Restrictive Practices Court alongside the High Court as a parallel superior civil jurisdiction.

There had been many years of uneasiness over the tendency of trade and industry to adopt restrictive practices. It can be argued that the English legal tradition was opposed to monopolies and restrictive trade practices, but in fact the common law left business

---

[1] R. O. Wilberforce, A. Campbell and N. M. P. Elles, *The Law of Restrictive Trade Practices and Monopolies* (1957), with Supplements, is a full treatise. J. Lever, *The Law of Restrictive Trade Agreements* is an excellent short account of the statutory provisions and of how they have been interpreted by the Restrictive Practices Court.

[2] See p. 7, above.

[3] In *re Hastings* (*No.* 3) [1959] Ch. 368 was a case where an applicant for *habeas corpus* who had been refused by a Divisional Court of the Queen's Bench Division applied to a Divisional Court of the Chancery Division, only to find that a Divisional Court's decision is the decision of the High Court and that decision had already been given: the High Court is one and indivisible despite its trinity of Divisions. On applications for *habeas corpus* see p. 228, below.

[4] See p. 319, below.

[5] See p. 328, below.

and industry reasonably free to make such arrangements as they pleased. That can be seen most clearly in the technique of stop-lists. If a manufacturer wished to secure that his products were not sold below specified list prices, he could not do so directly because the intervention of at least one middleman in the chain of distribution meant that there was no contractual bond between manufacturer and retailer. The process was for the manufacturers to form a trade association and to enforce their price system by all of them refusing to supply goods to any dealer who did not keep to the list prices, or similarly boycotting anyone who supplies to the offender; he was put on a 'stop-list'. Further, the association could exact a sum of money as the price of resuming supplies. There came into existence what were popularly called 'trade courts', sitting in secret and fining people for not observing the conditions laid down by the trade association. The polite term is 'collective enforcement'. The validity of such arrangements was contested in the courts, and it was upheld by the House of Lords.[1]

In most other countries monopolies and restrictive trade practices have long been regarded as undesirable and against the public interest and there is some form of legal restraint. The obvious method is to define the arrangements and practices that are regarded as undesirable and to prohibit them. The prohibited practice is put into much the same position as if it were a criminal offence; somebody has to ascertain the facts, bring the prosecution, prove that the alleged monopoly or restrictive practice comes within the definition laid down by law, and so get a verdict against those responsible. That method, which is accepted in the United States and Canada, has not been followed in this country. When it was decided after the war that there should be machinery for dealing with monopolies and restrictive practices it was believed that it would be more efficacious to have a case-by-case inquiry, taking particular instances and deciding whether there was anything undesirable in the particular circumstances. Hence when Parliament set up the Monopolies and Restrictive Practices Commission in 1948 it created what was essentially a standing body for investigating and reporting upon matters referred to it by the Board of Trade. If a report disclosed grounds for taking some action it was for the government to take administrative action or to bring the matter before Parliament for approval of an Order. The Commission was enlarged in 1953, but its functions were not substantially altered.

[1] *Thorne* v. *Motor Trade Association* [1937] A.C. 797.

The Commission could also be asked to investigate any practice generally, and one of their most important Reports was on a reference as to Collective Discrimination which covered a wide variety of restrictive practices.[1] There was no doubt about the undesirability of many kinds of restrictive practices, but the Report was not unanimous as to the best method of exercising control. The choice, broadly put, was between a general legal prohibition combined with some way of allowing exemptions, and a system of registration with case-by-case examination. Much discussion and public controversy ensued on which line should be followed, and on the extent to which the adjudicating body should be linked with administration or be independent and judicial. The solution was an acceptance of the registration of restrictive agreements with a judicial body to do a case-by-case examination and annul those that are undesirable, but with an out-and-out prohibition of collective enforcement. The Restrictive Trade Practices Act 1956 therefore creates an entirely new and unprecedented kind of jurisdiction. It sets up two new institutions. In the first place there is a Registrar of Restrictive Trade Agreements who is an independent official. The Act requires persons carrying on business in this country who have entered into a restrictive agreement (that is one between firms, suppliers or buyers and containing restrictions as to prices, quantities, qualities of goods or methods of distribution) to register the agreement. It does not cover the export trade and it does not cover labour or personnel conditions. The Registrar has extensive powers of calling for information, with powers in the High Court to make appropriate orders against anyone in default. Any dispute as to whether an agreement should be registered is also a matter for the High Court.

The second institution created is the Restrictive Practices Court. The Court consists of five judges, three from the High Court, one from the Court of Session in Scotland and one from the Supreme Court of Northern Ireland. The Lord Chancellor selects one of these judges to be President. In addition there are not more than ten other members appointed by the Crown on the recommendation of the Lord Chancellor from persons qualified by virtue of their knowledge of or experience in industry, commerce or public affairs. These members are appointed for a fixed period not less than three years and they may be paid. They are removable by the Lord Chancellor for inability or misbehaviour or on the ground of any

[1] Report on Exclusive Dealing, Collective Boycotts, Aggregated Rebates and other Discriminatory Trade Practices. Cmd. 9504 (1955).

employment or interest incompatible with the functions of a member of the court. The Court may sit as a single court or in two or more divisions, and in private or in open court, the quorum being a presiding judge and two of the lay members. On a question of law the judge's opinion will prevail, whilst on other matters the decision of the court is by a majority vote. On questions of law there is appeal to the Court of Appeal or to the equivalent court for Scotland or Northern Ireland.

The only kind of restrictive agreement that is directly forbidden is one for collective enforcement of conditions as to resale prices: the 'trade court' and the 'stop-list' are prohibited. A manufacturer has, however, been given a new right, for conditions of sale can now 'run with the goods', so that any wholesaler or retailer who gets the goods knowing of the conditions must observe them or run the risk of being sued by the manufacturer. A manufacturer must now come out into the open and bring an action in the High Court if he wants to enforce a price maintenance condition. The principle governing other forms of agreement containing restrictions is that they are liable to be considered by the Court and declared invalid if they are found to be against the public interest. Proceedings are initiated by the Registrar, who in effect challenges an agreement that has been registered and presents the case against it. Cases are heard much as they would be in the High Court, with counsel appearing for the Registrar and for the parties to the agreement, with the calling of evidence, submissions, and a reasoned judgment.

When an agreement comes before court the Act says that a restriction shall be deemed to be contrary to the public interest unless the court is satisfied of circumstances set out in the Act. The parties to an agreement have a twofold burden of proof. First, they must show that a restriction comes within one or more of seven conditions. These are broadly as follows: (a) that it is required to protect the public against injury; (b) that it gives the public substantial benefits or advantages; (c) that it is required for protection against restrictive practices by others; (d) that it is required so that proper terms can be made with buyers or sellers who may dominate the market; (e) that without the restriction there would be serious and persistent local unemployment; (f) that it is required for export business; (g) that it is required to maintain other restrictions that are allowed by the court. If the court is satisfied under one or more of these heads, the second consideration arises, the need for 'balancing'. The advantages of the restriction must be weighed against any disadvantages it will bring to the public or to sellers or producers of similar goods, and on balance the restriction must not be unreasonable. These principles do not mean that the court simply has to apply a rule, because it is still necessary to decide what particular weight is to be attached to any of these grounds in any particular case. If the court finds against an agreement it is declared void, and in appropriate cases a restraint order may be made to forbid it being carried out on pain of imprisonment for contempt.

The Act had to be brought into operation by stages to allow the Registrar's office to be built up and to provide for an orderly sequence of registrations. The first sitting of the Court for the hearing of a case was in October 1958, the Court consisting of two English judges, one Scots judge and four other members. The judges were not robed but counsel and the clerk of the court were wigged and gowned.

Before this legislation we could say that matters of general economic regulation were the concern of business and industry, subject to the control of government and Parliament. Now over a substantial field the decision rests with this independent Court. It is easy to see why this change commended itself to a number of people. To business interests it seemed preferable to have a judicial body making such decisions rather than have them made by the government, that is to say by civil servants and ministers. From the government point of view there was continual trouble in taking action that was resented by the interests concerned as being clumsy or biased political interference. It has, however, created a situation that may turn out to be impossible to maintain. The decision to vest this jurisdiction in an independent court with judges always presiding has produced results much like the common law. Cases are reported in the Law Reports and there is already a substantial amount of case-law. The essence of the jurisdiction is that the court has to apply conceptions of social and economic values. Whether some restriction is 'reasonably necessary' may well be justiciable by ordinary legal methods, but other questions and particularly the 'balancing' provisions are matters of national policy and decisions can be 'right' or 'wrong' only in terms of political and social ideas. The basic concept of the whole jurisdiction is that industry, trade and commerce should always be conducted in conditions of competition, as if competition is good in itself; it is in effect part of a political creed of the early 1950's. Ideas of that period may well become less acceptable in changed political and business conditions, but the court can hardly adapt itself because of its very nature; it is almost certain to go on behaving as if it were a common law court because of the judges and the law reports. Businessmen now have agreements drafted in the light of the decided cases, and no lawyer cares to upset that which is built on precedent. In current opinion the government of the day has an overall responsibility for the welfare of the country, including the economic organisation, and it cannot get out of all its responsibility by setting up a new court. The government cannot, of course, interfere with the court, but if there should at any time be a clash between the policy of the court and the government's view of the needs of the country there would have to be amending legislation.[1]

7. THE COURT OF APPEAL AND THE HOUSE OF LORDS

From County Courts and from the civil side of the High Court there may be appeal to the Court of Appeal.[2] This tribunal, which is concerned solely with appeals in civil cases, was established by the Judicature Acts 1873–5. The notion of an appeal as we understand it, that is, a review of a case on the grounds that the trial court came to the wrong conclusion, is alien to the common law. Common law developed a cumbrous system known as writ of error, whereby a judgment could be reversed for error on the official record of the case, but if the record was in order there might be no remedy. This was supplemented by orders for new trials and other devices. The simpler idea of going over the case again was introduced by the practice of the Chancery Court. The Court of Appeal has as *ex officio* members the Lord Chancellor, any ex-Lord Chancellor, Lords of Appeal in Ordinary, the Lord Chief Justice, the Master of the Rolls, and the President of the Probate Divorce and Admiralty Division. Of the *ex officio* members the Master of the Rolls is the only one who customarily sits in the Court of Appeal. The full-time

[1] The decision *In re Yarn Spinners Agreement* [1959] 1 W.L.R. 154 shows that the Court may annul an agreement despite the fact that unemployment and other upsets will occur. This decision affected Lancashire, where there has been so much depression over cotton that a little more could be accepted as being in keeping with the times, and a general election was not imminent. Yet a decision of this kind, affecting another trade at a more critical time in the life of a government, might well become a major political issue. A good note on this case is in [1959] *Public Law*, p. 105.

[2] Some lectures on the Court of Appeal by members of that court are now available: Lord Evershed M.R., *The Court of Appeal in England* (1950); Lord Cohen, 'Jurisdiction, practice and procedure of the Court of Appeal', 11 *Cambridge Law Journal* (1951), p. 3; Lord Asquith, 'Some aspects of the work of the Court of Appeal', *Journal of the Society of Public Teachers of Law* (1950), p. 350.

judges appointed to staff the Court of Appeal are called Lords Justices of Appeal. For a number of years there were five Lords Justices. Three judges are required to sit together for this court, so that we had two divisions of the Court of Appeal, one division consisting of the Master of the Rolls and two Lords Justices, and the other division consisting of three Lords Justices. The work of the court increased and, as is usual in our system, there was delay in increasing the judicial strength. A third division was for a time constituted from *ex officio* members and by diverting judges from other courts[1] until an Act in 1938 allowed three additional appointments. Under an Act of 1948 the court could sit in four divisions but again the increase in divisions had to be staffed by temporary arrangements. The Administration of Justice (Judges and Pensions) Act 1960 raised the number of Lords Justices to eleven, so that, with the Master of the Rolls, there is now a working strength of twelve which suffices for sitting in four divisions. Courts are normally so constituted that if the appeals to be heard are from the Chancery side then there will be two members of the court with Chancery experience and one with Queen's Bench experience, whilst if the appeals are to be common law there will be two members from the Queen's Bench side and one from the Chancery side.

Taking first the principles of appeals from the High Court, it should be noted that an appeal is described as being a rehearing of the case but that this is a very misleading term. The Court of Appeal does not hear the case again in the sense of listening to the witnesses. The evidence is taken from a shorthand note made in the trial court.[2] There are two main things than an appellant may ask for. *First,*

---

[1] Under the Judicature Act of 1925 judges and ex-judges of the Court of Appeal might sit in the High Court if requested to do so by the Lord Chancellor, with a proviso that the Lord Chief Justice or the President of the Probate Division should consent in the case of their divisions. The Judicature (Amendment) Act of 1938 provides that the duties of ordinary judges of the Court of Appeal appointed after this Act shall include the duty of sitting in the High Court if the Lord Chancellor requests them to do so, subject to the proviso of the 1925 Act. Ex-judges cannot be called upon to assist unless they consent. A High Court judge must, under the 1925 Act, sit in the Court of Appeal upon the request of the Lord Chancellor. The Lord Chancellor is President of the Court of Appeal, but for practical purposes that dignity falls to the Master of the Rolls. The vice-presidency has formerly fallen to the senior Lord Justice, but the Judicature (Amendment) Act 1935 enables the Lord Chancellor to appoint a vice-president from among the Lords Justices, the statute being so worded that claims by seniority existing at that date should not be disregarded (see p. 267, below).

[2] There is power to receive fresh evidence. The circumstances in which that power will be exercised were clearly stated in *Braddock* v. *Tillotsons Newspapers* [1949] 2 All E.R. 306.

he may ask for the judgment to be reversed, as when he contends that it is wrong in law. Here the notion of a 'rehearing' comes in, for the Court of Appeal can make any order that the trial court could have made, which enables the judgment to be reversed or varied and some other judgment substituted for it. *Secondly*, there is no direct appeal from the verdict of a jury, and hence if the real ground of complaint is that a jury's verdict ought not to stand, the appellant must ask for a new trial. An appellant may contend that the judge misdirected the jury as to the law or as to the evidence, or that the damages are excessive or inadequate, or that there was no evidence upon which the jury could have come to their decision, and many other grounds. If the Court of Appeal allows the appeal, then the case must be retried before some other jury; assuming the case goes no further, the losing party will have to pay the costs of two trials and one appeal. In the case of a trial before a judge alone, the Court of Appeal is very chary of questioning the facts as found by the judge, but they may, of course, find that he drew wrong inferences from the facts or that his application of law to the facts was incorrect: just as a judge may unfortunately misdirect a jury so may he in the language of the Court of Appeal 'misdirect himself' when sitting without a jury.

Appeals from County Courts may be brought as of right on questions of law if the amount of the claim exceeds £20 or the remedy is an injunction: otherwise leave of the judge is required. The County Courts Act 1955 introduced appeals from County Courts on questions of fact, limiting such appeals to cases which, before the 1955 Act, would have been outside County Court jurisdiction, as where the claim exceeds £200. There is no shorthand note in County Courts, but the judge makes a longhand note, copies of which are available to the parties and the Court of Appeal.

The procedure in the Court of Appeal was reviewed by the Committee on Supreme Court Practice and Procedure in its Final Report in 1953.[1] The major points were, first, that notices of appeal did not have to state the grounds, so that the respondent had to prepare to meet every possible objection. Rules of Court have since been made requiring an appellant to state the grounds. The second point was the reading aloud of the judgment of the court below and the various documents and passages of the evidence; for hours, and sometimes days, counsel would read aloud. Obviously the judges could read the material for themselves in a much shorter time than

[1] Cmd. 8878, pp. 188 *et seq.*

it takes to read it aloud, and there was an overwhelming case (strongly supported by solicitors) for changing the practice, but the Bar opposed the suggestion, and no immediate action was taken. In 1961 and 1962 there was a novel exchange of visits between 'teams' of judges and practising and academic lawyers of England and the United States so that each could examine the work of appellate courts in the country of the other. It was clear to the English lawyers that the methods of the United States appellate courts would not be suitable for adoption in England,[1] but the arguments in favour of the judges doing 'home-work' were reinforced. The Court of Appeal decided to experiment, and a Practice Statement was made: 'For the purposes of such experiment each member of the court will have read (a) the pleadings or the originating summons (or their equivalent), (b) the order under appeal, (c) the notice of appeal and respondent's notice (if any), and (d) the judgment of the judge together with any cases cited by him in his judgment.'[2] A similar practice is followed in the Restrictive Practices Court, and it works satisfactorily. By making documents available to the press and others there is no disregard of the principle of open court.[3]

The survival of the appellate jurisdiction of the House of Lords in the re-organisation of the courts in 1875 was only possible if adequate provision was made for legal strength. A statute of 1876 provided for the appointment of Lords of Appeal in Ordinary, commonly known as Law Lords, who are paid professional judges with life peerages. At first there were two Law Lords, but the number was gradually raised until there were seven. The Appellate Jurisdiction Act 1947 raised the number of Law Lords to nine, appointments beyond the number of seven requiring the Lord Chancellor and the Treasury to be satisfied that the state of business requires such appointments to be made. To do appellate work the House of Lords must consist of at least three persons from among the Law Lords, the Lord Chancellor, and peers who hold or have held high judicial office. The Lord Chancellor rarely sits[4] and the Law Lords form the normal personnel. Ex-Lord Chancellors are in receipt of a pension and commonly do something to earn it by

---

[1] Lord Evershed M.R. led the English team, and gave some account of the visits in *The Times*, 12 April 1962. D. Karlen, *Appellate Courts in the United States and England* (1963), is a study that grew out of these visits.

[2] [1962] 1 W.L.R. 395. The Court also pointed out that the new Rule requiring the grounds of appeal to be stated was not always observed with a real regard for its purpose.

[3] See p. 21, above.   [4] See p. 411, below.

sitting in the House of Lords and the Privy Council,[1] but an ex-Lord Chancellor who loses office by what he considers political jobbery is at liberty to sulk if he thinks that is the more dignified course. The House of Lords is the final appeal court not only for England but also for Scotland[2] and Northern Ireland. In the English system, appeals go from the Court of Appeal to the House of Lords. By the Administration of Justice (Appeals) Act 1934 restrictive measures were enacted, whereby there can be no appeal to the House of Lords unless either the Court of Appeal or the House of Lords gives leave. The form of an appeal to the House of Lords is by petition, and the hearing is quasi-legislative in form. There is no rule of law that lay lords may be excluded, but there is a rigorous convention excluding them; on one occasion a lay lord attempted to take part in the hearing of an appeal, but he was just ignored. So that the House of Lords sitting for judicial purposes is quite distinct (both in personnel and in time) from the ordinary sittings of that House.[3] It used to be the practice for the hearing of the arguments and the delivery of the decision to take place in the House itself, counsel being heard from beyond the bar; physically it is about the most inconvenient court room in the country. But a more serious inconvenience was that a sitting for judicial purposes could not be held whilst the House was in ordinary session, because the House could not be sitting in two places simultaneously. In 1948 the device of an Appellate Committee was adopted. This means that arguments can be heard before Law Lords sitting as a Committee (which can sit when the House is sitting), and then the decision is taken before Law Lords at a time when they are sitting as the House of Lords. In 1963 two committees were authorised and appeals may now be heard in two divisions sitting simultaneously. The separate judgments that may be given are technically speeches (which may these days be printed and handed down instead of being read aloud), the matter being eventually put before the 'House' as a vote.

It will be noted that both the Court of Appeal and the House of Lords are situated in London. This centralisation of appeal work is resented by those who live in the more distant counties and see no reason why important centres such as the Tyne should not have local hearings of appeals.[4] The Frenchman has local courts of appeal

---

[1] See p. 266, below.   [2] See footnote 1 on p. 86.
[3] Law Lords may sit and vote in the House of Lords in its ordinary sittings. By convention they should not take part in matters of political controversy, but they may and do contribute to debates such as those leading to the Criminal Justice Act 1948.   [4] Muir, *Justice in a Depressed Area* (1936), ch. III.

as well as local courts of first instance.[1] A further matter that has been much discussed is the duplication of appeals. It is difficult to justify two appeal courts. It may well be argued that at any given time either the Court of Appeal or the House of Lords is the better tribunal, or they are both equally good, so that on neither hypothesis is there any need for both of them. The result upon litigants is that an appeal to the Court of Appeal is not necessarily final, so that if the case is taken on to the House of Lords the whole of the costs in the Court of Appeal appear wasted. It is also sometimes disquieting to find that a litigant may lose a case, although the majority of judges find for him: if the trial judge finds in favour of A and against B, and then B appeals to the Court of Appeal where all three judges uphold the decision in A's favour, B may yet win in the House of Lords because out of the five judges sitting there three may be in his favour and two may be against him; the result is that altogether six judges favour A's case and three judges favour B's case, yet B wins. It is not possible to justify this state of affairs by assuming that the personnel of the House of Lords is superior to that of the Court of Appeal, for no such grading of judicial ability will stand investigation. If the rationalist spirit that led to the Judicature Acts should again lay hands upon our legal system it is possible that one Court of Appeal would be considered sufficient. The House of Lords is an expensive tribunal; the rules used to require all documents to be printed and bound into volumes. In one appeal the printing bill alone exceeded £800, and that was before the great rise in the cost of printing. New rules made in 1959 allow duplicating of documents and avoidance of much printing. Abolition of the Court of Appeal, so that all appeals would go direct to the House of Lords, would require so much re-organisation to deal with the volume of work that the character of the House of Lords would be lost in the process. Abolition of the appellate jurisdiction of the House of Lords, so that the Court of Appeal would be the final court, would offer less difficulty and to the English lawyer it might seem the simplest step. It must, however, be remembered that the House of Lords is a United Kingdom court. There are always some members appointed from Scotland and from time to time someone from Northern Ireland. Some important parts of law, including much of commercial law and law relating to road traffic, is the same all over the United Kingdom, and it is most desirable that there should be a single appellate court whose decisions are authoritative in every

[1] Ensor, *Courts and Judges* (1933), pp. 92 *et seq.*

part of the kingdom.[1] It is arguable that we have gained greatly from having Scots lawyers in the House of Lords, for there is perhaps no better stimulus to legal thought than contact with other systems of law. If the rabid nationalism that is afflicting the world should reach England, we may see a rebellion against a state of affairs in which two Scotsmen and one Welshman may lay down the law of England, but so far we have escaped such adolescent neuroticism. It may be that an overhaul of procedure and costs on appeals[2] would remove the chief grievances.

8. THE JUDICIAL COMMITTEE OF THE PRIVY COUNCIL[3]

The downfall of the conciliar courts as a result of the constitutional conflicts in the Stuart period deprived the King's Council of jurisdiction that it had previously exercised. The position was that the Council had jurisdiction in any matter unless jurisdiction had been taken away or had become vested in some other tribunal. Practically the only jurisdiction left to the Council was the hearing of petitions on judicial matters from the King's dominions beyond the seas. As the British Empire increased this jurisdiction became substantial. The cases were handled by a committee of the Privy Council, who generally acted judicially. In 1833 the committee was re-organised by statute, the general idea being to reconstitute it as a body drawn from the superior judges. Subsequent statutes broadened the composition, so that it included judges from dominions and British India and some colonies, and allowed the Crown to make two special appointments carrying salaries. In fact the judicial personnel of the House of Lords has supplied much of the working judicial strength. A somewhat belated widening of the membership of the Judicial Committee was the appointment in 1962 of nine Commonwealth judges to be Privy Councillors, namely six from Australia,

[1] Appeals in criminal matters do not come from Scotland, so that the Scots have escaped some deplorable decisions that the House of Lords have made in English criminal law (see pp. 117, 273, below).

[2] See p. 301, below. New scales of costs were introduced in 1962. Security for costs was raised from £700 to £1000, but transcripts from the court below no longer have to be lodged if the case has been reported, which may mean some economy ([1962] 1 W.L.R. 490).

[3] An excellent description of the Judicial Committee in its grander days may be found in 7 *Cambridge Law Journal* (1939), p. 2, by Sir George Rankin, a member of the Committee. See also Wade and Phillips, *Constitutional Law*, pt. x, ch. 4.

one from New Zealand, one from Nigeria and one from the Federation of Rhodesia and Nyasaland, following on decisions of the Conference of Prime Ministers. These judges will not all sit regularly, but will attend when they can be spared from their own courts. For many years the greater part of the work of the Judicial Committee was the hearing of appeals from Dominions and from India, but the general changes that have taken place in the Commonwealth have resulted in those countries preferring to keep appeals within their own judicial systems, and there are but a few remnants left of that jurisdiction. It continues to be the ultimate court of appeal from the Channel Islands, the Isle of Man, colonies, protectorates and trust territories.[1] There is no right of appeal (unless given by statute), the process being a petition to the Crown for leave to appeal. It is in practice much easier to get leave to appeal in civil cases than in criminal cases. In England it is the final court of appeal from ecclesiastical courts, now virtually confined to matters of ecclesiastical fabric or discipline of the clergy. In time of war the Admiralty Court has a prize jurisdiction, appeal lying to the Judicial Committee. There are also some oddments of jurisdiction. The form of proceedings is a petition to the Crown, the deliberations of the Committee being a prelude to advising the Crown. Since it is unconstitutional for the Crown to receive contradictory advice, the 'judgment' of the Judicial Committee is in the form of unanimous advice, which, of course, is always accepted and acted upon by the Crown. The rule of one judgment only is a simplification of case-law, for the practice of the Court of Appeal and the House of Lords of giving separate judgments may mean that an appeal has been allowed or dismissed, yet on investigation there appear to be many varying grounds that are inconsistent. The one 'judgment' of the Judicial Committee avoids these troubles, but it may create the impression of settled law when in reality the judges were hopelessly at variance in their ideas.

It is hard to say whether the Judicial Committee has been a satisfactory tribunal. When the last Canadian appeal was heard in May 1951, Canadian legislation having abolished appeals for the future, kind things were said on behalf of the Canadian Bar. Lord

[1] The changes can be seen from the statistics of cases. In 1937 the Judicial Committee heard 122 appeals, 58 of them from India. In 1949, 82 appeals were heard, made up of 56 from India, 8 from Dominions, and 8 from Colonies. In 1961, 49 appeals were heard: Australia 3, Bahamas 1, Ceylon 9, East Africa 4, Ghana 6, Hong Kong 2, Malaya 3, New South Wales 2, New Zealand 1, Nigeria 4, West Africa 9, West Indies 5.

Simon, in replying, explained that for many years his view had been that the Judicial Committee should have been partly appointed by dominion governments and should have gone on circuit: 'It might have been, if those ideas had prevailed in time, that they would have created a new kind of Supreme Commonwealth tribunal.'[1] Yet the very English character of the Committee has been a strength, for it has enabled a steady consistent body of common law principles to be applied. It seems clear from appeals from some territories that this process is needed; it is seen best in appeals in criminal matters, for these are not allowed unless some important principle of the administration of justice is involved. As one of the major problems of our legal system is to ensure that people can make use of it irrespective of their capacity to pay costs, one cannot help but wonder how accessible the Judicial Committee really is for a poor aggrieved inhabitant of a distant place, but following up these questions would go far beyond the scope of this book.[2]

9. ARBITRATION

We have seen that it is possible for the court to refer a dispute to a referee for decision. Arbitration is usually used to signify a voluntary submission by the parties of their dispute to the judgment of some person who is neither a judge nor an officer of any court. The agreement to arbitrate is generally made in writing, and it may be made either after the dispute has arisen or in anticipation of any disputes that may arise. Clauses providing for arbitration are common in many commercial contracts and in insurance policies. The agreement, known as the 'submission to arbitration', will normally name the arbitrator or provide for some method of appointing him. The type of arbitrator chosen will depend upon the nature of the case: for some cases a barrister with a commercial practice may be suitable, whilst in others it may be desirable to select an arbitrator who has technical qualifications or knowledge of the conduct of a particular business or trade. In commercial contracts it is often provided that the president of the appropriate trade organisation shall nominate an arbitrator. Although arbitration is an extra-judicial proceeding, the High Court (usually in the Queen's Bench Division) may exercise considerable control either actually or

---

[1] *The Times*, 3 May 1951.
[2] New rules came into force in 1958, but they do not go very far in helping a litigant.

potentially. Thus, if there is no arbitrator because the method of appointment cannot operate, the court will appoint an arbitrator. An arbitrator may be removed by the court if he acts improperly. An important effect of a valid submission to arbitration is that actions in the courts are generally stayed; the court is not bound to refuse to allow an action to be brought, and if it appears to the court that judicial proceedings are desirable the action may be brought, but, as a general rule, a submission to arbitration precludes the parties from litigation. An arbitrator may obtain the opinion of the court on a point of law that arises during his conduct of the case, and he may frame his award with alternative directions in order that the court may determine a legal point. The parties can insist upon an arbitrator putting proper matters before the court. The award of the arbitrator is binding upon the parties, subject to the power of the court to set it aside for misconduct or palpable error of law. There is also mechanism for enforcing the award, so that by order of the court it is equivalent to a judgment as far as execution is concerned. It is obvious that with so many ways in which an arbitration may involve application to the court there need be little fear that arbitration may be conducted in an irresponsible manner.

There is no doubt that for some years arbitration has been increasingly favoured in business and trade circles. A decline in the volume of business before the superior courts is often ascribed to an increase in the number of arbitrations. Some lawyers regret the present tendency, saying that the ordinary courts are in the long run the most satisfactory tribunals. The opinions of lawyers are here of no great importance, for, if disputants show a marked preference for arbitration, we can safely assume that their opinion is the one that matters.[1] It is, however, a mistake to think that all agreements to arbitrate are truly voluntary. The practice of insurance companies leaves the citizen with no option. It is prudent to insure certain risks, and essential to insure others. The insurance of third-party risks for motoring is compulsory. Yet the form of policy that the citizen may take out is, in practice, prescribed by the insurance companies. To drive my car I must insure, and to insure I must take what policy the various companies offer, and if I find that all the companies insist upon an arbitration clause, then I must agree to arbitrate or

---

[1] The Evershed Committee, Final Report, Cmd. 8878 (1953), para. 895, were 'much troubled by this trend to arbitration'; their prejudice in favour of law courts not being put out of business was at variance with a halting realisation that perhaps the consumer had grounds for going elsewhere.

give up the motor-car. In other directions the extensive use of standard form contracts put forward by business interests pursuing a common course of business leaves the citizen with no true freedom of contract: the citizen must either accept a service upon the terms that are offered to him, or do without the service. If the service is virtually essential, he may find that, among other things, he is compelled to agree that he will not resort to the law courts. The insurance companies have in fact said that they will not insist on the clause if the insured prefers to have the question of liability (as distinct from amount) determined by a court, but that does not alter the legal position. There is, however, one rule of law that cannot be evaded: an arbitration clause must stand or fall with the validity of the contract in which it is included. If an insurance company say that a policy is void they are contending that the contract does not exist, and therefore the term providing for arbitration is avoided, leaving the insured free to bring an action in the courts.

When the Lord Chancellor asked the business community in 1960 about the Commercial Court,[1] everyone said that the court ought to continue and that it needed several improvements, yet the memoranda show quite clearly that arbitration is much preferred. According to one group, taking a case to court can easily cost at least ten times as much as arbitration. Arbitration is far quicker. In arbitrations it is normal for documents to be put in, and oral evidence is not often given, whereas in court documents have to be proved and witnesses called. The atmosphere of commercial arbitration is friendly. Questions of quality are better decided by someone who is expert. Foreigners prefer arbitration, and awards are easier to enforce abroad than judgments, and, perhaps above all, arbitration is private. Not all these advantages are always present. Some arbitrations involve complicated issues and dispute about facts. Arbitrators do not usually act for nothing, and the fee of a good arbitrator may be substantial. The service of solicitors and barristers is frequently necessary, and their charges may be as high for an arbitration as for an action. As is explained later,[2] a large part of the cost of litigation is the collection of evidence and its presentation in court; if an arbitrator is to have the same evidence that would be required by a judge, then the cost will be much the same. One great advantage of

---

[1] Report of the Commercial Court Users' Conference, Cmnd. 1616 (1961) (see p. 63, above).

[2] See p. 300, below. But an arbitrator may use his own knowledge (see p. 402, below).

arbitration is that the hearing can be arranged for a time and date and place that suits the parties. In litigation it may be possible to get a date fixed for the trial of a case, but even then the date is primarily fixed by reference to the work of the judge. It is possible for the parties to an arbitration to telephone the arbitrator and make a suitable appointment.[1] I have known an arbitration conducted in instalments between 5 p.m. and 7 p.m. on successive days, a time that suited everyone concerned. Proceedings that can be varied to suit the needs of the parties are bound to have considerable advantages over proceedings that must be shaped to fit a common mould. A troublesome matter is the provision for getting a ruling from the High Court. The technique of stating a case[2] requires a good measure of legal skill: if it is not done adequately the High Court has to send it back for further findings, and it becomes a slow and expensive process. But that is seen as requiring improvement of the legal procedure and not as a reason for abandoning arbitration.

[1] On the High Court's aversion to telephones see p. 291 below.
[2] See p. 112, below.

CHAPTER III

CRIMINAL JURISDICTION

I. COURTS WITH ORIGINAL CRIMINAL JURISDICTION

Jurisdiction over serious crime had become a matter for the King's judges by the fourteenth century. This jurisdiction was exercised primarily in the counties where the offences were committed, the court being that of the itinerant judge with a commission of oyer and terminer and gaol delivery. The civil work done by the itinerant justice was under the commission of assize, and the name of 'assizes' became the common term for the court of the itinerant judge for both civil and criminal work.[1] Lesser crime was dealt with in surviving local and franchise courts. The system was hardly satisfactory, since the jurisdiction of the inferior courts was limited, and too much of the time of the itinerant judge was taken up in hearing criminal cases of no great importance. The remedy was found in the office of justice of the peace. This office has late twelfth-century origins, but the important steps were taken in the fourteenth century. A statute provided that 'worthy' men were to be appointed to keep the peace and hear and determine felonies. Further statutes enacted that they were to hold their sessions four times a year. Before these statutes these worthy men were more conservators of the peace than justices; the duty of hearing and determining felonies made them 'justices of the peace', or more simply 'justices'.[2]

The justices were appointed for counties. Four times a year, according to the statute, the justices assembled to form the court known as Quarter Sessions. The jurisdiction was not precisely defined: Quarter Sessions could try felonies, with the proviso that difficult cases were to be reserved for the judge at Assizes. No definite provision was made for dealing with lesser offences. The powers of justices were extended somewhat in the fifteenth century, and increased greatly in the sixteenth century. *First*, a number of petty offences were created which were not of sufficient importance to warrant a trial before Quarter Sessions. Power to hear and determine these in a summary fashion was given to the justices. There was no system. The statute creating the offence generally specified whether one, two or three justices should hear the cases:

---

[1] See p. 5, above, for the status of an itinerant judge.
[2] They are also known as 'magistrates' (see n. 4 on p. 94, below).

no court was prescribed, and the justices heard the case more or less where and when they found convenient. *Secondly*, a great deal of administrative work was given by Parliament to the justices. The Elizabethan poor law especially needed some local administrative system. The normal technique was to entrust duties to parish officers and provide that the justices should see that the parish did its duty. *Thirdly*, the justices were instructed to hold preliminary inquiries into allegations of crime that might lead to trial at Assizes or Quarter Sessions. This was in the nature of police powers in 'getting up' a case, not really a judicial activity and suitable only for a society that lacked an adequate police force. No substantial change took place until the middle of the nineteenth century.

In the early nineteenth century the ordinary course was for an accused person to be brought before one or more justices, generally in a private residence. If a petty offence was alleged, then the case would be dealt with summarily, there being virtually no rules of procedure except that the statutory minimum number of justices must be present. If the case was of a more serious nature, the justices would proceed to hear the evidence for the prosecution in order to determine whether there was a *prima facie* case against the accused. If such a case was made out, the accused would be 'committed for trial' at the next Assizes or Quarter Sessions. The convention had grown up that Quarter Sessions could not try cases that carried the death penalty, which in the earlier nineteenth century meant that a very wide range of cases was excluded from Quarter Sessions and had to be tried at Assizes. Whether the trial was to be at Assizes or Quarter Sessions, the subsequent procedure was much the same. A 'grand jury' of twenty-three men of substantial position was summoned. A 'charge' or address to the grand jury was given by the visiting judge, bills of indictment, that is, formal written accusations against persons, were then put before the grand jury. Most of the bills of indictment related to persons who had been committed for trial by the justices after preliminary inquiry, but it was possible for anyone (including members of the grand jury) to put forward such an accusation. The grand jury, deliberating in secret, heard as much of the evidence for the prosecution as they wished to hear, and on that decided whether the accused ought to be tried; they were said to find a true bill or no true bill. If they found a true bill, then the accused 'stood indicted' and the trial proper would proceed before an ordinary trial jury. Grand juries were abolished in 1933, and persons are now sent for trial direct from the preliminary inquiry by justices.[1]

Criminal offences are for some purposes classified as treasons, felonies and misdemeanours. Where this classification still has any meaning it will be found to be nothing but a thorough nuisance. The classification from the point of procedure is into (1) offences triable summarily by the justices, and (2) offences called 'indictable', triable before a jury at Assizes or Quarter Sessions.

Whilst various important changes have been made the system is in essence much the same. Justices are still local, that is, they have jurisdiction only within their area, the units being the counties and most of the larger boroughs. There are:

(1) Ordinary justices, appointed by the Lord Chancellor on the advice of local advisory committees.[2] There is no qualification, except that they must reside within fifteen miles of their area, and there is no pay.

(2) *Ex officio* justices consist of some high Officers of State and the judges (who are justices in all parts of the country), some ecclesiastical and university dignitaries, some lawyers engaged in the work of justices, and mayors of boroughs, and chairmen of county councils, urban district councils and rural district councils.[3]

(3) For the County of London (other than part of Hampstead) there are up to thirty-five Metropolitan Stipendiary Magistrates, who are full-time paid officers, recruited from practising lawyers.

(4) In some of the larger boroughs outside London there are stipendiary magistrates,[4] who in qualifications and pay are in much the same position as the metropolitan stipendiary magistrates. There are only thirteen of these stipendiary magistrates, and many populous centres rely entirely upon the unpaid services of the lay justices.

Instead of the old haphazard method of hearing petty offences it was provided by statutes of 1848 and later that justices must sit in a regular court house and follow a definite procedure. The name Petty Sessions came to be given to these courts, which must consist of two or more lay justices or one paid magistrate. Counties are divided into Petty Sessional Divisions, so that courts are held at a number of places, the county justices being assigned among the

---

[1] See pp. 96, 132–4, below.   [2] See pp. 160–2, below.
[3] See p. 165, below.
[4] These paid lawyers are called 'magistrates' in the statutes, and some people think it right to keep the term 'magistrate' for those who are paid and to use 'justice' for the ordinary unpaid, but there is no rigid distinction: a magistrate is a justice, and all of them (paid and unpaid) may belong to the Magistrates' Association, and they all sit in Magistrates' Courts. The Justices of the Peace Act 1949 s. 44, will eventually standardise some of the terms. In literature and in common speech the terms 'magistrate' and 'justice' are synonymous. On the question of extension of the use of paid magistrates, see pp. 174–6, below.

various divisions. In boroughs that have separate justices the borough forms one division. The number of sittings varies greatly; in a few county divisions it is sufficient if a court sits one day a month, whilst in great cities it is necessary to have six or more courts sitting simultaneously every day. Where there is a stipendiary magistrate in the Provinces he does not exclude lay justices: where several courts sit simultaneously it is obvious that the stipendiary can only take a proportion of the work. The system of lay justices exists in the County of London, but there the professional magistrates do the bulk of the ordinary work,[1] though the juvenile courts[2] are largely manned by lay justices. The City of London is peculiar in that the Lord Mayor and Aldermen sit alone. In the rest of Greater London all the work is done by lay justices, except for East Ham and West Ham, which have a stipendiary magistrate. Where there is a stipendiary magistrate the lay justices can sit with him and vote on an equality with him, for the stipendiary is only chairman of the bench; a metropolitan stipendiary magistrate is, however, sole judge in his court.[3] Until recently the metropolitan stipendiary magistrates were known as police magistrates.

The use of the word 'police' in connection with magistrates was unfortunate; it derived from the peculiar history of police and magistrates in the metropolis, and in statutory language a metropolitan police magistrate sat in a metropolitan police court. Partly because of that and partly through the prominence of police in proceedings before justices, the term 'police court' became common. The correct term was Court of Summary Jurisdiction (often shortened to Summary Court), and that includes Petty Sessions and special sessions known as Juvenile and Matrimonial Courts. Changes in the values of words led to criticism: 'summary' suggests something hurried, whilst 'petty' has come to carry a derogatory meaning. Hence it was proposed to do some renaming.[4] The Justices of the Peace Act 1949 introduced the new terms. A Magistrates' Court means a court of summary jurisdiction or examining justice or justices, and it is a Metropolitan Stipendiary Magistrate who sits in a Metropolitan Stipendiary Court.

The chief work of Magistrates' Courts is the hearing and deter-

---

[1] See p. 174, below.   [2] See p. 184, below.

[3] This is the Home Office view, based on an unpublished opinion of the Law Officers of the Crown given in 1855; it has been acted upon and I think never doubted.

[4] Report of the Departmental Committee on Justices' Clerks, Cmd. 6507 (1944), paras. 205–7.

mining of charges of lesser offences. As there are over 1000 Magistrates' Courts and so few stipendiary magistrates it is right to think of lay justices as being the normal tribunal. These justices are judges of fact and law. In the event of a disagreement they must decide by a majority. The procedure will be discussed later. Magistrates' Courts also hear matters that are really civil, such as certain rate cases and matrimonial and affiliation cases. Few administrative functions are now entrusted to Magistrates' Courts; the most important relate to liquor and betting licences.[1] Certain functions including the granting of summonses, warrants for arrest and search, and the taking of declarations and witnessing documents, are performed out of court, either in private at the courthouse or at a justice's private address. Preliminary inquiry into indictable offences need not take place in a court house, but normally these inquiries are made as if the proceedings formed part of the work of Magistrates' Courts, and sittings elsewhere are only used in exceptional cases: if, for instance, a witness is in a hospital and unable to be brought to the court house, the justices might see fit to hold their preliminary inquiry at the hospital. Since the creation of efficient police forces during last century the nature of preliminary inquiries by justices has changed. It is no longer any part of the justices' duty to 'get up' the case. Their duty is to ascertain judicially whether the prosecution has produced evidence on which the accused ought to be sent for trial at Assizes or Quarter Sessions. Subject to a qualification given later, the justices cannot try a person accused of an indictable offence, and hence the accused need not put forward any defence. In some cases it may be good tactics to announce the defence at the earliest possible time, but generally the defence is reserved until the trial on indictment. Even when the defence is disclosed the justices are not supposed to hold the balance between the prosecution and the defence: if there appears to be a substantial case against the accused he must be sent for trial. Before following up the course of events when a person is sent for trial it is necessary to consider a further possibility.

The division of offences into petty offences and indictable offences was too rigid. In many offences commonly committed it is impossible to say whether the matter is sufficiently important to warrant trial before a jury unless the whole circumstances of the offence are

[1] Magistrates' Courts authorise the temporary carrying on of a licensed business, grant extensions of hours, and occasional licences for premises not ordinarily licensed. The transfer of licences is done at a special session. Under the Betting and Gaming Act 1960 justices license bookmakers, betting offices and betting agents.

considered. Hence, by statutes from the middle of last century onwards, a large number of offences may be tried either on indictment or summarily. The modern division of criminal offences is:

(1) Indictable offences that must be tried on indictment before a jury; all the most serious crimes are in this category.

(2) Indictable offences that can be tried either on indictment or in Magistrates' Courts.

(3) Offences that are both indictable and summary.

(4) Summary offences in which the accused can demand trial on indictment.

(5) Summary offences triable only in summary courts.

Group (4) requires little mention. When an offence (other than assault) triable summarily is punishable with more than three months' imprisonment, the accused must be present and, before the charge is gone into, he must be told of his right to jury trial; if he wants a jury then the Magistrates' Court cannot determine the matter, but must treat the case as a preliminary inquiry to see if they should send for trial on indictment. Thus when a summary offence carries four instead of three months' imprisonment, it may be an advantage to an accused person, for he will then have an option as to the mode of trial. In the debate on a Bill there is sometimes an amendment to increase penalties, as there was when the Public Order Act 1937 was before Parliament, for the raising of a maximum sentence to four months' imprisonment gives an accused person the advantage of choosing the mode of his trial.

The cases in group (2) are very numerous. Piecemeal legislation, culminating in the Magistrates' Courts Act 1952 as amended by the Criminal Justice Administration Act 1962, has created a list of offences that are primarily indictable, but that can be dealt with summarily. The most important are cases of stealing and allied offences. Other legislation has resulted in all offences, other than homicide, by persons under seventeen being triable in summary courts. The decision whether an indictable offence that can be tried summarily should be so tried depends upon several factors. The accused (if not a child, for whom summary trial is obligatory) must be informed of his right to be tried by a jury and allowed to make his choice between that and summary trial. If the justices hear the case without putting this choice to the accused they would be acting outside their jurisdiction, and the proceedings would be quashed by the High Court and possibly costs given against the justices personally.[1]

[1] Thus when a person was charged with dangerous driving under the Road Traffic Act 1930 s. 11 (1), and the justices heard the case without informing the

The justices must also feel satisfied that the case is suitable for summary trial. This created difficulty because there were three factors, the offence itself, the punishment that could be imposed and the character and antecedents of the accused, and whilst the offence (say stealing a bicycle) and the possible punishment must obviously be known to the court, there is a principle of our law of evidence that a person's previous convictions should not, as a general rule, be mentioned until after that person is convicted in the case in question. When justices came to consider the 'antecedents' of an accused person who elected summary trial they were in a dilemma: if they inquired about his previous record and found that it was bad, there was matter of grave prejudice if they still considered that the case should be handled summarily; if they proceeded to hear the case and convicted and then learned that the previous character was bad, it was too late to send the case for trial by jury, since the accused had been tried and could not be tried again for the same offence. The Criminal Justice Act 1948 resolved the difficulties by providing new procedure.[1] When an offence is indictable but triable summarily, and the accused desires summary trial, the justices do not now inquire into the character and antecedents of the accused. If the justices proceed to try the case summarily and after trial and conviction they find that the accused has a bad record they can, instead of themselves sentencing him, commit him to the next Quarter Sessions for sentence. Quarter Sessions can impose any sentence that could be given if the offender had just been convicted on indictment. For example, if a man is charged with stealing a bicycle, the justices might, with the consent of the accused, see fit to try him summarily. If after conviction the justices learn that he is a confirmed stealer of bicycles, and they feel that the maximum they can impose (six months) is insufficient, they can commit to Quarter Sessions, for that court can impose up to five years for larceny, or in view of the prisoner's previous record it may impose corrective training or preventive detention. If Quarter Sessions imposes a sentence that the Magistrates' Court could not have passed, then the prisoner can appeal to the Court of Criminal Appeal against sentence.

Group (3) comes from the many instances of statutes creating offences and specifying the maximum punishment for conviction accused of his right to jury trial, the Lord Chief Justice made strong comments (*Rex* v. *Leicester Justices, ex parte Walker, The Times,* 31 October 1935).

[1] This is now contained in the Magistrates' Courts Act 1952. The Criminal Justice Administration Act 1962 allows justices who have begun to try such a case summarily to discontinue the summary trial and proceed as examining justices.

summarily and the maximum punishment for conviction on indictment. Such legislation clearly makes the offence both summary and indictable, leaving us without any guidance as to who decides whether a particular case shall be taken summarily or on indictment. The Magistrates' Courts Act 1952 lays down procedural rules, the effect of which is that the prosecutor makes the initial decision, but the effective decision is made by the justices hearing the case. If such a case is tried summarily, there is on conviction a power to commit to Quarter Sessions for sentence.

An offence may be both summary and indictable, and also carry more than three months' imprisonment on summary conviction (thus falling into group (3) and group (4)), as in the offence of dangerous driving, and hence the formulation of the law is complicated.

Trials on indictment are at Assizes, Quarter Sessions and special courts in London and Lancashire. The Assizes have been described under the heading of civil jurisdiction; the judge is a Queen's Bench judge, or a commissioner (a Queen's Counsel of adequate standing) if through illness or other causes a judge is not available. Three, and in some cases four, Assize Courts for criminal work are held each year in the various centres. Quarter Sessions are held at least four times a year for each county and for such of the larger boroughs that have their own Court of Quarter Sessions. In the boroughs where there is no separate borough Quarter Sessions, the work is done by the county Quarter Sessions. County Quarter Sessions have until recently consisted of the justices for the county assembled together. If all the justices had attended it would in some counties have amounted to a few hundreds; no such vast concourses did occur, but it was not unusual to find Quarter Sessions with twenty or more justices on the bench. It is not satisfactory to do judicial work with such large benches, and the Justices of the Peace Act 1949 provided for limiting the number; the present rule gives a maximum of nine justices. In borough Quarter Sessions the position is very different, for instead of the justices there is a Recorder, who is a barrister of at least five years' standing appointed by the Crown and paid for his services. A recorder is sole judge in borough Quarter Sessions. It is not a full time office, and thus leaves the holder free for private practice; he may also be in Parliament, though not for the borough of which he is recorder. In most recorderships the salary has not been large enough to be profitable to the holder after he has met his expenses; it has in fact been an office of honour rather than of profit, and recorderships have generally been held by many of those who are appointed to the Bench. Salaries have recently been reviewed with the idea of establishing a rate for the job.

Greater London has a special system.[1] The Central Criminal Court, commonly called the Old Bailey, acts as the Assize Court for the whole area. There are twelve sittings a year, which gives what is virtually a continuous court. As in the other Assize Courts, the judges sit by virtue of a commission. This commission is given to a number of people, including the Lord Mayor and the City Aldermen, but in practice the work is done by a judge of the Queen's Bench Division, the Recorder of the City of London, the Common Serjeant, the Judge of the City of London Court and specially appointed additional judges. Each of these sits separately, so that there may be several courts (eight in 1963) sitting simultaneously. The most serious offences are put into what is called the 'judge's list', which means that they come before the Queen's Bench Division judge. The Recorder and the Common Serjeant are salaried judges paid by the City corporation. The City of London Court is described elsewhere; its judge is, of course, legally qualified and salaried. The Central Criminal Court also acts as Quarter Sessions for the technical City of London. The rest of Greater London consists of parts of the counties of Essex, Hertford, Surrey and Kent, which are served by Quarter Sessions of the county pattern, and of the Counties of London and Middlesex. The County of London Sessions sits at Newington, twenty-four sessions a year. The Middlesex Sessions sits monthly at Westminster. Both these courts have the same jurisdiction as other courts of Quarter Sessions. They each have a salaried and legally qualified chairman and deputy chairman.

For over a hundred years the higher criminal courts have been Assizes, the Old Bailey, County Quarter Sessions and Borough Quarter Sessions, the courts in Lancashire (described later) having been established in 1956. The weakest of these courts used to be County Quarter Sessions. The justices elected their own chairman, and he was usually a layman. Conducting a jury trial is far more difficult than presiding over a magistrates' court. The Royal Com-

---

[1] Changes will soon be made. The Royal Commission on Local Government in Greater London, Cmnd. 1164 (1960), in making recommendations for sweeping changes in local government, did not consider the administration of justice except to say, in para. 865, that the Council for Greater London should be responsible for expenses. The London Government Act 1963 establishes a new structure of local government and does not deal with arrangements for courts, lieutenancies and associated matters. These, including metropolitan magistrates' courts (p. 174 below), will be covered by a separate Act.

mission on the Despatch of Business at Common Law was 'very strongly of opinion that all chairmen of Quarter Sessions should possess legal qualifications',[1] and an ensuing Committee on Quarter Sessions reported that it could not recommend any increase in jurisdiction of Quarter Sessions until all chairmen of these courts are legally qualified.[2] With odd perversity the government chose to introduce a measure of great complexity. The Administration of Justice (Miscellaneous Provisions) Act 1938 sets up a category of 'legally qualified chairman', and that term has an unusual meaning. It does not mean just having legal qualifications, which is what anyone would expect it to mean. 'Legally qualified' means either appointed by the Crown or falling into certain categories. The Court of Quarter Sessions of any county may apply to the Lord Chancellor for the appointment of a legally qualified chairman or deputy chairman. The Crown, acting on the advice of the Lord Chancellor, may make the appointment from barristers or solicitors of not less than ten years' standing, taking into account the legal experience of such person and the desirability of appointing a person who resides in or is connected with the county; the appointment may be for a term or subject to provisions as to retirement. A qualified chairman or deputy chairman may receive a salary agreed upon between Quarter Sessions and the county council and approved by the Lord Chancellor. The other course is that the justices in Quarter Sessions elect as chairman or deputy chairman a person who is or has been a member of the Judicial Committee of the Privy Council, a judge of the Supreme Court, a County Court judge, or holder of certain other legal offices. Thus if Quarter Sessions elects a County Court judge as chairman (which some Quarter Sessions have done) he will automatically be a 'legally qualified chairman'. Chairmen and deputies appointed under special Acts for London, Lancashire and Middlesex, and recorders of boroughs also count as legally qualified. When a legally qualified chairman was sitting the Court of Quarter Sessions had an extended jurisdiction. But there was no necessity for having such a chairman, and hence the question of offences triable at Quarter Sessions was complicated by there being two lists of offences, one for lay chairmen and the other for legally qualified chairmen. In fact this horrid piece of legislation worked passably well, for very soon virtually all counties came to have legally qualified chairmen; this was made obligatory in 1962.[3]

---

[1] Cmd. 5065 (1936), p. 71. [2] Cmd. 5252 (1936).
[3] See p. 104 below.

When justices send a person for trial they commit him to Assizes or to Quarter Sessions according to the circumstances. Assizes can try any kind of indictable offence, whilst Quarter Sessions are debarred from hearing certain kinds, notably any homicide. Hence a murder or manslaughter case *must* go to Assizes. If the case is not within the category reserved for Assizes, either Assizes or Quarter Sessions can deal with it, and the justices must decide which is the appropriate court. The rule was that cases triable at Quarter Sessions should be sent there unless 'the justices for special reasons think fit otherwise to direct', the idea being that the Assize Court judge should be relieved of as much of the less important work as possible. In practice most justices regarded the dates of Assizes and Quarter Sessions as being 'special reasons' and committed to the next in date. The Administration of Justice (Miscellaneous Provisions) Act 1938 provided that justices were not to commit a case triable at Quarter Sessions to Assizes unless 'they are of opinion that there are circumstances which make the case an unusually grave or difficult one, or that serious delay or inconvenience would be occasioned by committal to Quarter Sessions'. Powers were given to commit to the Assizes or Quarter Sessions of an adjoining county if this would avoid undue delay.

This system of higher criminal courts would doubtless have sufficed if criminal work had continued at the level of 1938. What happened was that from 1945 onwards the number of criminal cases went up and up. By 1959 Assizes were dealing with about twice as many criminal cases as in 1938, whilst the cases in Quarter Sessions had increased more than threefold. Criminal Courts were getting through their lists, but at some cost. Assize judges, giving priority to criminal work, had scant time for civil cases so that justice was intolerably delayed. Prisons had to house a vast array of men waiting to be tried, waiting far longer than was necessary because of an antiquated system of the sittings of courts. The worst conditions were in South Lancashire, and a special solution had to be found. Two new Courts were established by statute in 1956,[1] called the Crown Court at Liverpool and the Crown Court at Manchester. They do the work of Quarter Sessions for the cities of Liverpool and Manchester and the Assize cases for the two divisions which comprise the whole of South Lancashire. Each court has a full-time judge, called the

[1] Criminal Justice Administration Act 1956 following (though not completely) the recommendations in the Report of the Departmental Committee on a Central Criminal Court in South Lancashire, Cmd. 8955 (1953).

Recorder, with a salary of £5,250, the courts being in constant session. The civil side of assizes is taken by a High Court Judge, and he also takes a few of the very serious cases, but the bulk of assize cases in South Lancashire go to one or other of the Crown Courts. Ordinary Assizes continue for the Northern Division at Lancaster.

Further inquiry was needed, and in 1958 a Committee on the Business of the Criminal Courts was appointed, with Mr Justice Streatfeild as Chairman.[1] There was virtually no accurate information about the length of time that elapsed between committal for trial and trial, although various people could adduce instances of men waiting in prison for three or four months. The Home Office Research Unit made a special investigation, published in 1960 as *Time Spent Awaiting Trial*. This survey showed that at the continuous courts the bulk of the cases were heard within eight weeks whereas at Assizes and Quarter Sessions a substantial number had to wait for three or four months and a few for even longer. The Magistrates' Association advocated a system under which one month should be regarded as the normal limit, but the Committee felt that eight weeks would be a more realistic figure. Some alteration in the sittings of courts was obviously necessary. The Committee did not accept suggestions that there should be an extension of Crown Courts. Admittedly the two new Crown Courts had been expeditious in getting through the lists and had relieved the judges and left them free to attend to the civil work, but there are disadvantages. The judge of such a court is in a position where he may easily become stale and prosecution-minded: unlike other judges he does not get spells of civil work, or spells of private practice and he has an unusual professional and social isolation. On balance the Committee thought that the best solution was not to extend the Crown Court system but to improve the organisation of Assizes and Quarter Sessions and make some alteration in jurisdiction.

The Committee's recommendations were accepted and the necessary changes in the law were made by the Criminal Justice Administration Act 1962. The Act provides for five more High Court judges, so that the itineraries of the judges can be re-organised. In effect each of the seven circuits is to have two itineraries so that Assizes can be held simultaneously at more than one town. It is a fairly rational re-organisation, assuming that the circuit system is to

---

[1] The Report is Cmnd. 1289 (1961). The Committee's terms of reference also included a review of the arrangements for providing the courts with information about offenders for the purpose of sentencing (see p. 224, below).

continue, but the firm attachment to obsolete trappings appears in the provisions for the Sheffield Assize Division: it would not be proper if there were not a High Sheriff (even though these officers have for many years been no more than picturesque embellishments of the legal scene),[1] and as the High Sheriff of Yorkshire might be tied up with an Assizes elsewhere, the Act creates a new county, Hallamshire, for the sole purpose of having a High Sheriff. Clerks of assize are not surrounded with flapdoodle, and assistant clerks may be appointed to cover Assizes being held simultaneously. Quarter Sessions in counties and in boroughs may now arrange their sittings to give a convenient sequence of courts. County Quarter Sessions must have a Chairman legally qualified under the Act of 1938, and in boroughs there are better provisions for having deputy and assistant recorders. The Lord Chancellor has new powers: he may give directions about the sittings of courts, he fixes the remuneration of recorders and chairmen and deputies and assistants and has other regulatory powers. There are changes in jurisdiction. Some offences, notably bigamy and sexual intercourse with a girl between thirteen and sixteen, are now triable at Quarter Sessions, and some offences that were indictable only have been made triable summarily with consent, the most important being 'breakings' where the building is not a dwelling house. There are important alterations in committal for trial. If a trial is likely to be a long one, justice can send the case to Assizes notwithstanding that the charge is one that would ordinarily go to Quarter Sessions. The power to commit to a court for another area to secure an earlier trial is extended: such a committal may be made if it appears unlikely that the person would otherwise be dealt with within one month, and the case must be sent to another court if the normal court would not deal with it within eight weeks. Whilst these changes should result in the better administration of justice, the law has become more complicated and safeguards, qualifications and exceptions abound.

Whether the trial is at Assizes, Quarter Sessions, Central Criminal Court or Crown Court at Liverpool or Manchester there will be a jury. Criminal procedure is discussed later.

In practice the majority of indictable offences capable of being tried summarily are tried summarily. In 1854, before the Criminal Justice Act of 1855 introduced the first large measure of indictable offences triable summarily, the number of persons for trial on

---

[1] A small book, *The High Sheriff*, published by *The Times* (1961), described the traditions, customs and ceremonies of the Shrievalty.

indictment was over 29,000: the annual average for the 1930's was a little over 9000. Since the war there has been a great increase, there being some 19,000 cases a year, rising to 33,009 in 1962. In the earlier years of this century the proportion of indictable cases tried by jury was about 20 per cent; this fell to 15 per cent between the wars[1] and the proportion is still much the same. Since a number of the trials on indictment relate to offences not triable summarily, it will be seen that summary trial is adopted in most cases where that course can be followed. Since the choice of summary trial lies with the accused (subject to the justices approving), the explanation lies in the advantages of that course as seen by accused persons, and here it must, I think, be recognised that the scales are weighted in favour of summary trial. The maximum punishment on summary trial is six months' imprisonment,[2] or a fine not exceeding £100, or both imprisonment and fine. Most accused persons are guilty of some offence (although it may happen that the offence charged is not the most appropriate accusation), and know that a conviction by the Magistrates' Court is likely to result in lighter punishment than a conviction on trial on indictment. Summary trial is perhaps more likely to result in conviction, but there will be no delay. If trial on indictment is chosen, the accused must wait (often in prison) until Assizes or Quarter Sessions; he will then be tried by a jury who are probably more lenient than the justices would have been, but against this advantage must be offset the fact that punishment after conviction on indictment normally has a far larger maximum. It is sometimes thought that the willingness of accused persons to be tried summarily shows confidence in the Magistrates' Courts. The commonest of all indictable offences is larceny, punishable with up to five years' imprisonment on indictment, or up to six months' imprisonment on summary trial. The ordinary defendant who knows he may well get convicted does not show 'confidence in the justices' when he prefers to take his chance of a prompt and short sentence rather than the evils of waiting for a possibly longer sentence after trial by jury. It must also be remembered that the choice between summary trial and 'going for trial' is not always properly understood by defendants who are not legally represented. It is noticeable that when drivers of motor vehicles are charged with being 'under

[1] I made an analysis of this change in 1 *Modern Law Review* (1937), p. 132.
[2] If there are two charges of indictable offences there may be sentences of six months on each to run consecutively, but if there are more than two offences the maximum aggregate remains twelve months.

the influence' and have legal advice they often elect to go for trial by jury: experience shows that a jury is more likely to acquit in those cases, and as the chief fear of the accused is being disqualified from driving, which follows equally from conviction by a Magistrates' Court or conviction by a jury, there is little risk in going to the higher court.

A further matter, upon which it is not easy to be certain, arises from the natural desire of the police to get prosecutions over as soon as possible with the minimum of trouble and expense. It often happens that a charge that could properly be made against a person, such as housebreaking, is triable only on indictment, whilst larceny in a dwelling-house is triable summarily. This develops a tendency to put forward only some lesser offence, knowing that summary trial is likely to follow. In many cases this is a sensible procedure, for the state of our criminal law is such that grave charges can sometimes be supported technically in circumstances that do not really call for any such serious view of the case. The discretion is in practice exercised by the police, and the place of the police in the administration of justice is a matter discussed later. From time to time allegations are made that bargains are struck between prosecutors and defendants: the prosecutor agrees to make only a lesser charge in return for a promise that the defendant will elect summary trial or plead guilty. If this does happen it is exceptional. Counsel do discuss cases, but all the charges are before the court and if the prosecution want to drop a charge they must ask leave of the court.

Whilst all criminal cases are now tried in the courts described above,[1] mention must be made of the High Court and the House of Lords.

[1] The system of criminal courts often appears confusing to students. Table V on p. 119, below, and this note (which ignores exceptions) may help to clarify this section. The functions of justices are:

1. *Out of sessions*, which means not in Quarter Sessions.

(*a*) Granting of process (summonses and complaints), bail, warrants for arrest and search and other similar work: usually done in the justices' private room at the court-house, but may be done at a justice's house or anywhere. Preliminary inquiries (pp. 96, 147–51) are usually taken in open court.

(*b*) *In Magistrates' Courts* consisting of one paid magistrate or two but not more than seven lay justices: hearing and determining of petty offences and indictable offences that are tried summarily; no jury. Special sittings as *Juvenile Court* (pp. 184–196), and as *Domestic Courts* (pp. 177–183). There are some administrative functions (see p. 96, above).

2. Courts of *Quarter Sessions* are of two kinds, county and borough. Every county has *County Quarter Sessions*, consisting of up to eight lay justices attending by rota and a legal chairman. Some boroughs have their own courts, and those *Borough Quarter Sessions* have a recorder (p. 99) as sole judge and lay justices do not take part. Boroughs that have not got their own Quarter Sessions are served

The old Court of King's Bench had a wide jurisdiction in criminal matters, although in practice most of that jurisdiction was rarely exercised. The jurisdiction passed to the High Court by the Judicature Acts, and it is there assigned to the Queen's Bench Division. The Administration of Justice (Miscellaneous Provisions) Act 1938 has made minor alterations. The criminal jurisdiction now is:

(1) A divisional court of the Queen's Bench Division has appellate jurisdiction on appeals on points of law from Magistrates' Courts.[1]

(2) There is supervisory jurisdiction over all inferior courts.[2]

(3) The Queen's Bench Division can order that a case which would ordinarily be tried at a particular Assize Court or Quarter Sessions shall be tried at some other Assizes or Quarter Sessions.

Before 1939 such an order was made on a writ of *certiorari*, but this can now be effected by a simple direction of the court. The normal use of this power is to move a case from a locality where prejudice is likely to result in a biased jury to a less inflamed atmosphere. Provinical towns are sometimes divided into factions over pending cases, and when there is a tension resembling that of a parliamentary election, the jury are likely to be convinced of the truth long before they have heard any of the evidence. The power to move a case is usually exercised in the interests of the accused, and the case of Professor J. S. Lewis, the Rev. L. E. Valentine and Mr D. J. Williams caused some resentment. These gentlemen set fire to a Royal Air Force depot near Pwllheli 'for the defence of Welsh civilisation, and for the maintenance of the Law of God in Wales', according to their own account of the episode. They were tried at Carnarvon by County Quarter Sessions. The main function of Courts of Quarter Sessions is the hearing of cases on indictment (other than those indictable offences heard at assizes); jury trial. Also the hearing of appeals from Magistrates' Courts (pp. 112–113, below) and the sentencing of convicted persons committed for sentence (p. 98, above); no jury.

A petty offence is tried in the Magistrates' Court for the area where the offence is committed.

A person charged with an indictable offence is brought before justices for that area for preliminary inquiry. (1) If the offence is indictable but triable summarily with consent, the justices may (with consent of the defendant) try the case summarily. (2) If trial on indictment is necessary or preferred, the justices cannot try the case but will conduct a preliminary inquiry; if on the evidence of the prosecution there is a prima facie case they commit for trial either to Quarter Sessions or to Assizes according to the nature of the offence and the need for a speedy trial.

If the trial is at Assizes the court will be the Assizes for the county where the case arose, the judge being a Queen's Bench Division judge on circuit; jury trial.

In the London area, Quarter Sessions cases go to London or Middlesex Sessions (courts with professional judges) or to Quarter Sessions for surrounding counties, and Assize cases go to the Central Criminal Court (Old Bailey) (p. 100, above). Crown Courts at Liverpool and Manchester (each with a professional judge called a Recorder) do Quarter Sessions work for the two cities and Assize work for south Lancashire.

[1] See p. 112, below, and p. 118 for appeals to House of Lords.

[2] See p. 113 below.

Assizes in 1936 for arson and malicious damage to property, but the jury disagreed and could not come to a verdict. The King's Bench Division ordered a second trial to take place at the Central Criminal Court. A London jury was unable to take the view of the case that had presumably appealed to some of the Welsh jury, and the prisoners were duly convicted.

(4) The Queen's Bench Division can order that any trial on indictment shall be tried 'at bar' in that division.

A trial at bar takes place before three judges and a jury. It was used for cases of great public importance, including trials for treason in the 1914–18 war. Under the 1938 statute the court can order trial at the Central Criminal Court before three judges instead of trial in the Queen's Bench Division. The Treason Act 1945 assimilates the procedure in all cases of treason and misprision of treason to the procedure in cases of murder. Trial at bar is still possible, but it was not used for treason trials following the war of 1939–45. Joyce was tried at the Central Criminal Court by a single judge and jury.

(5) The King's Bench was the proper court to try treasons committed abroad, offences of colonial governors committed in their colonies, offences committed by persons in the public service abroad, offences against the Official Secrets Acts committed abroad, and the dreadful misdemeanour of wilfully neglecting or delaying to deliver or transmit writs for the election of Members of Parliament.

The 1938 Act provided that the court could order trial at the Central Criminal Court and that the trial need not be before three judges, but the Criminal Justice Act 1948 has abolished the peculiarities that clung to these offences. These cases are now dealt with as if the offence had been committed in the place where the accused is apprehended or is in custody.

(6) Misdemeanours (as opposed to treason and felony) may be tried in the Queen's Bench Division on Information.

An information is a written allegation of the misdemeanour, the document being filed with the court. There used to be two kinds of such informations. A private person could apply to the court for leave, and if this was granted an official called the Master of the Crown Office formally filed the document. Such cases had become exceedingly rare, and the procedure was abolished by the 1938 Act. The Attorney-General has long had a right to file an information *ex officio*, without getting leave of the court, and this right is left unaltered by the 1938 Act. Procedure by information dispenses with the need for a preliminary inquiry before justices and thus puts the accused on his trial very quickly. It is considered to be very disadvantageous to the accused. In ordinary trials on indictment the defence is greatly helped by the preliminary inquiry, for this must disclose the evidence upon which the prosecution are going to rely. This evidence, in the form of depositions, is available for the defence; if the prosecution intend to produce further evidence they must give notice to the defence. The form of an information is that of an indictment, so that the accused knows the charge, but the first indication of the evidence upon which the prosecution relies will be the 'opening' of the case for the prosecution. The defence will find far more difficulty in effective cross-examination of witnesses, and in preparing to meet this evidence, for the defence must be planned extempore in court instead of being planned in advance on a study of the depositions. The convention has been that trial on information should be confined to cases where the aggrieved person is in an official or exalted position. The last case of an information filed *ex officio* by the Attorney-General was that of one Mylius, in 1910, for libelling the King by asserting that the King had committed bigamy. Procedure by information was also used for some civil proceedings at the suit of the Crown.[1] There is always a chance that the law of criminal libel may be invoked for political purposes, and since libel is a misdemeanour the Attorney-General (who is of course a political partisan) is in a position to cause some embarrassment to opponents by resorting to informations instead of proceeding on indictment. However, if conditions arose in which unscrupulous use was made of this procedure, it is probable that there would be far more serious things to complain about.

Before the Criminal Justice Act 1948 all peers, and the wife or widow (until remarriage) of a peer, charged with treason or felony, had to be tried by peers. For misdemeanour the trial was in the ordinary courts, although under a statute of Elizabeth a peer had to be tried by peers for the misdemeanour of disturbing public worship after two previous convictions. If Parliament was not sitting the trial could take place before the Lord High Steward with a panel of peers to act as a jury. The last case was in 1686. If Parliament was in session, the trial was in the House of Lords. The court consisted of such of the lords of Parliament who cared to attend during the whole of the proceedings, and they were judges of both fact and law. The last case was in 1936 for manslaughter in the driving of a motor-car. The proceedings were published.[2] The arguments for and against that peculiar mode of trial may be studied in a debate in the House of Lords on a proposal by Lord Sankey that the practice should be abolished.[3] There was no opposition to its abolition in 1948.

[1] An English Information was an information in equity on the revenue side of the King's Bench Division, whilst a Latin Information was a proceeding by the Crown in the nature of a common law action. *Attorney-General* v. *Goddard* 45 T.L.R. 609 was a case where the Crown used an English Information. Goddard was convicted in 1929 of receiving bribes whilst carrying out his duties as a metropolitan police officer. Large sums of money were found in his possession. The objection to procedure by information was that, in the words of the judge, 'the Information simply charged Goddard with certain misdemeanours and asked him if he had committed them'. Commentators who referred to 'the refurbishing of rusty Stuart weapons' perhaps showed undue alarm. English and Latin informations were abolished by the Crown Proceedings Act 1947.

[2] Proceedings on the Trial of the Lord de Clifford, H.M.S.O. 1936.

[3] House of Lords debate, 4 February 1936 (99 H.L. Deb. 5. ss. 381–418). The trial of Lord de Clifford was held before eighty-five peers. Counsel for the Crown were the Attorney-General, the Solicitor-General and two Treasury counsel. Four King's Bench judges attended to advise, according to custom, although the House included five peers who held high judicial office. The cost of

The coroner's court may be mentioned in connection with criminal courts, for although it is not a criminal court it has some connection with criminal proceedings. There are some 350 coronerships in England and Wales. It is a very old office, originally designed for protecting the fiscal rights of the Crown. Violent deaths were a concern of the coroner because in the past they sometimes brought revenue to the Crown through fines, deodands,[1] and forfeiture of the chattels of a convicted person. The coroner also had the custody of many records. In the course of time the holding of inquests on sudden deaths became the substantial part of the work of coroners. The office has perhaps more survivals of past ages than any other part of our system. Important changes were made by the Coroners (Amendment) Act 1926. Except where there are special rights, coroners for counties are appointed by county councils and those for boroughs by borough councils, the appointments being made from barristers, solicitors or legally qualified medical practitioners. The amount of work, and the salary, varies considerably in different localities. Cases are brought to the notice of the coroner by the police, by various public authorities, and by members of the public. The coroner, with the assistance of his officer or the police generally, makes enough inquiries for the coroner to decide whether an inquest is necessary. An inquest must be held when the dead body of a person is lying in the jurisdiction and there is reasonable cause to suspect that such person has died a violent or unnatural death, or a sudden death of which the cause is unknown, or has died in prison or in other places or circumstances mentioned by statute. In the case of a sudden death of which the cause is unknown, the coroner can order a post-mortem examination, and if the result shows death from natural causes the coroner may dispense with an inquest. The coroner's court is a court of law, but it cannot be fitted into any classification of courts. Law courts are primarily concerned with *issues*, that is, the decision of points as between contesting parties.[2] The coroner's court is a

the prosecution was £700 exclusive of the time of the judges. A trial at the Central Criminal Court would have taken far less time to hear, and would have cost the prosecution £35. The House of Lords passed the motion condemning trial of peers by peers.

[1] An object that caused a death was forfeited. 'Horses, oxen, carts, boats, mill-wheels and cauldrons were the commonest of deodands' (Pollock and Maitland, *History of English Law*, II, 471–2). The object or its value was often devoted to pious uses. The rule of deodand represented a survival of very early ideas. Abolition came in 1846, hastened, it is said, by fears that whole railway trains might get forfeited.

[2] Law courts perform many functions (see pp. 358 *et seq.*, below).

fact-finding body, incapable of trying any issue, civil or criminal. If the result of a coroner's inquest is a verdict that *A.B.* met his death through the careless driving of *C.D.*, this in itself has no effect upon *C.D.* A subsequent prosecution of *C.D.* for an offence under the Road Traffic Acts, or a civil action against *C.D.* for compensation brought by the dependants of *A.B.*, are quite separate proceedings depending in no way upon the verdict of the inquest. Obviously the police and the dependants may find the inquest useful as a preliminary survey of the evidence. But there is one point of some importance. If the verdict at the inquest is one of murder, manslaughter, or infanticide by a named person, then that person is committed for trial. Ordinarily if the police think there is evidence of homicide they will charge the suspected person and there will be a preliminary inquiry before justices and, if a *prima facie* case is made out, a committal for trial. To prevent inquests being a concurrent pre-liminary inquiry the Act of 1926 provided that a coroner should adjourn his inquest if he is notified that any person has been charged before the justices with homicide (including causing death by reckless or dangerous driving); the coroner may later resume his inquest, but the verdict must not be inconsistent with the result of the criminal proceedings. If, however, the police have not charged anyone, either because they have not completed their inquiries or because on the evidence they do not think that a charge should be made, there is nothing to stop a coroner from holding his inquest. This may be very unsatisfactory, for the coroner's court does not have to observe any rules of evidence and may place some suspected person in a difficult position. There have been instances where an inquest has appeared very like an ill-conducted trial for murder. The coroner's jury is not drawn from the ordinary jury list: the practice of drawing a jury from the local workhouse, or of keeping a standing jury for all cases, has occurred. A Committee on Coroners made some recommendations in 1908, some of which were carried out in 1926. Another Committee made further recommendations in 1936.[1] The present position is that the police or the Director of Public Prosecutions will prosecute for any homicide where the evidence appears worth taking the case before the justices. A committal by a coroner is a relic of the days before police forces, and today it serves no useful purpose. The 1936 *Report* should receive the attention it deserves, and the power of the coroner to commit for trial should be abolished.

[1] Cmd. 5070 (1936).

2. COURTS WITH APPELLATE
CRIMINAL JURISDICTION

The remaining part of the system of courts for criminal matters is concerned with appeals. Starting with the lowest of the trial courts, the Magistrates' Courts, there is a complication in that an appeal may be made in either of two ways. An appeal can be made either to the High Court or to Quarter Sessions and then from Quarter Sessions to the High Court. An appeal direct to the High Court can be made only on a point of law, and is by the process called a 'case stated'. The aggrieved party asks the Magistrates' Court to state a case, which means that an account of the case giving the findings of fact and the decision made by the Magistrates' Court is drawn up, and on the basis of this document the legal point that arises is argued before the High Court. For this purpose three judges sit together, the court being known as a Divisional Court of the High Court. If the Magistrates' Court refuses or omits to state a case when required, it can be compelled to do so. This method of appeal is used when a binding decision on a point of law is required, the point usually being the interpretation of a statute or regulation, and the proceedings usually being in the nature of a test case. In the majority of instances the cost of going to the High Court is far greater than the amount of the fine imposed by the Magistrates' Court; unless the legality of a course of conduct is really in question it is generally far cheaper to accept the ruling of the Magistrates' Court rather than to challenge it in the High Court. The prosecution as well as the defendant may appeal in this way: in fact, local and other authorities who have prosecuted unsuccessfully are often more interested in getting authoritative rulings than are private individuals who have been convicted. When the prosecution appeals successfully, the High Court sends the case back to the Magistrates' Court with directions to convict.

The other method is to appeal from the Magistrates' Court to the local Quarter Sessions.[1] As a general rule this type of appeal cannot be made by a prosecutor who has failed to get a conviction. A convicted defendant can appeal against his conviction provided that he did not plead guilty. The appeal can be on the ground that

---

[1] There are special provisions for the composition of Quarter Sessions on an appeal from a Juvenile Court. In County Quarter Sessions not less than half the justices sitting must be on juvenile court panels and one must be a man and one a woman, whilst in Borough Quarter Sessions the Recorder is to be assisted where practicable by two members of a Juvenile Court panel who sit with him as assessors.

the justices came to a wrong conclusion as to the facts, or as to the law applicable, or as to both. An appeal on fact is a true rehearing of the case: the witnesses are heard again, and the appeal is like a new trial before a different tribunal. An appeal to Quarter Sessions on law alone is useless if an authoritative ruling is required, for the views of a recorder or legal chairman do not carry much weight in other jurisdictions. Whereas the original jurisdiction of Quarter Sessions necessitates the use of a jury, the appeal work is done without a jury. As well as appeals against conviction, it is now possible to appeal against the sentence imposed in the Magistrates' Court; this appeal may be made whether the defendant pleaded guilty or not guilty at the original trial. The powers of Quarter Sessions on an appeal are very wide. They can confirm, reverse or vary the sentence; they can send the case back to the Magistrates' Court for further hearing; they can do anything that the Magistrates' Court could have done. It should be remembered that the power to vary the sentence includes the power to increase it.

Prior to 1933 an appeal to Quarter Sessions was hedged with restrictive procedural rules, including the necessity of giving security for costs or finding friends who would stand surety for this: the result was to make appeals quite impossible for the average defendant. As the result of the Report of a Committee,[1] the Summary Jurisdiction (Appeals) Act 1933 abolished the security for costs and made provision for free legal aid in proper cases payable out of county or borough funds.[2] An appeal aid certificate may be given by the Magistrates' Court or by Quarter Sessions. The Act of 1933 came into force on 1 January 1934. The result can be seen from Table IV. The total number of appeals has increased considerably, but when the number of appeals is considered in relation to the total number of convictions it is apparent that appeals are still relatively uncommon.

From Quarter Sessions an appeal lies to the High Court (Divisional Court) by the technique of case stated, which, as in the use of this method described earlier, is limited to points of law. From the Divisional Court there may be an appeal (subject to conditions that are described later) to the House of Lords.

Another proceeding that is akin to an appeal is the use of orders of *prohibition* or *certiorari* to bring proceedings of inferior courts before the Queen's Bench Division for review. An appeal is a complaint that the inferior court decided the case wrongly, by being mistaken as to the facts or the law or both. The above-mentioned

[1] Cmd. 4296 (1933).　　　[2] On legal aid see pp. 140–7, below.

Table IV. Appeals to Quarter Sessions and legal aid

| | Number of persons seventeen and over, convicted in Magistrates' Courts | Total number of appeals to Quarter Sessions | Appeal aid certificates | | | | | |
| | | | By Magistrates' Courts | | By Quarter Sessions | | Total | |
			Granted	Refused	Granted	Refused	Granted	Refused
1934*	534,000	521	117	109	33	19	150	128
1935	615,778	712	114	96	47	40	161	136
1936	674,828	702	139	89	57	41	196	130
1937	656,953	884	93	100	51	32	144	132
1948	584,953	1,785	238	38	106	15	344	53
1950	602,416	1,819	286	70	126	19	412	89
1957	786,330	2,046	185	91	152	41	337	132
1961	1,002,423	3,241	467	158	266	38	733	196

* The total number of appeals to Quarter Sessions before the 1933 Act changed the law were:

1930	267	1932	289
1931	281	1933	313

orders are used when the inferior court acts outside its jurisdiction or acts in some irregular fashion. If the proceedings of the inferior court are not yet over, *prohibition* lies to prevent any or further proceedings, whilst if the proceedings have been concluded *certiorari* is a method of getting those proceedings quashed. For instance, if justices hear a case when they have no right to do so (as on p. 97, above), or if justices are personally interested in a matter before them, the Queen's Bench Division will set aside the proceedings.[1] Magistrates' Courts and Quarter Sessions are inferior courts, but Assizes are not in this category.

From Assizes or the original jurisdiction of Quarter Sessions the appeal in criminal matters is to the Court of Criminal Appeal. It is an astonishing fact that until 1907 there was no system of appeals in the more important criminal matters. There was an institution called the Court for Crown Cases Reserved, set up by a statute in 1848 to regularise a practice of the judges, but cases could only come before this court if a judge or chairman of Quarter Sessions saw fit. The court consisted of all the judges, with a quorum of five, and it was entirely within the discretion of a judge or chairman of Quarter Sessions whether he would reserve a point for the consideration of this court. The appalling miscarriage of justice which resulted in Adolf Beck serving years of sentence for an offence that he could not have committed resulted in the creation of the Court of Criminal Appeal in 1907. Unlike the Court of Appeal which is staffed primarily by Lords Justices engaged solely in appellate work, the Court of Criminal Appeal consists of the Lord Chief Justice and the judges of the Queen's Bench Division, that is, of judges normally engaged in original hearings. The court must consist of an uneven number of judges, three being the quorum. If a particularly important point is to be decided there may be a 'full court', which consists of five or seven judges. For many years the court usually consisted of the Lord Chief Justice and two judges, sitting on Mondays, but this became insufficient as the number of cases rapidly increased. In 1961 the court sat in three divisions, kept abreast of the work and found time to revert to the old practice of giving reasons for all its decisions.

There can be no appeal against an acquittal: if a jury says 'not guilty', that is the end of the matter. After a conviction:

(1) there is a right of appeal on any point of law;

(2) with leave of the trial judge or of the Court of Criminal Appeal, there may be an appeal on fact or law or both, or any other sufficient ground;

[1] See also pp. 40-3, above, and pp. 394-404, below.

(3) with leave of the Court of Criminal Appeal there may be appeal against the sentence (unless it is fixed by law, as in murder).[1]

The powers of the court are wide. They can dismiss the appeal, quash the conviction, alter or vary the sentence (including increase of sentence) when the sentence is appealed against, substitute a conviction for another offence if it appears that the accused ought on the evidence to have been convicted of that rather than of the offence of which he was actually convicted. The court may refuse to quash a conviction even when the appellant shows some technical fault in the proceedings if the court thinks that no miscarriage of justice has taken place. There is no power to order a new trial.[2] Whether there should be such a power was discussed in the House of Lords in the debate on the Criminal Justice Bill in 1948; judicial opinion was divided, and the Act did not include any such provision.[3] The Court has power to grant legal aid.[4]

There can be no doubt that the Court of Criminal Appeal has exercised a wise and liberal course in controlling procedure and evidence in criminal trials. It is, however, difficult to escape the feeling that the Court has done little to develop substantive criminal law. If the Court of Criminal Appeal is compared with the Court of Appeal, we find great differences; criminal appeals are dealt with more briefly, a reserved judgment being almost a rarity. Personally

---

[1] The Court of Criminal Appeal will not revise a sentence merely because its individual members might have given a lighter sentence. The court only interferes (1) when the sentence is not justified by law, or (2) where the length or severity of the sentence shows that the trial court erred in some matter of principle, or (3) where matters had been taken into account that should not have been taken into account (*Rex* v. *Barker* (1937) 81 Sol. Journ. 719).

[2] If there has been a mistrial the court can order a *venire de novo*, which means that there will now be a trial. This only happens if the first trial was not really a trial at all, as where a recorder appointed as a deputy someone who was not a barrister and therefore could not be a deputy, so that what everyone thought was a court of borough Quarter Sessions was not a court at all. But where a man was properly arraigned before a jury and acquitted without there being a real trial because the chairman took it upon himself to lead the jury into acquitting, the Queen's Bench refused to hold that the trial was a nullity; it was 'deplorably irregular', but it was a trial (*R.* v. *Middlesex Justices, ex parte D. of P.P.* [1952] 2 All E.R. 312). There is power in the Court to hear fresh evidence but the conditions are narrowly defined and it is only rarely that this is allowed (*R.* v. *Parks* [1961] 1 W.L.R. 1484).

[3] A Committee under the Chairmanship of Lord Tucker recommended that there should be power to grant a new trial on grounds of fresh evidence (Report of the Departmental Committee on New Trials in Criminal Cases (Cmd. 9150, 1954)). This is included in government proposals for legislation in 1963–4.

[4] This rests with a judge of the Court, who acts on a report from the registrar in accordance with the Criminal Appeal Rules; it is independent of the other forms of legal aid, and no particulars appear in the *Criminal Statistics*.

Table V. *System of courts exercising criminal jurisdiction*

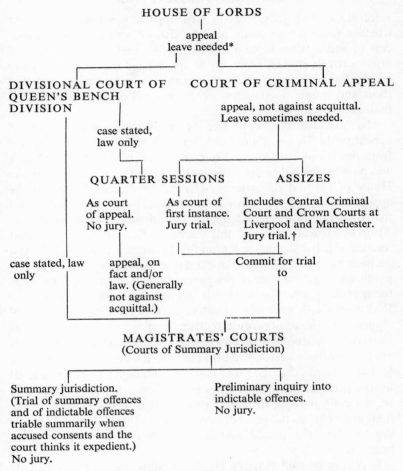

HOUSE OF LORDS

appeal
leave needed*

DIVISIONAL COURT OF
QUEEN'S BENCH
DIVISION

COURT OF CRIMINAL APPEAL

appeal, not against acquittal.
Leave sometimes needed.

case stated,
law only

QUARTER SESSIONS   ASSIZES

As court   As court of   Includes Central Criminal
of appeal.   first instance. Court and Crown Courts at
No jury.   Jury trial.   Liverpool and Manchester.
                               Jury trial.†

case stated, law   appeal, on   Commit for trial
only   fact and/or   to
                    law. (Generally
                    not against
                    acquittal.)

MAGISTRATES' COURTS
(Courts of Summary Jurisdiction)

Summary jurisdiction.   Preliminary inquiry into
(Trial of summary offences   indictable offences.
and of indictable offences   No jury.
triable summarily when
accused consents and the
court thinks it expedient.)
No jury.

* Administration of Justice Act 1960 s. 1 provides:

'(1) Subject to the provisions of this section, an appeal shall lie to the House of Lords, at the instance of the defendant or the prosecutor

    (*a*) from any decision of a Divisional Court of the Queen's Bench Division in a criminal cause or matter;

    (*b*) from any decision of the Court of Criminal Appeal on an appeal to that court.

(2) No appeal shall lie under this section except with the leave of the court below or of the House of Lords; and such leave shall not be granted unless it is certified by the court below that a point of law of general public importance is involved in the decision and it appears to that court or to the House of Lords, as the case may be, that the point is one which ought to be considered by that House.'

† Before the Administration of Justice (Miscellaneous Provisions) Act 1933 cases in these courts required the finding of a grand jury before the actual trial could take place.

I sometimes find judgments in civil appeals too long, and doubt whether some points really need be flogged so hard, but the process of writing does force one into a more careful consideration of arguments. It should, however, be appreciated that there are many criminal appeals in which there is nothing worth arguing, and that short and simple points come up in criminal cases far more often than in civil actions.[1]

The Administration of Justice Act 1960 has given new rights of appeal to the House of Lords. Before this Act there was no appeal from the Divisional Court. From the Court of Criminal Appeal it was possible for either the defendant or the prosecution to go to the House of Lords if the Attorney-General gave a certificate that the appeal was on a point of law of exceptional public importance, and that it was desirable that a further appeal should be allowed. The Attorney-General exercised this discretion fairly though somewhat restrictively, but the major reason for a change was the belief that a decision as to further appeal ought not to lie with a person who is a politician and a member of the government. The 1960 Act provides for appeals by defendants or by the prosecution from decisions of the Divisional Court in criminal matters or from the Court of Criminal Appeal with leave according to these two requirements: *first*, the court below must certify that a point of law of general public importance is involved; *second*, it must appear to the court below or to the House of Lords that the point is one which ought to be considered by that House. So that if the court below says 'No' to the first requirement, nothing further can be done; if they say 'Yes' to the first, and 'No' to the second, one can go to the House of Lords to say 'Yes' to the second and if they will do so, the appeal can proceed.

It cannot be said that the House of Lords have made adequate contributions to criminal law. There have been instances where the law badly needed clarification. For example, when there was an appeal against a conviction of manslaughter arising from a road accident, the public, and certainly the legal profession, hoped for a general restatement of the law, but the opportunity was missed.[2]

---

[1] See D. Seaborne Davies, 'The Court of Criminal Appeal: the first forty years', in *1 Journal S.P.T.L.* (n.s., 1951), 425. A most valuable account is 'The Working of the Court of Criminal Appeal' by Lord Goddard, then Lord Chief Justice, in *II Journal S.P.T.L.*, (n.s., 1952), 1.

[2] *Andrews* v. *Director of Public Prosecutions* [1937] A.C. 576. Juries would not convict and so the Road Traffic Act 1956 created a new offence of causing death by reckless or dangerous driving of motor vehicles.

Of two recent decisions the kindest thing that can be said is that they are so reactionary that if they should be applied we could expect reform by legislation.[1]

3. THE PROCESS OF PROSECUTION[2]

In any criminal proceedings someone has to make an investigation in order to formulate a charge, and someone has to exercise a judicial function in deciding whether the charge is substantiated. In England we divide these functions, so that the judicial process in our criminal law is commonly called accusatorial.[3] All prosecutions are nominally at the suit of the Crown, which means that the case against the accused must be presented by one party, called the prosecutor or the prosecution, and met by the other party called the defendant or the accused or the prisoner. The work of investigating, preparing and presenting the case for the prosecution falls upon the prosecutor and not upon the magistrates or judges.[4] An issue must be presented to a tribunal that is unacquainted with the matter, and that tribunal must try the issue between the two contesting parties. The general rule is that it is the duty of the prosecution to establish the charge against the defendant, and hence the 'defence' need be no more than a demonstration that the prosecution has failed to show beyond all reasonable doubt that the defendant is guilty.[5] If the prosecution can show that one of two men, who were not acting together, must have committed a murder, then both men must be acquitted since the case is not proved against either of them.[6] It is, however, convenient to speak of the 'defence', remem-

[1] Seaborne Davies, 'The House of Lords and the Criminal Law', VI *Journal S.P.T.L.* (1961), p. 104, is an article that should be read by everyone who cares for the traditions of liberal jurisprudence.

[2] Devlin, *The Criminal Prosecution in England* (1960) is the best general study. C. Williams, *Prosecuting Officer* (1960) is a delightful guide for police who conduct cases in Magistrates' Courts.

[3] See p. 18, above.

[4] The preliminary inquiry by justices is not an exception. A preliminary inquiry sees whether a man ought to be tried for a definite charge made against him; the process is not intended to ascertain whether *some* charge will lie or to help in 'working-up' and preparing a prosecution.

[5] Statute has made many exceptions to this rule. Parliament may say in effect: 'It shall be an offence to do so-and-so, or to be in possession of such-and-such objects, unless the accused can show a reasonable (or some specified) excuse.' In effect the onus of proving the excuse is then on the accused.

[6] This logical conclusion does not always produce satisfactory results in some matters not of a truly criminal character that are entrusted to Magistrates' Courts. In proceedings for an affiliation order (p. 177, below) to obtain weekly

bering that this may mean no more than a submission that no 'defence' is needed.

Although prosecutions are in the name of the Crown, this does not mean that public officials are the only persons who can prosecute offenders. There is a Director of Public Prosecutions, and his small department is responsible for conducting the most serious cases, but the cases handled in this way are relatively few in number. The basic principle of prosecutions in England is that it is open to any member of the public to institute criminal proceedings, there being no need for such person to have any interest whatsoever in the subject-matter of the charge.[1] It is convenient to examine the application of this principle and then return to the activities of the Director of Public Prosecutions. When we say that 'any member of the public' may prosecute, this expression covers persons in public employment; a police officer, or an official in a local government office or in Whitehall, is none the less a citizen and a member of the public. When 'the police' prosecute, the correct analysis is that some individual has instituted proceedings, and the fact that this individual is a police officer does not alter the nature of the prosecution. If William Styles is the name of a prosecutor, the law is quite indifferent as to his occupation: he may be a grocer, or a police or excise officer, but he remains William Styles the prosecutor. The real difference of course is that William Styles the grocer will only prosecute if he is adequately annoyed about something, whereas William Styles the policeman will prosecute on the instructions of his local chief of police. For most purposes we can talk about police prosecutions, or Board of Trade prosecutions, or prosecutions by some other authority, and contrast these with 'private prosecutions'.

Usually people who are aggrieved by criminal acts of others are quite content to leave the conduct of criminal proceedings to the police. There are, however, cases where the police are reluctant to

payments for the support of a bastard child the complainant may fail because she can only show that one of two men must be the father. The object should be the obtaining of support for the child, and personally I cannot see why an order should not be allowed so that a proportion of the expense is borne by each man who might be the father. At present a premium is set on unhallowed polyandry; it is far safer for a man to share a mistress than to have her entire affections.

[1] There are exceptions. For some offences no prosecution may be brought (except by the Director of Public Prosecutions) unless the leave of the Attorney-General or of a Secretary of State has been obtained. Charges under the Official Secrets Act are in this category.

prosecute, or the aggrieved person may feel that he can put up a more vigorous prosecution. For a proper appreciation of this position it is necessary to examine what is involved in prosecuting. Suppose that John Doe, who was in a bad temper, struck William Styles (grocer). Styles, who did not provoke the attack, feels that some proceedings should be taken; he may complain to the police and they may take proceedings, but Styles may well feel that the police will regard the case as trivial and so not press the case against Doe as much as Styles's outraged feelings require. If he likes, Styles can go before the justices and 'lay an information', which is a statement of his allegation. Unless the complaint appears frivolous, the magistrates will grant a summons against Doe; this summons, which will be served on Doe by a police officer, specifies the time and place at which a Magistrates' Court will hear the case. On the hearing of a summary case the prosecutor may conduct the case, and so Styles need not employ a solicitor. The witnesses who are to support Styles's story must be interviewed, and arrangements must be made for their attendance at court. Many a private prosecutor pilots such a case through the Magistrates' Courts without professional assistance, although those who can afford to employ a solicitor usually do so. If the charge against the accused is serious, and the case instead of being tried summarily is to go for trial at Assizes or Quarter Sessions, the position of the private prosecutor is that he has embarked upon a course that will involve him in some expenditure. It is no longer possible to dispense with a solicitor, for the conduct of cases by prosecutors is confined to Magistrates' Courts. Solicitors may appear in some Quarter Sessions, but in most Quarter Sessions and at all Assize Courts the right of audience is confined to barristers, and barristers must be instructed by solicitors. The prosecutor will have to pay a solicitor and probably a barrister as well. The greater seriousness of the case will involve more preparation: all the witnesses must be interviewed, and a full note made of the evidence they will give; expert testimony, as of medical specialists, may have to be sought. All this costs money, and the prosecutor becomes liable to pay what may be substantial sums. There is power in the trial court to order that the reasonable costs of a prosecution shall be repaid to the prosecutor out of public funds, but there is no certainty that the court will make such an order, and even when an order is made the prosecutor never recovers as much as he has spent, for the sum to be repaid as costs is calculated on a basis of the minimum work that need have been done and the cheapest of professional services. It is quite safe to say that a private prosecutor must expect to be out of pocket to some extent even in the most favourable circumstances.[1] As might be expected from this state of affairs, private prosecutions are not normally instituted unless the prosecutor has some substantial interest. Public corporations, the larger commercial undertakings, banks, insurance offices and so forth, frequently prosecute for offences that interfere with their business.

Most prosecutions are 'police prosecutions'. From their own knowledge, or from complaints made by aggrieved persons, the police decide that a criminal charge should be made. Unless it appears that the complainant is both able and willing to run a prosecution, it falls to the police to do this, and some police officer becomes the nominal prosecutor. There is in general no legal distinction between a private prosecution and a police prosecution: the police are expected to give their services to the private prosecutors in such matters as tracing witnesses and general co-operation in preparing the evidence; before the court private and police prosecutors and their legal advisers are in exactly the same position. In the *Criminal Statistics* no distinction is made between private and police prosecutions, but there can be little doubt that the latter are far more numerous.

In the provinces there are separate police forces for each county, local control being vested in a Standing Joint Committee, which consists of persons appointed by the County Council and by the magistrates in Quarter Sessions. County boroughs have their own police forces, placed under a Watch Committee appointed by the Borough Council. The Royal Commission on the Police have recommended that county and borough forces should come under committees consisting of two-thirds members of the local council and one-third justices of the peace.[2] There are also some forces for combined areas, with a specially constituted police authority. It is likely as a result of the Royal Commission's Report that there will be further amalgamations to secure forces of adequate size. The metropolitan police are under the direct control of the Home Office. The police for the technical City of London are a separate force under a commissioner appointed by the City. Although the provincial

---

[1] A private prosecutor may get advice from the Director of Public Prosecutions (see p. 127, below), and the Director may authorise special expenditure which must then be counted as proper expenditure to be reimbursed out of local funds.

[2] Cmnd. 1728 (1962), Ch. VI.

police are not directly under any central government office there is a good deal of control by Whitehall, exercised primarily through the grants of money that are made. The local character of police forces is in some respects steadily declining, but in the matter of prosecutions we still have marked effects of the system of local organisation. The various county and borough forces, each under its chief constable, follow no uniform pattern in the way they handle prosecutions.

There are some Magistrates' Courts where a solicitor generally appears to take the cases that the police have instituted, but it is more common to find the police taking their own cases except when the importance or difficulty of a case is thought to warrant legal representation. While the informant or complainant is entitled to conduct his case in the Magistrates' Court that may not give him all the rights of an advocate. Hence the police officer who lays an information may conduct it in court; he does this as the informant, and if the chief constable wants this to be done by a particular officer he must arrange for that officer to lay the information. There has for many years been controversy over what is called 'police advocacy'. No one doubts that a police officer may call witnesses, let them tell their story and if necessary ask them questions to see that all the facts are brought forward, and that in most cases this is all that is required. If we add an 'opening' of the case, cross-examination of the accused and his witnesses, making or answering a submission or making a speech for the prosecution, we have advocacy. Now advocacy is a peculiar thing, for it is subject to many conventions, particularly in the realm of prosecuting. An advocate for the prosecution is supposed to be there to help the court, and to be personally quite indifferent as to the result of the case; the Crown never 'loses', for it is no loss to the Crown if one of Her Majesty's subjects is found not to have committed an offence.[1] There are, of course, definite rules on a number of these matters, but the conduct of advocacy is even more dependent on a trained sense of what is allowable; no rule can, for instance, set out when it is right to press a point that is damaging to an accused and when that would be improper. Police officers may acquire all the merits of the good advocate, but conditions are somewhat against them. The relation of prosecutor to witness is hard to reproduce within a

---

[1] Anyone who reads *The Trial of Lady Chatterly*, a Penguin book, edited by C. Rolph, based on the transcript of that astonishing affair, will never again swallow all that lawyers say about the uninvolved and detached attitude of counsel for the prosecution.

disciplined force when the witness is being examined by his superior officer. Above all it is hard for members of a police force to have that detachment that the lawyer tries to cultivate. Hence it is not surprising that police advocacy has been strongly criticised; judges have condemned the method and the legal profession does not conceal its dislike of the practice. Where these views are held, the police present all the simpler cases and avoid all advocacy except that which is essential to get the case before the court, a solicitor appearing if anything further is required.[1] Whilst I think that that is the right solution, it is only fair to say that chief constables have some ground for complaint. A lawyer must learn his work somewhere, and it is not unknown to regard appearing for the police before Magistrates' Courts as a suitable opportunity for juniors to get experience. Some chief constables say that they have seen a succession of inexperienced young solicitors fumbling with their cases, and that as soon as the young man becomes any good he goes off on to other work and another learner appears.

Where an accused person is committed for trial it is necessary for the police, like any other prosecutor, to have professional legal assistance. In the middle of last century it often happened that no preparation was made of a prosecution; the accused was committed for trial, and at the trial court the clerk simply handed a copy of the indictment and of the depositions to a barrister, who did the best he could on this last-minute instruction, or even in some cases no barrister appeared at all and the judge piloted the case from the depositions. At the present day this lack of preparation would be considered unsatisfactory, but we still have no general system. Except in cases where the Director of Public Prosecutions is involved (a matter dealt with later) the practice varies from court to court.

At the Old Bailey the simpler police prosecutions used to be carried out without a solicitor; the magistrates' clerk sent all the papers to the Clerk of the Central Criminal Court. The barristers practising in the Central Criminal Court were members of the 'Bar Mess', and the Clerk of the Court gave them briefs in rotation. No solicitor acted in the preparation of these briefs: it was no more than sending the papers to counsel, who would if necessary confer directly with the police. Such briefs have long been called 'soups'. If a police case presented difficulty a London firm of solicitors, Messrs

[1] The Royal Commission on the Police, Cmnd. 1728, para. 381, think it undesirable that 'police officers should appear as prosecutors except for minor cases' and 'deplore the regular employment of the same police officers as advocates'.

Wontner and Sons, acted for the Commissioner of Police and briefed counsel. At the County of London Sessions and the Middlesex Sessions the more difficult police cases were also handled by Messrs Wontner and Sons 'as solicitors for the Commissioner of Police'. The lighter cases were dealt with by a system of 'soups', and Messrs Wontner and Sons distributed the cases. In 1935 a Solicitor's Department was set up as part of the organisation of the Metropolitan Police.[1] The Solicitor to the Commissioner of Police is responsible for representing the police in all cases in which legal aid is required before all the courts in the Metropolitan Police District. Members of his staff who are solicitors appear before magistrates, but for cases tried on indictment he must brief counsel, selecting them from a list approved by the Commissioner of Police. At the Old Bailey most Metropolitan Police cases have legal representation, and there are few 'soups'. The solicitor has also been appointed as court prosecuting solicitor for the County of London Quarter Sessions and for the County of Middlesex Quarter Sessions. In the more important police prosecutions at these Sessions the solicitor represents the police and instructs counsel. The simpler cases are handled as 'soups' and the distribution is entrusted to the solicitor to the Metropolitan Police, who acts on the instruction of the Courts.

Outside London a distinction must be made between boroughs and counties. In boroughs there is a strong tendency for the management of prosecutions of indictable offences to be placed in the hands of a solicitor employed as an official by the borough corporation. Most town clerks are solicitors, and should that not be the case there are bound to be solicitors in the town clerk's office. The town clerk or his subordinates may do the work, or a solicitor (not an official) may be given a salary; in the latter event, the solicitor may or may not be under the general direction of the town clerk. In some boroughs the chief constable gives the work to a few local solicitors. The clerk to the borough justices is not allowed to act in this capacity, but in the counties this prohibition does not apply. When a case is committed for trial from county justices, the police frequently instruct solicitors, either sharing the work between various local firms or else giving it to one firm. The tendency is towards giving all the work to one person, who becomes the 'county' or 'police solicitor'. If the police do not instruct a solicitor, then the

---

[1] The *Reports of the Commissioner of Police of the Metropolis* (published each year by H.M.S.O.) give information on the work of the Solicitor's Department.

clerk to the justices may manage the prosecution, but that is not a course that can be called satisfactory; the clerk to the committing justices first appears as an officer of a court, and it is contrary to all principle that he should then change to the role of prosecuting solicitor. This point was considered by the Justices' Clerks Committee, which recommended that the prohibition on clerks to borough justices acting as solicitors for prosecutions at Assizes and Quarter Sessions should be extended to clerks to county justices.[1] The law has not been changed, but the practice has been so largely abandoned that it can be called dying if not quite dead.

The Director of Public Prosecutions holds a key position in the administration of criminal justice,[2] and as with so many of our institutions his office has to be explained by reference to its development. In the middle of last century very serious or difficult criminal matters were often reported to the Home Office. The Home Office might give advice, or it might decide to give active assistance by handing the case over to the Treasury Solicitor[3] to prosecute. Counsel would have to be briefed, and if neither the Attorney-General nor the Solicitor-General took the brief it would go to one of a small group of counsel who became known as Treasury Counsel. In 1879 the office of Director of Public Prosecutions was created, but it was then merely advisory; he handed the conduct of cases to the Treasury Solicitor. A Committee considered the matter in 1884, and the office of Director was merged with that of Treasury Solicitor, and regulations were made as to the cases in which he should prosecute and the cases that should be reported to him. This merger was not satisfactory, and in 1908 the offices were separated.

The Director of Public Prosecutions is an official, appointed by the Home Secretary from barristers or solicitors of ten years' standing. His department has a professional staff of some thirty-

---

[1] Cmd. 6507 (1944), paras. 67, 68, 230.

[2] A short account of the office is given by Sir E. Tindal Atkinson (formerly Director of Public Prosecutions) 'The Department of the Director of Public Prosecutions', in the *Canadian Bar Review* for May 1944; Sir Theobald Mathew (the present Director of Public Prosecutions), *The Office and Duties of the Director of Public Prosecutions*, a lecture delivered before the University of London, 1950, and *The Department of the Director of Public Prosecutions*, two lectures delivered at the Law Society, 1952.

[3] The Home Office and other Departments have 'legal advisers' on their own staff, but these do not practise; if there is conveyancing to be done, or proceedings to be brought or defended, it must go to the Department's solicitor, and the Treasury Solicitor was appointed solicitor to the Home Office in 1842. The Treasury Solicitor acts for several government departments, and some have their own solicitor.

five barristers and solicitors, and an ordinary staff from the civil service. The Director acts under the general direction of the Attorney-General who is the political minister responsible to Parliament. The duties of the Director, and of the police and others in regard to him, are contained in statutory rules made by the Attorney-General with the approval of the Lord Chancellor and the Home Secretary, the present Regulations having been made in 1946.[1] The Director is not concerned with criminal investigation; police and other agencies do the detecting, arrests and collection of evidence. The Director's main functions are:

(1) He gives advice if he thinks it right to do so to those who apply, whether government departments, police or others. He may give advice orally.

(2) The police must report to him certain offences that are specified in the Regulations; there is quite a substantial list, which includes many offences because they are serious or because they are difficult.

(3) The Director prosecutes:

(a) In all offences punishable with death.

(b) In cases referred to him by government departments, if he thinks there should be a prosecution. The Home Secretary can require him to prosecute.

(c) In any case which appears to him to be of importance or difficulty or which for any other reason requires his intervention.

The actual steps in prosecuting are taken either by members of the Director's staff or by a solicitor appointed by him. The Attorney-General nominates counsel who are to receive briefs at the Central Criminal Court (where they are still called Treasury Counsel) and for cases at Assizes. In 1962, the Director prosecuted 1438 people for indictable offences (out of 215,534), his cases including 132 cases of murder, 41 of manslaughter and 19 of causing death by dangerous driving; he prosecuted 537 people for summary offences (out of 1,095,609). Thus, in relation to the total number of prosecutions, only a small proportion are taken by the Director. But the Director has an importance far greater than these figures suggest, for he is in fact the co-ordinating and controlling element throughout all prosecuting. This comes about through the interlocking nature of the first three of his functions listed above. Because cases listed in the Regulations must be reported to him he will be aware of cases of any category that he wishes to notice. He can advise for or

---

[1] These were made to replace Regulations made in 1886 which included a reference to cases 'hitherto undertaken by the Treasury Solicitor', a matter of some obscurity when there were no survivors of pre-1886 practice.

against a prosecution. If his advice in favour of a prosecution is not taken, he can himself prosecute. If his advice against prosecuting is ignored, he cannot directly prevent proceedings,[1] but he could report the matter to the Attorney-General who can stop a criminal case by entering a *nolle prosequi*. He has considerable power and influence, but it would be wrong to stress the element of coercion, for however much he may be left to exercise a discretion he is an official working within a parliamentary system, and that implies not only a minister responsible to Parliament but also that powers are exercised after argument and discussion among those concerned. The Home Office is the department primarily concerned with public order, police and the administration of the criminal law; policy at the official level is a matter for that department consulting with any other department particularly concerned and the Director, and, where matters of execution arise, of consultation with the police. Above that comes the ministerial level, Cabinet and Parliament. We could not keep our apparently chaotic method of prosecutions being run by police forces and others if it were not for this co-ordinating system. An interesting recent example is the offence of Public Mischief. In the case of *Manley*[2] in 1933 a woman had falsely reported that she had been robbed with the result that police officers wasted their time and persons came under suspicion; she was convicted and her conviction upheld on appeal, the court saying that 'all such acts or attempts as tend to the prejudice of the community are indictable'. This was an alarming decision, for anything might be a public mischief; it flouted the great tradition against undefined crimes and looked singularly like something of Hitler's.[3] Charges of public mischief were generally confined to circumstances like those in *Manley*, but there were a few cases of a different nature, including the publication of anti-Jew propaganda. It would have been a most

---

[1] The Director may of course take over a case and try to prevent it going any further. Thus when a private person obtained a warrant to arrest a person on a charge of murder, in circumstances in which the Director had already examined the results of investigations and decided (on the advice of Senior Treasury Counsel) that the evidence did not justify a prosecution, the Director took over the case and his representative invited the justices to decline to commit the accused for trial. The Attorney-General, in written reply to a Question on 23 October 1950, gave these facts and approved of the course that was taken.

[2] [1933] 1 K.B. 529.

[3] The decision in *Manley* was much criticised at the time: see comment in 49 *Law Quarterly Review* (1933) at p. 153, and an article by Stallybrass at p. 183. I examined the history in 'Common Law Misdemeanours', 6 *Cambridge Law Journal* (1937), p. 193, reprinted in *The Modern Approach to Criminal Law* (1945).

tricky thing to control by legislation, but it seemed to have been handled effectively by being placed in 1946 on the list of offences that must be reported to the Director: prosecutions were confined to suitable cases.[1] The future is, however, far from secure, for the Law Lords in the *Ladies' Directory Case*[2] have re-instated the Hitlerian principle of undefined crime by asserting that any conduct that is 'prejudicial to the public welfare' is a criminal offence.

We still keep to the rule that expenses of criminal cases fall on the county or borough where the trial takes place, and just as a private prosecutor is entitled to be repaid a sum that is supposed to represent the cost of prosecuting, so does the Director recover from local authorities some of his costs of prosecuting in their areas. The rest of the Director's costs and the general expenses of his department are met by money provided by Parliament.

In addition to prosecutions by private prosecutors, the police, and the Director of Public Prosecutions, there are many prosecutions each year by some government departments and local authorities. These bodies have their own legal departments, and, unless the nature of the case leads them to call upon the Director of Public Prosecutions, it is customary for the appropriate legal department to prepare any prosecutions. Departments that commonly prosecute include the Ministries of Labour, Pensions and National Insurance, Transport, Agriculture and Fisheries, Power, and the Customs and Excise. Local authorities prosecute for infringements of the Weights and Measures Acts and many other matters entrusted to their surveillance. No recent figures are available to show the numbers of these and similar prosecutions, but they account for some thousands of cases.

In the event of a person convicted at Assizes or Quarter Sessions appealing to the Court of Criminal Appeal it is desirable that counsel should be briefed to argue if necessary against the appellant's contention. Except when a prosecution is instituted by a government department that wishes to appear on an appeal it is usual to find the Director of Public Prosecutions appearing for the Crown in the Court of Criminal Appeal. Private prosecutors are not prohibited from appearing in the Court of Criminal Appeal to defend the conviction that has been obtained, but they are discouraged from doing so; the discouragement includes a rule that

[1] The Court of Criminal Appeal reviewed the offence of public mischief in *Newland* [1954] 1 Q.B. 158 and considered that it should be limited to conspiracy.
[2] *Shaw* v. *Director of Public Prosecutions* [1962] A.C. 220; this report of the appeal in the House of Lords incorporates a report of the appeal in the Court of Criminal Appeal.

they cannot get reimbursement of any of their costs, and a provision that the Court can at any time order the Director or solicitor to a department to take over the case. Obviously few people want to defend an appeal at their own expense when for the asking it can be done very competently at the public expense.

It is rare to find counsel for the Crown in the Court of Criminal Appeal doing anything that could be called pressing for the conviction to be upheld: in this court the principle that in criminal cases the Crown cannot 'win' or 'lose' is patent. Counsel for the Crown, normally the same counsel who appeared at the trial, are frequently not called upon to address the court; when they do address the court it is more in the nature of assisting the judges than defending the appeal.

4. CRIMINAL PROCEDURE

Practically all criminal cases come before the justices, either to be heard summarily or for preliminary inquiry. Most of the summary cases and a few that are more serious are begun by the prosecutor 'laying an information' on which a justice is asked to issue a summons which will be served on the defendant. A summons states the alleged offence and gives the date and place where the defendant is to appear. In the case of a person who would probably disregard a summons the prosecutor may ask for a warrant for arrest as the initial step; this application must be made upon a sworn statement. The granting of summonses and warrants need not be done in open court; in the case of warrants for arrest it would often be unwise to advertise the steps that are being taken. In a number of cases there is neither summons nor warrant, for the accused has been arrested and appears before the Magistrates' Court already in custody. The power to arrest without warrant is a very complicated topic; a police constable has very wide powers of arrest whereas a private citizen's powers are so limited and illogical that he is well advised not to try arresting anyone.

A defendant must be present in court during committal proceedings and at a trial on indictment. Personal attendance is also necessary in a number of summary cases, principally where a defendant may choose jury trial. In other summary cases the apparent command to the defendant 'to appear' is misleading. First, the defendant has a right to appear by solicitor or counsel. Secondly, the court may, on proof of service of a summons, either require the defendant to appear (and may issue a warrant for his arrest) or may hear the case in his absence. Minor offences, principally relating to road traffic, have for long been mostly heard in the defendant's absence. A new procedure for these cases was introduced in 1957.[1] The defendant gets, together with the summons, a brief statement of the police evidence, and a form on which he can if he wishes plead guilty, say that he does not intend to appear, and set out any mitigating circumstances. He need not reply, and if he wants to defend the case he must appear. Most defendants under this procedure plead guilty by post, and the statements are read out in court, without any witnesses attending. This saves a great deal of the time of police and others, at the cost of additional typing and office work.

In a summary case with the defendant present the substance of the charge is read out and he is asked whether he pleads guilty or not guilty. If he admits it, that is, 'pleads guilty', the court may wish to hear the more important evidence, but more often it is thought sufficient for the police officer in charge of the case to give a short account of the facts. The defendant may also address the justices, or evidence may be given by himself or by others in the hope of inducing the bench to impose a light or nominal sentence.

If the defendant pleads not guilty, the trial proceeds. In describing this procedure it will be convenient to assume that both prosecutor and defendant are represented by a solicitor. Actually, most summary cases are heard without professional assistance, and then it cannot be said that this procedure is always observed: by describing what happens when legal advisers are present we can get a sketch of what is supposed to happen in all cases. After the plea of 'not guilty' the solicitor for the prosecution will 'open the case', that is, he will describe the prosecution's allegations and indicate the way in which this story is going to be substantiated. This 'opening' is not evidence, and the advocate must be careful not to make statements that cannot be supported by the evidence he is going to call. The witnesses for the prosecution are then called. Each witness is first questioned by the prosecution, this process being the 'examination in chief', then 'cross-examined' by the defence, and then sometimes 're-examined' by the prosecution. A large mass of rules of evidence restrict the questions that may be asked: these rules are highly technical and difficult to understand. On the whole the rules of evidence are meant to protect the defendant. After the prosecution has called all

---

[1] Magistrates' Courts Act 1957 based on recommendations of the Departmental Committee on the Summary Trial of Minor Offences, Cmd. 9524 (1955).

the evidence that is to be given, the defence may submit that there is no case to answer, that is, that the prosecution has not proved the commission of the offence. The justices must then consider this submission, and if they decide that there is a case to be answered the defence must be put forward. The defendant's advocate may 'open the defence', and call witnesses, including the defendant himself: these witnesses will give their evidence in the same way as the witnesses for the prosecution, except that the examination in chief is now conducted by the defence and the cross-examination by the prosecution. It is possible, with certain restrictions, for the prosecution to call witnesses to rebut the evidence given for the defence. If the only evidence for the defence is that of the defendant himself, instead of 'opening' the case the defendant's advocate must call the defendant and address the Court afterwards. When there are other witnesses besides the defendant the justices may allow an address to the court after the evidence for the defence instead of the 'opening'. Further speeches are not allowed unless there is a point of law to be argued. The justices must then decide whether to convict or acquit: for this purpose they frequently retire to their own room so that they can discuss the case freely. If they decide to convict, the police officer in charge is usually asked to state what he knows about the defendant. During the hearing of the case the prosecution is generally speaking not allowed to give evidence to the effect that the defendant is of bad reputation or has been previously convicted of some offence. Such evidence is irrelevant to the question of whether he has committed the offence for which he is being tried, but after conviction it is relevant to assist the court in determining the sentence that should be imposed.

In the course of the hearing of a summary offence it may be necessary to adjourn the proceedings. In this case the justices may allow the defendant to go at large, or cause him to enter into a formal promise, called recognisances (with or without sureties), to pay a sum of money if he does not appear at the adjourned hearing, or keep him in custody.

If the offence charged is one that must be tried upon indictment, then the justices do not try the case but hold a preliminary inquiry. The nature of this preliminary inquiry, which may be before a single justice, has been described in discussing the criminal courts. The procedure consists of an 'opening' by the prosecution, followed by the calling of witnesses for the prosecution. These witnesses give evidence in exactly the same way that they would do in a trial. The clerk to the justices takes the evidence down in writing, reads it over to each witness, who then signs it. These statements of evidence are called 'depositions'. If the justices think that there is a *prima facie* case against the defendant, the charge must be read over to him and he must be asked if he wishes to say anything in answer to the charge, telling him that he need not say anything, but that if he does say anything it will be taken down in writing and may be used in evidence at the trial.[1] The defendant may give evidence, and may call witnesses; if this is done, there may be cross-examination. Any evidence for the defence is also recorded. Throughout the preliminary inquiry the defendant must be present.

If the justices decide to commit for trial, the question of bail will arise. Bail may not be given in treason, or in murder, but otherwise it is discretionary. Bail in our courts rests on recognisances, which are really promises; there are no deposits of money or the pledging of property or bondsmen. It used to be thought that bail should be granted if it seemed probable that the defendant would surrender to stand his trial. As experience has shown that very few people who are released on bail do 'jump bail', most observers of our system had been more concerned at bail being often refused than at bail being granted, and thought that the police view too often prevailed. However, the judges have taken strong exception to justices granting bail when the accused is a person with previous convictions of the 'professional criminal' type, on the ground that such a person may commit further offences whilst awaiting trial.[2] It has always been customary for the justices to inquire of the police whether they objected to bail, and now it is necessary to inquire about the accused's record, but as this is not part of proceedings that have to be in open court it can be done by handing in a written list so that it will not be published in the press and the accused would not be prejudiced at his trial. The amount of bail is discretionary, the Bill of Rights prohibiting 'excessive' bail. A recognisance by the defendant should be a sum reasonably within his capacity to pay; it is more important that he can name sureties, usually two, who will stand for him. A proposed surety may be in court, and be questioned about his means by the justices, or the police may be asked to inquire into the apparent

---

[1] Writers of detective stories sometimes render the caution, whether given by justices or police, as 'anything you say will be taken down in writing and will be used in evidence *against you*': the last two words are improper, for the statement made may go in favour of the defendant.

[2] *Rex* v. *Phillips* (1947) 32 Cr.App.R. 47, and Lord Goddard L.C.J. at Cambridge Assizes (*The Times*, 20 May 1947).

standing of the person. If the defendant cannot there and then produce acceptable sureties, he can be committed in custody with a direction that he is to be released if sureties acceptable to the police come along and enter into recognisance for a specified amount. If bail is refused, or 'excessive' bail demanded, there may be an application to a High Court judge. Before the war there were fewer than 100 applications annually, but of later years there has been a great increase; in 1956 the total was 1665 of which 7 per cent were granted.[1]

The depositions, and a copy of any statment that the defendant may have made, are transmitted to the clerk of the Assize Court or Quarter Sessions. The indictment is usually drawn up by the clerk to the court of trial. Since the abolition of grand juries it is now only necessary for the clerk to the court to sign this indictment, and at the next sitting the defendant can be put on his trial before a jury. There is a reserve power in the judges. An application supported by written statements of evidence may be made, and a judge may then give leave for an indictment to be filed. A trial on indictment follows the lines given for a summary trial. Counsel will certainly appear for the prosecution and also for the defence in nearly all cases. In these trials before a jury counsel are allowed to make second speeches. If the defence is calling evidence, the defence will open the case, call witnesses, and conclude with a summing up of the defence. The prosecution may then reply with a speech.[2] If no witnesses for the defence are called, or the only evidence is that of the defendant himself, then his counsel has the last word. Some value is set on getting the last word, although the truly last word always comes from the judge, recorder or chairman as the case may be. The judge's summing up is essentially in the form of 'if you find such and such allegations to be true, your verdict must be so and so', although to enable the jury to come to their conclusion the judge may review any of the evidence and comment upon it. If the jury return a verdict of 'not guilty', that is final; no appeal lies against an acquittal, and the defendant cannot be tried again for the same offence. If a defence of insanity is accepted by the jury, the verdict is 'guilty of the act (or omission), but so insane as not to be responsible, according to law, for his action at the time when the act was done (or the omission made)'. This curious verdict, devised by Queen Victoria, is treated as

---

[1] Devlin, *op. cit.* p. 72. Lord Devlin deals at length with the working of bail.
[2] The Fourth Report of the Criminal Law Revision Committee, Cmnd. 2148 (1963), recommends that the defence should always have the right to the last speech.

one of acquittal, with the result that no appeal can be made, although the effect is detention in Broadmoor or some other mental hospital.[1] From a verdict of 'guilty' there may, as described above, be an appeal to the Court of Criminal Appeal.

The principles governing indictable offences that are triable summarily have been discussed on pages 97–9. If the justices take the view, either at the beginning of a case or after it has been started as a preliminary inquiry, that it is one that can properly be tried summarily the charge is read to the defendant and he is asked whether he wants to be tried by a jury or whether he wants summary trial. He is also told about the possibility of committal to Quarter Sessions for sentence. If jury trial is chosen, the proceedings continue as a preliminary inquiry. If the defendant elects summary trial, he is asked to plead, and the subsequent procedure is that of a summary trial.

5. THE DEFENCE OF CRIMINAL CHARGES

So far prosecutions have been considered from the viewpoint of the prosecutor. How does the system appear to work when viewed by accused persons? The general atmosphere of complacency that surrounded our legal system settled more upon our criminal administration than upon our civil law. Mr Claud Mullins in his admirable book, *In Search of Justice*, focused his attention upon civil law, considering that there was not much wrong with the criminal law: shortly after the publication of this book Mr Mullins was appointed a metropolitan stipendiary magistrate, and he soon changed his views, finding that the criminal law is no subject for complacency. There is plenty to praise in the English administration of criminal justice; a danger is that this may lead to blindness towards the less satisfactory features.

In the early nineteenth century the English criminal law was the most brutal and savage of any civilised country. Great reforms were made, both in the rules of law and in matters of procedure, but traditional behaviour dies hard. An illustration may be taken from the Memoirs of Sir Henry Hawkins (Lord Brampton). Hawkins was called to the bar in 1843, and the events he described must have occurred soon afterwards when he was attending Old Bailey

---

[1] See 'A note on Broadmoor patients', by me in *11 Cambridge Law Journal* (1951), p. 57; and pp. 209–211, below. The Third Report of the Criminal Law Revision Committee, Cmnd. 2149 (1963) recommends some procedural changes and rights of appeal.

trials. The prisoner Jones, accused of picking pockets, pleaded 'not guilty'.

The accused having 'held up his hand', and the jury having solemnly sworn to hearken to the evidence, and 'to well and truly try, and due deliverance make', etc., the witness for the prosecution climbs into the box, which was like a pulpit, and before he has time to look round and see where the voice comes from, he is examined as follows by the prosecuting counsel:

'I think you were walking up Ludgate Hill on Thursday, 25th, about half past two in the afternoon, and suddenly felt a tug at your pocket and missed your handkerchief, which the constable now produces. Is that it?'
'Yes, sir.'
'I suppose you have nothing to ask him?' says the judge. 'Next witness.' Constable stands up.
'Were you following the prosecutor on this occasion when he was robbed on Ludgate Hill? and did you see the prisoner put his hand into the prosecutor's pocket and take this handkerchief out of it?'
'Yes, sir.'
Judge to prisoner: 'Nothing to say, I suppose?' Then to the jury: 'Gentlemen, I suppose you have no doubt? I have none.'
Jury: 'Guilty, my lord', as though to oblige his lordship.
Judge to prisoner: 'Jones, we have met before—we shall not meet again for some time—seven years' transportation. Next case.'
Time: two minutes fifty-three seconds.
Perhaps this case was a high example of expedition, because it was not always that a learned counsel could put his questions so neatly; but it may be taken that these after-dinner trials did not occupy on the average more than *four minutes* each.

A sentence of seven years could not be given today in such a casual way, but it is as well to keep the not too distant past in mind, for continuity of institutions may lead us to take for granted some practices that should be questioned.

The troubles of an accused person may begin whilst he is in the hands of the police, before he is ever brought to court. The next problem is to get legal aid. Lastly come certain characteristics of the trial, varying according as it is on indictment or summary.

(i) *The interrogation of suspected persons*

Most of the investigation of crime falls to the police. It is accepted that police must be allowed to ask questions of anyone they think may give information, but police have no power to compel a person to answer; a witness may be compelled to attend a *court* and there give evidence, but before proceedings are actually brought he can refuse to say a word. Also the police have no power to detain a person for questioning. They may ask someone to go to a police station to help them, and he may remain for many hours, with long periods of interrogation. There are rules laid down by the judges, which are not in themselves law but are cited in law courts, for the guidance of police officers. These rules say that as soon as a police officer makes up his mind to charge a person, he may not interrogate him any more; equally if the person is in custody (that is, under arrest whether yet formally charged or not) he may not be interrogated. The principle is that inconsistencies in anything he may already have said may be resolved, but when a person ceases to be a suspect and becomes an accused, a police officer cannot cross-examine him; a justice or judge cannot examine an accused, and *a fortiori* a police officer cannot be allowed to do so. There is much controversy over whether the rules are generally observed, whether the police could do their work adequately if they kept to the strict letter of the rules, and as to what (if anything) ought to be done about it.[1] The Lord Chief Justice and his colleagues are considering whether the rules should be redrafted or altered in some respects. The Royal Commission on the Police carefully avoid saying whether police do use guile and other inducements in order to obtain confessions (which some responsible and well-informed witnesses thought did happen from time to time) and contented themselves with the conclusion that 'Practices of this kind, if they exist (and evidence about them is difficult to obtain and substantiate) must be unhesitatingly condemned.'[2] I had occasion to go through much material, and I agree with those who regard abuses by the police as being isolated instances, but to my mind a major question has hardly been tackled. Police officers, acting within the accepted canons of fairness, may interrogate a person at such length that, combined with the various strains induced by tension in a police station and anxiety about the whole outcome, the person may come to say almost anything. Dr Sargant has shown[3] that those who interrogate may feed in supposed facts which eventually come back to them in the form of a confession in such a way that they regard it as spontaneous. The process of excessive interrogation may be misleading to those who do the questioning as well as being

---

[1] Much has been written on this of late. The principal contributions are Williams, *The Proof of Guilt*, 2nd ed. (1958); Devlin, *The Criminal Prosecution in England* (1960); Articles on 'Police Questioning' [1960] Crim. L.R. 298; a Report of a Committee appointed by 'Justice' reprinted in [1960] Crim. L.R. 793; and evidence given to the Royal Commission on Police.

[2] Royal Commission on the Police, Final Report, Cmnd. 1728 (1962), para. 370.

[3] *Battle for the Mind* (1957).

unfair to the victim of the process. The result may be that at the end there is an apparently voluntary confession that the police are firmly convinced is true and yet the confession is retracted by the accused at a later date. When a defence lawyer gets on the scene he may find that his client has already made his conviction a virtual certainty; it rarely matters, but one cannot be too sure after the cases of Evans and Riley.

When a person has been arrested he is taken before a Magistrates' Court as soon as is reasonably possible, which normally means within 24 hours, or longer if the next day is a Sunday. The justices may remand him in custody, or give him bail. The justices cannot at that stage learn much about the case, and they must rely to a considerable extent on police statements. Legal aid can be granted. If the remand is in custody, the accused goes to prison, where he can be visited by his lawyer and where the police can have no further interviews with him unless he positively consents.

(ii) *Legal aid in criminal courts*

If a defence is to be properly prepared and adequately presented it is virtually necessary to employ legal advisers. A few men, like Horatio Bottomley, can present their case in person, but this is rare. The need for competent legal assistance exists at all stages of a criminal charge. The defendant who is able to pay for a solicitor will usually consult with him before the case is heard. For a non-indictable offence the solicitor will generally conduct the defence. If the charge is one that must be tried before a jury, careful cross-examination by solicitor or counsel at the preliminary inquiry may be a great help in preparing the defence. It is also a matter for expert advice as to whether the defence should be disclosed at that stage: disclosure may induce the justices to refuse to commit for trial, or it may strengthen the prosecution's case by warning them of the weak points in their case. If the charge is of an indictable offence that can be tried summarily, the solicitor will advise his client as to whether he should consent to summary trial or elect to go for trial before a jury. The defendant who is not legally represented is not usually sufficiently acquainted with the procedure to understand the choice he is asked to make. It is far less trouble for the justices and their clerk to try the case summarily than to hear it with a view to committal for trial, since the latter involves the taking of depositions, a slow and laborious business. Many defendants do not understand about bail, and assume that if they elect to go for trial they will have to wait in prison. Other considerations have been mentioned above.

Most defendants at trials on indictment succeed in raising some money to pay for their defence, generally at the expense of their friends and relatives. I have been told of one prosecution in an industrial area where a considerable sum was raised by a collection of sixpences and coppers. In prosecutions that are likely to carry publicity value for the popular newspapers it is by no means unknown for defence funds to be provided by a newspaper, the prisoner providing a 'life story' as recompense. I have been present at an interview where an 'exclusive life story' was sold to a Sunday paper for a sum that enabled the defence to brief the best-known counsel of the day. Whilst it is undoubted that competent legal assistance is practically necessary, it must not be assumed that very expensive counsel are proportionately better than cheaper men. The whole question of counsel's fees is discussed elsewhere in this book. In criminal cases a certain responsibility rests on the prosecution; if famous and fashionable counsel are briefed for the Crown, the defendant and the public are apt to feel that counsel of similar standing should appear for the defence. When expert evidence is required, particularly of a medical or a scientific nature, it is often necessary to spend a good deal of money. Juries are more impressed by dogmatic statements from well-known persons than by the more cautious conclusions of the research worker. The ability to make proper use of experts is one of the signs of the good administrator, and it is not a faculty that is highly developed in the legal profession or that is common among jurymen. Money is a great asset to the defence, and the sensible solicitor will help his client to raise money by any legitimate method.

The reality of the costs of defence has received more publicity since motor-cars have become more numerous. Many comprehensive motor policies include free legal defence, and the motoring organisations offer similar facilities. In 1936 the Automobile Association extended the free legal defence of their members to include charges of manslaughter, pointing out that: 'The legal costs in these cases can easily amount to three or four hundred pounds—a serious matter for persons of moderate means.' Both costs and incomes have risen since then, but there is still a large class of the community for whom a half or a quarter of such a sum is not just a 'serious matter' but is an absolute impossibility. A person who cannot afford to pay for professional assistance and who cannot obtain it through any organisation to which he belongs must rely upon such assistance as is provided at the public charge.

The provision for legal aid in defending criminal charges began with the Poor Prisoners' Defence Act 1903 which was limited to trials on indictment. Under that Act a factor to be considered in deciding whether to grant legal aid was the nature of the defence as disclosed before the committing justices, a provision which compelled a poor prisoner to disclose his defence at a stage at which other prisoners and their legal advisers might see fit to say nothing. A Committee was appointed in 1925 to inquire into the subject of legal aid, and a Report dealing with criminal matters was published in 1926.[1] It was recommended that legal aid should be extended to preliminary inquiries and to cases heard summarily in Magistrates' Courts, though there can be few Reports in which recommendations have been put forward quite so half-heartedly.[2] The Poor Prisoners' Defence Act 1930 incorporated the Committee's recommendations and provided a comprehensive system for summary trial, preliminary inquiry and trial on indictment.

The 1930 Act did not work well in the period before the war. There was a reluctance to give certificates, some courts being apparently unaware that the requirements of a defence being disclosed had been repealed. The justices were not doing their duty. The whole subject of legal aid came to be reviewed during the war, and the Committee on Legal Aid and Legal Advice (Rushcliffe Committee) produced a comprehensive report in 1945,[3] which was implemented by the Legal Aid and Advice Act 1949. The 1949 Act established a wholly new system for civil matters,[4] but for criminal cases the Poor Prisoners Defence Act 1930 was left in force though amended. The position has been complicated because the operation of parts of the Legal Aid and Advice Act 1949 was postponed as a measure of national economy.[5] Nearly all the remaining parts affecting criminal law came into operation in 1960. The changes that have taken place are mentioned in the following paragraphs.

There had been doubts as to how far the facilities under the 1930 Act were known to defendants. Administrative steps were taken in 1945 as a result of the Rushcliffe Report to see that notices

---

[1] Cmd. 2638.

[2] 'The substance of our view upon the whole question is that in criminal cases the present system works satisfactorily and that no alterations are urgently or imperatively required. But in the course of the exhaustive evidence to which we have listened matters have emerged which we think show that, satisfactory as the system is, it is not incapable of improvement' (para. 22).

[3] Cmd. 6641 (1945).   [4] See pp. 280 et seq., below.

[5] See p. 310, below.

should be displayed at courts and in police and prison cells. There are two main kinds of certificates that may be granted. *Legal aid certificates* may be granted by justices either for the defence of a charge heard summarily or to assist the accused at a preliminary inquiry in indictable cases. This certificate entitles the recipient to a solicitor or, in the case of a preliminary inquiry into a charge of murder, a solicitor and counsel. *Defence Certificates* are for trials on indictment, and provide both solicitor and counsel. Defence certificates may be given by the justices who commit for trial, or by Quarter Sessions or by Assize Courts. It is also possible for Quarter Sessions or Assizes to ask counsel to undertake a defence without issue of a Defence Certificate.[1] The test for granting a legal aid certificate has been whether it appears that a defendant's means will not allow him to provide for his own defence, and that *by reason of the gravity of the charge or of exceptional circumstances* it is desirable in the interests of justice that he should have free legal aid. A defence certificate could be granted on the same conditions except that the words placed in italics above were not included. The 1949 Act provided for repeal of the words in italics, but this was not brought into force until 1963. The test is now the same in all cases, namely 'whether it is desirable in the interests of justice'. In the case of murder charges the defence certificate must be granted if the accused has insufficient means. There are provisions for legal aid on appeals. The legislation is now an untidy clutter of statute and rules and regulation. Table VI shows how the whole field is covered.

The Committee recommended that doubts about giving a certificate should be resolved in favour of the applicant; the Home Office commended that course to justices, and it is now a legal requirement under the 1949 Act: 'If...there is a doubt whether his means are sufficient to enable him to obtain legal aid or whether it is desirable in the interests of justice that he should have free legal aid, the doubt shall be resolved in favour of granting him free legal aid.' There is no prescribed test of sufficiency of means, but an applicant can be required to make a written statement in prescribed form as to his means and can be punished for false statements.

Counsel and solicitors who are prepared to take these cases put their names down on a panel. When a certificate is granted, the clerk

---

[1] There is also the system of dock-side briefs. Any prisoner who can produce £2. 4s. 6d. is entitled to select any of the counsel robed and present in court, and (irrespective of the means of the prisoner) the counsel selected must conduct the defence for this fee. This method gives very little time for the preparation of the defence.

Table VI. *Provision for legal aid in criminal cases*

Nature of proceedings	Application to be made	Certificate of authorisation	Assistance provided
Summary trial Preliminary inquiry	By letter to Clerk to Justices, when single justice may grant, or apply at Magistrates' Court	Legal Aid Certificate	Solicitor: on murder charge, solicitor and counsel
Trial at Assizes or Quarter Sessions, and on committal to Quarter Sessions for sentence	Apply to committing justices, or to judge or chairman at trial court or	Defence Certificate	Solicitor and counsel
	judge or chairman (on application or of his own motion) may request counsel to undertake defence	Order of the court as to costs	Counsel only
Appeal from Magistrates' Court to Quarter Sessions	Apply to Magistrates' Court, or if refused, by letter to Clerk of the Peace, or to Quarter Sessions	Appeal Aid Certificate	Solicitor and counsel; no counsel where solicitor can appear in Quarter Sessions
Appeal to Court of Criminal Appeal	Apply to Registrar (who may act on his own motion), Registrar reports to judge	Direction by Judge of C.C.A.	Usually counsel only
Appeal from Divisional Court in criminal matters, or from Court of Criminal Appeal, to House of Lords	Apply to Registrar of Court of Criminal Appeal	Direction by Judge of C.C.A.	Usually counsel only
On case stated to Divisional Court, or application for prerogative order	Proceed as for a civil claim: see pp. 310 *et seq.*, below	—	

of the court assigns a solicitor from the panel ordinarily by rota but the clerk takes into account any preference that the defendant may have for a particular solicitor. When counsel is to appear the solicitor usually selects a barrister who is on the panel and sends the brief to him, although some clerks prefer to apply a rota to counsel. When counsel appears at the instance of a judge, the court selects the barrister.

Counsel and solicitors have always been paid for conducting these defences, but so poorly paid that sometimes their expenses were not even covered. It is a principle of the Legal Aid and Advice Act 1949 that amounts payable to lawyers 'shall have regard to the principle of allowing fair remuneration according to the work actually and reasonably done', the cost falling on public funds. The 1949 Act applies this principle to legal aid in criminal cases, but the operation of this part was postponed until 1960. The Regulations lay down scales of basic remuneration, with additional allowances, and an 'escape clause' to cover cases that are unusually difficult or lengthy.[1] For work done under Legal Aid Certificates the Law Society, through its Area Committees established for the civil side of the Legal Aid Scheme, tax the solicitor's bill.[2] For Defence Certificates the bill comes before the clerk of Assize or the clerk of the Peace according as the trial was at Assizes or Quarter Sessions. Costs in Appeals to Quarter Sessions are dealt with in the same way as for trials in those courts. The sums due to solicitors are paid direct from the Legal Aid Fund[3] for work under Legal Aid Certificates, whilst for Defence Certificates and Appeal Aid Certificates the payments are made from the funds of the local county or borough, which is then re-imbursed by money from the Exchequer. When these complex regulations came into force in 1960 the Home Secretary said that he would appoint a Working Committee to keep the position under review. The First Report was published in 1962,[4] so that there is available a detailed account of how the scheme has worked out in practice. In the financial year 1960–1, the cost of Defence Certificates, Appeal Aid Certificates and legally aided cases in the Court of Criminal Appeal came to £610,135 for 12,111 cases, that is an

[1] There is a convenient memorandum, giving the various rates and scales, and explaining the procedure, in *The Law Society's Gazette* for March 1960, p. 194.
[2] See p. 310, below, on the Legal Aid Scheme; 'taxing' bills is explained at p. 296, below.
[3] See p. 310, below.
[4] First Report of the Working Party on Legal Aid in Criminal Proceedings (1962), H.M.S.O.

average cost of £49. 12s. 8d. a case. Legal Aid Certificates cost £91,862 for 4915 cases, giving an average of £18. 13s. 9d. a case. The Report gives in Appendices an analysis of the fees paid, so that the range of fees for the different kinds of work, distinguishing between counsel and solicitors, can be seen. It seems that in general the scheme is resulting in fair remuneration though some adjustments and extensions are needed.

As regards the extent to which applications are granted, Table VII shows that the bulk of certificates are granted by justices. The new ideas of the 1949 Act brought a change in the attitude and practices of the courts, with a striking increase in the granting of certificates. That was followed by a decline in numbers, and then by a rise to figures higher than ever before. The explanation is, I think, that justices have a certain reluctance to grant legal aid unless they see a real need for it, but they are also accustomed to pay attention to the attitude of the judges and particularly to the views of the Lord Chief Justice. In October 1951, Lord Goddard, Lord Chief Justice, said that, with the approval of his brethren, he wished to make a statement in court.[1] The tenor of the statement was that legal aid was being granted unnecessarily in many cases, particularly where there was no possibility of any defence. These views were not only expressed in court but were also put before meetings of justices. Lord Parker became Lord Chief Justice in 1958, and after an interval he began to say that legal aid is not given as often as it should be. Speaking of cases committed for trial he has said: 'There are of course occasions when a prisoner can conduct his defence or make a plea in mitigation more effectively in person and without legal representation. But such a case is of course rare. In almost every case the interests of the prisoner can only be safeguarded by legal representation....'[2] Justices appear to have taken note of the new policy. In 1963 the Act of 1949 came fully into force, with the removal of the restriction of Legal Aid Certificates to cases where the 'gravity of the charge' or 'exceptional circumstances' were shown. With a greater readiness to grant certificates, and wider grounds on which they may be granted, we can expect a substantial rise in the number of grants, with a corresponding rise in the expenditure of public money.

[1] *The Times* 2 October 1951.

[2] His address was attached to a Home Office circular to courts, in May 1961; it is reproduced in the First Report of the Working Party on Legal Aid in Criminal Proceedings (1962), H.M.S.O. Lord Parker also points out that a Defence Certificate is the proper procedure; asking counsel to conduct the defence is intended to be used when it is too late to use the ordinary procedure.

In considering the extent to which legal aid should be given in criminal cases we must have regard to its purpose. If the assumption is that legal aid is to ensure that any defence there may be is adequately presented and that in the event of a conviction or plea of guilty all the relevant information is before the court, there can be no doubt that legal aid is often given, as Lord Goddard said, quite unnecessarily. It can hardly be otherwise so long as justices or a court have to deal with applications, because they must act on insufficient information. Take, for example, a case of a young man charged with unlawful sexual intercourse with a girl under sixteen. The only defence is that he is under 24, has not been charged with such an offence before, and had a reasonable belief that the girl was over sixteen. A committing justice cannot put questions to the accused, and the only way that he can ensure that the possibility of a defence is properly examined is to give a Defence Certificate, although the result may well be that over £40 of public money is spent on a case where there is no defence. Everyone who knows what goes on in Quarter Sessions has listened to scores of cases where the prisoner is legally represented and pleads guilty; counsel is concerned with mitigation of sentence. Occasionally there really is something to elicit, particularly if there is some mental disorder,[1] but in the usual run of cases it is only too apparent that counsel have a job to think of anything worth saying. Police and other reports are already before the court;[2] even apparently useful points, such as a willingness of an employer to continue the man in his job, are normally in a probation officer's report. Many words can be expended in reviewing the dates of previous convictions to suggest that the prisoner did go straight for several years, and so on, but the bench has the list and has the intelligence and experience to have seen all that already. The bench listens attentively, or tries to appear to do so, and then imposes exactly the same sentence that they would have imposed if £40 or £50 of public money had not been spent in this way. But what is justice? The prisoner has had his innings, and he and everyone in court and outside the court through the press, can see that he had as good a chance to put forward his side as the prosecution had when it was their turn. Of course there is something in this, but it is exaggerated. Men in prison often brood on what happened in court, and blame their counsel, and effects on the public are not always what they are supposed to be. A social service requires a careful balance, for discredit can come from giving benefit when it is not needed as well as from not giving it when

[1] See p. 209, below.   [2] See pp. 223 et seq., below.

Table VII. *Legal aid under Poor Prisoner's Defence Acts*

| | Applied for by prisoner | | | | | | | | Offered by the court without application by prisoner | | | | | | | |
| | Granted | | | | Refused | | | | Accepted | | | | Declined | | | |
	1938	1950	1957	1961	1938	1950	1957	1961	1938	1950	1957	1961	1938	1950	1957	1961
Legal Aid Certificates:																
(a) by magistrates' courts for cases heard summarily	293	2586	2028	3980	113	268	962	1776	34	416	126	142	2	117	43	45
(b) by justices for preliminary inquiry	495	2497	1840	3169	180	190	689	1083	83	279	125	144	4	59	15	14
Defence Certificates:																
(a) by justices on committal for trial	1099	5870	3973	7675	400	684	1415	1749	112	626	243	382	7	120	51	88
(b) by Quarter Sessions	450	1205	1485	2592	282	575	989	1317	37	177	236	344	3	15	31	51
(c) by Assize Courts	240	264	427	450	154	58	164	239	30	22	83	28	3	10	12	2

Defences undertaken, without Defence Certificates being granted, at the request of the court

	Quarter Sessions	Assizes
1938	65	134
1950	238	244
1957	447	234
1961	946	422

it should be given. The weak point in legal aid in criminal cases is the blindfold way that aid is given or refused. The sequence in legal matters should begin with legal advice; the decision whether he ought to be aided should depend on professional opinion of his needs based on knowledge of the facts. This is achieved in the system for civil cases;[1] that scheme could not be applied to criminal cases without substantial modification, particularly on the assessment of means, but something needs to be worked out so that the same principles govern all forms of legal aid. This would also enable better provision to be made for advising convicted persons on possible grounds of appeal. An appeal against sentence is, for example, a tricky matter, for the sentence may be increased, and although independent professional advice is by no means infallible it should always be available.

(iii) *Trials on indictment*

The matters that require attention here are perhaps those that occur before the trial rather than the trial itself. Preliminary inquiries are usually completed fairly quickly, although there have been some periods of serious delays before metropolitan stipendiary magistrates.[2] Delay is a great hardship on an accused person, for there may be successive remands in custody until the committal proceedings are finished. Adjourned hearings also greatly increase the cost of the defence. Bail may be refused and the defendant committed to prison to await his trial, a course which, however proper in the circumstances,[3] will make the preparation of the defence more difficult. It is often difficult enough to get a full statement from a client when the interview takes place in the solicitor's office; when the interview is under prison conditions it is sometimes nearly impossible. It is far easier to prepare a defence when the defendant is out on bail.

Considerable criticism has arisen in the last few years from the publicity accorded to preliminary inquiries. Although this function of the justices need not be exercised in open court it is in practice performed under the conditions required for summary trials, and the

[1] See p. 310, below.

[2] *Report of the Departmental Committee on Courts of Summary Jurisdiction in the Metropolitan Area* (1937), p. 14. This *Report* gives other illustrations of the serious delays that occur. The Metropolitan Magistrates' Courts Act 1959 authorises the appointment of up to eight additional Metropolitan Stipendiary Magistrates but serious delays still occur; a protest was reported in *The Times* 8 October 1963.

[3] See p. 133, above.

10-2

press treats such inquiries as a normal judicial process. The trial of Rouse for murder in 1931 attracted great attention. Rouse gave a lift in his car to a man he found walking along a road, killed the man, and set fire to the car. The object was to create the impression that he, Rouse, had perished in an accident. At the preliminary inquiry, a good deal of evidence was given to establish Rouse's motive for staging his own death, the evidence showing that Rouse had several mistresses as well as a wife and children, and that the claims of these women were becoming highly inconvenient. Rouse's matrimonial and extra-matrimonial affairs were freely reported in local and national newspapers. At the trial it was held that this evidence must be excluded. In the past juries were allowed and even supposed to know about cases that came before them, but it has long been the theory that a jury decides from the evidence given at the trial, and today it would not be considered proper for a juryman to have outside information about a case. So here, Rouse was tried by a jury at Northampton Assizes, and that jury was supposed not to know anything beyond the evidence given at the trial. What chance is there of getting a jury who have not read the flaming headlines and perhaps have already decided that a prisoner is a bad lot? The general attitude induced by such a preliminary inquiry can be seen from a newspaper placard exhibited whilst Rouse was awaiting trial; the placard read 'Another burning car murder', and Rouse's advisers found it necessary to apply to the High Court to prevent such public assumptions of the guilt of their client. Proposals that there should be restrictions on reporting were met by an assertion that the court's power to punish for contempt is sufficient protection against publication of prejudiced statements. Thus in March 1949 the editor of the *Daily Mirror* was committed to prison for three months and the newspaper company ordered to pay a fine of £10,000 and costs for contempt of court in publishing material about a man who had been charged with murder. That example certainly shows that the power is a reality, but it does not help where the publication is a bona fide piece of reporting.

The trial of Dr Adams in 1957 raised the point again. At the committal proceedings on a charge of murder of a patient the prosecution led evidence of the circumstances in which two other patients had died. That evidence, which had of course been widely reported, was not given at the trial. Mr Justice Devlin in his summing-up expressed the opinion that it would have been wiser if the committal proceedings had been held in private. A few months later a committee was appointed under the chairmanship of Lord Tucker to consider whether committal proceedings should continue to take place in open court, and if so whether there should be any restriction on reports of such proceedings. The committee's report[1] is an excellent examination of the problem. It is not possible to prove that trials are prejudiced by reports of committal proceedings, but there is a widespread belief that they may be. The proper course is not to extend sittings *in camera*, but to restrict publication. The recommendation is that when the accused has been discharged or until the trial is ended, any results of committal proceedings should be restricted to particulars of the name of the accused, the charge, the decision of the Court, and the like. As to the views of the press the Committee said:

> We realise that any restriction on the reporting of what occurs in court was believed by the representatives of the press who gave evidence before us to infringe that freedom of reporting which they regard as essential to the proper administration of justice. We agree that freedom to report trials is essential, and we re-affirm the right of the press to report proceedings which result in the discharge or conviction of the accused; but we draw a clear distinction between reporting the trial itself and reporting preliminary proceedings. It is in our opinion illogical and wrong to permit such latitude in the reporting of preliminary proceedings that confidence in the fairness of the trial is undermined. That in our view is the crux of the matter.

I doubt whether any press man will recognise the distinction between a preliminary inquiry and a trial. Anyone who urges restrictions on reporting committal proceedings will find his views distorted (as I know from personal experience) under headings that refer to 'secret trials', 'secret courts' and similar misrepresentations. The proposals do not relate to trials and the courts would not be secret: the proceedings would be open to the public. In fact there is no part of the administration of criminal law that is less likely to be abused, for there is a constant check by the higher courts. If the justices do commit, then obviously the trial court can consider the conduct of the committal proceedings. If the justices refuse to commit, the prosecution can put the matter before a judge and he may authorise the indictment. Nevertheless, it will require a courageous Home Secretary to introduce a Bill to carry out these recommendations.

The mechanics of committal proceedings have been much criticised.

[1] Report of the Departmental Committee on Proceedings before Examining Justices, Cmnd. 479 (1958).

The evidence has to be written down, read over to the witness and signed by him. In some courts it is written down in long-hand, though in other courts silent typewriters are used or recording machines or shorthand writers who rapidly produce transcripts. A deposition is not a verbatim transcript but is in parts a shortened version putting everything of importance into few words and in parts verbatim when the actual words ought to be recorded. It requires a trained court-clerk to make a deposition, and the work cannot be left to a skilled noiseless typist or shorthand-writer. A Committee was appointed in 1948 to inquire into the practice with regard to the taking of depositions and whether there ought to be any change in the law. The Committee considered the suggestion that the taking of depositions is now an anachronism and is merely a waste of the time of the justices and of the labour of the clerk, and firmly rejected it; the Committee recommended the retention of the present system with, however, a number of minor changes.[1]

In February 1962 it was announced that the Home Office would review the whole subject of committal proceedings. At present the pre-trial processes have a number of different functions: (i) a decision as to bail or custody pending the inquiry; (ii) a review of the evidence of the prosecution to see if the case against the defendant is such that he ought to be put on his trial; (iii) to record the evidence so that (a) the defendant knows the case that he must meet, (b) an indictment can be drawn up, and (c) the judge or chairman of the trial court can learn the nature of the case, which is desirable for arranging the work of the court and conducting the trial, and essential on a plea of guilty; (iv) a decision as to the court to which the defendant is to be committed, and whether he is to wait on bail or in custody. These functions could be arranged differently, but the substance of the work has got to be done by someone if trial courts are to get their cases neatly packaged. One suggestion is that the prosecution should prepare a statement of the evidence that each of their witnesses would give, and hand these statements to the defendant who could either agree to be committed for trial or require some form of committal proceedings. A lawyer for the defence, in doubt as to what he can do for his client, often says: 'Let us see what the prosecution witnesses look like. It is not just a matter of what they say, but of whether there may be weak spots and some hope of shaking their evidence at the trial.' Few lawyers think that they can do that on a bundle of papers. And indeed the high proportion of

[1] Cmd. 7639 (1949).

defendants that plead guilty at trial courts is partly due to the nature of the committal proceedings: a preview of the prosecution's case shows that it is not worth fighting. It is in the long and involved case, which is going to be fought, that committal 'on the papers' would be particularly useful.

The process of the actual trial on indictment is on the whole satisfactory, the hearing being patient and careful. Cases are disposed of without adjournments (other than from day to day) except in a very few cases, yet the proceedings are not hurried. The impression given to most lay observers is distinctly favourable. Of course the character of the judge, recorder, or chairman is of vital importance, and I do not mean to suggest that every trial is all that it should be. County Quarter Sessions is a tribunal that used to enjoy a poor reputation in professional circles, but since having a legally qualified chairman became usual, and now compulsory, this criticism has disappeared. Apart from the problem of giving sentences, discussed in section 9 of this chapter, the major question is whether judge and jury constitute a satisfactory tribunal. The method of appointment of judges is discussed elsewhere. The problem of judges in criminal trials is exactly the same as in civil cases, being, in the words of Lord Davey, that: 'All English Judges are impartial, but not all have the power of divesting themselves of prejudice.' This personal factor is inevitable, since our tribunals must be composed of men and not machines. One judge, who was a great authority upon ecclesiastical law, will be remembered for his severity in all bigamy cases: as a pillar of the church he considered that all infringements of morality were necessarily serious offences. Whether a trial was held before this judge, or before one of his colleagues who was an agnostic, might make a great difference to the result. The extent to which a body of men, judges or others, are prejudiced is always a matter of dispute; the ecclesiastical lawyer and the agnostic doubtless considered each other to be hopelessly prejudiced. Trial by a single judge is perhaps not the best method; if ten out of a dozen judges can appear unprejudiced, the other two judges may well discredit the whole system. In most countries it is the practice to have three or more judges together, with or without some system of jury. The traditional English method in criminal cases has been the single judge with jury, except in a very few cases heard at bar before a bench of judges and a jury. The use of three judges in superior courts in England would be too expensive for there to be any chance of such an innovation. Juries are discussed in a later section.

(iv) *Summary jurisdiction*

A defendant in a case that is to be tried summarily in a Magistrates' Court is likely to have some difficulty with the procedure. Apart from certain minor matters prescribed by statute, a summary trial is supposed to be on the same lines as a trial on indictment.[1] With a competent bench and solicitors or barristers appearing for the parties, the system works tolerably well. It is not quick, and often appears unnecessarily laborious. When parties are not legally represented, the rules of procedure and evidence may not be observed so carefully, and a great deal of time is thereby saved. This is rarely a disadvantage to defendants: the correct procedure is difficult to understand, and the more correct a Magistrates' Court tries to be the less chance is there of a layman succeeding in presenting his case properly. In the ordinary case where advocates are not employed, the prosecution commences with the evidence for the Crown, usually a police constable. As soon as this witness finishes his statement, the defendant is asked if he wishes to ask any questions. Generally the defendant takes this as an invitation to state his own case, and he is promptly stopped by the chairman or the clerk and told that he can only ask questions; he must confine himself to cross-examination, that most difficult part of advocacy. Further witnesses will mean a repetition of the scene. By the time the case for the prosecution is finished the defendant may have made half a dozen attempts to give his version, and have been stopped on each occasion. He is then told that he can make a statement or give evidence. By this time he has often become convinced that he will be stopped if he tries to say anything that disagrees with the prosecution's evidence, and so he maintains a sulky silence. Those who come into contact with poorer people who have been summoned hear the same grievance over and over again: 'They wouldn't listen to me; every time I tried to say anything I was stopped.' The need for changes in procedure so that a defendant can tell his story at an early stage, without interruptions, has now been recognised for matrimonial cases: the Committee on the Social Services in Courts of Summary Jurisdiction[2] found the existing procedure unsuitable, but their terms of reference did not enable them to make recommendations except in matrimonial cases.

The change introduced for matrimonial cases before the justices is that instead of cross-examination the parties are to be allowed 'to tell their story in their own words, and it should be the duty of

[1] See p. 131, above. [2] Cmd. 5122 (1936).

the Court after hearing the story to put to the witness on behalf of either party any question which it may consider necessary by way of cross-examination'.[1] Some wise justices have been in the habit of following some such course, and there is something to be said for making it the standard procedure when there is no legal representation. The procedure would be that the justices would find out the case for the prosecution from the first witness, and then hear what the defendant has to say, allowing him to 'run on' with as little interruption as possible. The first witness would remain in the witness box, and if it appeared from the defendant's statement that any questions should be asked of the witness the bench would help the defendant to put the questions, the aim being to clear up any points of difference that have arisen in the statement of the respective cases. With subsequent witnesses the bench would be in a position to see that relevant questions were asked.

Such a change of procedure would remove the grievance of 'not being allowed to have my say', which is a matter of first-class importance, but it would not remedy all the present evils. In matrimonial cases it may be very successful, for there the parties are on an equal footing; in the ordinary prosecution the police and the defendant (both without advocates) are ill-matched adversaries. Can we rely upon the justices to redress the balance? This is a matter of great difficulty, for it involves the relation of the justices to the police and to the defendant.

There is undoubtedly a tendency in Magistrates' Courts for the police to have a special position or status. In principle a police officer is present like any other good citizen for the purpose of doing his public duty in prosecuting or giving evidence as a witness. But it would be surprising if justices could look upon the police in quite that way. The police, because they bring most of the prosecutions, are constantly in court and become well known to the bench. The police case is presented briefly and in a business-like way, whilst the defendant without an advocate is likely to be nervous and to react by being fumbling and slow, or truculent and tiresome. The police are a public service and so presumably have no interest in false or biased testimony, whereas the defendant obviously stands to gain by producing a plausible story. In the counties the justices, through the Standing Joint Committee, are partly responsible for the appointment and control of the county police force, and it is not surprising

---

[1] Cmd. 5122 (1936), p. 32. The Summary Jurisdiction (Domestic Proceedings) Act 1937 carried out these parts of the Committee's proposals (see p. 181, below).

that some justices feel that they must 'support the police' because they are 'our men'. These are all very natural feelings, but the administration of justice often requires one to examine natural feelings by seeing where they lead to, and here they can lead justices badly astray. Those who have been closely acquainted with the administration of summary justice over a number of years know of courts where the police have had a dominating position. In the next section I put forward the view that Magistrates' Courts have improved immensely in the last few years, but some practices die hard, and it is always worth looking at what happened recently because it may not really be dead and anyway it can so easily come to life again. There have been courts where advocates for the defence considered that an attack on the veracity of police witnesses would be unwise, for the justices would at once come to the rescue of the constable and show strong resentment to the suggestions that had been made. That attitude was frequently accompanied by an open incredulity towards anything that the defendant or his witnesses had to say. If the bench showed a disinclination to accept police evidence without query, it was not unusual for some police officer to say that the police would not bring such prosecutions in future if the justices were going to dismiss the cases.[1]

I do not mean to suggest that police evidence is always unreliable, but that police veracity is no lower and no higher than that of the average respectable citizen. It is rare for a County Court or High Court judge to show unswerving faith in the police, for their professional experience has taught them that a desire to get convictions and an internal *esprit de corps* may well result in untrue or biased evidence. It is sometimes clear that police evidence may be substantially true but inaccurate in detail. Thus in one trial four policemen gave evidence that they had each made an independent shorthand note of parts of a speech, and denied that they had compared notes afterwards. Each version included the expression 'Dictatorship *on* the proletariat', and with typical obstinacy each denied that the speaker might have said 'of' and not 'on'. The jury was apparently

---

[1] Mr Justice Swift: 'There is a marked tendency on the part of the police who bring charges and come into conflict with the magistrates—when they decide against them—to bring them to this court [High Court] on some pretended point of law in the endeavour to get their views upset.' Mr Justice Goddard (later Lord Goddard L.C.J.): 'This looks to me...like an impudent attempt to come here [High Court] to try to get the quarter sessions appeal committee scolded or put right because they had the temerity not to accept the evidence put forward by the dissatisfied police' (*The Times*, 16 January 1937).

better acquainted with the stock phrases of Communism, and acquitted the prisoner; some justices would have swallowed the police evidence without qualms or doubt.

On the whole the police do their work fairly well, but abuses do occur. A generation ago people were shocked by the Savidge case,[1] the Report of the Royal Commission on Police Powers[2] and a Report on Street Offences.[3] The year 1958 saw an exceptional number of prosecutions of police officers, including that of the Chief Constable of Brighton. It is inevitable that a large body of men with wide powers should need constant control. The present position is not satisfactory. The Home Secretary is responsible to Parliament for the Metropolitan Police, but he is not answerable for provincial forces. An aggrieved citizen can bring legal proceedings against a constable who has committed an unlawful act, and against his superior officer if he was acting under instructions. Neither the chief constable nor the police authority are liable in law, for although they may look like employers the constable is not their servant. If our would-be plaintiff has not been able to identify the constable, he cannot take proceedings. Apart from legal proceedings, a complaint can be made to the chief constable or to the police authority; the complainant will be told that the matter will be investigated, and eventually he will receive a further reply, but there is no tribunal or formal hearing that he can attend and satisfy himself that an adequate inquiry really has been made. The position is not in fact as bad as may be supposed, for sensible administration can often overcome the inadequacies of the law, but reform is needed. The Royal Commission on the Police has examined these problems of organisation and control and has made a number of recommendations, some of which will require legislation.[4]

In addition to the actual relationship of justices and police there is the matter of appearances; a Magistrates' Court must both be and appear to be independent of anything that could be construed as police authority. There were a few courts before the war in which the chief constable (who prosecuted) sat side by side with the clerk just in front of the bench, where he appeared to be an official of the court. There may now be no instances of a police officer being allowed to occupy such a misleading position, but there are still

[1] Cmd. 3147 (1928). [2] Cmd. 3297 (1929).
[3] Cmd. 3231 (1928), para. 59: bribery of police by prostitutes 'must inevitably occur'.
[4] Final Report, Cmnd. 1728 (1962). For some pertinent comment see J. Hart [1963] *Public Law*, p. 283. Legislation is expected in 1963-4.

places where the senior police officer present acts as if he were in charge of the court in such matters as telling a defendant or witness to stand upright and take his hands out of his pockets. It is a pity that many court-rooms have been built as part of a police station, a course which is favoured by many local authorities and by chief constables, for it is hard for the public not to think of it as a 'police court' when it is apparently part of a police station.

Justices who are conscious of the difficulties of defendants who are not legally represented may easily go too far in their desire to help. This is a danger that would have to be guarded against if procedure were altered to let a defendant 'run on'. It is a cardinal principle in our criminal trials that a defendant cannot be compelled to make any statement or give evidence. He must be asked if he wishes to do either, and told that if he does give evidence he may be cross-examined. Often a defendant asks the court what he should do, but a wise bench will not give him a hint and certainly will not advise him because (quite apart from any question of whether that is any part of the court's duty) the bench does not know what his evidence would be like and so might lead him into doing something very damaging to himself. There is no greater myth in the administration of justice than that the bench can look after the interests of a defendant. To help the defendant the bench must start asking questions, often overlooking the rule that if the defendant makes an unsworn statement or says he does not want to make any statement he should not be questioned at all. The trial ceases to be a contest[1] and becomes an inquisition. There should be nothing shocking in that, for it is a theory of trial that is more widespread than any other. The judge as inquisitor does, however, produce its own particular troubles, one being that the very system that allows the judge to protect the defendant also enables the judge to pursue the defendant and clinch the case for the prosecution. If we were to change our procedure so that it became inquisitorial we should need some new method of protecting defendants. Some years ago the provision of a 'Public Defender' was mooted, but it was generally felt that officialdom would settle upon his activities and defeat the object of the appointment.[2]

Doubtless some improvement in procedure can be made and the

[1] See pp. 18, 70, above.
[2] A pamphlet published in 1926 by the Howard League, *Counsel for the Defence*, preferred legal aid on existing lines, and the Committee on Legal Aid for the Poor, Cmd. 2638 (1926), para. 21, also disliked the idea of a public defender.

lot of a defendant not legally represented can be made easier, and that should be sufficient for most of the cases before Magistrates' Courts. But frequently Magistrates' Courts have before them defendants who ought to have seen a solicitor. A charge of 'no insurance' in respect of a vehicle no longer means that on conviction there is an automatic suspension of a driving licence, but disqualification from driving can still be ordered or come about through the complicated provisions of the Road Traffic Act 1962. It is true that there is commonly no defence to that charge, and indeed to many other offences, but a risk of being disqualified is generally of vital importance to the defendant; the justices will consider that matter, but the defendant should have legal advice and he cannot expect to get it from the bench. Fortunately we are in a period of an expanding service of free or cheap legal aid and advice, for if help is needed there is no satisfactory substitute for the legal profession.

6. LAY JUSTICES AND STIPENDIARY MAGISTRATES

There is at first sight something odd in the office of justice of the peace continuing in an age that has been steadily turning away from the amateur in favour of the professional. One might have expected that in the years since 1945 the unpaid justice would have been replaced by paid magistrates, yet the system of lay justices not only continues but is more firmly established today than it was before the war.

In the 1920's and 1930's there was a growing body of criticism of justices. Some people thought that there had been a deterioration in the standards of Magistrates' Courts, but a more likely explanation is that a more vocal type of defendant had been appearing in those courts. An important factor was the rise in the number of cases under road traffic Acts: in 1910–14 road traffic cases were under 10 per cent of the total number of cases but they had risen in 1930–4 to 45 per cent and by 1938 had reached 60 per cent. Other legislation had tended to place numerous obligations upon the citizen, enforcing these by fines imposed by Magistrates' Courts; sooner or later the average man forgets about his dog licence, wireless licence, car licence, or some other permit to live, and finds himself summoned to attend before the local court. Parallel with these changes there had been a great decline in charges of drunkenness, from 203,038 in 1913 to 53,402 in 1938, and striking reductions in charges of assaults, begging, sleeping out and offences against the

Education Acts. The justices of an earlier age had dealt mainly with the poorer classes, but motor-cars and the new social legislation brought the middle and upper classes into contact with institutions that they had not previously known, and they did not like what they found. It is no new thing for indignation to arise when a wealthier class comes into contact with institutions previously confined to poorer classes. Prison reform has always been stimulated by the protests of political prisoners. A number of ladies, sent to prison for their violence in the suffragette movement, refused the regulation prison bath, pointing out that the baths were caked with half an inch of dirt from innumerable previous occupants; unbathed but triumphant, these ladies secured some improvement in prison conditions.

For most people 'the law' means the police, Magistrates' Courts and County Courts. Respect for law and confidence in the judicial system depend very much upon the conduct of cases in inferior courts. One might have expected that the government would have shown some response to the criticism, but there seemed no awareness of the damage that was being done by the increasing loss of confidence in the administration of summary justice. The period before 1939 had an atmosphere of unwillingness to face facts. Some of the facts about justices and their courts were disturbing; writers then had hard things to say and put an edge on their comment.[1] A change came from that strange stirring and awakening that war brings into the social field.

The mobilisation for war of the population of this country and its resources was carried out through a code of Defence Regulations, with orders, rules and by-laws, and these were enforced through the ordinary machinery of the courts. The usual penalty for a Defence Regulation offence was three months or a fine of £100 or both on summary conviction, and two years or a fine of £500 or both on conviction on indictment, though some Regulations carried more severe penalties. The majority of these offences were dealt with summarily. For 1939–45, Assizes and Quarter Sessions found 1754 persons guilty, whereas in Magistrates' Courts 1,275,889 persons were found guilty. Black-out offences accounted for 928,397 of

---

[1] The student of the near past may look at *English Justice* (1932) by 'Solicitor' (the late C. L. Hodgkinson, a practising solicitor); Charles Muir, *Justice in a Depressed Area* (1936); the first edition of this book (1940). J. W. Robertson Scott, then editor of *The Countryman*, made great efforts to persuade his fellow-justices and the public that reform was necessary: a letter from him to *The Times* of 23 October 1935 was a notable contribution.

these convictions, and doubtless there were many other offences that were not particularly heinous when considered separately, but the load of serious cases was substantial. The effect of Magistrates' Courts having an important place in the war effort was twofold. It stimulated many justices into taking their duties very seriously, and it led to the government finding time for some reforms even during the war.[1] The prevalent view at the end of the war was that Magistrates' Courts had carried a heavy burden and that they had done their work reasonably well. At the same time there was a greater awareness of the need for some reform. The days when it seemed impossible to get an inquiry into an apparently well-founded allegation of misconduct of justices had gone: such instances were met by the appointment of a judge to hold a local inquiry.[2]

A Royal Commission on Justices of the Peace was appointed in June 1946, with wide terms of reference, covering in particular the selection and removal of justices, matters of qualification and disqualification, *ex-officio* justices, chairmen of benches, juvenile court panels, expenses of justices, and stipendiary magistrates. The Minutes of Evidence were published during the course of the Commission, and the Report[3] was published in July 1948. This Report and Minutes, together with the Report of the Justices' Clerks Committee,[4] gives an authoritative account of the system of justices over the preceding generation, and it is material that will be of value to students of the development of our institutions.

A striking feature of the Royal Commission was that all the associations and virtually all the individuals who tendered evidence were agreed that the system of lay justices should continue, although there was a general acceptance of the view that there might well be an increase in the number of stipendiary magistrates. It was left for a member of the Commission, Lord Merthyr, to say in his Minority Report that it is merely a question of time before lay justices disappear, and that it would be better if we came gradually to have a system of stipendiaries. All the other members accepted the desirability of the continuance of lay justices, with the result that the main Report is concerned with improving the present system. Both

[1] The Justices (Supplemental List) Act 1941; the Justices' Clerks Committee reported in 1944, Cmd. 6507: these are discussed below. There were some changes under emergency legislation, and much administrative action.

[2] Reports of such inquiries are: Cmd. 6485 in 1943, Inquiry at Stoke-on-Trent in 1945 (H.M.S.O. but not a command paper), Cmd. 6783 in 1946 and Cmd. 7061 in 1947.

[3] Cmd. 7463.   [4] Cmd. 6507 (1944).

these Reports were well received, and the principal recommendations requiring legislation were carried out by the Justices of the Peace Act 1949. The matters that were dealt with fall under a number of headings:

(i) *The appointment of justices*

Each county and each borough having a separate body of justices has a Commission from the Crown, the names of the justices being placed in a schedule. A person becomes a justice by having his name added to the schedule (being 'put on the Commission'), the appointment nominally being by the Crown but in fact being made by the Lord Chancellor.[1] Anciently there was a property qualification of land to the value of £20 a year, raised to £100 in 1732, but all property qualifications were abolished in 1906. Since 1919 women have been eligible. Originally justices were paid four shillings a day during their sessions, that pay being about sixteen times the wages of a day labourer, but the decline in the value of money led to the office becoming unpaid; by the end of the seventeenth century the remuneration merely provided a free dinner for the bench, and today their services are entirely gratuitous. It became the practice during the eighteenth century for the Lord Lieutenant of a county to make recommendations to the Lord Chancellor for the appointment of justices, but Lord Chancellors have always considered that they could act on any information from any source. Appointments have long been influenced by political considerations. Those who read Surtees will find in *Hillingdon Hall* that Mr Jorrocks became a justice because he was a Whig and the Lord Lieutenant thought that there were too many Tories on the bench. In the late years of the nineteenth century and the early years of the twentieth there was great dissatisfaction with the political aspect of the magistracy. A Royal Commission on the Selection of Justices of the Peace, who reported in 1910,[2] found that the county benches were largely Conservatives, due to the politics of Lords Lieutenant. The *Report* recommended that the Lord Chancellor should set up advisory committees in counties and in boroughs with a separate commission of the peace, and that these committees should advise the Lord Chancellor as to

[1] Within the Duchy of Lancaster the Chancellor of the Duchy performs these functions that are elsewhere performed by the Lord Chancellor.

[2] Cd. 5250 (1910). The way in which the justices might be alien to the ways of thought of the ordinary people is seen in the figures for Wales; Appendix VI to the Minutes of Evidence, Cd. 5358 (1910). Despite the enormous preponderance of Non-conformists in Wales, the justices were made up of 478 Non-conformists and 1006 members of the Church of England.

appointments. In the case of counties the Lord Lieutenant was to continue his advisory functions but was to act through the committee. These committees were set up, and appointments came to be made through their advice. The composition of those committees was in the hands of the Lord Chancellor, and their constitution and membership was supposed to be kept secret. It was common knowledge that the political parties dominated. In the first stage the Liberals secured their share and then the Labour party made good its claims. There were some areas where such committees worked well, but in many places the recommendations were made on party lines. At the worst the practice was for the committee to decide upon the quota of new appointments that should go to each party, so that each party produced the names of its nominees on the basis of 'If you agree to our names we will agree to yours': under that system there was little serious inquiry into the suitability of persons to be appointed, and it is not too much to say that the office was used as a reward for faithful political service.

The Royal Commission of 1946–8 thought that the Lord Chancellor and the Chancellor of the Duchy of Lancaster should continue to exercise their present powers in regard to the appointment of justices. Local advisory committees should be retained under the chairmanship of the Lord Lieutenant in a county and of someone nominated as chairman in boroughs. These committees must continue to be advisory and be appointed by the Lord Chancellor and their membership should not be disclosed to the public. The principal controversy was over politics in the appointment of justices. There was agreement that too much attention in the appointment of justices had been paid to political opinions, and that the politics of a person who is to be considered for appointment should be ignored in the sense that politics ought not to be regarded as either a ground for appointing or as a ground for not appointing. Three members of the Royal Commission thought that all regard to politics should be ignored in selecting persons to serve on advisory committees, and that there should be a similar disregard in considering names for appointments. The majority, however, took the view that this is not practicable. So long as the political parties show a keen interest in appointments being given to their own supporters, it remains necessary to guard against a 'spoils system' or a calculated exclusion of adherents of any particular party. The majority recommendation was that advisory committees should be less political in their composition and that members should understand that they are not present to push party claims. It was also recommended that the name of the secretary to the committee should be made public and that it should be generally known that individuals or organisations can submit suggestions to the committee through its secretary.

In public discussion there has perhaps been so much preoccupation with the matter of politics that there has been insufficient appreciation of the very real difficulties that advisory committees may have in finding enough suitable men and women to become justices. Such persons must be suitable in character and temperament, they must come from various sections of the community, their distribution geographically is important, particularly in counties, and they must be able to attend court with reasonable regularity. The task is made harder by the need for making more appointments from among younger men and women. Some justices are of course drawn from those people who are already active in public affairs, but it is not desirable that a very high proportion of justices should be members of local authorities, for these authorities and their committees and officers are concerned with many prosecutions and matters of summary jurisdiction and a justice who belongs to the authority may be disqualified from sitting on such cases. Advisory committees must try to draw in people from a wider field. The Lord Chancellor expressed his agreement with the general principles put forward by the Royal Commission, and presumably the advisory committee system has been adjusted; the composition of these committees remains secret, and it is not therefore publicly known exactly how far the Lord Chancellor has gone.

Under the Justices of the Peace Act 1949 the travelling expenses of justices are payable out of public funds, but, unlike members of local authorities, justices have no right to receive either subsistence allowance or any payment for loss of earnings. The payment of travelling expenses is a help to many justices in rural areas, but it does not go far to widen the field of selection. The Royal Commission considered whether Magistrates' Courts could be held in the evenings, for if that were feasible it might enable many people to act as justices who simply cannot manage to sit during ordinary working hours, as well as permitting many parties and witnesses to attend without interruption of their work. After the most careful examination the Royal Commission found that no general change from day-time courts is practicable.

New justices will usually at the time of their appointment know very little about the duties they are to perform, and hence something in the way of training is required. The Royal Commission considered that as the facilities for study and attending the sittings of higher courts and so on vary greatly over the country it would not be reasonable to lay down a rigid national scheme. The Justices of the Peace Act 1949 carries out the recommendations by making it the duty of Magistrates' Courts Committees[1] to make and administer schemes (subject to the approval of the Lord Chancellor) for courses of instruction for justices of their area. The result has been uneven, partly through varying degrees of zeal and partly because justices are appointed at irregular intervals, each place being treated separately, so that training schemes for an area are difficult to operate. The problems are being considered and it is hoped that better arrangements can be made for at present this is a serious weakness of the system.

(ii) *The removal of justices*

The position has for long been that justices are appointed for life but have no security of tenure, being liable to be removed from the commission if the Lord Chancellor sees fit. By convention the Lord Chancellor must exercise this power in a judicial manner and justices are not removed except for good cause.[2] The trouble in the past has not been the retention of justices guilty of misconduct or scandalous behaviour, but the retention of justices who were ineffective. Once a person was appointed a justice he might neglect his duties, or go away to another area, or become infirm and yet continue to sit. The somewhat deaf, doddering and senile justice could in the past be found adjudicating, and quite often as chairman of his bench. There is now nothing to be gained by giving instances of that scandalous state of affairs. Doubtless there are justices still sitting who would be better off the bench, but the improvement has been considerable.

The Lord Chancellor endeavoured to see that each justice did a fair share of work and that they resigned from the commission on certain changes in residence, but these were difficult to enforce. In 1938 the Lord Chancellor sent out a circular suggesting that justices who were incapacitated by old age or infirmity should have their names placed on a Supplemental List; they would then no

---

[1] See p. 168 below.
[2] The Lord Chancellor is not required to hold a formal hearing, and the merits of his decision may be publicly canvassed. The most difficult cause is perhaps the drawing of the line between a justice expressing strong disapproval of part of the law (which is permissible) and allowing his administration of the law to be affected by his disapproval of it.

longer be summoned to attend courts, but they would remain justices and could 'sign papers' for people and do similar work: other justices who were non-resident or did not attend courts should, it was suggested, resign. In some districts there was a good response, whilst in other areas justices who had not sat for years (and who were perhaps wise not to have sat) regarded the circular as a threat that they would be removed if they remained inactive, and they quickly returned to active service; in those parts the circular was known as the 'Resurrection Circular'. The original supplemental list was voluntary; a justice on the list could still as a matter of law adjudicate, and the Lord Chancellor could not put a justice on the list. Hence the Justices (Supplemental List) Act 1941 made the list statutory. The Royal Commission found that, in addition to some deficiencies in the legislation and other minor matters, there were two matters that needed consideration. The first was whether there should be a retiring age for justices, and here it was decided that there should be, and that 75 should be prescribed. The other related to the machinery for informing the Lord Chancellor about justices who ought to go on the Supplemental List; the Lord Chancellor had adequate powers, but he was badly informed as to the particular instances in which he should use his powers. The recommendation was that periodical reviews of benches ought to be made by the advisory committees.

The Justices of the Peace Act 1949 re-enacts, with amendments, the law as to qualification of justices and the Supplemental List. A justice must now reside within fifteen miles of the county or borough for which he is a justice unless the Lord Chancellor gives him a dispensation.[1] The provisions about the Supplemental List now incorporate the retiring age. The name of a justice will be put on the Supplemental List when he reaches 75[2] or if the justice wishes to go on the list. The Lord Chancellor can direct that a name be put on the list if he is satisfied 'either (i) that by reason of that person's

---

[1] There are now disqualifications in certain cases of justices who are members of local authorities. A solicitor who is a justice has restrictions upon his practice in proceedings before justices.

[2] The 1949 Act made a special exception for anyone who holds or has held high judicial office: as there was then no retiring age for judges it would have been anomalous if they were barred from acting as justices but could sit in superior courts. Now that new judicial appointments are subject to retirement at 75 (see p. 264, below) the exception loses its point. The Home Secretary wanted the retiring age for justices to be fixed at 70, but there was a Parliamentary accident; an expected amendment was not moved and the Bill went through as drafted.

age or infirmity or other like cause it is expedient he should cease to exercise judicial functions as a justice for the area; or (ii) that the person declines or neglects to take a proper part in the exercise of those functions'. The Lord Chancellor of course retains his power to remove a justice, and presumably for a contumacious refusal to act it might be thought better to remove a justice than to apply the gentler course of the Supplemental List.

(iii) *Justices* ex officio

The Royal Commission considered all the classes of persons who were justices *ex officio* and came to the conclusion that chairmanship of a local authority ought not to make a person a justice *ex officio,* though they wished to retain the mayor as a justice though not the ex-mayor. Some efforts were made to get this carried out by the Justices of the Peace Act 1949 but the views of local authorities prevailed and the *ex officio's* were all saved except for the ex-mayor. In some small boroughs it used to be a regular thing for the mayor and the ex-mayor to sit as a court for cases arising in the borough, and as the mayor was often changed each year that gave a court in which neither justice had had much experience.

(iv) *Size and chairmanship of benches*

A large bench is disturbing to parties and advocates as it is difficult to address, and it renders rapid consultation between the chairman and the members almost impossible. The Royal Commission agreed with the Committee on Justices' Clerks that whereas three or five is the best number the legal maximum should be seven. For Quarter Sessions it was thought that four or six justices in addition to the chairman is best, but that eight and the chairman should be the maximum. The Justices of the Peace Act 1949 leaves the numbers to be determined by Rules made by the Lord Chancellor, and he has made rules adopting the maximum of seven for Magistrates' Courts and eight and the chairman for Quarter Sessions.

The chairmanship of justices has had a not too happy history. In boroughs the mayor was by statute entitled to take the chair, and in smaller boroughs he commonly did so. It was a ridiculous thing because the mayor might never have been in a Magistrates' Court before. In county divisions the justices elected their own chairman. Seniority was often the criterion. There was no reason in law why benches should not have reformed their own practices, but junior justices felt diffidence and senior justices were not disposed to change. Following on the recommendations of the Royal Commission there are now Rules made by the Lord Chancellor under powers given by the Justices of the Peace Act 1949; the Act deprives the mayor of his right to preside, and there is now no difference between boroughs and county divisions. The Rules prescribe that a chairman shall be elected by an absolute majority by secret ballot, without any nominations; one or more deputy chairmen are elected also by secret ballot but with no need for an absolute majority. One would have thought that justices would not have needed such an elaborate set of rules for electing chairmen and deputies, but much of the elaboration is due to requests from justices. There is still some confusion over this matter of chairmanship because the conditions of benches vary so much. There are three kinds of chairmanship that arise. First there is the chairman of the justices of the county division or borough; he, or in his absence a deputy chairman, is needed for occasions when the justices act as a body, as when they have meetings for business. If two or more courts sit simultaneously, there should be a chairman for the day; that is, a justice who presides over all those attending in order to arrange the different courts, the allocation of cases and such matters. In each court-room there must be a chairman of the court, who will preside there and sign the register to certify the result of proceedings. The Rules under the Act leave the justices to follow their customary practice as to chairmanship for the day and chairmanship of courts in the absence of the chairman of the justices or his deputy.

(v) *Justices' clerks, areas of commissions of the peace and the organisation of Magistrates' Courts*

A justices' clerk was originally the personal clerk to an individual justice. Justices were entitled to take fees for some of their acts, and whilst some justices did their own clerical work and kept the fees, when a justice had a clerk it was customary for the clerk to take the fees due to his master. During the eighteenth century and first half of the nineteenth there was a tendency for the justices of a district to share the same clerk, and an Act of 1851 made it permissible to pay the clerk a salary; he became the clerk to the bench. The Justices' Clerks Act 1877 required that clerks should be either lawyers or men who had worked as assistants to a justices' clerk. Each bench (county division or borough) was left to appoint its own clerk. The clerk was paid an inclusive salary, which meant that he engaged his own assistants and paid them and all other expenses out of his salary; thus the more he paid out in wages, office expenses, stamps and stationery and so on, the less there was left for his personal remuneration. Some slight central control was introduced, and there were provisions for the Home Office to settle any disputes between the local authority and the justices about the appointment of a clerk or the amount of his salary. In busy places the clerk was likely to be a whole-time officer, but most clerks were solicitors in private practice who held the clerkship as a part-time appointment.

A Committee which reported in 1934 on *Imprisonment by Courts of Summary Jurisdiction in Default of Payment of Fines and Other Sums of Money*[1] found it necessary to discuss the position of justices' clerks, since the recovery of fines and other payments (and imprisonment in default) depend so much on proper office work. It was shown that the obsolete method of paying clerks could result in needless imprisonment. In 1938 the Home Secretary appointed a Committee to inquire into the subject of justices' clerks, and that Committee, after some suspension of its work in the earlier part of the war, reported in 1944.[2] The Committee on Justices' Clerks found that the provision of a satisfactory system of clerks is bound up with the whole organisation, administration and finance of Magistrates' Courts; hence the Report covered a much wider field than might be expected from its title. The recommendations have in the main been carried out by the Justices of the Peace Act 1949.

It is better to have whole-time clerks than part-time clerks if that can be arranged conveniently. A part-time clerk is likely from time to time to find that the duties of his clerkship and the calls of his private practice conflict. The work of justices has increased in quantity and still more in complexity, so that a fair amount of reading and study is needed to keep oneself up to date, and naturally a part-time clerk who has even greater difficulty in keeping up with matters affecting the general practice of a solicitor is hardly going to find enough time for study in connection with a part-time appointment. Wherever the work of a court warrants a whole-time clerk there is no difficulty, but many courts have insufficient work to warrant such an appointment and the services of a whole-time clerk can be obtained only by grouping two or more courts; a clerk then becomes clerk to whatever number of courts is needed to make up whole-time employment. In considering the principles on which courts should be grouped the Committee on Justices' Clerks found it necessary to consider the areas of commissions of the peace. No

---

[1] Cmd. 4649; it is an excellent Report.   [2] Cmd. 6507.

particular point arose over counties, but boroughs with separate commissions included many quite small towns. A separate commission of the peace is a Crown grant, as is having a separate court of Quarter Sessions, and whether a town had a grant depended on its history, on its size and importance and bargaining ability in the past quite as much as on the reasonable needs of the present day. Hence the 1949 Act says that there shall be separate commissions for counties, county boroughs, and non-county boroughs if at the end of 1948 the non-county borough had a separate commission of the peace and (a) 35,000 population or over, or (b) also had its own Quarter Sessions and 20,000 population or over, or (c) also had its own Quarter Sessions (but population under 20,000) and was specially saved by the Lord Chancellor.[1] All the boroughs under these limits lost their separate commissions and their separate Quarter Sessions where those existed, and became merged in the county.

The Committee on Justices' Clerks recommended that there should be special committees of justices to look after the administrative side of Magistrates' Courts. These are set up by the Act of 1949, and are called Magistrates' Courts Committees. The ordinary rule is that there is a Committee for each county and for each county borough, but there are eight non-county boroughs with separate commissions and populations of 65,000 or over which may have their own Committees.[2] These are statutory Committees, appointed by the justices for the area in question.[3] All justice's clerks are now appointed by these Committees and not by the various benches. The whole-time office staff are employees of the Committee, though they work under the direction of the Clerk. Clerks are paid personal salaries, the Committee being responsible for the salaries of assistants and other office expenses. This has not meant much change in practice in the larger boroughs which have had 'office committees' for years, but in counties it started a process of re-organisation.

The traditional basis of petty sessional divisions is the Hundred, which is a division of the county that existed before the Norman Conquest and which the Normans used for administrative and judicial purposes. There was a way of altering these divisions,

---

[1] Abingdon and Barnstaple were so saved.

[2] There is provision for counties that are customarily divided, and also provision for combination of areas.

[3] The details are partly in the Fourth Schedule to the Act and in Regulations made under the Act. Each county petty sessional division has a right to have one representative on the Committee.

through Quarter Sessions, but it was clumsy and is replaced by a review by Magistrates' Courts Committees and an Order of the Home Secretary. The divisions of a county, re-arranged if that is found desirable, continue to be separate units for jurisdiction, but the arrangements for clerk, staff and court-house are made by the Committee, which must consult with the justices on all of the more important matters. The general plan is that instead of having a local solicitor as part-time clerk to a single division, using his private office and his own staff, there should be whole-time clerks with whole-time staff arranged so that each clerk is responsible for sufficient courts for the work to add up to a full-time job. It is recognised that some part-time clerks and assistants will continue. Where the population is sparse and distances large it would require a vast amount of travelling to different courts to make up employment for a whole-time man, and a local solicitor using one of his ordinary office staff to help him will be more suitable. The 1949 Act also gives to Magistrates' Courts Committees duties, mentioned above, in connection with courses of instruction for justices.

The Committee on Justices' Clerks felt that the time had come when long service with a clerk should not be a qualification for appointment as a clerk, and that after a transition period only barristers or solicitors should be eligible. The 1949 Act is framed on that principle, confining the appointment to barristers or solicitors of not less than five years' standing, but for a limited period preserving existing interests and making it easier for some experienced assistants to become solicitors. An appointment of a clerk requires the approval of the Home Office, and the Committee can be required to submit particulars of any other candidate for the appointment so that the Home Office may see what choice was before the Committee. A clerk holds office at pleasure, but in counties the matter must come before the Home Office if the justices for the division do not agree with the Magistrates' Courts Committee. Whole-time clerks and staff are subject to a retiring age and are superannuable on the lines of the staffs of local authorities.

An important development since the Act of 1949 has been the growth of national joint negotiating machinery. Scales of salaries for clerks and their assistants and other conditions of service are now settled by two bodies of Whitley type. The Management side is made up of representatives of Magistrates' Courts Committees, and of the paying authorities, with the Justices' Clerks' Society or the National Association of Justices' Clerks' Assistants as the

Officers' side. Clerks, whether whole-time or part-time, are paid in accordance with scales varying with the size of the population of the place, whilst assistants are graded according to the nature of their work.

(vi) *The justices' clerk as adviser to the justices*

As the ordinary Magistrates' Court consists of lay justices it is obvious that the clerk holds a most important position, for he must guide them in all matters of practice and advise them on points of law. Much criticism of justices has centred round the clerk and the way he performs his duties. There is a serious difficulty in discussing such a matter, and that is that there are over 1000 Magistrates' Courts. 'Each of these courts is a separate and independent unit. Its decisions are liable to review on appeal, but otherwise its work is not subject to supervision by any superior or co-ordinating authority.... One consequence of the independent position of the Justices is that there is no central source from which authoritative information can be obtained about the methods adopted by the numerous Courts up and down the country....'[1] No one can know the practice of all the Magistrates' Courts. Solicitors are the best informed people, but their knowledge is mostly limited to the courts within a moderate distance of their office, supplemented, of course, by discussions with other solicitors. Further, solicitors are naturally chary of saying anything that might appear as adverse criticism of the courts before which they will doubtless continue to practise. Most statements made about Magistrates' Courts are true of some court some time.

The principal trouble has come from the clerk accompanying the justices when they retire to discuss a case. It has long been recognised that justices may consult their clerk in private, but this has to be reconciled with the principle that it is the justices who make the decision. If the clerk always retires with the justices, or apparently decides for himself whether he goes out with them, or if he stays with them until they come back, a defendant or an advocate may believe that the clerk takes part in their decisions, or even tells them what to decide and what sentence to impose. Suspicion may also arise even when justices having retired send for their clerk, and he returns into court before they do; a defending solicitor may assert that there was no point of law or anything in the case on which the justices could have needed their clerk and deduce from that that the clerk had gone in to tell the justices what to do. In 1952 Lord God-

[1] Cmd. 4649 (1934), p. 5.

dard startled justices and their clerks by appearing to rule that clerks could not join justices in their retiring room except when there was a point of law.[1] He subsequently made a statement in court explaining that there are two questions which arise.[2] First, on what matters may justices consult their clerk: it is clear that they may seek his advice on questions of law or mixed law and fact, or the practice and procedure of the court. In no circumstances may they consult their clerk as to the guilt or innocence of the accused so far as it is simply a question of fact, though they may ask whether facts found by them do constitute the offence charged. The clerk has a note of evidence, and they may wish to refresh their memory. They may not ask his opinion as to the sentence, but they may ask about the penalties that the law allows them to impose and consequential matters such as disqualification from driving. They may also ask for information as to the sentences which have been imposed by their bench or by neighbouring benches in respect of similar offences to that which they are trying. This must not be understood as an exhaustive list, although it undoubtedly covers the instances that commonly arise. The second question is the manner in which justices may consult their clerk. This is largely a matter of appearances: a clerk should not retire with his justices as a matter of course, but only when he is asked to do so, and he should return to his place in court as soon as he is released by the justices, leaving them to complete their deliberations in his absence and to come back into court in their turn. A statement was later made about the application of these principles to cases heard in the matrimonial jurisdiction of justices.[3] One would have thought that the principle had been made so clear that there would have been no more trouble, but cases still come before the courts.[4]

The relations between justices and clerk cannot be regulated entirely by rules. Some wise guidance can be given, as the Committee on Justices' Clerks did in their Report, but it must remain guidance. The conduct of public affairs in England rests on the ability of paid officials and amateurs to work together. A good clerk and a good bench seem to go together. The court is run in such a way

---

[1] *R. v. East Kerrier Justices* [1952] 2 Q.B. 719.

[2] Practice note (Justices' Clerks) [1953] 1 W.L.R. 1416.

[3] Practice note (Justices' Clerks) [1949] 1 W.L.R. 213.

[4] Notably a case where a clerk said, in reply to protests by counsel, that 'that case (*East Kerrier*) is as dead as the dodo': 16 *The Magistrates* (1960), p. 73. In *R. v. Stafford Justices* [1962] 1 W.L.R. 456, the clerk handed a note to the justices as they were about to retire; the principle is that justice must not only be done but must manifestly appear to be done.

that no one can think that the clerk dictates to the bench or that there is anything sinister in the clerk retiring with the justices. New justices are led into good ways, and so are staff. There is no short cut to a harmonious and well-run court, but it is really no harder to achieve than a comparable state of affairs on committees and councils and other manifestations of our way of life.

(vii) *A Rule Committee*

There is a considerable amount of law governing procedure in Magistrates' Courts and allied matters of administration. It has been contained partly in many statutes and partly in subordinate legislation. The experience of the civil courts is that procedure should be by Rules capable of more rapid adjustment to changing needs than can be provided by statute.[1] The 1949 Act follows recommendations of the Committee on Justices' Clerks and the Royal Commission in authorising the Lord Chancellor to appoint a Rule Committee to consist of the Lord Chief Justice, the President of the Probate Divorce and Admiralty Division, the chief metropolitan stipendiary magistrate and such other persons (including at least one justices' clerk, one practising barrister and one practising solicitor) as the Lord Chancellor may determine. Great labour has gone into clearing the jungle. By 1952 the procedural provisions in over forty statutes had been consolidated into a Magistrates' Courts Act, a Rule Committee had been appointed and a set of Magistrates' Courts Rules had been drafted, so that instead of a confusing mass of Acts and rules there can be a single statute and one set of rules. The problem now will be to reconsider and amend as need arises without allowing a new jungle to grow up.[2]

(viii) *The finance of Magistrates' Courts*

The expenses of a Magistrates' Court consist of the salaries of the clerk and staff and the general cost of the upkeep of the office and court-room, together with the salary of a stipendiary where one has been appointed. From early times the rule has been that these costs are to be borne locally, which means that they fall upon county or borough funds.[3] The court, however, receives sums for

---

[1] See p. 63, above.

[2] There are already many changes; see, for example, p. 131, above.

[3] The metropolitan stipendiary magistrates are paid out of the Consolidated Fund, and their courts are maintained out of the Metropolitan Police Fund: for the history of this, see the Home Office Memorandum to the Royal Commission on Justices of the Peace, 1946-8, printed as an Appendix to the Minutes of Evidence.

fees and for fines, and the disposal of these became complicated by numerous Acts of Parliament, the main principle being that (after the repayment of any fees incurred) the fine is to go into the county or borough rate fund unless statute directs the fine to go elsewhere.[1] Thus fines for customs and excise offences go to H.M. Customs and Excise, and fines for road traffic offences have since 1920 gone to the Exchequer. The result in the past was that the total fees and fines exceeded the cost of all the courts, but as the Exchequer took the road traffic fines most local authorities were not able to support the courts out of the fees and fines that they retained and had to make good a deficit out of the rates: a few places did, however, find that they covered and even exceeded their expenses. The Justices of the Peace Act 1949 instituted a pooling system. Fees and fines (other than a few exceptions) are now paid to the Home Office, which deducts the amount of fines due to the Exchequer and then divides the rest among the authorities in proportion to their respective expenditures: the pool does not cover the whole expenditure, so that every authority has a deficit, and there is a grant from central funds of up to two-thirds of the deficit.

The primary responsibility for fixing the salary of the clerk and staff and determining other matters of expenditure is on the Magistrates' Courts Committee for the area, though the Committee must consult the local authority, and in the event of disagreement the matter is determined by the Home Office. Naturally a local authority dislikes having to pay for something that is not run by the council, and there is a tendency for councils to suppose that as they pay they must have some control. Now that there is a government grant towards deficits the amounts to be paid out of local rates are small, and it might have been much simpler to finance the whole thing from central funds. The cost of County Court staff, offices and buildings are provided by the central government. The accounts of fines have for years been audited by the Home Office and all the accounts of Magistrates' Courts Committees are audited; there can be no repayment or grant on 'expenditure not properly incurred'. The retention of the local authority as the paying authority does not really give greater local autonomy, for the independence of justices has to be maintained against local authorities quite as much as against central departments.

[1] An explanation of the system before the Justices of the Peace Act 1949 may be found in ch. VII of the Report of the Committee on Justices' Clerks, Cmd. 6507 (1944).

(ix) *Stipendiary magistrates*

The system of paid magistrates had its origin in the two great defects of the administration of justice in the metropolis in the eighteenth century, namely, the poor quality of the justices and the absence of any adequate police force. An Act of 1792 set up seven public offices with paid magistrates, in addition to an existing office at Bow Street. Several Acts amending and extending the system followed. These paid magistrates were in charge of a few constables, and when the Metropolitan Police were established in 1829 they were placed under two magistrates. In 1839 the police were placed under a Commissioner and separated from the metropolitan magistrates: remnants of the older system can be seen in the Commissioner of Police still being a justice of the peace, though of course he does not sit in court, and in the magistrates being styled metropolitan police magistrates until the Justices of the Peace Act 1949 renamed them metropolitan stipendiary magistrates. The 1839 Act required these magistrates to be appointed from barristers, and that Act as amended in 1840 forms the basis of the present system. Lay justices were not prohibited from hearing cases, but there was a prohibition on taking fees except at these stipendiary courts where all fees went into public funds.[1] The result was to stop the activities of 'trading justices', and later to prevent the lay justices from paying their clerk except for licensing work. The Justices of the Peace Act 1949 removes the rule as to fees, but allows the Home Secretary to specify by Order the classes of case which should or should not be taken by them. Lay justices do liquor and betting licensing business, and hear a large number of cases brought by local authorities. For some years a court at Bow Street has been manned by lay justices, and sittings at other Metropolitan Magistrates' Courts began in 1959. The two systems have separate statutory requirements, and they cannot be integrated until the law is changed. The policy of integration has been accepted, and the details worked out, but all re-organisation of courts in London is to wait until the new system of local government in Greater London has been settled.[2]

---

[1] The Home Secretary continues to be responsible for the administrative arrangements of the Metropolitan Stipendiary Magistrates' Courts.

[2] Report of the Departmental Committee on Courts of Summary Jurisdiction in the Metropolitan Area (1937); Report of the Royal Commission on Justices of the Peace, Cmd. 7463 (1948), p. 73. The measures needed for integration are examined in the Report of the Interdepartmental Committee on Magistrates' Courts in London, Cmnd. 1601 (1962). On the re-organisation of Greater London, see note 1 on p. 100.

An Act of 1813 allowed the appointment of a stipendiary for the Manchester area, and then a general power was given by the Municipal Corporations Act 1835 which was substantially re-enacted in 1882. The essence of the provisions is that a borough can ask for a stipendiary, and if that request is granted (as it normally has been) the Crown makes an appointment. When a vacancy occurs there can be no new appointment unless the borough makes a further request. The result has been that the number of stipendiaries has varied, some towns having had stipendiaries and then not asking for any further appointment.[1] Similar legislation in 1863 allowed places that are now urban districts to ask for a stipendiary. If a stipendiary was wanted for a wider or special area it was necessary to have a special Act of Parliament. In recent years there have been twelve places with stipendiaries under the general Acts and five areas with special Act stipendiaries. The borough or place pays the salary, and some people think that that has been the chief reason why so few places have asked for stipendiaries. The cost of a stipendiary is, however, trifling in the budget of a big city, and other reasons may be more important. In the past stipendiaries in the provinces have not had a retiring age or a pension, and some towns have had the experience of a stipendiary continuing to sit when increasing age and infirmity should have led to his retirement. The Justices of the Peace Act 1949 removes difficulties of that nature. The main feature of the law is retained in that appointments, whether original or on a vacancy, may not be made except at the request of the locality. The changes are:

(1) A county as well as a borough may petition, or there can be a joint petition.

(2) The Lord Chancellor now advises the Crown, and appointments may be made from barristers of not less than seven years' standing or solicitors of the like standing.

(3) The amount of the salary is determined by the Lord Chancellor in consultation with the local authority (who continue to pay the salary), but it may not be greater than that for metropolitan stipendiaries.

(4) There is a compulsory retiring age and superannuation.

(5) The Home Secretary may give directions as to places, days and times of sittings of stipendiaries.

I doubt whether these changes will lead to any substantial increase in the number of stipendiaries. It is not that there is an objection to stipendiaries so much as a lack of enthusiasm for them. One of the weak points of paid magistrates is that few men have the ability

---

[1] I have given the names of these towns and some other information in an article 'Stipendiary Magistrates and Lay Justices' in 9 *Modern Law Review* (1946), p. 1.

to remain good tempered and patient when they take courts day after day. The sheer boredom of much of the work sooner or later produces foolish remarks, and if the particular stipendiary is not on good terms with the press his momentary lapse gets much publicity. Should a stipendiary, under the peculiar irritations of summary jurisdiction, develop signs of crankiness there is nothing to be done about it. A lay justice by not sitting nearly so often is less likely to develop an occupational disorder, but if he should get 'difficult' he can be controlled and outvoted by his fellow-justices. Stipendiaries in the provinces sit alone more commonly than they sit with lay justices, whilst metropolitan stipendiaries always sit alone for ordinary summary jurisdiction: these are the only people who administer criminal justice without any diffusion of responsibility, for judges, chairmen of Quarter Sessions and recorders all have juries, and at least two lay justices must sit to form a Magistrates' Court. Experience of other tribunals suggests that a lawyer chairman and two lay members may be a good composition,[1] and the General Council of the Bar suggested to the Royal Commission that a number of stipendiary magistrates might be appointed to visit various benches and sit with the lay justices. This suggestion was not supported by other bodies of opinion, and indeed the whole tenor of the evidence supported the conclusion of the Royal Commission:

In our opinion the system calls for improvement, not for radical change. It is, as we have already insisted, desirable that justices should be encouraged in the desire which most of them have manifested for further opportunities of instruction. They would not be so encouraged if their responsibility were to be reduced. The greatest care must be shown in the appointment of justices. They must be appointed for the right reasons, and not for qualities which, however meritorious, are irrelevant to the duties of a magistrate. Finally, they must have the advice of a well-qualified clerk, who knows how to distinguish law from fact and to confine his advice to the legal aspects of the case.[2]

In the preceding pages I have explained the steps that have been taken by administration and by changes in the law to improve the system of lay justices and their courts. The remaining question is whether justices are showing an interest in their duties and a desire to study and learn more about the matters with which they have to deal. I think that there has been a marked improvement.[3] Of course

[1] See pp. 343 and 348, below, for examples.
[2] Report of the Royal Commission on Justices of the Peace, Cmd. 7463 (1948), para. 216.
[3] A mixture of views can be found in a special issue of *Criminal Law Review* (October 1961), on magistrates.

there are still some justices whose attendance is poor and justices who have learned little and will never learn more, but a large body of justices do take the opportunities available for instruction. The membership of the Magistrates' Association has increased very considerably: it is a voluntary body, financed almost entirely by subscriptions paid by justices out of their own pockets. Numerous conferences in different parts of the country, some of one day and others of two or three days, have been well attended. As well as the Magistrates' Association meetings there have been, since the war, a number of occasions on which a judge on circuit has addressed justices. It is hardly possible to have attended such functions without feeling that justices have the desire and the will to learn. The prospect now looks fair, better indeed than in other parts of our legal system, but it is not like building in bricks and mortar where at some stage the building is finished; the effort has to be continuous.

7. AFFILIATION AND MATRIMONIAL JURISDICTION OF JUSTICES

A man has a legal obligation to maintain his wife and his children, whether legitimate or illegitimate. On ordinary principles these matters are part of civil law and not of criminal law and we should not expect justices to have jurisdiction, but there is a long history behind this jurisdiction. It goes back to the Poor Law of Elizabeth I; if a man does not maintain his children they would have to be maintained by the parish, and therefore the parish could enforce the obligations. Poor Law was under the superintendence of justices, and hence the jurisdiction. In more recent times the normal purpose of proceedings is to obtain weekly payments of money to help the mother to maintain a child or a wife to maintain herself. The old purpose is, however, still important, for if a woman does not take steps to compel the payment of maintenance, so that she or a child become supported by public funds, the National Assistance Board or other public authority can proceed against the man in the same way that the mother or wife could have done. For some years the tendency has been to treat the law as being primarily for the support and protection of children and deserted wives, and to add on a few other allied matters.

Pride of place historically goes to affiliation proceedings.[1] Either

---

[1] 39 Eliz. c. 3, and see Bl. *Comm.* 1, 458. The Affiliation Proceedings Act 1957 (a consolidating statute) is the present authority.

before the birth of the child, or within a year after its birth, the mother may apply for a summons against the alleged father. If the justices are satisfied that the man charged is the putative father, they will make an order called a 'bastardy' or 'affiliation' order, which may not exceed 50s. a week and stays in force until the child is aged sixteen and may be extended to twenty-one to cover education and training. Whilst some such provision is obviously necessary, it cannot be said that this part of our law works very well. Paternity is a singularly difficult thing to prove. The trouble is that sympathy with the woman can easily lead to an attitude insufficiently critical of the evidence; benches have been known to act as if the prime object were to find a father rather than to try the issue as to the particular man before the court.[1] It is some protection for men that the evidence given by the mother must be corroborated in some material particular by other evidence, but a requirement of corroboration is sometimes construed to mean that if there is corroboration the order must be made. If the question of introducing compulsory blood tests is raised among a gathering of justices it is likely that they will be sharply divided. It is beyond doubt that a negative result of blood tests is conclusive in showing that the defendant cannot be the father. On the other hand, a positive result merely shows that it is possible for the defendant to be the father and leaves the question of whether he is the father to be decided by other evidence. The result is that blood tests may help a man to escape but can never help the woman, and that seems shocking to a number of people (including many justices) who are conscious of the fact that when things go wrong a woman suffers more than a man. It is hard to get people whose emotions have been stirred to see that all that the man could 'escape' is the possibility of a wrong decision.

The statistics for bastardy orders show that in the earlier years of this century there were over 6000 cases a year; in 1920 the figure exceeded 9000, followed by a steady decline; in 1924 the figures were down to the pre-1914 level, and since then there has been a decrease. In 1938 there were 4313 orders, and 6,050 in 1962. The middle or upper class girl does not usually resort to the justices. It is possible for the father of a girl who has been seduced to bring a civil action against the man. This is a curious action. Nominally it rests upon the principle that he who wrongfully deprives another of the services of his servant commits a tort. If a father can establish that his

---

[1] An instance of an advocate being asked 'If your man is not the father, who is?' is cited in the *Journal S.P.T.L.* (1936), p. 19.

daughter performs some services for him, then she is *de facto* a servant and on this slender basis he may get substantial damages for being deprived of his daughter's services. A learned lawyer said that this fiction 'affords protection to the rich man whose daughter occasionally makes his tea, but leaves without redress the poor man whose child is sent unprotected to earn her bread amongst strangers'.[1] The published statistics of civil proceedings do not distinguish the different types of action, and so it is impossible to say whether seduction actions are still popular among those who can afford costs in the High Court.

The matrimonial jurisdiction of justices is a relatively recent growth. A statute of 1878 empowered justices to make orders of non-cohabitation, maintenance and custody of children, where a husband had been convicted of an aggravated assault upon his wife. Subsequent statutes extended the jurisdiction, and now the law has been amended and consolidated by the Matrimonial Proceedings (Magistrates' Courts) Act 1960.[2] The grounds for obtaining relief are now substantially the same for a husband as for a wife. The principal grounds are desertion, persistent cruelty, adultery and wilful neglect to maintain; a wife's obligation to maintain her husband and children is limited to cases where the husband's earning capacity is impaired and it is reasonable in all the circumstances to expect the wife to provide or contribute. The obligation to maintain children is extended by the 1960 Act to a 'child of the family', a new expression which means any child of both parties and any other child of either party who has been accepted as one of the family by the other party. The court may make an order, now called a 'matrimonial order', for one or more of the following:

(1) That the spouses be no longer bound to cohabit, which has the effect of judicial separation. This does not enable either party to marry again, and since spouses cannot these days be compelled to live together there is generally little to be gained by such an order. Indeed, since there cannot be desertion if the parties are judicially separated, such an order may prevent the complainant subsequently getting a divorce on the grounds of desertion. If, however, there is any reason to think that the husband may molest the wife, her position is more easily protected if there is such an order.

(2) Custody of children under sixteen. In the past this was normally

---

[1] Note to *Grinnell* v. *Wells* 7 Man. & Gr. at 1044. Seduction actions may not be brought in County Courts.

[2] The Act follows the Report of the Committee on Matrimonial Proceedings in Magistrates' Courts, Cmnd. 638 (1959).

12-2

awarded to the successful party, but the primary concern of the courts is now the welfare of the child. If no other suitable provision can be made, a child can be put into the care of the childrens' department of the local authority or placed under supervision.

(3) Payment of sums of money for the maintenance of the other spouse up to £7 10s. a week and for the maintenance of children of the family up to 50s. a week for each child. Maintenance for children is up to the age of sixteen, but the court may extend the period by two years at a time up to the age of twenty-one if the child is receiving education or training. The order may also provide for payment of costs of the application.

No adequate statistics are available. In 1938 Magistrates' Courts made 11,177 maintenance orders (an unknown number of which contained specific separation orders) and 185 separation orders with no provision for maintenance. The only figures available now are for matrimonial orders, of which 18,082 were made in 1962. The obtaining of maintenance is the main reason for the bulk of these cases. The figures do not, however, give a proper idea of the volume of work that this jurisdiction gives to Magistrates' Courts. Either husband or wife may apply at some subsequent date for the order to be varied or discharged. Then there is the matter of enforcing the order. Payments are commonly made through the court, and if the husband does not keep up the payments he may be brought before the court to be examined as to his means. The ultimate sanction is committal to prison. Thus a single case may come before the court many times over a period of years.

Although a husband may apply to a Magistrates' Court on nearly all the grounds upon which a wife may apply, husbands do not often do so. If a wife's conduct has been such that it would be good grounds for an application the husband can refuse to live with her and refuse to maintain her, and should she take proceedings he can set up her conduct as a defence. He will, of course, still be liable to maintain children of the family whether they are in his custody or his wife's.

Matters arising out of the guardianship of infants may come before the High Court or a County Court or a Magistrates' Court. The powers extend to making orders of custody and of access, and of maintenance.[1] In 1962 there were 4,995 orders made on these and similar matters. The court is required to have regard to the welfare

[1] The jurisdiction of justices is limited: they cannot deal with infants who have reached sixteen unless the infant is physically or mentally incapable of self-support, or deal with the administration of property, or order maintenance in excess of 50s. a week.

of the infant as the first and paramount consideration. Where a parent or guardian refuses consent to the marriage of an infant there may be an application to the court to give consent.

The practical working of the matrimonial jurisdiction of Magistrates' Courts was considered by a Departmental Committee which reported in 1936.[1] Most of the difficulties that have arisen have been due to the fact that Magistrates' Courts are essentially criminal courts, whereas their matrimonial jurisdiction is essentially non-criminal. The recommendations of the Committee received legislative form in the Summary Procedure (Domestic Proceedings) Act 1937. 'Domestic proceedings' are applications for affiliation orders, and matrimonial and guardianship proceedings. Legal aid is now available.[2] The court must consist of not more than three justices, to include where practicable both a man and a woman. The hearing is to be separated from proceedings for other business, and the public is excluded as in juvenile courts. Newspaper reports are limited to a bare recital of the parties, the grounds for the application, legal submissions and statements made by the court. Rules of evidence have been relaxed, so that a probation officer may (subject to certain safeguards) report in writing to the court the result of his inquiries. The use of probation officers to attempt a reconciliation between the parties is recognised. Certain changes in procedure where the parties are not legally represented have also been made; these have been mentioned on p. 152 above. There can be little doubt that this has been an improvement. How well it works depends largely on the type of justice who sits in domestic courts and the skill and wisdom of probation officers. It must not be forgotten, as the Committee point out, that too much zeal for conciliation by probation officers or by justices may mean that parties are persuaded to forgo their legal rights.

The matrimonial jurisdiction of Magistrates' Courts grew up to deal with the affairs of poor people. Until 1949 the limits of maintenance were £2 a week for the wife and 10s. for a child. Larger maintenance or a divorce meant the High Court, and the provision for legal aid was most inadequate.[3] Those who go to the High Court have never been much interested in judicial separation. In 1938 there were 71 petitions for judicial separation and 9970 for divorce, the figures for 1962 being 215 and 33,818. Judicial separation, whether ordered by a Magistrates' Court or decreed by the High Court, sends

---

[1] Report of the Committee on the Social Services in Courts of Summary Jurisdiction, Cmd. 5122.   [2] See p. 316 below.   [3] See p. 305, below.

the parties forth to a life of enforced celibacy or unhallowed unions. Now there are reasonably adequate facilities for poor people and people of modest means to take divorce proceedings,[1] and the two jurisdictions no longer correspond to the distribution of wealth. It is open to doubt (not much assisted by the Royal Commission on Marriage and Divorce) whether there is need to maintain two separate jurisdictions, and whether it is socially desirable that separated spouses should have their affairs settled by court orders that do not permit either party to marry again, however long a separation has lasted and however remote is the chance of any reconciliation. There are, however, some points about Magistrates' Courts that may be overlooked. A wife whose husband leaves her and will not maintain her needs a very quick and cheap way of getting an order for maintenance. In England we have a tradition of speed and absence of delays in criminal cases. We are used to an arrested person having to be brought before a justice within twenty-four hours, and of remands for not more than a week. Civil courts may move fast in a few matters, such as *habeas corpus* and some applications for injunctions, but the ordinary speed is slow. Hence Magistrates' Courts do provide a quick and cheap tribunal. It would be idle to contend that Magistrates' Courts deal with those cases to the general satisfaction of those concerned, but it is not always appreciated that it is virtually impossible to give general satisfaction. In most cases there is nothing very difficult in deciding whether there is or is not liability to maintain; the difficulty comes when there is liability and the court has to fix the amount of payments. When a husband and wife separate and the wife through having children or other causes is not earning money, then the husband's earnings have to be divided, and an income that sufficed for a joint household just will not meet the expenses of separate establishments. After justices have gone carefully into the figures it often happens that the man reckons that after he pays for his lodgings there is nothing much left for clothes and odd necessities, and that he cannot be expected to work hard if he cannot ever smoke or have a drink and so on: the wife says the amount allowed to her will not pay for rent and food and other needs. Each of the parties (and their friends and relatives) may blame the justices for making such an order. There are in our prisons always a number of men who have been committed for failing to pay under maintenance orders. Some of these men are wilful defaulters, who go to prison rather than pay on orders which they regard as

---

[1] See pp. 310 *et seq.*, below.

unjustifiable. Some are victims of unreasonable orders.[1] Some have been trying to do their duty by the women with whom they now live and their children, at the expense of the women who are still their lawful wives. Every year some two or three thousand men have gone to prison, arrogant and resolute, weak-willed and shiftless, and ordinary men caught in what seems a hopeless struggle. Better facilities for appeals[2] and a more careful procedure before making a committal order[3] can reduce the number of these wretched cases, but that is no solution. One of the most effective methods of ensuring that payments are duly made is attachment of wages: a notice is served on the man's employer, who must then deduct from the man's wages (somewhat as he deducts tax under P.A.Y.E.) and pay the amounts to the court. Such a system has long been in use in Scotland, but its introduction to England was resisted by trade unions and by employers and found no favour with Home Secretaries. The overcrowded state of prisons apparently led to a change of view, for the Maintenance Orders Act 1958 provides for the attachment of wages.

The furniture and household effects in a home usually belong, as a matter of law, to the husband, and he is usually the tenant if the house is leasehold. There is a widely held view that a wife should be entitled to a share of furniture and effects, and in some circumstances that she should have the tenancy. One thing that is quite clear is that Magistrates' Courts should not be entrusted with a jurisdiction that must involve the intricacies of property law; only lawyers can handle such matters, and incidentally it is only lawyers who see all the difficulties.

[1] A very bad case is cited in Cmd. 4649 (1934), p. 41: a man in receipt of unemployment benefit of 15s. 3d. a week, 2s. for his child, and 8s. for his wife was ordered to pay 15s. maintenance a week to his wife, and was expected to continue that payment when the 8s. was disallowed because his wife obtained employment, thereby leaving him 3d. a week to live on.

[2] Appeal against the making or refusal of an order, or revocation or variation of an order, lies to the Probate Divorce and Admiralty Division. The appeal may be on law or fact or on both. It is conducted on the notes made by the justices' clerk at the original hearing. There is some difference of opinion as to whether this is better than the usual method of appeal from Magistrates' Courts by a complete rehearing in Quarter Sessions or by case stated (see p. 112, above). By going to the Probate Divorce and Admiralty Division the law as to matrimonial causes is kept more consistent and Magistrates' Courts get authoritative rulings. But the individual who wants his case reconsidered would do better by a rehearing at Quarter Sessions.

[3] See note 2 on p. 227, below.

8. JUVENILE COURTS[1]

Until the middle of last century there was no special provision for the trial of children; if the offence charged was indictable the trial would be before a jury at Assizes or Quarter Sessions, whilst a petty offence would be tried summarily before justices in the usual way. An Act of 1847 allowed offenders under fourteen to be tried summarily for stealing. This policy was widely extended by the Summary Jurisdiction Act 1879 with the result that offenders under sixteen could be tried summarily for nearly all the indictable offences. These changes merely simplified proceedings against young offenders, who were still tried in the same courts and subjected to the same conditions as adults. The Children Act of 1908 represented the success of a long agitation, and established the principle that young offenders must be treated differently from adults. Offenders under sixteen had to be tried in a juvenile court, which was a court of summary jurisdiction sitting in a different place or at a different time from the ordinary sittings of the court, thus avoiding bringing the juvenile offender into contact with older professional criminals and undesirable persons. Prison for children was abolished, except in exceptional circumstances for those between fourteen and sixteen, in favour of methods aiming at reformation of the offender rather than punishment. The courts that tried young offenders were still the ordinary benches of justices. The practice of selecting certain justices for this work began in the London area under an Act of 1920, whereby a juvenile court consisted of a metropolitan stipendiary magistrate and two lay justices (of whom one had to be a woman); the Home Secretary nominated the justices, taking into account their suitability for the work.

In 1927 a Committee on the Treatment of Young Offenders issued a *Report*[2] which led to statutory changes in 1932. A consolidating statute, the Children and Young Persons Act 1933 with subsequent amendments, is the present authority. Those under fourteen are 'children' and those over fourteen and under seventeen are 'young persons'. For the courts the inspiration was drawn from the practice

---

[1] For reference on this topic and other matters relating to children the best book is Clarke Hall and Morrison, *Law Relating to Children and Young Persons*; the current edition is kept up to date by supplements. The Report of the Committee on Children and Young Persons (Ingleby Report), Cmnd. 1191 (1960) contains an examination of the system. John A. F. Watson, *The Child and the Magistrate* (1950), gives a clear account and much wise guidance to those concerned with juvenile courts.   [2] Cmd. 2831 (1927).

of the metropolitan juvenile courts.[1] The justices in each area make up a panel among themselves of those justices who are thought to be most suitable for work in juvenile courts; every three years the panel must be reconsidered, existing members still being eligible. Rules made under the Justices of the Peace Act 1949 provide that no justice shall be a member of a juvenile court panel after he has attained the age of 65 years, with an exception for stipendiary magistrates and any justices specially exempted by the Lord Chancellor. The Lord Chancellor, in considering the appointment of new justices, may give special attention to the needs of the juvenile court panel. The panel arranges for the courts and appoints a chairman. A juvenile court consists of not more than three justices drawn from this panel.[2] For many years it was a requirement that 'as far as practicable' the court must include one man and one woman, and this was made obligatory in 1954. Juvenile courts are still Magistrates' Courts, but they must hold separate sessions, preferably in a different room from the ordinary court-room; if an ordinary court-room is used, the juvenile court must not be held within an hour before or after its use for another court. Because of its evolution a juvenile court is a tribunal for the trial of young offenders, but on to that has been grafted the idea that the State must look after children who need care whether there has been delinquency or not. Hence there are two reasons why a child or young person may be brought before the court; it may be alleged that he has committed an offence, or that he is in need of care, protection or control. This duality affects the procedure and the powers of the court, but the two sides have much in common.

The Children and Young Persons Act 1933 laid down a main principle that is to be applied by all courts:

Every court in dealing with a child or young person who is brought before it, either as being in need of care or protection or as an offender or otherwise, shall have regard to the welfare of the child or young person and shall in a proper case take steps for removing him from undesirable surroundings, and for securing that proper provision is made for his education and training.[3]

---

[1] The metropolitan practice was altered in 1936. It was thought that there was no necessity for having metropolitan stipendiary magistrates as chairman of juvenile courts, and in 1936 the work passed almost entirely to lay justices.

[2] For the composition of Quarter Sessions on appeals from juvenile courts see p. 112, above.

[3] Applications for adoption orders can be made to the High Court, to County Courts or to Magistrates' Courts, in which case they are assigned to Juvenile Courts because of this general principle of securing the child's welfare. In 1962 juvenile courts made 6,947 adoption orders.

Throughout the proceedings care is taken to see that the juvenile does not come into contact with adult offenders. This is necessary both before and after the case is tried. A juvenile who is remanded, or who is committed for trial without bail, must ordinarily be sent to a remand home.[1] It is the responsibility of county councils and county boroughs to provide remand homes, either by themselves providing such homes or by making arrangements with other authorities or bodies. The Home Office inspects and exercises a general control. A remand home is a place of custody but it also has the important purpose of being an observation centre from which reports can be furnished to assist the court in deciding the best course to adopt for the welfare of the child or young person. A remand home is not, however, suitable for receiving every type of young person, and it has been the rule that if the court certifies that he is too unruly or depraved to be sent to a remand home then he could be committed to prison. The Criminal Justice Act 1948 authorises the Home Secretary to establish remand *centres* which will be able to cope with difficulties of custody and which will be equipped to provide expert reports on the physical and mental condition of those committed to a centre. Those who are fourteen and under seventeen will continue to go to remand homes as the ordinary committal, but if the court certifies that they are too unruly or depraved for a remand home they will be sent to remand centres: committal to prison remains possible until the court for an area is notified that a remand centre has been established, and after such notification committal must be to the remand centre and not to prison.[2] On remand for inquiry into physical or mental condition a person of fourteen and under seventeen may be sent to a remand centre if the local remand home cannot provide necessary facilities. Only one remand centre has so far been established; others are on the way.

In the case of young offenders the court has many powers varying with the offence committed and the age of the offender.[3] Table VIII shows the age limits for imposing various sentences or making other

[1] A child under fifteen may be sent to a special reception centre if the local authority provides one.

[2] Remand centres are also to be used for remands of those between 17 and 21 instead of using prisons.

[3] A full account of the powers of the court would be very lengthy; there are qualifications to practically every statement. A useful short account is given in a Pelican Book, *The English Penal System* (1957) by W. A. Elkin. See also the Report of the Committee on Children and Young Persons, Cmnd. 1191 (1960).

Table VIII. *The ages at which various court orders may be made*

	Child													Young person															
Age	2	3	4	5	6	7	8	9	10	11	12	13	14	15	16	17	18	19	20	21	22	23	24	25	26	27	28	29	30	31

Cannot be guilty of any offence — Doli incapax

Absolute or conditional discharge

£10 max.   Fine £50 max.

No consent to Probation requirements — Consent to requirements

Care of a fit person

Approved school

Detention in remand home

Attendance centre

Detention centre

Borstal

Prison

Hanging

Corrective training

Preventive detention *

Hospital or guardianship order †

† Under Mental Health Act, 1959

Conviction of an offence allows compulsory powers to be used in respect of psychopathic disorder and abnormality in a person of any age which would apart from a conviction not be available above age 20 and which would ordinarily lapse at age 25

But may be brought before juvenile court by local authority, police or authorised person (N.S.P.C.C.) on need for care, protection or control and an order may be made for supervision, care of a fit person, approved school, or hospital or guardianship order under Mental Health Act.

Age	2	3	4	5	6	7	8	9	10	11	12	13	14	15	16	17	18	19	20	21	22	23	24	25	26	27	28	29	30	31

This Table is taken from Appendix II of the Report of the Committee on Children and Young Persons, Cmnd. 1191 (1960), revised to take account of later legislation and showing the position at the passing of the Children and Young Persons Act 1963. Reproduced by kind permission of the Controller of H.M. Stationery Office.

orders in both juvenile and adult courts. The principal courses that a juvenile court may now have to consider are:

(1) A fine may be imposed on the offender.

(2) A limited measure of restitution or compensation may be ordered.

(3) There may be absolute or conditional discharge. This has developed out of recognisances, which are explained in the next section.

(4) A probation order may be made: the next section deals with probation.

(5) The parent or guardian may have to pay a fine, or be made to give security for the future good behaviour of the juvenile, but this must not be done if the parent or guardian has taken proper care of the juvenile.

(6) Whipping has ceased to be a penalty that can be ordered by a court. The remainder of the courses that may be taken all involve the element of compulsory detention, and hence the principle is applied that these orders may not be made unless the offence is one that carries liability to imprisonment when committed by an adult.

(7) The offender may be committed to the care of a 'fit person', and that person then has the rights and duties of a parent. The expression a 'fit person' includes a local authority, and most of the fit person orders put juveniles into the care of county and county borough councils. These are the authorities under the Children Act 1948 for the care of children who for a variety of reasons are deprived of a normal home life, and the children may be boarded out or may be in a 'home'.[1]

(8) An offender may be sent to an Approved School. The old Reformatories or Industrial Schools became known as Home Office Schools, which was a misnomer as they were not provided or run by the Home Office, and they are now known as Approved Schools. Such schools may be provided and administered by local authorities or by voluntary bodies; in 1963 there were 28 under local authorities and 95 under voluntary managers. The Home Office inspects and approves. When a court orders a child to be sent to an approved school the order is for his detention for three years or until four months after he ceases to be of compulsory school age whichever is the later; with a young person under sixteen it is for three years, and if he is older it is until he becomes nineteen. The managers of each school are required to consider from time to time the progress made by each boy and to place him out on licence as soon as he has made sufficient progress, and the managers are also responsible for after-care. The principal development in the last dozen years has been an increase in the number and variety of schools.[2] Juvenile courts used to select a particular school, but now the effect of their order is that the juvenile goes to a classifying school or centre which tests and observes and then assigns to a school of a type thought to be most suitable. A

[1] The Eighth Report on the Work of the Children's Department of the Home Office 1961 gives an account of the working of the Children Act.

[2] A review of the aims, methods and achievements of approved schools is given in a booklet, *Making Citizens*, prepared for the Home Office and published in 1945 by H.M.S.O. J. Gittins, *Approved School Boys* (1952), published by H.M.S.O. but not an official report, gives more detailed information.

difficult question is the course to be taken for absconding or serious misbehaviour in an approved school; the maintenance of discipline in these schools was considered by a Committee which reported in 1951.[1]

(9) There may be committal to a remand home for a period not exceeding a month. This is a mild form of punitive detention, and it is obviously hardly consistent with the main purpose of remand homes. For young persons it is replaced by detention centres when they are available, and will eventually continue only for children.

(10) No person under seventeen may be sentenced to prison by any court though for grave offences the higher courts can order detention.

(11) If the offender is over fifteen and under twenty-one there may be grounds for sending him to Quarter Sessions with a view to a borstal sentence; most borstal sentences do not originate in juvenile courts, and the sentence is discussed later.[2]

(12) The Criminal Justice Act 1948 provides for *detention centres* to be set up by the Prison Commission. If the offender is not less than fourteen but under twenty-one, the court can order him to be detained in a detention centre. This is being brought into operation gradually as such centres are established. By the beginning of 1963 there were thirteen centres, two junior, ten senior and one for girls, and others being prepared. For the younger group the period is three months, and three to six months for the older ones. The intention is to provide a short but sharp punishment, with hard work and brisk discipline. If a substantial period of training is required, the sentence should be approved school or borstal according to circumstances. To help in securing that this treatment is used in the right cases there are some restrictions; an order may not be made if the offender has been in prison or borstal unless the court thinks there are special circumstances, and before making an order the court must consider any report on the offender made by the Prison Department.[3]

(13) The Criminal Justice Act 1948 provides for another new kind of

---

[1] Report of a Committee to Review Punishments in Prisons, Borstal Institutions, Approved Schools and Remand Homes; parts I and II, Cmd. 8256 (1951). If serious breaches of discipline or absconding are treated (as they may be) as offences before a juvenile court, the court may send him back to an approved school with a new maximum age of nineteen and a half, or if he is over fifteen sentence him to borstal; the latter course may under the Criminal Justice Act 1948 be abolished when detention centres become available. Recommendations on powers to deal with misbehaviour were made in a Report on disturbances at the Carlton Approved School, Cmnd. 937 (1960), and the subject was further considered by the Ingleby Committee, Cmnd. 1191 (1960), p. 140. Criminal Justice Act 1961 gives powers to remove temporarily any person not less than fifteen years old who is seriously unruly or subversive, this requiring a justice's warrant, or application may be made to a Magistrates' Court for an order removing him to borstal.

[2] In 1962 there were 279 committals from juvenile courts and 1,188 from Magistrates' Courts to Quarter Sessions for borstal sentences. In addition there were 2,677 borstal sentences on cases tried at Assizes and Quarter Sessions. In some circumstances justices can commit direct to borstal; there were 371 such committals in 1962. On borstal generally, see p. 207, below.

[3] On Prison Department, see p. 206, below, and on reports to courts see p. 223, below.

institution called an *attendance centre*. The order here is that the offender aged not less than ten but under twenty-one is to attend for certain hours at the centre, the hours being such as to avoid interference, so far as practicable, with his school hours or working hours. The number of hours must not be less than twelve except that for children under fourteen the court can order less, and may exceed twelve if the court thinks twelve inadequate, but may not exceed twenty-four. An attendance order cannot be made in the case of anyone who has been previously sentenced to prison, borstal, detention centre or approved school. By 1963 there were fifty-one of these centres for boys up to seventeen, and one centre for boys aged seventeen to twenty. The regime is to provide 'physical exercise and useful occupation'.[1]

If a child or young person brought before the juvenile court is not an offender but is shown to be in need of care, protection or control, the powers are to send to an approved school, commit to the care of a fit person, or take security from the parent or guardian for the exercise of proper care in the future; in addition to the two latter courses, or instead of them, the juvenile can be placed under the supervision of a probation officer.

Generally speaking the hearing before a juvenile court is less formal than in an ordinary Magistrates' Court; for many courts an ordinary room is used, so that the justices sit at a table and there are no special 'court furnishings'. Policemen may be instructed to attend in plain clothes. Legal representatives may appear, but if they do not a parent or guardian, or in their absence any relative or other suitable person, may conduct the defence. There is a very sensible provision that if a child or young person 'instead of asking questions by way of cross-examination, makes assertions, the court shall then put to the witness such questions as it thinks necessary'; but unfortunately this does not apply to parents and other lay advocates who must apparently know how to cross-examine. The courts are not open to the public; press reporters may be present, but all other persons must be connected with the case or authorised by the court to be present. Newspaper reports of the cases must not give the name or anything that will reveal the identity of a child or young person who appears before these courts, whether he appears as defendant or as a witness unless the court gives permission. Since one of the objects of the Act is to bring home to parents their duties to their children it is provided that parents must ordinarily attend the court. The co-operation of local authorities is also an important element, and hence notification of proceedings must be sent to the County or Borough Council when juveniles are involved. Except in trivial

[1] L. W. Fox, *The English Prison and Borstal Systems* (1952), p. 339.

cases the court is required to take into account a number of things affecting the juvenile, such as his medical history, home surroundings, school record, and any report of the probation officer or local authority. The court may inform the parent or guardian of what the court proposes to do and then allow the parent to give his views about the proposed course. 'Sentencing'—a word that, along with 'conviction', is no longer to be used in juvenile courts—may thus resemble a consultation upon the best way of handling a difficult problem.

In the few years following the coming into force of the Children and Young Persons Act in 1933 there was considerable controversy about its effects. Some of the criticism was based on a failure to appreciate statistics. For instance, the number of boys under sixteen found guilty of indictable offences rose from 13,471 in 1933 to 21,189 in 1935, and this apparent wave of juvenile crime was ascribed to the new juvenile courts. As there had been an unusually high birth-rate after the 1914–18 war there were about a quarter of a million more boys in this age group, and when the figures were reduced to a rate per 100,000 in the age group the result was less alarming. It is also a mistake to assume that an increase in the number of convictions necessarily indicates a corresponding increase in the amount of crime.[1] If proceedings are thought to be too clumsy, expensive, and unsuitable for the nature of the offence, then many offenders will not be prosecuted at all. When the Summary Jurisdiction Act of 1879 allowed summary trial for many offences that previously required jury trial, there was an immediate sharp rise in the number of convictions. Similarly, the Children Act of 1908 was followed by a sharp rise in the convictions of juveniles. If the efficiency of a court is increased there is a greater readiness to resort to that court; in criminal cases this will appear superficially as a wave of crime. The indication in the 1930's was that some rise in juvenile delinquency was occurring, but it was not of such dimensions as to show that the methods adopted were unsuitable. The critics were on sounder ground when they commented upon the composition of the juvenile court panels: some benches put all their members on the panel, whilst a few regarded it as a privilege to which the junior (and so younger) justice could expect to attain when he had acquired some

---

[1] The only figures available are those for *proceedings*, for these are recorded and counted. We cannot know the number of instances when an offence could be proved but those concerned decide not to take proceedings. Also we cannot know the number of offences committed by juveniles who are not caught: we have the number of crimes 'known to the police', but unless the police catch the offender they do not know his age.

seniority. Most benches were doing their best to work the Act properly.[1]

Since 1939 there has been a strong movement to improve the welfare of children: whether we look at the steps taken on nutrition or at the Education Act of 1944 or the Children Act of 1938 we see evidence of a new awareness of needs. It would be surprising if juvenile delinquency had not also been a matter of great interest, but the figures have been such that the subject could hardly have been overlooked. It was to be expected that war-time conditions would result in a substantial increase in delinquency, and this of course occurred. Taking 1938 as an index figure of 100, the number of boys under 14 found guilty of indictable offences was 155 in 1945 and for boys of 14 and under 17 it was 150. The figures then began to drop, suggesting that a process of settling down had begun, but hopes were not fulfilled. After considerable fluctuations, with peaks in 1948 and 1951 and a relatively low level in 1954, 1955 saw the beginning of another period of rising figures. The figures are still rising. Policy must be decided on the assumption that the present high level will continue unless more effective methods of prevention or cure can be applied.

There has been a vast amount of inquiry during and since the war into problems of juvenile delinquency. More money has been available for research, and a concerted scheme of work is emerging.[2] There are serious difficulties, not the least being that the supply of properly trained research workers is insufficient. Much of the work has been directed towards finding the causes of juvenile delinquency, and whilst such work should continue it is not likely that results of practical utility can be obtained at all soon.

The field of inquiry into causation is of dismaying size, but until it has been fully explored, it is unlikely that a satisfying answer can be found to the problem of 'susceptibility'—the question, in other words, why, of a number of children with apparently similar personal problems, physical and mental make-up, and environment, some break down into delinquency, others into other forms of irrational behaviour, and others do not break down at all.[3]

---

[1] A good study of that period is Winifred A. Elkin, *English Juvenile Courts* (1938). See also the *Fifth Report on the Work of the Children's Branch of the Home Office* (1938).

[2] Some account of this is given in the *Seventh Report of the Work of the Children's Department of the Home Office* (1955), paras. 210–221 and *Eighth Report* (1961), pp. 34–36 and in Appendix B to *Penal Practice in a Changing Society*, Cmnd. 645 (1959).

[3] *Sixth Report of the Children's Department*, para. 217.

The Children Act 1908 came into force on 1 April 1909. We can now look back to over fifty years of a new system, of innovation and experiment, marked midway by the Children and Young Persons Act 1933. It seems a proper time to take stock of the position and to try and formulate the main currents of opinion. That is all the easier to do because there has been an extensive inquiry; the Committee on Children and Young Persons (Ingleby Committee) was appointed in 1956 and reported in 1960.[1] The following observations are based on the material that was before that Committee.

It is generally recognised that there is no great dividing line between delinquent children (here used in the general sense, to include 'young persons') and children in need of care, protection or control. Children who are not being properly looked after, who are disobedient, truanting, staying out late at night and so on, may appear before a juvenile court as being in need of care, protection or control because those factors are provable: defer action for a short while and the chances are that the appearance in court will be for an offence. These children shade off into those who are merely 'deprived' of a normal or satisfactory home, who may be received into care by a county or county borough under the Children Act 1948 without any court order.[2] The community provides a wide range of services, educational, health, welfare and custodial, dealing directly with children, and further services relating to the family and its environment.

The first problem is one of administration: what is the best way of ensuring that the right service comes into action where and when it is wanted. We have a national vice of departmentalism. A family in difficulties may become a concern of several departments of the local authorities, notably Education, Health, Children and Housing, as well as of a Probation Officer, N.S.P.C.C., and National Assistance Board. There has been a matching departmentalism in Whitehall, with meticulous control of details. Some people think that there should be a unified Family Service. There is much to be said for that, but each special viewpoint produces a different concept of how services should be organised. The only way to meet the complex and varying demands is to have much better co-ordination of services, and a clear rule as to responsibility. For the public this means that there should be 'one door on which to knock'. The Children and Young Persons Act 1963 imposes on county and county borough

---

[1] Report of the Committee on Children and Young Persons, Cmnd. 1191 (1960).
[2] For an understanding of the scope of the problem see Donald Ford, *The Deprived Child* (1955), and *The Delinquent Child* (1957).

councils a duty, in addition to their existing duties, to make available such advice, guidance and assistance as may diminish the need for children to be received into care or kept in care or be brought before a juvenile court as being in need of care, protection or control. Whether this will lead to satisfactory co-ordination between the departments of local authorities and with local voluntary bodies remains to be seen. There is provision for local authorities to report to the Home Secretary, so that the position will be kept under review. The 'one door on which to knock' is obviously envisaged, but it is not a requirement of the new Act.

The next major question is whether juvenile courts ought not to be replaced by some form of child welfare committees, as in Scandinavia.[1] A committee could deal with the whole range of needs and avoid nearly all the disadvantages of court proceedings. My own feeling is that it would be better to adopt a committee system at least for the younger children, but it is not worth canvassing. English opinion, as shown in the evidence of all kinds of organisations, political, social, professional, specialist and general, appears to be overwhelmingly in favour of retaining judicial process. The argument is that compulsory powers may have to be used; the personal liberty of the child and the rights of parents are involved, and such matters should be decided by a court. So juvenile courts will continue.

Accepting, as we must, the argument for retaining judicial process there is still the question of how far such process can be reconciled with the over-riding requirement to have regard to the welfare of the child. Virtually all care, protection or control cases fit in with the welfare concept, but the bulk of juvenile court work is concerned with offences and here there are difficulties. Judicial process is based on the defined issue. If, for example, a boy is accused of stealing, the court must try that charge. If, and only if, that offence is established may the court consider the welfare of the boy. It may be that the episode, of small moment in itself, uncovers a bad family situation, bad personal habits and other factors that make removal from his surroundings essential and an approved school the only place where he is likely to get the training he needs. Or it may lead to a diagnosis that the boy is subnormal mentally and aggressive, and needs hospital treatment. The boy is likely to believe that he was 'sent away', the most severe punishment, *because* he committed a

---

[1] A comparative study of the Swedish Child Welfare Board and the California Juvenile Court System is made by O. Nyquist, *Juvenile Justice* (1960), vol. XII in *Cambridge Studies in Criminology*.

trivial offence, and the parents may also feel a sense of injustice. To a kindly observer it can look like a legal pretext for doing something that wanted doing anyway, and unfortunate that it may not be done without a pretext. The Ingleby Committee recommended a new procedure for children under twelve who commit offences and all children in need of care or control that would make it plain that (*a*) parental duties are concerned, and (*b*) that the totality of the need for corrective or remedial action is the avowed issue. These proposals were, I think, quite workable, but they were not well received. When figures for offences and criminal proceedings are rising, one might expect a willingness to try new ideas, but that does not happen; the popular clamour is to try stiffer doses of medicines of which the efficacy is to say the least doubtful. The Ingleby proposals got mixed up with arguments about the 'age of criminal responsibility', which is a phrase that requires understanding rather than incantation.[1]

The upshot of all this is that not only are juvenile courts likely to continue but that they will continue with procedure and practice very much as they have been in recent years. The Children and Young Persons Act 1963 makes a few changes. The combination of petty sessional divisions for the purposes of having a single panel of juvenile court justices is simplified and may be carried out by the Home Secretary. The age of criminal responsibility is raised to ten. Under the earlier law proceedings for 'care or protection' were brought by police, local authorities or authorised persons, whereas complaints that a child was 'beyond control' had to be brought by parents or guardians, so that they had to take their own child to court and give evidence as a legal opponent thus appearing to reject the child and spoiling any hope of re-establishing a good relationship. The 1963 Act amalgamates 'beyond control' and 'care or protection' cases, redefining the grounds to give a single category of 'care, protection or control' cases to be brought by local authorities, police or authorised persons. A parent who thinks that a court order is necessary must ask the local authority to take proceedings, and if they will not, can ask the court to order them to do so. As

---

[1] The Ingleby proposals are Cmnd. 1191 (1960), pp. 31 *et seq*. They are explained more clearly by Lady Adrian in 17 *The Magistrate* (1961), pp. 109, 126. *The Times* leader, 22 February 1961, did understand what was proposed, and opined that 'the Government has deliberately chosen to side-step this issue and in view of the mixed reception this part of the Ingleby report was accorded it is understandable'. Lady Wootton, in [1961] Crim. L.R. 669, made one of the few reasoned cases against the proposals.

regards attendance of both parents and any legal guardian at court, the law is redrafted to cover circumstances where it would be unreasonable to require their presence, but there is little to emphasise parental responsibility and nothing to deal with the totality of the child's problem. The idea of a trial court and the idea of a child welfare centre must continue in such peaceful co-existence as may be possible. There are several minor improvements. No radical change is at all likely in the present climate of public opinion.

9. THE PROBATION SERVICE[1]

The process of placing an offender on probation grew out of the older practice of recognisances. A recognisance is in form a written undertaking made before a court whereby the person entering into the recognisance promises to pay a specified sum of money to the Crown, with a clause that if a certain condition is complied with the bond shall be void. If, for instance, the condition is that the defendant shall 'keep the peace' during the ensuing year, the effect is that if he does commit a breach of the peace the sum mentioned in the recognisance becomes due immediately. This technique, commonly called 'binding over', is used for many purposes. Persons may be bound over to prosecute, or to attend to give evidence. By way of preventive measures, an apprehended breach of the peace may be avoided by requiring persons who it is thought will commit some offence to enter into recognisances.[2] Often the court requires that the defendant must produce sureties who will be bound in the same way; since the court will expect the sureties to be persons of adequate means it is obvious that the man with poor friends may

---

[1] The standard book is now *The Probation Service* (1959), edited on behalf of the National Association of Probation Officers by J. F. S. King. For a short description, see *The Probation Service*, prepared by the Home Office (H.M.S.O.). There is a comprehensive survey in the Report of the Departmental Committee on the Probation Service, Cmnd. 1650 (1962), which is the main Report, and Second Report, Cmnd. 1800 (1962) on the probation hostel system.

[2] This power has been abused. If *A* threatens to beat *B*, it is a sound plan to get *A* bound over to keep the peace; it would be thought absurd to bind over *B* so that *B* should have the responsibility of answering for any assault that *A* might make upon him. Yet political speakers have been bound over (and in effect prevented from holding their meeting) because the police have anticipated that a breach of the peace might occur: the proper course is to bind over the speaker if it is apprehended that *he* will cause a breach of the peace; to make speakers responsible for disorder irrespective of the source of the disorder encourages organised hooliganism. There may now be an appeal (see n. 2 on p. 199).

be at a disadvantage. Wisely used there is much to be said for binding over offenders, for the suspended penalty often acts as a useful deterrent. In theory a recognisance is a voluntary thing on the part of the promisor, for he need not enter into the bond if he does not wish to do so; in reality he enters into the bond because if he does not do so the court may impose something more unpleasant.

It was realised during the last century that many persons bound over for offences would be more likely to conduct themselves properly and be less likely to commit further offences if during the period for which they were bound over they could be placed under the supervision of some person. Probation emerged as a combination of binding over an offender with provision for his supervision, but although the value of this course was realised there was a serious difficulty in that the courts had no system of officers or other facilities for undertaking the supervision of offenders.

In the last quarter of the nineteenth century some religious bodies began to appoint 'police court missionaries', a movement that grew rapidly and provided many courts with a useful and trustworthy handyman. Statutes of 1879 and 1887 empowered the courts in many cases to discharge convicted persons upon their giving security to keep the peace and come up for judgment. Many Magistrates' Courts used to inform such offenders that they would be under the supervision of the police court missionary, thus in effect introducing probation. By the beginning of this century the practice of placing on probation was common, but it was informal, and its use was confined to those courts where there were police court missionaries. The Probation of Offenders Act 1907 gave statutory effect to probation, and empowered the courts to appoint paid probation officers. Considerable use was made of this statute, but a Committee that reported in 1922[1] found that 215 courts had not appointed any probation officer, and that the conditions of service of many probation officers were unsatisfactory. The Criminal Justice Act of 1925 made the appointment of probation officers compulsory in all Magistrates' Courts. Many courts did not understand the value of good probation work, and they merely made appointments because they had to; they satisfied the letter of the law by appointing part-time probation officers at the cheapest rate. In 1934 there were 213 officers receiving salaries of £20 a year or less, while 83 were paid £5 or less. Cases of three or four days a week of work at salaries of

[1] Cmd. 1601 (1922).

£25 a year could be found.[1] In fact, the probation service was in a transitional state, passing from voluntary service to a public paid service, complicated, however, by the factor of its origin in missionary zeal. In 1907 a compromise was reached whereby voluntary societies (the chief of which was the Police Court Mission, a Church of England organisation) might select and provide probation officers by paying one-third of their salaries and expenses, the remainder being paid out of public funds. The missionary spirit is valuable, but there are disadvantages: a willingness to accept poverty is traditional (if not universal) in the religious, but it may spoil the market for other recruits, and it seems hard and ungenerous to criticise the efficiency of someone whose labour is a true personal sacrifice. In the London stipendiary magistrates' courts the Missions gave up in 1938, and began directing their attention towards providing hostels and homes. The tendency in the provinces was similar. At the time of the Criminal Justice Act of 1948 the probation service had become a lay professional service. A number of defects had appeared in the law and practice, and the 1948 Act repealed the existing legislation and recast it in a somewhat different form.

The Probation of Offenders Act 1907 grouped together three separate things, namely, discharge, binding over and probation. As regards the first, there are circumstances in which there is properly a conviction, but the infliction of punishment does not seem appropriate; the offender is in fact 'let off'. The second, binding over, did not impose any penalty but required the offender to be of good behaviour for a period that was commonly fixed at twelve months; if during that period the offender committed any offence he would thereby 'break his recognisance' and so (in addition to any punishment inflicted for the new offence) render himself liable to be punished for the original offence. A person bound over was thus 'let off', but conditionally. The third course, probation, calls for the active co-operation of the probationer, and it may well impose upon him quite onerous obligations. An unfortunate result of grouping these three things together was that people became used to the phrase 'discharged under the Probation of Offenders Act', and 'letting off' and 'probation' were often thought to be much the same thing. Under the Criminal Justice Act 1948 the court may discharge an offender if it is thought inexpedient to inflict punishment and

[1] The principal source for the state of the probation service in this period is the Report of the Committee on Social Services in the Courts of Summary Jurisdiction, Cmd. 5122 (1936).

that a probation order is not appropriate. Discharge may be absolute, which carries no actual or potential punishment,[1] or conditional. Conditional discharge replaces the old binding over or recognisances to be of good behaviour[2] by substituting a simple condition that the offender commits no offence for a specified period not exceeding twelve months. There is now no verbal connection between discharge and probation.

The 1907 Act provided that when a Magistrates' Court ordered discharge or probation the court did so 'without proceeding to conviction', although at Assizes and Quarter Sessions there had to be a 'conviction' before these powers could be exercised. It was an illogical position. One school argued that an offender who is trying to redeem himself by being of good behaviour or fulfilling his probation is greatly helped by the knowledge that if he succeeds he will avoid conviction, and therefore there should not be 'conviction' at Assizes or Quarter Sessions. The other view was that a spade should be called a spade, and that circumlocution is not only silly but often inconvenient. The Act of 1948 provides that in all courts there must be a conviction, but for non-procedural purposes this is not to count as a conviction if the person discharged or put on probation behaves sufficiently well not to be brought up and sentenced for the original offence.

The Act of 1948 ends the old method by which probation was secured by inserting conditions in a recognisance. Probation is now secured by an order made by the court requiring the person to be under the supervision of a probation officer, and containing such other terms, now called 'requirements', as may be specially appropriate. It is still necessary for the court to explain in ordinary language the meaning of a probation order and its requirements, and if an offender is over fourteen he must express his willingness to comply with the requirements. The name of a probation officer is no longer inserted in the order: the supervision is to be by a probation officer assigned to the petty sessional division in which the offender resides or will reside. There may thus be two courts involved; the

---

[1] Discharge may, however, be accompanied by an order for payment of costs or of compensation of limited amount for loss caused.

[2] This change relates only to an order after conviction. Preventive measures, and the procuring of persons to prosecute and to attend a court, still fall under the old style of binding over. The Magistrates' Courts (Appeals from Binding Over Orders) Act 1956 provides a right of appeal to Quarter Sessions, but the form of a recognisance is still, to any ordinary citizen, a piece of mumbo-jumbo whereby he has to admit that he owes say £10 to his Sovereign Lady the Queen.

court that made the order (Assizes, Quarter Sessions, or Magistrates' Court) and the supervising court. The court that made the order can discharge it, whilst the supervising court (which is always a Magistrates' Court) can amend it.

A distinction now has to be made between breach of the requirements of a probation order and conviction for a fresh offence during the period of probation. A fresh conviction may itself be a breach of requirement, but it must be dealt with as being a fresh conviction. (1) For *breach of requirement* the probationer is brought before either the Magistrates' Court that made the order or before the supervising court (whether the order was made by a Magistrates' Court or a higher court). If the magistrates are satisfied that there has been a breach of requirement, they can

> (*a*) fine up to £10, or
> (*b*) order him to attend at an attendance centre if that is applicable, or
> (*c*) if the probation order was made by a Magistrates' Court, deal with the offender for the original offence in any way that they could have done if he had just been convicted; if the probation order was made by Assizes or Quarter Sessions, commit him to Assizes or Quarter Sessions, which court can then deal with him as if he had just been convicted.

Courses (*a*) and (*b*) leave the probation order still in force, whereas course (*c*) ends the probation order. (2) The *commission of a further offence* is dealt with similarly for both probation orders and orders of conditional discharge. The provisions are complicated, but the ordinary working is this: the new offence is tried before an appropriate court and the offender sentenced for that offence; this fresh conviction makes the offender liable to be sentenced for the offence for which he was put on probation or discharged conditionally, and any complication is merely as to the court that should deal with it. If the same court made the probation or conditional discharge order and subsequently convicts of a further offence there is no difficulty. Where different courts are concerned, the principles are:

> (*a*) if the order was made by a Magistrates' Court and the new conviction by Assizes or Quarter Sessions, then Assizes or Quarter Sessions can sentence for the original offence after they have sentenced for the fresh offence;
> (*b*) if the order was made by a Magistrates' Court *X* and the new conviction is by a Magistrates' Court *Y*, then court *Y* after sentencing for the new offence can sentence for the original offence if court *X* agree to that course;
> (*c*) if the order was made by Assizes or Quarter Sessions, and the new conviction is by a Magistrates' Court, the Magistrates' Court sentences for

the new offence and commits the offender (in custody or on bail) to Assizes or Quarter Sessions to be dealt with there for the original offence;

(*d*) if the order was made by Assizes or Quarter Sessions and the new conviction is by Assizes or Quarter Sessions, there is machinery for securing the production of the offender before the court that made the order but no statutory machinery for enabling one higher court to sentence on behalf of another higher court, but it may be that the higher courts will 'take into account' the original offence in sentencing for the new offence.

Whether probation is likely to be successful depends upon many factors. The court must have adequate information about the offender's antecedents, character and other relevant matters, but this is required for all intelligent sentencing and is not peculiar to considering probation; it is discussed further in the next section. If it seems that probation would be a suitable course the court must consider whether there should be any special requirements. The probation officer will 'advise, assist and befriend' the probationer, but if it is desired to enforce some specific rule, such as that the probationer shall abstain from alcoholic liquor, or not associate with some named person, that must be made a requirement. The range of possible requirements is thus immense, which on the whole is a good thing, although it does allow of unsuitable requirements being made on occasion.[1] There are some limitations upon a requirement relating to residence, including a rule that residence in an institution may not extend beyond twelve months. An important new power given by the 1948 Act is that on suitable medical evidence a probation order may contain requirements for the treatment of

[1] The following illustrations come from several years ago, but they are worth remembering. 'Extravagant conditions [now called requirements] are sometimes inserted such as are hardly likely to win the respect and co-operation of the probationer. The following are a few examples of many which were brought to our notice:

A young man of eighteen charged with attempting to steal one shilling's worth of cigarettes was bound over on the condition that he should not smoke cigarettes for twelve months, that he should be in the house winter and summer at nine o'clock, and that he should go to church at least once every Sunday.

A man of forty-two charged with stealing a handbag from his wife was bound over, a condition being that he must not speak to his wife for twelve months.

Two boys placed on probation for theft were ordered not to attend a cinema for two years.

Our attention was drawn to one case where a man and a woman who were charged jointly were forbidden to speak to one another. The condition was apparently more honoured in the breach than in the observance as they were married within a month' (Cmd. 5122 (1936), p. 54).

The Act specially provides that the payment of sums of money by way of damages for injury or compensation for loss shall not be made requirements of a probation order.

mental conditions, and this may include residence in an institution. It is assumed that the National Health Service will provide the necessary facilities for examinations and reports and for treatment.

From the time of the 1907 Act probation officers have been officers of the court. Originally each court made its own appointment, and in large and populous places a single court is still the unit whilst elsewhere there has been a steady process of combining a number of courts.[1] The administration is in the charge of a probation committee appointed by the justices or in a combined area having members appointed by the justices for the constituent divisions. There must also be one or more case committees for each court to consider the progress of probation in individual cases. Both probation committees and case committees can now have some co-opted members. Probation officers and any clerical staff needed are employed by probation committees, the expenses falling upon the local authority, the protection to the local authority being an appeal to the Home Office. There is an Exchequer grant towards probation expenses, including the running of hostels and homes, with the usual concomitant of central control. The Home Office inspects and audits the service. The Home Office also has a training scheme for those who wish to enter the service, the Home Secretary having a general Advisory Committee and a Probation Training Board for the training scheme for candidates. The probation service is thus organised and run on a basis of Magistrates' Courts or combinations of such courts. Assizes and Quarter Sessions also have need of probation officers, and it is the duty of probation committees to see that a proper service of officers is available in those courts.

The greater part of the work of probation officers is the supervision of offenders, but they now have so many other activities that the name is somewhat misleading. In the matrimonial jurisdiction of justices the recognition of conciliation has added to the official duties of probation officers. They may act as conciliators, and they may report to the justices. The amount to be inserted in a maintenance or bastardy order may be determined after an investigation by the probation officer. The same process may be used for the amount of fines. There are many other matters in which the court can be assisted by information or miscellaneous activities. A good

---

[1] The London service is directly under the Home Office, the actual control being exercised through the London Probation Committee, a body consisting of Home Office officials, a judge, metropolitan stipendiary magistrates and a few others. The metropolitan police fund makes the contribution that would ordinarily fall on local authority funds.

probation officer is invaluable to the court to which he is attached. He is also very useful to the people of his district, who apply for advice on all manner of questions. Fear has been expressed that probation officers may become too much of general handymen to the courts and general advisory bureaux: 'some limit must be set to the activities of an official who is paid from public funds.'[1] It is to be hoped that the limit will remain elastic; it is better (and far cheaper) to prevent disputes and delinquency than to deal with the results. The 1948 Act has, indeed, added that they are to undertake after-care of persons discharged from custody if they are required to do so, thus giving statutory authority to what was generally accepted. Since 1957 they have acted as welfare officers in divorce proceedings. The recent Committee on the Probation Service emphasise that the supervision of probationers constitutes the bulk of the work of the service, but they did not recommend any narrowing of the range of functions which probation officers undertake.[2] The whole tenor of the Report is that the service has in all its aspects to be made capable of carrying the demands, and that these may well increase.

For many years a major trouble of the probation service has been the scale of salaries. The scale is determined by the Home Secretary. A recent development is the setting up of machinery of the Whitley Council type, with the employers' side made up of representatives of local authorities, justices and Home Office, and employees' representatives from the National Association of Probation Officers, though the Home Secretary still has the responsibility of fixing the scales. An aura of missionary days has clung to the service. The salaries paid before the war appeared ample, or even large, to those who thought in terms of the pittances paid to the old court missionaries, whilst to the trained officer the salaries appeared to be beyond all doubt lower than those for comparable work in other branches of the public service. Some progress has been made since the war in combining areas, thus giving an increase in the number of senior and principal officers and there were substantial increases in the salary scales. But the service was so far behind other social services that substantial improvement became necessary. The Committee on the Probation Service[3] accepted the general pattern of the administration except for two matters of structure. They recommended that the London area should cease to come directly under the Home Office

---

[1] Cmd. 5122 (1936).
[2] Cmnd. 1650 (1962), p. 10. Reports to courts are becoming more important; see p. 225 below.   [3] Cmnd. 1650 (1962).

and should have a committee made up of representatives from the courts. They recommend that salaries should be settled by negotiating machinery, without the Home Secretary prescribing the amounts. There are many recommendations for improvement of organisation, recruitment, training and conditions of service, and an emphatic recommendation for a considerable increase in pay. Negotiations took place in 1962, and after an indignant rejection of an offer of a small increase, more reasonable figures were put forward. The new scales, which became operative in 1963, are phased so that the full increases take effect in 1964. Salary goes by age up to 29, with a maximum of £1005; over that age it depends on length of service, rising to a maximum of £1350 at over six years service. After 1964 there are to be biennial reviews. The higher grades have received substantial increases, senior officers going to £1650 and principal officers, varying according to the area, rising to £1750–£2600.

10. THE PROCESS OF SENTENCING[1]

The process of sentencing an offender must be sharply distinguished from the process of a trial. In the case of a trial on indictment, the verdict is that of a jury whilst the sentence is given by the judge, a distinction which does not, of course, hold good for Magistrates' Courts, but whether the trial is on indictment or summarily there are certain principles that must be observed: there are strict rules of evidence, the burden of proof must be satisfied, and the issue to be decided is clearly formulated. If the result of the trial is a conviction, or if the offender pleads guilty, the court must then decide whether a penalty is to be imposed, and if so the nature and extent of the punishment. For every offence the law prescribes the penalties that may be imposed. For most offences other than murder the law prescribes a maximum punishment, the court being free to impose a less amount. The court thus has a free hand within the limits laid down for the offence in question.[2] In exercising the available choice

---

[1] Leo Page, *The Sentence of the Court* (1948); L. W. Fox, *The English Prison and Borstal System* (1952); W. A. Elkin, *The English Penal System* (Pelican Book, 1957); C. Mullins, *The Sentence on the Guilty* (1957). The booklet *Prisons and Borstals*, 4th ed. (1960), H.M.S.O., and *Penal Practice in a Changing Society*, Cmnd. 645 (1959), give an account of the present position and of the policy that is being followed. E. Green, *Judicial Attitudes in Sentencing* (1961) and R. Hood, *Sentencing in Magistrates' Courts* (1962) are studies in sentencing practice. Articles of current interest can be found in the *Howard Journal*, published for the Howard League for Penal Reform.

[2] Minimum penalties are not customary, although there are some instances. For 'black market' offences under Defence Regulations the fine had as a minimum

the court is in a very different position than it is during the trial: for the process of sentencing, the court is left to exercise its discretion. Before discussing this process it is desirable to mention the various penalties and other orders that may have to be considered other than discharge and probation which have been explained in the last section. The age limits for various sentences and orders are shown in Table VIII on p. 187.

(1) *Fines*. In the early days of our law fines were not imposed: the defendant was ordered to be imprisoned, whereupon he bargained for his release on payment of money and made an end (*finem facere*) of the matter. For many years now the courts have fixed the amount of the fines, and they do not necessarily end the matter, for they may be in addition to other penalties. When statute imposes a liability to fines the maximum amount is fixed in the statute, but where there is a common law power to fine there is no limit to the amount. Magistrates' Courts have long been empowered to impose fines on convictions for those felonies, such as larceny, that are triable summarily. Assizes and Quarter Sessions had power to fine for misdemeanour, but no general power in felony, until the Criminal Justice Act 1948 gave those courts a general power. The court can allow time for payment, or order payment by instalments, and can fix a period of imprisonment in default of payment.

(2) *Whipping*. The 1948 Act abolishes this as a penalty that can be ordered by a court.

(3) *Death*. This is now confined to murder,[1] treason, certain forms of piracy, and setting fire to Royal ships and certain other Crown property.

(4) *Attendance centres* and *detention centres* have been explained in the section on juvenile courts. As centres become available they may be used for offenders who are seventeen or over and under twenty-one.

(5) *Imprisonment*. Before the 1948 Act came into force it was necessary to distinguish between penal servitude and imprisonment.

the amount that would secure that the offender derived no benefit from the offence. For a few road traffic offences there is 'automatic' disqualification from holding a driving licence; the disqualification arises on conviction, without any pronouncement by the court, although where there are 'special reasons' the court may prevent this happening. This automatic disqualification is not a penalty that can be altered by the prerogative of mercy; it arises from direct operation of law on *conviction* and not from the *sentence* of a court.

[1] The Homicide Act 1957 has altered the law of murder and also restricted the death penalty: see A. Ll. Armitage in *Cambridge Law Journal* for 1957, p. 183. The Act was founded to some extent on the Report of the Royal Commission on Capital Punishment, Cmd. 8932 (1953).

For many years there had been no difference in the treatment of persons serving these two kinds of sentence. The minimum period for penal servitude was three years, and persons serving such sentences were convicts; remission of a portion of the period could be obtained by good conduct, and the convict was then released on licence. For imprisonment the minimum was five days, and the usual statutory maximum was two years. The court specified to which 'division' the prisoner should go, and 'hard labour' might be ordered.[1] Remission could be earned, and the prisoner was then simply discharged, the 'ticket of leave' applying only to convicts. For many years there had been no difference in the treatment of convicts and of prisoners except differences attributable to the difference in the length of the sentence. The power of courts to specify hard labour and first, second or third division never worked well: the courts never seemed able to grasp that they were supposed to classify prisoners by their antecedents and character and not by the offences they had committed, and that the triviality or serious-ness of the offence or the health of the prisoner was not to determine the question. The 1948 Act abolishes all these distinctions. Powers to send to penal servitude are converted into powers to send to prison, and if the court wants to send an offender to prison it simply fixes the length of the sentence, and the classification, disposal and treatment of the prisoner is determined by the Prison Department[2] in accordance with the Prison Rules made by the Home Secretary

[1] The first division was meant for political prisoners, but as assaults, woundings and so on arising from disturbances are regarded in criminal law as ordinary offences, irrespective of whether the disturbance had a political origin, there were very few first division prisoners. The second division was intended for 'persons who are not depraved and not usually of criminal habits'. The third division and imprisonment with hard labour had become substantially the same, except that in hard labour the prisoner was not allowed a mattress for the first fourteen days. The second and third divisions involved the same prison regime.

[2] The Prisons Act 1877 set up the Prison Commission as a Board, and as a matter of law the Commission owned the prisons and was responsible for the custody and treatment of prisoners. The Commissioners were appointed by the Crown, and dealt directly with the Treasury as if they constituted a separate department of government. In fact the Commission was staffed on normal civil service lines, and was responsible to the Home Secretary 'for the formulation and application of policy relating to the establishments under their control, and for their inspection and administration' (F. Newsam, *The Home Office*, 1954). Changes in the organisation of government made it desirable to transfer these functions to the Home Office, and that was authorised by the Criminal Justice Act 1961 and carried out in 1963. All the work in connection with running institutions, reporting to courts and so on, continue to be done by the same people or their successors in similar positions, and for practical purposes it is convenient to refer to the Prison Department and ignore the technicalities.

under statutory powers. The First Offenders Act 1958 requires a Magistrates' Court not to pass a sentence of imprisonment on a first offender unless the court is of opinion that no other method of dealing with him is appropriate, and they must state their reasons and enter them in the court register and on the committal warrant. The sentencing of young offenders has become so interlocked with borstal that they must be considered together.

(6) *Borstal and imprisonment of young offenders.* The training at the original Borstal Institution was designed as something more suitable than prison for the young offender who was in danger of becoming a professional criminal. The term *borstal* has become attached to a number of institutions that vary in their characteristics, from maximum security to 'open', but all carry an emphasis on training and rehabilitation rather than on mere custody. One of the objects of the Criminal Justice Act 1948 was to favour borstal sentences and discourage sentences of imprisonment. The old law was that a borstal sentence might be given 'by reason of his criminal habits or tendencies, or association with persons of bad character...'. There were difficulties when an offence was serious and the offender's character was only good in the sense that he had not previously been convicted. Hence the 1948 Act provided that the court must be 'satisfied having regard to his character and previous conduct, and to the circumstances of the offence, that it is expedient for his reformation and the prevention of crime...'. All sentences were to 'borstal training', with a standard maximum period of detention of three years, subject to release not earlier than at nine months, followed by supervision lasting for four years from the sentence.

Imprisonment of young offenders was restricted by the 1948 Act. For offenders under twenty-one, all courts were required not to impose imprisonment unless no other method seemed appropriate; the lower age limit was seventeen for Magistrates' Courts, and fifteen for the higher courts. An Assize judge did not have to give reasons, but Quarter Sessions was required to do so and a Magistrates' Court had to enter its reasons on the court register and on the committal warrant. Courts continued to send many young offenders to prison. Proposals for changes were considered by the Home Secretary's Advisory Council,[1] and new provision made by the Criminal Justice Act 1961. The minimum age for imprisonment is raised to seventeen. To deal with exceptionally serious offences by juveniles, the existing power of the higher courts to order detention

[1] *The Treatment of Young Offenders* (1959), H.M.S.O.

of a juvenile for a few of the gravest crimes is extended, and the minimum age for borstal is fixed at fifteen. For a person seventeen to twenty-one convicted at Assizes or Quarter Sessions of an offence for which imprisonment may be given, the court has now to consider the following courses if a custodial sentence is to be imposed:

(*a*) Send him to a detention centre[1] for not less than three nor more than six months.

(*b*) Send him to prison for a term not exceeding six months. It is intended to stop these short prison sentences as soon as there are sufficient detention centres.

(*c*) A sentence of borstal training may be given 'where the court is of opinion, having regard to the circumstances of the offence and after taking into account the offender's character and previous conduct, that it is expedient that he should be detained for training for not less than six months'. The court must consider any report on the offender made by the Prison Department. The maximum period is reduced to two years, followed by two years of supervision running from the date of his release.

(*d*) If the court thinks that borstal would be an inadequate sentence, they may (where the court has power to pass such a sentence) sentence him to prison for not less than three years. Thus for causing bodily harm, where the maximum is five years, a young offender could be sent to prison for up to six months, or for any term between three and five years. The only possible intermediate sentence is borstal.

The system is retained whereby a Magistrates' Court can on conviction commit an offender to Quarter Sessions with a view to that court giving him a borstal sentence.[2] Here, as in the court that sentences, the magistrates must consider any report on him made by the Prison Department. When a Magistrates' Court is in a position to commit to Quarter Sessions for sentence generally[3] that permits borstal or any other possible sentence to be considered.

(7) *Corrective training* and *preventive detention*. In 1908 special provision was made for persistent offenders. When a person with a bad record was convicted and given a sentence of penal servitude he could be charged with being a habitual criminal and be sentenced to preventive detention which was to follow the penal servitude sentence that he had just been given. It never worked well, and in late years it had become practically a dead letter. The 1948 Act abolishes it and in its place provides for two new kinds of sentence, corrective

---

[1] See p. 189, above.   [2] See footnote on p. 189, above.
[3] See p. 98, above.

training and preventive detention. Both require that the offender is convicted on indictment, that is, at Assizes or Quarter Sessions, of an offence punishable with imprisonment for two or more years.

Corrective training requires that the offender (*a*) is not less than twenty-one; (*b*) that he has been convicted on at least two previous occasions since he became seventeen of offences punishable on indictment with two years or more, although the conviction need not have been on indictment; then if the court is satisfied that 'it is expedient with a view to his reformation and the prevention of crime that he should receive training of a corrective character for a substantial time...', a sentence of corrective training for not less than two nor more than four years may be given in lieu of any other sentence.

Preventive detention requires (*a*) an age of not less than thirty; (*b*) three previous convictions on indictment since the age of seventeen of offences carrying at least two years' imprisonment, and that he was on at least two occasions sentenced to borstal, prison or corrective training; then if the court is satisfied that 'it is expedient for the protection of the public that he should be detained in custody for a substantial time', the court can impose a sentence of preventive detention for not less than five nor more than fourteen years.

The 1948 pattern of preventive detention has turned out to be as ill-suited for its purpose as that of 1908. The Home Secretary's Advisory Council has examined the position and recommended that preventive detention be abolished.[1] In effect this is another instance where it is thought that a sentence should be simply to imprisonment rather than to a specified variety of it; the classification and regime are better determined by the Prison Department.

(8) *Mental disorder.* Insanity as a defence, in the proper sense of avoiding a conviction, is virtually confined to murder cases. If a person was, at the time of his wrongful act, suffering from mental disorder to the extent that he did not know what he was doing, or, if he did know it, did not know that it was wrong, that constitutes a legal defence.[2] At a trial on indictment the jury bring in a special verdict known briefly as 'guilty but insane'. The Court than makes an order that he be detained and he becomes a 'Broadmoor patient' which means that he will be sent to Broadmoor or some other mental

---

[1] *Preventive Detention* (1963), H.M.S.O. See also W. H. Hammond and E. Chayen, *Persistent Criminals* (A Home Office Research Unit Report) (1963) and D. J. West, *The Habitual Prisoner* (1963).

[2] The best exposition and discussion of the test—known as the *M'Naghten Rules*—in ch. 4 of the Report of the Royal Commission on Capital Punishment, Cmd. 8932 (1953).

hospital, and consideration of his discharge rests with the Home Secretary. The only other circumstance in which mental disorder amounts to a defence is that, on a charge of murder, proof of 'diminished responsibility' can reduce the homicide to manslaughter. In all other cases mental disorder does not avoid conviction but it may lead the court to make an order that will secure care and treatment for the convicted person rather than giving a sentence of a penal nature. Magistrates' Courts have had powers for a number of years to make orders sending defendants to mental hospitals or to mental deficiency institutions. The Mental Health Act 1959 has recast the law, and extended the powers of the higher criminal courts. The present position is that:

'Where a person is convicted before a Court of Assize or Quarter Sessions of an offence other than an offence the sentence for which is fixed by law, or is convicted by a Magistrates' Court of an offence punishable on summary conviction with imprisonment, and the following conditions are satisfied, that is to say:

(a) the court is satisfied, on the written or oral evidence of two medical practitioners [one being on a panel of doctors having special experience in the diagnosis or treatment of mental disorders],

(i) that the offender is suffering from mental illness, psychopathic disorder, subnormality or severe subnormality; and

(ii) that the mental disorder is of a nature or degree which warrants the detention of the patient in a hospital for medical treatment, or the reception of the patient into guardianship under the Act; and

(b) the court is of opinion, having regard to all the circumstances including the nature of the offence and the character and antecedents of the offender, and to the other available methods of dealing with him, that the most suitable method of disposing of the case is by means of an order under this section,

the court may by order authorise his admission to and detention in such hospital as may be specified in the order or, as the case may be, place him under the guardianship of a local health authority or of such other person approved by a local health authority as may be so specified.'

The effect of a hospital or guardianship order is that the person becomes a patient and is treated as if compulsory powers were being exercised on grounds of mental illness on the system that has replaced being 'certified', except that the nearest relative cannot get him discharged. The period is one year, renewable if the responsible medical officer thinks that it is necessary in the interests of the patient's health or safety or for the protection of other persons. Discharge can be made at any time by the medical officer or hospital managers, or for guardianship by the local health authority. The patient is protected by rights of appeal to Mental Health Review Tribunals. It follows from these provisions that discharge is essentially a medical question. To meet cases where a court feels that detention should not be ended without full consideration of the interests of the public, the 1959 Act allows a court 'having regard to the nature of the offence, the antecedents of the offender and the risk of his committing further offences if set at large' to make a hospital order together with an order restricting discharge either without limit or for a specified period. Only Assize Courts and Quarter Sessions may make orders restricting discharge, but a Magistrates' Court can commit a person to Quarter Sessions with a view to such an order being made. The effect of this is to prevent discharge taking place except on the authority of the Home Secretary. It is not, however, intended that hospitals should have to keep anyone in custody after medical reasons for detention have ceased to exist: the person is a patient, not a prisoner, and although Mental Health Review Tribunals cannot direct release they are available to examine such cases and report their conclusions. It is important to appreciate that the Mental Health Act 1959 does not confer any new defence or remove any liability of an offender to be sent to prison or receive other penal treatment. If it is established by medical evidence in accordance with the Act that an offender is eligible to be treated under the Act, it is a matter for the court to decide whether to proceed under the Act or whether to exercise other powers of a remedial or penal nature.[1]

(9) *Consecutive or concurrent sentences.* A person may be tried and convicted of more than one offence and the court will then have to consider what to do in respect of each conviction. Punishments are normally cumulative: thus there may be a fine on each conviction or a fine and imprisonment, but obviously imprisonment renders conditional discharge or probation nugatory. In the case of prison sentences, the court may make them consecutive or concurrent. Consecutive prison sentences may be used to build up what the court regards as a sufficient total,[2] but most indictable offences have such a substantial maximum punishment that there is no need to do that. Larceny tried on indictment carries five years, but it is most unlikely that if, for example, there are convictions of four offences the court would want to use consecutive sentences to make the total more than five. It is more likely that the court would decide that, say, two years in all should be given, and arrange the sentences accordingly; four

---

[1] See p. 226, below.

[2] It must be remembered that Magistrates' Courts have limited powers; see n. 2 to p. 105, above.

sentences of six months consecutive would show that each offence was regarded as less serious than if there were four sentences of two years concurrent, but that is no more than a broad indication.

(10) *Taking other offences into consideration.* It often happens that when a person is charged with one offence he admits the commission of other offences. It would be possible to make each of these other offences the subject of a charge and to prosecute in respect of them all, but that would entail delay and considerable expenditure in preparing for a trial. On the other hand, it is regarded as most important that when an offender is dealt with there shall be nothing left outstanding: in particular, a man leaving prison should have a clear start again in life and should not have to face further criminal proceedings.[1] Hence the practice is to prosecute on a charge or charges in which the case is ready and for the defendant to ask the court to take into consideration in the sentence the other offences. The other offences are listed, and the judge must ask the defendant personally whether he admits them and wishes them taken into consideration. When a case is taken into consideration this does not constitute a legal bar to a subsequent prosecution, but he is ordinarily safe from such prosecution.[2] The practice depends upon the fact that the maximum of punishment that can legally be imposed on indictment is normally much more than the court would want to impose. The common offences to be considered are larceny, obtaining by false pretences and breakings and enterings, with maximum penalties for a single offence ranging from five years to life imprisonment, and the maximum is big enough to cover both the offence for which there is a conviction and the offences to be taken into consideration. If it should happen that the maximum available is regarded as insufficient, then the court should refuse to take other offences into consideration. Hence Magistrates' Courts can rarely follow this practice.[3]

---

[1] It may happen that a person is convicted and sentenced to prison and it is then discovered that he was responsible for some further offence. Unless that further offence is to be overlooked, he must be charged with it, brought from prison and tried and sentenced.

[2] If the conviction on which he has been sentenced should be quashed on appeal, it would be proper for him to be prosecuted for any of the offences taken into consideration.

[3] When a Magistrates' Court hears a case of larceny and convicts, the maximum sentence is six months; if the defendant asked for other cases to be taken into consideration the maximum sentence would still be six months, though the justices could send the offender to Quarter Sessions for sentence where the maximum would be five years.

On what principles does a court decide what the sentence should be?

In most ages there has been a widely held feeling that a criminal deserves and ought to receive a measure of punishment appropriate to the crime. That view, justified by some people on the ground that punishment should be expiatory or retributive, has moulded the attitude of our courts. The conception has been that every crime has a measure of punishment; the customary sentence may be mitigated or even increased for special circumstances, but in an ordinary case such and such an offence 'warrants' a sentence of such and such length. The Recorder of London told a Committee that reported in 1932 'that for larceny of a bicycle he would never feel justified in giving a longer sentence than twelve or fifteen months' imprisonment, no matter how often the offender had been previously convicted'.[1] Standardisation has never been rigid. In the early years of this century the judges agreed on a list of sentences that would be appropriate, in the absence of special circumstances, to the common kinds of criminal offences, and a copy of the list was given to judges on their appointment, but it turned out to be little use as a guide.[2] It is difficult to reduce the customary measures to writing, but those who are engaged in the administration of the criminal law soon learn the accepted limits. Hence if a barrister with some experience of criminal courts is given a judicial appointment he will know that is customary, and will do it with apparent serenity. An 'experienced judge' means one who is well used to trying defendants, and who, generally speaking, makes an excellent job of that side of his duty. But when we come to the passing of sentence, our 'experienced judge' is experienced merely in following a customary measure, and his experience does not extend to knowing what happens to those he sentences. Should we describe a man as being an 'experienced physician' if he ordered doses of medicine and never inquired what result they had on the patient? or, avoiding analogies that may be more striking than useful, is not the notion of gaining experience intimately bound up with the study of the *effects* of action?

This traditional method of sentencing has some merits. It is in accordance with the usual reaction of ordinary people and it appears to uphold the obligatory nature of the law. Uniformity is associated

[1] Report of the Committee on Persistent Offenders, Cmd. 4090 (1932), para. 21. Chapter III of that Report describes the common judicial attitude towards sentences.
[2] This has not been published but there have been public occasions on which judges have referred to the list.

with justice; when persons guilty of apparently similar offences are given dissimilar sentences there is apt to be a feeling that it is unfair.[1] Judges ought to do the customary thing, for then people know what to expect. The customary thing must of course alter as time goes by, but it should not alter too fast. Now the traditional principle of sentencing is altering and the real point is whether it is altering fast enough.

The more modern view is that the object of the criminal law is the protection of the community. As regards people who have already committed offences, that purpose can be served in three main ways. If an offender can be reformed he will no longer be a menace. He may be prevented from further harmful acts by being kept in custody. The thought of having to endure punishment may deter the person who has been punished or deter other people from committing offences. The question of what sentence to impose is then largely one of trying to forecast what would be the effect of each type of sentence that the court could impose. It is not until we look at the probabilities attendant upon each course of action that we can make the best choice. On this approach there is no need to ask what, say, is the customary punishment for the stealer of bicycles. Probation may meet one case whereas another offender might respond to a substantial period of training, as in borstal or, for an older person, a prison sentence of two years. Neither probation nor a two-year sentence would seem much good for a persistent stealer of bicycles; the prospects for reform look poor, and if several customary sentences ranging from six months to eighteen months have not deterred him it seems improbable that he will be deterred by two years. Possibly he could have been stopped if he had been treated differently earlier, but that is by the way; the choice now is between yet another traditional sentence or a longer period of corrective training or preventive detention. The treatment is made to fit the offender rather than to fit the offence. It is sometimes thought that this process of individualisation of treatment means that offenders get off more lightly; some do, but others get far heavier sentences.

The courts are at present in the process of endeavouring to consider the individual offender without, however, entirely aban-

---

[1] The most conspicuous instances come from fines. If a bench imposes the same amount of fine for a particular offence irrespective of the wealth of the offender it is obvious that the poor man is punished more severely than the rich man, and that looks unfair. If a bench does manage to fit the fines to the comparative wealth of different offenders there is criticism that it is unfair to treat the same offence differently for different people. A regular tariff seems to excite less criticism than an attempt to impose equality of burden.

doning their notion of each type of offence having a proper quantum of punishment. The traditional view is apt to be taken most firmly at the top and the bottom of the scale; a really serious offence must be visited with imprisonment appropriate to its gravity, whilst for a relatively minor offence it would be disproportionate and wrong to go beyond a light sentence. It is only when there is room to manœuvre, either because the offence does not clearly fall into the category of grave or minor, or because there are some exceptional characteristics, that a court feels free to look at the future needs of the offender.[1] It is not surprising that the sentencing policy of courts has often been at variance with informed opinion of those who see the effects of the sentences. A good example is the use of imprisonment. The Prison Department must receive all prisoners sent by the courts, and over a number of years they came to certain conclusions about the effects of prison sentences.[2] One conclusion is that prison conditions cannot be made suitable for the training of persons under twenty-one, yet the use of imprisonment for this age group increased substantially between 1938 and 1948. The Criminal Justice Act 1948 by imposing restrictions on the passing of sentences of imprisonment on those under 21,[3] led to an immediate drop in the number of such prison sentences. Unfortunately there was then a great increase in the number of youths convicted of indictable offences, and imprisonment again became a common sentence. The Prison Commissioners repeatedly called attention to the numbers of young persons received under sentence of imprisonment who had no previous proved offences. A further unsatisfactory feature has been the very many short sentences. In 1958, 905 boys received sentences of not more than three months; such sentences are nearly always useless. Apparently the only method of getting better sentencing is to alter the law. Under the Criminal Justice Act 1961[4] the court has no choice of an intermediate sentence; it must be borstal, and the Prison Department will then sort the recipients. Short prison sentences will disappear because the power to give them will disappear when detention centres are available.

Virtually nothing constructive can be done with prisoners serving

[1] E. Green, *Judicial Attitudes in Sentencing* (1961), p. 102, notes that disparity in sentences appears more noticeably in offences of intermediate gravity.

[2] These views have appeared piecemeal in the annual Prison Commission Reports; a most valuable statement is a Memorandum printed in the Report for 1945. See also *Prisons and Borstals*, 4th ed. (1960), H.M.S.O., and *Penal Practice in a Changing Society*, Cmnd. 645 (1959).

[3] See p. 207, above.   [4] See p. 208, above.

short sentences. The experience of those who administer prisons is that the principal thing with those serving short sentences is to see that they come to no harm, physical or mental. Table IX shows that sentences of one, two or three months account for a high proportion of receptions in prisons, and virtually no training is possible. The expectation of training in prison is a fairly high measure of success for a prisoner serving his first sentence, with a lower expectation for each previous sentence. When the record of convictions of a prisoner is examined it is often found that there has been a series of sentences ranging from a few days to three or four months, without a single sentence long enough for any effective training. Another familiar pattern of criminal record shows that the first prison sentence was of one month, the second was three months, the third was six months, and now he gets nine or twelve months. The first sentences were all useless for training him; he was in fact gradually acclimatised to prison, and when he has at last graduated to a sentence long enough to be of some use the chances of success have already been spoiled.

Table IX shows that short sentences are forming a slightly smaller proportion of receptions in prisons. The enormous reduction since 1913 was largely due to changes in the enforcement of fines, but the change since 1938 has been quite substantial. Yet in criminal records it is still common to find a string of short prison sentences, or gradually increasing sentences, all imposed during the last few years. It is probable that many short prison sentences are imposed simply because the bench has not learned enough about the effect of sentences, but that is not to say that all short sentences are due to ignorant and blundering benches. There may be a proper use for the short sentence: it is quite possible that the common notion of pulling a person up with a short sharp jerk is sound, though we do not know the kind of person for whom or the circumstances in which that is likely to be effective, and it may be that an ordinary prison cannot administer that jerk as effectively as it could be done in some other type of institution. But until there is some usable information on this I cannot see that a bench should be blamed for going astray when no one can be certain about the right course. Also, most of the offences with which we are concerned are thefts and similar acts of dishonesty, and most of them are small. On the common notion that a sentence goes by the size of the offence rather than by the offender, the court cannot impose a heavy sentence. It is true that our courts are less dominated by that notion and that they are prepared to go some way towards providing for each offender the treatment that is

Table IX. *Analysis of receptions in prison by length of sentences*

	1913		1938		1951		1961	
	Receptions on conviction	Percentage of total receptions on conviction	Receptions on conviction	Percentage of total receptions on conviction	Receptions on conviction	Percentage of total receptions on conviction	Receptions on conviction	Percentage of total receptions on conviction
Men								
Not exceeding 5 weeks	81,986	78·2	13,865	51·0	7,594	25·3	7,880	21·0
Over 5 weeks and not more than 3 months	13,932	13·3	6,518	23·9	7,945	26·5	9,424	21·0
Over 3 months and not more than 6 months	4,204	4·0	3,634	13·4	5,597	18·7	7,915	21·1
Over 6 months and not more than 12 months	2,651	2·5	1,770	6·5	4,168	13·9	5,769	15·4
Over 12 months and not more than 2 years	1,297	1·2	943	3·4	2,973	10·0	4,092	10·9
Over 2 years and not more than 4 years	570	0·6	360	1·4	1,312	4·3	1,891	5·0
Over 4 years and not more than 7 years	187	0·2	105	0·4	353	1·2	490	1·3
Over 7 years	19	—	13	—	36	0·1	62	0·1
Life sentences	8	—	—	—	—	—	48	0·1
Women								
Not exceeding 5 weeks	29,334	87·7	2,430	70·7	1,132	41·9	922	38·2
Over 5 weeks and not more than 3 months	2,930	8·8	525	15·3	714	26·4	826	34·1
Over 3 months and not more than 6 months	866	2·6	313	9·1	468	17·3	340	14·0
Over 6 months and not more than 12 months	222	0·7	111	3·2	233	8·6	200	8·3
Over 12 months and not more than 2 years	44	0·1	44	1·3	117	4·3	89	3·6
Over 2 years and not more than 4 years	32	0·1	14	0·4	34	1·3	36	1·5
Over 4 years and not more than 7 years	9	—	1	—	5	0·2	4	0·1
Over 7 years	—	—	—	—	—	—	2	0·1
Life sentences	4	—	—	—	—	—	3	0·1

likely to be effective, but, whilst they might go further than they do, it is quite unrealistic to urge that they should go the whole way. For a petty theft or act of dishonesty it may seem out of all proportion to impose a sentence long enough to allow of training in prison, and a court, moving as it must within the accepted limits of judicial action, could not impose a long sentence without appearing unjust.

The Home Secretary's Advisory Council on the Treatment of Offenders produced a report in 1957 on *Alternatives to Short Terms of Imprisonment*.[1] The only recommendations for new law were that the limit of time at attendance centres of seventeen to twenty-one year olds should be increased,[2] that there should be provision for attachment of wages for maintenance orders[3] and restrictions on prison sentences for first offenders.[4] The other recommendations were all within the present system, pressing for existing powers to be used for establishing remand centres and for extensions of attendance centres, and suggesting that courts should be reminded of some of their existing powers. The Council could not produce anything that looks like a solution.

However we look at it, the courts have not made as good a job of sentencing as they might have done. Suggested remedies can be divided into two broad categories. The most radical view is that the function of sentencing should be taken away from the courts and vested in some expert body. The alternative proposals are for varying degrees of training or instruction of judges and magistrates, and improvement of the process in the courts. There is, I think, no doubt that the latter course will be followed. The Committee on the Business of the Criminal Courts (Streatfeild Committee) had as part of their terms of reference 'to review the present arrangements... for providing the courts with information necessary to enable them to select the most appropriate treatment for offenders'.[5] The Committee was in fact asked to report on what improvements are needed on the supposition that the present system is in essence retained, and naturally the Report does not discuss the pros and cons of any basic alteration of functions. There is, however, a substantial case for a more radical change, and it is convenient to consider that first and then turn to the Streatfeild Committee's recommendations.

[1] H.M.S.O., not a Command Paper.
[2] Now in the Criminal Justice Act 1961, see p. 190, above.
[3] Now in the Maintenance Orders Act 1958, see p. 183, above.
[4] Now in the First Offenders Act 1958, see p. 207, above.
[5] Cmnd. 1289 (1961). On the other part of the terms of reference see p. 103, above.

At present the probation service is controlled by justices, and through the probation committee and case committees there is a direct relationship between the decision to place on probation and the process of probation. Courts may also exercise some control over extracting a fine from an offender. When, however, we look at committal to institutions, there is a clear division between the court that imposes the sentence and the authority that will be in charge of the person committed. Thus a court prescribes a period of imprisonment and has no responsibility for what happens to the prisoner: the prison authorities have the responsibility without having any say in determining whether the man should enter prison.[1] There is a clear distinction between the process of determining criminal responsibility and the process of sentencing, and the fact that the two processes are performed by the same agency is a result of history and not of any deliberate choice. Sentencing does in fact involve the exercise of a discretion in a way that is more associated with administrative functions than with judicial, and it is generally sound policy to ensure that administrative decisions shall be made by those who must take the responsibility for carrying out the work involved. The logical deduction from this is that all sentencing other than truly minor matters should be taken out of the hands of the courts and given to those persons who will be in charge of the treatment meted out to the offender. In such a scheme, after a plea of guilty or a conviction, the offender would come before an administrative body who would decide what to do with him. Such a body would be able to make a careful inquiry into the offender's record and all relevant circumstances, and having expert knowledge of the courses available they should be able to develop a technique far better than that of the courts. A number of people who have made a study of the administration of criminal law have come to the conclusion that 'the sentence-imposing or treatment function of the courts ought to be separated from the guilt-determining function',[2] and have made

---

[1] There are some executive powers to override the order of the court, but they can only operate in narrow limits. Imprisonment of a person under twenty-one may be changed to borstal, and an inmate of borstal may be transferred to prison. The prerogative of mercy, which includes pardon, commutation of sentence and remission in whole or in part, is vested in the executive.

[2] S. and E. T. Glueck, *Later Criminal Careers* (1937), p. 208. This is a theme that runs through several of the publications of Dr and Mrs Glueck: see *Unravelling Juvenile Delinquency* (1950). Margery Fry, *The Future Treatment of Adult Offenders* (1944), suggested a Treatment Authority. A general exposition is given in *After-conduct of Discharged Offenders* (1945), vol. v of English Studies in Criminal Science of the Institute of Criminology in Cambridge.

suggestions for the setting up of separate sentencing bodies. It is often supposed that the authority which sentences ought to have heard the case, but it is hard to maintain that as a vital principle since our law has long accepted the procedure of conviction in a Magistrates' Court and committal to Quarter Sessions with a view to a borstal sentence. The Criminal Justice Act 1948, now replaced by the Magistrates' Court Act 1952, extended this to a wider range of defendant who may be committed for sentence. If after a conviction a Magistrates' Court adjourns the case for inquiry before sentence the court that sentences need not consist of the same justices, though if it does not they must inquire into the case. There has been quite enough experience of these provisions to make it clear that a court that has not heard the case is not thereby hampered in considering the sentence, and it is not a serious argument against separate sentencing bodies to point out that they would not have heard the case. It is hard to know whether those who favour separate sentencing bodies are gaining ground. In the first edition of this book I felt that the right solution would be some form of sentencing body, but I have since changed my views. Since 1939 there have been many new occasions for decisions affecting the liberty and rights of the subject, and the experience to draw upon is now far greater than it was before the war. The old dispute was whether such decisions ought to be entrusted to bodies other than the ordinary law courts; that is now a dispute of the past, but there has, I think, emerged a strong conviction that a tribunal that decides issues of this kind ought to be independent of a Minister or that there should be an appeal to an independent body. This is examined later in a chapter on special tribunals where some mention is made of important recent examples. If the sentencing function were to be transferred to a special body, and that body were to be independent we should still have a divided responsibility; if those who run penal institutions were to be the deciding body, that would unify decision and carrying out the decision, but deprive the subject of the element of independence in the tribunal.[1] On balance there is a strong case for leaving the sentencing function with the courts.

The process of sentencing involves three main elements. The sentencer must (*a*) know what the various punishments and other courses actually involve and what they may or may not be expected

---

[1] The Prison Department is under the Home Secretary and he is responsible to Parliament. The issues, of course, are those of constitutional propriety and have nothing to do with the probity of individuals or departments.

to achieve, (*b*) appreciate that there is no single principle applicable to every case, and (*c*) have adequate information about the individual offence and about the offender. The only thing that we can be sure about is the first half of (*c*), that is about the offence, because courts always look at that. Knowledge of the other factors varies from ignorance to reasonable understanding.

In practice (*a*) and (*b*) tend to go together; anyone who makes a serious attempt to learn what, say, prison sentences do involve is almost bound to get on to the question of what they achieve and that leads to consideration of the reasons (good, plausible or manifestly absurd) that are advanced for imposing such sentences in such and such circumstances, and here I have no doubt in saying that the judiciary has in the past made a poor showing. For example, a good understanding cannot be acquired without visiting prisons, borstals, approved schools and other institutions. Records are kept of visits to institutions in the care of the Prison Department, and the Home Secretary has given information in reply to questions, and it is perfectly clear that it is exceptional for the lawyers who are professional judges to get first-hand experience of the places to which they send convicted people. There are many lay justices who make visits and who are well informed, but that is by no means universal. The Royal Commission on Justices of the Peace recommended that the instruction of justices should include the sentences that can be given and the orders that may be made.[1] Lawyers are just as much in need of instruction. In order to get legal qualifications it is necessary to make some study of criminal law with procedure and evidence, but the treatment of offenders is not included. Legal education has neglected some very important material about the administration of the criminal law. Every law student is expected to know how the system of law courts was altered during the nineteenth century, but he may be accounted legally educated without ever having heard of the Report of the Gladstone Committee in 1895, of the steps taken to carry out its recommendations, and the later developments. A barrister may acquire a substantial practice and be appointed a stipendiary magistrate, a recorder, a chairman of Quarter Sessions, a High Court judge, and be no better informed in these matters than any ordinary citizen. There is no more reason to suppose that because a person is a lawyer he is knowledgeable about the treatment of offenders than there is to ascribe such knowledge to a chartered accountant or any other professional man. At some time or other

[1] Cmd. 7463 (1948), pp. 23–4.

we in this country have committed most of the mistakes in penal policy that are still often advocated as a sovereign remedy. The account of these things should be part of education in public affairs.

Anyone who has to deal with offenders clearly ought to go further than that, but how far? It has often been suggested that a lawyer should become proficient in criminology and penology before he receives a judicial appointment that involves criminal work, and that a justice should be so equipped before taking part in decisions. The more naive reformers even believe that there should be compulsory examinations for those about to go on the bench.[1] It is unrealistic to expect a judge (who already has one specialist skill) to acquire proficiency in a wide range of social sciences. What we ought to expect of a judge is that he would regard sentencing as an ordinary subject to be studied as part of his professional equipment. Is it too much to hope that the legal profession may come to regard the subject of sentencing as being as important as, say, the rules of evidence?

The Streatfeild Committee were clear that sentencers must keep themselves informed by visits and by reading, but they also envisage an information service to be provided by the Home Office: there should be a handbook for sentencers which should contain not only information about all forms of sentences but also:

what they are designed to achieve and what they do achieve... there should be a standing booklet covering all forms of sentence and written specially for sentencers. The booklet may be regarded as a first step towards a textbook on sentencing. Sentencing is, in a sense, an emergent branch of the law, and it may be expected that, as in other branches of the law, the accumulated knowledge and experience will eventually reach a stage of development when a separate textbook is required. The booklet should be revised, as necessary, every few years, and supplemented every six months, say, by information about national trends in crime, together with additional research material as it becomes available.[2]

This is a most important recommendation; a service of that kind would be most valuable, though the passing on of the results of scientific work is not free from difficulties. Anyone who is aware of the amount of research that is being done and the possibilities that are opening up must feel that the results will some day lead to more rational and effective ways of preventing or curing criminal activities.

[1] Arguments have also been advanced for requiring judges to be trained, *inter alia*, in sociology, economics and psychology. Lawyers ought to feel flattered that their mental capacity is assumed to be unlimited.

[2] Cmnd. 1289 (1961), paras. 289–301.

Criminological research is, however, about the most difficult field in the social sciences: much of the effort has to go into background inquiries and the establishment of techniques. Some investigations do relate to particular sentences,[1] and it might be thought that the results merely have to be applied. To those concerned with policy, such studies are vital, for decisions of whether to increase facilities, alter age limits, maintain or revise the regime and so on ought to be based on factual evidence. But what so many people expect is something simpler, a dissemination of 'know-how' so that it can be applied to actual cases. That leads to the extent of a court's information about each particular offender.

Courts have generally had some information about offenders. There is a statutory requirement that before sentencing to borstal, corrective training or preventive detention the court shall consider any report on the offender from the Prison Department, but apart from that there is no regulation,[2] and judges and courts vary in the amount of information that is thought necessary. In Magistrates' Courts many of the lesser offences are heard in the absence of the defendant, and the court knows little about the offender; there used to be no satisfactory method of knowing whether there are previous convictions, and many a driver of motor vehicles was fined far less than he would have been if the court could have taken account of his record, but the new procedure under the Magistrates' Courts Act 1957 allows such evidence to be given. For the more serious summary offences and for all indictable offences the defendant is present, and the court may learn something about him. After conviction, the defendant being present, the police may be asked for any information they have including any previous convictions. For trials on indictment the police prepare an 'antecedents statement' which is given after conviction.[3] It includes some account of the defendant's

---

[1] For example, H. Mannheim and L. T. Wilkins, *Prediction Methods in Relation to Borstal Training* (1955); *Attendance Centres*, a Cambridge Study in Criminology (1961) by F. H. McClintock in collaboration with M. A. Walker and N. C. Savill; T. C. N. Gibbens, *Psychiatric Studies of Borstal Lads* (1963).

[2] It must be remembered that in dealing with a child or young person the court is not 'sentencing' and there are special rules (see p. 191, above).

[3] When justices try a man they are not supposed to know anything about him other than the evidence that is given; previous convictions must not (as a general rule) be mentioned until after conviction. At a trial on indictment the jury should be in a similar state of ignorance. It is the practice for the Assize judge or the chairman of Quarter Sessions to be given the depositions and other papers, including a list of any previous convictions, before the beginning of the case. This enables the judge to see that the prosecution do not ask questions that might disclose inadmissible evidence, and it also helps the judge to think about the

home circumstances, education, employments, service record, family position, and previous convictions. There was a tendency for these police reports to include views about the general way of life of the defendant unsupported by any evidence, and using phrases that made good headlines in evening newspapers.[1] In 1943 a case of that kind came before the Court of Criminal Appeal, and the principle was laid down that it is the duty of counsel for the prosecution to see that a police witness does not make allegations that cannot be substantiated.[2] Police reports improved after that case, but there were still some doubts as to what might or might not be included until a Practice Note was given in 1955.[3] Other reports might be available, and of course the defendant may produce witnesses who speak as to his character, employment, physical and mental condition or other matters. This somewhat haphazard state of affairs came about largely through the organisation of the higher criminal courts. There has been little difficulty in Magistrates' Courts getting information that they wish to have, because being continuous courts they can postpone sentencing so that, for example, a probation officer can interview the offender and can make a home surroundings report, and a medical or psychiatric report can be made, or indeed anything that seems relevant can be done, and all the material be available at an adjourned sitting. A similar procedure would often be hardly feasible for the higher courts because the Assize or Sessions might be over. The Streatfeild Committee took the view that at the higher courts it is important that the sentence should follow immediately on conviction. 'Many sentences are designed not so much to secure the reformation of the offender but, for example, to demonstrate

proper sentence he should give if the jury convict. If there is a conviction, this information is given in open court by the police. The Streatfeild Committee referred to the court having this information, and some members of Parliament in debates on 21 and 22 March 1962 described that as a 'disclosure' and a 'revelation for the first time to the public and even to a number of members of the legal profession' and sought to get it prohibited. It has never been a secret; my reference to it appeared in the first edition of this book in 1940, and it is mentioned in a Practice Note [1955] 1 W.L.R. 139, and doubtless in other places.

[1] After certain trials for unlawful assembly in South Wales in 1932, a police officer said of one of the accused (later the President of the South Wales Miners' Federation): 'He pays frequent visits to Russia, and, although the source of his income has not been ascertained, it is only to be assumed that he is well paid by Russia for his efforts to destroy the peace of this country which he has apparently determined to undermine.' At Birmingham Assizes in 1938 a person against whom no previous convictions were recorded was described as a blackmailer, a low-down cunning man and a confirmed drunkard; comment was made in the London *Evening Standard*, 23 July 1938.

[2] *Van Peiz* [1943] 1 K.B. 157. [3] [1955] 1 W.L.R. 139.

that persons who commit serious offences are punished; and the public impact of the sentence is much reduced if it is made known at a later date than the finding of guilt.'[1] On that basis the only feasible method is for reports to be prepared before the trial, provided that the defendant (who is of course not yet convicted and may be acquitted) does not object. The matter is complicated because if pre-trial reports from probation officers, Prison Department, medical and other services are to be made, there has to be an anticipation of what the court may need, and at the same time some limitation because full reports on every defendant, just in case the court needed them, would be wasteful. New arrangements came into force in October 1963. The Committee thought that probation officers' and Prison Department reports could properly express opinion on the likelihood of a particular sentence diverting the offender from crime.

Suppose that a court has got the results of research and that it has received the reports on a convicted person, can the two things be put together to produce a sentence that can be expected to have the desired effect; are we in a position anywhere near ordinary medical practice where knowledge and diagnosis can so often lead to effective treatment? The Streatfeild Committee went very near to suggesting that existing knowledge could be used in this way. Recent research can be an aid to sentencing, but even the most promising lines of prediction methods are not expected to reduce sentencing to a formula. When we go on to think about the effect of sentences that are intended to vindicate the law, to deter would-be wrong-doers, no one knows how effective such sentences are, and no one knows how to find out.[2] Of course we want more research, but it is hardly wise to pin all our hopes on scientific methods yet to be discovered, and anyway some of the difficult issues are ones of policy.

A good illustration of policy issues comes from some sexual offences, where judges are often criticised for what are thought to be stupid sentences. Sometimes the bench does appear ignorant,[3] but a judge may be well informed and yet appear to attach insufficient

[1] Cmnd. 1289 (1961), para. 310. Many sentences are so designed, but whether this is a piece of outworn tribal ritual or a technique that really does deter potential offenders is open to question.

[2] The Committee, Cmnd. 1289 (1961), paras. 282, 283, makes some suggestions, principally the collecting of opinion, but this is the weakest part of the Report.

[3] A good example is given by Havelock Ellis, 'The Eonist', contained in *My Confessional*. I was present at a meeting of law students to hear an address by a chairman of Quarter Sessions (legally qualified); at the close of the meeting one student asked about the sentencing of sexual offenders, and received the reply; 'I do not know any difficulty; a man like that is either insane or just vicious.'

importance to the psychological aspect of the case. Occasionally that aspect is less important than some commentators think,[1] but a common position is that a judge has to decide whether the interests of the community are best served by trying to reform or cure an offender or by shutting him up so that he cannot offend. If we take, as an illustration, a case where a man is convicted of sexual assaults, and the medical evidence shows some mental disorder and also indicates that medical treatment may be successful, the decision may be extremely difficult. Obviously the best thing for the community is to get the man cured so that he will not offend again, but doctors cannot guarantee a cure. Further, the best conditions for psychiatric treatment are apt to be those of personal freedom. If there is appropriate evidence the offender can be put on probation with requirements that ensure his receiving medical treatment, or under the Mental Health Act 1959 there could be a hospital or guardianship order. In the case of a hospital order there could be a restriction to ensure that he should not be released without the Home Secretary's authority, but that does not guarantee that he will be kept away from the public indefinitely or for a long period, because the Act clearly contemplates that if there cease to be any medical grounds for detention then the person should be discharged. The only way to be quite certain that he is unable to offend again for a time is to give him a substantial prison sentence. The facilities for psychiatric treatment within the prison system are being improved (the psychiatric prison at Grendon Underwood was opened in 1962), but prison conditions are commonly a bad environment for a sexual offender and not conducive to remedial treatment. Yet when a judge imposes a prison sentence in a case where there is clear evidence of mental disorder it is not necessarily a mistaken course. There are cases where the danger to the community is real and indeed very probable, and it may be better to give the community definite protection for a limited time rather than take a risk on curative methods.

Legislation may be used to restrict courses that are found to be undesirable. There is already power to prohibit courts from sending anyone under twenty-one to prison when the newer institutions become available. It may well be that the only way to prevent the passing of short prison sentences is to prohibit them, but that would not be practicable unless some other and more effective method of

[1] The amateur psychologist who thinks that he has the key to all penology should read *The Psychological Treatment of Crime*, prepared for the Home Office by Drs East and Hubert (1939), H.M.S.O.

treatment can be devised. Whipping was abolished as a court penalty because after careful examination it was found that it served no useful purpose.[1] Examination of results can assess the efficacy of a form of treatment, but there is no certainty about what will be the effect of a new course: it may work[2] or it may be disappointing.[3]

The great difference between the present time and pre-war days is that there is now an awareness of the need for sustained investigation, and there is permanent organisation to inquire and advise on whatever may be needed. In 1944 the Home Secretary set up an Advisory Council on the Treatment of Offenders, which is a standing body that considers matters referred to it by the Home Secretary. For example, a suggestion was made that the Citizen Training Centre in Boston, Massachusetts, offers a non-residential training for young offenders that might well be followed in this country. The Advisory Council examined the proposal;[4] suggestions that seem reasonable do get considered. As regards research, most of the work is done within

[1] See the Report of the Committee on Corporal Punishment, Cmd. 5684 (1938) and *Corporal Punishment*, a Report of the Advisory Council on the Treatment of Offenders (1960), H.M.S.O.

[2] The Money Payments (Justices Procedure) Act 1935 produced substantial results. It applies only to summary courts. When a person is fined and time is allowed for payment, the court may not (with exceptions) there and then impose a period of imprisonment in default of payment; a committal warrant must not be issued unless the court has subsequent to the conviction made inquiry as to the means of the offender in his presence. Where an offender is convicted in one area and resides in another, the inquiry as to his means is to be made in the area where he resides. When time is allowed for payment, or the defendant is not present in court, the offender must be provided with a written notice of the amount of the fine and particulars as to how it is to be paid. Instead of imprisonment there may be detention for a night at a police station. Where time is allowed for paying a fine, the court may place the offender under supervision; commitment is then not to follow unless the court has received and considered a report from the person supervising. An offender under twenty-one is not to be committed (with exceptions) unless he has been placed under supervision. In the enforcement of affiliation, maintenance and separation orders, and proceedings in default of distress for rates, the court must inquire in the defendant's presence as to whether his failure to pay was due to wilful refusal or culpable neglect, and if the court is of opinion that the default was not due to either of these reasons no committal warrant shall be issued. There are also provisions for reviewing orders for periodical payments. The Act came into force on 1 January 1936. There was an immediate reduction in the number of committals to prison: for offences other than drunkenness, the decrease was 43·6 per cent; for drunkenness, 23 per cent; for wife maintenance orders, 19·5 per cent; for affiliation orders, 33·8 per cent; for rates, 32·4 per cent. In 1936 there were 5081 fewer committals to prison for these causes than in 1935.

[3] The provisions for habitual criminals in the Prevention of Crime Act 1908 were the result of much deliberation, but they did not work well, and the same fate is overtaking preventive detention under the 1948 Act; see p. 209, above.

[4] *Non-Residential Treatment of Offenders under 21* (1962), H.M.S.O.

universities, with the Home Office sponsoring and assisting, although the Home Office has established a research unit of its own. The Home Secretary appointed a Committee in 1963 to review the arrangements for the recording, collection and presentation of criminal statistics. In 1958 the Home Secretary announced his desire to see a National Institute of Criminology in Cambridge, and the Institute was established in 1959. Criminology has become accepted as a university subject in degree courses. The biggest danger is that crime is 'news', and people expect too much; there is no prospect of revolutionary discoveries affecting the whole field of crime or its treatment.

We can, however, reasonably expect a series of improvements. A certain amount of human suffering and misdirection of human effort may be avoided, and we may have fewer warped personalities and fewer persistent offenders. A small gain here is worth some trouble to secure. An English criminal trial, properly conducted, is one of the best products of our law, provided you walk out of court before the sentence is given: if you stay to the end, you may find that it takes far less time and inquiry to settle a man's prospects in life than it has taken to find out whether he took a suit-case out of a parked motor-car.

II. 'HABEAS CORPUS'

Habeas corpus proceedings may be civil or criminal but it is convenient to refer to them in this chapter because many of them arise out of criminal cases and the rights of appeal given by recent legislation are defined in terms of appeals in criminal cases.

Habeas corpus is the most famous product of the common law for it ensures the basic liberty of freedom from unlawful imprisonment. It is procedural, a method whereby the High Court can inquire whether any person who is detained, either in prison or other official custody, or in private custody, is detained lawfully, and if the detention is not justified by law that person will be released. The machinery may be set in motion either by the person who is detained or by anyone else on his behalf applying for a writ. The conception is that if you get to know that someone is illegally detained (whether in one of the Home Secretary's prisons or one of the Minister of Health's hospitals or a feudal baron's castle or an ordinary dwelling where a baby is housed and guarded) you can get the matter before the court; presumably you will do this either on personal grounds, as where the alleged victim is a friend or relative, or to aid someone for whom there is political, religious or other special sympathy.

The rules about applying for the writ were altered by the Administration of Justice Act 1960. English lawyers have for generations been brought up to believe that an application can be made to a judge, and that if he refuses it you can go from judge to judge until you find one who is more merciful than his brethren. That was supposed to be the law, but a series of cases showed that we were all wrong, and had been wrong for years.[1] Nearly all cases of *habeas corpus* fall into one of two groups. The first relates to committals to prison, particularly from courts martial or from proceedings for extradition or relating to fugitive offenders when it is alleged that on jurisdictional or other grounds the committal is invalid. If the court went wrong on fact or law, but did what it lawfully could do, then the committal is valid; the remedy is to appeal and get the conviction set aside. The second group arises from custody of infants, who may be kept in the care of say one parent when a court has awarded custody to the other parent. This division has affected appeals. The Court of Appeal can hear appeals from the High Court provided they do not come from a criminal cause or matter, and so if an applicant was refused the writ for getting a child handed over he could appeal. In criminal cases there was no appeal because the Court of Criminal Appeal hears appeals only from convictions on indictment. It was, however, thought that this was not too bad because of the belief about being able to go from judge to judge. The 1960 Act had therefore to deal with both applications for the writ and appeals.

It is now specifically provided that when an application has been made no further application may be made to the same or any other judge or court, unless fresh evidence is adduced. Applications are to be made, in accordance with Rules, to the Divisional Court or to a single judge in court, except that (*a*) in vacation or when no judge is sitting an application can be made to a judge elsewhere, and (*b*) an application concerning a child is made to a judge in chambers. In civil cases the only alteration is that appeal now lies against an order for release as well as against refusal. So that if *A* seeks custody of a child who is with *B*, *A* may appeal if the judge refuses it, and *B* may appeal if the judge grants it, appeals going to the Court of Appeal and thence to the House of Lords as in other civil matters. In criminal matters, if application is made to a single judge: (*a*) he may grant it, but he will not do that unless it is a clear case; there is no

---

[1] The cases were successive attempts by the same person, who was in prison, to get his case before different judges. In *re Hastings* [1958] 1 W.L.R. 372; (No. 2) [1959] 1 Q.B. 358; (No. 3) [1959] Ch. 368; [1959] 1 W.L.R. 807.

appeal (e.g. by the Home Secretary) against an order for release; (*b*) he cannot refuse it, but may direct it to the Divisional Court. The Divisional Court can grant it or refuse it and either side may then appeal to the House of Lords if leave is given either by the Divisional Court or by the House of Lords. If the Divisional Court finds in favour of a prisoner, and the prosecution immediately give notice of appeal, the Divisional Court can continue the detention of the prisoner or release him on bail pending the outcome of the appeal. Once he is released he cannot be detained again.

What really happens with a man in prison who thinks that his imprisonment is illegal is that he applies in writing to the Divisional Court. The letter is considered by a judge (after it has been before an official) and if the court thinks that there is an arguable case and that the prisoner cannot instruct his own solicitor, the court sends it to the Official Solicitor who instructs counsel to apply on the prisoner's behalf.

In ordinary conditions *habeas corpus* is merely a background power as regards civil liberties, for the executive is not tempted to follow illegal or doubtful practices: it is safer to change the law. During a war there is likely to be special legislation that is judge-proof, so that if a man is detained by order of the Home Secretary his detention is legal and that is a complete answer to *habeas corpus*. Danger may come from an 'emergency' and a government that panics. We have lost our illusions about going from judge to judge, but we have got a much better system from the 1960 Act.

12. CONTEMPT OF COURT

Contempt of court has a long history with periods when it attracted little public interest.[1] After some years of quietude, the editor of the *Daily Mirror* was sent to prison for three months, the company fined £10,000 and the directors given a stern warning, for alleging that a man who was awaiting trial for murder had dissolved other victims in acid. Some cases in the next few years showed that contempt might be committed innocently, as by comment about a man without knowing that he had been arrested, or by distributing papers published abroad containing comment on a case *sub judice* in this country. *The Times* carried a powerful article *New Muzzle for Free Press*.[2] Lawyers were perhaps not entirely dismayed at seeing

[1] The standard text-book is Oswald's *Contempt of Court*, 3rd ed. (1910). Halsbury, *Laws of England*, 3rd ed. (1954), vol. VIII, with supplements, gives up to date material.   [2] 17 June 1958.

the courts belabour the press, but they were worried at liability without fault, and because (apart from certain civil matters) there was no appeal.[1] The Administration of Justice Act 1960 has dealt with these defects.

The subject is complicated because several different conceptions are brought under the same heading of contempt. There is contempt in the face of the court, which may be an affront to the judge or disturbance of the proceedings. A characteristic of these contempts is that in the superior courts they may be dealt with at once, the court acting on its own direct knowledge of the event. In such cases an appellate court may exercise first instance jurisdiction, as when a man threw tomatoes at the judges in the Court of Appeal and was promptly sent to prison. Conduct outside the court may consist of improper criticism or comment on the bench, or of interfering with officers of the court, as by obstructing a bailiff. Or it may be conduct that may affect the course of justice in a particular case, as by newspaper accounts that may affect the minds of jurors.[2] In all these cases that are not in face of the court, the proceedings are started in the Divisional Court of the Queen's Bench Division either by the Attorney-General or on behalf of the person aggrieved. The court learns of the facts from affidavits, counsel are heard and judgment given in the ordinary way. An offender may be imprisoned without limit, the period usually being fixed, he may be fined without limit and he may be bound over. There is obscurity as to the powers of lesser courts to commit for contempt in the face of court, though for county courts there is statutory power to fine up to £20 and commit for a period not exceeding three months. A Magistrates' Court has no such power, though a disorderly person may be removed, and if he has committed an assault or other offence he could be prosecuted. The important protection for inferior courts and for tribunals is that the High Court can punish anyone whose conduct is a contempt in respect of any jurisdiction.

The distinction between criminal and civil contempts is hard to define,[3] though most civil cases consist of disobedience to a procedural requirement, such as an order to produce accounts, which affects the other party. Imprisonment is generally for an unspecified time; when the person has become willing to do what he should, he

---

[1] The Bar Council made suggestions for rights of appeal, and *Justice* published a report *Contempt of Court*, 1959.   [2] See p. 148, above.
[3] See E. Harnon, 'Civil and Criminal Contempt of Court', 25 *Modern Law Review* (1962), p. 179.

Table X. *Appeals from orders or decisions in the exercise of jurisdiction to punish for contempt of court*

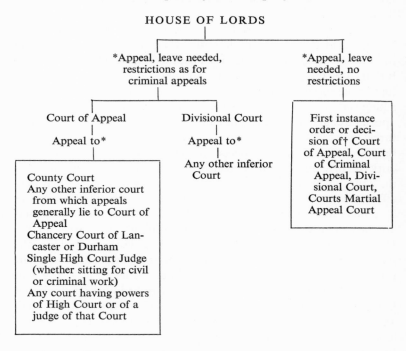

HOUSE OF LORDS

*Appeal, leave needed, restrictions as for criminal appeals

*Appeal, leave needed, no restrictions

Court of Appeal

Appeal to*

County Court
Any other inferior court from which appeals generally lie to Court of Appeal
Chancery Court of Lancaster or Durham
Single High Court Judge (whether sitting for civil or criminal work)
Any court having powers of High Court or of a judge of that Court

Divisional Court

Appeal to*

Any other inferior Court

First instance order or decision of† Court of Appeal, Court of Criminal Appeal, Divisional Court, Courts Martial Appeal Court

* Appeal lies in any case at the instance of the defendant and, in the case of an application for committal or attachment, at the instance of the applicant. The court to which an appeal is brought may reverse or vary the order or decision of the court below, and make such other order as may be just.

† All these courts have first instance jurisdiction in respect of contempts relating to themselves. The Divisional Court also hears at first instance some applications concerning contempts relating to other courts, especially newspapers prejudicing a trial.

apologises to the court, 'purges his contempt' and is released. Appeal has in fact existed in civil cases, for the contempt rests on an order that is appealable, but there was no appeal against the refusal of a court to enforce something by committal. Fines or binding over are not applicable to civil cases. The 1960 Act gives an appeal against refusal to commit, but otherwise does not affect the position: as in other civil matters, appeal is to the Court of Appeal and then, with leave, to the House of Lords.

The 1960 Act alters the substantive law by giving a defence for cases of innocent publication and distribution, and it clarifies the position of publication of legal proceedings that are not in open court.[1] Provision now exists for appeals. The person to be punished may appeal, and a person who has applied to the court to get someone punished and been refused may appeal. Table X shows the new system. The principle is that where a contempt relates to a court of first instance, appeal follows the usual course, namely to the Court of Appeal if the court is in the civil hierarchy of courts, otherwise to the Divisional Court. Further appeal, to the House of Lords, is restricted in the same way that it is in criminal cases.[2] On the right-hand side of the diagram are courts that ordinarily are appellate only, but they may exercise first instance jurisdiction when their own dignity or proceedings are involved as in the throwing of tomatoes: in those cases appeal lies to the House of Lords, with leave but with no particular restrictions.

The working of this can be seen from the proceedings against three journalists who refused to tell the Vassall Tribunal the source of their information. The chairman, in accordance with the Tribunals of Inquiry (Evidence) Act 1921, certified these offenders to the High Court. The Attorney-General then moved the court, and the cases thus came before the Divisional Court. In the first case the court decided upon six months' imprisonment but suspended the order in case Mr Clough should relent;[3] as his informant came forward, no further steps were taken. The other two journalists received sentences of six and three months imprisonment. They tried to appeal to the House of Lords, but leave was refused.[4] In view of the public interest aroused it is perhaps a pity that the House of Lords did not hear the case, though it is hard to see that much could be added to what the Lord Chief Justice had said in the other case in the Divisional Court.

---

[1] There are occasions on which a court may properly sit in private (see pp. 21–23 above) and some matters are normally dealt with in chambers. Suppose that an account of what happened in court or in chambers is published, is that contempt? It would be absurd to say that it should always be contempt for that would prevent publication of innocuous information such as directions as to trial in London or at Assizes (pp. 39–40, above) with or without a jury (p. 67, above). The 1960 Act distinguishes the circumstances where harm is most likely to result if the proceedings are published and limits contempt to such instances.

[2] See p. 117, above.

[3] *Att.-Gen.* v. *Clough* [1963] 2 W.L.R. 343.

[4] *Att.-Gen.* v *Mulholland, Att.-Gen.* v. *Foster* [1963] 2 W.L.R. 658.

CHAPTER IV

THE PERSONNEL OF THE LAW

I. SOLICITORS[1]

The most striking thing about the legal profession in England is the division into solicitors and barristers. As the solicitors far outnumber the barristers, and the layman has more contact with solicitors than with barristers, the junior part of the profession may be described first. The profession of solicitor took its present form relatively recently. In earlier times the barristers practically constituted the whole profession, the clerks who eventually evolved into solicitors being then far more lowly members of society. The old courts of King's Bench and Common Pleas had attached to them a number of attorneys who were appointed and controlled by the judges. These attorneys represented their clients and so could take many of the formal steps required for litigation. Some measure of legal ability or knowledge of procedure was required before a judge would admit a man as an attorney, but on the whole the attorneys were not sufficiently learned for the more important work of framing and then presenting a case; the more skilled work fell to the barristers. The rise of the Court of Chancery led to the need for a class of men corresponding to the common law attorneys; the counterpart of the attorneys were the solicitors of the Chancery Court, whose chief work was perhaps to 'solicit' (worry or bribe) the officials so that the customary delays of Chancery proceedings were reduced as far as possible. The ecclesiastical and admiralty courts had a similar class of men called proctors. In the fifteenth century the attorneys had often been housed in the Inns of Court where the barristers were organised, but in the later sixteenth century the barristers ejected the attorneys. The barrister was a gentleman, with the rank of esquire, and he could not be expected to mix with a mere attorney. The humbler branch prospered, and there was founded in 1739 the

[1] Enactments relating to solicitors were consolidated in the Solicitors Act 1957: there is an annotated edition by L. J. D. Bunker and P. J. Bunker (1958). An admirable and authoritative brief account, *The Solicitors' Branch of the Legal Profession*, was prepared by the Law Society as a Memorandum for the Royal Commission on Doctors' and Dentists' Remuneration, and is now to be found in the Annual Report of the Law Society's Council for 1958–9. T. Lund, *The Professional Conduct and Etiquette of Solicitors* (1960) is an authoritative guide. A small paperback, H. J. B. Cockshutt, *The Services of a Solicitor* (1961), explains the profession to the general public.

Society of Gentlemen Practisers in the Courts of Law and Equity as a body to which attorneys, solicitors and proctors could belong. The London attorneys generally became solicitors as well; the decline in the courts having proctors led to a virtual disappearance of proctors as a separate body, so that there emerged a combined profession that adopted the name of 'solicitor' instead of the more dignified name of attorney. In 1831 the Society of Gentlemen Practisers and other smaller societies were merged into the chartered body called the Incorporated Law Society, renamed the Law Society in 1903. It has always been a voluntary organisation, and this principle is still maintained, solicitors joining the Law Society or not, according to their inclination. The Society provides some club facilities for its members, but its activities in looking after the interests of solicitors are of course of benefit to all members of the profession whether they belong to the Society or not. Hence there is the position found in many organisations that those who do not belong (and do not pay subscriptions) get the benefit of something paid for by others, but there is a special point about the Law Society in that it is more than an ordinary professional organisation: the Society has been entrusted with statutory duties affecting members of the public as well as solicitors. The Solicitors Act 1941 provided that membership of the Law Society may be made compulsory for all practising solicitors by Order of the Lord Chancellor if he is satisfied on a poll of all practising solicitors that at least two-thirds of those voting are in favour of that course. Since that Act the Society has increased its membership and steps for making membership compulsory have not been taken.

Since the earlier eighteenth century admission as a solicitor has depended upon a combination of the idea of apprenticeship with that of examination. In 1877 the control of examinations was given to the Law Society, although the formal admission of solicitors remained in the Master of the Rolls. Substantial changes came into operation in 1963. The pattern before then was a period, varying from five to three years for a graduate, to be served under written articles with a solicitor. During that period the candidate had to take an Intermediate Examination (or part of it if he were a law graduate) and a Final Examination. There also had to be a period at a Law School for those who had not previously studied law. As candidates naturally had to take some time off to prepare for their examinations, the period of articles was much interrupted. The new scheme[1] now

---

[1] Briefly described in *Becoming a Solicitor* and explained more fully in *A Guide for Articled Clerks*, both published by the Law Society, 2nd ed. 1962.

in operation has rearranged the elements of articles, law school and Part I and Part II examinations. There are four categories of entrants. All students must have a prescribed minimum of education and produce referees as to their character to the satisfaction of the Law Society before enrolment. There is a fee of £20 for the various services and expenses of the Law Society. A non-graduate may attend a recognised law course, pass Part I, then enter into articles and serve four years, or he may enter into articles for five years, attend law school whilst in articles, and pass Part I; in either case he must pass Part II at the end of his articles. A graduate in a subject other than law must pass Part I before articles, then serve two and a half years and pass Part II. A law graduate will normally get exemption from Part I, and he may then take Part II before articles and serve two years, or serve two and a half years and take Part II at the end; the total time is much the same, as he must prepare for Part II whether he takes it before or at the end of articles. The law graduate gets an advantage because he can be taking Part II or serving articles, whilst the non-law graduate is struggling with Part I. The position of law schools is discussed later in the section on legal education.

Articles are normally arranged privately through family, school or other connections, although the Law Society is always ready to help. A solicitor must himself have been in practice for five years before he is allowed to have an articled clerk. Solicitors are frequently in partnership, and although the clerk is articled to a particular solicitor and not to the firm he will usually have the advantage of seeing something of all the work done by the partners. The conditions of articles will obviously vary with the solicitor or firm; a good mixed practice will give the articled clerk an all-round training, whilst a specialised practice will mean that he gets little or no experience of some kinds of work. There is discussion from time to time on the value of articles, because of the varying degrees of trouble that principals take over their articled clerks, and suggestions are made for a clearer definition of what articles should entail or for a staff course type of training.[1] Of course there are some principals who neglect the needs of their articled clerks, just as there are professional teachers whose performance is dismal. Articles are not intended to include 'training' in the sense of any course of instruction, but an opportunity to work with an experienced man, to see what goes on, and gradually to take on part of the work. I think that

[1] J. C. Hall, 'The Training of a Solicitor', 7 *Journal S.P.T.L.* (1962), p. 22.

the problem may solve itself through the financial aspect. It used to be customary for an articled clerk to pay a premium usually of £200 to £300, but that practice has been generally abandoned. The present trouble is about whether articled clerks should be paid a living wage. Some articled clerks are paid enough to live on, particularly when they are articled to solicitors in public employment. Solicitors in private practice generally say that they simply cannot afford to pay an adequate salary to someone who is not yet of much use in the office, but there is much variation. As the new scheme gets going the pattern for the able man will be a university education at public expense, six months at the College of Law (for which local authorities will pay fees and a maintenance grant) to pass Part II, followed by two years' articles with no more examinations to distract him; such a man is a valuable assistant and it is worth paying him properly. Complaints about having nothing to do and of not seeing or learning anything do not seem to arise when there is a decent salary.

In the past there were heavy stamp duties upon becoming a solicitor. Articles of clerkship had to bear a stamp of £80 and the admission of a solicitor £25. As an admitted solicitor it is generally necessary to have a practising certificate, which must be taken out annually, and which meant an annual £9 for public revenue and £1 for the Law Society, or for provincial solicitors £6 for revenue and £1 for the Law Society. The money thus received by the Exchequer from articled clerks and solicitors was not earmarked in any way for the regulation or improvement of the profession; it was simply a tax. Acts of 1947 and 1949 did tardy justice by reducing the stamp on articles to that imposed on all articles of apprenticeship, namely 2s. 6d., and abolishing the stamp duty on admission and on practising certificates.[1] After admission the young solicitor commonly obtains a position as salaried assistant or managing clerk. Before the war the newly admitted man could not expect a salary much in excess of £200 a year, and that salary was not likely to be greatly increased for two or three years; a substantial salary or profitable partnership was generally postponed until the solicitor was in his late twenties. There was a great shortage of solicitors at the end of

[1] By the Solicitors Act 1950 the fee for a practising certificate is a sum not to exceed £5 determined by the Master of the Rolls with the concurrence of the Lord Chancellor and the Lord Chief Justice. The obligation falls on nearly all solicitors, and the money goes to the Law Society, irrespective of whether those paying are members or not, in order to pay for the performance of the public duties of the Law Society. The other activities of the Law Society, as a club and as a professional association, are met by subscriptions paid by members.

the war, and much higher salaries have been paid in the last few years; in 1958 the Law Society said the range for newly qualified solicitors was £600 to £700 but that as an assistant solicitor in private practice he would be unlikely to rise to more than £1000 to £1500; perhaps around £1000 rising to £2000 is now nearer the mark for London and big cities. A number of solicitors go into public employment. The clerks of all but the less important local authorities are solicitors, and there are other solicitors on their staffs. Those wishing to enter the local government service often serve articles with the clerk to an authority, but some appointments are made from solicitors who served articles in private practice. The central government departments, nationalised industries, the larger trading and industrial concerns and various public bodies all have legal departments; barristers may be preferred where the writing of legal opinions forms a large part of the work, as in some government departments, but there are many more solicitors in these salaried positions than there are barristers. With so many openings there is little chance that the admitted solicitor will fail to make a living. A few solicitors make large incomes: if clients will bring their work to a man, he can employ assistants to do the work, until finally the office staff numbers a hundred or more. But very large firms with correspondingly large incomes are exceptional.

Solicitors may act as advocates in Magistrates' Courts and in County Courts, but (apart from a few Quarter Sessions) the advocacy in all other courts is confined to barristers. Probably half the work of solicitors is concerned with conveyances of land, which includes negotiations preceding sales and leases, with the drawing up of the appropriate documents and the arrangement and carrying out of mortgages. In earlier times a solicitor would not have drafted a will, settlement, or perhaps any other document that involves high technical knowledge; he would have gone to a barrister. Nowadays, it is only when there is considerable difficulty that a solicitor takes such a case to a barrister, the barrister being a specialist in such matters. Newer kinds of work, such as the formation and affairs of limited liability companies, have given solicitors profitable employment. In contrast to the barrister, the solicitor is more a business man, having an office to run and a substantial correspondence to deal with. Only in the larger firms can a solicitor confine his work to particular topics; the fact that solicitors are consulted directly by their clients means that they must at least present the appearance of being ready and able to conduct any ordinary kind of legal work.

The organisation and running of solicitors' offices used to depend to no small extent on a class of unadmitted managing clerks. Many of these men were highly skilled in the more routine processes, so that the commonly expressed view was that the firm just could not get on without them. Many of those men worked all their lives in the same office; they had security rather than substantial salaries. Economic and social changes have made it easier for clerks in an office to become solicitors, but there are still a number of unadmitted men. There was an Association, with an examination scheme, which gave some measure of status, and this was replaced at the beginning of 1963 with an Institute of Legal Executives. The senior grades are associate membership and fellowships, both obtainable by way of examinations. It is a good development, though the choice of title is unfortunate for 'executive' is coming to mean a man at the top.

Solicitors, being traditionally officers of the court, are amenable to direct discipline by the judges, but, whilst instances still occur of judges rebuking solicitors and making them personally liable for particular costs, the systematic regulation of the profession is divided between the Discipline Committee and the Law Society.[1] The Discipline Committee consists of present or past members of the Council of the Law Society, but it is appointed by the Master of the Rolls. From its inception in 1888 until 1919 the Discipline Committee investigated charges of misconduct and reported to the High Court, but in 1919 the Discipline Committee were empowered to make an order that the solicitor's name be struck off the Roll, or that he be suspended. In 1933 the Committee was given the further power of imposing a fine up to £500, the penalty going to the Crown, for offences against certain rules, and in 1941 for all cases where striking off the Roll is not obligatory. From the decision of the Discipline Committee there is an appeal to the Queen's Bench Division, from whom leave may be given to appeal to the Court of Appeal, and with leave to the House of Lords. In the exercise of this jurisdiction before the Discipline Committee the Law Society is usually the complainant, but there is no duality of function. No person who is a member of the Discipline Committee acts as a member of the Law Society's committee for considering complaints and, if there should be a prima facie case, pursuing them before the Discipline Committee: there is a complete separation of personnel.

[1] An authoritative brief account is T. G. Lund, 'The Professional Discipline of Solicitors', an article in *Administrative Tribunals at Work* (1950), ed. R. S. W. Pollard.

When the Discipline Committee hears a case it is usually constituted of three out of its twelve members; it follows a procedure similar to that of a law court, the complainant and respondent being represented by solicitors or counsel. The hearing is private, though the findings and order are announced in public.

The Discipline Committee has to consider whether the facts established constitute conduct unbecoming an officer of the Supreme Court or a member of an honourable profession. Thus a conviction of an offence involving fraud or scandal, unconnected with the respondent's practice as a solicitor, may be ground for disciplinary action. The obligations of a solicitor in the conduct of his practice are derived from precedent and partly defined by legislation; breach of either is professional misconduct which may come before the Discipline Committee. In 1933 the Council of the Law Society was given power to make rules for regulating the professional practice and conduct of solicitors. These rules must be approved by the Master of the Rolls. The particular occasion for this change was the need for better practices as to the keeping of accounts, and rules relating to this were made. Statutes of 1941 and 1956 added to the powers of the Law Society. Solicitors now have to produce an accountant's certificate annually, and they pay a small levy which provides a fund for the compensation of those who suffer from defalcations by solicitors. The Law Society also exercises control over articled clerks and over the employment of clerks who have been guilty of improper conduct in previous employment.

Thus whilst solicitors are virtually a self-governing profession, the disciplinary power over its members is wielded by a specially appointed body.[1]

2. BARRISTERS[2]

Barristers, known collectively as 'the Bar' and also collectively or individually as 'counsel', have a long history as a profession. The distinction between attorneys and those who pleaded in court can be seen under Edward I, but the settlement of the bar as a definite organisation probably took place later. Fortescue, writing in the middle of the fifteenth century, describes the Inns of Court as

[1] For some points on discipline in other professions, see pp. 350–2, below.
[2] W. W. Boulton, *Conduct and Etiquette at the Bar* is an excellent brief guide. R. E. Megarry, *Lawyer and Litigant in England* (1962), gives one of the best accounts of barristers in action, but it is so well written and the arguments so smooth that a reader may be hardly aware that it presents a case—the case of the successful Q.C. that everything is for the best and change is quite impracticable.

well-established institutions. Lincoln's Inn, The Middle Temple, The Inner Temple, and Gray's Inn, together with lesser Inns that have disappeared, existed as bodies with an organisation much like Oxford and Cambridge colleges. The governing body was the Benchers, who were senior members who themselves filled any vacancies that occurred. One function of the Inns was legal education, conducted by lectures and arguments. In rank below the Benchers came the Readers, who delivered lectures which were followed by arguments in which the next rank, the Utter-barristers, disputed with the Readers. The lowest rank of learners were Inner-barristers. In the more formal arguments, called moots, the Benchers acted as judges and the cases were argued by two Utter-barristers and two Inner-barristers. It was a tense training, tending to keep the narrow requirements of procedure well to the fore. The other function of the Inn was the 'call to the Bar'. The exclusive right of the bar to act as advocates in the superior courts rests on nothing but the attitude of the judges. A judge can allow a solicitor, or presumably anyone else, to conduct a case, but by convention this is not done. The judges have been content to accept the verdict of the Inns, so that a person becomes a barrister by the act of the Inn to which he belongs, subject to a rarely used supervisory power in the judges. The more successful barristers might rise to the rank of serjeants-at-law, an order that appears to have arisen by the end of the fourteenth century. The Chief Justice of the Common Pleas, with the consent of the other judges, could present names to the Lord Chancellor of barristers of eminence who had been sixteen years in the law. If the Lord Chancellor called upon a barrister to become a serjeant, he had to do so, for it was a public office. It was, however, far more advantageous than burdensome to be a serjeant, for according to Fortescue: 'Neither is there any man of lawe throughout the universal world which by reason of his office gaineth so much as one of these serjeants.' Becoming a serjeant was a necessary prelude to becoming a judge. The serjeant ceased to be a member of his original Inn and joined Serjeants Inn. The judges and the serjeants were therefore in close contact, forming an order quite apart from the rest of the barristers. The most momentous occasion in the career of a successful lawyer was becoming a serjeant. Thereafter he had the virtual certainty of becoming a judge, which was a trifling change compared with the gulf between ordinary barristers and serjeants. In the most important of the medieval courts, the Common Pleas, the serjeants had an exclusive right of audience. The relation between serjeants and judges was symbolised by the term of address, for they were 'brother' to each other; in this capacity a serjeant could intervene in a case and as *amicus curiae* assist his brothers on the bench by contributing his observations. This early history has profoundly affected our legal system, giving it the peculiarity of judicial office being more an activity of the legal profession than an aspect of the public service: this antithesis does not imply any necessary antagonism between the two ideas.

During the eighteenth century lethargy overtook the Inns, legal education ceasing and the emoluments of the Inns merely fattening the privileged few. By the earlier nineteenth century call to the Bar depended upon a student paying the fees and keeping twelve terms, of which there are four in each year, by eating the prescribed number of dinners each term. There were no examinations. The only instruction given was that students should 'read in chambers' with a barrister, and a student had to produce a certificate that he had pursued this type of study. This state of affairs was severely criticised in the era of reform that followed the Reform Bill of 1832. Change came in 1852, when the four Inns set up the Council of Legal Education. Instruction for students was re-introduced, and in 1872 a system of examinations replaced the certificate given by a barrister. Call to the Bar now depends upon keeping terms according to the practice of the eighteenth century, and passing examinations together with paying the fees. The cost varies with the Inn chosen, the minimum cost being £58 upon admission as a student and a further £100 upon being called, together with a deposit of £100 or a bond given for such a sum. During the three years in which terms are kept no attempt is made to see that students study law or learn anything of practice. The system of lectures (mentioned later) is voluntary. Provided a student can get through the examinations, he can be called and becomes a barrister-at-law, without any requirement of practical training or experience. This deficiency has traditionally been cured by voluntary pupillage with a barrister, called 'reading in chambers'. A new rule began in 1959 whereby anyone who is going to practise in England and Wales must undertake to complete a period of twelve months pupillage unless his Inn gives him dispensation. A pupil pays a fee of about a hundred guineas for twelve months. A conscientious barrister will give his pupils papers to inspect and documents to draw, and then go over them with the pupils. A great deal may be learned from attendance in court when the case has already been studied; the pupils see cases from the inside. Like all forms of private tuition, it is excellent when the 'tutoring' is done competently. When the period of reading in chambers is over, the young barrister sets up in chambers and waits for work. Barristers may not work in partnerships. Several barristers group together to form chambers, which means that they have rooms or share rooms adjoining each other, and employ a clerk in common. Each barrister pays his proportion of the rent and guarantees to the clerk a specified sum. The clerk, who receives commission upon the fees earned by each barrister, is rather a business manager than a clerk. Except in a few matters it is contrary to established usage for a barrister to be instructed by a lay client: the lay client must go to a solicitor, and the solicitor instructs the barrister. Hence barristers are dependent upon solicitors for substantially all their work. In some cases the lay client tells the solicitor that he would like a particular barrister to be briefed, but in most cases the lay client leaves the solicitor to select a barrister. Whether the barrister is asked to advise, or to draft some document, or to appear in court, he is sent a written brief, with the fee marked on it.[1] The amount of fees is settled between the solicitor and the barrister's clerk, it being against etiquette for the barrister himself to discuss his remuneration. A skilful clerk can help his barrister immensely by a wise acceptance or refusal of suggested fees. Since chambers may consist of several barristers, ranging from the very successful down to the beginner, it often happens that a brief intended for Mr A may, at the suggestion of the clerk, be given to Mr B if Mr A cannot take the case or if Mr A is now in a position to demand higher fees. Specialisation at the Bar means that solicitors never keep to one barrister or chambers for all their work; a firm of solicitors with a general practice will usually keep to a small circle of barristers for briefing in ordinary cases, sending their special cases to those with a specialised practice or of greater reputation. Until a barrister acquires a considerable reputation he is dependent upon his 'connection' with certain solicitors, yet a large part of bar etiquette is concerned with maintaining the superior status of the bar. Last century some barristers still lived in Lincoln's Inn Fields, and within living memory there could be seen a plate on the side door of one of these houses reading 'Tradesmen and Attorneys'. This spirit is not quite dead. Solicitors are still expected to go to the barrister's chambers: a busy solicitor with a large practice must wait upon a junior barrister who has virtually nothing to do. Of course the rules

[1] For practice under the Legal Aid and Advice Act, see p. 314, below.

16-2

are not always observed. The old class distinction between the two branches of the legal profession has broken down. The chance of success at the Bar is far more problematical than the prospects for a solicitor. Hence those who go to the bar intending to practise must have a larger financial backing, tending to confine the Bar to the children of wealthier families. A father who can afford to pay for his son to become a solicitor can equally pay for him to become a barrister, but whereas the young solicitor should be able to fend for himself the young barrister is unlikely to make enough to live on; the young barrister must be maintained for a few years, and even then there is no certainty that he will succeed in even a modest way. Many men who would in the past have become barristers now become solicitors. The social distinction cannot survive a state of affairs where many of the entrants into both sides of the profession have the same type of family, education and money.

The position of the bar is due partly to its close association with politics, the judiciary and high positions, and partly to the large cash rewards that come to those who are very successful. The average earnings at the bar are appreciably less than among solicitors, but it is possible for a barrister to achieve a considerable income fairly soon and a big income somewhat later. £25,000 a year is reached by a few men. The great financial success that comes to a few has a dazzling effect upon both the profession and the public; the influence of the very successful barrister upon our system is discussed later.[1] The conditions of a barrister's work make it necessary for him to do the bulk of it personally; juniors can 'devil' for him, and by judicious management he can sometimes appear in two cases that are heard more or less at the same time; naturally clients do not like a barrister to leave part of their case to a junior. If a practice increases there comes a time when the barrister has more work coming in than he can deal with. He will then consider becoming a Queen's Counsel,[2] commonly known as 'taking silk', because he may then wear a gown of silk instead of a stuff gown. Originally Queen's Counsel were appointed for the work of the Crown, but by the end of the eighteenth century it became a regular practice for successful men to apply for the appointment. The appointment is made by the Lord Chancellor; there are no qualifications, but it is understood that at least ten years' standing is required, together with an indefinable degree of success

[1] See pp. 256, 266, 426 et seq., below.
[2] A King's Counsel (K.C.) automatically becomes a Queen's Counsel (Q.C.) when the Sovereign is a Queen.

as a junior. The purpose of becoming a Queen's Counsel has for long had nothing to do with Crown work; the old rule that he must not appear against the Crown now means that leave to do so must be obtained, as when he appears for the defence in a criminal case, but the leave is given automatically. A number of conventions give Queen's Counsel the position of a superior grade of barrister. To some extent they replace the order of serjeants, which decayed and died out during last century, but unlike the serjeants the Queen's Counsel remain members of their old Inns. Queen's Counsel are generally known as 'leaders', because they must not appear unless an ordinary barrister, called a 'junior', appears with them. The junior must receive a fee equal to two-thirds of the leader's fee except where the leader's fee exceeds 150 guineas. If Mr *A* is a successful junior with an increasing practice he may become overworked. 'Counsel is bound to accept any brief in the courts in which he professes to practise at a proper professional fee dependent on the length and difficulty of the case, but special circumstances may justify his refusal, at his discretion, to accept a particular brief'[1] is a basic principle governing practice at the Bar. So Mr *A* cannot avoid overwork by taking only those briefs that he would like to have. He can increase his fees, but he cannot become too expensive because if litigants are going to pay large fees they may prefer to have a cheaper junior and leader. If Mr *A* takes silk, he may find that his practice declines unpleasantly, for whereas his fees as a leader will be a little higher the litigant must now pay for a junior as well. If Mr *A* has chosen wisely, clients will still brief him, and he will get higher fees and avoid doing the lesser and ill-paid work that overburdened him as a junior. If he has made a mistake, he cannot go back to being a junior; he must either wait and hope, or accept any offer of a minor judicial appointment.

The Attorney-General and the Solicitor-General (who is always a barrister) are in precedence at the head of the bar; after them the Queen's Counsel and the junior bar take precedence according to seniority. Discipline is still vested in the Benchers of the Inns. To assist in disciplinary matters, and to keep a watchful eye on the interests of the bar, there has existed since 1894 a body called the General Council of the Bar. It is composed partly of leaders and partly of juniors, elected by all the practising barristers. The General Council cannot itself take any disciplinary measures, but it can

---

[1] Rule 1 (1) of Rules as to Counsel's Fees. This, the 'cab-rank' principle, is discussed at p. 254, below.

report a case to the Inn to which a barrister belongs and the Benchers can then take appropriate steps. In 1949 it was decided to set up a Bar Secretariat financed by subscriptions from practising barristers, and the Bar is now in a better position to act as an organised profession with a wider range of interests than has been shown in the past. In 1962 an Inns of Court Executive Council was established so that matters of common interest may, when referred to the Council, be settled and be binding on the Inns.

3. LEGAL EDUCATION

In most countries the education of a lawyer is necessarily linked with a university degree. In England there is no such necessary link. A man may be called to the Bar, or be admitted a solicitor, without going to a university at all. If he does go to a university and obtain a degree, that degree (even though it be specifically a law degree) does not amount to a professional qualification. A university student can keep Bar terms by eating three dinners a term instead of six.

A degree in any subject reduces the period of articles. A degree in law may give exemption from part of the Bar or solicitors' examinations, and it is now an advantage in the period of articles and the time when examinations may be taken.[1] University law schools exist in their own right, and not as adjuncts to professional requirements.

Apart from universities and university colleges there are two law schools, that of the Council of Legal Education and the College of Law established by the Law Society. The Council of Legal Education is appointed by the four Inns of Court, and subject to the control of the Inns it prescribes the examinations that must be taken by bar students and arranges lectures upon legal topics. The teaching is almost entirely confined to the subjects prescribed for the examinations. The Council regards its law school as being primarily for non-university students or those who have not attended a law school, but attendance is voluntary and a Bar student may complete his qualifications without having attended any law school. The Law Society has followed a somewhat different policy. After many years of experimenting a system was introduced in 1922 under which every student who intended to become a solicitor had to attend a law school for at least one year before he presented himself for the final examination. This requirement could be satisfied by attendance either at the Law Society's own law school or by attending 'approved

[1] See p. 236, above.

law schools', which meant those in the universities. It did not work at all well. It was exceptional for universities to be able to provide special courses so that articled clerks generally had to take parts of courses designed for other students. To get through their examinations articled clerks often went to coaches, and particularly to Gibson and Weldon in London and Guildford. Hence an articled clerk who went to the Law Society's own law school in London might feel that it was a waste of time since Gibson and Weldon could teach him law and get him through the examinations. The new scheme[1] does not require a period of law school except for non-graduate entrants. They must attend full-time for eight months, and at present the only law school for this purpose is the College of Law, which was formed in 1962 by the merger of the Law Society's school and the tutorial business of Gibson and Weldon. The new College has a Board of Management appointed by the Council of the Law Society. There have been loud complaints from the provinces, for now non-graduate articled clerks must go to London or Guildford and incur the expenses of lodging and (according to some complainants) the wickedness of the great city. It will be seen that graduates do not have to attend law school, irrespective of whether they read law or some other subject to get their degree. The argument is that they have had training in orderly thought, mental discipline and all the other things that are associated with University work, and can catch up on law.

English law and its administration through the courts is dependent upon the legal profession, and if our system is to work well and develop in a satisfactory way the legal profession must be properly educated. It must be realised that the legal profession has public responsibilities: the Inns of Court and the Law Society are entrusted with public duties, the judges are drawn from the bar, and some appointments carrying lesser judicial functions are made from solicitors. A narrow training in nothing but the technique of legal work is unlikely to produce the right type of men. The widest possible outlook is wanted. Lawyers too must see their work in its social setting: they must learn to test their rules and practice by examining the function that they are fulfilling. The obvious prescription is that every law student should attend a law school, but that alone would hardly provide immunity from legal ills. There is no order of the universe to guarantee that a law school is a place of enlightenment. Law schools vary in place and time; the teaching in them is like any other teaching, that is to say, it is sometimes excellent and sometimes

[1] See p. 236, above.

dreary and useless. The staff of law schools are recruited almost entirely from university men who have obtained professional qualifications; some of them have seen very little practice, some have practised for years and then taken to teaching, whilst others combine practice with teaching. A closed circle, wherein only lawyers (themselves trained in law schools) teach in law schools, must be carefully watched, for a taught tradition may continue to be taught long after it is obsolete. Further, the division of law teaching between the universities and the profession may result in a partnership or in splendid isolation or even hostility. Unless there is co-ordination a law student may have his legal education spoiled by being over-lectured and over-examined.

Co-ordination of the work done by the universities and by the professional bodies was examined by a committee under the chairmanship of Lord Atkin that reported in 1934.[1] No great changes were recommended. It was assumed that the bar and the solicitors must continue to control the conditions of entry into the profession, which certainly includes the examination system. The tendency has been for the professional bodies to adopt examinations that test proficiency in the more technical matters. The teaching has tended to follow the habits of the examiners. The universities have partly followed the professional bodies and partly reacted against them. If the universities say 'The professional bodies are so severely practical that to get a balance we must continue to be theoretical', the professional bodies say 'The universities are so woolly and wide of the mark that we must insist on something useful'. The Legal Education Committee led to a better measure of co-ordination of teaching and examining, but the Council of Legal Education, the Law Society and the universities remain independent bodies; they consult and take heed of each other, but there is no tradition of pursuing a common policy.

The legal profession is concerned primarily with private practice. There are five or six solicitors in private practice for every one in public or similar employment, whilst a practising barrister is necessarily in private practice, for he cannot carry on any other profession or business or be a salaried official or servant. Training has naturally been directed principally to the needs of the practitioner. It is more difficult to devise a good system for solicitors since they have their offices in towns all over the country, and articled clerks are similarly dispersed, than it is for the bar which is so largely concentrated in

[1] Cmd. 4663 (1934).

London. It may well be that the Law Society is going to get into some difficulties in either compelling all non-graduate entrants to go to the College of Law in London or in setting up adequate Colleges in the provinces, and some adjustments may have to be made. The Law Society, like other professional organisations, has bouts of narrow-mindedness, but in the matter of training the Society has made great efforts and is constantly reviewing the position.

I doubt if anything can be said in praise of the Inns of Court in respect of legal education. Over a substantial period they have been wealthy bodies, possessed of good libraries and other facilities. They have been in a better position to run a law school and foster advanced studies than any other organisation in the country. The traditional pattern of a man being called to the Bar and then going into pupillage for a year meant that in fact there was a measure of training. For many years the majority of Bar students have been from overseas. In 1951 the intake was 1251, of whom 842 came from overseas, 438 being from Africa. Virtually nothing was done to see that these entrants were capable of the course of study, or to look after their welfare, or to see that they received adequate training. Pupillage is voluntary, and anyway the chambers of practising barristers could not offer pupillage to such numbers, and there was, and still is, no rule requiring them to get any experience or see anything of practice. Courses of practical instruction, lasting for three or four months, have been provided for newly called barristers, but useful as these may be to men from overseas who cannot find a vacancy as a pupil in chambers, the training still compares unfavourably with that of other professions. For men who are going into pupillage or have recently completed pupillage there are short courses, begun in 1962. Also begun in 1962 is a scheme whereby men from overseas may get some contact with practising members, but it does not amount to much. Overseas countries would have been much better served if the Inns of Court had had some sense of public responsibility, and now a solution is being found in other ways.[1] The Inns are close

[1] The Inns maintained that it was for the local Bar to make requirements as to practical training or pupillage, although it was perfectly well known that no such local requirement could be made. If a student from overseas could go to London, pass examinations in medicine and immediately be given qualifications to practise as a doctor, leaving him to do his practical and hospital work as a voluntary addition (perhaps in a place where it is known that there are no facilities) we should, I think, hardly accept the view that the London end had no responsibility. An inquiry was at last made, Report of the Committee on Legal Education for Students from Africa, Cmnd. 1255 (1961), chairman Lord Denning. The upshot is that much of the training must be done in Africa. *The Times*, 24 May 1962,

corporations, and their finances are their private concern. Any attempt to investigate this state of affairs would be bitterly resented. The Oxford and Cambridge colleges were in a similar position years ago; they resented criticism and regarded inquiry as a monstrous interference with private property, yet Royal Commissions were forced upon them and substantial reforms were carried out. The changes are now regarded as beneficial, and the idea of private property is less prominent than that of public responsibility.

University law schools are not all of one pattern, for professors and lecturers are not regimented or required to work to any national specification. If we look at the subjects that are taught we naturally find that there is a core of contract, tort, property, criminal and constitutional law. Beyond that there is an assortment to taste. There has been endless discussion about curricula, but no clear conclusion has emerged because the process of selecting subjects very soon leads to the fundamental question: what is a university law school trying to do? The underlying assumption of the past, still dominating the present, is that the purpose is to produce future lawyers with a liberal education based on legal studies, so that they will have a wider outlook and be better equipped intellectually. The argument is that the profession needs educated men, and a university is connected with education, not with the techniques of a profession which can and should be acquired elsewhere. The common expression of law teachers is that they are concerned with teaching men 'to think' or 'to think like a lawyer'. The highest expression of this ability is the handling of a problem. A set of facts must be examined to see what is relevant and where the uncertainties lie. A mass of law, principally contained in decided cases, must be examined, correlated, formulated into rules and principles, and applied to all the possible interpretations of the factual position. It is a form of training that has been evolved over the years and it has great merits, but it gets stressed far too much. The field of law has become much wider. A vast amount of modern legislation is concerned with the benefits and obligations and burdens of social services and the use of the resources of the community. Legal education largely ignores these great changes. The legal profession has also failed to come to terms with the society in which we now live, though whether the

reporting the appointment of Prof. L. C. B. Gower as adviser to the recently created Nigerian Council of Legal Education, observed that 'The Africans, in fact, unlike the legal profession in England, are implementing the spirit of the Denning Report with lightning rapidity.'

failure is due to the taught tradition[1] or to other causes is hard to say. There is a strong case for reviewing the work of university law schools solely for the future good of the legal profession, but the course of social events has added a further reason. The old assumption was that most of the students in law schools were going to practise. Nowadays a large proportion do not intend to practise; they are going into the public service, into accountancy and other professions, and into business, and in some law schools they are the majority of the students. It is an admirable development, but if a man is to have an education based on study of the law and institutions of this country and of the international order (which seems to me to be a very sensible thing to do in a university) he needs a school that is more concerned with contemporary society.

It is often thought that the way to widen a training is to put in some other subjects, and that a lawyer should make some study of political science, economics, psychology, sociology and maybe other things. Apart from limitations of time and of capacity, we cannot design a law course except in relation to the rest of higher education. If we could make a new start we might say that the social sciences all deal with man in society, and hence there should be a common basic education to precede specialisation in any particular branch. If that were the approach we should discover the extent of the common ground and how to teach it, but specialisation from school onwards takes us further away from such ideas. Inasmuch as our law schools suffer from this, so do other schools of social science, and we can get no cure for our deficiency by turning to people who are similarly afflicted. The major problem of law schools is that of the law: the making of adjustments between stability and change. The trouble is not an absence of new ideas but the dominance of the old men of the law, the supporters of outworn tradition, for they are to be found in law schools as well as on the Bench and among the practitioners.

Teaching in universities is largely influenced by the type of research work done by the teaching staff. Our law schools have been dominated by the traditional attitude to common law simply because most of the research of law teachers has been in that field. Until recently there has been very little research from law schools in this country on matters of administration of law, although work done in American universities has shown that a law school may be an excellent centre for such inquiries. In the Second World War it is not too much to say

[1] See pp. 356 et seq., below.

that problems of social policy became matters upon which winning or losing the war might depend, and their importance has hardly lessened in the post-war struggle for existence.[1] The result was that money became available for social studies. The Legal Education Committee of 1934[2] found a great dearth of facilities for the promotion of legal research and advanced legal studies, and recommended the founding of an Institute of Advanced Legal Studies. Such an Institute was established by the University of London in 1948. The post-war period has also seen the beginning of field studies into the administration of the law.[3] If this kind of work continues (as it certainly will if money is available) there will be an increasing number of law teachers who have been concerned with such research, and their interests will lie more in the effects of law and its administration than in the evolution of legal rules. But the common lawyer of traditional pattern is in no danger; he needs to be supplemented rather than ousted, which is after all a process for which there are weighty precedents from the old Court of Chancery.

4. SHOULD THE PROFESSION CONTINUE TO BE DIVIDED INTO BARRISTERS AND SOLICITORS?

The distinction between the bar and solicitors is on the face of it somewhat odd. There is nothing peculiar in having specialists within a profession, but it is unusual to find that the citizen is obliged to employ two men to do the work that he would willingly entrust to one of them. The process of specialisation occurs among solicitors; the practice of some firms is virtually confined to a few matters, whilst in others one partner is a specialist. Advocacy in the lower courts may be the special work of a solicitor just as advocacy in higher courts may be the only strong point of a barrister. As well as the general division between the common law and the

---

[1] *Problems in Social Policy* (1950) by R. M. Titmuss, a volume of the official History of the Second World War.

[2] Cmd. 4663.

[3] The Department of Criminal Science, now the Institute of Criminology, in the Law Faculty of Cambridge, has been engaged upon work of this nature. The results of a study of *Detention in Remand Homes* (1952) (vol. VII of *English Studies in Criminal Science*) were circulated by the Home Office to all Magistrates' Courts with a letter saying: 'Reliable factual information regarding the outcome of treatment has hitherto been difficult to obtain; and the conclusions of this research will, the Secretary of State hopes, be not only of interest to all Juvenile Court Justices but also of practical value to them in selecting the appropriate form of treatment to secure the welfare of those appearing before them.'

chancery bar, there is further specialisation. For consultative work there is no reason why the specialist should be a barrister, or even have any legal qualifications. A layman who wants legal advice may have to go to a solicitor in some cases, whilst in others he can consult other people such as tax experts and accountants. If a solicitor wants expert advice he can go to anyone he likes; one of the tax experts in London who is often consulted by solicitors is a man without any legal qualifications. The advantage of 'taking counsel's opinion' is that the barrister who advises takes a certain responsibility, in that he may be called upon to argue the case if it should go before the courts. Where advocacy is concerned, there is generally some advantage in the case being presented by a man who has not prepared it. In working up a case a solicitor may lose objectivity in outlook; when you know your client and are quite certain that he is telling the truth it may become difficult to realise that a court may see the matter in an entirely different light. In litigation the most important faculty, from the viewpoint of the client's interest, is ability to forecast what a court will do. In fact, law itself can be described as the bases of predictions of what judges will say and do. The best estimate of the probable course of a case can be made by a man who looks at it in an impersonal way. If the greater efficiency of separate persons to prepare and present a case is admitted, this does not settle the question, for we must consider the cost. This is most difficult, for cases vary so much. I should say that looking at this from the solicitor's end one might distinguish three kinds of case. (a) There are small cases, in Magistrates' Courts and in County Courts in London and some other areas where it may be cheaper for the client if counsel is briefed; the fee of junior counsel not yet established in practice is low, the solicitor does not himself have to waste hours in waiting about but can send a clerk to 'Hold the brief', and the client may be as satisfied as a litigant can ever be. (b) There are many cases that a solicitor knows he could handle perfectly well, such as undefended divorces and the general run of Quarter Sessions cases, but which he is not allowed to take. In cases of no more complexity than these a solicitor with a case at his finger tips could deal with it without all the preparation of a brief that has to take place when counsel must be briefed. The rules here are as arbitrary as in trade union demarcation disputes in shipyards. (c) There are the more difficult cases. Of course it sometimes happens that a solicitor who has spent a long time over an involved case is in a better position to present it, and then he may have the mortification of seeing counsel floundering badly. In such a case the solicitor will nearly always be in court whilst the case is heard, and he must in practice spend nearly as much time over the case as he would do if he were able to conduct it altogether. Here the use of counsel does put up the cost, but it may well be worth it on the basis that counsel is a specialist in presenting cases.

If the bar and the solicitors were fused, it is probable that there would be a slight reduction in cost. I doubt if the saving would be as drastic as some people think. Specialisation would still be needed. Either firms would become much larger, so that the more common forms of specialised work would be done by a particular partner, or else the specialist in one firm would be 'briefed' by another firm. If the total number of professional men is to remain about the same, and their standard of living is not to be lowered, the cost to litigants will hardly change. There may be a certain saving in overhead costs when a particular type of legal work is done on a larger scale; at present most solicitors regard litigation as profitable if they have many actions to conduct and rather a nuisance if litigious matters only come to their office occasionally. Large firms in a combined profession might effect some further economy, but this would not solve the problem of the cost of litigation; in any case the payments to witnesses and other heavy out-of-pocket expenses would not be affected by such a re-organisation of the legal profession.[1]

The objection to fusion is nearly always made on the ground that specialisation is necessary. But the present system, regarded as providing specialists, is absurd. Medical, engineering and other specialists are men who acquired general practitioner qualifications, and then specialised. A young barrister is only too glad to get any work, yet solicitors (who may themselves be specialists) are supposed to regard him as a specialist. If all lawyers had to go through the same training, and they all had to become general practitioners, some of them later leaving general practice to become specialists, the arguments would be a bit more convincing.

There is one reason for maintaining a separate bar that is not much discussed, and that is connected with the 'cab-rank' principle.[2] Where there is only one profession, a firm of lawyers (like solicitors here) is free to decline to act for a particular person; some one who is unpopular for social, political, racial or other grounds, or who wants to attack some trade or industrial interests, may find that the legal

¹ See p. 300, below.
² See p. 245, above.

254

firms of great reputation all regret that they cannot help him because of the interests of their other clients. In our system such a man can always have the service of eminent counsel (if he can afford it); the 'cab-rank' principle means that counsel who appear on one side might just as well have been on the other side if their brief had got in first. In criminal courts a small number of counsel may be found sharing the work, sometimes prosecuting and sometimes defending. It is a merit, though like the merit of offering specialised services it does not imply that the whole of the existing state of affairs must be maintained.

It is sometimes said that an advantage of having a separate Bar is that it consists of a relatively small number of men, less than 2000 altogether. Barristers are often well known to the courts before which they practise, and often the proper conduct of an action depends upon the judge feeling that he can trust the barrister; in cases that are uncontested such as most divorce cases, or are more in the nature of applications to the court for assistance or leave, as in many chancery cases, the judge must largely rely upon the integrity of counsel. The inference is not that barristers are more honourable than solicitors, for there are no grounds for such a supposition, but that a small number of practitioners is more easily known than a large number. The limitation of numbers also facilitates the selection of judges. These objections are not fatal to the idea of a combined profession.

The public gain from fusion is so problematical that compulsion by legislation could hardly be justified, and fusion by agreement seems most unlikely. The Bar means practising barristers, and that means private practice, and the successful men do not ordinarily want any changes. Every now and then there is a depression at the Bar; there was, for example, great moaning in the latter part of 1959 when it was being said that incomes were down and young men were not going to the profession. The Lord Chief Justice said that partnerships for counsel might be a good thing.[1] Since then there has been almost a boom at the Bar; legal aid in civil and criminal cases has increased, and costs risen, putting hundreds of thousands of pounds more a year into legal pockets. There have been an unprecedented number of appointments to the Bench and to lesser judicial positions that carry better pay. Reforms are forgotten, and any successful barrister is ready to explain precisely why the present structure is best for litigants, best for the public and must not be altered. Solicitors

[1] *The Times*, 11 November 1959. Correspondence followed, and a *Times* leader on 10 December 1959 came out roundly in favour of reform.

are in a different position. There are some 17,500 in private practice, 1550 in local government, and a substantial number (perhaps 1800)[1] in industry and trade. The salaried posts include many very important positions. The salaried men are as much members of the profession as those in private practice; in 1962 the President of the Law Society and four members of its Council held full-time appointments outside private practice. To judge by articles and correspondence in the *Law Society's Gazette*, there are a number of solicitors who would favour fusion, some of them having had experience of law practice overseas, but most solicitors are not much interested either way, for it is seen as hardly a live issue. An issue that is alive is the possibility of a common legal education and examination system; it is possible at present to change from being a solicitor and be called to the Bar, and for there to be transfers the other way, but examinations are different. A better solution, hardly practicable in the present climate of opinion, would be a common training from which everyone would become a solicitor to begin with; from that general profession some members would become specialists, advocates and consultants, and they would be the Bar with their own organisation and code of conduct. If we had gone into the Common Market there might have been a flare up, because solicitors would have asserted that their position is similar to that of some continental lawyers who have a right of audience.

5. JUDGES

The judges of the High Court, the Court of Appeal, and the House of Lords, commonly called the superior judges, are appointed by the Crown acting upon the advice of the appropriate minister. For practical purposes the appointment can be regarded as being in the hands of the minister concerned, who may of course consult his colleagues. The Lord Chancellor, who is nominated by the Prime Minister, occupies an anomalous position. For some purposes he is the head of the judiciary and his powers are extensive, yet he is invariably a member of the cabinet. As a cabinet minister the Lord Chancellor holds office upon the usual political terms, which means that ordinarily he will vacate office if the government changes. Hence when there is a change of government the new Prime Minister will have to fill the office of Lord Chancellor just as he has to fill the

---

[1] There is an estimate of the number of lawyers in legal positions in an Appendix to G. S. A. Wheatcroft, 'The Education and Training of the Modern Lawyer' in 7 *Journal S.P.T.L.* (1962), p. 1.

office of Chancellor of the Exchequer, Home Secretary and so on. The choice of a Lord Chancellor must be made from among those barristers who have adequate standing, but within this range the choice is governed by political considerations; the Prime Minister wants someone who will perform the judicial functions adequately and who will also be a welcome addition to the cabinet. A barrister who has rendered service to a political party may find his reward in being made Lord Chancellor when his party gets into office. That monumental work, Campbell's *Lives of the Lord Chancellors*, is as much a political as a legal history of England. An ordinary judgeship is a permanent appointment, whereas he who achieves the Lord Chancellorship may rejoice in his peerage, his salary of £12,000, and his great dignity, only to find that his political party is turned out of office and that he is now an ex-Lord Chancellor with a pension and a conventional obligation to make himself useful in judicial work. A departure from strict two-party politics may give somewhat different results. When Ramsay Macdonald formed a Labour government in 1929 he chose Lord Sankey (a Liberal) as Lord Chancellor; when that government became a coalition predominantly conservative Lord Sankey remained as Lord Chancellor; later, on a cabinet reshuffle, he was replaced by Lord Hailsham. Lord Sankey at the time of his appointment was a Lord Justice; he had not at any time been noticeably active in party politics. Lord Maugham, appointed in 1938, and Lord Simonds, appointed in 1951, were Law Lords who had never been particularly active in politics. Such appointments provide Lord Chancellors who are already experienced in judicial work but who lack that experience of government that comes from the more usual course of party and the House of Commons. Of course a Lord Chancellor who is primarily a lawyer and secondarily a politician must at least be in sympathy with the political views of the cabinet in which he serves; a Lord Chancellor can never be 'non-political'. A fuller account of the position and duties of the Lord Chancellor is given later;[1] I have here emphasised his connection with political circles because of its bearing upon other judicial appointments. The nominations to all vacancies among the superior judges are made either by the Prime Minister or by the Lord Chancellor. The Prime Minister nominates the Law Lords, the Lords Justices of Appeal, the Lord Chief Justice, the Master of the Rolls, and the President of the Probate Divorce and Admiralty Division. It is commonly assumed that the Prime Minister is guided by the

[1] See p. 411, below.

Lord Chancellor. The ordinary judges of the High Court, often called puisne judges,[1] are nominated by the Lord Chancellor. The Lord Chancellor is responsible for the lesser judicial appointments.[2]

A puisne judge of the High Court must be a barrister of at least ten years' standing. A barrister of at least fifteen years' standing, or an existing High Court judge, qualifies for appointment as a Lord Justice of Appeal. The qualifications for a Lord Justice of Appeal, or being a judge of the Court of Appeal, qualifies for appointment as Lord Chief Justice, Master of the Rolls, or President of the Probate Division. The Lords of Appeal in Ordinary (the Law Lords) must be appointed from barristers or advocates of fifteen years' standing or persons who have held high judicial office in England, Scotland or Northern Ireland for two years. Since most barristers begin to practise when they are still young men, and judges are never appointed from those under forty and quite often from those over fifty, the requisite standing at the Bar is usually attained many years before there is any chance of judicial appointment. All the superior judges other than the Lord Chancellor hold office 'during good behaviour subject to a power of removal by His Majesty on an address presented to His Majesty by both Houses of Parliament', this being the provision of the Judicature (Consolidation) Act 1925 which derives through the 1875 Act from the Act of Settlement of 1701. There may be a petition to either House, or the matter may originate with a member, there being some authority for saying that it must be in the Commons. The charge against the judge must be formulated and he must be given an opportunity to answer the charges. As no English judge has been removed since the Act of Settlement there is little authority for stating the procedure, and the interpretation of the statute is by no means certain.[3] On any

---

[1] Before the Judicature Acts 1873–5 the Courts of King's Bench and Common Pleas each had a Chief Justice, whilst the Court of Exchequer had a Chief Baron. The other judges of these courts were called puisne judges. At present each division of the High Court has its head, so that the puisne judges are the High Court judges other than the Lord Chief Justice, the Lord Chancellor, and the President of the Probate Divorce and Admiralty Division.

[2] For county courts, see p. 28; for recorders, see p. 99; for lay justices, see p. 160; for stipendiary magistrates, see p. 174; see also p. 387 on appointments to special tribunals.

[3] Judges are appointed by letters patent under the Great Seal. If there were no mention of an address by both Houses, it would appear that an appointment could be terminated only by cancelling the letters patent, and that had to be done by a judicial process called *scire facias*. That writ was abolished by the Crown Proceedings Act 1947 and presumably the procedure would now be by motion in the Queen's Bench Division. In that judicial process the ground for cancellation

interpretation the provisions do what they were intended to do when they were first formulated in the Act of Settlement, that is, secure the independence of the judges from the executive. The judges are not protected in any way from change made by statute; Parliament can alter the terms upon which they hold office, alter their salaries, or make any other change. The cabinet system of government has for some years meant that the distinction between executive and legislature is thoroughly blurred. The cabinet, considered as a group of ministers of the Crown, cannot interfere with the judges; the cabinet considered as the leaders of a political party with a sufficient majority can interfere with the judges by causing the passing of appropriate legislation. By convention a judge may not be criticised in Parliament unless there is a motion for an address for his removal: a decision of the courts may be criticised, but only upon the supposition that the complaint is about the law and not about the conduct of the judge. Statute also lays down the number of judges that may be appointed and their salaries and pensions. The numbers of judges have been mentioned in describing the various courts. The prescribed amounts are: Lord Chancellor £12,000 (£8000 as a judge and £4000 as Speaker of the House of Lords), Lord Chief Justice £10,000, Lords of Appeal and the Master of the Rolls £9000, whilst the Lords Justices of Appeal and the other superior judges receive £8000. These amounts are charged upon the Consolidated Fund, the older constitutional law books explaining that this secures the payment of the judges even if Parliament does not meet. The point today is that the statute providing for these payments remains in force until it is repealed, so that the payments to judges, unlike the payment of the civil service and the armed forces, do not have to be discussed each year and be authorised by annual votes.

Appointments to the bench are in the long run largely controlled by conditions at the Bar. The pattern was formed in days when professional earnings were higher, taxation much lower, and money appeared to have a stable value. The old conditions still haunt the

would be 'misbehaviour', which means (a) in the execution of office, as by failure to attend or refusal or neglect of duties, or (b) scandalous behaviour in his private capacity. It is not clear whether the power to remove after an address replaces the common law meaning of 'good behaviour', in which case there must always be an address, and it is for Parliament to decide what constitutes 'misbehaviour'. I think that the power to remove after an address is additional to the common law. It is a principle of construction that judicial process is not abolished except by clear words, and the word 'but' in the Act of Settlement and the words 'subject to' in the later statutes are quite consistent with the power upon an address being separate from and additional to the common law process.

Inns and the Law Courts. From the barrister's point of view a judgeship was not necessarily desirable. A successful barrister might well be making a good deal more than a judge's salary, and when he was approached with the possibility of a judgeship he might feel that he could not face a substantial drop in income. On the other hand, the successful man is working to the limits of his capacity and sooner or later he must relax the tension. It is, however, singularly difficult to reduce a practice without causing the practice to collapse; practices are apt either to grow or decline. At the age of forty-five a judgeship may be unattractive, whereas at fifty-five the position may be very different: the extra years of earning high fees would have put the barrister into a good financial position, and life on the bench would be a welcome relief and at the same time constitute an insurance against the inevitable decline in practice that must occur if a man continues at the Bar when he is growing old. Of course some appointments were made from among men who were earning less than a judge's salary, but it is the conditions of the more successful men that have settled the normal practice. It is sometimes thought that the substantial salaries paid to our judges were designed to lessen the chance of corruption by putting a judge into a position where he is not likely to be tempted. There is no evidence that the far lower salaries of French judges lead to corruption; the French judge by entering the judicial profession when he is under thirty belongs to a State judicial service, and his salary is fixed in accordance with the salaries paid in other forms of the public service. In England we have had to tempt men to leave private practice of a lucrative nature, and this is the reason for the salary; corruption is eliminated by professional tradition, which is perhaps the only effective method under any system.

The Bar has been having a difficult time financially since the war. In common with other people who live by fees and similar payments, the tax structure has been disadvantageous. A barrister may have one or two lucky years, though his average may be modest, but the good years are taxed at too high a level to let him eke out the lean years. He cannot be in a firm or partnership, and hence he cannot build up a capital asset. Employers could provide superannuation schemes for their employees, but the 'self-employed' had no such advantages until a tax concession was given in 1956. It is difficult to be sure about earnings at the Bar but such figures as are available[1]

[1] A review of common law chambers was published in *The Times*, 13 August 1953 and the Attorney-General said that the position 'had not much improved'

suggest that the analysis in the last paragraph is still applicable. Barristers have a much greater range of income than solicitors and medical men; the not particularly successful barrister does not do as well as those in other professions whilst the successful barrister does a lot better. Another difference is that solicitors and medical consultants tend to have a steady rise in income all the way through their working years whereas barristers (like dentists) begin to earn appreciably less when they get past about fifty-five. A successful middle-aged barrister may still drop in income after he accepts a judgeship, but the gap is smaller than it used to be. He cannot save as his predecessors did during the years of high earning in practice, although he may since 1956 provide for his own retirement. What he has to think about is not so much his position at present as what it will be in ten or fifteen or more years time. High Court judges' salaries were fixed at £5000 under William IV, and remained unaltered until the Judges' Remuneration Act 1954 raised the figure to £8000. A judgeship used to be regarded as a very highly paid position, whereas it is now in the higher level of salaries but carries no more than is paid to, say, the chairman of a national board. But to a barrister the old balance has altered in favour of a judgeship; the prestige and dignity still count, whilst the income and the high security of the superannuation are better than he would have achieved if he had stayed in private practice.

An important question is whether politics enter into the appointment of judges, not in the sense of appointing a man simply because of his politics, but of whether the choice between possible candidates has been influenced by party considerations. Here it seems quite impossible to deny that in the past there has been much attention paid to the claims of party. Out of 139 appointments made between 1832 and 1906, eighty of those appointed were members of Parliament at the time of their appointment, and of these sixty-three were appointed whilst their party was in office, leaving a mere seventeen appointments made from those in political opposition.[1] The obituary notices of judges published in *The Times* have pointed out whether the judicial appointment was due to professional standing or political

two years later (*The Times*, 12 July 1955). Much information is given in the Report of the Royal Commission on Doctors' and Dentists' Remuneration, Cmnd. 939 (1960). Some of this material is given in a convenient form by R. E. Megarry, *Lawyer and Litigant in England* (1962), p. 184.

[1] These figures are given by H. J. Laski in an essay on 'The Technique of Judicial Appointment' published in *Studies in Law and Politics*: it is the only thorough investigation that has been published.

services: we find that 'The Bar, however, did not regard him as a likely candidate for judicial honours till his astonishing Parliamentary success at the General Election...', or that 'On its merits the appointment was welcomed by the Bar...moreover he had some political claim on the party in power'.[1] The most obvious use of judgeships as political rewards arose with the Law Officers. Each government appoints an Attorney-General and a Solicitor-General, who are practising barristers normally with Parliamentary seats. The functions of the Law Officers are to advise the government in legal matters and to conduct important litigation. The job of an Attorney-General is to support his party in power; he is avowedly a partisan who is expected to fight for the government with all the zeal he can show. Yet an absurd convention of relatively modern origin gave the Attorney-General a first claim on the highly coveted office of Lord Chief Justice if that office became vacant.[2] The fierce opponent of a minority might in the course of a week shed his counsel's wig and gown and appear in scarlet robes to hold the scales of justice between those he had so recently denounced and those he had so recently supported. The practice has undoubtedly changed, and for some years there has been no sign of party politics in judicial appointments, though in respect of the Lord Chief Justiceship it can be said that political appointments lasted longer than for other offices: a long series of appointments of persons holding the office of Attorney-General or other government office was broken in 1946 when Lord Goddard was made Lord Chief Justice, for he was then a Law Lord who had been in turn a King's Bench judge and a Lord Justice. This new precedent was followed on Lord Goddard's retirement in 1958, for his successor, Lord Parker, was a Lord Justice. It must not be supposed from these references to party politics that there ought to be any ban upon the appointment of barristers who have been in the House of Commons or otherwise active in politics; it is even the other way round, that our bench

[1] *The Times*, 21 August 1934 and 26 July 1938.
[2] When the Lord Chief Justiceship fell vacant in 1921 Gordon Hewart was Attorney-General, but the state of Lloyd George's government was such that he did not care to lose his efficient Attorney-General and risk losing a by-election. Hence a High Court judge aged 78 was appointed to keep the place warm, and on his retirement in 1922 Lord Hewart was appointed. He was followed in 1940 by Lord Caldecote, who had filled a succession of offices, including that of Co-ordination of Defence. Lord Caldecote as Lord Chief Justice did remember (as Lord Hewart sometimes failed to do) that he was on the bench and not still at the Bar, and as a judge he earned the respect of many people who in the days when he was co-ordinating defence were apt to refer to Caligula's Horse.

gains from having some judges who have been much concerned with political life.[1] There are really two propositions. The first is that politics should be disregarded in making appointments, and the second is that a man should not be taken from the office of Attorney-General or other ministerial office to go straight upon the bench if that can reasonably be avoided.[2] There is no evidence that disregard of these principles will lead to biased decisions. It is implicit in the notion of political debts that accounts can be settled. A judgeship means the end of a career at the Bar or in politics; there is no recent instance of a judge resigning and going back to practice or to politics, although it can hardly be said that he may not do so. There has been no apparent connection in the last hundred years between the political antecedents and the decisions of judges. The point is primarily one of public confidence, that people may feel sure that those on the bench have been appointed for legal eminence and suitability and not for political reward or by way of disposing of an embarrassing colleague.

There is no regular practice in England of promoting judges. Since the creation of County Courts in 1846 there had been only one County Court judge who had been promoted to the High Court until the immediate post-war years when three County Court judges and the judge of the Salford Hundred Court were appointed to the High Court. Among the superior judges there may be promotion from the High Court to the Court of Appeal, or from the High Court or the Court of Appeal to the House of Lords. The scale of salaries given above shows that there is little financial gain, except in the case of the Lord Chancellor and the Lord Chief Justice, whilst between the High Court and the Court of Appeal there is no change in salary.[3] An appointment may be made direct to any of the courts, or the vacancy may be filled by promotion. Since the High Court judges are mostly engaged upon the original hearing of cases and the other judges are confined to appellate work there may well be sound reasons for filling a vacancy in the Court of Appeal or the House of Lords by an appointment from the Bar rather than by a promotion from the High Court: a good trial judge does not neces-

[1] Lord Haldane thought experience in the House of Commons helped 'in checking the danger of abstractness in mental outlook' (*Autobiography* (1931), p. 69).

[2] In 1962 Sir J. Simon, then Solicitor-General, was appointed President of the Probate Divorce and Admiralty Division; a good appointment may be unfortunate as a precedent.

[3] There is a traditional story that when the Judicature Act was being framed the judges were consulted as to whether the judges of the Court of Appeal should be distinguished from those of the High Court by having an extra £500 a year or by being made Privy Councillors, and they chose the latter.

sarily make a good judge of appeals, and vice versa. There is much to be said for not having a system of promotion. When a man is on the bench he should be as independent as possible: there is a tendency, for historical reasons, to suppose that the sole need is to make it impossible for the executive to interfere with the judiciary, and to overlook other possibilities. The desire for promotion has probably been the weakest part of the French judiciary; a lesser judge may feel that unless he does something to attract the heads of his service he may be passed over and left in his present grade.

Until the Judicial Pensions Act was passed in December 1959, there was no retiring age for our superior judges. For new appointments there is now a retiring age of seventy-five, with corresponding changes in the entitlement to pension; judges appointed before this Act may continue under the old law or opt to come within the new provisions. The question of a retiring age for judges has been discussed for a number of years. County Court judges have for long been subject to a retiring age of seventy-two with possible extensions to seventy-five. Justices of the peace now retire at seventy-five. Retirement at sixty-seven, sixty-five and sixty, with extensions, has been adopted for university professors and other officers, local government officials and civil servants. It is hard to find a generally acceptable figure. Some retiring ages were fixed in the past with one eye on the state of employment and the other on facilities for promotion. With full employment it seems that sixty-five gets rid of too many men who are still good at their work. Observation suggests that among the professional class it is common to find people who carry their full faculties past seventy, but often not as late as seventy-five. There is much to be said for seventy-two, but as Parliament has accepted seventy-five as the maximum for County Court judges and justices of the peace it was hardly possible to go to a lower figure for the superior judges.

A superior judge could be removed on an address if he became incapacitated by senility, but apart from this before the new Act there was nothing to stop him sitting in extreme old age. Lord Hewart, a former Lord Chief Justice, was reported as saying: 'I shall never resign or retire as long as I live.'[1] The introduction of a retiring age was discussed by the Royal Commission on the Despatch of Business at Common Law 1934-6.[2] The Commissioners pointed out that there was some inducement for an elderly judge to retire,

---

[1] *The Times*, 24 November 1933.
[2] Cmd. 5065 (1936).

since he became entitled to a pension after fifteen years' service, and that the Lord Chancellor may privately urge a judge to retire. With two dissentient members the Commission recommended the introduction of a compulsory retiring age of seventy-two. A discretion to extend the age, such as exists for County Court judges, was thought unsuitable for the superior judges because it would involve invidious distinctions. In his evidence before the Commission, Lord Hewart vigorously opposed a retiring age, pointing out that it would deprive the bench of such men as Mr Justice Avory. Anyone who listened to Mr Justice Avory in his last years—he continued to sit on the bench until a few days before his death at the age of eighty-three—must admit that he retained his faculties unimpaired. The greatest judge there has ever been in the common law countries was Oliver Wendell Holmes of the American Supreme Court, who was nearly ninety before he retired from the bench in 1932. A retiring age is bound to exclude men who have years of good work before them, and at the same time it is no guarantee that men whose faculties become dimmed at an earlier age will not retain an office that they ought to relinquish. The sound argument for a retiring age is that judges must inspire confidence, and that on the whole people do not care to be judged by those who belong to a generation that is generally inactive. It was difficult to escape the feeling in Mr Justice Avory's court that a man so old should have no place of power in society. But a retiring age, at whatever figure it is fixed, is no guarantee that men whose faculties become dimmed at an earlier age will not retain an office that they ought to relinquish. The old provision for a pension after fifteen years' service, or earlier in the case of disability, was unsatisfactory, for a judge whose health and vigour was impaired, but who was still able to sit, was naturally inclined to struggle along until he qualified for pension. Under the 1959 Act pensions are on a graduated scale, starting with one-quarter of the last annual salary in the case of a judge who retires after five years' service or less, and rising by annual increments of one-fortieth to a maximum of one-half of the last annual salary after fifteen years.[1] A judge may elect to retire when he becomes seventy, and he will then receive the graduated pension to which his length of service entitles him. The pension payable to an ex-Lord Chancellor is increased from £3750 to £5000, irrespective of the length of time that the recipient held office: the explanation is that an ex-Lord

[1] There is also a lump sum and a measure of security for dependants (see p. 29, above).

Chancellor cannot go back to private legal practice, and there is, as the Solicitor-General explained, a 'moral compulsion' on him to sit in the House of Lords in its judicial capacity and as a member of the Judicial Committee of the Privy Council. When, however, Lord Kilmuir ceased to be Lord Chancellor in 1962 and soon afterwards accepted a commercial appointment, the Prime Minister took the line that an ex-Lord Chancellor who does not choose to receive his pension may accept such a post, and that Lord Kilmuir was not drawing pension.

English conditions tend to produce a certain measure of uniformity in the outlook of the judges. It is the most difficult thing to analyse. Judges are of different political faiths, different religions or agnostic, and have varying degrees of intelligence and cultural attainments. Yet there is something that enables us to talk about the judges almost as we do about the cabinet, tacitly postulating a body of men whose varying inclinations will appear homogeneous. This is not strange when we remember that the judges have had careers that are in outline similar. Generally there has been a period at a university, followed by call to the Bar, perhaps some politics, becoming a King's Counsel, and then the Bench. Invariably there has been success at the Bar. Now the Bar is one of the few openings left in which a man with a few hundred pounds may possibly rise by his own personal exertions to a position of great eminence. The vigorous individualism by which men in a small way could become great manufacturers largely belongs to a past economic order. The classic Victorian precepts for success in life survive at the Bar. Other professions tend to produce individualists, but the conditions are less propitious (except for film stars). Successful barristers, and hence the judges, are not likely to be very critical of the legal order. The existing system has brought them large incomes and position and has produced a disposition to resent change. The appointment of judges fairly late in life, and their continuance on the bench as elderly men, strengthens this tendency. A noticeable trait is 'touchiness' about their own position. The House of Lords debates on 11 and 14 December 1934 may be instanced. The Lord Chancellor moved the second reading of a bill to increase the strength of the King's Bench Division and to allow the Lord Chancellor to appoint a vice-president of the Court of Appeal. The Court of Appeal had for years been sitting in two divisions, one presided over by the Master of the Rolls and the other by the senior Lord Justice. It was clear that Lord Justice Slesser might soon come to preside over one of the courts. Hence if the bill went through it would be possible for the Lord Chancellor to nominate another Lord Justice as vice-president and so deprive Lord Justice Slesser of the dignity due to his seniority. Since Lord Justice Slesser was appointed by a Labour government it might produce the impression that the bill was designed to enable the government to secure a political sympathiser as vice-president. Clearly this aspect of the bill required discussion, but it did not necessitate the charges that were made by Lord Hewart, the Lord Chief Justice.[1] Lord Hewart appeared to take the view that there had been a long-standing plot (hatched among part of the civil service and fostered by Royal Commissions) to alter the position of the judiciary. The Royal Commission on the Despatch of Business at Common Law, which had dared to suggest some changes in the organisation of the courts, was placed foremost among the sinister influences. Apparently Lord Justice Slesser had consulted Lord Hewart, who declined to advise him; Lord Hewart did, however, say that if he were placed in such a position he would not retire but would just decline to sit. In the whole of this remarkable outburst there was no appreciation of the fact that the judiciary exists for the public service and not for its own glorification. It may be said that the temper of the judiciary cannot be judged by the views of one particular judge. The reader may draw his own conclusion from this: the Judicature Act 1873–5 provided for a conference of the judges to be held from time to time, the idea being that the judges might make proposals on matters where change is needed; in over fifty years not a single suggestion for change has come from the judiciary as a body.[2]

A more serious matter is the clash that has often occurred between the ideas of judges and modern social tendencies. For many years now Parliament has been passing legislation that is often called

[1] All the superior judges are summoned to the House of Lords, but the summons is merely 'to advise', and ordinary judges do not attend unless their advice is actually sought. The Lords of Appeal are life peers. The Lord Chancellor is a hereditary peer. Other judges may receive peerages, it being customary to give a peerage to the Lord Chief Justice; Lord Hewart's membership of the House of Lords was due to his peerage and not to his office. The title of the judges of the Court of Appeal, viz. Lord Justice, is misleading, for their office does not make them 'lords' in the sense of peers.

[2] In 1892 the judges set up a committee of themselves; the committee sat every day after court for four months, and its Report was adopted by the judges after a three-day debate. There were about a hundred proposals, and these were explained in two articles in *The Times* entitled 'The Judges' Reforms, by a Member of the Bench', the author being Lord Bowen. In later times individual judges have worked hard for law reform, and many Committees and Royal Commissions have produced better Reports for having a judge as chairman.

'social'. The common law is on the whole highly individualistic, upholding the liberty of men to enter into such contracts as they see fit and allowing property owners to do what they like with their own, subject of course to certain limitations. Modern legislation often cuts across these ideas: statutes regulating conditions of employment and statutes aimed at slum clearance and a better standard of housing obviously conflict with the policy of the common law. In interpreting such statutes the judges make a curious assumption. If a layman studies a statute aimed at slum clearance he would come to the conclusion that Parliament meant what it said, and that the core of the matter was an explicit intention to interfere with property rights by compulsory measures, with compensation. In fact, it is generally taken for granted that social legislation is meant to interfere or control; the political battles are about monetary compensation. Yet when one of these statutes comes before the courts the process is this: 'The common law upholds freedom of contract and rights of property; we presume that Parliament means to legislate in accordance with existing law; therefore we will start by assuming that Parliament did not intend to alter freedom of contract or rights of property.' It is not surprising that with such an assumption the courts have often succeeded in wrecking a statute.[1] This has been one of the results of a too rigid theory of precedent: the courts have applied canons of construction originally derived from a philosophy of individualism or *laissez faire* in a society that has abandoned that philosophy for over half a century. It is important to note that this has not been a matter of party politics. Some of the clearest instances of judicial interpretation contrary to what most people would have said was the obvious meaning of the Act came between the wars; it was legislation passed by Conservative votes that was interpreted in a way that was infuriating to a Conservative-controlled administration. One result was that certain types of legislation

[1] See Llewelyn Davies, 'The interpretation of Statutes in the light of their policy by the English Courts', 35 *Columbia Law Review* (1935), p. 519; Jennings, 'Courts and Administrative Law', 49 *Harvard Law Review* (1936), p. 426. In *Fisher* v. *Bell* [1961] 1 Q.B. 394, the defendant had displayed in his shop window a flick-knife with a ticket 'Ejector Knife—4s.'. Under the Restriction of Offensive Weapons Act 1959 it is an offence to 'offer for sale' such a knife. Lord Parker L.C.J. holding that no offence had been committed said: 'Parliament in its wisdom in passing an Act must be taken to know the general law...the display of an article with a price on it in a shop window is merely an invitation to treat. It is in no sense an offer for sale the acceptance of which constitutes a contract.' Some day a judge may go into a supermarket and find it very difficult to buy anything for he will know that nothing he sees is offered for sale, and the attendants may misunderstand him when he speaks of an invitation to treat.

became a curious battle of drafting. The attitude of the judges was; 'If you frame statutes properly we shall interpret them so as to carry out your meaning.' The administrator replied; 'When we drew a statute in plain language you misinterpreted it by making false assumptions; when we drew a statute in highly technical language you said it was unintelligible; now we will tell our draftsmen to try again.' In cases heard during and since the war there has been little complaint about the treatment by the courts of legislation of a collectivist nature. Presumably the judges, like nearly all sections of people, have come to accept some views about public action that would have seemed dangerously revolutionary not so many years ago. Another factor is that there has been less room for administration to come before the courts, for one reaction to certain decisions was to try to make new legislation 'judge-proof' by various methods, the chief of which has been the creation of special jurisdictions.[1]

The notion of a judge being 'impartial' needs more thought than it is commonly given. Strong views (as mentioned on p. 151) may obviously affect decisions, but general outlook and mental habits can have just as much influence without being so noticeable. Whatever the conscious effort to be impartial, and here our judges have a high standard, there is always the 'prejudice' or 'bias' or as Holmes called it the 'inarticulate major premiss' of the judge. The more thoughtful judges recognise the difficulty. Lord Justice Scrutton, in discussing the need for 'impartiality', said:

This is rather difficult to attain in any system. I am not speaking of conscious impartiality; but the habits you are trained in, the people with whom you mix, lead to your having a certain class of ideas of such a nature that, when you have to deal with other ideas, you do not give as sound and accurate judgments as you would wish. This is one of the great difficulties at present with Labour. Labour says: 'Where are your impartial judges? They all move in the same circle as the employers, and they are educated and nursed in the same ideas as the employers. How can a Labour man or a trade unionist get impartial justice?' It is very difficult sometimes to be sure that you have put yourself into a thoroughly impartial position between two disputants, one of your own class and one not of your class. Even in matters outside trade-unionist cases (to some extent in workmen's compensation cases) it is sometimes difficult to be sure, hard as you have tried, that you have put yourself in a perfectly impartial position between the two litigants.[2]

It is sometimes argued that the whole matter is one of social class, for people of working-class origin cannot afford the education and

---

[1] See ch. VI, below.   [2] I *Cambridge Law Journal*, p. 8.

the time of brief-less waiting in the earlier stages at the Bar. Our judges do on the whole come from homes that are not working-class; it would be harder for a working-class man to become a judge than for him to become a high official in a government department. The class factor cannot be ignored, but in its simple form it is not a complete explanation. If we seek for a body of men coming from much the same social class and having had much the same education and nurture as the judges, we may find it in the administrative group of the home civil service, but I cannot find that the administrative class as a whole have the habits of mind discernible in the judges. Similarity of social origin and education may produce similarity of outlook at the end of the first twenty-five years of life, but after a further twenty-five years he who has been at the Bar and he who has become an administrator will have developed a different cast of mind. The muddles over interpretation of the Public Health Acts[1] have been due primarily to the judges not realising what Parliament wanted to do; the conflict was not between employers and workmen but between judges and administrators. The history of the Workmen's Compensation Acts shows the effects of the judicial bias in favour of the common law, for the law of workmen's compensation involved interference with the contract of employment and the imposition of liability without fault. Where it is clear that the community must be protected, as in the provisions against selling adulterated milk, the judges have found no difficulty in interpreting statutes according to the intention of Parliament, even when the result is liability without fault.[2] The judge sees a compensation claim as an issue between two persons, and from this angle the bias is against making *A* pay money to *B* unless *A* is at fault. The administrative mind realises that if an injured workman is not compensated by his employer the cost will fall on public funds; whether it is better to make the employer pay (as under the Workmen's Compensation Acts) or to pay out of a fund partly contributed through weekly stamping of cards and partly from State funds (as under the National Insurance system now in force) is a matter of policy and that is not to be determined by ideas of 'fault'. Social legislation can rarely be comprehended by seeing its effects as solely an issue between two individuals, but the isolated issue is the centre of traditional common law technique. If we turn to the legal battles over trade union

[1] Jennings, 'Judicial Process at its Worst', 1 *Modern Law Review* (1937), p. 111.
[2] Jackson, 'Absolute Prohibition in Statutory Offences', 6 *Cambridge Law Journal* (1936), p. 83.

activity, the judicial record has been none too good,[1] the bias has been against organised labour. In issues where employees are in conflict with employers it is doubtful whether a judiciary trained and selected on the English pattern can be entirely satisfactory. I doubt if anyone who has not been somewhat intimately involved in industrial relations can appreciate the issues that arise; the nuances can be so easily missed, and points of enormous importance in the eyes of a party may seem small or even ridiculous. If the training of lawyers were to be broadened, and if the selection of judges were widened, we should still get this trouble.[2] The answer, I think, is that when we find something that the judiciary does not do very well the best course is to look for some other way of doing it. Industrial relations have evolved the machinery of joint bodies, representatives of employers and of labour, with an essentially negotiating technique. With a lawyer chairman that may be an excellent tribunal for disputes.[3]

It has been customary for lawyers and others to bestow fulsome praises upon the judiciary. Lord Hewart, speaking at the Lord Mayor's Banquet in 1936, said that: 'His Majesty's Judges are satisfied with the almost universal admiration in which they are held.' After making a generous allowance for the prevailing optimism at such functions it was really a remarkable public utterance.[4] Complacency is a dangerous thing. So also is indiscriminate disparagement. Our machinery of justice is likely to continue in much its present form for some years, and improvement is more likely to occur by investigation of its actual working than by apology or abuse.

[1] Jenks, *A Short History of English Law*, 3rd ed., p. 336: 'The decision in the *Taff Vale Case* [1901] apparently made a great change in the law; it threatened to ruin Trade Unionism, by making huge drafts upon its funds. The House of Lords [in its judicial capacity] had first invented a new civil offence ("civil conspiracy"), and had then created a new kind of defendant against whom it could be alleged.' Professor Goodhart's well-known essay on 'The Legality of the General Strike' can now be found in his *Essays in Jurisprudence and the Common Law*. I think most lawyers who have studied the subject accept the accuracy of Webb's *History of Trade Unionism*; this is a far more valuable guide than any purely legal account.

[2] Distinguished academic lawyers, who have seen a fair amount of practice at the Bar, might be appointed to the Court of Appeal. It is believed that this proposal was put before some judges, and that they disapproved of the idea. American experience suggests that such appointments may be very satisfactory.

[3] See pp. 332-8, below.

[4] This famous observation apparently began as an ironical suggestion from Avory J. In his memoirs *Not Without Prejudice* Lord Hewart explained that his 'natural caution' prompted him to insert the word 'almost'.

6. JURIES

Juries are used for some purposes other than the trial of actions. The most familiar instance is a coroner's jury, where the jury is required to make a finding of fact; there is no 'issue' to be tried, for there are no 'parties' before the court.[1] This section is confined to a discussion of trial juries. The middle-class man or woman who carefully avoids litigation, and who never commits a summary offence, not even with a bicycle or a motor-car, and who is in fact a model citizen, may nevertheless find that contact with the courts cannot be avoided: jury service is compulsory.

Opinion about juries has changed. The eulogies of Blackstone[2] are definitely unfashionable. The current opinion is perhaps on these lines: jury trial in civil cases is sometimes satisfactory and sometimes most unsatisfactory, and hence the restriction of jury trial[3] has been a wise development; however, there is much to be said for jury trial in criminal cases and (in the past at least) in cases where the liberty of the subject is concerned.[4]

In the late eighteenth century we get many professions of enthusiasm for trial by jury. Lord Camden said: 'Trial by jury is indeed the foundation of our free constitution; take that away, and the whole fabric will soon moulder into dust. These are the sentiments of my youth—inculcated by precept, improved by experience, and warranted by example.'[5] When Erskine was made Lord Chancellor in 1806 he took 'Trial by Jury' as his motto, although it was said that 'By Bill in Equity' would be more suitable for the Woolsack.[6] Erskine was so enthusiastic about juries that Lord Byron, after sitting next to Erskine at dinner and hearing about little else, felt that juries ought to be abolished.[7] Lord Loughborough, before his appointment as Lord Chancellor, declared that: 'Judges may err, judges may be corrupt. Their minds may be warped by interest, passion, and prejudice. But a jury is not liable to the same misleading influences.'[8] Even Lord Eldon, when he was Solicitor-General and found that for

[1] See p. 110, above.
[2] Bl. *Comm.* III, 379; IV, 343.   [3] See pp. 67–8, above.
[4] Lord Devlin, *Trial by Jury* (1956), is a good modern appraisal. G. Williams, *The Proof of Guilt* (3rd ed. 1963), has a chapter on jury trial, generally adverse. Lord Devlin writes from observation, Dr Williams from authorities ranging from *Law Reports* to the *Daily Mirror* and from *a priori* reasoning. As we none of us know what happens in jury rooms there is a big element of guess-work however one approaches the matter.
[5] Campbell, *Lives of the Lord Chancellors*, 5th ed., VII, 35.
[6] *Ibid.* VIII, 376.   [7] *Ibid.* IX, 94.   [8] *Ibid.* VII, 400.

political reasons he could not oppose Fox's Libel Bill, began his speech 'by professing a most religious regard for the institution of juries, which he considered the greatest blessing which the British Constitution had secured to the subject'.[1] The older constitutional law books are in the same tradition.[2] In two more recent works, intended for a wider range of readers, we get stress on the past value of juries.[3] Modern books on constitutional law, such as Wade and Phillips, make no comments upon jury trial.

The assertions that have been made can be tested against decided cases. If all the cases cited in Wade and Phillips, *Constitutional Law*, in the section on the Citizen and the State, are examined, it will be found that juries played an insignificant part. *First*, the divisional court of the King's Bench Division seems the most important court, whether for prerogative writs, appeals by case stated from summary courts, appeals from Quarter Sessions, or (until 1934) appeals from County Courts. These functions have always been exercised without juries. *Secondly*, where a jury was used, the jury either (*a*) answered questions so put that the jury cannot have known in whose favour they were finding, or (*b*) followed the judge's opinion. I should like to think that the traditional ideas of the jury as a safeguard of the liberty of the subject had been decently buried, but the Law Lords will not allow any outworn and discredited creature of the law to rest in peace. The House of Lords in 1961 proclaimed the doctrine that the 'Court of King's Bench was the custos morum of the people and had the superintendency of offences contra bonos mores...that there is in that court a residual power, where no statute has yet intervened to supersede the common law, to superintend those offences which are prejudicial to the public welfare',[4] a doctrine that might be acceptable if we still lived in the eighteenth century. In conformity with the historical age to which their views belong, the majority explained that the vagueness and the peril of the launching of prosecutions in order to suppress unpopular or unorthodox views

---

[1] *Ibid.* ix, 189.

[2] 'When questions evolved by political agitation are raised between the subject and the crown...it is conceived that, by the wit of man, no system could be devised more fitter' than jury trial (Broom, *Constitutional Law* (1885), pp. 156–7).

[3] Article on Jury in *Encyclopaedia Britannica*, 11th ed. (1911), and Jenks, *Book of English Law* (1936), pp. 97 and 167.

[4] *Shaw* v. *Director of Public Prosecutions* [1962] A.C. 220, the 'Ladies Directory' case. *D. of P.P.* v. *Smith* [1961] A.C. 290 resurrected a rule about murder that was thought to be dead, and *Sykes* v. *D. of P.P.* [1961] 3 W.L.R. 371 shows that misprision of felony goes further than lawyers had thought.

need not be feared because of jury trial.[1] So that traditional views of juries as a safeguard must be further considered.

Cases reported for their legal interest are not a fair sample of the cases that come before the courts. Pleasant chatty reports like Howell's *State Trials* give us a better indication, for we get all the political trials worth noting, irrespective of their legal interest. Many of these were sedition trials. Dr Jenks points out that the vagueness of sedition is 'a danger to the liberty of the subject.... Happily, in the days when this danger was greatest, the sturdy independence of juries was a real safeguard against oppression, and a strong justification of the jury system.'[2] I have examined many of the late eighteenth-century trials for seditious libel, and failed to find any justification for this view. In reading these cases I found it quite impossible to predict what the jury was going to do; for every acquittal there was a conviction to balance it. In 1792 Paine[3] was convicted for publishing the *Rights of Man*, whilst in 1793 his publisher Eaton[4] was virtually acquitted. The jury found Eaton 'guilty of publishing'; the judge pressed the jury to alter their verdict, but all the jury would agree to do was to alter it from 'Guilty of publishing' to 'Guilty of publishing that book'. As Fox's Libel Act had been passed, the effect was an acquittal. Poor Daniel Holt[5] was convicted in 1793, and completely ruined, for publishing suggestions for mild reform of the franchise and parliamentary constituencies, whilst the case of John Reeve[6] in 1796 is a standing warning of the danger of knowing too much legal history. The list could be continued. The only cure for admiration of these juries is to read the *State Trials*, and ponder over the possibility that if the printer put 'guilty' when he meant 'not guilty' and vice versa, you would not have noticed anything odd.

The explanation appears to lie in the qualification of jurors and mode of selecting a jury. Special juries could be ordered in all common law courts for civil or criminal cases other than treason or felony. Sedition trials, being for misdemeanour, were usually tried by special juries. The qualifications of special jurors have always

---

[1] Nuclear Disarmers who were prosecuted for felony for conspiring to commit an offence against the Official Secrets Act 1911 s. 1 (1) which everyone thought was meant to refer to spying, when they had organised a demonstration at an airfield, were convicted by a jury, although the use of such a charge in such a case produced comment in legal circles: it was upheld by the House of Lords, *Chandler* v. *D. of P.P.* [1962] 3 W.L.R. 694. [2] *Book of English Law* (1936), p. 167.
[3] 22 *State Trials*, 357. [4] Ibid. 754, 786.
[5] 22 *State Trials*, 1189. [6] 26 *State Trials*, 529.

been rather vague. The Juries Act 1825 s. 31 was probably declaratory in prescribing that they must be of the rank of esquire or higher degree, or be merchants or bankers. To get the panel, the sheriff attended before a master of the court, who selected forty-eight names from the list of special jurors. In criminal informations filed by the Attorney-General, the master of the Crown Office selected the names, and 'he was not bound to take the jurors as they occurred upon the Sheriff's books, but was to make a selection'.[1] When the panel of forty-eight names had been selected each party proceeded to strike out names, one at a time, alternately, until twenty-four names were left; these twenty-four special jurors later balloted to make the trial jury of twelve. By the Juries Act 1825 s. 32 the forty-eight names were to be obtained by ballot. The Juries Act 1870 ss. 16 and 17 provided that special jurors were to be selected from the panel by ballot, unless the court ordered that a jury be 'struck' in the old style. A case early this century illustrates the way in which 'striking a jury' might work. Mr Lygon, M.P. (Conservative) brought a libel action against Mr Greenwood, M.P. (Liberal) and a newspaper owned by Mr Winfrey, M.P. (Liberal). Mr Lygon had said that he was against feeding school children out of the rates, and he was cited as being against feeding school children, the words 'out of the rates' being omitted, so that a fearsome *innuendo* arose. The master ordered a special jury to be struck. The venue was Northamptonshire, so the sheriff of that county sent the special jury list to his London agent before whom the parties appeared and balloted for forty-eight names. Another appointment, a day later, was made for 'striking'. The plaintiff's solicitor at once set off for Northampton, followed by the defendant's solicitor, to find out the politics of the panel. The result showed thirty-five Conservatives and thirteen Liberals. The next day with 'unerring accuracy' the plaintiff struck out twelve out of the thirteen Liberals, whilst the defendant said he objected to the twelve 'most violent Tories'. That left twenty-three Conservatives and one Liberal. At the assizes the one Liberal got in on the ballot, and because he was a 'quiet, unobtrusive Liberal...we got him foreman of the jury, and he brought down the verdict from £500 to £100 by sticking out'. Mr Winfrey thought that thirty-five to thirteen was a fair average of Conservatives to Liberals on the special jury list. He looked at the Huntingdonshire list and found it much the same.[2]

---

[1] Tidd, *King's Bench Practice*, 9th ed. (1828), p. 789.
[2] Committee on Juries, Minutes of Evidence, Cd. 6818 (1913), Questions 2579 *et seq.*

It will be noted that the ballot for the panel gave a fairly representative selection, but that the method of striking would always change the proportion. Had that particular panel been thirty-six Conservatives to twelve Liberals, the trial jury would have been all Conservatives.

The Juries Act 1922 abolished 'striking' (except under the Lands Clauses Consolidation Act 1845), and this method of selecting jurors of the most convenient politics is now a thing of the past. Today it will depend on the lot of the draw. What are the chances? Under the Juries Act 1922 the Jurors' Book is made up by placing marks in the list of electors against the names of those who are qualified as jurors, 'J' for common jurors and 'SJ' for special jurors. Since the Juries Act 1949 we are only concerned with those who used to be 'common' jurors and are now simply jurors.[1] A juror must be (1) a £10 freeholder, or (2) a £20 long leaseholder, or (3) a householder in the valuation list of £30 in London and Middlesex or £20 elsewhere, or (4) occupy a house with not less than fifteen windows; qualifications (2), (3) and (4) are due to the Juries Act 1825.

The effective qualification for jury service has changed: the economic and social significance of living in a house with a rateable value of £30 or £20 has altered. It used to mean that jury service was largely confined to the middle and upper classes. A few years before the war I took as a sample a ward in Cambridge that consists partly of working-class houses, old and new, and partly of middle-class houses. There were just under 5000 parliamentary electors, and the list showed 187 jurors, which works out roughly at one juror to every 26 electors. It was only by some stretch of the imagination that a working-class prisoner could be said to be tried by 'twelve representatives of his countrymen'.[2] The views and prejudices of jurors were more apt to be those of the middle classes than those of the poorer classes. That was so obvious with special juries that they were felt to be indefensible when their abolition came in 1949.[3] In the

---

[1] Before the Juries Act 1949 the qualification for being a special juror were that he must (1) be an esquire or of higher rank, or (2) be a merchant or banker, or (3) occupy a dwelling-house in the valuation list at not less than £100 in larger towns or £50 elsewhere, or (4) occupy premises of the annual value of at least £100, or £300 if it is a farm; the qualifications (3) and (4) were added by the Juries Act 1870.

[2] Kenny, *Outlines of Criminal Law*, 16th ed., p. 501.

[3] If an employer and a trade union engaged in litigation with jury trial, the employer might well have asked for a special jury, hoping, perhaps not in vain, that the merchants, bankers and wealthier persons on the special jury would hold 'sound' (i.e. employers') views about trade unions. After trade unions had

Cambridge ward mentioned above, various elections showed a balance of five Labour supporters to eight Conservative supporters, whereas of the 187 jurors, ten were known to be Labour, sixty-two were known to be Conservative, and 115 had expressed no particular political allegiance.[1] It is true that the jurors appear to be far more Conservative than the electors generally, but this is perhaps of less importance than the attitude of the 115 'doubtfuls'. Now governments are put into power and driven out of office by the political 'doubtfuls'. My conclusion is that whilst a property qualification has tended towards Conservatism, the major tendency has been for a jury to be in sympathy with the party in power at the time of the trial. Since valuations were generally increased in the new lists that came into force in 1963, most occupiers are now jurors, and the major tendency is even more likely to be a sympathy with whoever is in the majority. This would be of great importance if we really were concerned with attempts by the government to use the courts to oppress their political opponents, but that belongs to a past age. Under modern conditions, civil liberties mean in practice the rights of small minorities, such as nuclear disarmers, communists and fascists, none of whom have the stature to be regarded as political opponents by Conservative, Labour or Liberal parties. When prosecutions are brought, these are not the machinations of political party, but an attempt to secure public order; no government can be indifferent to civil disobedience, tumultuous processions, disorderly meetings and injured policemen. Dislike for a tiresome minority may lead to oppressive prosecution in the sense of exaggeration, the inflating of rather silly behaviour into allegations of danger to the realm and so on. Now if we ask whether a jury is a protection to a defendant in such a case, I doubt whether the probabilities of political complexion are worth taking into account; the ability to be fair to people one does not like, perhaps to strain things in favour of the sincere but misguided defendant, is not a special attribute of party or non-party.

If it is agreed that juries perform no special and valuable function

obtained a better legal standing in 1875, they turned their attention to advocacy of reform of the law, for they had suffered badly under the English legal system. The measures advocated included reform of the jury system (Webb, *History of Trade Unionism* (1920 ed.), p. 367).

[1] These figures were obtained by going through the records of canvassers at election times; those acquainted with the organisation of election campaigns know that the estimate of votes definitely 'for' and definitely 'against' is reasonably accurate.

in political cases, then the future of juries must depend on their utility in ordinary cases. Liability for jury service has become even more peculiar than it used to be.

Jury service is obligatory, being one of the few survivals of the medieval principle of compulsory public office. If a person on the jury list is summoned and does not attend it is still the practice, in the absence of good excuse, to impose a fine. For centuries jurors have been unpaid, and there were many instances of jurors suffering considerable loss through having to attend for a case that lasted several days or even weeks. The Juries Acts 1949 and 1954 authorise payments for jury service. All persons who are summoned and attend, whether they actually serve or not, are entitled to draw travelling and subsistence allowances, and to receive compensation for loss of earnings or for additional expense incurred not exceeding twenty-five shillings for four hours or fifty shillings for a longer period in one day. In civil cases the cost falls on national funds whereas in criminal cases it falls on local funds. The argument that extension of jury service would be a grievous burden to poorer people has thus disappeared. When this legislation was before Parliament there was some demand for alteration of the qualification for jurors. It is difficult to defend a system whereby jury service depends on occupation of property of a given rateable value. A general liability for jury service might, politically at least, be a wise step in a country that proclaims equality before the law. Further, if we are to believe those who tell us that jury service is good for the jurors, broadening their outlook and uplifting them by allowing them to share in the dispensing of justice, and that the stale air of the law is refreshed by contributions from the uncloistered life of jurors, it is surely a little unfair to keep so much of the population from any share in these good things. In the debate on the Juries Bill in the House of Commons in 1949, the Attorney-General indicated some sympathy for proposals that jury service should be extended to those entitled to vote in elections, but this was not within the scope of the Bill. What has happened is that the revaluation of dwelling houses for rating, and particularly the new lists of 1963, has resulted in nearly all occupiers becoming jurors. In past years the property qualifications did give some selection that was defensible in a community where education and responsibility tended to go with wealth expressed in housing. Now the property qualification depends on social habits in housing. What constitutes 'occupation' of property is a highly technical part of the law. Generally with a married couple the husband is tenant or legal owner (Building Societies do not like lending to women) and goes down as occupier, thus excluding his wife and any grown-up children, lodgers or other inmates of the household from being put on the jury list. Liability for jury service has thus been extended not by deliberation on the needs of the administration of justice but by a sidewind of local government finance. The typical juror will be the male head of a family having a separate unit of housing, and apart from a bias against women and young adults (who have not yet got their own housing) the system is more representative of the population at large. But having got to this stage it looks as if the logical step would now be to extend jury service to those who are on the register of electors, which means substantially all of the adult population other than aliens and persons (such as persons mentally ill and persons convicted of various offences) who are disqualified.

'Qualification' means being on the list and aged over 21 and under 60; there are no tests of capacity. In 1961 in the course of a murder trial it appeared that one juror (a Jamaican immigrant) was of low intelligence and very small education and that he did not understand enough of the proceedings to follow the evidence; the judge thought that some amendment in jury service qualification is needed.[1] The list is made up automatically, and under the present law any prior examination of each person is out of the question. Some professions and occupations disqualify, and if the names are noticed they are crossed off, but otherwise the individual may point out his disqualification when called upon to serve. Temporary exemption is given for sickness and some other causes. The number of jurors to be summoned is not fixed, but depends on the amount of work before the Court; the number commonly varies from thirty-six to sixty, but as many as 300 have been summoned.[2] The panel is summoned by the sheriff, which in practice means the under-sheriff or deputy. No rules govern the selection of names. In some areas tradition dictates that the sheriff shall follow some method. Thus in London the method has been to take two districts, geographically apart such as Hampstead and Wandsworth, and make up the panel by taking names alphabetically from each district, working though each list until it is exhausted. In some areas the panel has been described as being

---

[1] *The Times*, 30 November 1961, reports the episode.
[2] Halsbury, *Laws of England*, 2nd ed., xix, 303; this large panel was summoned for the trial of Mile End Guardians in 1908. The proportion of women must equal the total proportion of women to men in the Jurors' Book.

selected 'at random'.[1] The theory is that if a prejudiced panel is selected, the party aggrieved can challenge the array.[2] Trial juries are called from the panel by balloting. Challenges, either to the array or to individual jurors, are not common.[3]

It is easier to see the weak points of the present methods of getting a jury than to be sure of the remedy. A Committee was appointed in 1963, with Lord Morris of Borth-y-Gest as chairman, to inquire into 'the qualifications for, exemption from and conditions of jury service, and related matters'. It is not an inquiry at large into trial by jury, and the main characteristics are unlikely to be altered.

We speak of jury trial when in fact we mean trial by judge and jury. It is accepted in our system that the judge not only rules on any matters of law but that he sums up the evidence and may comment upon it. The judge must be correct in his law and explain it in a way that is intelligible to the jury and not likely to be misunderstood. He need not review all the evidence, but he must sum up in a way that covers the case of each party. He must tell the jury what courses are open to them, with fine distinctions as to how far he can go in leading them so that they bring in a unanimous verdict, preferably the verdict that the judge thinks is right but at least a verdict that is legally possible in the circumstances. The court will not inquire into what happened in the jury room, a principle that is observed even when jurors are prepared to swear, after the case is over, that they did not come to a unanimous verdict,[4] or that the majority wanted to acquit the accused until one juror produced a list of the accused's previous

---

[1] *Report of Committee on Juries*, Cd. 6817 (1913), paras. 106, 107; Minutes of Evidence, Cd. 6818 (1913), Questions 1155 *et seq.*

[2] The fairness or otherwise of the panel can be considered beforehand, since the names (with occupations and addresses) are arranged alphabetically, and this list must be available for at least seven days before the sitting of the Court (Common Law Procedure Act 1852 ss. 106, 107; Juries Act 1870 s. 16).

[3] There were challenges in the *Podola* case in 1959 and the *Pen Club* case in 1960, both murder trials of notoriety, and in the *Lady Chatterley* case in 1960. The Criminal Justice Act 1948 reduced the right of an accused person to challenge jurors by providing that he may challenge not more than seven jurors without cause and any number for cause. On challenges for cause the judge (or chairman or recorder at Quarter Sessions) tries the issue. The purpose of limiting the right is to reduce the number of jurors that need be summoned; in the past an unreasonable number of 'spare men' had to be summoned just in case some prisoner should start challenging jurors. The Criminal Justice Act 1948 also gives the court power in all cases to allow the jury to separate at any time before they consider their verdict.

[4] *Ellis* v. *Deheer* [1922] 2 K.B. 113.

convictions.[1] The process of arriving at a verdict is thus an inviolable mystery which the Court will not penetrate. There appears to be no great objection to a juryman talking about his experiences, which are sometimes not entirely flattering to the bench and apt to be devastating about counsel, but I am sure that any attempt to collect an adequate sample by interviewing a number of jurymen would be stopped as being a contempt of court. Inquisitive lawyers or sociologists cannot be allowed to do that which judges themselves do not want to do. So that when lawyers say that the giving of reasons is essential to the administration of justice, that does not apply to jury trial. We have to make such estimates as we can, and in that way the abilities of judges and juries may be compared on two points:

(1) The problem of deciding whether a witness is to be believed or not.

Skill in estimating the characters of others depends to a considerable extent upon experience, provided that 'experience' means that conclusions are in some way tested. Most doctors ultimately *know* whether their patients have been telling the truth. College tutors also have to take responsibility for their estimates of character. Businessmen are also largely concerned with the same problem. When these people make mistakes they sooner or later know that they have made a wrong estimate. Now a judge, by the very nature of his office, is not accustomed to testing his conclusions. He can live in the firm conviction that he is a shrewd judge of character. To some extent as counsel, and almost certainly as judge, he will very rarely find out when he has been wrong. A man who never knows of his mistakes is apt to think that he is generally right. A judge does not always 'gain experience' on the problems of fact; he increases his self-assurance and his self-confidence.[2] A learned judge once said that: 'The average English jury can understand most things which are put to them in plain language.' What this really means is that when a judge explains to a jury, say the distinction between false pretences and larceny by a trick, and the jury find a verdict in accordance with the judge's views, the judge deduces that the jury understood his plain language. No law teacher would make that assumption, because he tries to find out whether the plain language of lectures, textbooks and learned judges has been understood.

I cannot see any reason for supposing that in the matter of assessing credibility a jury is likely to be any better or any worse than a judge.

(2) The application of common public opinion of sensible men.

In many cases this is irrelevant. 'You cannot have public opinion on questions arising on charter-parties and bills of lading.' The two chief fields where this is needed are defamation and negligence actions.

[1] *R.* v. *Thompson* [1962] *Crim. L.R.* 117; *The Times*, 14 February 1962, reports the refusal of the House of Lords to give leave to appeal. Unanimity is discussed by J. A. Andrews, 'Legal Realism and the Jury' [1961] *Crim. L.R.* 758, and old principles were reaffirmed by the Judicial Committee in *Shoukatalie* v. *The Queen* [1962] A.C. 81. [2] Cf. p. 213, above.

The problem is really one of evidence. An epithet is defamatory because people regard it as such. Can we assume that judges and juries know this, or must evidence be produced to show what ordinary people think? When chocolate manufacturers (Messrs Fry) published a caricature of a well-known amateur golfer (Mr Tolley) without his leave in order to advertise their goods, Mr Tolley brought a libel action. It is clearly not defamatory to assert that a golfer eats chocolate; the only possible libel was that the public would believe that Mr Tolley had been paid to allow himself to be caricatured, and hence he was not a bona fide amateur at all. There was, very naturally, no evidence that 'amateurs' receive money for the use of their names or portraits in advertisements. The jury found in favour of Mr Tolley. The Court of Appeal had to consider whether the jury were entitled to come to that finding, that is, the extent to which the jury could add their common knowledge to the evidence that had been given. Scrutton L.J. said that 'A jury is certainly allowed to know something not in the evidence'; Greer L.J. and Slesser L.J., who found that there was no evidence on which the jury could have acted, implied that advertising habits are outside a jury's knowledge.[1] The House of Lords thought otherwise,[2] except for Lord Blanesburgh, who said: 'Neither the belief nor its limitations were explored or made the subject-matter of evidence...neither could have been within the judicial knowledge of the judge or within the wordly experience of a Middlesex common jury.' The point was not whether persons whose portraits appear *are* paid, but whether the public *thinks* they are paid. Lord Blanesburgh thus objected to a jury acting without evidence, yet he was quite prepared to act without evidence in stating the wordly experience of others. As Viscount Hailsham said: 'It is always difficult to determine with precision the amount of judicial knowledge which is permissible to a judge or jury.' There is no more difficult task than the devising of a method for ascertaining what is common knowledge. Admittedly a jury is not a perfect method, but a random selection from the public at large is surely better than relying upon a select group such as the judges.

In negligence actions we get the complication that the standard of care may be assessed by common knowledge and practice, or by specialist knowledge and practice. Whether steel chains have been adequately inspected and tested must depend upon specialist evidence. When a pane of glass falls out of a garage door and

---

[1] [1930] 1 K.B. 467, Scrutton L.J. at 475, Greer L.J. at 481, Slesser L.J. at 491.
[2] [1931] A.C. 333, Lord Blanesburgh at 349, Viscount Hailsham at 339.

injures a chauffeur, and a question arises as to the proper measure and periods of inspection of such a building, is this common knowledge or specialist knowledge? The Court of Appeal took the view that it was not common knowledge, Scrutton L.J. saying: 'I do not think a county court jury, who are not as a rule people who keep motor cars, are entitled to find without evidence what is the ordinary practice as to examination of a garage.'[1] The jury here must apparently weigh evidence that is given, and not apply their common knowledge, because garage doors with panes of glass are much more abstruse topics than other kinds of doors.

When our jury system appears to give queer results it may be found that one or more of the following points is involved:

(1) Putting a matter of common knowledge before the jury, and then disputing their verdict by denying that they have that knowledge. This is discussed above.

(2) Expecting a jury to follow a long case without having any of the help that counsel and the judge rely upon.

In *Mechanical etc. Co. and Lehwess* v. *Austin*[2] the trial lasted fourteen and a half days. In the House of Lords, Viscount Sankey L.C. said: 'If the jury had had the same advantages we have had, in this long and complicated case, of having such a transcript of the evidence before them and the whole of the correspondence under their eyes, they could not have arrived at the conclusion that the licence agreement was made.' Lord Atkin observed that: 'It can hardly be said that the jury lose sight of the documents, for they barely see them.' I believe that the sole reason for not supplying the jury with copies of documents is a relic of the days when juries were illiterate, and that such a curious practice is quite indefensible today. A transcript of evidence is more difficult. A shorthand note is cheap, but the transcript is expensive, and it is often not made at all unless an appeal is entered. But in a long trial the note is often transcribed for each day, and when counsel find this indispensable it must surely be equally useful to the jury.

(3) Asking a jury to give positive answers to highly technical questions.

A jury may be asked to answer any question of fact. A plea of justification in libel may result in a jury being asked to say whether a particular method of contraception is or is not harmful and dangerous,[3] although it is probably safe to say that with the data then available the question was unanswerable when tackled as a scientific problem.

In the long run our judicial system cannot afford to adopt methods that would appear ludicrous outside the courts. We know that laymen cannot resolve matters upon which lawyers cannot agree. For medical questions we are getting nearer to a sensible technique, for judges now try to ensure that an agreed medical report is put before the court. The Rules of the

---

[1] *Cole* v. *De Trafford* (No. 2) [1918] 2 K.B. 523, Scrutton L.J. at 538.
[2] [1935] A.C. 346, Viscount Sankey L.C. at 356, Lord Atkin at 370.
[3] *Sutherland* v. *Stopes* [1925] A.C. 47.

Supreme Court, since 1934, make provision for a court expert to be appointed to report upon questions of fact or opinion, but this can only occur in non-jury cases. A suitable technique might be for the parties' experts to see if they can agree, with a court expert to act as moderator, and if no agreement can be reached the jury should, whenever possible, be exonerated from the burden of having to decide matters outside their competence. In personal injury cases it is necessary to arrive at some conclusion about the extent of the injuries, and if the experts cannot agree somebody must decide what is to be done. If a libel action arises because Mr Z has stated that Mr X's cancer cure is useless and dangerous, and the defence is justification, it is a curious course to ask a jury (or a judge) to pronounce upon the cure of cancer; it is, however, quite sensible to ask non-experts whether Mr Z held that opinion honestly and whether he had reasonable grounds for that opinion.[1]

(4) It is questionable whether the amount of damages should be left to the jury as it is at present, or whether it should be left to the jury at all.

The amount of damages is not a matter upon which a jury is likely to show any special ability; it does not depend upon estimate of character, nor to any large extent upon general knowledge. In libel cases the amount of damages given is a grim joke.[2] It may be far cheaper to maim a man for life by knocking him down with a motor-car than to call him an ass, unless, of course, the Court of Appeal holds that there was no evidence upon which the jury could have found that 'ass' meant a stupid fellow, for possibly the only judicial knowledge of an ass is that it is *equus asinus*. If it is felt that a jury ought to have the power of awarding damages,[3] then there is much to be said for taking first a verdict simply for plaintiff or defendant, with no amount stated. This would be followed by a further hearing on the amount of the damages. Questions of money can only be

---

[1] It may be argued that 'reasonable grounds' cannot be estimated by the non-expert; whether this is so or not, it seems hardly possible for courts to avoid such decisions.

[2] The Defamation Act 1952 has altered the law of libel, but it is hard to say what the effect will be upon the measure of damages. One wonders whether a film star might still get £25,000 for a suggestion that she had been raped by Rasputin, or, in view of the change in the value of money, whether it would be £50,000. In 1958 two newspapers published statements that the police were inquiring into the affairs of a limited company of which L was chairman. In an action for defamation brought by L and by the company, a jury awarded £25,000 against one newspaper and £17,000 against the other in favour of L, and £75,000 and £100,000 in favour of the company. The Court of Appeal ordered new trials on points of the law of defamation, and said that there would also have to be new trials because of the damages awarded (*Lewis* v. *Daily Telegraph* [1962] 3 W.L.R. 50). It was said at the trial (*The Times*, 6 March 1962), that the highest recorded figure for damages for defamation was £40,000 given to Lord Keyes nearly two years ago when the defendant made very serious charges and attempted to justify them.

[3] Lord Justice Singleton said in the Court of Appeal that it is desirable that in serious cases of personal injury the damages should be assessed by a jury, but he thought that the time of the courts would be saved in such cases if a tribunal of three judges of the King's Bench Division assessed the damages (*The Times*, 4 July 1951).

settled by talking about figures. To send a jury away with the idea that if they find for the plaintiff they are to give 'substantial' damages means very little. Some jurymen feel that £100 is substantial, whilst others plunge for £25,000. The wealthier jurymen naturally think in larger amounts.[1] The most elementary precaution in any other kind of business would be to ask the plaintiff how much he wants, and how he has arrived at that figure.[2]

There is no single certain cause for the decline in the use of juries in civil cases. I had thought that a major reason has been expedition: the non-jury cases have been easier to fit into court lists, so that they have been heard sooner, and have taken less time to hear, so that litigants, officials and judges have all favoured trial by judge alone. Lord Devlin has suggested other reasons, which may well have been more decisive. A large proportion of common law cases are actions for personal injuries, on roads or in factories. Lawyers want to forecast what the result of an action will be, and it is far easier to forecast what a judge will do, both as to liability and as to damages.

Juries in criminal cases have in general attracted less adverse criticism than juries in civil cases. This is partly due to the fair trial of criminal cases depending largely on those characteristics with which a jury is often adequately endowed. It is true that juries vary in quality, but so do judges and courts of Quarter Sessions. A point that is perhaps of some importance is that the Court of Criminal Appeal has far less powers over the verdicts of juries than the Court of Appeal; juries in criminal cases are allowed to do their job, so that the counterpart of *Tolley* v. *Fry* can hardly arise. There is a substantial volume of criticism of jury trial of charges of driving whilst under the influence of alcohol and of dangerous driving. The figures show that when drink cases are tried in Magistrates' Courts there is acquittal in around one case in twenty-five, whereas in cases tried before a jury there is acquittal in about one case in three. From that it is deduced that juries are too lenient to drivers, probably because

[1] In personal injury cases special juries were apt to give bigger amounts. Some years ago the London General Omnibus Company and the Railway Companies ceased applying for special juries and asked for common juries because on the average they awarded lower damages (Committee on Juries, Minutes of Evidence, Cd. 6818 (1913), Questions 2407 *et seq.*).

[2] A careful reading of *Mechanical etc. Co. and Lehwess* v. *Austin* [1935] A.C. 346 suggests that the jury gave the plaintiffs far more damages for the wrongful use of the invention than they had been prepared to accept for an out-and-out sale of the patents.

[3] Devlin, *Trial by Jury* (1956), 141–4. *Current Law*, which is the lawyers' stand-by for knowing what has happened each month, now gives brief notes on the amount of damages given in such and such circumstances.

they feel sympathetic to someone who has done little more than they sometimes do themselves. Too much must not be built on the figures, for it is only when there seems sufficient evidence to be worth a contest that the defendant chooses jury trial; the hopeless case or plea of guilty does not get beyond the magistrates. The Road Traffic Act 1962 has altered the wording of the offence, and made it easier and more effective for the prosecution to produce evidence of alcohol in the defendant's body fluids, and it may be that the proportion of convictions will rise.

Quite possibly the points I have been making are of far less importance than the subsidiary question of the convenience of the legal profession. When proposals were being discussed for extension of the hours of opening of a great library, the chief librarian opposed extended facilities, saying that 'Readers interfere so much with the work of the library'. A similar attitude is not unknown among judges and the profession. Sir Fitzjames Stephen[1] came to the conclusion that a judge and special jury was an excellent tribunal, but that a judge alone was better than a common jury. But he considered that the arguments in favour of jury trial were collateral advantages, the most important of all being that the jury saves the judge from sole responsibility. It is only judges at Assizes and recorders who must have a jury if they are to escape an 'intolerable responsibility', for with justices of the peace the sense of responsibility is diffused. Stipendiaries sitting alone must take the responsibility, remembering that the smallest case may be the beginning of a criminal career.

All I ask is that in any change that is made we try to give the right reasons, and that jury trial shall not be discredited because we work it badly or because we wish to avoid some re-organisation of the Courts.

7. COURT OFFICIALS

Perhaps the most astonishing chapter in the history of our law courts is that dealing with the official staff.[2] Medieval law had a poorly developed notion of contract and a highly developed law of property. Offices, such as the clerkships in the courts, came to be regarded as property; the official had a freehold for life in the office, just as he might have such a freehold in land. As the work of the

---

[1] *History of the Criminal Law*, I, 566 *et seq.*

[2] Holdsworth, *History of English Law*, I, 246 *et seq.*, with appendices taken from Parliamentary Papers, is the most accessible account. *The Black Book of Abuses*, 1819 and later editions, is a virulent contemporary exposure.

courts increased the staff was not increased accordingly, for that would have interfered with property: the process was for the office holder to continue to receive the fees, but for him to employ men to do the work. In the early nineteenth century the chief clerk of the King's Bench received on an average £6280 a year, and paid his deputy £200 a year. The patronage to these highly paid or sinecure offices was partly in the government and partly in the judges: 'The fact that many highly placed people both in the fashionable and the judicial world had an interest in these offices, made the system extraordinarily difficult to eliminate.'[1] Royal Commissions investigated, and a series of statutes ending with the Courts of Justice Salaries and Funds Act 1869 converted court officials into salaried officials with pension rights assimilated to the civil service. The Treasury was given some control over salaries and the establishment, but the methods of appointment remained substantially unchanged. Later legislation as the result of further Commissions and Committees brought the legal departments more under the control of the Lord Chancellor and the Treasury. The whole situation was reviewed by the Royal Commission on the Civil Service in their sixth Report in 1915.[2] They found that 'the present method of appointment in all the Legal Departments is nomination, subject, in the case of some of the higher officials, to certain qualifications imposed by statute, and in the case of the clerical staff generally, to a qualifying examination of an elementary character'. In general the head of each division nominated the appropriate officers, so that the appointments were made by the Lord Chancellor, The Lord Chief Justice, the Master of the Rolls, and the President of the Probate Division. 'After making full allowance for heredity in legal talent and for the tendency among members of certain distinguished families to adopt a legal career in successive generations, we believe that "influence", as it is commonly called, has had a considerable share in determining the appointments.' Of the seven King's Bench masters and two assistant masters, four were sons of judges and two or three were relations of judges. Of four Chancery masters, two were sons of dead judges and one was a nephew of the Lord Chancellor at the time of his appointment.[3] Of eight clerks of Assize, five were sons of judges. In evidence the following passage took place: 'The Clerk of Assizes Act was

---

[1] Holdsworth, *op. cit.* p. 250.

[2] Cd. 7832 (1915). My statements are taken from this Report except where other authority is cited.

[3] Minutes of Evidence, Cd. 8130 (1915), Question 50,660.

passed after the appointment of a Mr Bovill, who had been a cavalry officer. He really did not know much about it at first.' 'Was he the son of a judge?' 'He was the son of a Lord Chief Justice, and that raised rather a scandal, because his military methods did not quite accord with the practice.'[1] The Report notes that the Lord Chancellor had shown less tendency to appoint for family reasons; we might hazard the conjecture that he had more political debts to pay and put his party higher than his family. The higher official posts in the courts carried salaries up to £3800 a year, the qualifications of barrister or solicitor being necessary. The ordinary clerkships were paid at rates similar to those in the civil service. The Commission's conclusion is not surprising: 'In the appointment of clerks the part played by "influence" appears to be less than in the case of the higher appointments, perhaps, because, in Lord Loreburn's words, these posts are "not an object of very great ambition".' The Commission recommended that the power of appointment (except for the Pay Office and the judge's clerks and secretaries) should be vested in the Lord Chancellor with an advisory committee from his own department, the civil service commission and a solicitor. The majority thought that the clerkships should be filled by open competition except for certain classes that are generally filled from solicitors' clerks. A strong dissenting group advocated competitive examination for all clerkships, pointing out that when a man is going to spend forty years in a department he can be trained after his appointment. The Commission found that on the whole the court officials had been competent, but that the standard of efficiency in the legal service was lower than that in the civil service, although in the matter of hours of work, vacations, and to some extent salaries, court officials were better off than the civil service.

The old method of nomination no longer governs appointments, but there is still less uniformity than in ordinary departments of government. The financial officers in the Supreme Court Pay Office are appointed by the Treasury, and the clerks of that office through the civil service. Since 1954 Judges' Clerks are appointed by the Lord Chancellor. Clerks of Assize were appointed by the judge who was last on the circuit where the vacancy occurred. The Supreme Court of Judicature (Circuit Officers) Act 1946 provides that Clerks of Assize are to be appointed by the Lord Chief Justice and shall be officers of the Supreme Court. Other duties previously performed by special circuit officers become the duties of the general body of

[1] *Ibid.* Questions 51,452, 51,453.

Supreme Court officers. The district registrars of the High Court are appointed by the Lord Chancellor, and the district probate registrar by the President of the Probate Division. The Masters in the Queen's Bench and Chancery Divisions and the Registrars in the Probate Divorce and Admiralty Division are appointed by the heads of the Divisions, that is, by the Lord Chief Justice, the Lord Chancellor and the President, respectively.

It is inevitable that some of the superior officials should be drawn from barristers and solicitors. These masters have to perform highly technical functions, sometimes of a judicial nature, but they also have extensive administrative work; the 'establishment' is under their direction. Barristers usually have no experience of running an office; in barrister's chambers the 'staff' may be one clerk and two boys, and a good clerk has some of the characteristics of Jeeves. Solicitors have usually had experience as 'managing clerk' of running an office, although it may be upon a small scale. Efficiency requires 'establishment' matters to be dealt with by persons of experience. The allied proposal to appoint a 'business manager' to conduct part of the administrative work has been mentioned above.[1]

The position in County Courts was investigated by the Royal Commission on the Civil Service and by the County Court Staff Committee in 1920.[2] These investigations showed a thoroughly unsatisfactory state of affairs. Registrars of County Courts were appointed by the County Court judge subject to the approval of the Lord Chancellor. Registrars are not only the head of the office side of their courts but also exercise lesser judicial functions. The appointments are made from solicitors. In the busier County Courts the registrars were debarred from private practice, whilst in others it was a part-time job. Remuneration depended upon the number of plaints. Since it is often possible for a plaintiff to choose in which County Court he will commence proceedings, persons with a large volume of debt collecting could transfer their 'custom' to another court if a registrar was not sufficiently obliging; a registrar who wanted to keep his income at a satisfactory level had a strong temptation to lean in favour of creditors.[3] The clerks in County Courts were the employees of the registrar. They were paid either from an allowance made by the Treasury for clerk-hire, or by the registrars personally. Their conditions of work, pay, and security of

---

[1] See p. 46, above.   [2] Cmd. 1049 (1920).
[3] Minutes of Evidence, Cd. 7832 (1915), Question 51,908; Cmd. 1049 (1920), p. 5.

employments depended upon the registrar. In some cases decrepit and senile clerks were still employed, since no pension was available and kindly registrars did not care to dismiss men who would have to resort to poor relief. Other registrars were not so kind-hearted. The conditions in the Supreme Court were defended, as such conditions always are defended, by asserting that it works satisfactorily. For the County Courts it was impossible to contend that all was well, and despite obstructionist views held by the Treasury[1] some reforms were made by statute, now consolidated in the County Courts Act 1934. The fact that some County Courts have a small volume of business made it impossible to adopt a uniform system. All registrars are now appointed by the Lord Chancellor, who (with the concurrence of the Treasury) directs the salary that is to be paid and whether the registrar is to be whole-time or not. The tendency is for part-time registrars to be replaced by whole-time registrars who may serve more than one district. Whole-time registrars are subject to a retiring age of seventy-two and receive pensions. A registrar may still be paid a salary that includes the remuneration he must pay his clerks, in which case the registrar appoints the clerks. Where the salary is exclusive of paying clerks, the Lord Chancellor and the Treasury can appoint the clerks, who then become entitled to the benefits of the Superannuation Acts as civil servants if they can get the certificate of the Civil Service Commissioners. The latter system is obviously preferable, and it can be introduced by the Lord Chancellor when vacancies occur and offer a suitable opportunity.

The office of Clerk to the Justices has been explained above;[2] the new conditions have applied since 1953, and there thus passed away the chief institutional relics of older ideas of staffing courts.

No material is available for the whole of the administrative side but the organisation and work of chancery chambers and chancery registrars' office is the subject of a Report in 1960.[3] This showed a state of affairs that if it had existed in other parts of the public service would be regarded as intolerable. It is not a matter of corruption, or of personal incompetence, but of an addiction to the ideas and methods of a century or more ago. The drawing of orders 'takes weeks and may take months to perfect, and involve, just as we have seen they did in the years 1826 and 1874, unnecessary expense...'.

[1] Cmd. 1049 (1920), pp. 18 *et seq.*   [2] See p. 166, above.

[3] Report of the Committee on Chancery Chambers and the Chancery Registrars' Office, Cmnd. 967 (1960). The *Law Society Gazette* (May 1960) contains a memorandum to the Committee from G. S. A. Wheatcroft, who was a Chancery Master but had then resigned to become a professor of law.

Solicitors had to attend personally to collect documents that could have been sent by post. 'It seems likely that the telephone is less used in the High Court than in any other office in the Kingdom.' 'It is not surprising that these officials wish to maintain the quiet asylum in which they live.' This is understandable, as are many other things described in this book, on the assumption that the law exists to let lawyers do traditional things and keep ancient ritual unsullied by the demands of a vulgar age.

CHAPTER V

THE COST OF THE LAW

I. THE FINANCES OF THE LAW COURTS

In the past the growth of royal justice was partly due to the profits that accrued from exercising jurisdiction. The early itinerant justices were more concerned with safeguarding the King's fiscal rights than with the trial of ordinary actions. A law court was expected to pay for itself and show a profit for the King. It is some time since justice has been a substantial source of income, but the old idea survives in the idea that the courts ought not to be run at a loss.

The criminal courts are supported out of public funds, for there is no method of making the defendants pay the expenses. Relatively small receipts in the form of fines cannot balance the expenditure. The principle is that crime is tried locally and that the local authorities must provide court houses, salaries and other outgoings. Lay justices are of course unpaid, but stipendiary magistrates and recorders are paid by the local authority. Assize Court judges are paid (in their capacity of High Court judge) out of the Consolidated Fund. The exact incidence of the cost as between local authorities and the central government is complicated by the system of grants made from the Exchequer.[1] The cost of prosecuting also falls upon local authorities. The defendant may be ordered to pay a sum by way of costs, but this hardly affects the general situation. A private prosecutor may relieve the local authority of some expense, but here the private prosecutor may receive from the local authority part of the cost he incurs. The Director of Public Prosecutions recovers some of his costs from local authorities, the rest falling upon his department and being met by an annual vote from Parliament. The expense of prosecutions carried on by government departments is met out of their funds provided by Parliament. A good deal of the time of the police is taken up by attending courts. With so many different items to consider it is quite impossible to give any figures of the cost of our criminal courts. It is probable that the cost of trying a man on indictment (exclusive of the cost of catching him and punishing him if he is convicted) is quite substantial, and for practical purposes we can regard the whole costs as being borne by the community.

[1] For Magistrates' Courts, see p. 172, above.

In the civil courts a litigant has to pay for three main items: (a) the court fees, (b) the expense of collecting evidence and bringing witnesses to court, and (c) the charges of solicitors and counsel if briefed. It is as if a man rents a house; the court fees represent the rent, whilst items (b) and (c) are the expenses of occupying it, and they may vary from the irreducible minimum to riotous extravagance. The cost of the services given by the courts is made up of the salaries and pensions of the judges, the salaries, wages and pensions of the court officials, and the provision and maintenance of buildings and equipment. The principle adopted is that in the Supreme Court the cost of the judges should fall upon public funds and that all other expenses of the courts should fall upon the suitors. The Supreme Court fees are fixed by the Lord Chancellor and a committee of judges, with the concurrence of the Treasury. The schedule of fees fixed in accordance with the above-mentioned principle in 1884 (and subsequently varied a little) resulted in the receipts exceeding the expenditure (after deducting judges' salaries paid by the State) by a considerable sum. By 1910 the 'profit' amounted to well over a million pounds. The Treasury view was that the 'profit' should be off-set against the capital cost of building the Law Courts. The increased cost of administration due to the war of 1914 led to a distinct 'loss' on the Supreme Court, and the fees were accordingly increased after a committee had considered the matter.[1] Since 1922 there has in most years been a surplus over the whole of the expenditure including the judges, and in every year except during the war the receipts were substantially more than the expenditure other than the judges. Put in another way, litigants are supposed to get the judge free and to pay for the other services at cost price: in 1938 they had to pay £245,373, and in 1950, £97,697 more than the services actually cost. The Committee on Supreme Court Practice and Procedure came to the conclusion that 'there is scope for some reduction in court fees without injustice to the general body of taxpayers'.[2] On the figures given by the Committee there has been an excess of receipts over expenditure (excluding the cost of the judges) of over four million pounds since 1922, which amply supports such a moderately phrased conclusion. There are no longer any surplus receipts. On the 1958–9 Estimates the total cost was £3,142,243. The Judges' salaries and pensions, paid out of the Consolidated Fund, were £453,375. Court fees and other charges produced

[1] Cmd. 1565 (1922).
[2] Second Interim Report, Cmd. 8176 (1951), para. 151.

£1,907,400. Parliament had to grant £781,486 to cover the rest of the expenditure.[1]

Since County Courts are humbler institutions their finances are more favourable to the litigant. The court fees are fixed by the Treasury with the concurrence of the Lord Chancellor: 'in the opinion of the Treasury the balance between expenditure and revenue of the County Courts should be adjusted on the basis that the State should bear the cost of the Court buildings and the salaries, pensions, and travelling expenses of the Judges, and that the rest of the expenditure should be defrayed by the suitors' fees.'[2] In the earlier years of this century the County Courts made a modest 'profit' of about £30,000 a year from the suitors on the Treasury theory of the fees. From 1915 there was a deficit, becoming so substantial that votes of £200,000 or £300,000 a year were required. The fees were increased in 1924 and some staff economies made, so that by 1925 the courts became self-supporting again, and only a token vote came before Parliament. On the estimates for 1937 the total cost was put at £1,045,383 and the receipts at £800,000, the balance of £245,383 consisting of £98,000 for judges' salaries and pensions and various sums for the other items that are paid for by the State. On the 1950–1 Estimates the cost had risen to £1,221,198 (the cost of the judges being £144,868) and the receipts had fallen to £596,550.

Whether the major part of the cost of the civil courts should be borne by litigants has often been questioned. It can be argued that the services should be 'free', which means that everyone by indirect or direct taxes pays the bill. I do not see that it is possible to say what 'ought' to be done except in relation to some definite theory of social structure. Court fees are easy and cheap to collect. Provided that inability to pay court fees is never allowed to prevent anybody from having access to the courts, there seems no strong case against the present practice. The present reliefs from paying court fees, discussed later in this chapter, could be extended without introducing any new principle.

[1] When receipts were sufficient so that no grant was needed there was a token vote of £100 to give opportunity for debate. When grants are needed the votes come under several heads, some money (£108,692 in 1958–9) going direct to the courts whereas other money (£672,776 in 1958–9) goes to departments, such as the Ministry of Works who provide and maintain the buildings.

[2] Cmd. 1856 (1923), p. 5.

2. 'COSTS'

Solicitors have never had the freedom enjoyed in other professions of fixing the amount of their fees. From early times a person presented with a solicitor's bill has been able to get it 'taxed', that is, to have it examined by an official of the court who has power to disallow or reduce the amount charged for the various items. A bill is made up of disbursements and profit costs. Disbursements are payments made by the solicitor on behalf of his client such as court fees, stamp duties, counsel's fees, payments to witnesses, and so on. Profit costs are the solicitor's charges for his own work, but of course the solicitor has to meet his business expenses (the rent of his office, salaries and wages of his staff, and so on) before arriving at the net figure that is his real profit. For purposes of costs, a solicitor's work is divided into contentious, which means being concerned with proceedings in court, and non-contentious,[1] although for all kinds of work the traditional method of charging was by a string of items. It was most misleading because it suggested that a solicitor could not do anything, even answering the telephone to make an appointment, without noting it down and charging 3s. 4d., 6s. 8d. or some multiple of such fractions of a pound. There was often no item at all for doing the important part of the work. It was as if a surgeon made up a bill for making an appointment with the patient, inspecting the patient, attending the hospital, supplying swabs and so forth, and omitted to mention his performance of the operation. A new method of charging was introduced for conveyancing and similar work in 1883, when scale charges were adopted, the amount of the fees depending on the purchase price. For other non-contentious work a new system known as 'Schedule II' began in 1953, the essence of it being that the solicitor gives a general description of the work that he has done and makes a charge that has regard to the amount of work, its complexity and other relevant matters. A client may appeal against this to the Law Society or he may have the bill taxed. From 1 January 1960 the method of charging for contentious work has been changed to bring it more into line with 'Schedule II' practice. The items of profit costs in a solicitor's bill for litigation are now far fewer, because wherever a number of steps have to be taken for some stage in an action they

---

[1] The charges for contentious work are regulated by Rules of Court made through the appropriate Rule Committee (see p. 63, above). For non-contentious work there is a special committee under the Solicitors Act 1957 s. 56.

are now lumped together under a general heading instead of being made up of the traditional bits and pieces. Where a process is substantially routine the charges are fixed, but where something is a matter of professional skill and experience the charge is either left to be settled between a prescribed maximum and a prescribed minimum, or it is 'discretionary'. It is hoped that the new system will lead to professional charges being based, both in appearance and in fact, on the nature and amount of professional service instead of on the number of attendances, the length of documents and other crude pieces of calculation.

In ordinary litigation, where neither party is assisted under the legal aid scheme, the process is as follows. The client authorises his solicitor to bring, or defend, the action. The normal thing is for the winning party to be given his 'costs'.[1] But there are two kinds of costs to be considered. Any party, whether he has won or lost, must pay his own solicitor all the solicitor's proper charges and disbursements for conducting the litigation in the way that the client authorised expressly or impliedly. These are called 'solicitor and own client costs'. The costs that must be paid by the loser to the winner are calculated upon a different basis: the idea is that the loser must pay only such costs, charges and expenses as have been necessarily or properly incurred for the conduct of the litigation. In practice each party is likely to have spent more than was strictly necessary, because it will have been thought prudent to be prepared for all eventualities. To arrive at the sum that the loser must pay for costs, the winner's solicitor sends a bill to the loser's solicitor; this bill may be agreed to, in which case the loser simply pays the agreed sum. If the loser's solicitor disputes the amount claimed, and a compromise cannot be made, the solicitors 'tax' the bill. In the High Court there are taxing masters assigned for this work, whilst in County Courts the work is done by the registrar. Both solicitors attend before the taxing master, and go through the bill item by item, arguing for and against it. The taxing master disallows any item that he thinks is unjustifiable, and reduces sums that he thinks

[1] The court always has a wide discretion as to costs, but this is a judicial discretion exercised according to principles. If an action is won on a legal technicality, but is an utterly unreasonable or frivolous action, the winning party may get no costs awarded, or even have to pay the loser's costs. Costs can also be apportioned when each party wins on some issue. In some proceedings, particularly in the Chancery or Probate Divisions, where the subject-matter of the action is a fund or estate, the court may order all the proper costs of all the parties to be paid out of the fund or estate; the cost of an application to the court is regarded as being part of the expense of administering the estate.

excessive. Thus if the winner has briefed a leading counsel as well as junior, say giving the leader 60 guineas and the junior 40 guineas, the amount allowed may be 30 and 20 guineas, or the taxing master may say that there was no need for a leading counsel and allow merely a modest fee for the junior. This method ensures that a party who has conducted his case on extravagant lines cannot make the losing party pay for that extravagance. When the taxation is completed, the sum allowed is known as 'party and party costs'. The party and party costs are never as high as the solicitor and own client costs: the client must pay for every disbursement properly made by his solicitor and for all the solicitor's proper charges, irrespective of the party and party taxation. If the client considers that the solicitor and client costs are too high, he can have these costs taxed. Such taxations, which are not common, involve the element of the instructions given by the client; the point here is not the figure at which the work could have been done, but whether the solicitor has charged properly for the work he was instructed to do; work done by way of precautionary measures, and the securing of expensive counsel, must be paid for by the client if he expressly or impliedly authorised it. The actual taxation of a bill costs money, and this must be paid for according to the rule that if less than one-sixth of the bill is disallowed the costs of taxation fall on the person who challenges the bill, whereas if the bill is reduced by more than one-sixth the party claiming on the bill pays for the taxation.

It would be misleading to give any figures for an average difference between solicitor and own client costs and party and party costs because circumstances vary so much. The tendency has been for solicitors to be more careful and for taxing masters to be more generous, so that the gap has narrowed. If we take two examples of simple High Court actions we might get these results:

	Solicitor and own client cases *A* and *B*	Party and party	
		Case *A*	Case *B*
Solicitor's charges	£80	£75	£60
Disbursements:			
Court fees	£30	£30	£30
Payment to witnesses	£50	£45	£20
Counsel's fees	£70	£60	£35
Miscellaneous	£10	£5	£5
	£240	£215	£150

Case *A* is the common position.[1] The explanation of Case *B* may be

[1] According to the Report of the Evershed Committee, Cmd. 8878, p. 233.

that it did not seem so simple when the case was being prepared there was extra work, counsel advising, and some evidence obtained, only to find at the trial that the anticipated difficulty did not arise. In a heavy case there may be a substantial amount of costs for reviewing the situation and advising the client as to the wisdom of letting a case proceed or negotiating, and whilst that is properly chargeable against the client it is not within the scope of party and party costs.

The fact that a successful party must in practice always bear part of the costs he incurs has some curious results. Among persons with enough money to meet costs and damages there is always the knowledge that litigation has this effect. If *A* claims £600 from *B*, *B* can generally escape by offering say £550. The solicitor to *A* will have to advise him that if he sues *B* for £600 and wins there will be the matters of costs; *A* had better take £550 in settlement than get £600 on a judgment and pay out something between £25 and £75 in costs over and above what he can recover from *B*. If one of the parties is poor, the other party may be at a great disadvantage. Ordinarily there is little use in suing a poor defendant; if a person has no money there is no sense in trying to make him pay out that which he has not got. In an action for recovery of possession of property it may of course be worth suing a poor defendant, for getting possession of a house or valuable goods may be worth while even when the plaintiff can get nothing in costs from the defendant. A poor plaintiff raises other questions. As to how a poor plaintiff can manage to sue there are various means, explained in the next section. Suppose that *X*, a person without means, complains that he has been libelled in a newspaper, and threatens to commence an action. The solicitors to the newspaper will advise that the action will have to be a High Court action, and that if the newspaper defends the action the solicitor and client costs will be not less than say £250 (and may be very much greater), and that as *X* is a person without means there is little chance of recovering any party and party costs from *X* if the newspaper wins the case. Similar problems come before insurance companies every day. It is obviously cheaper to buy off such complainants with sums running up to £100 than to defend unsubstantial claims and pay still larger sums to lawyers. Every now and then the newspaper or insurance company will fight such a case and win, tax their costs, and bankrupt the plaintiff; this will cost more than buying off the particular claimant, but it will discourage other bogus or light-hearted claimants. Many companies pay out yearly considerable sums in settlement of claims that could be successfully resisted, simply because of the costs that would otherwise be incurred.

On the other hand, a wealthy litigant has a great advantage. As will be explained later, one party can to some extent set the pace in running up costs. There is also the matter of appeals. One party may be able to afford the cost of a High Court action, but he may hesitate to commence proceedings when he knows that his adversary is likely to go to the Court of Appeal and then to the House of Lords. Solicitors are not unacquainted with cases settled (sometimes on unfair terms) because of a threat to make litigation as expensive as possible. Many appeals are little more than gambling on the costs.[1] The present restriction on appeals[2] reduces the possibility of unjustifiable appeals, but it cannot eliminate that possibility.

[1] The case of *Sutherland Publishing Co.* v. *Caxton Publishing Co.* may be studied. The plaintiffs owned the copyright in a work entitled *Heating and Ventilating*. They sued the defendants, alleging that in a book called *Modern Plumbing* the defendants had infringed their copyright. The plaintiffs claimed damages for infringement and damages for conversion under the Copyright Act 1911 s. 7. The defendants admitted infringement and offered to submit to an inquiry into damages, but denied that the plaintiffs could get damages for both infringement and conversion. This point came before the court [1936], Ch. 323; the High Court found for the defendant, but on appeal the Court of Appeal found for the plaintiff. The case then went back to the High Court for the damages to be assessed on the basis that the plaintiff had two heads of damages. This hearing [1937], Ch. 294, took ten days, the judge eventually fixing damages at £150 for infringement and £50 for conversion. The defendants had, however, paid £251 into court at an early stage of the dispute, a fact of course known to the plaintiff but not to the judge. The result was that the defendants became entitled to the party and party costs incurred since the date of payment into court. The plaintiffs then appealed to the Court of Appeal, and the defendants cross-appealed [1938], Ch. 174. As Mackinnon L.J. said: 'It is obvious that by this time the costs of litigation were far more a matter of importance than any vindication of the originality of the literary work entitled *Heating and Ventilating*.' If the plaintiffs could induce the Court of Appeal to put the damages at more than £251 then the plaintiffs would get party and party costs for all the hearings, whereas if the defendants could induce the Court of Appeal to leave the figure at £200 (the cross-appeal to reduce the figure being perhaps a tactical move) then the defendants would get the costs. Mackinnon L.J. spoke of winning or losing the 'costs game', and observed that 'the spice of a gamble may now be added to the joys of litigation'. The Court of Appeal (Mackinnon L.J. dissenting) raised the damages to £495, with the consequent order for costs against the defendants. The defendants then appealed to the House of Lords [1938], 4 All E.R. 389. The House of Lords discharged the order of the Court of Appeal and restored the order of the trial judge, thus bringing the damages down again to £200; the order as to costs took account of the defendants' cross-appeal, so that finally the defendants were given the bulk of the costs in the courts below and two thirds of the costs in the House of Lords. The amount of the costs must be far greater than the sum in dispute, and neither party can have gained anything. Yet the plaintiffs had a genuine grievance which the defendants tried to meet in a reasonable way.

[2] See p. 84, above.

It is extremely difficult to get figures that correctly represent the actual cost of litigation. If we take typical types of action, there are immense variations in the costs. The most variable items are the obtaining and presenting of evidence, and counsel's fees. In a running-down case, for instance, the witnesses who testify to what happened may be prepared to attend and give evidence voluntarily without receiving any payment, or they or some of them may have to travel considerable distances and be recompensed for loss of earnings. Some witnesses exploit their position. A medical practitioner may insist on a fee that is excessive, and that will certainly be drastically handled by the taxing master, but the party may find it expedient to pay that fee rather than go without that evidence. A witness can of course be compelled to attend, the court fixing the proper sum to pay him, but a witness who is infuriated by such treatment may (with or without violating his own conscience) not be as satisfactory as if he attended voluntarily. Even when people are reasonably public spirited and reasonably honest it may be expensive to collect them together for a trial. Counsel's fees are more within the control of the parties. For a straightforward case there is considerable range of fees, according to the standing of the counsel briefed. In practice a solicitor conducts a case according to the amount of money his client is able or willing to spend. There is of course a minimum figure at which the case could be conducted, but unless the client can pay only that sum it may be well to spend rather more; it depends on the kind of case and the current attitude of the Bench. A solicitor can, for example, say what an undefended divorce should cost, the minimum being about £90. Yet some years ago the estimate would have been uncertain, for the judge might not have been satisfied by evidence that A and B shared a room for a night. Evidence of 'association', that A and B had been seen dining together, going to cinemas and so on, should be available in case the Bench was in a prickly mood. A client would then have been told that £60 might do, but £120 or more would be safer. Nowadays a substantial number of cases involve industrial processes, arising from accidents, infringements, contracts and other causes. Evidence of the safety of a process, of common usage, of special design or scientific nature is constantly needed, and there can be a great difference between the minimum cost and the best possible preparation of the case. The amount of costs is never certain except in debt-collecting, where the normal case is undefended and the costs consist of fees and scale charges. In the High Court a judgment in default of appearance for a sum of not less than £300 has costs endorsed on the writ for £8. 17s. as basic costs with additions in certain circumstances. The County Court scale is complicated, varying with the amount claimed and with the mode of service of the summons and other matters, but it may be taken that it is somewhat lower than that for the High Court. Of course an action may be defended, and in defended cases the costs may be very much higher.

In exceptional cases the costs are monstrous. Mr Claud Mullins in his book *In Quest of Justice* (1931) gives many examples, taken from his own experience, law reports, and biographies of lawyers. The most startling example is a claim for £40,000 against under-writers, where the taxed costs of one side came to £89,000. In normal cases it may be said that a person should not start a High Court action unless he can risk spending say £250 on his own costs and £150 for his opponents' costs. The Newcastle-upon-Tyne Law Society's *Report on the Cost of Litigation* put the cost of conducting an average commercial action in London at £400 for one party; this would mean about £700 costs for the party who lost. The cost of appeals would have to be added. In one case a firm engaged in litigation over a trade-name had set aside £4000 for costs in case they lost the action and possible appeals; they won in the Court of Appeal and lost in the House of Lords, the total bill coming to £4500. County Court proceedings are of course cheaper, but in relation to the sums recovered the position is quite as unsatisfactory. Mr Mullins gives figures that show that taxed costs in County Courts are about equal to half the sum recovered, which means that the total amounts spent by both parties is approximately the same as the sum in issue. This is probably a little misleading, since in the cases that have been easier to conduct the costs are more apt to be agreed and so do not appear in the registrar's records. Costs are now higher than they were at the time when these cases occurred. The costs expended upon workmen's compensation and rent restriction would have paid many times over for a special government department or independent statutory body to deal with these matters.

It must also be remembered that litigants have to pay for the mistakes of judges. If a judge misdirects a jury, or conducts a case in some irregular fashion, the Court of Appeal may order a new trial. A litigant who has spent a large sum is surely suffering from a grievance when he is told that he must now begin all over again because the original trial judge made a mistake. Many appeals are due to uncertainty in the law. The settling of some rules of common law, and the interpretation of some statutes, has cost litigants vast fortunes. Whenever a new trial or an appeal is due to error of a judge or uncertainty in the law, the litigant who suffers should not have to bear the cost. The best remedy would appear to be an 'insurance fund'; an additional charge of £1 on each proceeding commenced in the High Court would produce over £100,000 a year.

There is no section of the community that is satisfied with the present cost of litigation. A few lawyers find that it is to their advantage, but lawyers as a whole do not gain by it. There has been a decline in the amount of litigation, and a tendency (discussed in the next chapter) to create administrative machinery rather than extend the work of the law courts. Lawyers as far as litigation is concerned flourish best upon a large volume of relatively cheap work. High costs frighten away clients. As the volume of litigation has contracted the cost has risen. Most solicitors now regard fighting an action as a misfortune from which they may save their client; a good settlement is better than a victory in the courts, and a solicitor who ignored this would not be doing his duty to his client. But the real effect is that many just and proper claims are compromised because a verdict of the courts is too expensive.[1]

A great deal has been said and written about the cost of litigation during the last few years. Three observations may be made:

First, in most cases the various items of the costs are not unreasonable.[2] Solicitors' charges, taken as a total, are not excessive for the amount of work done if we consider the general level of remuneration in other professions. In fact solicitors have been under-paid rather than over-paid. Their charges were fixed before the 1914 war and permitted increases were 20 per cent in 1917, 33⅓ per cent in 1932 and 50 per cent in 1944. The new charges for contentious work are intended to give an increase of 50 per cent over the 1957 level. The expenses of running his office must of course be considered in

---

[1] A correspondent in *The Times*, 16 August 1934, wrote: 'In a claim for £1300, the hearing of which would involve one short witness on either side and the citation of three or four decided cases, an experienced solicitor estimates the costs payable to the defendants if the claim fails at £300. Consequently the plaintiff, who is not rich, feels compelled to accept a wholly inadequate offer.' The defendant would of course have had to pay his own solicitor as well as paying the defendant's costs. This produced another letter: 'In a recent action (in a county court) a plaintiff claimed a sum of £50, the plaintiff succeeded in his action and his costs have just been taxed at £85. The defendant's costs will probably amount to about £50 or £60, when I have the heart to send in a bill.'

[2] Sir W. Ball analysed the costs of an action in 1946 (207 *Law Times*, p. 185). He came to the conclusion that costs are not too high for the amount of work that is involved.

thinking of profits. The court fees have been discussed in the last section. The expenses of getting evidence must be fairly high so long as our courts insist on oral evidence. The Evidence Act 1938 is an attempt to allow a greater use of written evidence but it would have to be greatly extended if it is to have much effect in reducing the cost of evidence. Some oral evidence will continue to be necessary, and if the witnesses' losses of earnings are substantial we have an item that cannot be reduced. Counsel's fees are the most debatable subject. The general average of fees is far higher than it used to be. Sir Hardinge Gifford (later Lord Halsbury) caused much talk in the Temple when he received 450 guineas on a brief; in the last thirty years such a sum for a leader of such eminence would pass unnoticed. In 1929 Lord Justice Scrutton considered that it would be preposterous to pay £100 to a King's Counsel for an ordinary case, pointing out that when he was called to the bar (1882) the proper fee would have been 2 guineas for a consultation and 10 guineas for the brief. The present situation is that the majority of barristers make a poor living and a few make large incomes. As I have pointed out in the section on barristers, a man who is much sought after must charge large fees. Modern conditions of publicity enable a barrister to get 'a name'; he must not of course seek for this, but it may come upon him. Clients like to feel that their affairs are in the hands of well-known barristers, and often feel a sense of importance in having Sir Somebody Something to represent them. Solicitors often feel that they can escape responsibility for selecting counsel by suggesting a fashionable leader. If one party briefs expensive counsel, then the other party may feel that they should do the same. In most cases it is a vicious circle. Few solicitors (at least in London) think that the fashionable barristers of the day are really any better than many men who take more modest fees. If the expensive leader wins the case, then people say: 'It was worth the fee; nobody else could have done it.' If the case is lost, they say: 'If that great barrister lost the case, then nobody could have won it.'

Secondly, the subject of costs is regarded as merely technical and it does not attract the kind of study that is applied to tort, contract and other parts of the law. The men who influence our law most, the judges, the successful barristers and the publicists, all move in a world carefully insulated against the cold discomfort of bills of costs. In books about the law written for general reading, such as Lord Justice Slesser's *The Law* and the late Professor Geldart's *Elements of English Law*, the subject of costs is ignored; *The Book of English Law* by Dr Jenks has a bare two pages on the topic, from which a reader might think that all is well. The general attitude, fostered by law schools, is that 'the law' is a great body of principles to be studied and applied: to ask whether a man can in reality get any remedy if he cannot afford the costs is regarded as a vulgar and irrelevant intrusion. Now that we have a legal aid service (described in the next section) it may be thought that there is even less need to think about costs, for 'legal aid will take care of that'. The legal aid service does not cover all the needs of all people. Further, it is a most undesirable thing that the cost of something should cease to be a matter of concern because it becomes payable out of public funds.

Thirdly, it is doubtful if a satisfactory solution can be found so long as parties are entitled to spend what they like. The administration of justice is a public concern, and the public may well say that no individual is entitled to determine the scale of expenditure. A particular litigant may think that his case is of such importance to himself that he will spend a vast sum of money on it; it does not follow that a part of the machinery of government should be at his disposal on his own terms. The principle of limited expenditure is in force for Parliamentary elections. A candidate is allowed to spend up to a fixed sum, together with 2*d*. for each voter on the list in counties and 1½*d*. in boroughs. A statutory return of expenses must be made, and excessive expenditure is prohibited. An enlightened public may some day decide that legal contests must also be limited in costs. The Evershed Committee[1] considered the matter and concluded:

It is not possible, however, to recommend for adoption at the present time any of the suggestions made for restricting the costs which are chargeable or recoverable. It is hoped that the procedural reforms recommended in other Sections will have the desired effect of eliminating extravagances and securing economy in the conduct of litigation, but if this view proves wrong, further consideration should be given to the limitation of party and party costs by references to scales of costs or to the standard [applied on taxation] or otherwise.

That Committee sat in a period when optimism prevailed: the 'new approach' has fizzled out,[2] and some form of limitation of costs seems the only remedy. It should however be remembered that every great change in the administration of justice has been opposed by influential lawyers and public men on the ground that it would be 'unworkable'.

[1] Cmd. 8878 (1953), para. 763.   [2] See pp. 431–2, below.

3. LEGAL AID

There has been an age-long complaint that the cost of the law prevents the poor man from getting justice. Some facilities for free assistance have existed for many years, but they were inadequate. The Legal Aid and Advice Act 1949 provides a service based on new principles and it may ultimately cover the full range of needs. It is useful to look at the older system[1] because it helps to explain the new. The provision in criminal cases has already been explained,[2] and here we need be concerned only with civil matters.

(1) *Poor Persons' Procedure.* Before the 1949 Act this was the official provision. It was orginally worked through the office of the Supreme Court, but in 1926 it was handed over to the Law Society and Provincial Law Societies and run by some ninety committees, retaining, however, the characteristic that it related to High Court actions. An applicant had to satisfy a committee that he had reasonable grounds for taking or defending a case, and that his income did not exceed £2 a week or his capital £50, or in exceptional circumstances £4 or £100. If the committee gave a certificate the applicant would not pay court fees and he would be assigned a solicitor and counsel free of charge; the applicant could be required to pay actual out-of-pocket expenses, such as witnesses' expenses, and he would have to meet his own travelling and other expenses. There was no appeal against a refusal by a committee to give a certificate. Solicitors and counsel could put their names on a list as willing to do this work. There was no remuneration; the burden was carried not by the legal profession as a whole but by those individuals who felt moved to help poor people. There was a government grant to pay for the organisation and secretarial assistance needed, but that was all.

The main defects of the Poor Persons' Procedure were:

(1) There was no system whereby a person of moderate means need pay only part of the cost; it was a case of be poor and pay nothing or pay in full. The 'poverty line' for Poor Persons' Procedure was far too low. The rules appeared to be drawn on the supposition that a person with an income of between £2 and £4 a week could afford to take proceedings, so that free legal aid was only justifiable in 'special circumstances'. Mr Seebohm Rowntree's estimate in 1937 of the *minimum* family budget was 53s. a week, or 41s. a week in rural areas, as a figure for the lowest income

---

[1] Egerton, *Legal Aid* (1945), gives the position prior to the changes made by the 1949 Act.
[2] See pp. 138–147, above.

on which a tolerable standard of living could be maintained: where earnings fell below this line it was almost certain that there would be a shortage of some of the necessities of life. It was quite possible for an application under the poor persons rules to be refused because the income exceeded £2 a week although the applicant's income was actually insufficient (after paying rent and other outgoings) to provide the minimum standard of nutrition laid down by the British Medical Association.

(2) The procedure applied only to High Court matters other than bankruptcy and criminal causes. The chief use of the procedure was for divorce and actions for personal injuries. The majority of other civil matters that commonly affect working-class people come before County Courts and Magistrates' Courts. For instance, the law of landlord and tenant, and the Rent Restriction Acts, are notoriously difficult to understand, yet a poor tenant had no service to which he could turn for assistance. A Committee that reported in 1928 even rejected a suggestion that a poor litigant in a County Court might get the court fees remitted although the Council of County Court judges was in favour of such a step.[1] In 1949 the Committee on County Court Procedure recommended that such remission should be allowed in cases of hardship.[2]

(3) It asked too much of the solicitors and counsel who gave their services. Unlike medical men, who have always been at liberty to charge the wealthy as much as they think expedient, the lawyer cannot get higher fees from the rich to enable him to give extensive free service to the poor. The solicitor, like the taxi-cab driver, must not ask for more than the recognised fare, and anything he carries free is an addition to the running-costs of his office.

(2) *Poor Man's Lawyer.* The idea of lawyers attending at certain centres and giving free legal advice arose in connection with University Settlements in the East End of London. The work spread to other organisations of a charitable, religious, or social nature. Political parties have also made provision for this service at some centres. Poor Man's Lawyers have always been quite unofficial and need not be affiliated with any law society or be approved or noticed by any public body; it is quite possible for a centre to flourish without its existence being known outside its immediate locality. The National Council of Social Services keeps a list of these centres and information can be obtained. There have always been areas, including the whole of several large towns, in which there is no such centre. There has been no uniformity in their organisation or in the assistance they can give. The usual arrangement is that a voluntary rota of solicitors and barristers provides for lawyers to attend the centre on one or more evenings a week. Applicants generally give some particulars about themselves to a secretary who may decide whether the

[1] Cmd. 3016 (1928), p. 8.
[2] Final Report, Cmd. 7668 (1949), para. 121.

applicant's means justify resort to free assistance. The principal thing is the giving of advice. Help may be given with correspondence, but the centre cannot act as a solicitor and do legal work; the applicant must go to a practising solicitor. The financial arrangements for helping applicants have varied; the common element has always been difficulty in obtaining sufficient funds. These centres have found great difficulty in keeping going over the last few years and there is naturally some doubt about their future. The Legal Aid Service has expanded and the new arrangements for giving free or very cheap legal advice will presumably get more widely known and extensively used. It may be that there will be so little left for a Poor Man's Lawyer to do that this creditable chapter in voluntary service will come to an end.

(3) *Other agencies.* It is clear that the facilities mentioned above could not enable all persons to get legal aid when they cannot afford ordinary fees. To some extent free or cheap legal assistance is given by the various organisations to which people may belong. A man may be able to look to his trade union, or professional or trade association, or some other body for legal assistance. This will generally cover merely certain types of case.

One product of the cost of litigation has been the speculative solicitor. It is illegal for anyone to finance litigation in return for a share in the proceeds, the offence being known as champerty. Yet some solicitors conducted a good deal of business on semi-champertous agreements, the solicitor doing all the work for nothing, and paying all the disbursements, in return for which he would get costs from the other side if he won the action. If the action was lost the solicitor was out of pocket. Obviously a solicitor would only undertake cases on that basis if he expected to win, for it was 'no cure, no pay'. Accident cases were the chief hunting ground of such solicitors, who were often referred to as 'ambulance chasers', although the real prey was insurance companies. A solicitor could not go directly to an injured person and ask if he could act for him: the technique was to have a bogus organisation or so-called 'claims assessors' who would approach the prospective plaintiff and explain to him how he could be helped to obtain justice. It must not be supposed that the client always suffered: the speculative solicitor was a specialist in that type of case, and he worked with counsel and doctors who were skilled in what was needed and who did not expect to be paid if the case should be lost, but the welfare of the client was not the first consideration and he did not get disinterested advice. Since the

1949 Act any person with a reasonable case can be sure of getting assistance for a High Court action, and ambulance chasing, as a highly organised type of specialist practice, has lost the basis on which it rested. Every profession has some members who habitually engage in unprofessional conduct, and doubtless there will continue to be some scope for speculative actions. Lawyers of the greatest respectability quite often see fit to help a client by acting for him knowing that they are unlikely to get adequately paid unless he is successful; the distinction is that they do not make a business out of such arrangements.

There were a number of people before the war who were endeavouring to get some improvement in the facilities for legal aid. The true position had been explained in a few books, and some proposals were put forward and discussed at the Provincial Meeting of the Law Society in 1938,[1] but there was insufficient pressure to lead to any action. There was an opposing body of opinion which objected to improved facilities on the ground that litigation is not a thing to be 'encouraged', a view that was held by the Committee which rejected any analogy with Health Insurance by saying that 'It is manifestly in the interests of the State that its citizens should be healthy, not that they should be litigious'.[2] Then in the years following 1939 came a rapid change.

At the beginning of the war it was realised that people would want information and advice, and about a thousand Citizens Advice Bureaux (mostly under the auspices of the local Council of Social Service) were set up covering the whole country. Many of the queries were about legal matters, but no general legal service could be arranged. Poor Man's Lawyer centres suffered from the general disturbances, black-out and raids making evening sessions too difficult, and this led either to the cessation of their work or to day-time opening which necessitated the employment of paid legal advisers. The next development was the realisation that army morale suffered when men, especially those overseas, were bothered about their private affairs. In 1942 an Army Legal Aid Scheme was started, and this was soon follwed by an R.A.F. scheme and then a Navy

---

[1] The proposals, together with a summary of the discussion, were published in 186 *Law Times* (October 1938), p. 296.

[2] Report of the Committee on Legal Aid for the Poor, Cmd. 3016 (1928), para. 17. It is a Report compounded of ignorance and stupidity. The critics had no desire to *encourage* litigation any more than to encourage surgical operations: the contention was that people who really needed professional services should not be debarred by poverty.

scheme. The Service schemes gave advice, and did the preparatory work for litigation. The actual conduct of litigation was either through local solicitors or under the Poor Persons' Procedure.

The war took away from private practice about two-thirds of the solicitors and a higher proportion of their staff, and the Poor Persons' Procedure could not continue on the old basis. The rigid means test would have excluded too many service men, and it was accordingly relaxed. Most of these cases were petitions for divorce, and the solution adopted was for the Law Society to set up a Services Divorce Department; salaried solicitors and staff were engaged, and the Law Society soon had a huge and unprecedented legal practice. But civilians also needed Poor Persons' Procedure, and as solicitors became unable to handle all that work a Civil Section was set up by the Law Society. The Law Society, which received a Treasury grant for running this service, did the work very cheaply. Counsel received nominal fees for taking those cases.

The war-time experience showed that we could not go back to the old system. A Departmental Committee under the chairmanship of Lord Rushcliffe was appointed in 1944 to examine the matter, and its Report appeared in May 1945[1] recommending what is in effect a new public service of legal aid and advice. The Association of Municipal Corporations, the Labour Party and the Trades Union Congress and several other organisations opposed the idea of a service being run by a central or local government authority for these authorities are often parties to disputes with private citizens. The Committee shared that view, and recommended that the service should be run by the legal profession and primarily by the Law Society. The Report was accepted in principle by the government, and the Legal Aid and Advice Act 1949 is based on that Report.

The 1949 Act does not itself directly set up a system of legal aid, but says that 'it shall be the responsibility of the Law Society to make arrangements, in accordance with a scheme made by them with the approval of the Lord Chancellor and with the concurrence of the Treasury, for securing that legal aid and legal advice are available... and generally to administer...this Act'. So that the backbone is the Law Society's Scheme together with Regulations made by the Lord Chancellor.[2] In fact the Law Society had prepared a scheme to

[1] Cmd. 6641.
[2] E. Sachs, *Legal Aid* (1951), describes the beginning of the service and gives the text of the Act and the subordinate legislation.

put before the Rushcliffe Committee, and had worked out a further detailed scheme for the Lord Chancellor before the Bill was introduced, so that although the Act is merely a framework the filling-in of detail could at once take place.

The country is divided into twelve areas, each with an area committee and subdivided to give a network of local committees. The committees are composed of solicitors and some barristers, who are paid small fees, with a salaried staff. The cost of the service is paid out of a Legal Aid Fund established and administered by the Law Society; this Fund is supplied by contributions from assisted persons, costs that are recovered and from the Exchequer.[1]

The Rushcliffe Committee made a distinction between the need for advice and the need for aid consisting of taking steps to assert or resist a claim or in litigation. Hence the Act has separate provisions for advice and for aid. The aim is to provide a wide and generally available system of virtually free legal advice, whereas legal aid is subject to certain conditions and a means test. When the Act was passed it was intended that the legal advice service and the legal aid service would start together although legal aid would at first be limited to the Supreme Court and before long be extended to other jurisdictions. Before that could happen the government announced in October 1949 a number of measures of economy, and these included postponing the full operation of the new Act. The provisions for legal advice were shelved, and aid was restricted to the Supreme Court or High Court cases remitted to County Courts. The scheme therefore started in a mangled form, and came into operation by instalments.[2]

The first step for a person in doubt or difficulty is to seek legal advice. When the Act was passed it was intended to establish a number of centres where legal advice would be given by solicitors employed whole time or part time for that purpose. The postponement of establishing such centres gave time for second thoughts, and in 1958 the Law Society proposed a different system, which the Lord Chancellor adopted and brought into operation in 1959. There are two schemes, one statutory and the other voluntary, but they are interlocked. Solicitors may put their names on a panel, and a person

---

[1] As solicitors and barristers do not receive the full amount of their costs for Supreme Court and House of Lords cases they do in effect contribute to the fund (see p. 315, below).

[2] The present position is explained in simple terms in an excellent pamphlet prepared by the Law Society, *Legal Aid and Advice: How to Obtain the Help of a Lawyer.*

who wants legal advice can go to any solicitor on the panel. The statutory scheme is available for clients who pass a simple means test: they then pay 2*s*. 6*d*.[1] for an interview of up to thirty minutes. The solicitor keeps the 2*s*. 6*d*. and gets 17*s*. 6*d*. from the Legal Aid Fund. But a client can get advice under the voluntary scheme, where there is no means test but a fee of not more than £1. The two schemes together should give people an ordinary professional service at a known (and very reasonable) cost. Legal advice is often all that is needed, but if more help is required the case becomes one for legal aid.

There are broadly speaking three situations in which legal aid may be sought. An applicant may want to make or dispute a claim, or he may want to bring or defend a case in the courts, or he may want to appeal or defend an appeal. We must first consider the types of matter in more detail.

(*a*) Aid to assert or dispute a claim relates to the stage where there is not yet any question of litigation; it is essentially for negotiations, which may lead to a settlement that ends the matter, or may fail and be followed by litigation and come under the next paragraph.

(*b*) Legal aid for proceedings covers most matters in the County Courts, other local courts of civil jurisdiction and the High Court. It is not available for libel, slander or breach of promise of marriage, nor for the ordinary processes of debt collecting or debtors wanting to pay by instalments.

(*c*) Appeals in the Court of Appeal or the House of Lords are covered.

(*d*) What are ordinarily called the civil cases in Magistrates' Courts come under legal aid, namely, matrimonial proceedings, affiliation proceedings, proceedings relating to the guardianship of infants and for the recovery of small tenements. Appeals in affiliation cases to Quarter Sessions are covered under this heading, whereas appeals in the other matters are to Divisional Courts and covered as being in the High Court.

An applicant whose needs fall within these categories has to get across two hurdles, that is, merits and financial position.[2]

In all cases the applicant must show that he has reasonable grounds for asserting or disputing a claim, or for being a party to

---

[1] No fee is charged to a person who is in receipt of national assistance.

[2] Where it appears that an applicant is likely to fulfil the conditions and it is in the interests of justice that legal aid should be given as a matter of urgency, an Emergency Certificate can be given.

proceedings, and he may be refused assistance if it appears unreasonable that he should receive it in the particular circumstances of the case. The principle which has been adopted for deciding this is for the Committee, who are themselves lawyers in private practice, to ask themselves a hypothetical question: 'What advice would I give to the applicant if he were a private client possessed of means sufficient to pay his own costs?' Legal aid should be made available to the extent to which it is necessary to enable that hypothetical advice to be acted upon.

For (a) and (d) above the Secretary of a Local Committee can decide in favour of an applicant, but if he does not do so the decision is made by the Committee. Applications under (b) are decided by the Local Committee, and if they refuse there can be an appeal to the Area Committee. Applications under (c) must go to Area Committees for decision.

The applicant's means must be within the prescribed limits. The principle here is that a person of small means should receive assistance free of charge whereas a person of moderate means should make a contribution in accordance with his ability to pay. In working out this principle we get complicated rules because in order to get a fair result it is necessary to look at the money a person has after meeting his proper commitments; we are concerned with 'disposable income' and not gross income. Similarly, we cannot assume that capital assets are available; a house in which a man lives (unless the value, after deducting any mortgage, exceeds £3000) and his furniture are not 'disposable capital'. The assessment of disposable income and capital is governed by Regulations which deal with deductions for maintenance of dependants, interest on loans, income tax, rent and other matters for which the person must or reasonably may provide, the value of a house in which the applicant resides and a number of other matters. The assessment is made by the National Assistance Board. The financial conditions of legal aid were laid down in the 1949 Act, and as the value of money declined the effect was to exclude from the scheme people whose position would, in 1949, have qualified them for assistance. In 1959 a Committee recommended[1] a raising of the limits, and substantial increases were made by the Legal Aid and Advice Act 1960.

If disposable income does not exceed £250 a year, and disposable

[1] Report of the Advisory Committee upon the Financial Provisions of the Legal Aid and Advice Act 1949 and the Legal Aid (Assessment of Resources) Regulations 1950 (Cmnd. 918, 1959).

capital is not over £125, legal aid is free. For aid in proceedings the top limit of disposable income is £700, and the rule is that the maximum contribution payable from income is an amount equal to one-third of the excess over the 'free' limit: if, for example, an applicant has a disposable income of £600, his contribution is £600 less £250, divided by three, namely £116. 13s. 4d. For capital, the maximum contribution is the amount by which disposable capital exceeds £125; if disposable capital exceeds £500 the applicant is outside the scheme unless it appears that he cannot afford to proceed without legal aid. If the applicant with disposable income of £600 also had disposable capital of, for example, £200, his maximum contribution would be £116. 13s. 4d. for income and £200 less £125 for capital, a total of £191. 13s. 4d. When these figures of income are translated from 'disposable' back into actual, the top limits are an income of about £1200 for a single man to £1600 for a married man with three children.

The cost of asserting or disputing a claim is far less than that of litigation, and lower limits apply, namely that disposable income is not more than £325 and disposable capital not more than £125. If negotiations fail and litigation arises, an application can be made for legal aid for proceedings and the higher financial limits will apply.

The procedure is that the applicant fills up a form and sends it to the Secretary of the Local Committee. In many applications for assistance in claims or for proceedings in Magistrates' Courts the Local Committee can assess disposable income and capital, but otherwise the applicant will have to be seen by the National Assistance Board. If the Local Committee approve the application on merits, and the applicant is within the financial limits, he receives a form setting out the terms on which the Local Committee are prepared to issue a civil aid certificate. If we take the example given above, where £191. 13s. 4d. was the maximum contribution, the Local Committee will estimate the cost of the proceedings and they may offer a certificate provided he contributes the maximum, or less, say £100, he being liable up to a further £91. 13s. 4d. if the actual cost is so high; if it is less than he contributes, he gets a refund of the excess over the actual cost. Contributions from income are normally payable by instalments. It may seem that when a maximum contribution exceeds the estimated cost, as it often does in undefended divorce cases, there is no point in having a civil aid certificate. The advantage is that whatever happens the litigant knows the maximum amount that he can be called upon to pay for his own costs: a case that is expected to be undefended may be defended, and other complications may arise; he may win and have to face an appeal, and the costs of that are covered.

There is, however, the question of what happens if he loses and is on ordinary principles ordered to pay the costs of his successful adversary. Here it is provided that 'his liability by virtue of an order for costs made against him with respect to the proceedings shall not exceed the amount (if any) which is a reasonable one for him to pay having regard to all the circumstances, including the means of all the parties and their conduct in connection with the dispute'. Thus it seems that the taking or defending of proceedings in proper cases has become a real possibility for people of small or moderate means, and that the risk of being ruined by losing and having to pay costs has largely disappeared, but except to the poorer people it is by no means a 'free' service.

The 1949 Act continued the Divorce Department of the Law Society for matrimonial causes where the contribution payable was £10 or less. A process of winding-up the Department began in 1960 and all cases now go to solicitors in private practice. All practising solicitors and barristers can have their names on panels either for doing any work under the scheme or limited categories of work for which there are special panels. Virtually every firm of solicitors with the exception of some large city firms have joined the legal aid and legal advice panels and nearly all barristers have joined the legal aid panels. A person who becomes entitled to legal aid must select a solicitor and (where this is required) may himself select a barrister from an appropriate panel, or he may leave his solicitor to select counsel. Solicitors and counsel must accept the legal aid client unless there is good reason to refuse. The fact that the services of solicitor and counsel are given under the scheme does not affect the ordinary relationship between solicitor, counsel and client. Legal aid cases are thus conducted in the same way as cases in which parties are not legally assisted, except for costs. For legal aid for claims, matrimonial and other civil cases in Magistrates' Courts and relatively small matters generally, the solicitor applies to the Area Committee, and the Area Committee do the equivalent of taxing a bill. For other matters, which include substantial County Court cases, and proceedings in the High Court and Appellate Courts, the solicitor's bill is taxed by a taxing master. Here there are some peculiarities. Briefs to counsel are not marked with any fee, but marked 'Legal Aid' so that the Taxing Master allows what he regards as a proper fee for the work done. For claims in Magistrates' Court and County Court proceedings solicitors and counsel are paid out of the Legal Aid Fund the full amount allowed on taxation. For work in the higher courts counsel receive 90 per cent of the amount allowed on taxation and solicitors receive disbursements in full and 90 per cent of the amount allowed as profit costs. The Rushcliffe Committee[1] thought that this work ought not to attract the full remuneration, and they recommended 85 per cent; the estimate was that 70 per cent of profit costs were office expenses, so that 85 per cent really meant 50 per cent of true profit. The 1949 Act started off with 85 per cent, which was changed to 90 per cent in 1961. Since the money is paid out of the Legal Aid Fund there are no bad debts or trouble and delays in collecting costs, and that is some compensation for the percentage deduction.

No money passes between the assisted person and solicitor or counsel. The assisted person pays his contribution into the Fund. If he loses, then his contribution goes on his own costs; he may be ordered to pay his opponent's costs but the court must consider what it is reasonable to order him to pay; if he is defendant, he will of course be liable to satisfy any judgment given against him. If he wins, any costs from his opponent and any damages recovered are paid into the Fund. For example, suppose the actual cost of an action was £90, and £400 damages and £70 costs were recovered from the defendant. The Fund is then £20 down on costs. If the plaintiff made no contribution, then the £20 comes out of the damages, and he gets £380. If his contribution had been £50, then £20 of that stays in the Fund and he gets £30 back and £400 damages. The Fund is therefore fed in part by costs recovered from the other side and in part by the contributions of the persons who are legally aided. These two sources yield well over half the cost of the litigation; the balance, and money to cover administration, advice and criminal cases (where no money comes in), is covered by grant from the Exchequer. In 1960–1 the grant was £1,800,000 and in 1961–2 £2,575,000.

The Legal Aid and Advice Service has become established as part of our legal system. It is now regarded as part of a solicitor's duty to consider whether his client would be assisted by facilities of the scheme and to advise him accordingly. Having legally aided clients has become an ordinary incidence of practice. The number of cases is still mounting. The advice service began in 1959. In 1960 legal aid for claims began, and legal aid in the House of Lords in civil and

[1] Cmd. 6641 (1945), p. 35.

criminal cases. Also in 1960 the financial requirements for applicants were altered, in effect substantially raising the level at which assistance can be obtained. In 1961 matrimonial and other civil cases in Magistrates' Courts and Quarter Sessions came within the scheme. In 1960–1 applications showed an increase of 42·5 per cent over 1959–60, and in 1961–2 an increase of 82·2 per cent over 1960–1, that is, an increase of 159·6 per cent in two years. In 1961–2 there were 103,723 applications for assistance, and 74,834 Civil Aid and 1668 Emergency Certificates were issued. Analysis of the cases shows that divorce and matrimonial and allied cases in Magistrates' Courts head the list, with 29,624 and 28,515 cases respectively. The next largest group is that of common law actions, mostly personal injury on roads and at work, of 12,218.

The enlargement of the scope of legal aid and the range of incomes that enable people to receive assistance brings into greater prominence the matter of costs as between parties. In a case of Assisted person A against Unassisted person U, if A wins he gets costs (that is, ordinary party and party costs), but if he loses, then any order is limited to such amount as the court finds to be a reasonable one for him to pay having regard to all the circumstances, including the means of all the parties and their conduct in connection with the dispute. There has been debate over what the law should be. It can be said that the State by assisting A to bring his action puts U into danger, and the State should indemnify U; if A loses and appeals, and U wins the appeal, U will probably get nothing or a negligible sum from A and so have to bear his own costs below and those on appeal. On the other hand, there has always been a risk of not getting payment of costs (whatever order for them is made) when the unsuccessful plaintiff is a poor man,[1] and the legal aid service creates no new risk. Further, the unassisted U may not suffer at all; the defendants in most personal injury claims are covered by insurance and there are other pockets that do not need lining with public money. A compromise was proposed in a government Bill introduced in March 1963. The court, after considering what contribution an assisted person could make to the costs, would have had a discretion in some circumstances to order costs to be paid out of the Legal Aid fund to a successful unassisted litigant. Some difficulties arose, and the Bill was dropped on the understanding that the government would introduce a Bill in the next session of Parliament.

There are obvious dangers in entrusting the legal aid service to the

[1] See p. 298, above.

legal profession, for any close body may become insensitive to public needs. One of the problems of our day is how to bring the views of the consuming public effectively before those who run public enterprise. The legal aid service is under the general control of the Lord Chancellor, who as a minister is responsible to Parliament.[1] He has an Advisory Committee, appointed by him from persons with 'knowledge of the work of the courts and social conditions'. The Law Society is required to make an annual Report on the operation and finance of the civil side of the legal aid service, and this Report and any comments of the Advisory Committee must be laid before Parliament. These annual Reports are most informative and contain valuable statistics.

The student of social services should make a close study of the legal aid scheme and its working. It secures the services of professional men without there being any feeling of regulation or control of their activities, and it goes a long way to ensure that assisted persons will be treated like ordinary clients. If assistance is needed it is provided free or subject to contributions according to a means test, and that test works on a basis not of gross income or gross capital but of what is 'disposable'. If it succeeds in all these things it will be no mean achievement.

[1] Parliamentary control is also secured through finance. In the Session 1955–6 the Select Committee on Estimates examined the legal aid service, and much information is given in their Report and Minutes of Evidence. There is virtually no room for economy if legal procedure remains in its present state. Reform, particularly in divorce jurisdiction, would save an appreciable amount of public money.

CHAPTER VI

SPECIAL TRIBUNALS

I. THE CREATION OF SPECIAL TRIBUNALS

England has for centuries had a large number of courts that can be called 'special'. A 'court' was a place for doing business of a public nature, judicial and otherwise, and wherever we find places with any peculiar standing (Royal Forests, Staple Towns, Cinque Ports) or certain industries (lead mining in the Mendips, tin mining in Devon and Cornwall) or classes of men differentiated from the general population (merchants, soldiers, ecclesiastics) we find historically a special body of law with special courts. The development of the courts described in earlier chapters resulted in most of the special jurisdictions becoming absorbed in the common law system. Courts-martial and ecclesiastical courts are the chief survivors of the ancient special courts. Courts-martial are now entirely governed by statute, the Army Act, with jurisdiction confined to those in military service. A similar system exists for the navy and air force. Ecclesiastical courts are now largely statutory, and their jurisdiction is in practice confined to discipline of the clergy and matters affecting the ornamentation and fabric of churches. The constitutional position of the armed forces of the Crown and of the Church of England can be studied in works on constitutional law.[1] There are other old jurisdictions that survive.[2] In 1954 the Court of Chivalry sat again, not having sat for 223 years, to try a complaint by the City of Manchester against a theatre company for unauthorised use of the armorial bearing of the city.[3] The modern distinction between 'ordinary' and 'special' takes little notice of these survivals, for it is concerned with the development of administrative law. Decisions about many of the common affairs of people are made by bodies other than the law courts. A citizen disputing with his landlord, claiming benefit under National Insurance, objecting to an assessment for rating or taxation, wanting to develop his property or involved in many other matters, may find that his case is heard by some tribunal or that he

---

[1] Wade and Phillips, *Constitutional Law*, pt. IX, pt. XI.
[2] Halsbury, *Laws of England*, title *Courts*.
[3] *The Times*, 22 December 1954, describes the ceremonial of this picturesque affair: the case is in the Law Reports [1955] P. 133.

must appear at some inquiry. These are the jurisdictions that are now contrasted with the courts that have been described in the preceding chapters.

Whilst it is usual to speak about 'the ordinary courts' as if they are clearly distinguished from special jurisdictions, there is less of a clear-cut division than is often supposed. The most marked characteristic of special tribunals is that they are a very mixed lot. For many people, including a number of lawyers, the word 'tribunal' evokes a Rent Tribunal,[1] a body that in many of its features is the very opposite of a law court. Yet we have the Transport Tribunal[2] and the Lands Tribunal,[3] both independent judicial bodies with lawyer chairmen, and virtually High Court status: appeal is to the Court of Appeal. The Patents Appeal Tribunal and the Registered Designs Appeal Tribunal consists of a High Court judge, with appeal to the Court of Appeal. The Court of Protection is virtually a part of the High Court consisting of the Lord Chancellor and the judges of the Chancery Division, for dealing with the estates of persons who are mentally disordered. The work is done by the Master and Assistant Masters, with reference or appeal to a judge. Particulars of the work of these bodies is given in the annual *Civil Judicial Statistics*, the Tables appearing after those for the ordinary superior courts and before those for County Courts and other civil courts. The latest addition is the Restrictive Practices Court,[4] consisting of High Court judges and other persons, with appeal to the Court of Appeal. If we looked at the activities for which Parliament grants money under the heading of the Supreme Court we should see that it includes the Courts-Martial Appeal Court, because as regards England it has the same composition as the Court of Criminal Appeal and uses the same building and general facilities; there is also an item for Pension Appeals, for they go to a High Court judge but are not High Court matters. A special jurisdiction may, however, be of a high level and yet be unconnected financially or by association of ideas with the High Court, as for example the Commissioner who has appellate jurisdiction under the National Insurance Acts.[5]

At a lower level comes a bewildering variety of tribunals and inquiries, each limited to some special field, with no uniformity of composition, area of operation or procedure. The only common element is that all these bodies are statutory and are exercising

---

[1] See p. 340, below.   [2] See p. 328, below.   [3] See p. 349, below.
[4] This new jurisdiction is better classified as a law court (see p. 75, above).
[5] See p. 344, below.

functions laid down by particular Acts of Parliament. Institutionally there is nothing that we can put alongside the hierarchy of ordinary civil and criminal courts that have been described in earlier chapters, to give a parallel hierarchy of administrative jurisdiction. We can look at specimens of tribunals and inquiries and make some broad distinctions, but that will not give us much in the way of a system. There is another difference from the law courts in that we have to ask rather different questions. There is no need to go into the reason why the civil and the criminal courts exist: we simply take it for granted that people have disputes that have to be determined and that criminal cases have to be tried. Our principal concern is whether our ordinary courts do their work competently, expeditiously and at a reasonable cost. With special tribunals and inquiries we may well ask similar questions, but there is the further and often much more difficult question of why they were established: why, already having a system of courts, should we provide a variety of additional and unrelated institutions instead of using the established machinery? The first public inquiry concerned with these questions came at a time when the problem was seen as being that of Ministers' Powers[1] under the two headings of delegated legislation[2] and judicial or quasi-judicial decisions. The Committee on Ministers' Powers pointed out that some people believe that the delegating of legislative power and the conferring of jurisdiction on Ministers and tribunals is wholly bad and should cease, but the Committee thought differently and stated their general conclusion:[3]

But in truth whether good or bad the development of the practice is inevitable. It is a natural reflection, in the sphere of constitutional law, of changes in our ideas of government which have resulted from changes in political, social and economic ideas, and of changes in the circumstances of our lives which have resulted from scientific discoveries. In this connection we call attention to the following passage in the Report (June 1931) of the Committee on Finance and Industry:[4]

'The most distinctive indication of the change of outlook of the government of this country in recent years has been its growing pre-occupation, irrespective of party, with the management of the life of the people. A study of the Statute Book will show how profoundly the conception of

---

[1] The Committee on Ministers' Powers was appointed in 1929. The Chairman, Lord Donoughmore, resigned for reasons of health, and Sir Leslie Scott, who became a Lord Justice in 1935, was chairman when the Report was being drafted. The Evidence and Memoranda was published, and they provide the best material for study of that period. The Report, Cmd. 4060, was published in 1932 and has been reprinted. Many references to the Report are made later in this chapter.

[2] See p. 42, above.   [3] Cmd. 4060, p. 5.

[4] Cmd. 3897 of 1931. Pt I, ch. I, para. 8, pp. 4 and 5.

the function of government has altered. Parliament finds itself increasingly engaged in legislation which has for its conscious aim the regulation of the day-to-day affairs of the community, and now intervenes in matters formerly thought to be entirely outside its scope. This new orientation has its dangers as well as its merits. Between liberty and government there is an age-long conflict. It is of vital importance that the new policy, while truly promoting liberty by securing better conditions of life for the people of this country, should not, in its zeal for interference, deprive them of their initiative and independence which are the nation's most valuable assets.

This statement is still, I think, representative of the attitude taken by lawyers. The chairman of the Committee on Finance and Industry, Lord Macmillan,[1] was a Law Lord, and there is a touch of the legal precedent about the way it was cited by a Committee that also had a distinguished legal chairman, and thus endorsed it stands like a great decided case.[2] It suggests a single, relatively simple analysis with 'interference' as the principal factor.

The period since the middle of the nineteenth century has seen a vast growth in the scope of government activities. In the eighteenth and early nineteenth centuries it was generally thought that the government should maintain order and see to the protection of property and the enforcement of contracts, but that it should do as little else as was possible. Those views slowly changed, until in the modern welfare state we accept a governmental or public responsibility for the general economic condition of the country and the principal social needs of the population. This amazing transformation has not been achieved solely by a concept of 'interference', for the provision of 'works' (water, drainage, houses, transport, power, schools, hospitals and so on) and of 'facilities' (such as education, health services and social security) do not seem to be essentially interferences except to a one-track mind. Even a law student stuffed with Dicey and the latter-day legal saints is conscious that there is some difference between the legislation and administration that provides funds for his going to a university and the bureaucratic control of London taxi-cabs.

The best example of direct interference is to be found in the Factories Acts. Regulation of trade and of employment by statute was no new thing, but the Factories Act 1833 went much further by establishing an inspectorate. The pattern of regulation by law,

---

[1] In a *Man of Law's Tale* (1952), p. 196, Lord Macmillan says that the introductory chapter was largely his composition, whereas Keynes took charge of the drafting of the technical parts.

[2] As in Wade and Phillips, *Constitutional Law*, pt. VII, ch. 2.

backed by an administrative system for checking and enforcing, has been applied to other needs for improving working conditions, accuracy of weights and measures, cleanliness of food supplies and many other fields. All these measures have had to provide for some method of adjudication: prosecution in Magistrates' Courts is the most usual procedure, but a special tribunal or Minister's decision is prescribed for some matters.[1]

A large group of powers relate to the acquisition of land. There is here no element of Naboth's Vineyard: the position is that certain works are needed, in the sense of civil engineering, for the making of roads and bridges, water supplies and sewerage, and for what we now regard as the normal physical equipment for the essential services of a modern community. Once it is settled that, say, a new sewerage system is required, then the use of some land for that purpose is a consequence. Until the later nineteenth century Private Acts of Parliament[2] were used to give powers for the making of turnpike roads, canals, railways, water and drainage works and various kinds of town improvements. Where there was profit to be made, as with canals and railways, the powers were given to the promoters to form and run a commercial undertaking: where there would be no profit the general practice was to set up an *ad hoc* authority, such as Improvement Commissioners for an urban area, and authorise them to finance the work by levying a rate. When our local government authorities took their present shape in the nineteenth century they owed more to these *ad hoc* statutory bodies than

---

[1] See p. 357, below.

[2] Ordinary legislation starts by a Bill introduced by a member of the government or by a private member, which gives 'government Bills' and 'private members' Bills'; when passed they become ordinary statutes. A private Bill is quite different and it must not be confused with a private member's Bill. A person or body outside Parliament may petition Parliament to alter the law relating to a locality or to confer rights on or relieve from liability some particular person or body of persons, and the Bill to carry out this proposal is a private Bill. It used to be necessary for the promoters to get some well-disposed members of each House to help the Bill along, but in the middle of the nineteenth century that became unnecessary, the Bills being divided between the two Houses and brought forward as a matter of routine. Persons who object to the Bill may, if they have sufficient interest, be allowed to oppose. The most distinctive part of private Bill procedure has always been the Committee stage, for before the Committee (which now numbers five in the Lords and four in the Commons) the promoters and opponents of the Bill appear by counsel, produce witnesses if appropriate, and in fact prove their case for or against. Private Bills used to be used for really private purposes, as for divorce, naturalisation, and settled estates, but for many years the petitioners have been local authorities and statutory undertakers.

to earlier forms of local self-government. The principal need was to convert the crowded and insanitary town of the Industrial Revolution into something that was not a menace to health, and to prevent a recurrence of the evils of uncontrolled building and use of premises. The local elected council had a number of services to run, much of its work being the building and engineering requirements for public health. The new problems created new services, and then in turn the new services created new problems. The insistence upon properly made-up roads, adequate sewerage, and clean water supplies meant that civil engineers and administrators had to work together. Decisions in such matters involve the rights of individuals, for it is not possible to put through any large scheme without interfering with private property or compelling property owners to take certain steps. Conflicts, generally between local government authorities and individuals, were inevitable. The usual position has been this: the local authority wants to do something, say lay pipes across A's land, and A objects; is the local authority right in its contention? Right or wrong seems to depend not upon morals but upon two questions of expediency: *First*, is this proposed layout of pipes sound from a technical point of view, and what alternative layouts are possible; these are questions for civil engineers to answer. *Secondly*, is the scheme worth carrying out from the point of view of the public; the cost to the ratepayers and the disturbance of A's property (for which he will receive compensation) have to be weighed against the communal gain; this is a question that the local authority, an elected representative body with technical advisers, must answer. But is the property owner, or other interested person who objects, to be helpless against the local authority? The earlier answer was that the power would be given by Parliament through private Bill procedure and that procedure ensured that conflicting interests were thrashed out in a kind of judicial process in Committee whilst considerations of public policy were determined by Parliament. That was a very good answer, but private Bill procedure has always been expensive. An attempt was made to cheapen the process by statutes authorising the use of Provisional Orders. The local authority asked the appropriate Minister to confer the required power by an Order; the Minister then caused a local inquiry to be held, and on the result of that inquiry decided whether to make the order; if he did make the order, it was 'provisional' because it had no legal effect until it had been confirmed by Parliament. Several provisional orders were scheduled to a Provisional Orders Confirmation Bill, but this would not necessarily go through in the ordinary way, for if an order were opposed that part would be dealt with as if it were a private Bill. The result was that provisional order procedure could be quite as expensive as private Bill procedure. For a local authority to force through the compulsory acquisition of a small piece of land for allotments or for building a school would cost many times the value of the land. The application to the Minister, the public inquiry and the Minister's decision did not cost much; the expensive part was a contest in Parliament. Hence the obvious way of cheapening the process was to take away the need for going to Parliament at all by providing that the order of the Minister should be absolute[1] and not provisional. The debates in Parliament on proposals to give such powers to Ministers generally turned on whether Parliament ought to divest itself of duties that it had previously performed, and the proposals were accepted because it was felt that the next best thing to Parliament doing that work was for it to be done by a Minister responsible to Parliament. It was not thought of as essentially judicial work that should or even could be given to the judges, but it did provide a pattern for giving Ministers power to decide various kinds of disputes. The judges had certainly not welcomed having to decide many questions that arose from State control over railways, for they soon learned that they were in effect asked to pronounce judgment upon the management of railways. Lord Campbell, when Lord Chief Justice, complained that Parliament was trying to turn the judges into railway directors. A separate tribunal (described later) was established.

The third line of development has been the emergence of services that are essentially a matter of financial and administrative organisation. The typical example is National Insurance. These began with the Liberal government in the years before the 1914 war, and have expanded until the period after the Second World War resulted in a nation-wide system of social security. In such services there is a constant flow of claims for the various benefits, and inevitably there are disputes as to whether an applicant is entitled or as to the amount that is due to him. It is here that special tribunals have been particularly favoured.

These three lines of development are not separate, either in nature or as historical stages. The completion of a sewerage system is likely

---

[1] The nomenclature changed, and by later statutes the local authority makes the order (which is really a draft order) and submits it to the Minister, who, after an inquiry, may confirm it.

to result in direct interference with property rights, for when facilities are available occupiers can be compelled to provide modern sanitation. The educational system needs land for schools, and it interferes with parents who do not see to the schooling of their children. National Insurance makes contribution compulsory, so that those who ought to put stamps on cards and who do not do so are prosecuted. It is possible to pick out the element of interference in virtually every aspect of modern life, but to regard this as the main feature is to get so many things out of proportion. The field of law has expanded, but attitudes are still governed by the conditions of a past age. People still think of law as being essentially a set of commands: the law says you must do this and not do that or you will get "had up" before a court.

This simple concept of commands and sanctions does give a reasonable analysis of criminal law and of contract and tort, for in these matters the courts are concerned with punishment and with the giving of damages and other remedies. Property rights are protected by criminal law and by actions in law courts against people who interfere with those rights. It is generally true to say that the older and traditional part of our law rests upon this idea of sanctions, although there have always been a few legal topics, such as the law of wills, where there is difficulty in finding either command or sanction. The law lays down how a will is to be made, and if the requirements are not observed the document cannot be accepted as a will. No evil falls on the testator for he has died before it is realised that the document is not valid. The persons who thought they were going to receive some benefit, and now discover that they are not, may consider that they suffer an evil, but that does not arise out of anything that they have done or not done: the sanction, if any, is not related to the actions of the would-be testator. It is better to drop the ideas of command and sanction and to recognise that the law provides a facility for those who want to make testamentary dispositions.

A great deal of social legislation is designed to give an extension of opportunities. A simple example is the provision of municipal libraries. The law does not require local authorities to provide libraries, but they may do so; and the law does not require any citizen to use the library, but he may do so. He cannot decide entirely for himself how and when he will take out books; he must go through the prescribed procedure for being accepted as a borrower and he must observe the rules. The same kind of analysis can be made of the Health Service. You do not have to make use of it, but if you do you have to observe a number of rules and regulations. Many of the rules and regulations of modern law are in a sense compulsions, in that they control people's conduct, but they are really procedural. When an institution has grown up over a long period of time, as for example banking, we accept the procedures. Customers make out cheques in particular ways because they know that that is how it should be done, and whether that rests on the custom of bankers or is required by statutory provision is of little importance. If by some queer chance we had no banking system, and decided to create one as a national service, there would be a whole apparatus of rules and regulations, and customers would have to use the prescribed forms, all to provide a facility. Much of the structure and working of public services is not thought of as being 'law', because 'law' is associated with lawyers and law courts, and people do not go to lawyers for guidance and assistance over the whole range of the services. One's doctor is commonly the adviser on what can be obtained under the Health Service and a Trade Union Secretary may advise and assist on claims under the National Insurance Acts. Indeed one of the unforeseen difficulties of the Welfare State is to ensure that the citizen does get on to the right part of the right service. But whether people go to lawyers for advice or go elsewhere, all this is law, and it is an expanding field.

A result of these processes is that we now have a great variety of persons and bodies performing functions that are judicial, or that at least have some element or appearance of being judicial. There is no publication which describes all these jurisdictions, and indeed an up-to-date list of them cannot be found,[1] so that a comprehensive

---

[1] The principal source is to be found in the *Memoranda and Minutes of Evidence* of the two official inquiries. The material from the *Committee on Minister's Powers* (whose Report is Cmd. 4060, 1932) is now important for the history of these matters. The published papers of the *Committee on Administrative Tribunals and Enquiries* (The Franks Committee, whose Report is Cmnd. 218, 1957) give a mass of information. Each government department was asked to supply particulars about each kind of tribunal, inquiry or hearing with which it was concerned, and the resulting six volumes of Memoranda give a complete list as things stood in 1955. The actual working of all these bodies is not described, and although many of the bones can be clothed from the Minutes of Evidence there is no convenient synthesis. The Report is discussed at pp. 384 *et seq.*, below. The Annual Reports of the Council on Tribunals (see p. 386, below) list the Tribunals under the Council's general supervision, with the number of cases heard. A description of some tribunals is given in *Administrative Tribunals at Work*, ed. R. S. W. Pollard (1950). C. K. Allen published material on particular tribunals in the first number of *Public Law* (1956), subsequently reprinted in book form. The best general account is still W. A. Robson, *Justice and Administrative Law*, 3rd ed. (1951).

account would be a formidable undertaking. In some instances a tribunal's jurisdiction is virtually a self-contained subject, as with the new Restrictive Practices Court: the tribunal and its work give us the whole story. In other instances a tribunal or inquiry before an inspector is merely a part of a large and involved subject, and there is a very real chance of seeing things in a wrong perspective by looking at the jurisdiction as if the whole subject were the determination of disputes. Despite these complications we have to look at these tribunals and inquiries to get a balanced view of our machinery of justice. A comparison of the law courts and these newer jurisdictions is made later, and a further section deals with the control exercised over them by the law courts, but before considering these matters it is useful to take a number of these tribunals and give a brief account of their salient features. The following tribunals have been selected in order to give a general view of the kind of bodies known as administrative or ministerial or special tribunals, and of the range of matters with which they are concerned.

2. EXAMPLES OF SPECIAL TRIBUNALS

Transport

One of the earliest needs for a special regulatory body was in connection with canals and railways. The rise of road transport provided new problems. Now nationalisation, and some measure of de-nationalisation, are superimposed on a structure that was already complicated.

The Railway and Canal Commission. The trend towards monopoly by the railway companies led Parliament in 1854 to compel railway companies to afford reasonable facilities and to prevent them from giving preference to particular traders. Complaints were to be made to the Court of Common Pleas, but this proved unsatisfactory, and a tribunal of Commissioners was set up in 1873. In 1888 the tribunal was re-formed as the Railway and Canal Commission, consisting of two persons (one of whom must be experienced in railway business) appointed by the Home Secretary on the recommendation of the President of the Board of Trade, and a High Court judge nominated by the Lord Chancellor.[1] The Commission was by statute a court of record, which meant that it had its own seal and that other courts would take cognisance of its proceedings. The judge, who presided,

---

[1] The Commission also acted for Scotland and Northern Ireland, in which case the presiding judge and appeal court were different.

gave a ruling on any point that the Commissioners decided was one of law, and on points of law there was a right of appeal to the Court of Appeal. The Railways Act 1921 added to the work of the Commission by giving it power to require a railway company to afford reasonable railway services and facilities. This in effect gave the Commission the right to settle some questions of railway policy. The jurisdiction over many kinds of disputes, particularly undue preference and traffic facilities, was continued. At the same time the Commissioners were relieved of their duties of considering railway charges by the creation of the Railway Rates Tribunal.

The Railway Rates Tribunal. This Tribunal consisted of three permanent members appointed by the Crown on the joint recommendation of the Lord Chancellor, the President of the Board of Trade, and the Minister of Transport. One had to be a person of experience in commercial affairs, one a person of experience in railway business, and the president had to be an experienced lawyer. The Tribunal was a court of record, appeals on points of law going to the Court of Appeal. The Tribunal was formed in connection with the re-organisation and amalgamation of the railway companies that arose out of the situation after the 1914–18 war. The first duty of the Tribunal was to settle standard terms of carriage of goods for all railways; for this purpose goods were classified and terms and rates for each category were drawn up. After having brought the new system into operation the Tribunal was engaged primarily upon controlling its operation. The fares, rates and charges in connection with the road transport service of railway companies, and many matters connected with the London Passenger Transport Board, were also placed under the jurisdiction of the Tribunal.

The Transport Act 1947 set up a new public corporation, The Transport Commission, to take over the railways and associated services and to run other undertakings that might be brought within the scheme of nationalisation. This involved some re-organisation of tribunals. The Act set up a temporary *Transport Arbitration Tribunal* to assess compensation and other matters concerned with the transfer of undertakings to public ownership, and *The Transport Tribunal* as a permanent body, being in effect the old Railway Rates Tribunal reconstituted. In jurisdiction it took over that of the Railway and Canal Commission (which was abolished in 1949), that of the High Court over tolls and the work of the Appeal Tribunal under the Road and Rail Traffic Act 1933. It also had new work, such as appeals in the licensing of persons to carry goods and provide port facilities in competition with the Transport Commission. Rules of procedure are similar to those for the old Railway Rates Tribunal, which had been modelled on those of the High Court. On a point of law there is an appeal to the Court of Appeal.

The Transport Act 1947 did not directly transfer road haulage or passenger road transport to the Transport Commission, but provided for road haulage to be taken over and for passenger transport to be dealt with by schemes. Long distance road haulage was taken over, but a substantial measure of de-nationalisation was carried out under the Transport Act 1953. The 1953 Act also repealed the provisions for taking over passenger transport. The Transport Act 1962 divided the Transport Commission into the Railways Board, Docks Board, British Waterways Board and a Holding Company. The Transport Tribunal continues, with an increased membership; it has now a lawyer president, two persons of experience in transport business and two persons of experience in financial matters or economics. It now sits in two divisions each of the president and two members. The London Fares and Miscellaneous Charges Division deals with passenger fares in London, and charges for carriage of mail and armed forces. The Road Haulage Appeals Division hears appeals on road carriers' licences, which are explained later. For these hearings the president may appoint one or more persons from a special panel, either to sit alone or with a member or members of the Road Haulage Appeals Division; when the president does not himself sit he directs which person is to preside.

The present Transport Tribunal has lost the main work of dealing with rates and charges all over the country that occupied its predecessor the Railway Rates Tribunal, for only London passenger fares are now determined in this way.

The Licensing Authority for Public Service Vehicles. The Road Traffic Act 1930 set up a system of special licensing of buses and motor coaches. The statutes have been consolidated and the Road Traffic Act 1960 is the present authority. A public service vehicle is a motor vehicle for carrying passengers for hire or for reward, other than taxi-cabs, ordinary cars that are hired, trams and trolley-buses. There are three classes of public service vehicle: (1) stage carriages, where stops are made to pick up and set down passengers and separate fares of under 1*s*. are charged; (2) express carriages, where all fares are 1*s*. or more; (3) contract carriages, where the vehicle is hired as a whole. The control of public service vehicles is through a system of special licensing. England and Wales are divided into ten traffic areas, and for each area there are three Traffic Commissioners (except in the Metropolitan area where there is one Commissioner). The members are appointed by the Minister of Transport, two of the members being appointed from panels nominated by the local authorities in the area. The chairman for each area, selected by the minister, must give his whole time to the work; he holds office on the same terms as the civil service except for a later retiring age of seventy. The other two members for each area are appointed for three years and may be re-appointed. The Commissioners issue various kinds of licences. The licence for the vehicle itself (which is additional to the Road Fund licence required by all motor vehicles) specifies whether it is a stage, express or contract carriage; stage and express carriages may be used as contract carriages, but a contract carriage may never be used as a stage or express carriage. There is also a certificate of fitness designed to secure the road-worthiness of the vehicle; the granting of this depends on the reports of inspectors and examiners. Drivers and conductors of public service vehicles also require special licences, the aim being to secure competent men. The crux of the matter is the road service licence. Contract carriages do not require a road service licence, but stage and express carriages are unable to operate at all without such a licence. The Commissioners must take into account the suitability of the routes proposed, the existing services, whether the proposed service is in the public interest, and the needs of the area as a whole in relation to traffic and the co-ordination of all forms of passenger transport, including transport by rail. If a road service licence is granted there may be conditions attached. It is usual for a time-table and schedule of fares to be attached. In determining the fares to be sanctioned the Commissioners must see that the fares are not unreasonable, and that where it is desirable in the public interest the fares shall be so fixed as to prevent wasteful competition with alternative forms of transport. Where a service is to operate outside the area of the Commissioners who give the licence it is necessary for the Commissioners of another area or areas to back the licence. The result of this system is that the Commissioners are in complete control of passenger carriage on the roads: they may deprive an omnibus proprietor of his business by refusing a licence, or ruin him by the limitations of the licences they grant. The hearing of an application for a licence, or the backing of a licence, must be in public; counsel may appear, and there are a number of rules of procedure. Drivers and conductors to whom licences are refused may appeal to a Magistrates' Court.

Applicants for other licences, or persons who have unsuccessfully opposed the grant of such licences, can appeal only to the Minister of Transport. 'This system of appeal from one semi-judicial, semi-administrative authority to another, the minister himself, has never been popular. The officers appointed by the minister to hear appeals have fulfilled their duty with conspicuous ability and irreproachable fairness; yet complaints were never altogether silenced.'[1] The system was considered by a Committee which reported in 1953 in favour of appeals continuing to lie to the Minister.[2]

The Licensing Authority for Goods Vehicles. The Road and Rail Traffic Act 1933 instituted the control of goods vehicles on the roads by a system of special carriers' licences, known as A, B or C licences, and gave the work of issuing these licences to the Chairmen of the Traffic Commissioners who had been established by the Road Traffic Act of 1930 for road passenger vehicles. Vehicles used in connection with the applicant's own trade, such as delivery vans, require a C licence, which is issued as a matter of course. Vehicles used solely for the carriage of goods for profit require A licences, whilst vehicles used partly for the applicant's own trade and partly to carry goods for profit require B licences. A and B licences are not granted as a matter of course. An early effect of the Transport Act 1947 was to nationalise long distance road haulage, C licences being unaffected but A and B licences for private operators being restricted to a distance of 25 miles from the operating centre. Changes away from nationalisation were made by the Transport Act 1954, the 25-mile limit being repealed as from the end of 1954. The principles on which the licensing authority is required to act appear to remain unchanged. The licensing authority takes into account 'the interests of the public generally, including those of persons requiring, as well as those of persons providing, facilities for transport', and they may grant or refuse licences, or grant for particular numbers or types of vehicles. Certain conditions as to the maintenance of the vehicle and the observance of regulations are inserted. Notices of applications for licences are published, and any person who is already providing facilities (by road or otherwise) can object. Objection can be made, *inter alia*, on the ground that if the application is granted there

[1] Mahaffy and Dodson, *Road Traffic Acts and Orders*, 2nd ed. (1936), p. lxvi. Since the whole object of Parliament was to interfere with individual freedom to run buses where and as the owner saw fit, it would be strange if there were no complaints.
[2] Report of the Committee on the Licensing of Road Passenger Services (1953).

331

would then be transport in excess of the requirements of the public. An application that is opposed will mean a hearing of the contentions by the licensing authority, which must sit in public and follow the other requirements as in hearings of applications for passenger road service licences.

The Road and Rail Transport Act 1933 provided a special Appeal Tribunal for appeals on carriers' licences. It consisted of three members appointed by the Minister of Transport. One of them, the chairman, had to be a person of legal experience, and before appointing him the Minister of Transport was directed to consult the Lord Chancellor. The other members were appointed in consultation with the President of the Board of Trade and the Secretary of State for Scotland. The members held office on the same terms as the Traffic Commissioners. The Transport Act 1947 abolished that Appeal Tribunal and transferred such appeals to the Transport Tribunal.

Tribunals for Industrial Disputes

The provisions for the settlement of industrial disputes vary from industry to industry, but the chief features can be seen by considering the three main forms that have emerged and the more recent developments that have taken place.[1]

Voluntary provisions in particular industries. The report of the Whitley Committee in 1918 considered that industrial peace is largely a matter of proper understanding and knowledge between employers and workmen. Proposals were made for Councils to provide this co-operation. The original form of Councils was soon modified, and the chief form has been National Joint Industrial Councils. Each of these covers the whole of an industry, the Council consisting of representatives of employers and of the trade unions in the industry. The Councils are not statutory, but the government encouraged them by providing money and help in the staff, and by letting it be known that the government would regard such Councils as authoritative bodies to speak on behalf of the industries concerned. These Whitley Councils, through regular meetings to discuss industrial questions, have played a large part in conciliation and settlement of disputes. In some cases definite arbitration machinery has been set up. The original idea of consultative bodies that could prevent disputes has not been dropped, and Whitley Councils must be regarded as having far wider functions than that of arbitration.

[1] The *Industrial Relations Handbook*, prepared by the Ministry of Labour and published by H.M.S.O. is a most useful source for detailed information.

Some industries had already created machinery for dealing with industrial questions, and these industries continued with their own arrangements and did not follow the Whitley model. Where the machinery devised through Whitley Councils or other organisations breaks down there is always the Industrial Court available if the parties can agree to such a reference.

The Industrial Court. The Industrial Courts Act 1919 provided for voluntary arbitration and inquiry in industrial disputes. It differs from earlier forms of arbitration in that it is a standing body with continuity of practice. The Minister of Labour appoints the members, of whom some are independent persons, some represent employers, and some represent workmen. The minister appoints a president and chairmen from among the independent persons. The purpose of having chairmen is to allow the court to sit in divisions. The president and some of the other members are full-time officers. When either party to an industrial dispute reports the matter to the minister, the minister may refer it to the Industrial Court if (*a*) there is no machinery in the trade or industry for settlement of disputes or such machinery exists but it has been tried and has not succeeded, *and* (*b*) the consent of both parties has been given. The Industrial Court does not therefore take the place of machinery devised in particular trades, although it may supplement such machinery in the case of a deadlock, and it preserves the principle of voluntary submission. When a matter is referred to the Industrial Court, the president decides whether the court will consist of one or more members and whether there shall be assessors. The usual practice is for the court to consist of three members, the president or one of the chairmen and two members representative of employers and workmen respectively. The court can within large limits regulate the procedure. The cases are usually presented by officials of the employers' and workmen's organisations, but legal representatives can be heard with leave of the court. There are no court fees, and no costs are awarded. The hearings are usually in private. Oral evidence (if taken at all) is not on oath, and the attendance of witnesses is not compulsory. The court, unlike most arbitrators, gives reasons for its decision, and volumes of these decisions are published by the Stationery Office. An award of the court cannot be directly enforced (except where statute has so provided), but it may affect legal rights, for an award that has been acted upon may be taken in a law court as showing the terms of service of a workman. The minister may refer a matter to the court for advice (as opposed to a reference for settlement), or he may use the court as a court of inquiry; in the latter instance there are powers to compel attendance of witnesses and production of documents.

Wages Councils and similar systems. What are now called Wages Councils were known before 1945 as Trade Boards. They arose out of 'sweating', the chief instances being the employment of women under unconscionable terms. As the Factory Acts and the Public Health Acts gave a remedy (in theory) for hours of work and sanitary conditions, the need was for administration and enforcement of these Acts and the question of wages. The Trade Board Act 1909, amended in 1918, provided for Trade Boards in a number of trades where low wages were notorious; the Acts could be extended by the Minister of Labour to any trade where there was no adequate machinery for regulation of wages and where the wages paid made it desirable that there should be a Trade Board. The essence of Trade Boards was that they should fix minimum rates of wages and that those rates would be compulsory. The explanation of the contrast with the voluntary principle is that the workers in some trades are badly organised. Where there is strong trade unionism the representatives of organised labour feel that they can get better terms by direct dealing with the employers, and compulsory adjudication would be resented; where unionism is too weak to bargain the position is different. The original idea was that Trade Boards would be composed of elected representatives of employers and workmen with a number of impartial persons known as 'appointed persons'. Actually the trades concerned were too unorganised for the elective system to work satisfactorily, and the system adopted was for the Minister of Labour to appoint all the members, the representative members being appointed from nominations put forward by individuals or organisations. When the Wages Councils Act 1945 came into operation there were 52 trade boards in existence, and they automatically became Wages Councils. The 1945 Act makes little change. The composition is the same, the representatives of employers and of workers and the independent members all being appointed by the minister. The councils deal with wages and with holidays and holiday remuneration. A council makes such investigation as it thinks fit. If discussion does not produce agreement then the representative members may vote by sides; the independent members do not then vote, but if after voting by sides it is found that the two sides cannot agree the question may be decided by the independent members. The result is a 'proposal', which is normally circulated in the industry so that representations may be made. After any further inquiry or consideration that seems needed, the proposal is sent to the minister, who may refer it back to the Council or make it into an order. The 1945 Act also sets out the conditions under which the minister may establish Wages Councils in industries where such organisation is needed.

As well as this general legislation there have been statutes applying to particular industries and providing machinery for fixing minimum wages. Agricultural wages have been so regulated since 1924 (with amending Acts in 1940 and 1947), and the Road Haulage Wages Act of 1938 brought road haulage workers within the ambit of minimum wage regulation. The Catering Wages Act 1943 set up special boards, which were turned into councils by the Terms and Conditions of Employment Act 1959. A statute that needs special mention is the Coal Mines (Minimum Wages) Act 1912, for that was not an instance of compulsory wage fixing being due to weak trade unionism, but arose as the result of a deadlock between exceedingly well-organised parties.

In all these instances of Wages Councils and similar bodies[1] the employer is under a legal liability to pay at least the minimum wage applicable, and if he has paid below that rate the workman can recover the difference between what he has received and what he would have received at the minimum rate. There is a further sanction in that the employer may be prosecuted and fined for paying less than he must. There are officials appointed to supervise the working of the schemes, with statutory provision for them to take criminal proceedings and conduct the prosecution. The expenses of the Councils are paid out of public funds.

Compulsory arbitration. There is nothing to prevent an agreement within an industry providing that disputes must go to arbitration, and such agreements do exist. Legislative provision is a very different thing, for, if the law requires submission to arbitration, that cuts across the traditional position of labour and employers and raises difficult questions of enforcing the law. Compulsory arbitration was introduced in 1940 and after eighteen years' experience it has been abandoned. Some account of these measures is worth noting, for the idea of compulsory arbitration is by no means dead and attitudes built up over eighteen years of a compulsory system are bound to affect future practice.

---

[1] Railway Wages Boards were set up by statute, but that embodied an agreement between railwaymen and the companies, awards having no legally binding force, and the Boards can properly be regarded as a form of voluntary organisation.

In the early part of the war it became apparent that the industrial effort was hindered by defects in the machinery that then existed for settling disputes. In the first place, if a dispute arose there was no obligation to submit it to the Industrial Court or to some other tribunal; the facilities were there for the contestants to use if they wished, but they could not be compelled to go to court if they preferred to fight by strikes and lock-outs. The second was that if the contestants did get an adjudication upon their dispute, the decision could not be legally enforced. On ordinary legal principles a collective bargain (that is, an agreement or award between representatives of employers and of workers) is not a contract between employers and workers, and however it might be framed it could not bind persons who were not parties because they were outside the associations or trade unions engaged upon the negotiation or adjudication. There was an interesting provision for the cotton industry,[1] but the enforceable compulsory adjudication resulting in an enforceable award did not appear until the needs of war led to the National Arbitration Tribunal being set up in 1940 under Defence Regulation. The purpose was to supplement the Industrial Court, but to leave that body still functioning. The Tribunal was continued by the Supplies and Services Acts until it was superseded in 1951.

The Tribunal had panels of persons appointed by the Minister of Labour and National Service, of representatives of employers and of representatives of employees. The jurisdiction was:

(1) Existing or apprehended trade disputes might be reported to the minister. Where he was of opinion that there was agreed machinery between employers and workpeople he had to refer the dispute to that machinery, but if there was no such machinery or it failed to produce a speedy settlement, he might refer it to the Tribunal and had to do so if there was no settlement in twenty-one days unless there were special reasons for delaying the reference. A settlement (whether by negotiation, agreed machinery or award of the Tribunal) was binding on parties by being incorporated into the contract of employment. Strikes or lock-outs were illegal unless the dispute had been referred to the minister and he had failed to refer the dispute to existing machinery or to the Tribunal within twenty-one days. By this curiously roundabout way nearly all strikes were made illegal, for the minister was not likely to legalise the strike by delaying to refer it for settlement.

[1] The Cotton Manufacturing Industry (Temporary Provisions) Act 1934; both sides of the industry could ask for an order to enforce a collective agreement, and after reference to a Board unconnected with the industry and on a unanimous report in favour the minister could make such an order enforceable against all employers and workers throughout the industry.

(2) The minister could refer anything he liked to the Tribunal for advice.

(3) Employers were required to observe 'recognised terms and conditions of employment' or the trade of industry, and to provide such terms and conditions or something not less favourable. If any question arose as to the nature or existence of such terms and conditions, or whether an employer was observing his obligations, the matter could be referred to the minister, who was then to refer it to the Tribunal, which made an award as if it were a trade dispute.

The system of the National Arbitration Tribunal rested in the last resort on the criminal law. In 1946 the Attorney-General pointed out that the government could not enforce the specific prohibition against strikes even when the unions were opposed to the strikers and the whole community was united in hostility to the strikers: 'You might as well try to bring down a rocket bomb with a pea-shooter as try to stop a strike by the processes of the criminal law.'[1] Yet prosecutions were tried and it was the failure of a prosecution of dockers in 1950 that led to negotiations and the recasting of the system. The Industrial Disputes Order 1951 ended the prohibition of lock-outs and strikes, thus taking away the sanction of the criminal law. The Industrial Disputes Tribunal consisted of three appointed members (one of whom was chairman) and one person from a panel representing employers and one to represent workers. Matters began with a report to the minister, and the principle was retained that the minister should send the matter to be dealt with by any existing machinery within an industry for negotiation or arbitration: the minister referred a matter to the Tribunal only if there was no established machinery or if there had been a failure to reach a settlement. If a strike or a lock-out had actually begun, the minister was not required to refer the matter to the Tribunal. The principle was that there should not be arbitration whilst direct action was continuing. The Tribunal was essentially for 'terms of employment' and could not deal with such a matter as reinstating a worker after a strike. A decision of the Tribunal became a term in the contracts of employment to which it relates, and thus enforceable as a civil obligation.

In 1958 the government decided to allow the Industrial Disputes Order to lapse. There had been no breakdown, but the Employers' Confederation were opposed to some aspects of the jurisdiction, whereas the Trades Union Congress were in favour of the Tribunal continuing. It certainly was a little odd having two arbitration courts, with labour on the whole preferring the Industrial Disputes

[1] Debate in the House of Commons on the Trade Disputes Bill, on 12 February 1946.

Tribunal. Now the old position as regards agreeing upon terms and conditions of employment is restored, and apart from particular agreements or *ad hoc* inquiries ordered by the minister, cases go to the Industrial Court if the parties consent. There is, however, provision under the Terms and Conditions of Service Act 1959 for enforcing a wage structure. If terms and conditions of employment are established in a trade or industry by agreement or award, and a claim is lodged with the minister that an employer is not observing those terms and conditions, the minister can take steps to get the claim settled; in the last resort the minister can refer the claim to the Industrial Court, and if the Court is satisfied that the claim is well founded an order may be made that the recognised terms and conditions become implied terms of employment, and so enforceable. The staff of national and local authorities come within this Act. In this somewhat round-about way the Industrial Court can enforce collective bargaining.

Tax Commissioners

The Land Tax Commission consists of Commissioners named by statute from time to time, the last occasion being in 1938, the names being published in the *London Gazette*. The Commissioners act for local districts, together with the justices of the peace for that district. They hear and finally determine any disputes concerning the assessment and collection of land tax.

The General Commissioners of Income Tax were appointed by the Land Tax Commissioners from their own number, their activities being confined to their own district, but since 1958 vacancies are supplied by persons appointed by the Lord Chancellor. The Special Commissioners of Income Tax are appointed by the Treasury; the Special Commissioners go in pairs on circuit to do their judicial work; when not engaged as a tribunal they act as administrative officials engaged in the assessment of taxation. Persons dissatisfied with assessments may appeal to the Commissioners; in some cases there is an option between appealing to the General Commissioners or to the Special Commissioners, but in a considerable number of cases the appeal must be to the Special Commissioners. The taxpayer may present his case in person, or by a solicitor, barrister, or accountant. The Crown may be represented by an Inspector of Taxes or a representative of the Commissioners of Inland Revenue. From the decision of the Commissioners of Income Tax there is an appeal by case stated on points of law to the High Court. In some cases the appeal may be to the Board of Referees, and from them to the High Court. This Board, appointed by the Treasury, consists of professional and business men with special qualifications for dealing with the matters within their jurisdiction; the chairman is a Queen's Counsel. From the High Court there is an appeal to the Court of Appeal, and thence, with leave, to the House of Lords. In no part of our legal system is there such lavish provision for appeals as in income tax matters.

War pensions

The Pensions Appeal Tribunals Act 1943 provided for Tribunals to be appointed by the Lord Chancellor. The members may be paid such remuneration as the Treasury determines and they may be removed if the Lord Chancellor thinks fit. Claimants for pensions fall into four groups: members of the naval, military or air forces; mariners; civil defence volunteers; other civilians. One member of the Tribunal must be of the same sex as the applicant and belong to the same group. For the armed services, this member must be discharged or demobilised, with the rank of officer or without reaching such rank, according to the rank of the claimant. For mariners and civil defence volunteers, the member can be a person who is or has been in such an occupation, whilst for other civilians the member may not be a member of the armed forces. The other members are barristers or solicitors of not less than seven years' standing, and medical practitioners of similar standing. A Tribunal consists of three members. If the appeal is against assessment of the extent of disablement, the composition is two medical members and a member of the applicant's group. In other appeals the composition is a lawyer, a medical man and a member of the applicant's group. When there is a lawyer sitting he is chairman, and when there is no lawyer the chairman is one of the medical members so appointed by the Lord Chancellor.

If the appellant or the Minister of Pensions is dissatisfied with the decision of the Tribunal as being erroneous in point of law, he may appeal to a High Court judge who is nominated by the Lord Chancellor for that purpose, provided he gets leave of the Tribunal or of the judge. There have been many appeals to the judge, and there can be little doubt of the value of this provision. One effect of getting authoritative decisions is that earlier determinations may be seen to be erroneous and need review. In 1947 the Lord Chancellor set up a War Pensions (Special Review) Tribunal to deal with certain earlier

22-2

cases, the minister undertaking to accept its recommendations. Decisions of the judge are reported in the ordinary series of law reports and the Stationery Office has published selected material for the guidance of claimants.

Rent Tribunals

The Furnished Houses (Rent Control) Act 1946 provides for the setting-up of Tribunals to assess rents for dwellings that are let with furniture or with services, including attendance, heating, lighting or hot water supply. If the Minister of Housing and Local Government is satisfied that the Act should apply to an area (either on representations by the local authority or after consulting them) he can set up a Tribunal. The Tribunal consists of a chairman and two other members and persons to act in their place in their absence or illness. No qualifications are prescribed.[1] Each Tribunal appoints its own clerk and other necessary officers. The minister and the Treasury determine all matters of remuneration and allowances.

The Rent Restriction Acts, extended in 1939, had the general policy of pegging the rent of a house to the figure at which it was let (the standard rent) when the Acts first applied to the particular house, which might be the beginning of the war of 1914 or of 1939 or the date of the first letting. For first lettings since 1939 the rent (and hence the standard rent) might be inflated. By the Landlord and Tenant (Rent Control) Act 1949 the Tribunals could fix a standard rent for such property. Some other defects of the Rent Restriction Acts were also dealt with by allowing reference to these Tribunals. The Housing Repairs and Rents Act 1954 sought to improve housing by allowing increases of rent on account of better repairs and to encourage modernisation of houses: Rent Tribunals had a substantial increase of work on rent increases and in fixing standard rents for houses improved by the help of grants. The Rent Act 1957 effects a substantial measure of decontrol. Houses with rateable values of over £40 in London and £30 elsewhere, and furnished lettings of houses over those limits, are released from control. Where control remains, the maximum rent is twice the 1956 gross rateable value, subject to adjustments for the responsibility for repairs, rates, and a reasonable charge (as agreed or determined by a County Court)

---

[1] Preference is given to legally qualified persons as chairmen. Under the Tribunals and Inquiries Act 1958 the minister appoints chairmen from a panel appointed by the Lord Chancellor, and no chairman or other member can be dismissed except with the concurrence of the Lord Chancellor (see p. 387, below).

for services or furniture. The effect on Rent Tribunals is to take away part of their jurisdiction whilst the changed limits of control will of course reduce the volume of work.

Probably no other Tribunals have been so often adversely criticised by the High Court and few lawyers have had a good word to say for them. The Tribunals were introduced in the period after the war when accommodation was scarce and the Rent Acts could be dodged by a landlord providing some furniture. It naturally shocked the legal mind to find Parliament determined to prevent landlords from exploiting the scarcity value of houses and to do so by avoiding the law courts on the ground that people have 'a great dread of ever having to go to court to get a decision'.[1] The state of the law about rent restriction and control, and in fact about virtually the whole subject of housing, has been an appalling mess, due to the inability of successive governments to find a solution to conflicting policies. These Tribunals have to determine what is a 'reasonable' rent, and that notion, which would give trouble enough in any circumstances, is affected by the whole course of rent and housing legislation. Since the First World War the rent that a tenant has paid for an unfurnished dwelling has depended on the category of the tenancy and not upon prices derived from a free market. If the house was rent controlled, the amount depended on the date when the control arose and the past rent; the rent of a Council house has reflected the subsidies of different periods and the changing conceptions of managing the Council's property; on an uncontrolled letting, which may be on a long or short term, the rent reflects the price level of some particular period. The result has been that people have ideas about what rents 'ought' to be, but the ideas are not based on any coherent principle of economic price or of social needs. In the circumstances Rent Tribunals have probably given as much satisfaction as could have been given by any form of adjudication. The Council on Tribunals made an examination of Rent Tribunals during 1961, and found that most of the complaints received from members of the public amounted to no more than a grievance about a particular decision. It may be that there should be a right of appeal on merits as well as on law.

---

[1] The Act was based on recommendations in the Report of the Inter-Departmental Committee on Rent Control (Ridley Committee), Cmd. 6621 (1945). There was no appeal on a point of law until it was given by the Tribunals and Inquiries Act 1958.

The social security legislation

The broad pattern is that the Family Allowances Act 1945, the National Insurance (Industrial Injuries) Act 1946, the National Insurance Act 1946 and the National Assistance Act 1948 provide for certain benefits which are generally payments, the amount of which is either precise or variable within strict limits. The normal dispute is whether benefit is payable and how much the benefit should be. The claim is made in the first instance to an official and the important provisions relate to appellate tribunals. The National Health Service Act 1946 is different; the need is for examination of complaints about the quality of the service, including the conduct of practitioners in the service.

The Family Allowances Act was originally operated by giving some powers of decision to the minister, but the basic question of whether there is a 'child' and whose 'family' he belongs to for the purpose of the Act, was on dispute a matter for a referee drawn from a panel. The referee could state a case for the decision of the High Court, but otherwise his decision was final. The National Insurance Act has a different system, described below, of local tribunals and a Commissioner who is in effect an appeal court. When these different methods of settling disputes were reviewed by the Franks Committee[1] it was clear that the National Insurance system, which is later in date, is the better, and in 1959 it was provided by statute that questions under the Family Allowances Act and corresponding questions under other Acts should be decided by the national insurance tribunals and Commissioner. This change extends the scope of appeals, for the Commissioner is not limited to questions of law but can also go into the merits of a case.

The National Insurance Act provides for a unified scheme of national insurance whereby insured persons (that is, practically everyone in the country) becomes eligible for benefits for sickness, unemployment, maternity, widowhood, guardian's allowance, retirement pensions and death grants. The machinery for determination of claims and disputes is modelled on that of the old Unemployment Insurance. Certain questions, including whether the contribution conditions are satisfied, are determined by the Minister, with an appeal to the High Court on a point of law. Apart from these special points, the claimant can go to the Local Appeal Tribunal. The old Court of

---

[1] Report of the Committee on Administrative Tribunals and Enquiries, Cmnd. 218 (1957), para. 184.

Referees under the Unemployment Insurance consisted of an appointed Chairman[1] (usually a lawyer) and two members, one drawn from a panel representing employers and the other from a panel representing work-people. The new National Insurance retains the appointed chairman and one member drawn from a panel representing work-people, but instead of the other panel representing employers only it must now represent both employers and insured persons other than employed persons. The reason for this change is that the Act covers people who work on their own account and people who are not gainfully employed, and hence wider representation is needed. From the Local Appeal Tribunal appeal lies to the Commissioner who is described below under the Industrial Injuries Act.

The National Insurance (Industrial Injuries) Act will eventually replace Workmen's Compensation. Accidents that occurred before the new Act came into force will continue to be dealt with under the old law, but for injuries that occur subsequently the new provisions apply.[2] The old law required disputes to go to County Courts, with appeal to the Court of Appeal and the House of Lords, and that medical matters be ascertained by the calling of medical witnesses. The new law takes all this right out of the field of the law courts. It becomes national insurance, employers and employees being required to contribute (in addition to contributions to ordinary national insurance). The machinery for disputes is derived from the old Unemployment Insurance with some additions:

(1) Certain matters, including 'insurability' and contributions, are decided by the minister with an appeal to the High Court.

(2) Medical matters are referred to Medical Boards and Medical Appeal Tribunals.

(3) Subject to these special points, claims are made to an insurance officer, with an appeal to the Local Appeal Tribunal.

This Tribunal is of the familiar pattern of an appointed chairman (usually a lawyer) with one member from a panel representing employers

[1] By the Tribunals and Inquiries Act 1958 the Minister of National Insurance and Pensions must appoint the chairman from a panel of persons appointed by the Lord Chancellor (see p. 387, below).

[2] This is a compulsory insurance scheme to provide benefits in cases of personal injury, disease or death due to employment, and it operates irrespective of whether the employer or the workman was to blame or not. An injured workman may, and generally does, bring an ordinary action against his employer if the injury was due to the employer's negligence or breach of duty; if he succeeds he gets damages. A convenient account of employer's liability and of the National Insurance (Industrial Injuries) Act is in W. M. Cooper and J. C. Wood, *Outlines of Industrial Law*, 4th ed. (1962), chs. IX and X.

and one member from a panel representing work-people. There are provisions for adding medical practitioners either as members or as assessors. Appeal lies to the Commissioner.

The National Insurance Commissioner and the Industrial Injuries Commissioner and their deputies are distinct offices created by the separate Acts, but the same people have been appointed to both offices. They are all Crown appointments with a statutory qualification of barrister or advocate (in Scotland) of at least ten years' standing. The intention of the Acts is that the Commissioner should be a lawyer of the standing of a High Court judge. There are at present seven deputy Commissioners. The Commissioner or a deputy may sit separately or for determining a point of law there can be a tribunal of three who may decide by majority. In effect we have a new jurisdiction run by lawyers, and precedent grows apace. Selected decisions are published by the Stationery Office, there being one series for Industrial Injuries Act cases and four series for different kinds of National Insurance Act cases.

The National Assistance Act ends the old poor law; it is now a function of the central government to provide aid, mainly financial, to those in need and whose needs are not met by national insurance or otherwise. The local authorities are to provide residential accommodation for the aged and the infirm and special services for certain handicapped persons. The aid given by the central government is administered by a National Assistance Board. The Board's local officers give decisions on claims in the first instance, with an appeal to a local Appeal Tribunal. This Tribunal has a chairman and two members, the chairman and one member being appointed by the minister and the other member being drawn from a panel of persons representing work-people. There is no further appeal.

The disputes that arise in the *Health Service* are essentially matters of the standard of the service: medical treatment is not like benefits under national insurance: benefits depend on whether one is entitled to them, whereas medical treatment depends on medical need and there is no limit to its extent or cost. The machinery for hearing complaints is through the Executive Councils which exist for counties and county boroughs or for a few combined areas. An Executive Council is a body representative of the local doctors, dentists, chemists, the local health authority and persons appointed by the minister. Complaints go first to a Service Committee of an Executive Council. A Service Committee consists of equal numbers of lay and professional members, with a lay chairman, and the Committee investigates and reports to the Executive Council its finding of facts and its recommendation. If the Executive Council considers that no action should be taken, or that the practitioner was at fault but that some less penalty than removal is called for, both the complainant and the practitioner have a right of appeal to the minister, whose decision is final. If, however, the Executive Council consider that the practitioner should be removed from the service, the Executive Council makes representations to the National Health Service Tribunal, which then hears the case. The chairman of the Tribunal must be a practising barrister or solicitor of not less than ten years' standing and is appointed by the Lord Chancellor. The two other members, appointed by the Minister of Health, are a layman appointed after consultation with the National Association of Executive Councils, and a professional man belonging to the same profession as the person whose case is being investigated. The 'practitioner members' are appointed after consultation with the appropriate professional organisations. If the Tribunal finds in favour of the doctor, etc., that decision is final; if, however, the Tribunal finds against him, he can appeal to the minister. The minister can thus overrule the Tribunal in favour of a doctor, etc., but never against him.

Agriculture

During the war agriculture, which had been in a generally depressed state, became a vital national concern. A great deal of public money was spent in bringing land into cultivation and on the improvement of land and its equipment. Extensive powers were conferred on the Minister of Agriculture by Defence Regulations, and to exercise these he set up in each county a War Agricultural Executive Committee consisting mainly of farmers who worked with Ministry officials. Some land was requisitioned and farmed directly by the committees, but they were also concerned with assisting and if necessary coercing farmers and landowners to improve production. After the war it was feared that there would be a collapse of agriculture, and the Agriculture Act of 1947 and the Agricultural Holdings Act of 1948 were passed with the agreement of the political parties and all sides of the industry. There were three principal matters to be dealt with. First, land under requisition had to be reviewed to consider whether it should be returned to its owners or should be retained, and other tracts of land were to be considered with a view to their acquisition in order to increase their productivity. Secondly, the farming industry was given a guaranteed market at guaranteed prices for the staple farm-products and, in return for that, an obligation was placed on the owners and occupiers of agricultural land to maintain a reasonable standard of estate management and of good husbandry. Thirdly, tenants who were farming their land properly were to be given a high measure of security against being evicted by their landlords.

The land held under requisition was duly reviewed, some of it being purchased for permanent retention and the rest of it being returned. A new body, the Agricultural Land Commission, considered various tracts of land and reported upon whether they should be acquired by the State in order to increase productivity.[1] It came, however, to be realised that in the post-war conditions such large-scale interventions by the government were not appropriate, and that policy has been abandoned, and the Commission no longer exists.

For some years the main interest centred round the methods of enforcing a satisfactory standard of farming and estate management. These disciplinary powers were repealed in 1958, but the provision made for exercising these powers had certain characteristics that should be of interest in the study of special jurisdictions, and hence a brief account is given here.

The 1947 Act provided for the setting up of *County Agricultural Executive Committees*.[2] The minister appointed the members, three representing farmers, two agricultural workers, two landowners, one county councillor and four other members. The Committees were intended to be local agents of the minister, carrying out his functions either by delegation of powers or by providing a report on which the minister might act. These Committees were primarily executive, farming land that was still under requisition, providing facilities for cultivations, drainage and other services and administering various schemes, but they also had judicial functions. In their general duty of securing a high level of agricultural production they had to advise, persuade and, if necessary, coerce those who were inefficient. Compulsion began by making a supervision order which was followed by directions. A farmer or landowner could thus be told

---

[1] This was intended to apply to substantial areas, commonly divided among several owners, where drainage work, access roads and fixed equipment was needed to make the best use of the land, and there seemed no way of surmounting the difficulties of separate ownerships and interests, or of financing the necessary work, except by the State taking it over.

[2] I described these committees in an article 'County Agricultural Executive Committees', 68 *Law Quarterly Review* (1952), p. 363.

what he had to do. There were elaborate provisions for affording an opportunity to make representations and for a hearing before the committee, with a right for the farmer or landowner to appear in person or by counsel or solicitor or anyone else. There was no appeal against the making of a supervision order or against a direction, except where the direction was to a landlord to provide expensive equipment. If a farmer or landlord did not follow the directions a move could be made for dispossession. That carried a right of appeal. Committees also acted as a court of first instance on whether a landlord should be allowed to give a notice to quit to his tenant.

These Committees were much criticised. A common legal view, apparently accepted by the Franks Committee,[1] was that their composition and informality of procedure made them insufficiently judicial. It was suggested that this form of judgment by one's farming neighbours did not provide an unbiased and impartial tribunal and that personalities mattered too much. It was also said that many irregularities occurred. There were undoubtedly a number of difficulties in administering this jurisdiction. There was a consistently hostile press often filled with urban ignorance, and the feelings of urgency and the subordination of the individual to the common good were giving place to an ordinary peace-time outlook. The disciplinary powers slowly fell into virtual disuse, and their abolition in 1958 was little more than a recognition of changed circumstances. There were, however, some other reasons why the jurisdiction of the committees gave trouble, and it is because of these reasons that we should not forget this small part of our judicial history. The prime function of the Committees was 'parental': they were to help, advise, persuade and lead into better ways those farmers and landowners who were not making the best use of their land; the compulsory powers lay behind that process but they were only used in a relatively small number of cases. There is a difficult problem in knowing how to impose sanctions after a period of advising, persuading and attempting to educate. We have this problem over children. Both domestically and in schools we assume that the process of guiding and educating must be backed by a power to discipline, and that a parent or schoolmaster who finds it necessary to use compulsion should do so within a continuing relationship of child and parent or of boy and master. The moment we begin to put the exercise of disciplinary powers into a judicial mould we run into trouble. Before the law was changed in

[1] Report of the Committee on Administrative Tribunals and Enquiries, Cmnd. 218 (1957), paras. 145–52.

1963[1] a child could be brought before the Juvenile Court as being 'beyond control', which gave an impartial tribunal that heard both sides and decided on the evidence whether a case had been proved. The result was often wretched, for the parents gave evidence and so appeared to turn against and reject their own child, and probably spoiled any chances of a satisfactory relationship in the future. Judicial honour was satisfied, at the cost of human misery and social inefficiency. If an Agricultural Executive Committee had had to prosecute an inefficient farmer or landowner before an independent tribunal (which is what the lawyers and the Franks Committee supposed to be the right solution) the Committee would have assumed a role that would have made it most unlikely that they could continue advising and assisting after the proceedings were over. I think the answer is that we have not had enough experience of problems of this kind to be at all sure what is the solution.

The Agricultural Land Tribunals are impartial bodies originally set up to hear appeals from decisions of Committees or of the minister. The country is divided into eight areas, each with a Tribunal. The chairman and deputy chairman must be barristers or solicitors of not less than seven years' standing and are appointed by the Lord Chancellor for three years and may be re-appointed. They are removable by the Lord Chancellor for infirmity of body or mind or bankruptcy (and not for 'unsuitability'). The members, two for each sitting, are drawn from panels appointed by the Lord Chancellor representing farmers and landowners. Two assessors can be added, and these must be drawn from a panel nominated by the President of the Royal Institution of Chartered Surveyors. The independent lawyer chairman is in effect the permanent element, with the other members varying with the sittings and the places in the area where sittings are held. When the disciplinary powers of the minister and Committees were abolished in 1958 the position of the Tribunals as courts of appeal in farming came to an end. There remain, however, the questions of notices to quit. A landlord has to satisfy a Tribunal on one or more of the grounds specified in the Act before a notice to quit can take effect. If a tenant is farming badly enough the landlord may not only get rid of him but may avoid payments that are normally due to an outgoing tenant. The Land Drainage Act 1961 added a jurisdiction to try complaints by an owner or occupier that his land is suffering through the failure of someone to cleanse a ditch, and to order that the necessary work be carried out. For this

---

[1] See p. 195, above.

purpose the Lord Chancellor makes a panel of persons experienced in land drainage, and when a Tribunal is constituted it consists of a chairman, one member from either the farmer panel or the landowner panel, and one member from the land drainage panel.

Under these Acts persons affected are always notified that they have a right to make representations. There may be written representations and alternatively or in addition there may be oral representations, the parties having a right to appear in person or by legal representatives or by other persons.[1] The Tribunals sit in public and normally follow a procedure similar to that of a law court. The Tribunal usually inspects the land after the hearing. Appeal lies on a point of law to the High Court.

The Lands Tribunal

When in the later eighteenth century Parliament gave extensive powers for the compulsory acquisition of land, it was the practice to provide that the compensation to be paid should, in the absence of agreement, be determined by a jury. Later, and notably by the Lands Clauses Act 1845, there was introduced the alternative of arbitrators. Each side appointed its own arbitrator, and the two arbitrators appointed an umpire who would decide if the arbitrators failed to agree. Then towards the end of the nineteenth century statutes began providing for a single arbitrator appointed by a government department. The next step came from the provisions of the Finance Act of 1910 for the taxation of land values; this required an independent arbitrator to determine values, and the method adopted was to make a Reference Committee of the Lord Chief Justice, the Master of the Rolls and the President of the Surveyors' Institution, who appointed persons to act as official arbitrators. This was followed for the determination of compensation for property taken during the First World War, and then adopted in 1919 for the settlement of disputed compensation on acquisitions by government departments or a public or local authority, and later extended to a number of similar matters. The official arbitrators were a satisfactory tribunal on valuation but legal questions so often arise in these matters that it was decided to create a tribunal that would have professional skill in law as well as in valuation. The Lands Tribunal Act 1949 provided that

---

[1] This includes friends and relatives, officials of the National Farmers' Union or other organisations, and land agents; expert evidence and advocacy tend to get mixed up when lawyers do not appear. These cases can be of enormous importance to the parties, and to brief counsel before the Tribunal (the land agent being an expert witness) may be a prudent course.

the Tribunal should consist of a President who must be either a person who has held high judicial office (not necessarily in England) or be a barrister of at least seven years' standing, and other members who must be barristers or solicitors of like standing or persons experienced in the valuation of land appointed after consultation with the President of the Royal Institution of Chartered Surveyors. All appointments are made by the Lord Chancellor who has power to dismiss if in his opinion the person is unfit to continue in office or incapable of performing his duties: subject to that, appointments are on terms and conditions determined by the Lord Chancellor with the approval of the Treasury. The jurisdiction of the Tribunal may be exercised by any one or more of its members, so that the composition of the Tribunal can be adjusted as between legal and valuation experts according to the nature of the case.

Procedure is governed by rules made by the Lord Chancellor. From a decision of the Tribunal appeal lies to the Court of Appeal. The intention is that the Lands Tribunal shall deal with all matters of valuation of land and allied matters, and whenever some new occasion for assessing compensation arises the jurisdiction is usually given to the Lands Tribunal. Decisions of the Tribunal are reported in *Planning and Compensation Reports*.

Domestic tribunals

There are a great number and a great variety of groups of persons formed for their mutual benefit: societies, clubs, associations, professions, trade unions and so on. It is of their nature that they should be largely self-governing, and this must involve some jurisdiction over their own members in such matters as imposing fines for breaches of rules and suspension or expulsion from the society. There are instances, as in some professions,[1] where Parliament has intervened and provided for a judicial organ. The powers of the Discipline Committee to fine solicitors, or to suspend them or to strike them off the Roll (subject to an appeal to the High Court)[2] and of the Inns of Court to control barristers[3] have already been

---

[1] On the common law position, see D. Lloyd, 'The Disciplinary Powers of Professional Bodies', 13 *Modern Law Review* (1950), p. 281.

[2] See p. 239, above.

[3] See p. 245, above. There is no appeal from the Inns of Court to the law courts. The judges, who in the days of Serjeants had their own Inn and acted as Visitors to the four Inns, are now members of those Inns. There is an appeal from an Inn to the judges sitting as a domestic tribunal. The case of Marrinan excited much public interest because of the resort to tapping of telephone

mentioned. Architects have since 1931 been subject to the control of the Architects' Registration Council. There is a Discipline Committee consisting of one member appointed by the Minister of Works, one by the Minister of Housing and Local Government, two by the president of the Law Society, and four by the Architects' Registration Council. Appeal lies to the High Court. Until the Medical Act 1950 a medical practitioner's name could, after due inquiry, be removed from the Medical Register by the General Medical Council without there being any appeal to the law courts; the system then introduced is that there is a statutory disciplinary committee, and appeal lies to the Judicial Committee of the Privy Council.[1] A similar system was provided in 1956 for dentists and in 1958 for opticians. Statutes also regulate the professional discipline of midwives, nurses, pharmacists and veterinary surgeons, giving a right of appeal to the High Court. The Professions Supplementary to Medicine Act 1960 provides machinery for registering chiropodists, dieticians, medical laboratory technicians, occupational therapists, physiotherapists, radiographers and remedial gymnasts and for their professional organisation and conduct. Disciplinary powers are vested in a Committee for each profession, with an appeal to the Privy Council. When this legislation was before Parliament there was debate over a case in which the British Medical Council in the exercise of their disciplinary powers had received a script made by the police listening in to a doctor's telephone conversation by consent of the other party to the conversation. Whilst that was not 'telephone tapping' as understood when the government accepted the Report of the Committee of Privy Councillors in 1957,[2] it did raise some difficult questions, and a Committee was appointed on the Powers of Subpoena of Disciplinary Tribunals. The Committee[3] recommended that a statutory disciplinary tribunal should have statutory power to secure the issue of writs of *subpoena* to compel the attendance of a witness and

conversations, and the Benchers followed an unusual course by sitting in public, their judgment being reported in *The Times*, 4 July 1957. For Marrinan's appeal to the judges, see *The Times*, 3 October 1957.

[1] The Privy Council has long been associated with medical matters. It was Sir John Simon, who in 1848 was the first medical officer of health for the City of London and later Medical Officer of the Privy Council (and so not to be confused with a later Sir John Simon who became Lord Simon and Lord Chancellor), who took a most active part in organising the medical profession as well as in shaping our law of public health. His book, *English Sanitary Institutions* (1890) is far more interesting than its title or appearance suggests.

[2] Under the Chairmanship of Lord Birkett, Cmnd. 283 (1957).

[3] Cmnd. 1033 (1960).

the production of documents, and that they should be issuable to secure the production before such tribunals, subject to all proper exceptions, of evidence obtained by police officers whether in the course of criminal investigation or otherwise. Where there is no specific legislation, the Queen's Bench has a discretion to issue writs of *subpoena*. The Committee also pointed out that every disciplinary tribunal should have legal advice available, and that seems to be accepted practice as recent legislation has provided for legal assessors to assist the disciplinary tribunals for medicine and allied professions.

In professions that are not so regulated by statute a member has a far more limited right to go to the law courts, for all that he can do is to ask for review on the grounds covered by *certiorari* or allied remedies,[1] which in effect means that he can get the disciplinary proceedings set aside if there has been a failure in the basic requirements of a judicial process or other errors of a strictly limited kind. It is only where a right of appeal is definitely given that the merits of a decision can be examined by the courts.[2]

In addition to regulating some professions, which were in origin voluntary societies, Parliament has created some groups and made special provision for their control. One of the most important is the Milk Marketing Board, which is not only a large undertaking with a cash turnover larger than that of the budgets of some countries, but is also a body for disciplining producers and distributors of milk by trying them for breaches of the scheme and imposing substantial penalties upon those who are found guilty. This jurisdiction was considered by a Committee which reported in 1939;[3] the Committee found substantial merits in this system and did not see any good reason for following a different principle.

Ministers

Ministers of the Crown in charge of government departments have many statutory powers that may be called judicial. A mere list of these powers would be lengthy, and its composition would require some criterion for deciding what should be included, for it is

[1] See pp. 394 *et seq.*, below.

[2] The distinction can be seen in *Hughes* v. *Architects' Registration Council* [1957] 2 Q.B. 550, a precedent containing much wisdom on the rationale of the discipline of professional bodies. J. G. Miller, 'The Disciplinary Jurisdiction of Professional Tribunals', 25 *Modern Law Review* (1962), 531, examines the grounds on which disciplinary action may be taken.

[3] Cmd. 5980, Report of the Departmental Committee on the Imposition of Penalties by Marketing Boards and Other Similar Bodies.

principally in connection with ministers' powers that the dichotomy of 'judicial' and 'administrative' becomes of importance. All that is considered here is the general pattern of these powers, and that depends on the enabling statute. The power may be given without any procedure being specified. Thus the Home Secretary settles disputes between Magistrates' Courts Committees and local authorities if those bodies should be unable to agree upon the salary of a justices' clerk or other expense of the court. The practice under similar legislation has been for the parties to put the facts and contentions forward by correspondence, and for there to be no oral hearing or formal inquiry. A minister may of course provide for a formal inquiry if he so wishes. Several statutes require a minister to cause a public local inquiry to be held; the origin of this, as has been explained, was in provisional order procedure, and hence it is pre-eminently in the type of matter that would have required a private Bill a hundred years ago that the minister now has to order a formal inquiry, as for compulsory purchase of land and interferences with property rights. The inquiry is normally held by an official of the ministry who possesses professional qualifications in architecture, engineering or surveying. Whether the case is one from a local authority or from the activities of the ministry, there is no decision announced by the person holding the inquiry; he makes a report, which is for the assistance of his ministry, and the decision is given in an official letter on behalf of the minister. A formal inquiry may be an expensive proceeding, and recent legislation on the compulsory acquisition of land allows the minister, as an alternative to a public local inquiry, to afford to a person who objects an opportunity to be heard 'by a person appointed' by the minister.

It should be noticed that all the special tribunals that have been mentioned have a publicly known composition, the decision being given by the body that heard the case, whereas the exercise of powers given to a minister follows a different pattern. This is discussed later in this chapter.[1]

Royal Commissions and committees of inquiry

There are a few Royal Commissions that are permanent bodies for administration, and there are many Standing Committees in connection with government departments, but the ordinary Royal Commission or Department Committee is temporary, being appointed to inquire into a particular matter and ceasing to exist as soon as it

---

[1] See pp. 388 *et seq.*, below.

has made its Report. The distinction between a Royal Commission and a Departmental Committee is largely one of dignity and standing. A Royal Commission is appointed by the Crown, which means that the proposal for the inquiry comes before the government, and the names of the members are put forward by the Prime Minister. It is in constitutional position independent of any government department. A departmental committee is appointed by a Minister, or by two Ministers jointly. The purpose in either case is to have an inquiry that is official in the sense that it is paid for out of public funds and has available the resources of the public service, yet is independent of the government and of Parliament. The persons appointed may be expert, or they may be persons of experience in public affairs. To be a member of one of these bodies is a form of part-time voluntary work, similar to that of justices of the peace.

There are occasions when an official inquiry is set up to investigate allegations of public maladministration or of some supposed scandal, but that is not the usual situation. These inquiries are usually into some part of the public service or of social institutions where it appears that developments or a new departure may be desirable. What is needed is a survey of the facts, assessments of relative opinion, specialist and general, and a set of recommendations that can form a basis for new legislation or new administrative practices. Such inquiries do not form any part of the machinery of justice: they are not concerned with the rights of individuals between themselves or as against the State, but with the policy that ought to be adopted for future action. There would be no need to mention these inquiries if it were not for one characteristic of their procedure, namely the taking of evidence.

The usual practice of Royal Commissions and of Departmental Committees is to receive evidence from organisations and individuals who may be expected to be able to contribute relevant information or opinions. A Royal Commission usually sits in public to hear such evidence, and publishes a verbatim transcript and the memoranda. A Departmental Committee generally does not do that, but some committees (notably the Ministers' Powers Committee and the Franks Committee[1]) have taken evidence in public and published their material. The procedure does, however, strongly suggest a judicial proceeding. Witnesses are examined on statements that have been made, and the questioning or cross-examination is obviously based on the practice in law courts. But the purpose is to inform the

---

[1] See note 1 on p. 326, above.

354

Commission or Committee about the general situation and of the opinion of the organisations and individuals who are called to give evidence, and however much the calling and questioning of witnesses resembles judicial procedure it is not in fact a judicial or quasi-judicial function.

There are, however, some occasions when an inquiry is needed into allegations of misconduct or into some supposed public scandal. Usually that kind of inquiry is needed because there are insufficient grounds for bringing legal proceedings or because the conduct that is alleged is not legally wrongful. The establishing of such an inquiry raises an important point of law. There is no doubt that the Crown, or a Minister of the Crown, can appoint persons to make an inquiry, for that is no more than asking for advice, but there is no power in the Crown to set up any new kind of jurisdiction. The Act of 1641 which abolished the Star Chamber specifically prohibited the Crown from setting up any new kind of court. In ordinary inquiries by Royal Commissions and Departmental Committees this problem does not arise because the organisations and people concerned are quite happy to give evidence voluntarily. If, however, an inquiry is to be made into allegations of malpractice or misconduct it may be desirable that the Commission or Committee should be armed with compulsory powers. The Tribunals of Inquiry (Evidence) Act 1921 was passed for that purpose: it provides that, if a resolution is passed by both Houses of Parliament that a tribunal be established for inquiring into a definite matter of urgent public importance, then the Tribunal has the powers of the High Court as regards witnesses. Witnesses can then be summoned to attend, compelled to give evidence and to produce documents, and they are entitled to the same immunities as they would be if they were witnesses before the High Court. There have been only fourteen tribunals of inquiry under this Act, but the occasions have generally given rise to a great deal of public interest and discussion. Recent instances are the inquiry into an alleged leakage of information about the raising of the bank rate[1] in 1958, the inquiry into the case of John Waters[2] in 1959 and the Vassall inquiry in 1963.[3] These inquiries have been much criticised on the ground that the procedure is unfair to persons who

[1] Report of the Tribunal appointed to inquire into allegations of improper disclosure of information relating to the Raising of the Bank Rate (Cmnd. 350).
[2] Report of the Tribunal appointed to inquire into the allegation of assault on John Waters (Cmnd. 718).
[3] Report of the Tribunal appointed to inquire into the Vassall Case and Related Matters (Cmnd. 2009).

23-2

may be involved.[1] The ordinary rule in our civil and criminal courts is that witnesses are called by the parties, and the party calling a witness has the opportunity of eliciting his evidence. There are no 'parties' before a tribunal of inquiry. All the witnesses are called by the tribunal and examined by counsel for the tribunal. It is inevitable that some witnesses will say things that reflect upon other people, but it is not feasible to allow everyone who is mentioned to be regarded as a defendant and so be legally represented and allowed to cross-examine, for the proceedings would be endless. The usual practice has been to appoint a judge as chairman and to rely on his good sense to guide the proceedings as fairly as possible.

Whatever procedure a tribunal of inquiry follows the result can only be a report of the findings of the tribunal: that is to say, there cannot be a decision as to legal rights or as to criminal liability. It is therefore hardly right to regard these tribunals as being part of the machinery of justice for they do not make 'decisions' that are comparable in any way with those of the ordinary courts, or of special tribunals or of Ministers.

3. THE NATURE OF SPECIAL TRIBUNALS AND MINISTERIAL DECISIONS

The previous sections have shown that these jurisdictions are the product of national social policies, either regulatory or for the provision of services. They form part of a complicated pattern of public affairs, that is of our system of government in a wide sense, but when we try to define or describe their position we get into difficulties. One aspect, which is of considerable practical importance, concerns the arrangement of our law for the purpose of exposition and reference: ought this chapter to appear in a book dealing with the Machinery of Justice? Would it not be more logical to regard a number of the tribunals as being merely appendages of the civil service? Lawyers particularly feel that they must be able to classify anything with which they have to deal, for much of the working of the law depends on being able to tie the proper label on to a set of facts. Special tribunals and minister's decisions have more often than not been considered in relation to the Separation of Powers and the Rule of Law. This should be a helpful approach, for one of the first steps in making a classification is to see how far one's subject fits into existing categories. These are, however, matters where many lawyers

[1] G. W. Keeton, *Trial by Tribunal* (1960), is a study of some of these inquiries.

have strong views, and most legal writing has been advocacy, concerned to prove a case asserting: (*a*) these special jurisdictions should not exist; (*b*) alternatively, if they must exist they should be in the hands of lawyers; (*c*) alternatively, if they are not to be in the hands of lawyers, then lawyers should control them and ensure that they are properly exercised.[1]

We should expect to find a number of people who dislike the newer policies, or at least feel uneasy about them. These things have been the stuff of home politics: virtually all of them were fought through Parliament and carried against an opposition which claimed to be upholding the freedom of the individual. After each change there has been a process of settling down. The once intolerable interference with liberty in having to have modern sanitation, send children to school, and put stamps on insurance cards, has become generally accepted. Every control or service has naturally produced some friction and complaints at some time about some aspect, but these are usually seen as a ground for amendment or improved administration. There is no general dislike of these policies, or they could not have been introduced and could not continue. Dislike and opposition is sectional: there are die-hards, crusty with old-fashioned individualism; people who feel that the new order benefits every class but their own; landlords who consider that they have been unfairly treated since the Rent Restriction Acts began in 1915; and there are the lawyers with their tendency to be crusty and their vigilance in the protection of privilege and rights of property.

Suppose that we set out, with open minds, to devise some methods for securing greater cleanliness in food that is sold to the public. We should find two different systems at present in operation. For shops there is a detailed code of regulations about the packaging, storage and handling of food, with inspectors from the local authorities who visit shops and who prosecute before Magistrates' Courts for breaches of the regulations. For milk production we should find licensing and regulations, and also inspectors, but under the ministry. Non-compliance with regulations can lead to the minister depriving the dairyman of his licence (which puts him out of business) with, however, a right for him to appeal to an independent tribunal. The two methods could be examined and their relative merits be compared and assessed. That is the course that we should expect to be followed

---

[1] Compare the traditional defence to an action about a borrowed kettle: we did not borrow it; alternatively we returned it; alternatively it had a hole in it when we borrowed it.

in any of the social sciences, but it is not a course that comes naturally to the legal mind. Lawyers approach these matters with a bias against anything where a minister or a tribunal is concerned; there is a deep-seated suspicion of anything savouring of administration, and the instinctive reaction is to look for something that can be used in evidence against these newer procedures. One factor is that the new policies so often ignore the lawyers. Once a local authority has bought land for housing there is no more conveyancing, drawing leases or other bread-and-butter work for a solicitor's office. Statute may even lift a whole subject out of the hands of lawyers and courts, as when Workmen's Compensation was re-born as the Industrial Injuries Act,[1] and a workman goes before a tribunal accompanied by a trade union secretary. The legal profession is an interest, and it has been adversely affected, and that goes some way towards explaining the lawyers' attitude. It does not, however, give a complete explanation for there are other factors which are probably far more important. Lawyers are brought up to believe that the law enshrines certain fundamental values and that it is the lawyer's calling to preserve this heritage. The central theme is that the individual is protected by the law through the judicial process. Lawyers therefore start with an underlying supposition that judicial process is something separate and distinct, based on principles that have a special sanctity.

These ideas form the background to virtually all discussion of special tribunals and minister's decisions. It is an unsatisfactory approach, because the newer policies are reviewed in the light of the separation of powers and then measured against the rule of law, only to find that the separation of powers gives us no help and that the rule of law has so many different meanings that the phrase is a menace to clear thinking. Yet a student must tread this path, for official committees and judges have spoken in these terms, and habits of thought persist. A piece of legal doctrine may be thoroughly discredited and yet continue to be invoked. A case in the courts may still turn on a distinction between executive and judicial functions, with references to the rule of law, as if these are precise and universally accepted principles.

(a) The separation of powers

The doctrine of the separation of powers divides powers into three classes. The legislature enacts the general rules, called law, which the

---

[1] See p. 343 above.

community must observe. The executive sees that these rules are applied. The judiciary determines whether the conduct of persons and bodies is in accordance with the rules. The theory of the separation of powers[1] means more than this: it is a way of expressing the opinion that government activities not only can be so classified, but that they ought to be so classified and assigned to separate institutions. It is an old argument that if all the powers are vested in one man or body of men, then a tyrannical law may be enacted, it may be enforced tyrannically, and the legality of the action judged corruptly: in the language of Nazis, the Leader may shoot his opponents and then assert that they had contravened his law and that he had judged them and himself carried out the sentence. In a wide sense English institutions do perhaps represent the separation of powers. Parliament enacting, Whitehall administering,[2] and the law courts judging is a familiar picture. If one single institution could create a criminal offence, catch offenders, judge them, and punish them, we should feel that our traditional methods of government were not being followed. Yet even a cursory glance at our political institutions shows that the three powers are not exercised by separate bodies. In the legislature, the House of Lords exercises judicial functions, convention decreeing that lay lords must not take part in appellate functions, whilst the House of Commons has the right to try persons for contempt and to punish them. Statutes have conferred upon ministers (as the heads of administrative departments) powers to make rules, regulations and orders having legal force, and to decide certain disputes. The judiciary makes new law through precedent, has statutory power to make rules of court, and undoubtedly exercises administrative functions as in the licensing sessions of justices. The Lord Chancellor is head of the judiciary, the head of an administrative department, a cabinet minister, and presides over the House of Lords. The centre of the English political system, the cabinet, may sometimes work as if the distinction between executive and legislature did not exist. If the cabinet were to make a decision in policy as to road traffic, the

[1] A convenient brief account is Wade and Phillips, *Constitutional Law*, pt. II, ch. I, and somewhat more fully in Jennings, *The Law and the Constitution*, ch. I and appendix I.

[2] When Parliament passes a statute the executive must carry it out. If, for example, a salary is raised, the appropriate official must make the larger payment. In such cases 'executive' suggests the nature of the act, which is executing or carrying out a specific order. In very many instances the executive is given power to do certain things, with a wide discretion as to how it will set to work. The best term for these activities is 'administration'. The modern usage is to keep to the term 'the executive', but to use the term 'administer' in describing activities.

carrying out of that policy would be regarded as merely a technical matter; if the Minister of Transport already possesses adequate powers he could just make the appropriate orders, whilst if he has not got power to do this it would be necessary to pass a statute; the assumption is that any legislative proposals originating in government decisions will be passed by the House of Commons, for the alternative is a change of government. The more English institutions are examined the more confusing does the distribution of powers appear. It is in fact exceptional if we can take an institution and say: 'This body exercises one of the powers of government, and one only.' The more usual analysis will be: 'This body is primarily concerned with one of the powers, but it also exercises one or both of the other powers.'

This discussion supposes that the three powers are distinguishable. The Committee on Ministers' Powers assumed that such distinctions could be made, and in their Report they gave an analysis which has been regarded almost as an authoritative definition.

A true judicial decision presupposes an existing dispute between two or more parties, and then involves four requisites:
(1) The presentation (not necessarily orally) of their case by the parties to the dispute; (2) if the dispute between them is a question of fact, the ascertainment of the fact by means of evidence adduced by the parties to the dispute and often with the assistance of argument by or on behalf of the parties on the evidence; (3) if the dispute between them is a question of law, the submission of legal argument by the parties; and (4) a decision which disposes of the whole matter by a finding upon the facts in dispute and an application of the law of the land to the facts so found, including where required a ruling upon any disputed question of law.[1]

On this definition it is clear that the law courts are generally engaged upon making judicial decisions, but it will also appear that the various tribunals noted in the last section (or some of them) make true judicial decisions.

It is useful to look at these problems from a different viewpoint. When a government has decided to introduce certain kinds of legislation, such as extensions of social services, the general policy may often be quite simple and capable of expression in a short paragraph. The legislation must, however, be formulated with some precision. The Bill put before Parliament is likely to contain clauses giving the minister at the head of the appropriate department powers to carry out the changes, and other clauses will make some provision for

[1] Committee on Ministers' Powers, Cmd. 4060 (1932), p. 73. On this Committee generally, see p. 320, above.

settling disputes that may arise. Can we really distinguish between administrative and judicial powers, and, if so, will that enable us to say what bodies ought to exercise those powers?

Starting with judicial powers, there is the process of definition I have already used. Clearly we cannot use any such definition to tell us whether disputes under the proposed legislation should go to the law courts or to a special tribunal, for the whole result of that definition was to establish that judicial powers are exercised by special tribunals as well as by law courts. Another line of approach would give this argument: The law courts do certain kinds of work; presumably they know how to do it, and do it tolerably well; therefore any further work of that nature should be given to the law courts. To find the nature of the work of the law courts we must concentrate upon their usual activities. Many legal writers are primarily interested in the law courts as a mechanism by which the law is developed by precedents, and they would place law-making by the judges in the foreground of the picture. It is agreed that judges make law by their decisions, the current disputes being as to the exact nature of the process and the characteristics and quality of judge-made law. But if we take the *Civil Judicial Statistics* and the *Criminal Statistics* and look at the volume of the work of the courts, and then look at the relatively small number of cases that appear in the *Law Reports*, it is obvious that for every case that makes law there are thousands of cases that establish nothing new. The importance of functions cannot of course be assessed by a simple numerical method; a single judicial decision might cripple opposition political parties, whilst a (numerically rare) cabinet decision to go to war might be the end of all our present institutions. However we evaluate activities, the main function of the law courts is clearly the decision of cases: the judges themselves have always considered that their prime duty is to dispose of the case that is before them, subordinating their other activities to this end. But what does 'disposing of' a case involve? If we examine the work of the law courts it is clear that decisions in the sense of finding facts, applying law to those facts, and if necessary giving a ruling upon law, are part of the work. It is equally clear that a vast amount of the work does not involve these elements. In criminal cases, numbering well over half a million each year, the defendant pleads guilty, leaving the court with nothing to do except to decide whether to inflict a punishment or the nature of the punishment. In all criminal cases the sentencing process is the exercise of a discretion, except in a very few cases such as murder where only one sentence is possible.[1] In civil cases there is often no 'dispute'; the Chancery judge who sanctions expenditure for a ward of court, the Divorce Court judge who considers whether a decree should be granted, the County Court judge or registrar who decides the instalments that can reasonably be paid by a debtor, and many of the activities of the courts mentioned above are matters of discretion. Modern legislation tends more and more to emphasise this aspect of the law courts. Moneylenders and hire-purchase touts must not make unfair contracts, and cranky testators must not ignore their dependants, but formulation of these obligations appeared impossible; the technique is to leave it to the discretion of the judge. Can we say that the courts are exercising administrative powers?

In the case of the administrative decision, there is no legal obligation upon the person charged with the duty of reaching the decision to consider and weigh submissions and arguments, or to collate any evidence, or to solve any issue. The grounds upon which he acts, and the means which he takes to inform himself before acting, are left entirely to his discretion.[2]

On the first sentence of this quotation, the law courts are not acting administratively, for a judge is expected to listen to arguments in such matters as sentencing, although of course he can take no notice of what is said. The second sentence describes perfectly the position of the law courts in the exercise of many of their discretionary powers. Further, many statutes direct ministers to make certain inquiries before acting, but contain no direction that the minister is to take any notice of the result of those inquiries. An attempt has been made to escape these difficulties by making a category of quasi-judicial decisions, meaning that there is a dispute, the facts are ascertained, but the decision is then arrived at by the free choice of the official concerned: 'Indeed generally speaking a quasi-judicial decision is only an administrative decision, some stage or some element of which possesses judicial characteristics.'[3] There is often little reality in these distinctions. When a judge determines to send a convicted man to prison the judge exercises a free choice between courses that are open to him. When the Prison Department decide to which prison the man shall be sent, they exercise a free choice. The free choice does not mean that they can do exactly what they like; the Prison Department can no more send a man outside the realm than

[1] Under the Homicide Act 1957 the sentence for capital murder must be death and for other murders it must be imprisonment for life. See pp. 204 *et seq.*, above, for a discussion of the process of sentencing.

[2] Committee on Ministers' Powers, Cmd. 4060 (1932), p. 81.

[3] Committee on Ministers' Powers, Cmd. 4060 (1932), p. 81.

the judge can sentence to prison for longer than the law allows. The point is that the nature of the work is the same, and any analytical distinction turning upon the fact that the judge may hear counsel in court whilst the Prison Department consult their staff and advisers and do not listen to counsel, is a distinction that cannot be taken seriously.

It is doubtful whether any definition of judicial and administrative can be found that will properly delimit the sphere of the law courts and that of administrative bodies, for law courts do such varied kinds of work that we must either say that the judiciary has extensive administrative powers or that there is a wide no-man's-land between judicial and administrative functions. Analysis of the nature of powers does not give us a workable test for deciding whether a new power ought to be assigned to the judiciary or to the executive.

It may well be asked whether there is anything of substance that divides the law courts from the special tribunals. The special tribunals are 'special' in that each of them deals with one topic or a small range of topics, but this is true of the Probate Divorce and Admiralty Courts. It is sometimes said that law courts are manned by independent judges and special tribunals by civil servants who are not independent. This mixes up two points, namely the kind of people and their independence. A reference to the judges is usually confined to the judges of the superior courts, but even if it is taken to include County Court judges and registrars, legal chairmen, recorders and stipendiaries, that is still not the whole of the judiciary, for the lay justices of the peace are an essential part. Even more misleading is the supposition that special tribunals are usually manned by civil servants. Nor is there any clear dividing line based on tenure or conditions of office.

There are different degrees of security of tenure of judicial offices: the superior judges can be regarded as irremovable by the executive, County Court judges can be removed by the Lord Chancellor for inability or misbehaviour, whilst justices can be removed by the Lord Chancellor at his pleasure. It seems clear that no legal proceedings of a penal nature can be taken against benches or juries, and that words spoken by parties, witnesses and counsel in judicial proceedings are privileged. It also seems clear that the superior judges are immune from civil proceedings arising from anything they do or say in their judicial capacity.[1] The position of inferior judges

[1] The immunity certainly covers all acts within their jurisdiction, however malicious the judge's conduct may have been. It probably covers acts outside the jurisdiction if the act was in an intended execution of judicial duty.

depends on whether they have acted within their jurisdiction, which is by no means always an easy matter to determine.[1] If within their jurisdiction, they will not be personally liable if they have acted in good faith. If acting without or in excess of jurisdiction, they are liable if they act maliciously and without reasonable and probable cause, but good faith and reasonable conduct will not necessarily give them a defence. Justices were disturbed to find from *O'Connor* v. *Isaacs*[2] in 1956 that they may be personally liable 'as a result of a perfectly bona fide mistake of law made by them, or more accurately by their clerk...' in proceedings that took place some years earlier. This potential liability is for what, in our older legal system, was an action of trespass. Hence if a defendant was committed to prison (as was the plaintiff in *O'Connor* v. *Isaacs*), whether for non-payment of money or as a substantive sentence, he can sue the justices for false imprisonment. If he paid any sum to be released then that can be included in the damages. Again, if the defendant's goods had been seized under an invalid order, that would be trespass to goods and action would lie against the justices. Where, however, the justices make an invalid order for the payment of money, as for example an invalid order to pay money to the wife, the mere order does not amount to a direct interference with person or property; there is therefore no trespass, and hence no basis for an action against the justices. If the independence of inferior judges rested substantially on their immunity from legal proceedings they might well shiver at this formidable rigmarole based on forms of action that were abolished years ago. Justices are certainly not satisfied with the position,[3] but I am sure that it does not make a scrap of difference to

[1] Where there is a mistake or misunderstanding of the law, as where a single justice does something that requires two or more justices, or where an unlawful sentence is imposed, there is clearly an absence or excess of jurisdiction. The difficulty comes when jurisdiction depends upon the evidence. If there is in law no evidence upon which the justices could act, but nevertheless they have so acted, is that a wrong exercise of a jurisdiction which they have, or is it a usurpation of a jurisdiction which they have not got? The case-law gives no clear answer.

[2] [1956] 2 Q.B. 288. The action failed because it had not been brought within twelve months: the period of limitation is now six years.

[3] There are many difficult points: see L. A. Sheridan 'The Protection of Justices' 14 *Modern Law Review* (1951), p. 267, and D. Thompson 'Judicial Immunity and the Protection of Justices', 21 *Modern Law Review* (1958), p. 517. The Magistrates' Association and the Justices' Clerks Society fortified themselves with Counsel's Opinion, and discussions led in 1959 to the Lord Chancellor and the Home Secretary appointing a working party to consider the arrangements for meeting out of public funds the expenses incurred by justices of the peace, clerks of the peace and clerks to justices in defending actions and any costs or damages

anyone's decisions. The independence of inferior courts comes from habits of mind and tradition, and owes little to the forms of law.

A marked characteristic of special tribunals is the great variety in the persons who serve on these bodies and in the tenure of their offices. Civil servants are to be found, but their position may easily be misunderstood. It is common for statutes to provide that an inquiry must be held before a minister can take certain action, and in these cases a civil servant is sent to hold the inquiry, but he should not be regarded as a tribunal; he is collecting material for the use of the minister and it is the minister who is responsible for the decision.[1] There are a few instances in which civil servants are themselves vested with the power to decide: the Special Commissioners of Income Tax are Treasury officials, and the District Auditors are officials of the Ministry of Housing and Local Government but they act in their own name and not on behalf of the minister. High Court judges preside over tribunals for appeals on registered designs, patents, and pensions, and over the Restrictive Practices Court. The Crown makes some appointments, as with the National Insurance Commissioner and the lay members of the Restrictive Practices Court. The Lord Chancellor appoints to war-pension tribunals, agricultural land tribunals and the Lands Tribunal. The Master of the Rolls appoints the Discipline Committee for solicitors. There was at one time a tendency to provide for the minister concerned to have to consult with some other minister (Traffic Appeal Tribunal) or for an appointment to be made jointly (Railway Rates Tribunal), but this was clumsy and inappropriate to the status of ministers, and it has not been followed in recent legislation. It is now the common practice to give the Lord Chancellor the power to make appointments in all matters where a lawyer member or chairman is required. The usual statutory provision has been that members of special tribunals (other than any lawyer chairmen) are appointed by the minister concerned with the subject. Thus the Minister of Labour appoints the members of the Industrial Court and the Board of Trade appoints the non-legal members of the Performing Rights Tribunal. The tendency is clearly towards increasing the powers of the Lord Chancellor.[2] There may be restrictions on who may be appointed, either by requiring qualifications, as where lawyers or doctors are specified, or

awarded against them. The recommendations in the Report on Expenses of Legal Proceedings against Justices and Clerks (1961), H.M.S.O., have been accepted in principle by the government.

[1] See pp. 388–94, 403–405, below. [2] See p. 411, below.

by requiring appointments to be made from panels. For tribunals connected with industry it is often provided that one member is to come from employers and another from workers' representatives, and in agriculture there is a similar principle. The usual provision is that members of tribunals hold office for the period specified in the warrant or instrument by which they are appointed.

Some tribunals are regarded as being virtually law courts, but there is no clear dividing line. Halsbury, *Laws of England*, a work to which judges as well as practitioners are apt to turn when in difficulty, used to end a lengthy description of law courts with a section headed Judicial Commissioners. The Railway and Canal Commission, the Railway Rates Tribunal, the Land Tax Commission, the Income Tax Commissioners, the Road Traffic Commissioners, Industrial Courts and Tribunals of Inquiry constituted the list, without any indication of why these particular tribunals were given the rank of being Judicial Commissions; the new edition in 1954 has no such classification. Professor Robson draws a distinction between 'administrative tribunals' and 'judicial commissioners' by saying that the vital feature of administrative tribunals is that there is no appeal to the law courts.[1] That distinction did not fit the facts, for in the past rights of appeal to the law courts have depended upon the parliamentary history of particular statutes. Now that there has been a considerable extension of appeals[2] we cannot possibly look to this factor to help in any classification.

It may be thought that the right way to classify tribunals as being independent and so virtually special law courts, is not to look at the legal power of appointing members, or at the presence or absence of any right of appeal, but to look at the facts: does this tribunal act independently or are its decisions regarded as being departmental work under the control of the head of the department? The Committee of Ministers' Powers tried to mark off a number of tribunals as being 'specialised courts of law' on the ground that, although they may be appointed by, or on the recommendation of ministers, they 'are in fact absolutely independent of ministerial influence, and function as regularly constituted Courts of Law although exercising a specialised jurisdiction.'[3] The trouble with this distinction is that it is virtually impossible to apply. The Committee mentioned the Special Commissioners of Income Tax as being independent, and

---

[1] *Justice and Administrative Law*, 3rd ed. (1951), p. 90.
[2] See p. 394, below.
[3] Report of the Committee on Ministers' Powers, Cmd. 4060 (1932), p. 84.

the Court of Referees[1] under the Unemployment Insurance Acts as being ministerial, but it would certainly have puzzled the members of a Court of Referees (representatives of employers and of workers, with a chairman often a lawyer) to know why they were dependent and so ministerial whilst certain Treasury officials were independent and thus a specialised court of law. Whether any person or body is 'in fact independent of ministerial influence' cannot be ascertained without a close and intimate knowledge of each sphere in which the question may arise. It is a fairly safe guess that representative members and lawyer chairmen will show independence of mind and will not follow the dictates of any ministry. How hard it is to get at realities without having personal knowledge can be seen by considering County Agricultural Executive Committees. These are essentially a local executive of the minister, being his agents, and acting in his name. In administrative matters these committees are controlled by the ministry, yet when these committees heard a dispute, say a notice to quit case between a landlord and his tenant, the committee was as free of ministerial control as is a bench of justices.[2] A point that is often overlooked is that the people who serve on many of these tribunals are quite likely to have other public activities: the lawyer chairman may also be chairman of a county Quarter Sessions, and lay members of tribunals may also be members of local authorities and be justices. These things do not breed subservience to ministries.[3]

At first impression the doctrine of the separation of powers looks a useful theory for classifying tribunals and minister's decisions, and particularly useful for supporting the lawyers' claim that things judicial should belong to the judiciary. It turns out to be of little assistance either to a student who is looking for a guiding principle or to an advocate who is presenting a case.

(b) The rule of law

The doctrine of the separation of powers is regarded as being applicable to all developed communities, and the 'rule of law' may also be used as a general concept. There is, however, a more limited sense for this phrase, and when a lawyer in this country speaks of

---

[1] Now a tribunal under National Insurance (see p. 343, above).

[2] See p. 346, above. The Agriculture Act 1958 abolished the jurisdiction of Committees and they continue as wholly executive bodies.

[3] There is little published information about the kind of people who are appointed to tribunals; a good start has been made by S. McCorquodale, 'The Composition of Administrative Tribunals' [1962] *Public Law*, p. 298.

the rule of law he means a particular doctrine which, it is asserted, is a principle of the Constitution of the United Kingdom. But the particular doctrine, now identified with Dicey, is derived from more general ideas that have a long and respectable ancestry. In all ages men have pondered on the factors that make for good or for bad government. Of the many elements that go to make up the good there is regularity, order, justice and fairness: on the other side there is that which is arbitrary, an irresponsible use of power, unfair and unjust. The good elements are associated with law, for all communities have sought to associate law with religion or with some natural order. The train of thought obviously leads to the conclusion that the good community is the one that is governed by law. The rule of law is thus the protection against arbitrary behaviour and against tyrannic or despotic government.

This broad idea has, of course, to be interpreted, and if it is to be of much use it has to be translated into institutions, and, as we should expect, the interpretation and translation have varied considerably. In countries that have adopted written constitutions the practice has been to enshrine in the constitution all the principles that are thought to be fundamental, so that they become 'constitutional' in a sense quite different from the English use of that term. Constitutional provisions can only be altered or abrogated by amending the constitution, and all ordinary law must be made within the limitations that the constitution lays down. The law courts are accordingly given the power to decide whether legislation or executive acts are valid or not.

English history has led us to a very different position. The constitutional struggles of the seventeenth century, as they appeared in the law courts, were over the nature and extent of the royal power. The lawyers took their stand on the medieval conception of a legal order, saying, as Bracton had done, that 'The King is beneath no man, but beneath God and the law'. This assumes that there are legal principles that are fundamental and which must govern all human action. This conception of the supremacy of law led to a precise and practical conclusion: the fundamental principles were thought to be enshrined in the common law. Hence when a question arose of whether the King possessed some power, that is whether a particular executive or governmental act was legal or illegal, the matter should be determined by the law courts: the judges would thereby maintain the principle of government under the law. The royalist answer was that the law of the judges was a part, not the whole, of the law: prerogative was also law. The Revolution Settlement of 1689 accepted the claim of the courts to judge the legality of executive acts, but it also made it clear that the ultimate authority is an Act of Parliament.

The lawyers had both won and lost. There was to be no rival court, such as the Star Chamber had been. Executive acts could be challenged in the courts and the existence and extent of any alleged prerogative would be determined by the judges; legality must depend on decisions of the courts based on the law, that is to say on common law and statute. But the old ideas about the common law had to be reconciled with the supremacy of Parliament. Lawyers had been accustomed to the idea that the common law contained such fundamental principles that anything, even a statute, infringing them could be declared null and void. It is true that the courts had never gone as far as that, but then the occasion had not arisen. In fact the supremacy of Parliament put the common law beneath statute: an Act of Parliament might upset and alter any part of the common law, even to the extent of directly reversing some rule that earlier lawyers had regarded as fundamental. Lawyers are not, however, at all quick at absorbing new ideas, and they continued throughout the eighteenth century to speak and write as though the common law were still fundamental and the law courts might sit in judgment on statutes and if necessary hold any offending legislation to be null and void. In fact they knew they could do nothing of the kind, but it was not until the nineteenth century that it became customary to refer to the legal omnipotence of Parliament as if it were undoubted.

A new interpretation was needed, and that was given by Dicey in his *Introduction to the Study of the Law of the Constitution*, first published in 1885. He explained in his Preface that he 'deals only with two or three guiding principles which pervade the modern constitution of England', these being the Sovereignty of Parliament, the Rule of Law and Conventions of the Constitution. It is a singularly difficult book for a modern student to appreciate, for it consists of analysis that was only partially correct in 1885 and is now positively misleading, yet it cannot be ignored. For many years it was regarded as being an accurate and masterly exposition of the basis of our free institutions, not merely as an analysis of the present but as showing the principles that must be observed if the good in government is to prevail over the bad. Lawyers came to regard Dicey's rule of law as if it were fundamental law. That, I think, is the key to the enormous influence that Dicey has had on the development of public law. He created again in lawyers a belief in the high purpose of the common law: it could no longer control statutes but the common law was the foundation of civil liberties and of our national way of life. It was flattering to lawyers, and doubly acceptable because it seemed to reinforce by logical argument the tradition of how the common law had overcome the powers of arbitrary government under the Stuarts.

As regards Dicey's views about the sovereignty of Parliament, there is little that concerns the administration of justice. If we look at our law courts we can say that anything that is passed as an Act of Parliament is binding upon them. That is purely a matter of law about what is legally binding; it does not mean to imply that Parliament can, as a matter of practical politics, commonsense or so on, pass anything that it wants, or that anything it passes is morally binding or can necessarily be enforced. It is purely a rule about sources of law, limited to the law courts that come within the system that is subject to the Parliament at Westminster. The complications, and they are substantial, relate to other fields, including political theory, international law and the commonwealth.

It is not necessary here to examine the whole of Dicey's exposition of the rule of law or to go into the criticisms to which they have been subjected.[1] The propositions that have had so much influence on legal thought are contained in the following extract:

> The rule of law means, in the first place, the absolute supremacy or predominance of regular law as opposed to the influence of arbitrary power, and excludes the existence of arbitrariness, of prerogative, or even of wide discretionary authority on the part of the government. Englishmen are ruled by the law, and by the law alone; a man may with us be punished for a breach of law, but he can be punished for nothing else. It means, again, equality before the law, or the equal subjection of all classes to the ordinary law of the land administered by the ordinary law courts.[2]

Dicey was concerned with explaining why civil liberties were greater and more secure in England than on the Continent.[3] Now he was right in his general assessment of the facts; the English system *did* give better protection to the individual. Being a lawyer he treated

---

[1] W. I. Jennings, *The Law and the Constitution*, has an Appendix on Dicey's Theory of the Rule of Law, in which he subjects Dicey's propositions to a devastating criticism. E. C. S. Wade, who began editing Dicey in the 9th ed. in 1939, is far fuller and less destructive.

[2] 9th ed., p. 202.

[3] F. H. Lawson, 'Dicey Revisited', 7 *Political Studies* (1959), pp. 1, 208, is a fair account of Dicey's methods and objects.

this as a legal problem: his rule of law was a conclusion, a deduction from rules and principles of the legal system. The conception of regular or ordinary law fitted in quite well with the feelings of lawyers, for they thought of ordinary law as consisting of case-law and statutory provisions which together provide a body of definite and fixed rules. Lawyers also thought of rights and liabilities in terms of judicial process: any interference with a man or with his property must be justified by the ordinary law, to be established in the ordinary courts of civil or criminal jurisdiction. Dicey illustrated his thesis principally by examining the way in which civil liberties are protected against wrongful government interference. If we take the power to arrest, the Dicey analysis was valid and it remains valid. If a citizen maintains that he was arrested illegally he can sue the person who arrested and detained him, and any person who authorised such acts, bringing his case before the High Court. The court will ascertain the facts, apply a known and definite body of law to those facts, and so arrive at a judgment. The defendants may be constables or high officers of state, but they must submit to the court and the application of the law. The Dicey analysis suited a *laissez faire* conception of government, but government was already concerned with the living conditions of the people. If Dicey had considered the law of public health, which had been consolidated into a vast statute in 1875, he would have seen extensive discretionary powers being exercised by local authorities and the Local Government Board. He did, in later editions, note the growth of administrative action, but he never considered whether his celebrated propositions were still sufficiently accurate.

In the period between the wars all manner of things were happening that were not in accordance with the rule of law as expounded by Dicey. In particular there were growing areas of 'wide discretionary authority on the part of the government' and important parts of the life of the community appeared not to be regulated by 'the ordinary law of the land administered by the ordinary law courts' but to rest on administration, regulation and tribunal. The validity of the new developments could not be questioned, for they were statutory. It was impossible to maintain that Dicey's rule of law was still a valid deduction from the legal facts, but lawyers would not give it up; they shifted their ground, and came to regard the rule of law as expressing the ideal to which our institutions ought to conform. In that way lawyers could go on speaking of the rule of law as if it were present fact with an ascertainable content. Then in the

1950's there had to be a further adjustment. Lawyers could no longer regard wide discretionary powers and decisions by tribunals and ministers as things that should not exist; we might be better without them, just as the country might be a better place without motor vehicles and television, but they are here and will continue, and instead of bewailing a lost era the sensible course is to see that the use of such dangerous things is not abused. The rule of law was interpreted anew so that it has come to denote standards rather than specific rules. Discretionary powers, for example, may allow a local authority to forbid certain development of land without paying compensation, and other development with compensation, with an appeal to the minister whose decision may depend on unjusticiable concepts of artistic form or social desirability: but all along the line the processes must comply with standards of openness, fairness to all concerned, having regard to relevant considerations and ignoring the irrelevant, and of course observing all the specific procedures provided by law. Adjudication, whether by tribunal or ordinary law court, must observe the proper standards.

Lawyers have always been groping for some eternal and super-human basis for law. The new interpretation of the rule of law is only another way of expressing old ideas of natural law. One of our most distinguished judges, Lord Radcliffe, says: 'We must never, then, lose touch with the idea of Natural Law or give up the belief that all positive law bears some relation to it.'[1] Now whether these ideas are profound truths or are beliefs that compensate lawyers for the uncreative nature of their calling, does not affect the result, which is a lack of precision. In 1959 the International Commission of Jurists met in New Delhi.[2] The Congress 'recognises that the Rule of Law is a dynamic concept for the expansion and fulfilment of which jurists are primarily responsible and which should be employed not only to safeguard and advance the civil and political rights of the individual in a free society, but also to establish social, economic, educational and cultural conditions under which his legitimate aspirations and dignity may be realised.' Lord Denning proclaimed his conversion to the new content of the rule of law, though he spoke of its fulfilment as being a government responsibility.[3] This is

---

[1] *The Law and its Compass* (1961).

[2] 1 *Journal of Indian Law Institute*, p. 207. A full report of the conference has been published by the International Commission of Jurists.

[3] 'Lord Denning of England stated at one of the closing plenary sessions of the Congress that he had till then taken the Rule of Law as basically a negative concept to restrain the Executive from violating the rights and interests of individuals.

admirable. Lawyers have spent a good deal of their time delaying slum clearance schemes and obstructing the fulfilment of social policies and it is nice to know that they have at last seen the light. The Rule of Law, which is a fine sonorous phrase, can now be put alongside the Brotherhood of Man, Human Rights and all the other slogans of mankind on the march.

But suppose that our feet are quite firmly on the ground, that we have to produce an answer to some very practical question, what help do we get from the Separation of Powers and the Rule of Law? Take a problem that arose a little while ago: how should mentally disordered people be treated as regards compelling them to enter or remain in hospital; who should decide what ought to be done, and how can we be sure that abuses do not arise? The process is empirical; what particular points do we want to meet, and are these best secured by the practices and procedures of law courts or by hand-tailoring a special tribunal;[1] it is unlikely that the Separation of Powers or the Rule of Law will be helpful.

(c) The distinction between tribunals and ministers' decisions

We may get a more helpful analysis by looking at procedure and comparing the judicial and the administrative processes. It is no new thing in the English legal system to find that procedure gives us a key to distinctions that are baffling when considered as substantive matters.[2] The judicial process is well known because it can be seen in action: we have the judge, who is a known person and not associated with any party to the proceedings; the evidence tendered to the court

But he had now reason to believe that the concept was incomplete without incorporating a positive aspect also, viz. of assuming the existence of "an Executive invested with sufficient power and resources to discharge its functions with efficiency and integrity" and of endeavours by the Government to create "such social and economic conditions within a society as will ensure a reasonable standard of economic security, social welfare and education for the mass of the people"' (*Ibid.* p. 209).

[1] The arguments set out in ch. 7 of the Report of the Royal Commission on Mental Health (Cmnd. 169, 1957) led to the establishment of Mental Health Review Tribunals. For comparison of law courts and tribunals, see pp. 380–3, below.

[2] The most obvious example is 'equity'. The beginner in law, and the foreign student, commonly have difficulty over law and equity, for the common law courts and the chancery court often dealt with the same subjects (for example, contracts) and the Lord Chancellor though a minister has since the later seventeenth century appeared in court as being much like a common law judge. But the procedure was different. Even Blackstone missed the full importance of that difference. Equity also demonstrates better than any other part of our law the working of discretionary powers exercised by judges.

is available to all parties, and there are opportunities for testing and criticising evidence tendered by an opposing party; parties may be legally represented and put forward arguments on facts or on law. The judge is expected to base his decision on law and to explain what he has done by 'giving reasons'. The assumption is that some law must be applicable and that this law is ascertainable by a process of considering principles that can be found in books of authority. The judge often has to exercise a discretion, but he will generally find that there is some precedent and that he cannot do just whatever he thinks would be best. There are times when a judge does have such a wide choice that it is proper to say he can decide on the ground of what he thinks is the best policy, but that is regarded as the result of there being gaps in the law; he may have to make policy decisions, but that is not his real business.[1]

The administrative process, as, for example, the exercise of powers conferred on a minister as the head of a government department, is for the most part not open to public inspection. In a matter of any importance there is a first stage of collecting information on everything that appears relevant. The core of it is the file of papers, and the file gets bigger with correspondence, memoranda and minutes. If it is a matter in which a statute prescribes the holding of an inquiry, then the inquiry is held and the report of the inquiry is added to the papers. Other departments may be consulted, and the opinions of experts, including legal advisers, may be obtained. The mass of paper, which may be considerable, is made manageable by the preparation of analyses and summaries. Then comes the question, Who actually decides? Many people think that that is a most pertinent question and that if it were not for veils of secrecy they could get a clear answer. This idea comes from a lack of understanding of the structure and functions of the staff of a government department. It may be that in a particular ministry all matters of a certain kind go to a particular person or persons of a particular grade, and that that is where the decision is ordinarily made. But the decision is in form and in law the decision of the minister. A most important part of a civil servant's job is to understand the limits of what he should do without reference to a higher official or to his minister. Much depends on the extent to which a case falls within clearly settled departmental practice or raises a new issue on

---

[1] Out of the numerous writings on judges and their ways I think that B. N. Cardozo, *The Nature of the Judicial Process* (1921), and J. Frank, *Law and the Modern Mind* (1930), both reprinted recently, is the best short selection.

which a policy decision is required. The minister also must understand what he can do on his own responsibility and when he ought to go to the Prime Minister or to the cabinet. Some matters must clearly go to the minister, as when replies must be made in Parliament, but the governing consideration is that the minister is responsible to Parliament for everything done in his name irrespective of whether he had in fact authorised it or had even heard of the matter.[1] Hence the minister is entitled to expect from the staff of his department a very high standard of care and an acute sense of the level at which a decision should be taken. It may thus happen that a matter which is not of itself of much importance but which may have political repercussions will go to the minister whilst something that is intrinsically of far greater importance can properly be settled by an official of moderate position. The decision, given in the name of the minister and not disclosing the identity of the person who actually made the decision, is an inevitable result of giving a power to a minister, for such a power cannot consistently with ministerial responsibility be exercised in any other way.

Local government authorities have to decide many matters that affect the rights of citizens. Common instances are the control of development under the Town and Country Planning Acts and compulsory acquisition of land. These matters are thrashed out in committees, which either report to the council or make the actual decision under delegated powers, the committee members having the help of reports and advice from the council's officials and coming to a conclusion on grounds of policy. The notion of responsibility attaches to these decisions: if attacked, they must be defended in a council meeting, and the ultimate arbiter is the electorate. There is, however, in virtually all these matters, either a right of appeal to a minister or a necessity for the council to secure the approval of a minister, so that an aggrieved person complains to the minister. The centre of interest thus shifts to the minister and to the process that he follows, and hence in this section the decisions of local authorities need not be considered separately from decisions by ministers.

The administrative process is principally used for matters that are

[1] Responsibility really depends on the attitude of the House of Commons. Questions are not allowed on the decisions of law courts, and the House might accept a minister's contention that he should not answer for the exercise of a power that has obvious similarities with what is accepted as the business of law courts, but that does not extend to such matters as approval of slum clearance schemes or compulsory purchase orders even when in the circumstances the High Court would hold that the minister had the duty to 'act judicially'.

to be decided on policy, which means that the decision may be based upon any grounds or reasons that appear appropriate to the person who makes the decision, though ministers often have to decide issues by applying a known rule to facts established by evidence. The fact that the courts have more scope for policy than older writers recognised and that government departments often have a highly developed system of precedent, tends to blur the line between law and policy, but it does not remove the distinction.[1] The conception of law as being essentially fixed and binding runs through the judicial process. A judge is left virtually uncriticised and uncontrolled for the very good reason that he must work within well-understood limits; he must apply the law as he finds it, which includes doing his best to produce something intelligible and consistent when legal sources are confused or insufficient. The administrative process is free from those limits; a decision may be deliberately based on expediency, the state of the public finances, repercussions on other government policy, public opinion or any other of the numerous factors that determine the wisdom or practicality of the action in question. The ground that is thought to be good today may be altered tomorrow. It may be that the judicial process and the administrative process might with advantage borrow a little from each other, but we confuse them at our peril, for the values of liberal democracy are not so tough that they can stand unlimited maltreatment.

If we consider all the agencies mentioned in the last section and look at the process that they follow, I think that a sharp distinction should be made between ministers and the other deciding agencies. On this view all the definite tribunals and officials, such as district auditors, who act in their own name and not as agents of the minister, are regarded as belonging to one category of bodies that follow the judicial process. In nearly all these agencies there is a tribunal of known composition that hears a case, applies a known rule to the case as established and so arrives at a conclusion. There are some instances where this analysis seems hardly applicable. Rent tribunals

---

[1] There is a school of thought that regards law and policy as being substantially the same thing. Professor Robson, *Justice and Administrative Law*, 3rd ed. (1951), p. 432, says: 'In my view one can distinguish "policy" from "law" only in theory, and even then the distinction is doubtful.' Against this view H. W. R. Wade, 'Quasi-Judicial and its Background', 10 *Cambridge Law Journal* (1949), p. 216, has many pertinent arguments. I think that Professor Robson's contention comes to little more than that dividing lines are impossible to define and therefore they do not exist and therefore the two things are the same.

have been given an impossible task, for one cannot apply law to facts if the basic conception, that of a fair rent, is nebulous. Legal representation has not until recently been allowed before some tribunals. But these are anomalies rather than characteristics of special tribunals. There may be scope for policy, as there often is before law courts, but the typical instance is a tribunal applying Acts and subordinate legislation: a tribunal under the National Insurance Acts, for instance, could no more refuse a claim because of the state of public finances than a County Court could refuse a tenant the protection of the Rent Restriction Acts because those Acts have been an obstacle to a sensible housing policy.

It has been the general practice in the past to lump together ministers and special tribunals, as if they are merely different forms of the same kind of body. That has had a number of unfortunate results. It is the exercise of powers by ministers that attracts much criticism and often creates strong feeling, for it is the very nature of policy decisions that they should often turn on factors that are controversial. Policy often depends on conceptions of finance, priorities and allocations between competing claims, and whether the 'time is ripe', which are all matters on which dispute is commoner than agreement. If special tribunals are thought of as belonging to the same category as ministerial decisions then people will suppose that decisions of tribunals may also depend on the minister's view. This identification has been helped by the general use of the term 'administrative tribunal' and 'administrative justice'. I cannot see why a tribunal under the National Insurance Acts, or under other Acts that have been mentioned, is 'administrative': it is appointed by a minister and it applies a part of a great statutory system, but County Court judges and justices of the peace are appointed by a minister, and they apply parts of equally vast statutory systems. The high water mark of infelicitous phraseology is to be found in Professor Robson's book *Justice and Administrative Law* in which he uses the phrase 'Trial by Whitehall' as including decisions of ministers and determinations by special tribunals. 'Whitehall' means government departments, that is to say, ministers and civil servants. The term might be applied to Special Commissioners of Income Tax and to District Auditors (who are civil servants, though not acting on behalf of a minister) but it is wrong and misleading so to describe the great variety of men and women, professional and representative, paid and unpaid, who sit on these tribunals. When the chief point in creating a tribunal is to provide an independent body to

377

decide disputes, as for example Agricultural Land Tribunals, it is particularly important to avoid phrases that suggest that the tribunal is really Whitehall. The most satisfactory term seems to be 'special tribunal'.[1]

(d) The choice between law courts, special tribunals and ministers

Whether a dispute is to come before a law court or is to be dealt with in some other way is a matter for the provisions of the relevant statutes. It is sometimes possible to see from the debates in Parliament why a particular provision was made, but that only puts the question back to the drafting of the Bill. When proposals for new legislation are being prepared in a government department are there any principles for choosing between courts, tribunals and the minister? It is commonly believed that the Civil Service likes to keep as much as possible in their own hands and particularly want to by-pass the law courts. That is not borne out by the evidence tendered to various inquiries. Departments have quite enough to do and do not want to have the trouble and the responsibility of numerous decisions in individual cases if it appears feasible to pass that work over to some other agency. The cardinal point is that the minister is going to become responsible for some service or process, and the ministry must therefore keep in its own hands the making of all decisions that are vital to carrying out the minister's functions. If we take, for example, the compulsory acquisition of land, all the statutes vest the ultimate decision in a minister because if the power were vested in any independent body then that body could stultify the performance of the minister's functions. If it is decided as a matter of government policy that a new motor road is to be built between points A and B, it is obvious that land will have to be acquired, and that someone must have ultimate responsibility for deciding the route that the new road is to follow. If an independent court or body had the power to say whether any particular piece of land could be acquired or not, then that would be equivalent to deciding upon the route of the new road, and indeed upon whether there could be a new road at all. No minister can be expected to agree to legislation that would remove from his control the carrying

[1] The need for separate treatment of tribunals and minister's powers, which I put forward in the 1953 edition of this book and in an article 'Tribunals and Inquiries', 33 *Public Administration* (1955), 115, now seems accepted. The Franks Committee kept the two subjects properly apart (see p. 386, below). But the word 'administrative' is still applied to these tribunals, still suggesting to the unwary that the whole thing is a minister or his stooges.

out of projects and policies which rest upon policy decisions for which he has a responsibility to Parliament. When we look at the compensation to be paid we see that the government is concerned with the law that determines the basis for valuations, but that any particular valuation is left to the independent Lands Tribunal. In the same way the determination of whether a particular applicant is or is not entitled to benefit under the National Insurance Acts, or to how much benefit, is left to independent adjudication. So also is the question whether a landlord of agricultural land is or is not justified in getting rid of a tenant on grounds of bad or inadequate farming. There have been instances where a ministry has kept control of a class of decisions that were not, as events went, at all necessary to safeguard the working of a scheme, but those have been miscalculations due to excess of caution and not to any general objection to some independent adjudication.

If decisions in certain matters are to be retained in the ministry, there is a further question whether the statute should lay down any procedure to be followed or not. There is a fairly standard procedure for the holding of inquiries before an inspector, and this is required by a number of statutes. This procedure was devised in the past as a substitute for private bill procedure,[1] in order to save both money and time, but it is now so well established that it is used in matters that would never have justified a private Act. Planning appeals, for example, have run into some 6000 a year, which means that the ministry has to maintain a substantial staff of inspectors and other officials engaged upon this work. Where the matter is one of a different kind, without any aura of private bill procedure, a statute may very well lay down no procedure to be followed but simply confer upon the minister the power and the duty to make decisions. The minister may then establish some procedure which may include a public inquiry or hearing, but any such procedure is an administrative arrangement and is not obligatory. Alternatively the method by which the decisions are made may not be divulged; all that is known to the outside world is that applications are received and that a decision comes from the ministry.

If the disputes that are likely to arise are not of a kind that would have a direct effect upon the work of the ministry there is from the ministry's point of view a definite advantage in passing the work over to some independent body. Whether the work should be done by the law courts, or by a tribunal created for the purpose, rests upon a

[1] See pp. 322–4, above.

number of considerations. It is sometimes supposed that ministries set up special tribunals because they will carry out the ministry's policies, and some people even think that the minister, in selecting the members of such tribunals, deliberately looks for persons who will either be subservient to the ministry or can be relied upon to be sympathetic. There is no truth in that, and indeed it would defeat the whole object of establishing a tribunal, which is to provide an independent method of adjudication in matters where the ministry does not mind whether the decision in any particular case goes one way or another. The choice between law courts and a special tribunal is in practice made by considering their respective merits. Law courts have certain obvious advantages: they already exist, they have a known procedure, their behaviour is fairly predictable and they are eminently respectable. A minister who tells the Commons that disputes under his Bill are to go to the law courts does not have to argue that point; all the lawyers and some other people will accept that as being obvious, whereas proposals for creating a special tribunal have to be supported by arguments in favour of some special provision. Inevitably these advantages have to be considered in comparison with the characteristics of law courts.[1]

1. Special tribunals may make provision for deciding cases at very little cost to the parties. The cost of the officials and the buildings used comes out of public funds. Where poor people are chiefly concerned, as in some matters under the National Insurance Acts, the applicant merely has to attend; witnesses are not usually needed, but if the applicant has to call a witness (other than a full-time salaried trade union official) the cost is paid by the Treasury. An appeal from a tribunal to the umpire costs the applicant nothing at all. A party may employ a solicitor and be represented by counsel, in which case the costs may be substantial. In some tribunals there is far less need to employ lawyers than there is in the law courts, and parties are often unrepresented professionally. In tribunals such as the Special Commissioners of Income Tax and the Agricultural Land Tribunals the parties are generally represented. Of course part of the saving of cost to the parties is at the expense of the taxpayer, but taking this into account there is still an absolute saving in cost, for

---

[1] There is a full discussion in the last chapter of Robson, *Justice and Administrative Law*. A study of the working of some special tribunals, together with the reasons for retaining such tribunals rather than hand the work over to law courts, is contained in the Report of the Departmental Committee on the Imposition of Penalties by Marketing Boards and Other Similar Bodies, Cmd. 5980 (1939).

the salaries are lower than in the judiciary, and the buildings and so forth are not specialised.

2. There may be less delay before cases are heard. If there is an increase in the number of cases the minister may be able to expand the service to deal with it. In 1925 the Courts of Referees were dealing with nearly 12,000 claims a month; the figures vary with trade conditions, and the personnel can be varied to meet the circumstances. This flexibility is also a characteristic of magistrates' courts, where extra courts can be held to deal with a pressure of cases.[1] An increase in the work of professional judges generally means delay in hearing cases, for an increase in the number of judges has not in the past been made until at least two years after the need for that increase had become acute. In some cases special tribunals have been more dilatory than law courts.

3. The procedure of law courts is very difficult for litigants in person.[2] Special tribunals can adopt a more informal method, rendering it far easier for the inexperienced to present their case adequately. Even when solicitors are engaged there are great advantages, the saving of time and trouble being due to factors much like those mentioned for arbitrations. In the preliminary work before the hearing of an action in the law courts it may be necessary to apply to the court over some point, whereas for a special tribunal the telephone can be used and arrangements made in the way that is used for ordinary business affairs. Officials of the law courts are so afraid of telephones that they generally conceal their telephone numbers.[3] The 'majesty of the law' is to some extent a policy of 'splendid isolation'.

4. Special tribunals can avoid the rigidity of precedent that often hampers law courts. There is sometimes a need for a break with past practice. It is not uncommon for judges in law courts to regret that they cannot make a new start in interpreting a statute or a line of cases. A special tribunal is unlikely to achieve the futility of saying that a conclusion is 'ridiculous' and yet necessary because of precedent.[4] Much of the law depends upon standards or measuring rods: negligence is measured against a hypothetical 'reasonable man', whilst various words, such as 'in repair' for houses and 'sea-worthy'

---

[1] Stipendiary magistrates, being fully engaged already, cannot expand in that way, and hence the Metropolitan Magistrates' Courts Act 1959 provides for the appointment of temporary acting stipendiary magistrates (see p. 147, above).

[2] See p. 152, above.   [3] See pp. 290–1, above.

[4] Lord Justice Scrutton found himself in this position in *Hill* v. *Aldershot Corporation* [1933] 1 K.B. 259.

for ships, have come to denote an ascertainable standard. It does not matter if some standards cannot be stated until we have a dozen precedents reported in the course of twenty years. If the standard of public health works had been left to the judges to evolve through precedents we might still be living in fear of cholera epidemics. The more rapidly changes are occurring the more quickly must standards change or new standards be established. A special tribunal may escape the baleful influence of precedent upon precedent.

5. Special tribunals can be staffed by men possessing expert knowledge in particular fields. The specialisation that exists among High Court judges could never extend to all the subjects covered by special tribunals. A High Court judge who was called upon to take the Commercial List although he was not accustomed to such work made the following comment:

> It is useless to have a list labelled 'Commercial' if the Judge who has to deal with it has no special experience which qualifies him for trying Commercial cases, and if such a Judge is entrusted with the list it is not too much to say that it is a fraud on the important class of litigants who are concerned. Having entered the case in the belief that it will be tried by a specially skilled tribunal, they find that they get nothing of the sort. ...I think I am entitled to make it clear that I do not willingly take part in such arrangements, and also I think that I am right in calling attention publicly to what is a serious public mischief.[1]

It would, I think, be contempt of court for an ordinary member of the public to express those sentiments in such vigorous language. It may be said that there is not such a difference between ordinary Queen's Bench Division work and the Commercial List as there is between 'lawyers' law' and many of the topics handled by special tribunals. We may also remember that the judges themselves disliked hearing certain kinds of railway cases because they felt ill-equipped to handle such work.

6. Special tribunals have been able to work out their own procedure[2] and for many matters they have made good use of the expert knowledge of their members. Suppose that we have to decide whether a field is foul with twitch. In a law court the judge would hear expert evidence on each side, which means one or more witnesses saying that the land is foul and other witnesses saying that it is clean. An Agricultural Land Tribunal would also hear such evidence, but then the members would inspect the land. The tribunal would almost

---

[1] Mr Justice Talbot, reported in *The Times*, 8 December 1934.
[2] They may be forced into a Procrustean legal bed (see pp. 386–7, below).

certainly come to the right conclusion, whereas the law court, by clinging to its conception of a trial and evidence, may easily go wrong on the simplest of facts.[1]

The strong points of special tribunals cannot be ignored. This is not a claim that special tribunals are always better than law courts, either generally or in the particular points mentioned. It is impossible to discuss whether one tribunal is better than another unless we know the kind of work it has to do. The most important thing is a personnel with adequate knowledge and experience and opportunity to use that knowledge. There is no reason why law courts should be more expensive, dilatory, and hidebound than special tribunals. But reform of these matters would not do away with the need for special tribunals. Public law has become far too complex for any one group of men with a similar training to handle it all: the work has got to be spread over different institutions to secure efficiency.

4. THE NEW COMPROMISE

The years following the end of the war in 1945 saw a steadily mounting volume of dissatisfaction with some of the results of the new policies and their administration. There has been a feeling that in many matters the citizen is helpless against the power of the state, having no effective method of getting justice. Such ideas are extremely difficult to examine because they jumble together all the frustrations, exasperations and difficulties arising from a diversity of causes. A period following total war, with economy everywhere upset, and a cold war in the offing, would have been disturbing in any event, but the period was also one of vast social changes. Many people found that some control cut across their expectations: it seemed to them that some power, commonly called 'they', possessed unlimited power. 'They' would not allocate sufficient petrol, or grant a licence to build. 'They' would not allow a site to be used as its owner wished, often because 'they' wanted to acquire it at a great deal less than its real value. There was a great deal of substance in many of the complaints, particularly the attempt to control the use of land without paying compensation for restrictions, the price paid on compulsory acquisitions, and the too rigorous interference with the inefficient use of agricultural land. People who were

---

[1] A substantial amount of commercial work goes to arbitration for similar reasons: on the quality or nature of goods an expert arbitrator can use his own knowledge (see p. 402, below).

disgruntled, justifiably or otherwise, found plenty of lawyers ready to champion their cause. Lawyers were able to reduce the discontents to apparent order: 'they' were the executive, and the trouble came from 'decisions' which ought to be made by the courts or at least in accordance with certain basic principles. The normal legal assertion was that if only the lawyers were allowed to handle these affairs, then all would be well. Well-known lawyers even went so far as to assert that if there were better provision for judicial review the courts would have prevented interference with agricultural land and the payment of inadequate compensation, although that could not have been done except by disregarding Acts of Parliament.[1]

In fact there was no great volume of well-informed criticism of special tribunals as opposed to minister's powers. Rent Tribunals and Agricultural Executive Committees came in for attacks, but then they were set up to control the use of property in what was thought to be the public interest, and had the members been uniformly angelic they would have met with hostility. The best evidence for the view that special tribunals were acceptable to the public is that statutes continued to create new tribunals, irrespective of the political colour of the government. It has also been noticeable that when workmen and employers set up machinery for disputes they also adopt the pattern of a special tribunal and show no hankering after law courts.[2] The real difficulty arose over minister's powers. It was becoming apparent that a general inquiry by Departmental Committee or Royal Commission was needed when a special impetus came from the affair of Crichel Down. That story of muddled administration when it appeared in 1954[3] promptly became authority for all sorts of things that in fact were not present, but a myth may be most potent in stirring men into action. In 1955 the Lord Chancellor appointed a Committee on Administrative Tribunals and Enquiries under the Chairmanship of Sir Oliver Franks, and the Committee reported in 1957.[4] Most of the recommendations were

[1] I examined some of these claims in 'Judicial Review of Legislative Policy', 18 *Modern Law Review* (1955), 571.

[2] Mr Charles Muir, *Justice in a Depressed Area* (1936), p. 86, considered that the Northern working man regards special tribunals as being fairer and more efficient than the ordinary law courts.

[3] Report of the Inquiry held by Sir Andrew Clark, Cmd. 9176 (1954) and Report on whether civil servants should be transferred, Cmd. 9220 (1954). J. A. G. Griffith 'The Crichel Down Affair', 18 *Modern Law Review* (1955), 557, is a most useful account.

[4] Cmnd. 218 (1957). The Evidence was taken in public and published, along with Memoranda from departments. See also E. C. S. Wade, 'Administration

accepted by the government and they have been carried out by administrative direction and by new legislation, the Tribunals and Inquiries Act 1958.

The Franks Committee was appointed:

To consider and make recommendations on:

(*a*) The constitution and working of tribunals other than the ordinary courts of law, constituted under any Act of Parliament by a Minister of the Crown or for the purposes of a Minister's functions.

(*b*) The working of such administrative procedures as include the holding of an inquiry or hearing by or on behalf of a Minister on an appeal or as the result of objections or representations, and in particular the procedure for the compulsory purchase of land.

The Committee was thus limited to the 'constitution and working' of tribunals and the 'working' of minister's decisions where a formal procedure had been prescribed by statute. Minister's powers in respect of administration and ordinary decision were outside the terms of reference. So that, for example, the Crichel Down affair or the allocation of petrol during rationing could not be considered because no statutory procedure was applicable to either of them. Nor was the Committee's work a general inquiry into the whole subject of adjudication and decisions by agencies other than law courts. The Committee did have to consider the general background, and took refuge in constitutional piety. Parliament decided that various decisions should not go to the ordinary law courts but should have special procedures: 'This must have been to promote good administration'. The special procedures must be generally acceptable.

It is clear that there are certain general and closely linked characteristics which should mark these special procedures. We call these characteristics openness, fairness and impartiality. Here we need only give brief examples of their application. Take openness. If these procedures were wholly secret, the basis of confidence and acceptability would be lacking. Next take fairness. If the objector were not allowed to state his case, there would be nothing to stop oppression. Thirdly, there is impartiality. How can the citizen be satisfied unless he feels that those who decide his case come to their decision with open minds?[1]

The Report goes on to explain that the method of adjudication

under the Law', 73 *Law Quarterly Review* (1957), 470; W. A. Robson 'The Franks Report' [1958] *Public Law*, 12; G. Marshall 'The Franks Report' 35 *Public Administration* (1957) and 'Tribunals and Inquiries: Developments since the Franks Report' 36 *Public Administration* (1958), 261; J. A. G. Griffith 'Tribunals and Inquiries', 22 *Modern Law Review* (1959), 125. There is a useful note by H. W. R. Wade on the Tribunals and Inquiries Act 1958 in [1958] *Cambridge Law Journal*, 129.

[1] Franks Report, para. 23, 24.

by tribunals is the application of rules, and that they are thereby distinguished from minister's decisions. 'Tribunals as a system of adjudication have come to stay.' They 'are not ordinary courts but neither are they appendages of Government Departments'. 'Tribunals should properly be regarded as machinery provided by Parliament for adjudication rather than as part of the machinery of administration.'[1] Hence the Committee dealt with tribunals and minister's decisions separately, but applying to each the principles of openness, fairness and impartiality. The greater part of the Report is accordingly concerned with improvements and safeguards within the existing structure. The principal recommendations, with the action that has subsequently been taken, fall under the following headings:

The Council on Tribunals[2]

This is a permanent body of up to fifteen members appointed by the Lord Chancellor under the Tribunals and Inquiries Act 1958. It is similar in many ways to a Departmental Committee; its members serve in their spare time as a form of voluntary public work, meeting monthly and of course making visits and doing home-work; there is an official full-time secretariat, and the functions are advisory. It is required to keep under review the tribunals specified in the Act, and new ones that may be added to the list, to report on any matters referred to it concerning tribunals or statutory inquiries, or to report of its own initiative if the Council thinks that something is sufficiently important. The Council must be consulted before procedural rules are made. The Council makes an annual Report on its work, and that is published. It is too early to form definite views about the Council, but I think that some tendencies can be seen. It was intended to be a consumers' watch dog, and its membership has few lawyers, but its Reports have a familiar ring to anyone who has followed the lawyers' views over several years. The lawyers got nearly all they wanted from the Franks Committee, and then the government enacted most, but not quite all, of the Franks recommendations. The pressure to let the lawyers run everything is still at work. The Council on Tribunals has a majority of non-lawyer members, but a singularly active and persuasive minority, and a legal chairman, a legal secretary and legal assistants. The judicialising of

[1] Franks Report, para. 37, 40.
[2] See 'The Council on Tribunals' by H. W. R. Wade [1960] *Public Law*, 351. Professor Wade advocated such a body in his evidence to the Franks Committee, and he is a member of the Council.

some procedures has had bad effects,[1] and if the Council is to achieve the position to which it aspires it must be something more than a handmaiden to the Temple.

The members and chairmen of tribunals

There was criticism of the general position whereby the minister concerned with the subject-matter of a tribunal appointed the chairman and members and could dismiss them. It is essentially a question of appearances: there is no evidence that ministers want members of tribunals to be subservient or that any attempt has been made to exercise any kind of influence. Nevertheless, when a tribunal sits to adjudicate between a citizen and a minister it is possible that the citizen may doubt the impartiality of the tribunal if it is appointed and liable to be dismissed by the minister. On the other hand, members have to be appointed by someone, and in theory all ministers are part of the same institution: a prisoner tried by a magistrates' court for an alleged offence against the Crown is brought before a bench appointed and dismissible by the Crown. The Committee thought that members should be appointed by the Council on Tribunals, but the government could not accept this, and the Act leaves appointment of members to be made as hitherto with, however, a right for the Council to make general recommendations. Dismissal is, however, now restricted: no member or member of a panel can be dismissed except with the concurrence of the Lord Chancellor, and also with that of the Lord President of the Court of Session and of the Lord Chief Justice of Northern Ireland for tribunals that sit in all parts of the United Kingdom.

The Committee recommended that all chairmen should be appointed by the Lord Chancellor, but the Act does not so provide. For an important group of tribunals the Act requires the Lord Chancellor to appoint a panel and then the appropriate minister selects a chairman from that panel. There is some extension of requiring legal qualifications in chairmen, but no general rule.

It is hardly likely that the composition of tribunals will be noticeably different. Everyone who has had experience of making appointments knows that the trouble is to find enough suitable men and women for the magistracy, tribunals and other forms of public service, and good chairmen are harder still to find. If lawyers are appointed simply on the basis that it is a good thing to have lawyers, the standard of tribunals may not be altered for the better.

[1] See pp. 403–4, below.

25-2

Reasons are to be given for decisions

The Act provides that tribunals and ministers who make decisions after statutory inquiries shall, if requested, give reasons for their decisions. The reasons may be given orally or in writing, and they then form part of the record. There are a number of exceptions, but the general effect is to introduce a requirement that is regarded as essential to sound methods of adjudication. In asserting that reasons should always be given, lawyers have over-stated their case. Law courts do not *always* give reasons, and juries never do so. The giving of reasons for a decision is primarily applicable to points of law and the relevance and bearing of findings of fact. The majority of cases turn on simple questions of fact, such as whether a vehicle was exceeding 30 m.p.h., or was parked in a street, or had no lights, and reasoned judgments can hardly be expected. The interest of lawyers in making tribunals and ministers give reasons is twofold. First, there is a belief that people will accept decisions against them if they are told the reasons why they have lost their case. There is some truth in that, but it is somewhat naive to suppose that people are always so easily satisfied. Secondly, if reasons are given, then the High Court can look at the record and decide whether the reasons are good reasons; this has to be considered in connection with other grounds for judicial review.[1]

Representation before tribunals and public sittings

The Committee recommended that the ordinary rule should be that parties may be legally represented and that sittings should be held in public, as has been the case in most tribunals and inquiries. These matters, together with other procedural points, can usually be regulated by rules made after consultation with the Council. Some sets of rules have already been made. Little difficulty arises over legal representation, which is now generally allowed, and the practice is to provide for public hearings except in those instances where personal and financial details of applicants must be examined.

Inquiries and minister's decisions

Most of the statutory procedures to be considered under this heading relate to land. There are compulsory purchase orders for a variety of public purposes, slum clearance which may result in either an order to the owner to demolish the buildings or in a com-

---

[1] See p. 398, below.

pulsory purchase by the local authority, so that it may clear and then develop the area, and there are appeals to the minister against the refusal of planning permission, or against conditions that have been attached to a consent. The procedure is derived from that for Private Bills in Parliament,[1] the essence being that the decision is vested in the minister but there is a statutory procedure that must be observed. If we take as an example the compulsory purchase of land by a local authority for the purpose of building houses, the first part of the procedure is concerned with resolutions of the local authority, notices to people concerned, and advertisement, and submission of the order (really a draft) to the Minister. The purpose is to inform all who may be concerned so that persons who object can oppose the order. If there are objections the minister must cause a local public inquiry (or in some circumstances a less formal hearing) to be held. The inquiry is conducted by an official of the ministry, called an inspector, and it is conducted much like a trial. The inspector, however, does not make or announce a decision: he makes a report to the minister, and in due course the minister's decision is conveyed in a letter. For many years there has been controversy over this procedure. Before considering the recommendations of the Franks Committee and the changes that have been introduced it is useful to consider why there should have been such diverse views. The explanation is that there are two ways in which one may look at these matters.

One view is that of the administrators, by which I mean the local authority, with committees of its council and their officials, and the departments of the central government. They are seeking to provide the people with services that are wanted, and that the democratic system has approved and authorised. The administrator thinks primarily in terms of the object to be achieved, of housing, roads, schools and so on. Most of his problems are present even when the necessary land is available. Housing is not just a matter of sites and building: every other service is involved. The relief of traffic may call for a by-pass, or an internal circular route or some other lay-out. The cost must be considered, and the competing claims of other plans. The central government is vitally concerned with the level of capital expenditure. Projects may be held up for years because of such difficulties, even when the site is immediately available. Hence an administrator normally regards the obtaining of land as only one of the factors. If the public want motor roads,

[1] See pp. 322–4, above.

and the government decide that a new road is to be built, some people are going to lose some land. If the engineers and surveyors agree that a particular lay-out would be best, and that cuts across Blackacre, the procedure will allow the owner of Blackacre to object, and that objection and the grounds for it will be taken into account when the minister decides on the final plans.

The other view can be called that of the lawyers, for they have been so much concerned with these matters on behalf of landowners that a distinctive legal approach has to be recognised. The lawyer comes in to defend his client's interests, and he sees the matter as being a dispute between the public authority that wants the land and his client who does not want to give it up. Something is being demanded from a man, and if there is a public need then that ought to be properly proved. Great importance is therefore attached to the inquiry, which ought, on this reckoning, to be the equivalent of a trial. Yet when lawyers looked at the procedure they found that although it had some resemblance to a trial there were, in their view, some serious shortcomings.

They knew that the inspectors usually had professional qualifications in engineering, architecture or surveying, and experience showed that they conducted inquiries with fairness and competence. But they were commonly civil servants from the ministry concerned. If it is a local authority that is asking for compulsory purchase, then there are apparently two contending parties with the minister as judge. The local authority will have to call evidence at the inquiry to establish their case, and the owner of Blackacre can appear personally or by counsel or solicitor and cross-examine the witnesses, and himself give evidence, and call witnesses in opposition. If, however, it is the minister who proposes to acquire land, as when the Minister of Transport needs land for improving trunk roads or the Home Secretary wants land for a penal institution, then the minister did not prove his case: an official explained the plan, but he could not be cross-examined on the need for the works or the merits of the proposals. In either case, the inspector gave no judgment: he reported to the ministry, and in due course the minister's decision was given by letter. Lawyers wanted to know what happened in the ministry, and what was in the inspector's report: they were not allowed to see it. Did the department have evidence, such as a report from officials of another ministry, which was not mentioned at the inquiry? To what extent was the decision based on evidence or on policy? And behind all these questions lay the belief that the minister is not impartial. When a minister is given a power of a judicial nature it will be exercised honestly, for civil servants are honourable men, and to the best of their understanding,[1] but the principles of natural justice are hard or impossible to observe. The notion that a minister is always judge in his own cause is a gross exaggeration, for departmental policy does not prejudge individual cases; belief that slums ought to be cleared does not mean that anyone in Whitehall assumes that any particular area is a slum that ought to be cleared, any more than a dislike of thieves prejudices a court that hears a charge of larceny. It may be possible to see the minister as impartial where it is a local authority that is seeking to acquire, but where it is the minister who wants the land for his own departmental purposes there is no escaping the lawyers' contention. If the Ministry of Transport decide that a trunk road should have a roundabout, and that involves taking a piece of your land, you are given an opportunity to object and you must be heard, but then the ministry look at their own plans again and find in their own favour.

In effect lawyers assumed that these ministerial powers are judicial or near enough to judicial to require the observance of the basic principles of adjudication and from that premiss (which they took as being self-evident) they deduced quite logically that the procedure was bad. There were various sets of proposals for reform. Some lawyers thought that such decisions should go before a tribunal which would be both independent and impartial. Others thought that the powers of ministers should be subject to extensive judicial review: an aggrieved person should be able to force a minister to justify his decision before a law court, or a new Administrative Division of the High Court, or before some English version of the French *Conseil d'Etat*. More moderate lawyers proposed some changes in existing procedures that might remove the commoner grievances. The Franks Committee followed the obvious course, that is to say they rejected all claims to have decisions made by independent persons or for there to be extensive powers of review by the courts, and they also rejected the view that these decisions are purely administrative. The Committee sought for 'a reasonable balance', which meant meeting the complaints in so far as that could be done within the broad pattern of

---

[1] Those who like to see hard things said about civil servants found delight in *Blackpool Corporation* v. *Locker* [1948] 1 K.B. 349. Scott L.J. produced an astonishing doctrine that a power to delegate power to requisition is a legislative power, and belaboured some officials for not understanding that, although it was contrary to existing legal authority and remains a curiosity of legal thought.

existing procedure. It appears as a victory for the moderate wing of legal opinion.

The changes in procedure for compulsory acquisition, slum clearance and planning appeals were introduced by the Ministry of Housing and Local Government in 1958 as a matter of practice. The Town and Country Planning Act 1959 added a section to the Tribunals and Inquiries Act giving power to the Lord Chancellor to make rules for regulating procedure in statutory inquiries, that is for all such inquiries and not just for planning. Rules of procedure for inquiries on compulsory acquisition by local authorities and on planning appeals were made in 1962 after consultation with the Council on Tribunals. Under these rules, and the practice where rules are not yet made, a local authority and a ministry must provide a full statement in writing of the reasons for any proposal. If a minister is himself the initiating authority, he will also provide a representative who will explain the proposal at the inquiry and answer questions on it. If the views of other government departments are part of the authorities' case (as, for example, where the Ministry of Agriculture support a refusal to allow the use of certain land for building) then a representative of that ministry will attend the inquiry to give evidence. There is no change in the general way in which inquiries are conducted. There has been much discussion over the position of 'third parties'; ought, for example, a neighbouring land-owner to have a right to appear as a party when the issue is the grant or refusal of a planning permission that may affect his property? After consideration, the practice is continued whereby such a person may be heard at the discretion of the inspector, but he is not a party.[1] The really important changes relate to the inspector's report and the decision. The minister must notify his decision in writing, giving his reasons. As regards the inspector's report, he may attach that to his decision, or summarise its conclusions and recommendations. In any case, the parties and persons who appeared are entitled to be supplied with copies. If the minister either (a) differs from the inspector on a finding of fact, or (b) receives any new evidence or takes into consideration any new issue of fact which was not raised at the inquiry, and is thereby inclined to disagree with the inspector's report, he must notify the parties and give them an

[1] A planning decision does not affect his private rights of property: a planning permission does not entitle anyone to obstruct rights of light or commit any nuisance (in the legal sense) against someone else's property. The Council on Tribunals in a special report, Cmnd. 1787 (1962), found they could not support a legal right for a 'third party' to be heard.

opportunity to make representations or ask for the inquiry to be re-opened. All this represents a large measure of 'judicialising' these processes.

These changes are in general agreement with the recommendations of the Franks Committee, without, however, accepting all their detailed proposals, except for two major matters. The Committee recommended that before an inquiry the minister should wherever possible provide a statement of the ministerial policy relevant to the particular case. It is hard to express policy in written statements, and the government felt that this was impracticable. The other recommendation was that there should be a general corps of inspectors placed under the control of the Lord Chancellor, but the government has preferred to leave the position virtually unchanged.[1] It must be realised that the arrangements for holding these inquiries and making decisions needs co-ordination between different sections of a staff. Planning appeals alone have been running at over 6000 a year, inquiries having to be held in all parts of the country. The volume of work far exceeds that of the Probate Divorce and Admiralty Division and the Divorce Commissioners, and the number of contested cases is over six times that of the ordinary actions heard in the Queen's Bench Division.

A substantial amount of the dissatisfaction with inquiries and minister's decisions came not from the procedure but from the law governing compensation. Between the wars the ordinary rule was that compensation was assessed on market value, except in slum clearance, where much lower amounts might be awarded. The result was much litigation over clearance orders, and, as lawyers could not attack the statutes that dealt with payments for unfit houses, they attacked the procedure and the minister's decisions. In other matters, where market value was the test, there was relative peace. When legislation of the war period and of 1947 laid down rules of compensation that would lead to awards below market value, often appearing derisory, much of the dissatisfaction was channelled by lawyers into criticism of the procedure. The supposition that people are likely to be satisfied with a decision if they are told the reasons looks threadbare when applied to the compulsory acquisition of land, for the landowner has always known the purpose for which his land is to be acquired: his point is the elementary one that he does not want to lose his land, and particularly not for an inadequate

[1] The Lord Chancellor is now consulted on the appointment and dismissal of inspectors, which means more minutes and files and nobody any the better for it.

payment. Nor is it any easier to see why such a landowner should be mollified if the inspector were to be a Lord Chancellor's man whose reports were made available. In 1958 the government announced a new policy, being substantially a return to paying market values, and this was carried out by the Town and Country Planning Act 1959. The law was consolidated by the Land Compensation Act 1961. The new law will probably do more to make people reasonably contented with inquiries than the whole of the Franks Committee recommendations, except in slum clearance where the old controversies are likely to continue.

5. CONTROL BY THE LAW COURTS

Judicial control is exercised either on appeal or by review. An appeal is a complaint that a decision of the inferior tribunal was wrong through mistake as to the facts or the law or both. There is no general right to appeal from a lower to a higher court, or from a special tribunal to the High Court. Hence, when dealing with a particular jurisdiction, it is necessary to look at the statutes to see if any right of appeal is given, and if so whether it is on fact or law or both. Within the hierarchy of ordinary courts a system of appeals has been in existence for many years, whereas until recently it has been exceptional for appeals to lie from a special tribunal to the High Court. There was a widespread feeling that there ought generally to be a right of appeal on a point of law, and following on recommendations of the Franks Committee the Tribunals and Inquiries Act 1958 provided for such appeals in respect of a number of tribunals. The first appeal under this Act came before a Divisional Court on 6 October 1959. Rules of court provide whether such an appeal is to be by way of case stated[1] or otherwise; the High Court may itself give the decision that the tribunal should have given, or send the case back to the tribunal with an opinion or direction as to the course to be followed. These provisions do not apply to tribunals under the National Insurance Acts, because they already have an appellate court in the Commissioner, who is virtually a judge.[2]

Control by review of proceedings does not rest upon statute but upon the common law power of the Queen's Bench to examine the extent and mode of exercise of powers. The subject of judicial review is extremely difficult. It rests upon a mass of case-law stretching from decisions on procedure long obsolete down to the present day. It is a growing body of law, and it illustrates the way in which

[1] See p. 112, above.　　　　[2] See p. 344, above.

common law adapts itself to new needs. But such adaptation is a somewhat painful process at the time, however satisfactory it may appear to a later generation of legal historians who escape the discomfort of living in the transitional periods that they describe so admirably, for case-law grows through illogicality, fine distinctions and sheer perversity as well as by sound reasoning. In the result we have not as yet got a consistent body of rules, but the main lines can be stated with a fair measure of certainty.[1] Two trains of thought can be seen. The first is the attitude that the superior judges developed towards the conduct of inferior courts. The inferior court ought to be kept within its jurisdiction, it should keep its records properly, and it should observe certain canons of judicial behaviour that have become known as the 'principles of natural justice'. The control was exercised principally by writ of error (abolished a century ago) and prerogative writs.[2] The writs that were used were *mandamus, prohibition* and *certiorari*. Now that these writs have been abolished and their place taken by orders it is necessary to speak of them as writs when describing the past and as orders when describing the present. The principles remain unaltered.

In theory there is no overlapping of appeal on a point of law and judicial review, so that if there are adequate provisions for appeals on law that does not affect the scope or the need for review. The best examples come from magistrates' courts, where both forms of judicial control are in constant use. In *Hill* v. *Baxter*[3] the defendant drove a motor-van across a road junction at a fast speed, ignoring an illuminated 'Halt' sign, and collided with a motor-car. The defendant contended that he had had a 'black-out', and the justices, accepting his evidence, found that he was not conscious of what he was doing

[1] The only full-length study is S. A. de Smith, *Judicial Review of Administrative Action* (1959). Shorter accounts are in Griffith and Street, *Principles of Administrative Law*, ch. v; Wade and Phillips, *Constitutional Law*, pt. vii, chs. 2 and 3.

[2] The different prerogative writs and orders have been mentioned at pp. 40–3. The subject forms part of the wider question of the control exercised by the courts over public authorities. In addition to the prerogative writs and orders there are other remedies. Interference with the liberty or property of a person is actionable unless it can be justified in law. In some cases the courts may issue an injunction or declaration of illegality where a public authority contemplates some conduct that would be contrary to law. It must be realised that public authorities want to observe the law; if the case can be brought before the courts and a pronouncement on legality obtained, it matters little what 'remedy' the court gives; the real remedy will be that the public authority will alter its conduct accordingly. The present fashion is for declaratory judgments (see Griffith and Street, *op. cit.*, p. 236, and I. Zamir, 'The Declaratory Judgment v. The Prerogative Orders', [1958] *Public Law*, 341).

[3] [1958] 1 Q.B. 277.

and was not capable of forming any intention as to his manner of driving, and so they dismissed the charges. The case went to the Queen's Bench Division on a case stated, that is on a point of law. The court held that the Road Traffic Act 1930 contained an absolute prohibition against dangerous driving and the defendant's intention as to the manner of driving was immaterial; that if the onus rested on the defence of proving a state of automatism they had failed to do so, and as the facts showed that the defendant was driving and driving dangerously, the justices had come to a wrong conclusion in law. But if in a similar case there had been a conviction, but (a) the magistrates' court had not told the defendant that he could choose jury trial on the dangerous driving charge,[1] or (b) the court followed the correct procedure but imposed a sentence in excess of the legal maximum,[2] or (c) the court had been correct in procedure, conviction and sentence, but one of the justices had a pecuniary interest in the case, then the appropriate remedy is judicial review, by *certiorari*, and not an appeal. There is no sound reason for this distinction. Instances (a) and (b) are called an excess of jurisdiction, but instance (c) can also be called an excess, since *that court* (as opposed to that type of court) should not have tried the case. But it would be just as sensible to say that the justices in *Hill* v. *Baxter* had no jurisdiction to do what they did, namely to acquit on an erroneous view of the law. The distinction comes from the historical development of the remedies, and it could hardly survive any thoroughgoing rationalisation of judicial processes. The distinction has, however, been of the greatest importance and it will continue to matter very much, because judicial review is available where there is no appeal on law. Before the extension in 1958 of rights of appeal from special tribunals, the only method of getting a decision of, for example, a rent tribunal before the High Court was by raising some point where review would be applicable. That was also the position in respect of minister's decisions or of any administrative act, and, since there is no appeal on law against such decisions and acts, the old position will continue. Obviously a litigant who wants to challenge some action taken by a local or public authority or by a government department will try to persuade the High Court that the principles of judicial review cover his case, for often that is the only way he can

[1] See p. 97, n. 1, above.
[2] It used to be a bit of luck for a defendant if a magistrates' court gave him a sentence it had no power to impose, for on *certiorari* the High Court would quash the sentence. The Administration of Justice Act 1960 allows the High Court to substitute any sentence which the court below had power to impose.

bring his complaint before the court. The court, having been bred in the common law tradition and nurtured on distrust of the executive, may be sympathetic. Nowhere in our case-law has there been more skill in the use of precedent, or sophistry and casuistry, than in judicial review. The process has gone so far that one may easily lose sight of its connection with inferior jurisdictions.

The connecting link between inferior law courts and administrative bodies is the justice of the peace. The justices exercised a very wide range of duties that are now performed by local authorities: duties to repair highways and bridges, and other administrative matters, were traditionally regulated by indicting the persons responsible and trying them at Quarter Sessions.[1] The standard judicial process used in criminal courts had to serve all purposes. Since all the activities of justices in court were in form judicial, the King's Bench could control all their activities by prerogative writs. Most of the administrative powers of justices were taken away from them and vested in County Councils in 1888. Newer administrative powers have been conferred on various bodies, but little on justices. The Queen's Bench Division has continued its control, transferring the notion of 'inferior court' to some of the activities of administrative bodies. The conception of judicial functions has been steadily expanded.

It is to be noted that both writs (*prohibition* and *certiorari*) deal with questions of excessive jurisdiction, and doubtless in their origin dealt almost exclusively with the jurisdiction of what is described in ordinary parlance as a Court of Justice. But the operation of the writs has extended to control the proceedings of bodies which do not claim to be, and would not be recognised as, Courts of Justice. Whenever any body of persons having legal authority to determine questions affecting the rights of subjects, and having the duty to act judicially, act in excess of their legal authority they are subject to the controlling jurisdiction of the King's Bench Division exercised in these writs.[2]

Thus a Rural District Council in permitting development pending the approval of a town-planning scheme, the Minister of Health in approving a housing scheme, or a County Council in licensing a cinema, were engaged upon work that was sufficiently 'judicial' for the King's Bench Division to review their decisions.[3] A decision may be

---

[1] See Webb, *English Local Government: The Parish and the County*, p. 307.

[2] Atkin L.J. (as he then was) in *Rex* v. *Electricity Commissioners* [1924] 1 K.B. 171, at 205; it is a passage that has often been cited.

[3] At the same time they are not sufficiently judicial to be 'courts', with the result that defamatory statements made in a London County Council meeting for granting music and dancing licences do not have the absolute privilege that attaches to statements made in a law court (*Royal Aquarium* v. *Parkinson* [1892] 1 Q.B. 431).

reviewed to see if there has been an excess of jurisdiction, and if it is found that the tribunal went outside its jurisdiction then its decision will be quashed. If a tribunal has a written record, then (because of the old notions of error on the record) the Queen's Bench will consider whether there is an error of law apparent from the documents.[1] The result is that if reasons are given for a decision, so that it is a 'speaking order', then the question of whether those reasons are good in law can be tested by *certiorari*, and this is not limited to questions of jurisdiction. A tribunal is also required to observe 'the principles of natural justice'. The conception of natural justice certainly covers two propositions. *First*, a man must not be judge in his own cause. Whenever there is a likelihood that a judicial body, or any member of it, may have a bias in favour of one of the parties, that body or person must not hear the case. This is interpreted to mean that if an observer might suppose that there would be bias, then the person concerned should not adjudicate, so that in the language of this part of the law a person may be 'interested' and there may be 'bias' when in fact the course of justice is not affected.[2] People who adjudicate must remember that financial interest, relationship, membership of committees and voluntary bodies, and a host of other 'interests', are all regarded as 'bias', *Secondly*, no party ought to be condemned unheard. But as a person cannot present his case unless he knows what it is that he has to meet, it follows that he must be informed of any charge against him and of any evidence and have an opportunity to contradict it. A special tribunal need not conform to the procedure of law courts, and in particular it need not adopt the process of an oral hearing, but both sides must be treated equally.[3] It is doubtful whether natural justice is considered as extending beyond these two propositions.[4]

In all these cases the matter investigated by the Queen's Bench Division is the *way* in which an inferior tribunal is going to act or has acted. If the inferior tribunal has made a decision, the superior courts are not concerned with its merits; it may be a decision in which the facts were correctly found and the law correctly applied,

[1] *R.* v. *Northumberland Compensation Tribunal, ex p. Shaw* [1951] 1 K.B. 711 affirmed on appeal [1952] 1 T.L.R. 161.

[2] Cases are cited in *Report on Ministers' Powers*, Cmd. 4060 (1932), p. 77. *The King* v. *Sussex Justices, ex p. McCarthy* (1924) 93 L.J.K.B. 129, goes very far. The Justices of the Peace Act 1949, s. 3, disqualifies a justice who is a member of a local authority from adjudicating in proceedings by or against the authority or any committee or officer of the authority.

[3] *Local Government Board* v. *Arlidge* [1915] A.C. 120.

[4] *Report on Ministers' Powers*, Cmd. 4060 (1932), p. 80.

but if the inferior tribunal ought not to have heard the case at all or if they heard it in a way that offends the judges' idea of the proper conduct of cases, then the decision is quashed.

It would seem to follow that if a tribunal has kept within its jurisdiction, has given no reasons or made a speaking order that shows valid reasons, and has observed the principles of natural justice, then its decision cannot be questioned unless Parliament has given a right of appeal. Often that is so, but here it is necessary to consider another train of thought. Virtually all the powers possessed by ministers and by local and public authorities have been conferred by statute, and therefore, if there is any dispute as to the existence or extent of such a power, it must be a matter for the courts to decide by interpreting the statutes. The court may find that an alleged power does not exist at all,[1] but if there is a power it will be assumed (in the absence of special provision) that Parliament intended that the power should be exercised in accordance with certain principles of common law. On this basis the courts will intervene if a power is exercised unreasonably, negligently, without taking into account all relevant matters and excluding the irrelevant, or is exercised for any purpose (proper or improper) other than that for which the power was conferred.[2] Further, if there are any conditions imposed, or procedure specified, then such requirements must be satisfied. These principles, relating as they do to all kinds of statutory powers, are applicable to powers to hear and decide, that is, to jurisdiction. Cases decided on administrative powers may be cited on questions of excess of jurisdiction, and vice versa. But the two trains of thought do not merge in other parts. The rules about speaking orders and observance of the principles of natural justice are applicable to judicial powers and not to administrative powers. Or, to put the position as it actually is, it means that if the court wants to apply the control that is peculiar to inferior tribunals, then

---

[1] A well-known case is *Attorney-General* v. *Fulham Corporation* [1921] 1 Ch. 440, in which it was held that a power to establish a wash-house where people could wash their own clothes did not allow the local authority to set up a municipal laundry and wash clothes for people.

[2] It would be necessary to cite many cases to support all these propositions, and that would not be appropriate to the brief account that is given here. The case of *Roberts* v. *Hopwood* [1925] A.C. 578, however, deserves special mention. The Poplar Borough Council, which had power to fix the rate of wages of its employees, decided to pay a minimum wage to men and women of £4 on the general ground of the amount needed for adequate living, though that sum far exceeded the rate for labour in the neighbourhood; it was held that that was not a lawful exercise of the power.

the court must first hold that the activity in question is 'judicial' or at least 'quasi-judicial'.

There is general agreement that judicial review is essential to our conception of government under the law, but the practical question is the extent to which a court that is inquiring into observance of the law may attempt to review the processes and policies of administration. The courts have vacillated: at times it has looked as if almost any administrative action could be reviewed, with decisions or dicta that suggest a goodly addition to the legal empire, and then soberer judgments have prevailed. Government departments, looking at the ways in which judicial processes have often been used, have tried to escape such risks by framing legislation that is 'judge-proof'. Thus it was thought that a ministerial decision could not be reviewed if the statute said that such decision 'shall be final and not subject to appeal to any court', but that does not exclude *certiorari*: the phrase 'shall not be called in question in any court of law' does appear to be judge-proof. These controversies have been removed, at least for the time being, for the Tribunals and Inquiries Act 1958 has followed a recommendation of the Franks Committee and provided that any such words in existing Acts shall not have effect so as to prevent review by the High Court on *certiorari* or by *mandamus*. This does not apply to ministers' decisions about acquisition of land and slum clearance where *certiorari* continues to be excluded but instead there may be an application to the court during six weeks following the confirming of an order, on the ground that the order is not within the powers of the Act or because the applicant has been substantially prejudiced by the requirements not having been complied with.

The whole tenor of the Franks Committee Report and the ensuing legislation and administrative action is to bring special tribunals and ministers' decisions nearer to lawyers' conceptions of the way that adjudication ought to be conducted. As regards special tribunals, we can expect to see an increase in the number of chairmen with legal qualifications, and parties may more often be legally represented. The government has not followed the Committee's recommendation that the Legal Aid Act be extended, but it is expected that this will be done in a year or two. Professional practice has already found profitable work at inquiries: there are better brief fees to be had on planning appeals than in much of the work before 'ordinary courts'. What is now happening is another great expansion of the common law. Is it going to resemble the time in the seventeenth century when common law took over the commercial jurisdiction of Admiralty and made a mess of it? In that expansion the common lawyers began by having no idea of what commercial people needed: lawyers could not or would not look at their common law principles afresh, and for a century the merchants suffered. Or is it going to be more like law and equity, where the long drawn out attacks by the common lawyers on the Chancery court resulted in the end in a widened and revitalised common law. It depends on how much lawyers are rigid and set in their ways. A lawyer who sails into a tribunal believing that he is bringing the light of law into outer darkness (a process that I have observed) is simply a menace: a menace to his client if he is an advocate, and to the tribunal if he is its chairman.

The strong point of lawyers is their notion of the *way* in which disputes should be decided. The ideas that lie at the back of a trial in our law courts represent a great contribution to civilisation. They are: (1) an adjudicator with an open mind, (2) a definite formulation of the issue that is to be decided, (3) parties must have a full and equal opportunity to present their cases, (4) the best available evidence must be produced, (5) all irrelevant material must be excluded, (6) a body of accepted principles must be applied, and (7) reasons for the decision must be given. It all sounds good and looks impeccable as a specification for producing satisfactory results. The trouble is that lawyers deal all their lives with words and tend to ignore realities. Further, lawyers are very critical of other people, particularly of officials, but they are almost incapable of self-criticism; the truth has been revealed to them, and they must infuse it into darkest Whitehall. The writer of one of the best recent books on administrative law speaks of the 'missionary spirit'.[1] The recipients of missionary zeal may recognise the sincerity of the person who would labour for their redemption and yet regard him as arrogant, bigoted and full of beliefs for which there seems to be no credible evidence. Let us look at some facts, and first on the vital point of evidence. Take (3) above, and see what is said: 'Of course, the right to a hearing has always been sacred in courts of law, and any legal decision given without proper consideration of both sides would be set aside on appeal'.[2] Yet consider the position of a prisoner not so long ago. He could be and often was interrogated. He could not see depositions against him until 1837 or have copies until 1849. It is true that he could bring witnesses by 1702, but he could not have counsel in felony

[1] H. W. R. Wade, *Administrative Law* (1961), p. 6.
[2] H. W. R. Wade, *op. cit.* p. 142.

until 1837. and could not give evidence until 1898. There was no right of appeal until 1907. But of course these bits of common law only dealt with trivial things, like hanging a man by the neck until he is dead, and hardly affected important matters like real property. Now let us look at the admirable proposition that the best evidence should be produced: what does that mean? Anyone might think that the best evidence would usually include the evidence of the parties, yet common law did not allow the parties to give evidence until 1851 in civil actions and, as mentioned above, until 1898 in criminal charges. These restrictions have gone, but the lawyers' rules on what is evidence are so fantastic that if a research worker were to follow them he would be rebuked for being silly and incompetent. For lawyers, we start with the proposition that what constitutes evidence is not based on reasoning or experiment but on authority; judges have laid down in decided cases what can and what cannot be evidence. Evidence means oral statements of witnesses or documents, subject to admissibility. If the question is whether a man's limb has been amputated, then that ought to be 'proved by evidence', and if a court has one or two medical members, and they inspect the person, and decide that he has lost his leg, there is still no 'evidence'. Or consider the process of fixing a 'fair rent'. If the parties before a rent tribunal produce someone who speaks, or produces admissible documents, that is 'evidence'. If a valuer gives an opinion (based on inspection and experience of property generally) that is 'evidence'. But if the parties choose to produce no oral or written statements, so that the tribunal acts on the result of its own inspection and experience of property generally, then the tribunal acts 'without having any evidence before them at all', and an eminent Q.C. asserts that this is 'a brutal repudiation of elementary justice'.[1] Fortunately the legal profession has always had some members whose mental horizon extends beyond the Law Reports, but special tribunals may yet have nonsense of this kind forced upon them: legalism begets legalism.

The important question is whether this judicialising process is having a good effect. On the whole I think that special tribunals will be all the better for some superintendence, in the same way that Magistrates' Courts and their working need to be kept under review: sensible rules of procedure, adequate and well-qualified staff and suitable buildings have to be provided, and memoranda on new

[1] This exhibition is displayed in [1956] *Public Law*, pp. 84–6, and the cases there cited.

legislation and so on help the administration of justice. The independence of the judiciary is not diminished one scrap by the activities of the Home Office, and the Lord Chancellor advised by the Council on Tribunals may perform a similar function in respect of tribunals. But when we turn to inquiries relating to the acquisition of land or use of land, the result of recent changes is from a national point of view deplorable. As the processes have become more judicialised they have become slower, subject to delays and uncertainties, and far more expensive.

The basic trouble is that a procedure that is substantially judicial is not suitable for these matters. In some cases there has already been a government decision that, for example, road construction or improvement is to take place. For some road work there is virtually no choice of site; if a cross-roads is to have a roundabout it must be at the cross-roads. For other works there may be a choice of site; if the new road is built someone is going to have to give up some land somewhere. For local authority proposals the elected local council has approved some scheme and the question now is whether that should be confirmed by the central government. Or there may be a question of whether an area should be redeveloped, and if so what kind of redevelopment should take place. The minister has to make the decision, and the original purpose of the inquiry was to make quite sure that all the facts and views would be collected. The inquiry was not an occasion for justifying a proposal: the justification was to be made to the popularly elected local council or by the minister if challenged in Parliament. These days, if we take the whole process of inquiry, inspector's report and the minister's decision giving his reasons, there is almost a public trial of the merits of a project. To use judicial forms for administration is not unprecedented, for the traditional method of administering the counties was by indictment in Quarter Sessions and verdicts of juries. The present inquiry system involves a vast amount of oral evidence, with the cumbersome habit of counsel repeating everything once or twice. To establish that, if shops are pulled down and new shops are built, the rent of the new shops is likely to be greater than the rents of the existing shops, or some similar proposition, can take an astonishing time, and the guineas disappear as the clock ticks the minutes. The substance of a project is often a choice between different sites, plans or operations, and this, with the balancing of relative merits, is a very different business from adjudication in law courts. A lawyer naturally looks at things from his client's viewpoint: if the minister can be forced into

26-2

producing a reasoned case there is just a chance that he may slip up, or be deflected, and if his client does in the end lose his land (as he generally does) he has at least had a run for his money. The result is, however, that getting things done in England is becoming increasingly difficult. The Minister of Transport has said that it takes three years to get through the preliminaries for building a road; highway engineers say that the time is between three and seven years before the work can start. In the middle of last century it was possible for promoters to go by Private Bill, get Parliamentary authority to acquire land, get the land, build a railway and be operating it in less time than it now takes to be allowed to start the construction of major works. The problem of giving the individual a reasonable deal, and at the same time not taking too long to get on with public works, has not been solved. Private Bill procedure became too expensive and clumsy, and provisional order was tried as a substitute and was found to be little better; the ministerial inquiry system was much quicker and cheaper in its earlier days, and now we are badly in need of roads, docks, power plants and so on, and must wait years and years, on occasion for so long that when the project can be begun it is no longer adequate. An examination of this side of the problem is beyond the scope of this book. I mention it because I think it is of the greatest importance to realise that lawyers' ideas of administering justice are not applicable to running the business of the country. The legal discipline was evolved for deciding defined and relatively simple issues according to a body of accepted principles: it cannot be applied to issues of policy and it cannot be a substitute for the control that Parliament should exercise. The ideas of judicialising inquiries have led to increased opportunities for judicial review. Courts cannot control policy decisions (beyond securing that any requirements of procedure are satisfied) without a real danger that the judges may substitute their own ideas of policy for those of the minister. It is quite as necessary to provide against being ruled by judges as it is to guard against being judged by ministers.

There are people who would raise a monument at Stevenage to the memory of the doctrine of judicial control of policy, mortally injured in legal battle in 1948,[1] but it may be that all that has happened is that the courts are less willing to attempt to check policy than they

---

[1] *Franklin* v. *Minister of Town and Country Planning* [1948] A.C. 87, in which the House of Lords refused to hold that the minister in selecting the site of a new town, that of Stevenage, had a duty that was judicial or quasi-judicial, thereby disclaiming some possibilities of control by the courts.

have been in the past. If the courts can give up the vain task of trying to treat the policy decisions of ministers as if they are the proceedings of an inferior court it will make the way clearer for the development of special tribunals; freed from their link with the varied powers of ministers there will be a better chance of special tribunals coming more within the realm of the judiciary to take their proper place as courts with special jurisdictions.

CHAPTER VII

THE OUTLOOK FOR REFORM

Substantive law is concerned with rights and with the remedies for violations of rights. Procedural law is concerned with the process by which remedies are made available. The older English law books are concerned with procedure, propositions of substantive law being made in terms of procedure. Reform of procedure during the nineteenth century led to a new type of law book in which substantive law was the subject. This has been a great gain in that it has been possible for the principles of substantive law to be studied and developed without hindrance from the fog of procedure in which they were previously enveloped. Most of the modern major books upon such matters as contract and tort show some attempt to assess the reasonableness of the rules expounded. Legal thought has been directed primarily towards substantive law. For instance, the Harvard Tercentenary Celebrations included addresses from many distinguished lawyers, published in 1937 as *The Future of the Common Law*, in which it is clear that the future is thought of as resting upon the content of the law. It is noticeable that the Lord Chancellor's Law Reform Committee (described later) has so far been concerned largely with substantive law. There is no lack of interest in procedural matters, for they touch the day-to-day work of lawyers, and the frequent references to committees and commissions of inquiry cited earlier show that these matters are continually being reviewed.[1] Yet procedure is regarded as having an inferior status, being a field for technicians whereas substantive law is in the realm of learning. Books upon procedure consist of instruction either for practitioners or for students preparing for an examination in the retentiveness of their memories; there is nothing comparable with the scholarly works on contract, tort and other parts of substantive law. One consequence is that there is commonly a lack of appreciation of the bearing of procedure upon substantive law, for a rule may appear

[1] The situation appears to be worse in the United States: the Introduction to *Minimum Standards of Judicial Administration* (1949), edited by Arthur T. Vanderbilt, Chief Justice Supreme Court of New Jersey, begins by saying: 'One of the strangest phenomena in the law is the general indifference of the legal profession to the technicalities, the anachronisms, and the delays in our procedural law.' This is a large and authoritative book, but if an English student does no more than read the Introduction and looks at the maps he will become aware of the main issues.

sound and just and yet produce unfair results because of the conditions under which it may operate.

We may take as an example some matters between landlord and tenant prior to 1939. If a landlord served a notice on his tenant requiring the tenant to make extensive repairs, with the option of forfeiting the lease or buying the house at a stiff price, the tenant could dispute the landlord's claim. This is no more than saying that, if *A* makes a claim on *B*, then *B* can defend himself, which appears eminently reasonable. If the appropriate rules of court were studied they would, I think, appear equally reasonable. Yet the reality of landlord and tenant was that landlords could often exploit tenants by serving schedules of dilapidations where the tenant was a man of small means. To meet such a claim it was necessary to employ a lawyer and generally a surveyor as well; the man who could not afford professional assistance had to capitulate on the terms offered by the relatively wealthy landlord. Parliament certainly thought that the position was unsatisfactory, and so passed the Leasehold Property (Repairs) Act 1938. This Act in effect prevents the landlord from taking any steps without the leave of a court (normally a county court) where the house is of a rateable value of £100 or less. Parliament found that having the same law for the rich as for the poor simply did not work well enough, and so provided one set of rules for tenants with a rateable value of £100 or less and another set of rules for those with larger rateable values. When the law works badly it may be possible to effect a cure by altering either substantive or procedural law. Hence this section is concerned with the changing of any part of our law.

We cannot expect any substantial reform of our legal system through the operation of judicial precedent. Even if our judges were zealous for reform, which they are not, there are limits to the doctrine of precedent. Much of our legal system now rests on statute, and it is the fundamental postulate of our law that a statute is valid until it is repealed or altered by a subsequent statute. If reforms are to be made they must be made by Parliament. The real question is whether Parliament is likely to legislate on these topics, which involves consideration of the conditions under which proposed legislation does actually get passed. A bill introduced into Parliament by a private member is not likely to reach the statute book. The government makes such heavy demands upon the time of the House of Commons that a private member's bill usually dies for lack of attention unless an adequate measure of government support is given. In addition to finding time it is generally necessary to arrange for the private member to have the assistance of certain officials and particularly of parliamentary counsel[1] on the drafting. A notable example of reform by a private member's bill was the Matrimonial Causes Act 1937 due to the valiant efforts of Sir Alan Herbert. There are usually one or two Acts a year that begin in this way, but too much must not be expected from that source. Where there are obvious abuses or gaps the private member may be able to draw a bill and present a satisfactory case in its support. There are, however, parts of the law that do not work well but which it would be unwise to alter until there has been an adequate investigation, and this preliminary work can rarely be done by a non-official inquiry. Where the machinery of justice is concerned it is not easy to make proposals that do not involve the expenditure of public money, and a bill involving expenditure may not be introduced by a private member. The bulk of the changes, and particularly those that affect different branches of the law or its administration, must in practice come from the government.

Government bills are proposed by a minister, but under our system of cabinet government no minister may introduce a bill, or even announce that a bill will be introduced, without the sanction of the cabinet. The purpose of cabinet control is twofold. In the first place, all proposals for legislation must be examined to see that they are consistent with government policy or, where specific government policy is not affected, to consider the reception that the bill will have, the controversies it may raise and so forth. In the second place, the legislative programme of the government must be arranged with regard to the time available in the House of Commons, for there is more call for legislation than the House can handle by its present procedure. The cabinet exercises these controls largely through committees.[2] Sessions of parliament now last a year, beginning in late October or in November, and the programme for a session must be considered several months in advance. It is not customary to disclose the government's programme although there may be public

---

[1] See p. 420, below.

[2] The process of producing a bill is described by Sir Granville Ram in a paper 'The Improvement of the Statute Book', *Journal S.P.T.L.*, n.s., vol. 1 (1951), p. 442. Sir Noel Hutton, the present First Parliamentary Counsel, has also written about the process, with particular reference to law reform statutes: 'Mechanics of Law Reform', 24 *Modern Law Review* (1961), p. 18. These are the only published accounts of a most important process of government which is virtually unknown except to those who have taken part in it as ministers or as officials.

announcement about intentions in respect of certain bills and the major items will in any case be mentioned in the Queen's Speech on the opening of the next session. The legislative programme must include the annual legislation which governs the raising and spending of money, the maintenance of the army and other matters which require annual authority. There will also be bills to carry out the policy of the government; these, with much of the financial legislation, are the measures particularly associated with the government of the day and are pre-eminently the field of party politics. The remaining bills are not really party measures, though of course politically a government may be called to account for everything its members do, and virtually anything may become a party issue. Sometimes a minister has a project of the non-party kind in which he is personally interested, but the majority of these bills come from the civil servants in government departments. All departments find in the course of their work that some changes in the law are needed either to facilitate or extend the department's own work or in matters for which the department has a general responsibility. Even when a minister has a personal interest in a matter, as with Lord Birkenhead's well-known desire to reform the land laws, he is likely to find that much work has already been done: government is team work, of ministers and of a minister and his department, though the minister has the power and takes the glory. Some bills are designed to carry out the recommendations of commissions and committees, but here it must be remembered that the inquiry probably originated in a department, and that the Report of the inquiry must be accepted by the minister before it can be carried out. A minister with no ideas of his own will never be at a loss for projects if he thirsts for action. However they may have originated, the various legislative projects must compete for a place in the programme. A minister who puts forward a project must satisfy his colleagues that it ought to be included. Applying this to measures for law reform, we can examine the situation in this order: first, the minister who must move; secondly, the process of deciding what provisions are needed, which includes any prior investigation that may be required; and, thirdly, the arguments in favour of being assigned a place in the programme.

There is no single minister who has responsibility[1] for law in

---

[1] In strict use of terms a minister cannot be responsible for that which he has no power to control. No minister is responsible for any particular magistrate or judge or court, or rule of common law or of statute, for he has no power to control them, but the state of the judiciary and the law is a matter for which there is a general responsibility in the appropriate ministers.

general or for the machinery of justice. The Home Secretary and the Lord Chancellor share the responsibility, and it is hard to lay down any exact dividing line. The broad division is that the Home Office is concerned with the criminal law, preventing offences, catching offenders, part of the process of trying them, and virtually the whole of the treatment of offenders. The Lord Chancellor is concerned with the composition of all courts, criminal and civil, parts of criminal procedure, and everything relating to civil law and its administration.

The Home Office has a bewildering variety of matters in its care.[1] There is direct responsibility for the metropolitan police and a general responsibility for provincial police, particularly in the power to make regulations on conditions of service and organisation and in control of grants of money from the exchequer. The Home Secretary has some powers in respect of the Director of Public Prosecutions,[2] and various powers concerning criminal procedure, costs in criminal matters, and the organisation and finance of Magistrates' Courts.[3] Prisons and other institutions for custody or treatment of delinquents are either in the care of the Prison Department of the Home Office, or are provided by local authorities or other agencies and inspected and approved by the Home Office. There is a close association with the probation system. The care of Broadmoor patients (formerly called criminal lunatics) is under the Minister of Health, but the Home Office retains responsibility for releases. The prerogative of mercy, which includes pardons, commutations and reductions of sentences, is exercised on the advice of the Home Secretary. Other matters that may be specially noted are the powers relating to children and the general oversight of the jurisdiction of justices in matrimonial and affiliation proceedings. The Home Office sends many circulars to Magistrates' Courts for their information and guidance, particularly when there is new legislation coming into force.

The Home Office has responsibility, in a wide sense, for general policy in penal affairs and for introducing new penal legislation and revision of existing law. The courses to be pursued in penal matters comprise the whole range of preventive measures, of efficiency in detection, apprehension and prosecution, of the arrangements for trial (including the free defence of Poor Prisoners) and the punishments or other methods of disposal of those who are proved to have committed offences. In addition to the ordinary staff the Home Office has a research unit and makes considerable use of non-

[1] See Sir Frank Newsam, *The Home Office* (1954).
[2] See p. 126, above.   [3] See p. 167, above.

official, principally university, departments and research institutions. Since 1944 there has been a standing Advisory Council on the treatment of offenders, a body which, under the chairmanship of a judge, includes members bringing practical experience from many fields, and both tenders advice on questions referred to it by the Home Secretary and also makes proposals on its own initiative. In 1959 the Home Secretary set up a Standing Committee under the chairmanship of Lord Justice Sellers, called the Criminal Law Revision Committee, to examine such aspects of the criminal law as the Home Secretary may from time to time refer to them. The first major reference to the Committee is the law of larceny and kindred offences. The Committee is expected to submit a draft Bill showing their proposals for recasting of the law, and for that purpose they have the assistance of parliamentary counsel.

The duties of the Lord Chancellor are many and onerous.[1]

(1) He is Speaker of the House of Lords, which involves his attendance upon the Woolsack when the House is sitting as a legislative body.

(2) He is a member of the government, and is normally in the cabinet. As most heads of departments are in the Commons it may fall to the Lord Chancellor to present the government's view in the House of Lords in matters that are outside his special knowledge; this may be a heavy burden at times.

(3) He may preside over the sittings of the House of Lords in its judicial capacity, though in recent years he has been unable to do so at all frequently. It is too much of a strain to sit morning and afternoon, and then continue in the House of Lords in its legislative capacity, as well as performing his other duties.

(4) When he is able to do so, the Lord Chancellor presides over sittings of the Judicial Committee of the Privy Council.

(5) He is head of the Chancery Division of the High Court and *ex officio* a member of the Court of Appeal. He does not in practice sit in either court, and there is normally little work connected with this part of his office.

(6) He is president of the Supreme Court. This involves a considerable amount of work. He makes recommendations for the appointment of High Court judges and in practice advises the Prime Minister as to other judicial appointments.[2] Some of the higher officials of the courts are appointed by him.[3] He must also devote some time to the work of the Rule Committee.[4]

---

[1] A convenient summary of the Lord Chancellor's duties is given in the *Report of the Machinery of Government Committee*, Cd. 9230 (1918). Some further information, particularly on the office staff of the Lord Chancellor, may be found in Lord Schuster, 'The Office of the Lord Chancellor', 10 *Cambridge Law Journal* (1949), p. 175.

[2] See p. 256, above.   [3] See p. 288, above.   [4] See p. 63, above.

(7) He is responsible for the County Court system, which includes the appointment of the County Court judges and registrars.[1] In some matters the control is in the Treasury with the concurrence of the Lord Chancellor.[2]

(8) He makes recommendations for the appointment of legally qualified chairmen of Quarter Sessions and for the appointment of Recorders. The appointment and removal of justices of the peace (other than in the Duchy of Lancaster), and of the stipendiary magistrates, is exercised by the Lord Chancellor;[3] the institution of Advisory Committees has not prevented the Lord Chancellor from having to give a fair amount of personal attention to the questions that arise.

(9) He has a substantial amount of work in connection with special tribunals. It has been accepted policy since the war that the appointment of legally qualified chairmen should be made by the Lord Chancellor. The appointment by him of other members, or of panels, has been required by some statutes, now substantially extended by the Tribunals and Inquiries Act 1958. He appoints the Council on Tribunals under that Act, and, as the Council has no executive powers, its recommendations must come before the Lord Chancellor and be approved by him before they can be brought into operation.

(10) He has considerable ecclesiastical patronage, amounting to about one appointment a week; this is about three times the patronage of the two archbishops together.

(11) There are also duties in connection with the Land Registry, the office of the Public Trustee, and the care of lunatics.

It is not surprising that 'Successive holders of this office have testified that it is beyond the strength of any one man to perform the work that ought to be done'.[4] To help the Lord Chancellor there is a Permanent Secretary with a staff forming the Lord Chancellor's Department. It is a small department, but much of the heavy preparatory work for legislation is done by committees. There are three standing committees, namely the Statute Law Committee, the Law Reform Committee, and the Committee on Private International Law.

The Statute Law Committee is concerned with the form of our statute law rather than with its contents. The ordinary process of legislation produces a most inconvenient state of affairs: first, the law upon a matter is likely to be contained in several Acts which, with their repeals and amending provisions, must be read together; secondly, the statute book remains cluttered up with statutes that in whole or in part are no longer in force. The remedy for the first trouble is to consolidate statute law, whilst for the second there must

---

[1] See p. 29, above.   [2] See p. 294, above.
[3] See pp. 161, 175, above.
[4] Cd. 9230 (1918), ch. x, para. 3.

be revision, and to make the results really useful there must be suitable indexing and publication.

Consolidation is an enormous blessing to those who must refer to statute law, but it must not be confused with codification or with reforming or even with reviewing the law. The process is to take all the statutory provisions relating to a subject and to re-arrange them to form a single enactment. This requires far more than the method of scissors-and-paste, for new clauses must often be drafted, language must be harmonised and the bearing of one part upon another has constantly to be checked. If the case-law were to be reduced to statutory form we should then have partial codification. This has been done on occasions. When Sir M. D. Chalmers drafted the Bills of Exchange Act 1882 he found that the law was contained in some 2500 cases and 17 statutes; out of that mass came a bill of 100 sections, and it has turned out to be a very good Act. The reason why this process cannot normally be followed instead of the far more limited process of consolidation is that the more ambitious bill is apt to take up a lot of parliamentary time. When a serious beginning was made last century in the work of improving the statute book[1] a convention grew up that consolidation bills should be referred to a joint select committee of both Houses, and that the bills should then go through each House without debate. It is in practice virtually impossible to consolidate without making some amendments to meet inconsistencies or to resolve doubts that have arisen, and there has in the past been difficulty over this: if it can be accepted that the amendment is minor, then both Houses can accept the bill after the joint committee and spend no time on it, whilst if the amendments are of substance there can be debate. Two recent changes are of major importance. In 1947 the Lord Chancellor reconstituted the Statute Law Committee so that it is predominantly official and legal, with the addition of three peers (one a Law Lord) and three members of the Commons, and gave it the following terms of reference: 'To consider the steps necessary to bring the Statute Book up to date by consolidation, revision or otherwise, and to superintend the publication and indexing of Statutes, Revised Statutes and Statutory Instruments.' To assist in carrying out this work there was set up a special branch of the office of Parliamentary Counsel. New provision was made by the Consolidation of Enactments (Procedure) Act 1949. Under this statute the Lord Chancellor

---

[1] A description is given by Lord Jowitt, *Statute Law Revision and Consolidation* (1951), published by the Holdsworth Club of the University of Birmingham.

lays before Parliament a memorandum about corrections and minor improvements that he thinks should be made in connection with a particular consolidation bill. People interested may make written representations about these. The bill and any representations are then referred to a joint committee of both Houses, who must refer their conclusions on these points to the Lord Chancellor and the Speaker. The result is that any corrections or minor improvements that are brought forward must have the approval of the joint committee, the Lord Chancellor and the Speaker, and that they must all be satisfied that the proposals are not such that they ought to be enacted by the usual legislative method. When this has been done neither House can amend the bill, though the power to reject it is preserved. There can be no doubt that these changes have produced excellent results. Improvement of the statute book has become an accepted part of governmental activity, and not just something that received attention if there should be time to spare. A vast quantity of obsolete and spent statutory provisions have been repealed, and a new edition of Revised Statutes has appeared which contains in 32 volumes all the statute law in force at the end of 1948; the living statute law is now to be found in these 32 volumes together with the Acts passed since 1948. Reference is easier through improvements in indexing. Since the reconstitution of the Statute Law Committee in 1947 consolidation Acts have on the average amounted to nearly five a year. Whilst parts of the law are thus tidied up, other parts get worse through successive amendments, so that the need for consolidation will continue indefinitely.

In 1934 the Lord Chancellor set up a standing Law Revision Committee 'to consider how far, having regard to the Statute Law and to judicial decisions, such legal maxims and doctrines as the Lord Chancellor may from time to time refer to them require revision in modern conditions'. The Committee originally consisted of four judges, five barristers, two professors of law, one solicitor, and the Permanent Secretary to the Lord Chancellor. In 1937 two more academic lawyers were added to the Committee. Several matters were submitted to the Committee, which investigated the state of the law and published reports containing recommendations for reform. In most cases the recommendations made were adopted and legislation followed. The Committee was reconstituted in 1952, with a membership of five judges, four barristers, two solicitors and three academic lawyers. The new Committee, now known as the Law Reform Committee, has to consider, having regard especially to judicial decisions, what changes are desirable in such legal doc-trines as may from time to time be referred to it.[1] The Committee has power to work through subcommittees consisting of such number of its members as the chairman, after consultation with the Committee, may think fit, together with such other persons as the Lord Chancellor may approve. It was announced that anyone may suggest subjects for consideration by the Committee, so that although references to the Committee must come from the Lord Chancellor the initiative may come from the Committee or from any other source. The particular reference to judicial decisions suggests that the Lord Chancellor has rules of common law especially in mind.

In 1952 the Lord Chancellor set up a standing Committee on Private International Law. The Lord Chancellor may refer rules of private international law to the Committee for their consideration, and he may ask the Committee to undertake work in connection with international conferences on these subjects.

It is said that this division of duties between the Home Secretary and the Lord Chancellor leads to difficulties, and that this can be seen if we consider the position of a Member of Parliament who wishes to raise matters by asking questions in Parliament. If a question relates to some matter clearly within the scope of some department, then the minister for that department can be questioned. But if a question relates to say criminal or civil procedure it is by no means clear to whom the question should be addressed. In the Commons the Home Secretary may well say that it is not his business. The Attorney-General will probably say that it is not his business, perhaps adding that he will communicate with the Lord Chancellor. In the House of Lords the Lord Chancellor may intimate that it is not his responsibility, but that the matter will be considered. The conclusion of this line of thought is to say that when nobody is responsible for a thing the usual result is that there is consistent neglect, and therefore there should be a single minister who is definitely responsible. In other countries such minister is called the Minister of Justice.

Proposals to create a Ministry of Justice were brought before Parliament on various occasions during last century. The long story of corruption and inefficiency in the officials of the law courts[2]

---

[1] The work of the Committee is described by E. C. S. Wade, a member of it, in 'The Machinery of Law Reform', 24 *Modern Law Review* (1961), p. 3; it is some-what less encouraging than an outside observer might well have expected.

[2] See p. 286, above.

provided the chief argument. At the time of the Judicature Act of 1873 the worst abuses had been removed, but the framers of that Act found that further changes were needed in the appointment and control of court officials. A Commission was set up to report upon the Administrative Departments of the Courts of Justice. This Commission was primarily concerned with methods of recruiting the officials, but, in discussing the general problems of staffing the departments, the conclusion was that a Minister of Justice should be established. Details were outside their scope, but they made the suggestion that a re-organised Home Office might be the solution. In the absence of any larger scheme it was suggested that the Lord Chancellor should be responsible for the organisation of the courts.[1] When the topic of court officials came before the Royal Commission on the Civil Service, a Minister of Justice was advocated by Lord Haldane in the evidence he gave to the Commission.[2] The Machinery of Government Committee, under the chairmanship of Lord Haldane, reviewed the whole position of the administrative side of the legal system.[3] This Committee broke fresh ground in pointing out 'the difficulty of getting the attention of the Government to law reform', and added this argument to that of 'the total inadequacy of the organisation which controls the general administration of the very large staffs' to produce a most impressive case for the establishment of a Minister of Justice. The Committee proposed that the Home Secretary should become Minister of Justice, by the process of transferring some of the work of the Home Office to other departments, leaving the Home Office with its present duties connected with legal administration, and transferring to the Home Office the general work of administration in connection with justice that is now vested in the Lord Chancellor. This would leave the Lord Chancellor free to devote his energies to judicial work and to his position as principal legal adviser to the government. The proposals were not limited to a mere shuffle of existing duties. 'The Minister of Justice would probably sit in the House of Commons and he ought to be accessible to those who have suggestions to make. Besides his administration of the staffs of the various Courts in England, his Department should contain experts charged with the

[1] C. 949 (1874). The *Report* reviews changes in staff that had already been made, giving tables for comparing the position in 1874 with that of the earlier nineteenth century.

[2] Cd. 8130 (1915), Questions 60,907, 60,966–9. The *6th Report*, Cd. 7832 (1915), contains the Commission's conclusions on the staff of the courts.

[3] Cd. 9230 (1918), pt. II, ch. x.

duty of watching over the necessities of law reform, and of studying the development of the subject at home and abroad.'

It is unfortunate that the name Minister of Justice has a sinister sound to many English ears, despite the fact that such a minister is commonly found in the most respectable countries. The fear is that 'justice' would then come under his 'control'. In some countries that have a Ministry of Justice the appointment and promotion of judges is in the hands of the Minister of Justice. In England the question of a Ministry of Justice need not be complicated by this problem, for there is no necessary connection between creating such a ministry and an alteration in our technique of judicial appointment. In fact the Machinery of Government Committee recommended that judicial appointments should be concentrated in the Lord Chancellor who was not, under the Committee's scheme, to be Minister of Justice.[1] The fear that the process of justice would somehow be controlled is difficult to dispel because no critic has ever explained what it is that he thinks would happen. For many years County Court judges have sat in buildings and been assisted by staff all appointed and controlled by the Lord Chancellor's Department, and Metropolitan Stipendiary Magistrates have sat in courts and been served by staff appointed and controlled by the Home Office. There has been no bad result from taking away from judges the power to appoint staff in the courts, and not everyone appreciated the constitutional importance of retaining the right of a judge to appoint a relative to an office carrying £1500 a year (in the days when that was a comfortable salary) without there being any opportunity for public criticism of the appointment.[2] In fact the Lord Chancellor's Department has been taking over the administrative side of the law courts by a piecemeal process,[3] and it has not been suggested that any judge has a scrap less of independence. If the anticipated evil is that the Minister of Justice might sit in the House of Commons

---

[1] The Report of the Machinery of Government Committee, Cd. 9230 (1918), p. 73, suggested that all judicial appointments should be made by the Lord Chancellor, who should be required to consult a committee including the Prime Minister, the minister who would be Minister of Justice, ex-Lord Chancellors, and the Lord Chief Justice. The Lord Chancellor has already taken over the duties of the Home Secretary in the appointment of recorders and stipendiary magistrates (see p. 175, above).

[2] See p. 287, above.

[3] By 1925 the permanent secretary to the Lord Chancellor had become the Accountant-General of the Supreme Court (Schuster, 'The Office of the Lord Chancellor', 10 *Cambridge Law Journal* (1949), p. 183). Clerks of Assize are now officials of the Supreme Court and Judges' Clerks are now appointed by the Lord Chancellor (see p. 288, above).

and so be an ordinary political minister, without the legal standing and conventional aloofness of the Lord Chancellor, it must be remembered that the Home Secretary already performs many of the duties of a Minister of Justice, and that he no more controls or seeks to control criminal courts than the Lord Chancellor controls or seeks to control civil courts. Lord Birkenhead, who was Lord Chancellor from 1919 to 1922, expressed strong views against a Ministry of Justice, but he did little more than set up the usual Aunt Sallies and demolish them with an accurate aim.[1] Lord Birkenhead did, however, state very clearly the arguments in favour of not making substantial changes in the office of Lord Chancellor. That one man should fill so many roles, and be a chief exhibit for students of the doctrine of the separation of powers, is hardly a thing that would be deliberately created if we were to fashion a constitution *de novo*, but it is a most useful office:

In every democracy there arise from time to time occasions of jealousy and difficulty between the judiciary and the executive. Our present system, under which the head of the judiciary is also a prominent member of the executive government, has its disadvantages. But it has this great advantage—that it provides a link between the two sets of institutions; if they are totally severed there will disappear with them any controlling or suggestive force exterior to the Judges themselves, and it is difficult to believe that there is no necessity for the existence of such a personality, imbued on the one hand with legal ideas and habits of thought, and aware on the other of the problems which engage the attention of the executive government. In the absence of such a person the judiciary and the executive are likely enough to drift asunder to the point of a violent separation, followed by a still more violent and disastrous collision.[2]

No fresh arguments for or against a Ministry of Justice have been advanced since the days of the Machinery of Government Committee and the reply of Lord Birkenhead. There has been a change in the Lord Chancellor's Department, in that it is now run a little more on the lines of any other department. Lord Haldane knew far more about administration than others who had gone to the Woolsack, for he had been Secretary of State for War and had re-organised the War Office: when he became Lord Chancellor in 1912 he doubtless felt that his new department needed some attention, for it was then not far removed from being an interesting little museum. Things were changing when Lord Haldane again became Lord Chancellor in 1924, but he held office for less than a year and we cannot be sure

[1] Viscount Birkenhead, *Points of View* (1922), I, 92.
[2] Birkenhead, *op. cit.* p. 112.

whether his apparent indifference to his earlier proposals was due to a change in his views or to other circumstances. Many people who are anxious for law reform have continued to regard a Ministry of Justice as being most desirable, and think that such a ministry would resolve their difficulties. I was of that opinion when I first wrote this book, but I have since come to the conclusion that a ministry is not a matter of such great importance. There is often some gain in re-arranging departments. In the last few years the ministries responsible for health and housing have been rearranged, but that does not of itself ensure better health or more houses. Law reform can hardly be accomplished by having more efficient administration in a department of the central government: it requires legislation, and having a minister to propose a bill is merely one of the factors.[1] I do not know of any project for law reform that has failed to progress for lack of a minister. The fact that some suggested reform has not been taken up by either the Lord Chancellor or the Home Secretary does not show that a sound project has fallen between two stools, for who can say that a Minister of Justice would have been more receptive?

Turning now to the second factor, that is, the production of a Bill, there must generally be a great deal of preliminary work before drafting can start. There are some matters which arise from the work of a department which clearly call for legislation, and no special inquiry is needed before the minister approves of the line that should be taken, but there is not much scope for purely departmental Bills in the field of law reform. If the principal measures of law reform passed in the last hundred years are examined it will be found that they have been based on the reports of Royal Commissions or official committees. There are good reasons why that practice was followed and why it should continue to be followed. If law reform is to be successful it must be carefully considered by a wide range of people, many of them experts or concerned with the matters in question; it must command general approval, so that as far as possible it must be outside the sphere of party politics. These things can be secured more easily from an independent inquiry

---

[1] *Law Reform Now* (1963), a book sponsored by the Society of Labour Lawyers, edited by G. Gardner & A. Andrew, proposes a body of not less than five full-time Law Commissioners to review and bring up to date the general law; a Vice-Chancellor, who would sit in the Commons, would preside over them. The case for some expert body more continuous than *ad hoc* Commissions and Committees is well worth examining, but legislation would still be needed and that is where most of the trouble comes.

than from the work of the staff of a department. The evidence that is put before these commissions and committees contains the views of those who are specially concerned: organisations, such as professional bodies, trade unions, associations of local authorities and innumerable other bodies, often take great care in preparing their statements so that they may be taken as fully representative opinion. The proposals that come from one quarter are commonly put to other witnesses, and as the inquiry progresses there emerges a clear realisation of the measure of agreement and the nature of the opposition that should be expected if a particular course is followed. Suggestions get a critical examination, and the atmosphere of these inquiries is inimical to ill-prepared and vague propositions; some parts of a recent Report by 'Justice' would have been torn to shreds if they had come before a royal commission.[1]

The process of commission and committee builds up a reliable body of information and the solutions that are produced are commonly practical and workable. The recommendations that are made must of course be considered by the minister concerned, and if he and his colleagues feel able to accept the Report, it is then relatively easy for the minister to put the proposals before Parliament, for it is a great commendation of a measure to be able to say that it is founded on the recommendations of an independent body which had made a full inquiry; the proposals may be attacked, but not on the ground that they come from the politics of the minister or from the machinations of civil servants.

Commissions and committees do not usually draft the legislative changes that they recommend, as virtually all the drafting of govern-

---

[1] 'Justice' is the British Section of the International Commission of Jurists, a self-appointed body. In *The Citizen and the Administration* (1961) the sole example given of 'injustice caused by administrative action' is a case of a man who contracted mercury poisoning working for an electricity authority. He sued the Electricity Board but on the evidence he produced his claim was barred by the Statute of Limitations because of lapse of time. He applied for a gratuity, and refused to negotiate when the Board indicated that they would not pay much more than his loss of earnings. The Minister of Fuel and Power and the Prime Minister refused to intervene. The Board is a public corporation and it could not properly waive the Statute of Limitations, i.e. accept a legal liability to spend public money where no legal liability existed. If he had been in private employment he might have got a bigger gratuity, or he might not have been offered anything. The trouble lay in the law. The Report refers four times to corruption and maladministration in local government without even a wisp of evidence. For other comments see a special number of *Public Law* (Spring 1962) and A. W. Bradley, 'The Redress of Grievances' [1962] *Cambridge Law Journal* 82. The proposal for some kind of *ombudsman* was rejected by the Lord Chancellor on 7 November 1962.

ment bills is now done in the office of Parliamentary Counsel.[1] The aim of a department, whether it is putting forward its own proposals or proposals based on the Report of an inquiry, should be to state in ordinary language the provision that is to be made. Drafting is a difficult matter and very much one for experts, and it has its own problems, not the least of which is to know how the consumer controls the expert.

We now come to the third point: in addition to arrangements for investigation and preparation, the minister must try to get the Bill included in the list for the next session of Parliament. It is here that the real difficulty lies. The minister will probably have little difficulty in satisfying his colleagues on the merits of the proposed changes in the law, but every Bill that is included has the effect of excluding something else. As an example we can take the state of parts of the criminal law, where the need for reform has been apparent for years and yet no action was taken. The law of larceny began with a simple conception of taking someone else's thing and carrying it away; that has been elaborated, but as it would not stretch far enough to cover many forms of dishonesty a number of allied offences have been created by statute. Now when we take a common enough case of a rogue who gets someone to entrust to him a motor-car for sale, and the rogue sells the car (generally at a figure below the minimum specified by the owner) and does not hand over any, or all, of the proceeds of sale, we may have difficulty in naming the offence: false pretences, larceny, embezzlement, fraudulent conversion, false accounting, all have to be considered, and did he steal (or whatever offence it is) the car or the money, and whose money was it when he did whatever he did? It is all a horrible labyrinth which might well be cleared by substituting for the existing offences a single offence of dishonest dealing with property. If we were to examine the burglary and housebreaking group of offences, and the robbery, demanding with menaces and blackmail sections, we should find anomalies, obscurities and absurd distinctions. The case for remodelling is strong, but there is no urgency. Those who draw indictments often spend a long time in deciding how the charges should be framed. A rogue sometimes escapes through the fog engendered by the present law, but not often, for it is possible to charge various offences and it

---

[1] Chalmers drafted the Bills of Exchange Act, referred to at p. 413, above, on instructions from the Institute of Bankers and Associated Chambers of Commerce, but nowadays legislation has to fit into a more complicated pattern. Sometimes a committee is expected to produce a draft bill to accompany its Report, and then the practice is to assign one of Parliamentary Counsel to the committee. On producing a Bill, see n. 2 on p. 408, above.

matters little what the jury do provided they convict of something. This produces bad mental habits in those who administer criminal law, for common-sense leads one to support convenient results, and logic and legal principles are apt to get bent in the process, to the great distress of sensitive academic lawyers. When, however, these things were weighed against the proposals of other ministers it did not seem that there was a strong case for immediate action. Legislation about road traffic, or companies, or industry might produce more tangible results by reducing accidents, promoting enterprise and increasing output. Time has been found in the last few years for legislation on courts and procedure and methods of dealing with convicted people, for they were problems of some urgency. There are a number of other factors that may affect the priority to be given to legislative proposals. A vigorous minister who carries special weight with his colleagues may succeed where a weaker minister would fail. There is an element of getting to the top of the queue by being deferred year after year. The appointment of the Criminal Law Revision Committee,[1] with its assignment of the law of larceny, illustrates this process.

In this competition for getting Bills it is not to be expected that law reform will take any high place, for it is not usually urgent and it has little public appeal. It is non-political, which may smooth its progress but at the same time deprives it of the driving force of party. It may be so technical that it is hard to explain what it is all about, as in proposals for altering the law as to consideration in contract. Yet when proposals have a wide backing and there is general agreement among lawyers as to the change that is needed, time has generally been found for the necessary legislation.[2] We may grumble at the slowness with which these things happen, but they have been happening; a middle-aged lawyer who applied the law he learned as a young man would soon get into trouble. The problem is to speed up the process. The creation of a Ministry of Justice would not decrease the competition for Bills, nor can I see why a Minister of Justice should be a more successful competitor than the Lord Chancellor or the Home Secretary. It would be easier to get Bills for law reform if there were a stronger backing from lawyers and a wider general interest. One trouble is the persistence of certain ideas about law.

The technique of the English judges rests upon the idea that there

---

[1] See p. 411, above.

[2] For example, Law Reform (Enforcement of Contracts) Act 1954; Law Reform (Limitation of Actions) Act 1954; Occupiers Liability Act 1957.

is an accepted body of material from which a judge can deduce the answer to any legal problem. In the great majority of cases there is no difficulty, for the law is clear either from statute or decided cases. When the law is not clear the judge proceeds to pronounce the law avowedly as a deduction from some kind of legal authority. Even when a judge, in the last resort, says that he is deciding upon some 'general principle' he is purporting to follow authority. In reality the judicial process is complicated: behind the avowed basis of the decision there must lie a host of formative elements.[1] For forensic purposes the judicial process must generally be taken at its face value. Study of the law reports gives the impression of the law developing from precedent to precedent. The law appears to grow out of itself. Apart from an unnecessary modern rigidity in the theory of precedent our judicial process is more a common method of conducting public business than a peculiarity of the lawyers.[2] Fundamentally, as a working technique for judges, there is much to be said for the method; criticism is directed more at the way it is worked than at the basis of the method. The limitation is that it is a technique for *judges*, yet it has dominated other fields. Legal study in England has for over half a century been dominated by legal historians. Academic lawyers accepted the habits of the judges and proceeded to expound and teach the law in the judicial manner. The writings of the late Sir Frederick Pollock suggest that he would have been of the greatest value in the Court of Appeal or the House of Lords if those who nominate to judgeships had had the wisdom to make such an appointment. Most of the revered academic lawyers have had the outlook of the bench at its best. This has produced some unfortunate results. A judge must of necessity act upon certain assumptions. He must assume that there are certain fundamental legal concepts and that all law consists of regrouping these and making logical applications of them. He deals with a verbalistic subject, and when he handles such words as *contract, marriage, piracy*, he must assume that they represent immutable ideas or absolutes with an unvarying meaning that can be ascertained by consulting works of authority. For academic Anglo-American lawyers these judicial habits became the idea that fundamental concepts should be sought in the earliest records of our law.[3] The

---

[1] See also p. 373, above.   [2] See p. 11, above.

[3] J. B. Ames, who had a profound influence on the Harvard Law School, could even contend that because a notion was not present in the fourteenth and fifteenth centuries it has no business to exist in modern law (*Lectures on Legal History*, 1913, p. 119, the lectures being delivered in the 1890's).

relaxation from legal history has been a subject called Jurisprudence. In our law schools this has generally meant an assumption that 'law' has an ascertainable meaning quite apart from definition or linguistic usage, and that the concepts of 'law' can be studied on the same basis, for they are thought of as real entities eternally fixed in the order of nature. The bondage to medieval scholasticism may be studied in Salmond's *Jurisprudence*. Out of this historical school came magnificent research leading to the most barren of conclusions. Maitland stands out as a giant. He realised the futility of much of the legal thought of his time: he insisted that institutions and legal concepts are not ideas in themselves but are specific pieces of history.[1] In an age when Dicey dominated the field of constitutional law it was Maitland in the last part of his *Constitutional History* who showed what was really happening to English public law. Men who understood the detailed historical work of Maitland but lacked his deeper understanding used his plea for legal history as an argument to pile upon students still more history. The measure of under-standing may be gauged by the fact that the last part of Maitland's *Constitutional History* was the one part that was ignored and ex-cluded from the reading list in the very law school where Maitland had taught. Who cared what was really happening to English public law? It was not history, it was not jurisprudence, it was not the common law of judges. Men trained in our law schools have been taught that full understanding of the law comes from study of legal sources. Over 70 per cent of the judges have in the past come from Oxford and Cambridge, so that presumably the bulk of successful and influential lawyers have also been at the older universities: from my knowledge of the textbooks that have been in use and a more limited acquaintance with the contents of lecture courses, I feel confident that these men passed through a system of legal education that has been content to leave out of consideration the actual working of the law. The actual working of the law cannot be studied in statutes, law reports and legal textbooks, for the actual working of some part of the law means a study of the affairs of people who are affected by it. For many years the settlement of disputes under the Workmen's Compensation Acts was in the hands of lawyers and the ordinary law courts. Lawyers could say when compensation was payable and how much should be paid, but if we wanted to know whether the sums payable were sufficient, or showed curiosity as to

---

[1] See particularly the essay, *The Body Politic*, delivered in 1899, reprinted in *Selected Essays of Maitland* (1936).

what happened to a man who received a lump sum in settlement, or widened our query into the effect of the law in mitigating the results of an industrial accident, it was no use turning to the lawyers for an answer. There were further interesting questions about the cost of administering that part of the law, such as the relation between the legal costs and the sums paid as compensation, and the expenditure of an employer (or his insurance company) and a workman (or his trade union) for each pound of compensation recovered, and how this compared with foreign and commonwealth practice. Inquiry showed that the system was extravagant and inefficient, and it has been changed.[1] Similar questions might be asked about many common law actions and the damages that are awarded. But once one gets away from the rules of law and into the realm of the effects on people there are vast territories to explore. The lawyer's reply has been that these are not 'legal questions' at all, and if a thing is not 'law' he cannot be expected to know anything about it. It is so much more comfortable to build a snug nest, lined with the pure theory of law, than it is to see what is happening as a result of the law and its administration.

During the war there was an elaborate code of Defence Regulations and other subordinate legislation made under the Emergency Powers Acts. After the war came a spate of legislation. Lawyers had a hard time trying to master so much new law, for statutes of prodigious length and complexity have been accompanied by an even greater volume of Statutory Instruments and departmental circulars and memoranda. The cry was that there might be a pause and time for digestion before we got any more on our plate. But there has been no pause, merely a steady flow of legislation instead of a torrent. Enterprising law publishers have done much to ease the burden, and lawyers have come to feel a little less overwhelmed by the volume of new legislation without, however, finding that professional life is any more free from anxieties. Those in private practice have nearly all had a fair measure of personal worry over their earnings. The Bar had a boom after the war, then a depression and now a boom again. The tax structure[2] was particularly hard on the few men who were doing reasonably well. Solicitors have been struggling against the rising costs of running their offices. These conditions have tended to produce a pre-occupation with the difficulties of work and personal position, and the little energy left over

---

[1] Wilson and Levy, *Workmen's Compensation*, 2 vols. (1939, 1941). On the present position see p. 343, above.   [2] See p. 260, above.

has commonly gone into resentment at the apparent causes. Lawyers have been so acutely aware of the failings of others, especially of Parliament, of ministers, of civil servants, of local authorities and of special tribunals, that they have scarcely given a thought to whether their own house needs a spring-clean. In the social services and in general conditions of working and living there have been great improvements, in a continuous effort to meet the needs of our changing society. But new ideas have not penetrated to the law courts: in litigation the principle is that what was good enough a hundred years ago is good enough today and will be good enough in a hundred years time, because it is absolutely good. Lawyers really do believe that the common law has evolved a judicial process that is supremely good. Whether that view can be accepted, or whether it should be regarded as being akin to an advertiser's description of his own goods, depends on our approach. If we think of the principles on which our judicial process is based, there can be little doubt that they do, as I have suggested,[1] represent a great contribution to civilisation. If, however, we look at the process as it actually is, seeing the paper work and the preliminaries to the hearing, and listening to the conduct of the case, we may feel very differently about the whole business, or at least some of its aspects.

Consider some of the ordinary characteristics of legal proceedings as they may strike an observer who is not soaked in legal tradition. The first is that one side starts off with its case, and that has to be followed without our knowing where the controversy lies, so that we cannot concentrate on the facts or arguments that are really in issue. The pleadings and proceedings before trial of a civil case show the line it is going to follow, but this does not extend to evidence. In civil cases you will hear counsel inquiring at times whether certain points are disputed and so avoiding full evidence of that which is not disputed, but that cannot happen in criminal cases. Nearly everyone who has to deal with the pros and cons of some matter in business or administration wants to find out at the earliest stage how much is common ground. Legal procedure might well begin with a narrative agreed between the parties showing with specific reference to the evidence where the dispute actually lies. The conduct of cases has a large admixture of tiresome habits and mumbo-jumbo. Counsel's conduct is based on social conditions of past ages, when the literacy and mental capacity of counsel stood out in bright contrast to ordinary people. So these days we must be read to, as if we are still

[1] See p. 401, above.

illiterate, and counsel must repeat the answers that witnesses give so that our limited intelligence can take it in. At the same time a question to a witness may begin 'I put it to you that...' or some other expression that may puzzle people who are not used to such affectations. A common bit of mumbo-jumbo goes like this: a man is giving evidence as to why he remembered the time when he started to drive home. He says: 'I had to be home by ten, and it was getting very foggy, so at nine I rang up Muriel, and I says, "Muriel, what's the fog like your end?" and she says...'. He is stopped: what Muriel said is hearsay, and not admissible. The poor man is confused and bewildered, for his natural way of speaking is apparently taboo. The proper course is to go in for circumlocution whereby he makes it clear that in consequence of information that he received he decided to leave earlier than he otherwise would have done. Behind the irritations and sillinesses lies a really serious piece of humbug. The process is said to be the ascertainment of the truth, which in the oath of a witness is elaborated as the truth, the whole truth and nothing but the truth. The technique of cross-examination is supposed to be the great instrument for this purpose: its function is to sift, probe and test evidence. An easy way to check this is to listen to the trial at Quarter Sessions of a charge of driving a motor-vehicle whilst under the influence of drink. When the doctor called by the prosecution has given his evidence, he will be subjected to a standard series of questions from counsel for the defence. These questions are not designed to sift and test the evidence, for the evidence is usually an honest professional medical report: a particular line of questioning is adopted because experience shows that it is likely to confuse and mislead the jury. It is best to listen to more than one case, because the first time you hear this piece of advocacy you might get taken in by it, for it is quite plausible casuistry.[1] Some of the most devastating criticism comes from medical men. An eminent psychiatrist has observed that: 'The judicial process does not seem to be designed primarily for the ascertainment of fact: and if it is not so designed, it is hardly surprising that it is not very successful.'[2] A medical man,

[1] I am not here concerned with the ethics of advocacy. C. P. Harvey, *The Advocate's Devil* (1958), is one of the few practising barristers who does not conform with the tradition of smug complacency.

[2] 'The Judicial Process and the Ascertainment of Fact' by Dr Eliot Slater, 24 *Modern Law Review* (1961), p. 721. Dr Slater does not like the fancy dress used in court. It is commonly said that wigs and robes and some pageantry make the higher courts more impressive, though who is impressed and to what effect is unexplained: obviously criminals are not 'impressed' unless that means they come back to court again because they liked it so much on an earlier occasion.

like any other witness, is called by one side or the other, to be pushed by counsel as far as he can be made to go, 'and it is rare for him to retire from the box without being trapped into expressing an opinion with greater confidence or emphasis than in a cool moment he would think justified'. The idea that the witness is 'trapped' is I think wrong, and that what happens is a far more serious thing. Let us suppose that a witness was driving his car along a street towards traffic lights some distance away, when he was overtaken by a motor-cyclist who appeared to ignore the traffic lights and to crash into a van that was coming out with the lights in its favour. The car driver will be cross-examined on how fast he and the motor-cyclist were going, the distance he was away from the lights, the distance the motor-cyclist was from the road markings when the lights went amber, the other traffic that was about, the time of day, the weather and maybe other things. These questions may all be relevant, but on most of these points the witness cannot give a precise answer: men do not notice everything that happens particularly when it does not appear at the time to be unusual or in any way to matter to their own affairs. But the cross-examination is conducted as if the witness does know the answers and is concealing them: counsel must drag out the truth.[1] If a witness says he does not know, and keeps on repeating that, counsel can get no further, but most people cannot bear the strain of persistent questioning and clutch at any suggestion of certainty. The witness ends up by giving detailed evidence which he is now certain is the truth. If a similar cross-examination can lead another witness into details that cannot be reconciled with that of the car driver, then counsel has established that there is a conflict of evidence. I think that counsel do this, and often do it so well, in good faith; it is traditional truth-finding, which has in its day uncovered witch-craft, and that which is basic to the common law is not to be doubted.

One of the main conceptions of common law is the 'day in court'. Pleadings and other preparations lead up to a culmination when the trial will in a single process decide and settle the matter. Now the great majority of civil actions are for personal injuries on the roads or whilst at work. Liability and the amount of damages have to be decided at the hearing. If the extent or permanency of the injuries cannot be established until some time has elapsed, the hearing must

---

[1] Some representatives at the Commercial Court Users' Conference, Cmnd. 1616 (1961), referred to 'the atmosphere in a court of law where even their intimate business friends are liable to be examined and cross-examined as though they were liars'.

wait. In the meantime the injured person does not know whether he can establish his claim, and evidence may become stale or disappear. His recovery may be adversely affected by the uncertainties. We cannot have a quick investigation of the accident and a determination of liability with some damages on account and a final decision when the full extent of the injuries can be assessed, because the 'day in court' is another basic principle. Further, the nature and timing of these proceedings makes it virtually impossible to get a satisfactory tie-up between accident investigation and prevention and particular accidents. Even the famous common law system of precedent is working so badly that the House of Lords has found, in two cases within a few weeks of each other, that the mass of reported decisions is a hindrance to the administration of justice.[1] A writer who has recently analysed judicial decisions on the duty to fence dangerous machinery has shown how the doctrine of precedent can take control of events. He sums up the position thus:

Not only the intentions of Parliament, but all real considerations also can be displaced in court by the power of precedent, that is, considerations that are 'real' to non-lawyers who come to the courts in search of remedies and answers to their problems, and hear their cases being disposed of on the basis of considerations that have no significance or reality except for lawyers.[2]

Of course, the rules of evidence do not always produce such rubbishy results, and counsel do not always prevent the truth from emerging, and precedent is not always an impediment to justice, but these things happen often enough to be regarded as regular features of the system. People who can choose do not want the process: they prefer to go elsewhere. Mr Griffith, in writing about the growth of special tribunals, summed up the position:

The ordinary applicant for national assistance, national insurance, or industrial injury benefit, did not hanker after his day in court. The T.U.C.

---

[1] See *Davie* v. *New Merton Board Mills Ltd.* [1959] 2 W.L.R. 331. In *Qualcast (Wolverhampton) Ltd.* v. *Haynes* [1959] 2 W.L.R. 510, Lord Somervell said at p. 518, 'If the reasons given by a Judge for arriving at a conclusion previously reached by a jury are to be treated as "law" and citable (which is what has been happening), the present system will die from a surfeit of authorities'. The explanation of the reporting of so many cases is that counsel want ammunition because, whatever the case, an advocate must say something that appears relevant and if possible learned. If, as some lawyers urge, our courts should pay attention to other Commonwealth courts far more reports would be cited; see R. E. Megarry, *Lawyer and Litigant in England* (1962), p. 161. And why not all the law reports of all the common law jurisdictions of U.S.A.? Then some of the cases in our courts could go on for ever.

[2] A. D. Woolf, 'The Doctrine of Precedent at Work', *Law Society's Gazette* (March 1963).

certainly did not wish to have restored the supreme privilege of fighting cases to the House of Lords. Property owners did not like the basis of compensation but accepted the Lands Tribunal. The truth is that only a certain type of lawyer, politician and constitutionalist dearly loves our system of established courts. The man on the Clapham omnibus and the man in the company's Rolls are alike in this, that they would prefer to be driven in their respective vehicles to any arbitrator or tribunal rather than to the courts.[1]

The one explanation that lawyers will not consider is that perhaps the process they offer is not good enough. It represents outworn conceptions of how to go about the business of collecting and marshalling facts: any competent scientist, business executive or administrator is better equipped in this respect than Bench and Bar. Whitehall's methods of finding and applying the principle or rule appropriate for a particular case are years ahead of the lawyers' technique. The trial of cases in the law courts belongs to the horse and buggy period. To put things right we do not need a Ministry of Justice: we need a new attitude in the legal profession, particularly in the Bar. There have been several occasions in the last few years when it looked as if some major reforms would be made and then either nothing much happened or some outworn and inconvenient bit of legal paraphernalia has been patched up and given a coat of paint. Lawyers' myths and lawyers' interests combine to make a tough shield against a planned and efficient system.

Lawyers commonly talk about the common law as being a bulwark of the liberty of the subject and of themselves as the upholders and guardians of liberty. Yet a situation has existed in which men committed for trial have had to wait in prison much longer than need have been to suit the convenience of barristers. If courts of Quarter Sessions in an area had been co-ordinated, there would have been frequent courts, and much waiting in prison would have been avoided. Such arrangements could not be made in many areas because Recorders[2] fixed their sessions to suit themselves, sometimes fixing them for just after County Sessions thus giving themselves the minimum of work and prisoners the maximum time to wait for trial. Now as a result of the Streatfeild Committee and the Criminal Justice Administration Act 1962[3] Quarter Sessions have got to co-ordinate their sittings. But why do we have to have these separate courts, often sitting in the same town? why is there no planned system as there is for County Courts? The continuation of these different

[1] J. A. G. Griffith, 'Tribunals and Inquiries', 22 *Modern Law Review* (1959), p. 133. [2] See p. 99, above. [3] See p. 103, above.

Quarter Sessions, even when the dates of sittings are co-ordinated, means that each court has its separate clerk and staff. A single court, sitting at least monthly and at such places as are convenient, would remove most of the difficulties, but it would upset recorderships. It might even upset the restrictive practices of the Bar, for a barrister who belongs to one circuit has restrictions on appearing at a court on another circuit, and rationalised Quarter Sessions would spread across boundaries of circuits. The maintenance of bar etiquette has been far more important than personal liberty.[1] The Assize system was developed in the days of travel by horse. Now they have been re-organised, and together with the improvements we have Hallam-shire[2] as a monument to the retention in adult life of games of make-believe and paper hats.

On the civil side we have had inquiry after inquiry affecting the High Court, but no review of the system of civil courts as a whole. We might, for instance, get on better if we had local courts of first instance with unlimited jurisdiction: much of the High Court jurisdiction could be taken at a lower level and decentralised, and much of it transferred to an enlarged Court of Appeal. But what would poor barristers, most of them with chambers in London, do with a decentralised system? For the Bar there are supreme merits in what we have. Consider patents, a subject of some concern to an industrial economy. We can start with a tribunal of first instance (an examiner who acts for the Controller-General of Patents) and appeal to the Patents Appeal Tribunal which consists of a High Court Judge. Now we can say that his decision is erroneous on the face of it, and go for *certiorari* by applying to a Divisional Court of the Queen's Bench Division. Then on we can go to the Court of Appeal, and end up in the House of Lords. Our case can be argued on five separate occasions. Everything is for the best in the best of all possible legal worlds.

Between the wars there were Committees and Commissions, and hopes arose that perhaps something would be done to improve High Court practice and procedure. Very little was done. Then in 1947 the Evershed Committee was appointed.[3] High hopes were set on that Committee, for it breathed a new and welcome determination to make a brave new legal world in the Law Courts. Six years that Committee laboured, and the result of those six years is that every-

---

[1] I put this in the past tense because in 1963 the Bar set up a Special Committee on the circuit system, and hope springs eternal.
[2] See p. 104, above.　　　　　　　　[3] See p. 46, above.

thing goes on much as it did before. The high hopes have ebbed away. The delays, uncertainties and high cost are still there. Solicitors still have to explain to clients that a case may cost at least £600 in costs if it is fought and lost, and can tell of cases where the client was too rich for legal aid and too poor to pay for justice.[1] New rules have been made, and the machinery may creak less, but the pattern is unaltered. Table XI shows the number of ordinary actions entered for trial and the number actually tried in the Queen's Bench Division since 1935. It is clear that as the number of cases tried has declined the average time expended on a case has increased. The courts now sit for a longer time and get through about half the number of cases. It seems a plain example of Parkinson's Law, that work expands to fill the time available for doing it. But when a lawyer comes across some data that cannot be refuted, such as Table XI, he instinctively looks for an explanation that will show the wisdom or necessity of that state of affairs. It is not as if we live in a period generally averse to change; in other fields reform has not been unduly difficult. The Royal Commission on the Law Relating to Mental Illness and Mental Deficiency was appointed in February 1954 and reported in May 1957,[2] recommending far-reaching changes, and these were approved by Parliament in 1959. To be concerned with such reforms is invigorating; analysis of defect can lead to designing a new process based on realities: it was not necessary to invent a Hallamshire in order to provide hospital facilities.

There should be nothing surprising in legal institutions being cluttered up with the debris of years of social change; other services have been as inefficient and quite as exasperating. The peculiarity of the legal system is its blind devotion to its own shortcomings. The major fact is that the Bar as a profession is out of tune with our times. The only conditions under which its members are permitted to practise are those of complete individualism, each for himself alone; there is nothing of the modern pattern of trained men who work as a team. Nor are there any representatives of those in salaried positions in the public service or in private concerns: a career of public service disqualifies a man from ranking as a practising barrister and of having some say in the affairs of the Bar. Out of this peculiarly exclusive group of individualists comes the whole of our judiciary except for a few minor appointments. It is a completely

[1] See, for example, A. J. Harper, 'What Price Justice!', *Law Society's Gazette* (1960), p. 385.
[2] Cmnd. 218.

THE OUTLOOK FOR REFORM

closed circle. This is not to say that there is no hope. Bar and bench have in the past produced some bold reformers, but never I think without pressure from outside. Law and its administration is a far too serious business to be left to lawyers. There are limits to the effectiveness of a committee of distinguished lawyers, with a legal secretariat, for producing recommendations for reforming the law, nor is it apparently better if a number of non-lawyers are made members, for what will emerge will be lawyers' solutions based (like the matters they are reforming) on legal material. Wilson and Levy blew the old Workmen's Compensation system to pieces because they looked at social facts.[1] It is doubtful if the present way of handling personal injury actions could survive a thorough-going investigation of the social results; it would probably show a degree of hit and miss, inefficiency and cost that even a Q.C. explaining the merits of our system would find difficult to defend. But apart from a concern about particular fields of legal inadequacy, the importance of studies into the social effects of the law is that a ferment may be started. When there is a reasonable amount of available knowledge about the effects of some kind of legal proceeding, there can be public discussion and a building-up of opinion about what should be done. An approach of that kind does eventually get through into legal circles. But is there much chance of going beyond that, and having a legal profession that will actively work for a brave new legal world? We have reached a stage where the legal profession needs recasting into a new pattern. There are great possibilities, if there is enough vision, and enough courage.

The outlook for reform of substantive law is fair, for outsiders can push and jostle and the bottleneck of Parliament is no worse than for any other legislation. But the modernisation of the machinery of justice will be a very slow process unless the legal profession can cease to be backward looking and fit itself for the conditions of a changing society.

[1] A. Wilson and H. Levy, *Workmen's Compensation* (1939).

Table XI. *Actions in the Queen's Bench Division*

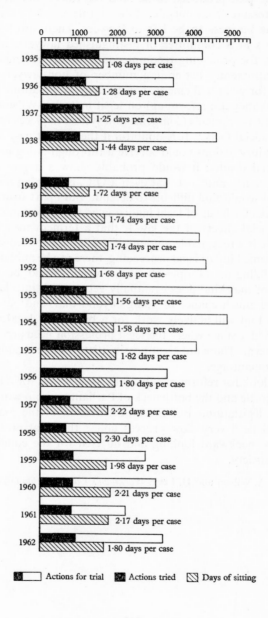

Actions for trial   Actions tried   Days of sitting

434

TABLE OF STATUTES CITED

Statutes used to be cited by the regnal year, as for example 15 & 16 Geo. V, c. 49, which means the 49th chapter in the statute book passed in a session of Parliament that began in the 15th and continued into the 16th years of the reign of George V. Even those whose accomplishments include remembering the dates of the Kings and Queens of England cannot be sure of the date, for that session began in 1924 and continued in 1925, and only a person with a remarkable memory could say what 15 & 16 Geo. V, c. 49 is all about. The Acts of Parliament Numbering and Citation Act 1962 provided that, beginning in 1963, the statutes are to be numbered by the calendar year and not by the session. Under this new system the statute '1963, c. 37' means the 37th statute in the Volume of Statutes for 1963, which is simpler and gives the year but still provides no clue to the subject-matter. The best method of citation is by the short title, and 15 & 16 Geo. V, c. 49 then becomes the Supreme Court of Judicature (Consolidation) Act 1925 and 1963 c. 37 becomes the Children and Young Persons Act 1963. Obviously the short title (which is actually longer) is generally more convenient than regnal years or calendar years and numbers.

TABLE OF STATUTES CITED

TABLE OF CASES CITED

TABLE OF STATIONERY OFFICE
PUBLICATIONS CITED

Official publications can be divided into two broad categories according to whether they come from the activities of Parliament or from other sources. Those arising directly from the work of Parliament include Bills, records of proceedings with reports of debates in each House and in committees, and Acts of Parliament. There are also Select Committees which are appointed each session to inquire into and report on Public Accounts and some other matters, and Select Committees appointed for particular inquiries: their proceedings and reports are published as Parliamentary papers. Powers of delegated legislation give rise to statutory instruments, which are published in a similar form to that used for statutes. The other type of publication can be subdivided into: (a) Statements on government policy, including material on foreign affairs and other matters; (b) Annual reports from government departments and bodies; (c) Reports from Royal Commissions and Committees of inquiry; (d) Pamphlets and books prepared by or sponsored by government departments on matters with which the department is concerned. Types (a), (b) and (c) are generally presented to Parliament by a minister (nominally by command of the Sovereign) and so are called Command Papers. Before 1870 they carried numbers without any prefix. In 1870 the numbering began again, with the prefix 'C.', these running on until the number was over 9000: the process was repeated in 1900 with the prefix 'Cd.', again in 1919 with the prefix 'Cmd.', and again in 1956 with the prefix 'Cmnd.'. These prefixes are often confused, and it is better to include the date as part of the reference. Eventually these papers form part of the volumes of Accounts and Papers for the year, and they may then be cited by the volume in which they are included, but it is not convenient to adopt that as the general system of reference because it cannot be known until some time after a paper has been published. Sometimes a report is published without being presented to Parliament, as for example a Report in 1937 on the Courts of Summary Jurisdiction in the Metropolitan Area, but that is not a matter of any importance. Royal Commissions and Committees are sometimes referred to by the name of the chairman, as for example the Peel Commission and the Donoughmore Committee, which is not really convenient because there is nothing to link the name with the subject-matter. On the format of these papers, those in type (a) are often short and have no cover except that on which they are printed, and so they get called 'White Papers'. Those in types (b) and (c) are apt to be longer, and traditionally appeared in covers of stouter blue paper, and so are 'Blue Books'. These are colloquial terms, and often all manner of official publications are called blue books. Apart from legislation, the most valuable sources for the administration of justice are to be found in types (b), (c) and (d). The relevant annual reports are: Civil Judicial Statistics, Reports of the Law Society on the Operation of the Legal Aid and Advice Act, Reports of the Council on Tribunals, Criminal Statistics, Reports of the Prison Commissioners, and Reports of the Commissioners of Police of the Metropolis and of H.M. Inspectors of Constabulary. It would serve no useful purpose to index every use made of these returns, and they are not included in the list below. The reports of Royal Commissions, official Committees and Advisory bodies represent the result of independent expert inquiries; a Royal Commission has more dignity and standing than a Committee, but there is no essential difference. It used to be the practice to publish the Minutes of Evidence of these inquiries, but since the first World War this has generally been restricted to Royal Commissions, though reports of Committees often have substantial appendices containing data that otherwise

441

would not be available. Type (*d*) is akin to ordinary book publishing; the pamphlet and books vary from somewhat slight and popular expositions to the severest kind of technical guide. The principal use of the publications on, for example, probation, prisons and borstals and approved schools, is the provision of an account that is shorter and simpler than that contained in specialist studies. There is no special method of reference to these publications, and they are best referred to by their title and date.

444

INDEX

INDEX

Magistrates' Courts and Quarter
Sessions, summary of, 106 n. 1
Magistrates' Courts
affiliation, 119 n. 6, 177–9
appeal from, 112–13, 183
chairman, 165–6
clerk as adviser, 170–2
committal for non-payment, 182–3,
227
committal for sentence, 98
committal for trial, 93, 96, 102, 104,
119, 132–3, 147–51
composition, 94, 95
contempt, 231
domestic proceedings, 22, 181
finance, 172–3
guardianship of infants, 180
jurisdiction, 95–9, 104–5
juvenile court, 184–96
legal aid, 140–4
London, City of, 95
London, County of, 94
magistrates' courts committees, 163,
168, 173
matrimonial jurisdiction, 179–83
money payments, 182–3, 227
petty sessional divisions, 94–5, 168–
9
petty sessions, 94, 95
probation orders, 200
rules, 172
sentences, 98, 105, 212
stipendiary magistrates, 94, 95
police 95, 153–6
probation service, 202
See also Justices of the Peace,
Juvenile Courts, Procedure in
Criminal Cases
Magna Carta, 2
Mahaffy, R. D., 331
Maitland, F. W., 10, 44, 110, 424
Manchester Crown Court, 29, 102
Mandamus, 41, 42, 395, 400; *and see*
Prerogative Writs
Mannheim, H., 223
Marshall, G., 385
Master of the Rolls, 48–9, 80, 81, 235,
237, 239, 240, 257, 258, 259
Masters, 39, 49, 287–9
Mathew, Sir T., 126
Matrimonial Causes, *see* Divorce,
Magistrates' Courts
Maugham, Lord, 257
Mayor's and City of London Court,
34, 100

Mental Health Review Tribunals, 210,
211, 373
Merrivale, Lord, 56
Merthyr, Lord, 159
Metropolitan Police, 122, 155
Solicitor to, 125
Metropolitan Sipendiary Magistrates,
94, 95, 174; *and see* Justices of the
Peace
Milk Marketing Board, 352
Ministerial Tribunals, *see* Special
Tribunals
Ministers
decisions by, 320, 324, 352–3, 360–3,
373–8, 378–80, 388–94
delegated legislation, 42–3, 320
distinguished from special tribunals,
373–8
legislation, 320, 408–9
responsible to Parliament, 317, 324,
375, 409
Missionaries, legal, 401
Monopolies Commission,76–7; *and see*
Restrictive Practices Court
Morrison, A. C. L., 184
Muir, C., 84, 158, 384
Mullins, C., 135, 204, 301

National Arbitration Tribunal, 336–7
National Assistance, 344
National Insurance, 319, 325, 342–3,
379, 380, 394
National Insurance (Industrial In-
juries), 343–4
National Insurance,Minister of,342,343
Newsam, Sir F., 206, 410
Nisi Prius, 4
Nolle Prosequi, 128
Norwich Guildhall Court, 34
Nullity, Decree of, 52–3
Nyquist, O., 194

Odger's *Pleading and Practice*, 64
Official Referee, 69
Old Bailey, *see* Central Criminal Court
Opticians, 351

Page, Sir L., 204
Parker, Lord, 144, 255, 262, 268
Parliament, Acts of, *see* Statutes
Parliamentary Counsel, 420, 421
Patents Appeal Tribunal, 431
Peel, Earl, 41
Peers, Trial by, 109
Penal Actions, 25–6

452